Praise for WHO CAR~~~ ~~~ ~ ~~~

"This is a really cool book that describes a San Francisco that was such a unique and creative place, and which will probably never exist in this form again. Great stuff documented with detail and respect!"
—BILL GOULD, FAITH NO MORE

"Some of the most interesting, if not always easily delightful, music and art comes from loons larking about on edges. The San Francisco-based art-terrorists, whose stories Will York captures, reveals a scene where every bizarre cranny both amuses and alarms, keenly giving the feeling of fascinated unease the musicians themselves inspire."
—BRIAN DOHERTY, author of THIS IS BURNING MAN & DIRTY PICTURES

"If your concept of San Francisco rock starts with The Jefferson Airplane and ends with The Beau Brummels, then good for you because The Grateful Dead were terrible. On the other hand, you're missing out on some of the oddest, most oddball, and downright oddballest music ever created. Thankfully, Will York is determined to introduce you to the sights, sounds, sites and wounds of excellent but under-heralded artists like Flipper, the Residents, Toiling Midgets, Caroliner, Pop-o-Pies, The Thinking Fellers Union Local 282 and even MTV's Faith No More. Great book!" —MARK PRINDLE, markprindle.com

"An evocative deep dive into San Francisco's leftfield post-punk underground, before it was quashed by the successive waves of dotcom booms that rendered the corporatization, unaffordability, and tech orientation of a boutique city. Through crucial first-hand testimony from some of the scene's prime movers, *Who Cares Anyway* illuminates the creative forces that sparked it, underpinned by an unprecedented blend of situationist thought, substance misuse, and psychosis." —DAVID KATZ

"A fascinating tale of self-made weirdo punk visionaries plotting revenge on the fine arts. Warning: Extremely Compelling."
—OWEN KLINE, director of FUNNY PAGES

[continues over]

WHO CARES ANYWAY

POST-PUNK SAN FRANCISCO AND THE END OF THE ANALOG AGE

WILL YORK

HEADPRESS

A HEADPRESS BOOK
First published by Headpress in 2023, Oxford, United Kingdom
headoffice@headpress.com

WHO CARES ANYWAY
Post-Punk San Francisco and the End of the Analog Age

Text copyright © WILL YORK
This volume copyright © HEADPRESS 2023
Cover design and layout: MARK CRITCHELL mark.critchell@gmail.com
Index: Edwin Canfield
The Publisher thanks Leigh Bushell

10 9 8 7 6 5 4 3 2 1

A CIP catalogue record for this book is available from the British Library

ISBN 978-1-915316-05-9   paperback
ISBN 978-1-915316-06-6   ebook
ISBN NO-ISBN hardback

HEADPRESS. POP AND UNPOP CULTURE

Exclusive NO-ISBN special edition hardbacks
and other items of interest are available at **HEADPRESS.COM**

Printed in Great Britain by Bell and Bain Ltd, Glasgow

WHO CARES
ANYWAY

WHO CARES ANYWAY

CONTENTS

CONTENTS

THE MID-EIGHTIES

THE LATE EIGHTIES

INTO THE NINETIES

END THE GAME

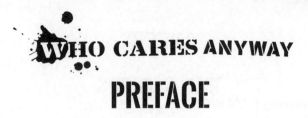

WHO CARES ANYWAY

PREFACE

"Tennyson said that if we could but understand a single flower we might know who we are and what the world is. Perhaps he was trying to say that there is nothing, however humble, that does not imply the history of the world and its concatenation of causes and effects."
—J.L. Borges, 'The Zahir'

In April of 1999, I ordered some items from the website of Amarillo Records in what must have been one of my earliest forays into the realm of e-commerce—if one can even call it that. A look back at the archived website (no, not amarillorecords.com, but members.aol.com/starleigh7/cat_al.html) tells me that I must have paid with a check, as the only other forms of payment they accepted were cash or money order.

Among the items in my order was the Three Doctors Band's *Back to Basics—"Live"* LP, which, at $4.50, had been priced to move. The blurb on the website called it "Beyond parody, beyond integrity, beyond conceptual...beyond listenable!" I may have taken that as a challenge. I remember being amused by the cover art and intrigued, if somewhat baffled, by the liner notes. Alas, when I put the record on, I discovered that it was warped—as in, physically warped, enough so that it wobbled on my turntable.

Sheepishly, I emailed the label to see about getting a replacement. To my relief, I received a prompt and courteous reply from label head Gregg Turkington, who also happened to be the lead vocalist for the Three Doctors. "Sorry about that!" he wrote, before parenthetically adding that "it may be a blessing in disguise that yet another copy of that album was somehow destroyed."

Pressing my luck, I sent a follow-up email to inquire about my odds of ever stumbling across a couple of out-of-print records by another of Turkington's bands, the Zip Code Rapists, at the local record store. "Not too good," he replied. "However, I do have a tiny quantity of *The Man Can't Bust Our Music* and *Sing and Play the Three Doctors and Other Sounds of Today* here; I would

PREFACE

sell you the EP for $10 and the LP for $4 (as it is a shitty, shitty later pressing on truly rotten vinyl)." It was a deal.

It's only a slight exaggeration to call the ensuing shipment—which also included an Amarillo Records sampler CD and a few back issues of Turkington's 1980s zine *Breakfast Without Meat*—the inspiration for this book. I could backtrack a little further—to the time a fellow DJ at WXYC-Chapel Hill introduced me to comedian Neil Hamburger or the time a listener called in and requested that I play something by a band called Faxed Head. But really, it was the one-two punch of *Back to Basics* and *Sing and Play the Three Doctors* that cemented my fascination with San Francisco, or at least the mythical version of it I was concocting inside my head.

In October of that year, I did what so many other loners, outcasts, and weirdos before me had done: I packed my bags and moved to San Francisco. It's not that I thought I was going to track down the Three Doctors or any of the other aforementioned acts, most of which were defunct or on hiatus by that point anyway. But I wanted to experience big-city life for a year or two while I got my act together after college, and though I'd never even visited the place, San Francisco seemed more appealing than New York or Chicago.

One thing led to another, and then another. After working (and getting laid off from) a couple of dotcom jobs, I managed in 2001 to get my foot in the door as a freelancer with the *Bay Guardian*, a free alternative weekly of the sort that every decent-sized city used to have. (San Francisco actually had two, with the other one being the slicker and better-financed *SF Weekly*.) I was into some pretty obnoxious music in those days—including a lot of metal, noise, and free jazz/improv—but before long, my editors at the *Guardian* were giving me free rein to write about basically whatever I wanted, especially if there was a local angle. And between the post-dotcom resurgence of the local scene and the steady stream of touring acts, there was no shortage of new music to write about—most of which had little or nothing to do with the stuff that had initially piqued my interest in the Bay Area.

That said, I did find the occasional opportunity to indulge my curiosity about Amarillo Records and related matters, and the more I did so, the more that curiosity grew. Between 2002 and 2005, I put together a handful of

retrospective/"where are they now?" articles that led me back in time, first to the mid-1980s (the Pop-O-Pies and the early, pre-Mike Patton version of Faith No More) and eventually the early 1980s (Flipper and Subterranean Records). After the fourth or fifth installment of this unofficial "series," I received a note of encouragement from Mr. Gregg Turkington himself: "I tell you, the more of these nostalgia articles you do, the more inevitable your destiny becomes: one day you're going to HAVE TO do a book, the history of San Francisco high-quality oddball bands from the '80s/'90s."

Somewhere in there, I had read *Our Band Could Be Your Life*, Michael Azerrad's then-recent tome on American underground rock in the 1980s. I loved it, especially the chapters on Black Flag and the Butthole Surfers. At the same time, I noticed it didn't include any bands from San Francisco. In the book's preface, Azerrad noted, "There are plenty more books to be written about this subject; I invite you to write one of them." So I did.

POST-PUNK SAN FRANCISCO AND THE END OF THE ANALOG AGE

A few words might be in order about the subtitle. By "Post-Punk San Francisco," I'm not referring specifically to post-punk as a genre, such as it is, or even to the immediate post-punk era (roughly 1978–1984, to use Simon Reynolds's definition), although both of those are certainly relevant. Rather, I'm referring to the whole trajectory of things that happened *after* punk—and that couldn't have happened *without* that initial gestalt shift. By the latter half of the 1980s, few of those things bore much of an outward resemblance to what one might consider "post-punk," let alone punk rock in the biblical sense of the term. But as I came to realize in backtracking my way through this era—from Amarillo to *Wiring Dept.* to Subterranean and, finally, the early Mabuhay Gardens era—it was all part of a continuum. In the words of Flipper "fifth fin" Bruno DeSmartass, "There was an explosion, and it went off, and it coalesced in different directions—in strange and ordinary combinations."

As for "The End of the Analog Age," it's worth pausing for a moment to

PREFACE

appreciate that in 1977, the cutting-edge technologies available to underground artists were things like Xerox machines, analog synthesizers (not cheap), and reel-to-reel tape recorders (also not cheap). Through the 1980s, most of the recordings discussed in these pages were still done on eight-track (or occasionally even four-track) machines, with sixteen tracks being a rare luxury. Apart from a few stray DAT recordings, most everything discussed in these pages was recorded on analog tape, up to and including Mr. Bungle's *Disco Volante*. I mention all of this not to stoke debate over the relative merits of digital versus analog audio, but to emphasize that this was simply a different era—a different world, even. In retrospect, it was a brief window in time, this era of pre-internet DIY culture that blossomed with the dawn of punk and proliferated via zines and fliers, records and tapes, dingy clubs on the wrong side of town, and college radio stations on the far end of the FM dial.

All the while, Silicon Valley was laying the groundwork for the increasingly virtual world we now find ourselves inhabiting. That it was doing so a mere thirty or forty miles from San Francisco adds a layer of irony to the narrative recounted here. With the benefit of hindsight, though, it's possible to detect premonitions of things to come, whether in the paranoid visions of Minimal Man, the subconscious ramblings of Ricky Williams, or the apocalyptic themes of Flipper songs like 'Kali' and 'One by One.' It's as if they could sense that this was somehow a last gasp for a certain age of humanity. Yet instead of fear and loathing, the overriding mood was one of desperation and urgency—especially early on, at the turn of the eighties. To paraphrase Flipper's Bruce Loose, "It was the dance to the death at the end of the world."

In his book *Black Sun*, author Geoffrey Wolff writes, "Myth-sellers sigh that the experience of Paris in the Twenties was at a pitch and intensity never again to be duplicated. Reason, and the enemies of nostalgia, argue against such limits and exclusions. Evidence supports the nostalgists." Perhaps you will feel the same way about the (not entirely mythical) era of San Francisco portrayed in this book.

THE PUNK ERA

1.

"THEY WANTED CABARET, AND THEN THE PUNKS CAME"

John Surrell: San Francisco in '74 was pretty much a dead town.

Tony Hotel: At that time in Haight-Ashbury, it was right at the end of the hippie movement. All the stores were boarded up. The people who were left there were, like, some hippies and a lot of junkies and street people.

Tom Wheeler: When I first got to San Francisco in '76, I saw people who'd been in Quicksilver; I saw people who'd been in Jefferson Airplane. They were in these kind of not-very-good bands. A lot of it was like disorganized blues jams. I saw the guitar player for Quicksilver trying to play, like, James Brown-type wah-wah guitar funk stuff—not very well.

Geoff Travis: San Francisco, for me, was this legendary city of Lenny Bruce, of Jefferson Airplane, of the City Lights bookstore. I was so excited about going there. But in fact, when we arrived, there was this massive air of desolation about it. There were the dregs of the Haight-Ashbury scene and, although the park was a great place to visit, the highlight turned out to be a free concert by Hot Tuna.[1]

Scott Davey: There was a huge influence from Marin County—these sort of cocaine/hippie bands. "Laid-back" was the term. It was sort of a self-satisfied, laid-back kind of scene. And not that much fun. Bands like Stoneground kind of personified that. And then there were top forty bands playing on Clement Street,

1   Neil Taylor, *Document and Eyewitness: An Intimate History of Rough Trade* (Orion, 2010).

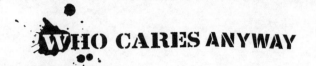

and then if you were even slicker, playing on Union Street. But outside of that, there was little or nowhere to play.

John Surrell: We had a couple of places on Haight Street: the Omnibus and the Cat's Cradle. But there had to have been maybe a dozen places in '74 to park your band. There was nothing. Because I think what had happened was, after the sixties, there was so much heroin and that stuff going on, which we weren't aware of at all when we moved there. We thought, "Well, we're here—this is great." But there was not a club scene at all.

Scott Davey: In the gap between the hippie ballroom years and all the punk/new wave venues that sprung up, there was a real void. Most of the music, or much of it, had corporate backing. Even the Bill Graham opening slots were never given to any kind of grassroots band. They were all corporate-subsidized. And there was also nowhere to rehearse for a grassroots band.

We played at military bases. There were actually a lot of military bases around the Bay Area at the time. We played once at the officer's club at the Presidio. And there was Treasure Island; there was Alameda Naval. And they were more open. At the other clubs, it had to be basically top forty. You might sneak in an original tune now and then if it sounded commercial, but the military bases were more open. You could slip in more originals.

Esmerelda: Right before punk rock was the Eagles. Fleetwood Mac, the Eagles—that was it. *Hotel California*. And that's what punk rock came out of—*that* music. And it was *so* bland—like the sixties and seventies packaged in a safe way and sold back to you.

Bob Steeler: The main rock scene was getting so tired and co-opted by commercial entities. The Eagles can play, and they've got a unique guitar sound and all that, but *so what*. It's just so middle of the road.

Ruby Ray: We did have one magazine called *Psyclone*, and they had pretensions of being—I wouldn't say "underground," but part of the scene or whatever. The disco scene was what was being promoted at that time. But the whole hippie thing was still not even fading out yet. Eagles, the end of the hippies. Hall & Oates. People like that.

THE NUNS AND CRIME

Punk arrived in San Francisco in the latter half of 1976, albeit with little fanfare. On August 19, the Ramones played the Savoy Tivoli in North Beach, where they opened for a comedy troupe called the Duck's Breath Mystery Theater in front of a few dozen onlookers. On Halloween night, Crime debuted before an unsuspecting audience at the Old Waldorf, where they made it through five songs before getting the proverbial plug pulled. And in December, the Nuns became the first punk band to play the Mabuhay Gardens, a Filipino supper club that would quickly develop into the local punk rock mecca—San Francisco's answer to CBGB's.[2]

"The Nuns really kicked it off," recalls Scott Davey. "They had an attack that music hadn't really heard until the Ramones, really." Yet perhaps more important than their actual music was their role in practically willing the Mabuhay punk scene into existence. As the story goes, the group had been trying in vain to get a gig at one of the more established rock venues when singer Jeff Olener came across a flier for the Mabuhay. Intrigued, he decided to approach owner Ness Aquino about renting out the club. "The only night that was available was Monday," he explained in James Stark's *Punk '77*, "because the other nights Ness had Filipino nite-club acts."[3] It took a leap of faith, as drummer Jeff Raphael recounted in the same book. "We rented out the Mab and printed up a couple of hundred tickets, and we just walked

2   The precise date of this show is seemingly lost to the sands of time. However, the December date is referred to in a few different sources, including *Punk '77* and the first issue of *Search & Destroy* (published in June of 1977). The Nuns' appearance at the Mabuhay was preceded by a November 1976 show by Mary Monday and Her Bitches, a sort of punkish burlesque group. It may have been a flier for the Mary Monday show that caught Olener's attention.
3   Stark, *Punk '77: An Inside Look at the San Francisco Rock 'n' Roll Scene* (RE/Search, 1999), p. 12.

around North Beach, saw people who were interesting-looking and just gave them tickets."[4]

While the Nuns were the first punk band to play the Mabuhay, Crime was the first SF punk band—indeed, the first one on the entire West Coast—to make a record. Their self-released debut ('Hot Wire My Heart' b/w 'Baby You're So Repulsive') was actually recorded before their Halloween debut at the Old Waldorf. Decades on, it is still an anomaly. Whereas the Nuns sound to modern ears like a competent band playing recognizably punkish music, the early Crime records still sound jarring. What stands out most about the first 7-inch is the sheer gall it took to make it. 'Hot Wire My Heart' sounds like the New York Dolls as interpreted by the Shaggs, with drummer Ricky Williams dropping beats left and right but somehow continuing unperturbed. ("We couldn't afford to go back and redo 'Hot Wire My Heart,'" bassist Ron "The Ripper" Greco later explained.[5] "Ricky really fucked up in the beginning but then he really came in hard.")

"I remember when that came out," says Bob Gaynor, who, like Williams, lived south of San Francisco in Palo Alto at the time. "Ricky gave me one, and I was like, 'This is the worst fuckin' thing I've ever heard in my life.' In retrospect, years later, it kind of grows on you, I guess. The band got better after that."

The Sleepers' Michael Belfer had a similar reaction. "At that time, in 1976, to make a record—that was something only artists signed to major labels did. The whole idea of DIY and making your own record was really new. So we were like, 'Let's hear it! Let's hear it! Put it on!' So he put it on, and it was the worst fucking thing I'd ever heard. They are out of tune; Ricky's timing is horrible; it's sloppy; it's a fuckin' trainwreck; they're all over the place. And I actually thought there was a rule: 'You can't make a record like that! You're not even in tune!' As if there was some *law*."

Crime's debut at the Old Waldorf was met with similar bewilderment. Their performance was part of a political fundraiser where they shared the bill with a mime troupe "dressed like Fruit of the Loom characters—like fruits and vegetables," as Sleepers bassist Paul Draper recalls. Crime singer/guitarist Johnny Strike would later recall playing to an audience consisting largely of "gay

4   Stark, *Punk '77*, pp. 13-14.
5   Michael Lucas, "Crime: San Francisco's First and Only Rock 'n' Roll Band." *Ugly Things* #14, 1995. http://www.dementlieu.com/users/obik/arc/crime/int_ut14.html

politicos [and] some people in wild fruit costumes and maybe ten friends of ours up front ... our friends were dancing and enjoying themselves, but a lot of people were running for the exits."[6]

At the time, everyone in Crime except for Ricky Williams was already pushing thirty years old. Even so, they often come across like teenagers playing dress-up in front of the bedroom mirror—and based on Johnny Strike's description of his early home rehearsals with fellow guitarist/vocalist Frankie Fixx, that wasn't far from the truth: "We had one mic taped to a bookcase, and one of us would sing and play rhythm guitar while the other made stabs at primitive lead guitar."

In those days, the duo were calling themselves the Space Invaders, and in keeping with the glam rock theme, Fixx took to "wearing a self-designed space suit complete with a battery-powered flashing belt." When they changed their name to Crime a year later, their look changed with it. Gone were the spacesuits, and in their place were various combinations of police outfits, leather jackets and caps, sunglasses, and gangster suits. Intentionally or not, their look reflected something of their surroundings—namely, the gay leather scene on Folsom Street's "Miracle Mile," not far from their South of Market rehearsal studio.[7]

More importantly, they looked good in black and white—the default medium of photographers like their friend James Stark, whose iconic images of the band are as central to their legacy as any of their recordings. He even accompanied the band to their first recording session—where, according to Johnny Strike, "Stark took some pictures of us recording, wearing headphones, and standing behind the board where it looked like we knew what we were doing." They didn't, of course, but they didn't let that stop them.

Scott Davey: There was a little bit of, "Wait a minute, they don't even know how to play." I mean, like, Crime were a terrible band to begin with. They got better

---

6   Ibid. All additional quotations from Johnny Strike are also taken from this source.
7   This stretch of Folsom Street was "one of the most extensive and densely occupied leather neighborhoods in the world" during the 1970s, according to Gayle Rubin ("The Miracle Mile: South of Market and Gay Male Leather, 1962-1997" in *Reclaiming San Francisco: History, Politics, Culture* [City Lights, 1998]). Several key punk locales—including Iguana Studios and the 1183 Howard Street apartment described in Chapter 4—were located on or near this part of Folsom Street.

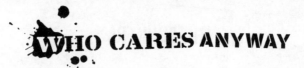
later, but to me, they were agonizing to hear. But a lot of the bands just had such a creative concept. I mean, Crime had a brilliant image. They dressed and looked the part. Their image was so solid that it kind of overcame their lack of musical ability.

Rozz Rezabek: Crime were kind of like poseurs. I mean, they had enough money to buy cop uniforms to wear onstage. And they had these siren lights that they would turn on. They weren't really well-respected in the scene. They really could play their instruments pretty good, and they *looked* cool. But people saw right through that. They wanted *new*; they wanted *wild*; they wanted outside the lines.

Debi Sou: Crime wasn't really punk. For me, they were more like a rock band with an image. And punks, to me, were people who weren't even that polished. They didn't even *have* an image. They were just kind of being weird. They were being themselves, so there wasn't an idea of, "Oh, we have to have an image."

Bruno DeSmartass: It was all costume, no content. But the thing was, that was just an elemental part of the scene back then. They were just early. So you can't disregard a band like that, even though they suck.

Paul Draper: Well, they were not the best musicians in the world. But I mean, I liked their feel. I liked what they were doing. I enjoyed them.

EDEN

"You might think it is impossible that a 'family-style supperclub' could exist in the heart of North Beach, where the topless still reigns supreme—and yet, there it is: The Mabuhay Gardens, at 443 Broadway, owned and operated by Ness Aquino, whose philosophy is simply: 'If you can't show it to children, don't book it.'"
—*San Mateo Times* (January 3, 1975)

THE PUNK ERA

MABUHAY CALENDER FEB 1977 – "THERE WEREN'T VERY MANY PUNK BANDS THERE BECAUSE THERE REALLY WEREN'T ANY." – JEFF OLENER, THE NUNS

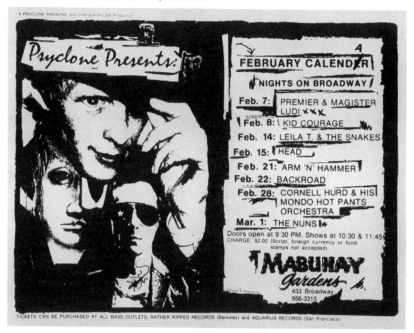

TICKETS CAN BE PURCHASED AT ALL BASS OUTLETS, RATHER RIPPED RECORDS (Berkeley) and AQUARIUS RECORDS (San Francisco)

By the spring of 1977, the Mabuhay had begun to open its doors to other punk bands—although apart from Crime, the Nuns, and the occasional touring act like Blondie or the Damned, the pickings were initially pretty slim. As the Nuns' Jeff Olener put it, "There weren't very many punk bands there because there really *weren't* any."[8]

In the meantime, the club played host to a motley assortment of acts, ranging from hard rock (Magister Ludi, Killerwatt) and power pop (Kid Courage, the Nerves) to oddball, yet not-quite-punk outfits like Novak, Mary Monday, and Leila and the Snakes. By the fall of 1977, however, the club was advertising "punk rock shows nightly from 11 p.m.," and there was no shortage of new bands to fill the calendar.

8   *Punk '77*, p. 13.

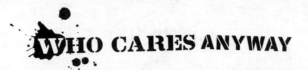

WHO CARES ANYWAY

Peter Urban: You first had Nuns and Crime, and that was pretty much it. I mean, you did have some others, but they weren't really major forces. And then the Dils and the Avengers were the next round, if you will. And the Readymades, I guess. Then after that, you get Negative Trend and the Sleepers and UXA. So it's still early, it's the early punk scene, but it's different phases of development, if you will.

Peter Belsito: Things moved really fast. I was what I would call a second generation to that scene. When I got to the Mabuhay, most of the people there knew each other already. There was already a thing going on, and I was kind of on the outside of that. It was before the Dead Kennedys but after the Nuns and Crime. I mean, I saw very early shows—I'm not sure how early, but I saw very early shows by the Mutants, the Avengers, Negative Trend, and the Sleepers at the Mab.

John Surrell: The Mabuhay was kind of like a place where you could take your new band and park it there. It was easy. But it was also like the alternative place to be. It was not like one of the established clubs that Bill Graham ran. You didn't have to be like a real legitimate, working, signed band. So the Mabuhay was a great place to be *because* of that.

Jeff Olener: What I loved about it is that it scared most of the regular people away because it was too bizarre for them, and it wasn't being hyped by the papers all the time. There was no media coverage at all. We made it totally unique, and no one knew about it. It was a well-kept secret, except for a few hip people. And for the first six months of 1977, it was fabulous because it was like your own private scene you had created.[9]

As the scene materialized, some unlikely benefactors emerged. Along with Aquino, there was Dirk Dirksen, a former TV producer who took over management of the Mabuhay's late-night bookings in the spring of 1977.[10] "He really wasn't out of the

9   Ibid.
10   As Dirksen explains in *Punk '77*, he had been involved with booking live acts at the Mabuhay on Monday and Tuesday nights as far back as 1974, but these were not rock bands. After the first Nuns show, *Psyclone*'s Jerry Paulsen took over booking punk/rock acts for a few months before Aquino and Dirksen nudged him out of the picture,

music scene," emphasizes writer Brad Lapin. "He was out of the TV scene—the old 1960s TV scene. He'd been around that long."[11] Dirksen not only booked the bands but also played the role of emcee—and his rambling introductions and announcements quickly became part of the show, whether audiences liked it or not. "He would be like, 'Get out of here, loser,'" recalls Mia Simmans. "He would come up and just be the bastard, and everybody would go, 'Fuck you!' And he'd just go, 'Yeah, tell your mama.' It was perfect. Couldn't have been better."

Dirksen's role as lead carnival barker was a product of both his showbiz background and the unexpected success of the new music. "They wanted cabaret, and then the punks came," summarizes Debi Sou, a dancer who sometimes performed across the street at the El Cid. "They made more money on the punk shows at eleven than they did on the cabaret. But I think Dirk was going for cabaret. That's why he liked it because he could do his little emcee bit, his little comedian skits. And the punks would go for it, because they liked art, and for them, 'Ah, it's all art.'"

NORTH BEACH, SEARCH & DESTROY, AND THE GHOSTS OF COUNTERCULTURES PAST

Long before punk came to the Mabuhay, North Beach had a reputation as a decadent nightlife hub. In the 1860s, the area was part of the so-called Barbary Coast, where prostitution, gambling, and opium dens thrived along a notorious stretch of nearby Pacific Avenue. In 1964, the country's first topless bar, the Condor, opened at the corner of Broadway and Columbus, and it soon had plenty of company in that department.

Yet the neighborhood wasn't merely a haven for sin and vice. In the 1950s, North Beach served as ground zero for the Beatnik movement, and by the early

citing erratic behavior on his part.

11 In a 1978 interview, Dirksen discussed plans to begin work on a TV show based out of the club (Michael Goldberg, "Punk Rockers," *SF Examiner*, September 3, 1978). The show came to fruition, but a similar idea would take root several years later in LA in the form of Peter Ivers's New Wave Theatre.

1960s, it was also home to prominent jazz clubs such as Basin Street West and the Jazz Workshop (both on the same 400 block of Broadway that the Mabuhay later occupied). As filmmaker Craig Baldwin explains, it was all still in the air, so to speak. "North Beach is drenched in Beat—or, you could say, *Bohemian* culture. Beyond the subculture of the Beats is this idea of living a little bit differently and not a bourgeois life and not a married life. Maybe living in a single-room occupancy and spending time in the cafes."

The Beats may have been old news by the 1970s, but there were still tangible reminders of their presence. Chief among them was City Lights bookstore, which made headlines in 1957 when it published Allen Ginsberg's *Howl*, prompting an obscenity trial. Two decades later, both Ginsberg and City Lights owner Lawrence Ferlinghetti would chip in $100 apiece as seed money for a new publication, *Search & Destroy*, which a City Lights clerk named Val Vale was busy assembling with the aid of an IBM typewriter in the store's upstairs office.

Ruby Ray: I think I met Vale in the early summer of '77. I was working at Tower Records, but the punk scene was so under the surface at that time that I didn't really even hear about it. I used to see Vale around North Beach, and I always wondered who he was. And then one day he came into Tower Records, and he had this stack of magazines, so I just ran after him, and I found out that he had put out the first issue of *Search & Destroy*. So that's pretty much how I found out about everything.

Richard Peterson: I had a job at a photo studio on Broadway, which was very close to the Mabuhay Gardens. I used to hang out at City Lights bookstore every day. While I was there, I met Vale. He told me that there was this new thing going on at a club down the street, and he was going to make a new magazine because he didn't know of anyone else making a magazine about it.

Search & Destroy published its first issue in June of 1977, and like the Mab, it quickly became part and parcel of the scene. Its role in both chronicling and curating punk in San Francisco—the look, the attitude, and the influences—can hardly be overstated. Along with LA's *Slash*, it alerted the rest of the world to the existence of West Coast punk, well before any of the bands were able to tour or put out records with any kind of widespread distribution.

THE PUNK ERA

Vale himself was the focal point of one of the first local newspaper exposés on the nascent punk scene, an October 1977 article in the *Examiner*. The piece's author, Ira Kamin, mentions Vale's past life as an organist for Blue Cheer during the Haight-Ashbury era before expressing bewilderment at his enthusiasm for the new music: "It's so loud that it's a white noise. So, of course, there's no discernible melody. No words. Just this very tense noise."[12] Describing the crowd at a recent Ramones/Nuns concert, Kamin adds, "This is not a drugged, barbiturate audience. No reveling in the mind and marijuana and psilocybin." Whether one was pro- or anti-punk, the shadow of the hippies and the 1960s counterculture still loomed large.

Denny DeGorio: Even though it was punk rock, it was kind of an extension of the hippie scene, in a way. I mean, there was something uniquely San Francisco about it. It was accepting.

David Swan: A lot of people in SF circumvented glam and disco and went directly from psychedelia to punk.

Richard Peterson: In the beginning, there were people who looked like they were right out of the sixties. If you look at my audience shots, it was all over the map. There was every kind of person there is, and there's no uniform look. People didn't know that they were supposed to follow anything yet. They just thought they were supposed to be themselves and do-it-yourself and be crazy and wild and free. It's the same as the root of the sixties and the same as the root of the Beat era. So all these things tie together. But they had a different personality. To me, they were each an evolution of something that was missing from the one before.

Esmerelda: The whole thing was a reaction to the sixties. I mean, a lot of us *were* hippies. And there was this whole period of time where people would go around—when people still had hair—and at parties, they'd cut your hair off at the parties. I had a 14-inch ponytail that got cut off at a party. It was like, "You can't be a hippie anymore. That's over. We're in the new world now. The new world is short

---

12 Ira Kamin, "It Started with Iggy Pop." *San Francisco Examiner*. October 2, 1977.

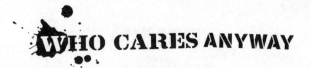

hair, bleached hair, looking like a zombie robot." Which made sense at the time. It was this sense that all that romanticism had *failed*. We'd believed in all of that, and we felt like suckers. Everybody was really angry, and all that anger came out in the music. Like, "Fuck that. Fuck *you*." But the thing that was so great about it was that it had such a great sense of humor. It had an enormous sense of humor.

Peter Belsito: I never felt negative about the Summer of Love. When I got to San Francisco, I had long hair. And it was gone within a year. I came back east to see old friends, and they said, "I knew your hair would be short, but I didn't think it'd be *that* short." The Summer of Love was a huge influence on my going to San Francisco in the first place. I had been to San Francisco before, in like '72. And I'd been down around the Peninsula, and the whole hippie thing was in full rage, especially down on the Peninsula. But I didn't come back again until '77, and that was all discredited by then. All the hippies had become businesspeople.

Denny DeGorio: As a kid, growing up near San Francisco like I did, I was really excited by the message of the whole hippie thing and the idea of revolution and all that. And as I grew up and that whole scene kind of turned into a cash cow for Bill Graham, I felt kind of cheated. I felt like they did a bait-and-switch on me. You know, they sold me revolution, but I ended up getting some bill of goods, some bullshit. I kind of saw 'em as sellouts and hypocrites. For some reason, we were young and knew it all, of course, and I thought *we* were gonna change the world.

Peter Urban: I think it's important, in terms of the various underground music movements that have followed the punk rock scene, to recognize the role that late-seventies punk rock played in just tossing out everything and allowing for these new forms to come in. It's not like no one else had been doing experimental music or whatever. You can cite all sorts of examples: Beefheart, the Stooges, the Velvet Underground. And that's why those frequently get credited as being grandfathers of punk rock because they didn't fit into any milieu of the day. But there wasn't really an organized movement, if you will, at the time. With punk rock, you had groups across the country and around the world, frankly, that were sort of putting forward the same *kind* of rejection of the mainstream, and it paved the way so that new things could emerge from it.

2.

"WE DON'T PLAY, WE RIOT" FROM GRAND MAL TO NEGATIVE TREND

Craig Gray: A friend of mine who was gay came to San Francisco, and he met Don Vinil and this guy Rico. Don said he needed a guitar player, so my friend called me and said, "This guy needs a guitar player." So I moved down with a guitar and 300 bucks.

Don Vinil: I met this guy from Canada who had a friend up in Vancouver who played guitar. So he wrote him, and he came down—Craig—and he and I and Vale, who later started *Search & Destroy*, picked up the pieces and started rehearsing. We had Todd for our drummer. Our first rehearsal was in his bedroom. He threw open the doors, and it turned into a street party. We all had a real good time. [13]

Craig Gray: Vale rehearsed with us. He never actually did a show with us. But he also gave me the instructions on how to write a song, which was "intro, verse, chorus, verse, chorus, middle eight, verse, chorus, outro," according to Vale. That was the songwriting formula … which I immediately threw out the window.

Don Vinil: Well, Vale quit because of *Search & Destroy*, and Jimmy from the Avengers introduced us to Will Shatter. He played three-string bass. We got this crummy little place to rehearse three times a week, five hours a day.

Will Shatter: I bought this guitar from Sears for $17. And I didn't know how to play it, but I was trying to learn. And I would go to the Mabuhay and tell people

---

13 *Damage*, Vol. 1, No. 5, pp. 26–29. All Don Vinil quotes in this chapter are drawn from this article.

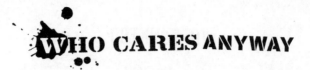

that … I could play guitar, and that I wanted to get a band together. And I was trying to get a band together. And … finally, Jimmy from the Avengers knew a band that wanted a bass player, and he told them to get in touch with me and that I would be willing to learn, but I didn't know how to play. I thought, "The only way I'm gonna hear any music I like is to play it myself."[14]

Craig Gray: When I first met Will, he couldn't play anything at all. He bought his first bass from this guy Linwood, who was the bass player for UXA. And then I started showing him root notes, and we went from there.

Debi Sou: I was kind of impressed with Will and how he developed as an artist and a musician from the early days when he really had to count "one two three." He just didn't have a good sense of timing. Craig always had to really work a lot.

Don Vinil: We rehearsed for about a month and got a twenty-minute set together. These friends of mine were having a party South of Market, which we decided to debut at. I was doing a movie with Penelope (Avengers) at the time, so I went there, changed my clothes, and threw on my makeup and stuff. Everyone who was anyone was there, all the bands and everyone coming to check us out 'cause we were like the first second-wave band to come out.

The aforementioned show—which took place on October 2, 1977, at the Safes, a makeshift storefront venue near Eighth and Howard—was one of just three that Grand Mal would play during their brief existence.[15] They didn't leave behind any recordings, and if not for the band members' subsequent endeavors, they

---

14 *In the Red* (1978, unfinished). Directed by Liz Keim and Karen Merchant.

15 As Gray recalls, Danny Furious from the Avengers sat in on drums at that first show. ("He'd never heard the songs before. But you know, punk rock.") The other two Grand Mal shows both took place at the Mabuhay: an October 27 date opening for the Avengers and the Dils and then a November 7 slot opening for the Dead Boys. Rozz recalls making his debut with his soon-to-be-bandmates at the latter show. "Don only wanted to sing half the set with Grand Mal. He was saving his voice because they thought they were gonna get a shot to open for Iggy Pop. Fat chance. He was okay with me doing a song, but I just was overeager. I didn't let Don finish. I gave him the bum's rush from the backstage area at the buffet and shoved him off stage and grabbed the microphone. Counted out '1-2-3-4' and started singing."

would scarcely be remembered at all.

Yet, in hindsight, the lineup was a remarkable assemblage of (admittedly raw) talent. It was also a good example of the strange bedfellows who sometimes found themselves as bandmates in the pioneering days of punk. "Craig was living in Don's house when I met him, and he moved in with me the next day," recalls Debi Sou. "Craig really wanted to get away from Don. Don was gay, and Craig wasn't. He had no money and no place to stay. So he kind of had to deal with Don every day, which wasn't easy for Craig."

Debi Sou had recently moved to town from Portland, and she persuaded a few of her friends—two fellow burlesque dancers and a tall, lanky musician named Rozz Rezabek—to follow suit. As Rozz recalls, "I was kind of like living as their houseboy [in Portland] and helping them around the house, and they were like, 'You should start a band.' Then when they decided to move to San Francisco, I moved with them. So I moved in right at the same time as Craig was moving in, into a little one-bedroom apartment on Pine Street."

Debi Sou: At one point, Will was living there, Rozz was living there, Craig was living there, two of my girlfriends—everybody was living there. But it was just a two-room flat.

Rozz Rezabek: I think it was the first or second night I was in town; Chip and Tony Kinman [of the Dils] came over. We had a little amplifier, and I had brought down a Flying V guitar, and then there was an acoustic guitar there. And Chip and Tony sat there with us—with me and Craig and Will, Debi Sou, Pam, probably Jimmy Wilsey, and a few other people—and started playing 'She'll Be Comin' Round the Mountain When She Comes.' And they had all these punk rockers singing along. It was like, "Oh wow, this is *all* there is to forming a band?" It was kind of like a folk song singalong. The Kinmans, way somewhere in their background, have a little bit of Pete Seeger and Woody Guthrie in 'em. They've got some real folky roots.

Debi Sou: I met Craig on Halloween in '77. But I had seen him in Seattle and in Vancouver at an Alice Cooper show. Because he was also into this glitter thing. A lot of the pre-punks were into the glitter thing.

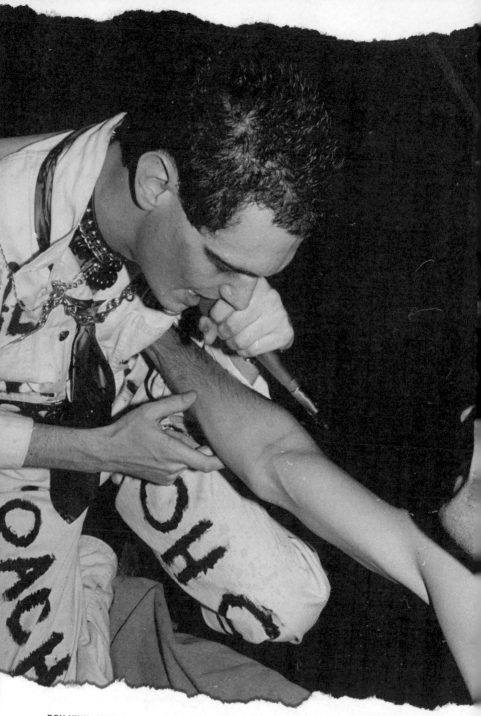

DON VINIL, LEAD SINGER FOR GRAND MAL. VINIL WOULD GO ON TO FRONT THE PUNK/REGGAE OUTFIT THE OFFS. PHOTO BY JAMES STARK.

THE PUNK ERA

Craig Gray: I was totally a little glam rock kid. I was really into Alice Cooper when I was fourteen. I saw the *Billion Dollar Babies* tour when I was fifteen. And then all the English glam rock stuff. I saw Slade when I was a kid. But Mick Ronson was the main guitar influence. And probably Glen Buxton and Michael Bruce from Alice Cooper would be the other two guys who were most influential. I wasn't really into all those sixties guitar hero dudes—you know, Hendrix, Clapton, all that stuff. Jimmy Page. My hippie uncle listened to that shit.

Debi Sou: So I walked into the Mab, and then there was this guy that was also at these other shows that I had been to all up and down the West Coast. I was like, "Oh, who the hell is that?" He had been a model for Crazy Colors when that first came out in San Francisco. You had Vidal Sassoon, and they were the first one who did Crazy Colors. So he had his hair in four colors. At the time, that was kind of amazing. In '77, that got a lot of reaction from people.

Rozz Rezabek: Debi Sou came from a working-class family. She was always the hardest worker and the most together, who kept food on the table and got us all to get the apartment rent together somehow. She was the rock of Negative Trend.

Debi Sou: It seems to me that I bought all their clothes—Will's too—but I bought all Craig's clothes at the Goodwill. That's what I did a few times a month. I would go to the Goodwill, and then I would come home with bags of stuff.

ENTER WILL SHATTER

Will Shatter grew up about an hour south of San Francisco in the towns of Gilroy (home of the annual Gilroy Garlic Festival) and Aptos. Yet he also spent part of his teenage years in London, where his father—an executive in the frozen food industry—had relocated for work. Will (or Russell Wilkinson, as he was still known at the time) attended high school at the American School in London, where he may have encountered the early stirrings of punk but definitely encountered some radical political ideas that were at odds with his well-heeled upbringing.

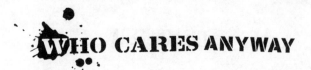

WHO CARES ANYWAY

He turned twenty-one in 1977, which made him several years older than his bandmates in Negative Trend.

Rozz Rezabek: It was funny because he was from Gilroy, but he tried to hide that fact, even from me. I didn't make any pretensions about where I was from, but he had been over in England, so that made him one up on all of us.

Debi Sou: I think Will, the exposure of Will and his adventures in England and his whole outlook on things, was a bigger influence on Craig than anything else. Because Will influenced all of us—me too. He had this really personable, human thing in him. He could get along with women, but he could get along with guys really well, too. He was just such a normal, friendly guy. He had so much empathy for people. Yet he had this really sharp, cynical, political edge to him—a very dark, dark edge to him.

Rozz Rezabek: I used to call him "the blueprint," because everybody would meet Will, and they'd be taken under his spell. If he had wanted to be evil, I have no doubt in my mind; he could have been like a Charles Manson or something. He had that kind of sway over people.

Peter Urban: Will had been, when he was in London, with the IWW—the Industrial Workers of the World—which is an anarcho-syndicalist group, so he was already orientated towards anarchism. I come from a left-communist background—like left of Leninism, in other words. We're closer to the anarchists. So we got along well politically.

Michael Belfer: Will was very well read, and he had some people who kind of mentored him. They were from Situationist International—SI. There actually was a chapter on the West Coast. It's the same world that Malcolm McLaren came out of.

Rozz Rezabek: Peter Urban was a fairly intelligent, educated guy. And Will—Will could talk the talk. But Will was more like me: he had all the good books by Nietzsche and Camus and everything on his bookshelf, but he hadn't read 'em. He just bought 'em at garage sales.

"I THOUGHT, 'THE ONLY WAY I'M GONNA HEAR ANY MUSIC I LIKE IS TO PLAY IT MYSELF.'" – WILL SHATTER. PHOTO BY JAMES STARK.

WHO CARES ANYWAY

Michael Belfer: I just remember Will talking about this couple. He would talk about going to these meetings with Paula and … the husband.

The couple, John and Paula Zerzan, were the founders of a small anarchist collective known as Upshot. Like Vale, John Zerzan had experienced the Haight-Ashbury era firsthand and was a good decade older than Shatter and company. Nonetheless, they hit it off, with the Zerzans enthusiastically imparting their ideas on Situationism and related topics.[16] "That was the whole context for some of us," says John. "The Situationist element and their critique, their style, their writings: if you were looking for the radical thing, that was what was going on. And then punk, which was its own thing."

As with the Sex Pistols and Malcolm McLaren, the influence of Situationism on Negative Trend wasn't so much theoretical as it was aesthetic.[17] "The Situationists, I think for punk people, probably had a graphic sense that was appealing," notes Brandan Kearney. "And of course, they were into street actions and graffiti of one sort or another and taking comic books and putting new dialogue in. All of this stuff was kind of DIY."

As Rozz recalls, he and Will were sitting up late at night making propaganda collages with the Zerzans when they stumbled on their new band name.[18] "I had a picture of a curfew bust at the Mabuhay, and then I took a headline from another story that said, 'Where America's Youth Is Headed,' and then another thing from the fashion page of the newspaper that said, 'The Trend Is Obvious.'

16 Upshot, in turn, was one of several Situationist-influenced groups in the Bay Area at the time, along with the Berkeley-based Bureau of Public Secrets as well as For Ourselves, whose 1974 book *The Right to Be Greedy* Zerzan cites as a major influence.
17 In Jon Savage's *England's Dreaming*, McLaren describes his encounters with Situationist magazines in the early 1970s: "The text was in French: you tried to read it, but it was so difficult. Just when you were getting bored, there were always these wonderful pictures, and they broke the whole thing up. They were what I bought them for: not the theory." (p. 30).
18 Debi Sou recalls things differently. "At one point, Craig's father came to visit us in San Francisco. This is like in '77, right when Negative Trend was just forming. And they needed a kind of logo. Craig's father made that logo, the arrow pointing down. Craig's father was a teacher. He really wanted to understand what this punk thing was. So I thought that was pretty cool, that his father would come and stay in our flat for a week or ten days or something and then get this whole idea about what was this whole punk thing was all about."

THE PUNK ERA

We drew the Negative Trend symbol sitting around that night. 'Negative Trend.' That was the name."

PUNK, POLITICS, AND NEGATIVE TREND

"The most important thing is to play for kids that aren't into anything, hate school, hate their parents, hate working, hate everything. Those kids have a lot of energy." —Will Shatter[19]

Negative Trend was just one of several politically charged bands in the early SF punk scene. Among the others were the pro-communist Dils ('Red Rockers,' 'Class War'), the anthemic and vaguely revolutionary Avengers ('We Are the One,' 'The American in Me'), and the conspiratorial UXA ('Paranoia is Freedom'). This is to say nothing of the Dead Kennedys, who came a little later. "The LA scene was much less political, much less in-your-face political," says Brad Lapin, who moved to San Francisco from LA in late 1977. "Politics was *not* considered cool. In San Francisco, it was considered very cool. You had *very* political bands. And the scene was very political. It was very utopian."

Exemplary of this utopian spirit was the Miners' Benefit, a two-day concert for striking coal miners held at the Mabuhay in March 1978. With the exception of Crime, practically every band in the scene showed up to play. "At the same time," notes Peter Urban, "when Negative Trend played—if you've seen the footage—Rozz starts off by basically insulting the working class.[20] So punk politics was never very straightforward. It's not like you're joining a left-wing party or something like that. It was a different sort of animal.

"I mean, mostly what you had was a sense of vague unease," he continues. "The punk scene was all about being outsiders. There was no positive reason to

---

19 *Slash*, July 1978, p. 14.
20 The 1979 short film *Louder, Faster, Shorter* (directed by Mindaugis Bagdon) is made up of footage filmed during the Miners' Benefit, although Negative Trend does not appear in the video. However, the audio portion of their set is included on the later compilation CD *Miners' Benefit* (along with UXA, the Sleepers, and Tuxedomoon).

go into it. It basically branded you as an outsider, and it made it difficult for you to succeed, quite frankly. So people who went into the punk scene in '76, '77 were people who were already at odds with mainstream society for one reason or another. It need not have been political. It could have been any number of

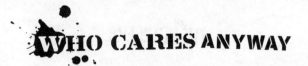
WHO CARES ANYWAY

things. But they were definitely at odds with mainstream America."

Adds Zerzan, "It was so nihilist that you couldn't really put a label on it." The nihilism and unease were by no means limited to the punk scene, either. The dawn of punk coincided with the tail end of a decade's worth of revolutionary political violence in the Bay Area, ranging from the Weather Underground (which maintained two safe houses in San Francisco during the early 1970s) to the Symbionese Liberation Army (which formed in Berkeley and made national headlines with the 1974 kidnapping of Patty Hearst). Then there was the New World Liberation Front, an amorphous group responsible for dozens of bombings from 1974 to 1978—most of them targeting public buildings such as power plants and courthouses, but at least a few of them aimed at local politicians. (While there were no casualties, there were some close calls: one bomb exploded in the front yard of a supervisor's neighbor, while another blew up a district attorney's car in his own driveway.)

The New World Liberation Front was the subject of an early Negative Trend song, simply entitled 'NWLF.' Will Shatter wrote the lyrics, which allude to a couple of September 1977 bombings, suggesting that the song was written soon afterward. If so, it would have been one of his earliest songwriting attempts, and the lyrics tend to bear that out. "They're gonna blow you up / Blow you up, blow you up / New World Liberation Front / I hope they blow you up" goes the song's chorus.[21] Clumsy lyrics aside, the song reflects something of Shatter's mindset at the time. Metaphorically, at least, there was a blurring of the lines between punk rock and revolutionary politics, between art and violence. This theme is underscored in a 1978 interview in *Slash*. "I'm not gonna do this forever," he says in response to a question about whether he considers himself a musician. "After it gets too easy, it won't be very interesting. I'll have to save up my money and buy a gun and become a terrorist."[22]

It was the sort of bluster one could still get away with back then. "In the

---

21 The recording appears on the Miners' Benefit compilation, which was recorded on March 20 and 21 of 1978. Coincidentally, the last known NWLF bombing occurred a week prior, on March 14. According to *Days of Rage* author Bryan Burrough, "a communiqué expressed support for a coal miners' strike" (p. 354).
22 As if to underscore the point, another early Negative Trend song was entitled 'Groovy Terrorist.'

24

THE PUNK ERA

seventies, the terrorist groups or the underground groups were kind of the *rock stars*," explains Rozz, putting his old bandmate's remarks in context. "Carlos the Jackal, people like that. Whereas Will and the people we hung out with, it was pretty lightweight."

Negative Trend caused enough trouble onstage to make any such extracurricular activities superfluous. The group quickly developed a reputation for its chaotic and, yes, anarchic live shows, which at times resulted in very real damage to life and limb. At one show, Rozz was maced by a fan. At another, he was doused with lighter fluid and almost set on fire before a Mabuhay doorman intervened. And at yet another, he went onstage with a broken arm, having left the emergency room earlier that evening without being seen by a doctor so as not to miss the gig. Taken together, these incidents reflected not only the increasingly rowdy audiences the Mabuhay was starting to attract but also the singer's willingness to put himself in harm's way for the sake of—what was it, exactly?

Bruce Conner: His very first gesture on the first night as the first chord was struck was to run full speed off the stage, land on the tops of the front tables, grab drinks out of people's hands, throw 'em down on the floor, and kick the chairs over.[23]

Will Shatter: Dirk's always saying to us that this isn't reality, that it's a theater of illusion. Like he'll tell us, "You put out too much for that show; you should have held back and teased the people." He treats it like pure theater, but we don't approach it that way. We go through this shit all week to get on stage so we can do as much as we can to bring chaos and disorder for our little half hour.[24]

Rozz Rezabek: When I was in Negative Trend, I was just moldable clay—to the Upshot people, to Will, to the crowd. "Who can be more outrageous? If the crowd's gonna do something crazy, well, I'm gonna do something crazy. Someone's gonna jump on stage and do something? Well, I'm gonna jump on *them*."

23 *Damage*, August/September 1979, p. 8.
24 *Slash*, July 1978, p. 14.

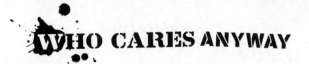

WHO CARES ANYWAY

When I finally had the nerve to ask Dirk about getting paid, he pulled a file out of his desk, and he said, "This is just a bill for microphones, for furniture, for tables and chairs, and for sundry items." He said, "You'll be playing here for another year before you're even with me." Because there was just so much destruction at the Negative Trend shows as they became more kind of antagonistic. It went to a *strange* place.

WINTERLAND

A mere month after Negative Trend's debut at the Mabuhay, they were added to the bill for the Sex Pistols' much-anticipated appearance at Winterland on January 14, 1978. The Trend was one of three local groups on the bill, along with the Nuns and the Avengers. "It's a mark of San Francisco's acceptance of punk that it's the only city [on the tour] that can come up with genuinely punk opening bands," wrote Noel Monk in *12 Days on the Road*, a chronicle of the Pistols' ill-fated American tour. It would have been Negative Trend's fourth ever show had they actually played.

Craig Gray: The night before, Will and Rozz went down to Winterland and spray-painted "Negative Trend" all over it. Then the next day, Malcolm asked Howie Klein, who at the time was a local critic and DJ—he hadn't started 415 Records yet—who the most outrageous band in San Francisco was. And we were, at that moment, kind of crazy, so he suggested us. So Malcolm decided he wanted us to play after the Sex Pistols.

Rozz Rezabek: Do you know what it's like to be seventeen years old and have Malcolm McLaren and the Sex Pistols on the radio, saying, "We're not gonna play unless Negative Trend headlines"? It was a very exciting thing in our lives. For thirty years, I'm thinking, "Wow, because we're such good anarchists or because we've got such a great cohesive band." No, it was because [McLaren] went to Howie Klein and said, "Who's the worst fuckin' band in town?" And Howie said, "Negative Trend, hands down."

THE PUNK ERA

Craig Gray: So we showed up at the show. Bill Graham was *furious* at us for spray-painting on the building. Malcolm got us all in somehow and gave us backstage passes. So we started to drink, and Malcolm and Bill Graham spent most of the evening arguing about letting us onto the stage.

Malcolm McLaren: They said, "We wanna play," and I said, "You're fuckin' right, you're fuckin' gonna play," and this cunt in charge of the stage said, "No, they can't go on, Bill Graham is professional, it's only these bands." … Fuck this professional crap. I said, "Find the cunt [Graham] and bring him." Eventually, he came up to me, and I said, "This band wants to go on, they're here, they're more important than the Pistols 'cos they're from this town, they should be taking over this shitty old joint." He said, "Okay, they can go on stage, but they'll have to go after the show." Great, they're gonna top the show! That was the whole idea. They would end it.[25]

Craig Gray: Then, just as the Sex Pistols were about to end, Malcolm took us all and marched us up to the edge of the stage, where Bill Graham was standing with a bunch of Hells Angels.

Malcolm McLaren: At the end, I said, "Listen, now this band is going on," and he said, "Well, I'm sorry, but everybody's leaving, it wouldn't be any good … " and there's all the bullshit of all these old assholes coming on stage to clear it up, the equipment, all that crap.[26]

Craig Gray: Bill Graham said we weren't getting on the stage, and Malcolm said, "Okay," and that was pretty much it. So we didn't get to play. But now I hear that we *did* play. I hear all sorts of stupid stories, but that's pretty much it.

25 *Slash*, May 1978, p. 14.
26 Ibid.

CRAIG GRAY ONSTAGE WITH NEGATIVE TREND. PHOTO BY JAMES STARK.

BLACK AND RED

The original version of Negative Trend lasted longer than Grand Mal, but not that much longer. By April 1978, Rozz had returned to Portland, mostly to recover from the litany of injuries he'd sustained diving around onstage. His tenure with the band lasted all of five months—an action-packed five months that included the non-appearance at Winterland, a brief Pacific Northwest tour, and a dozen or so shows at the Mabuhay. "It was like a supernova," says the singer. "It was a zenith."

With Rozz out of the picture, the band turned to Mikal Waters, an Australian native with a sedated crooning style. Meanwhile, Steve DePace was brought in to replace the enigmatic Todd Robertson on drums. It is this version of the band that appears on Negative Trend's self-titled EP, recorded that June at a low-budget studio in South of Market (just around the corner from the storefront space where Grand Mal had debuted the previous fall). Needless to say, it was their first time in a professional studio, and it was also the first time the studio had played host to a punk band. "We were told Todd Rundgren had built it, but the only guy we dealt with was a hippie dude named Stu, who was the engineer," recalls Gray. "We gave him *Aladdin Sane* to listen to and said, 'Yeah, kind of make it sound like that if you can.' And he did a good job. I mean, it was well recorded, well mixed for the time. Mikal paid for the whole thing. I think it cost him 300 bucks in 1978, which would have been a lot of money because no one *had* any money."

Released that fall, the record shows a band that had progressed by leaps and bounds in the few months since the Miners' Benefit (at which point none of the songs on the EP were even in their setlist).[27] Of the four songs, Shatter wrote the lyrics for two of them: the topical 'Mercenaries' and the more poetic

---

27 The record was originally released via Heavy Manners, a one-off label operated by a friend of the band, Debbie Dub (who later managed Flipper for a short time). It has since been reissued several times, including a 12-inch vinyl version (with the new title *We Don't Play, We Riot*) on Subterranean in 1983; a CD release on Henry Rollins's 2.13.61 imprint in 2005; and finally, a reproduction of the original 7-inch on Superior Viaduct in 2013.

'Meathouse,' which is either a metaphor for the entertainment industry ("I took a look into that meathouse / They package all our heroes there") or a reference to a certain apartment basement (more on which later; see Chapter 4). Though Shatter's best songwriting was still to come, 'Meathouse' in particular reveals a marked improvement over the likes of 'NWLF.'

Musically, however, the key track is 'Black and Red.' Built around a repeating, almost geometric riff, the song chugs along at around 100 beats per minute—not exactly dirge material, but still a good twenty BPM slower than anything on, say, *Never Mind the Bollocks*. "I think seeing the Sleepers had a lot to do with that—realizing that slower tempos were good as well," acknowledges Gray. In turn, both the song's discordant guitar breaks and bleak, self-loathing lyrics anticipate elements of Black Flag's *My War* by several years. More relevant to our narrative, the song's main riff directly inspired Flipper's '(I Saw You) Shine,' itself an influence on the later Black Flag as well as sludge mavens like the Melvins.[28]

"This goes all the way into a true-to-life nihilism that is the only alternative to arsenic in the morning coffee," wrote Chris Desjardins in a review for *Slash*, whose readers subsequently made the EP a staple in the zine's top ten chart. "If you can take it, better than anyone had any right to expect."[29]

28 Introducing '(I Saw You) Shine' at one of Flipper's early Sound of Music gigs circa 1980, Bruce Loose matter-of-factly says, "Craig, you've been ripped off."
29 *Slash*, March 1979.

3

LITTLE RICKY

"You're born to die. The minute you're born, like, old age just sets in. Oh well, it's part of life."—Ricky Williams[30]

Peter Belsito: Really, when you saw the Sleepers, you saw these guitarists, and you saw Ricky. I mean, Ricky *sounded* like David Bowie—in his best moments. He was obviously influenced by David Bowie.

Tommy Antel: He was really good. He could go through the rapids of a river and make it look fluid. He could be so fucked up and still sing, and it would be like, "How'd this guy do this? The words must be coming from a subliminal god into his brain because, obviously, his brain is not working." It was like a Morrison-type thing. The guy was really incredibly talented.

Tim Lockfeld: He was just kind of a fixture in Palo Alto. He was glam; he was glitter; he was … whatever was before punk rock. But he was also—with that mop of hair—kind of a throwback to the Beatles' look. The missing Beatle, Wrongo.

Ruby Ray: Ricky had such an incredible voice. He had a very strong presence, too, but he was … touched, I guess you could say. He would always swing the microphone—like swing it in a real big circle. So it was always dangerous to be up too close to the stage when the Sleepers were playing because Ricky could be unpredictable.

30 *Ego Magazine*, No. 7, 1983.

WHO CARES ANYWAY

Connie Champagne: Back then, the hangout at the Mabuhay was the girls' bathroom. Everybody kind of hung out there. So I met him in the girls' bathroom, and I said, "I thought your show was really good," like a seventeen-year-old from Sacramento would say. And he said, "Fuck you! Who the fuck are you?" I didn't know him at that point. I just thought, "Man, I just said something nice to you." He got right in my face, and I said, "Well, fuck you. You're just a dime-store imitation of Iggy Pop. Nobody cares about you."

Ricky Williams: I really hate when people say that about Iggy Pop. I've gotten that one too much … I don't like Iggy Pop at all.[31]

31 Ibid.

THE PUNK ERA

Connie Champagne: He followed me all over the Mab. He kept asking, "Why do you think that? Why do you say that?" I said, "I didn't mean anything by it. You're just being an asshole. I was trying to pay you a compliment." Then he was sorry about it and had some lucidity to talk to me about it. And then, of course, he tried to put the moves on me.

Paul Draper: Ricky was hanging out with Iggy Pop when Iggy was on one of his benders—one of his extended lost weekends during that period.

Connie Champagne: Ricky dated De De Semrau for a while, from UXA. But she was also dating Iggy Pop at the time. That's why he got so upset with me when I called him an Iggy Pop imitation. Apparently, De De would make Ricky get in the backseat and have Jimmy get in the front.

KOWALSKY

De De Troit: When I met Michael … he was mostly with people like Ricky from the Sleepers and hanging out on Polk Street at the Raven a lot and basically trying to get into a lot of trouble. He seemed to really like being notorious. He liked having a reputation of getting into the most fights. He'd run up to some fag on Polk Street and say "faggot, faggot, faggot" and just go wild trying to get this guy to really take him on. Because Michael didn't care if he got the shit beat out of him or not—it didn't matter to him. Mostly he knew that people would *not* take him up on it, so it didn't matter.[32]

Michael Belfer: Kowalsky was a real scenester. He didn't play any instruments, but he was super knowledgeable about records and different music styles. I mean, Kowalsky was the one that introduced us to all the music that we started listening to once I started hanging out with Ricky, which was John Cale, Eno's

32 *In the Red.*

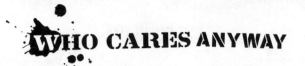

solo records, the Stooges, a lot of reggae. Kowalsky was really into reggae. He was always on the tip of what was going on with these different dub records, so he introduced us to dub. He acted as a big cultural influence. He'd throw a lot of stuff in front of us. And seriously, he wanted to influence us. That was his whole agenda. And some of it did influence us, and other stuff didn't.

Bob Gaynor: He was just kind of the non-musician jokester who looked like those guys. I always thought of Ricky and Draper and Kowalsky and a guy named Clem Smith as the guys who all sort of had a nexus look. Leather jackets, but not motorcycle jackets. A little Mick Jagger, a little Iggy Pop, a little Paul McCartney. I mean, he was sort of a cool guy, but he was also an asshole frequently, too.

Rozz Rezabek: He'd come up with ideas like prank calling the CIA. The guy would look in the white pages and find the FBI's number and call them from different telephone booths and stuff. I mean, insane stuff.

Tommy Antel: Michael was really an incredible antagonist. He and Ricky would get into it. They'd be fighting over this or that—kind of like when you see little kids fighting over a toy or something. They were just these antagonists. And a lot of times, it was their way of self-actualizing. But they were very talented.

"SOMETIMES, HE WAS VERY, VERY NUTS"

Tim Lockfeld: I don't know how close anybody gets to Ricky, but I would spend time with Ricky and do things with Ricky and have madcap adventures with him. One of several people I know where you go, "Wow, I'm hanging out with this really cool person who I admire," and then at some point during the event, you go, "Oh fuck, I wish I wasn't here."

Debi Sou: Sometimes Ricky came off really psycho. Like, he would come up and say, "I'm gonna kill you," and he'd walk off. But you'd just laugh and say, "Oh, that's Ricky." We had a lot of fun times with Ricky, too. But often, he was slobbering in the corner because he was so inebriated. Slobbering or puking, or he's got some dribble, drooling. I mean, it just didn't look attractive. But when he got on stage, he could perform. He had something—something to show people. But offstage, he just seemed often like a stupid idiot.

Rozz Rezabek: Ricky would walk around with the Satanic Bible for weeks on end and come right up to your face and say, "I'm gonna kill you," for no reason whatsoever. He would pick fights with Black guys for no reason whatsoever. You would always see him running down Polk Street with somebody chasing him. Or he'd try and buy drugs when he didn't have any money. He'd just get the drugs and throw 'em in his mouth and swallow 'em and then not bust out any money. People would beat him up, but he didn't care. He'd just lay there, loaded.

Boris Zubov: One thing that Ricky Williams was very much known and hated for is, he would spit at people. He was very intense, especially backstage. If you got in his way and you did something wrong, he would spit at you. My claim to fame is that Ricky Williams never spit at me.

Tommy Antel: Sometimes, he was very, very nuts. I mean, I saw him with this one nurse/girlfriend who left him in the car just a few minutes too long, and I came out, and you see his little pointed boots kicking her windshield out. He was left in the car too long, not in the car seat.

Paul Hood: The first time I met him, actually, was when I was with the Enemy, and we stayed at Howard Street. I think we were just arriving or something, and this kind of vampirey guy was sort of floating up the stairs. And then the guy who everyone paid rent to sort of said, "Oh, no you don't!" Next thing I know, Ricky's flying down the stairs.

Richard Peterson: I went to a lot of parties with him—the afterparties and all that. I remember he was kind of annoying in some ways because, at the parties, he would want to be the DJ playing the records on the turntable at the party, but he wouldn't play anything for more than fifteen or thirty seconds.

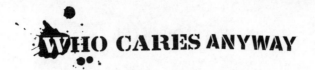

He'd start a song, and then he'd rip it off and put on another one, over and over again. That was his way of deejaying.

Sari Gordon: In his room, he listened to songs over and over: John Cale's 'Mr. Wilson,' Arthur Lee and Love, Syd Barrett—over and over. We'd go to parties, and he'd do the same thing until someone would get fed up with him hogging the turntable.

Michael Belfer: I just loved listening to Ricky deejay because he was so passionate about music. I mean, that was the whole thing Ricky and I clicked on, was that we both had an immense amount of passion for music. And Ricky was a *fanatical* Beatles fan. He loved the Beatles.

Tim Lockfeld: He'd say, "Listen to this song. What do you think? This is *fantastic*. I love this." I mean, he had very eclectic taste. I remember he was into this Thomas Dolby song, 'One of Our Submarines Is Missing'—something I didn't expect him to be really into.

Paul Hood: Ricky always wanted to play and record. It's what he wanted to do *all* the time. When you didn't want to do it, he would still hang out and bug you. He'd say, "Can I, uh, just use your tape recorder?" "Okay, Ricky, but do you have any of your own tape?" "Yeah, yeah." Not necessarily true.

Ricky Williams: I was in the hospital for asthma a lot, then I was in a mental hospital for a nervous breakdown. I had to rest … It was fun. I had my stereo there and this piano—I played piano and listened to records every day.[33]

Paul Draper: I don't know how long that lasted. They used to have the seventy-two-hour holds and then sometimes like a two-week hold for evaluation. I'm not sure. Maybe Michael Kowalsky also had that. I think I remember when he went in, but it was not for very long. It's not like he was institutionalized for a year or

---

33 *Search & Destroy #1-6*, p. 137.

anything like that. It's more like the police wanted it until they could figure out what to do with you.

Sari Gordon: I remember thinking he was super vain and not as crazy as he pretended to be. I have a Polaroid I took of him, and he used a pen to fill in a spot where good bangs weren't covering his forehead.

Tommy Antel: He was on SSI [Supplemental Security Income]. There was kind of this game where him and Raymond and all these people would just go in and know how to act lethargic.[34] Like, Raymond went in there, and he carried in an ashtray with a dead bird in it and just sat in the guy's office. And then he finally got SSI.

If you went in there really loaded, they weren't gonna give it to you. You had to act like you were mentally ill—not like, you know, an *addict*. So they all had these plans to just go in there and stare at the window. They'd just act nuts. After a while, the psychiatrist who was doing the evaluation would just say, "Give this guy a check—retroactive!"

Connie Champagne: Ricky told me that the time he spent in a mental hospital was all an act so he could get on SSI. I don't believe that. I think he *told* people that to have less embarrassment, to look like he was more in control. But you know, schizophrenia generally attacks people in their late teens, early twenties. That's when schizophrenia onset generally happens.

Boris Zubov: I can't say that he was a schizophrenic, but he sure acted like one. He could be the sweetest guy in the world, but he could also be the biggest asshole within moments. Never to me, but I saw that change of him just like becoming manic.

---

34 This is the same Raymond who later wound up sharing an apartment—and an informal meth-dealing operation—with the Nuns' Richie Detrick and the Sleepers' Michael Belfer circa 1984. The saga is recounted in Belfer's memoir, *When Can I Fly?* (HoZac Books).

WHO CARES ANYWAY

Connie Champagne: There was no question that he was diagnosed schizophrenic. My mom was a social worker in the state mental health system and absolutely checked that out. It was *not* an act. And I saw it. There are a lot of people who would argue with me about that, who would say it was an act. But I spent a lot of time with him, and I can tell you that it's not an act. He absolutely was damaged. Deeply damaged.

Paul Hood: Everyone was in awe of him, but people who got close to him would get pissed off because he was so needy. It was just a part of who he was, I guess, or what he was going through. I don't even know. He'd come up to you, and he'd tug on your sleeve or something, and then he'd get right in your face—"Hey, hey"—and then say what he was gonna say. It was like, "Yes, Ricky. Got it. I understand."

Connie Champagne: He was, in my opinion, probably the most charismatic and one of the most gifted people I've ever met, but he didn't have any survival skills whatsoever beyond learning how to con girls out of things. But you could see it. He would just self-medicate. Or even if he wasn't on drugs, you could see his schizophrenia just come over him.

THE NURSES

Johnny Strike: We started keeping Ricky prisoner before shows. We'd deliver him to Ripper's place in the Excelsior, where he lived with his parents in an old house which was full of clocks which Ripper's dad collected. Ricky hated going there; he'd always look terrified when we'd drop the two of them off.[35]

Paul Draper: Ricky was always, like, a problem. That's why he had these girlfriends who would drive around and make sure he got to the places he was supposed to be. Which they would nickname his "nurse," his "nurses."

35 Lucas, "Crime: San Francisco's First and Only Rock 'n' Roll Band." *Ugly Things* #14, 1995.

THE PUNK ERA

Michael Belfer: Ricky always needed a guardian. And a lot of the time, he had a girlfriend who played that role. "The nurses." They came and went. So those nurses, whether they realized it or not, were in kind of a partnership with me. *They wanted Ricky to be successful, so they would do what they could to protect him.*

Connie Champagne: When you say "nurse," it's not a nurse like a person who's an RN. That's not what it is. It's a person that's a caregiver because he can't drive or hold a job or pay a bill. He could barely wipe his ass—let's just put it that way.

Paul Draper: His childhood and home life was kind of messed up. And he wasn't like a rich kid. A lot of the other artists were kind of like upper-middle class. Ricky's grandmother, who doted on him—she had a comfortable middle-class existence. A lot of times, he would just go to his grandmother's house to recover because his parents were kind of messed up in different ways.

Michael Belfer: He would always go on about how his father had been institutionalized, but I never had any proof of that. That was never corroborated. His father was a sweet guy. Reputed to be bisexual. He was a really great singer. But he never really did anything with his singing.

Sari Gordon: I "dated" Ricky for a couple months. Lived with him and his mom in an apartment in Mountain View or Sunnyvale. He had an iguana. His mom had just started going to AA and was telling me all about it and was calling her sponsor and showing me all her new books and medallions. She was really shaky. He spent a lot of time in his room playing with his hair in the mirror. *Nosferatu* was playing at the Varsity, and for a long time, he wore a long, skinny black trench coat and held his hands like Klaus Kinski.

Connie Champagne: His mother was kind of like a crazed alcoholic. Beautiful woman at one time. Both his parents were beautiful. I mean, his dad looked like Clark Gable. They were great-looking people. But they just were a mess.

And Ricky's mom didn't want me to like his dad. So this is the story she told me. I'm sitting there on the couch; she's smoking cigarettes and drinking instant coffee. I don't know where Ricky is—probably in his room listening to records

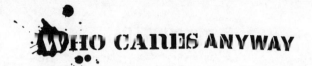

or something. She says, "Well, you should know something about Ricky's dad."
And I said, "Oh, really? Like what?"

Well, when Ricky was about four, he really wanted this snake at the pet store, and the parents had agreed that he was too young to have it. And they got into some sort of fight in the ensuing weeks, and then she ran off to her mother's trailer to sort of take a break from the husband. She left Ricky with his father to take care of him for the weekend, and then when she got home, he had that snake in his room, with a little cage and everything. She said, "I thought your dad and I agreed that you couldn't have this. What happened?" And he describes to her how he walked in on his dad getting a blowjob from some guy—like some strange guy. Which is *really* traumatizing, of course. And his father told him, "If you promise not to tell your mother, I'll get you that snake tomorrow." You know, Freud would have a field day with this.

4.

SEVENTH WORLD
INTRODUCING THE SLEEPERS

A s punk was raging at the Mabuhay, a different kind of revolution was quietly brewing some thirty miles to the south in Silicon Valley, as the area had recently come to be known.[36]

Much like punk, the ideas percolating in Silicon Valley were still obscure, if not totally unknown, to most ordinary Americans. The occasional newspaper report on the growing technology hub would invariably refer to newfangled concepts like "semiconductor" and "microprocessor." In an early 1978 interview in *Search & Destroy*, Sleepers guitarist Michael Belfer gave Vale a similar sort of briefing: "Down where we rehearse—it's called Silicon Valley because the Santa Clara Valley has the most advanced technology in the world as far as computer chips go. The biggest company that makes them, the world's largest distributor, is right by our studio—SILICONEX. All this technology in such a small, concentrated area!"[37]

Even before the advent of Silicon Valley, the Greater Palo Alto area had long been a hotbed of research and development—much of it funded by the likes of the CIA and the Pentagon—on phenomena ranging from LSD to artificial intelligence. It was also home to the Menlo Park Veterans Hospital, the inspiration for Ken Kesey's *One Flew over the Cuckoo's Nest*. Evidently, the utopian futurism that drove the computing revolution went hand in hand with an undercurrent of barely concealed madness.

Yet, for all that, everyday life in Palo Alto was peaceful and prosperous. "Palo Alto has a very liberal artistic community, but it's sort of a shell within itself,"

---

36 The term "Silicon Valley" began appearing in print as early as 1969, though it was not widely in use until the late 1970s.
37 *Search & Destroy #1-6*, p. 138.

explains Boris Zubov, who, in those days, was a DJ at KFJC, an influential college radio station operating out of nearby Sunnyvale. "It's so easy to not want to go anywhere from there because, especially in the mid-seventies through the early eighties and into the nineties, we had everything you could possibly want: great restaurants, an amazing nightclub called the Keystone Palo Alto. But what started happening was, the bands in Palo Alto started getting restless and started going up to the city, the Sleepers being one of the first ones that did that."

The Sleepers had something of a head start, given Ricky Williams's early involvement in Crime. Prior to that, he and bassist Paul Draper had been jamming together in Palo Alto and occasionally heading up to the city during the pre-punk glam days. "We were going up to the Polk Street area when I was in my glam band, Trigger," recalls Draper, who first met Williams at one of Trigger's shows circa 1975.[38] Unbeknownst to them, their eventual bandmates—Belfer and drummer Tim Mooney—had already been rehearsing together in a nearby garage for a couple of years by that point.[39]

Michael Belfer: I worked in an ice cream parlor on University Avenue, and Ricky came in one day. He wore a black leather jacket, and he just had that look: he looked like a rock musician. But to me, he looked like a great lead singer.

So finally, one day, we started talking more, and he invited me to come and

38 Tom Wheeler: "Polk Street had a very kind of runaway, street-urchin, guys-and-girls-selling-sex kind of thing. Miz Brown's was a coffee place on Polk Street where you'd see these guys who very much looked like they had just stepped out of *Ziggy Stardust*. I moved to town in 1976, and I saw some of the same guys hanging around that scene start showing up at the Mab playing in what became new wave and punk bands. I think that's a thread that's not recognized sometimes in what made up the Mabuhay scene."

39 Ricky made his last appearance with Crime on March 3, 1977, at the Mabuhay, where they opened for Blondie. He was subsequently booted as a result of his increasingly problematic drug use and general unpredictability—traits he would not outgrow with time. Johnny Strike: "The drummer for Blondie offered to play drums for our set. Ten minutes before we were supposed to go on, we started running through our songs for him; two minutes before we went onstage, Ricky showed up looking stoned (as usual). I can't remember if we were any good or not, but I do remember halfway through the set, in the middle of a song, not hearing any drums and looking back to see Ricky walking off the stage. We kept playing to the end of the song and then stalled for a bit. Eventually, much to our relief, Ricky walked back onstage as though nothing had happened. After the set, he told me that he had had to shit" (*Ugly Things* #14).

THE PUNK ERA

jam with him and Paul Draper, who was the bass player. Ricky was playing drums, and Paul was playing bass and guitar. So I went over and played with those guys, and they really liked my playing and wanted to keep doing it. And I somehow convinced Ricky, "Look, I've got a drummer that I've been playing with for years. Why don't we bring him in, and you try singing?" And I finally convinced him to do it. And that's how the Sleepers came together—the initial version of the band, the four of us.[40]

40 While Belfer recalls having to convince Williams to sing, Draper remembers things differently: "Ricky was already doing vocals when I was rehearsing with him and writing songs, even before he was in Crime. So no, I don't think he was planning on singing and playing the drums or anything like that. When Tim and Michael came around, we just said, 'This is great.'"

WHO CARES ANYWAY

Paul Draper: He and Mooney were still in high school together. They weren't going to that [Mabuhay] scene yet. They were playing hard rock—Montrose, Camel, that kind of stuff—when we met them. They were so young that they just kind of evolved right into it. Putting those two things together kind of made our sound because Ricky and I were coming more from punk rock, Iggy Pop, David Bowie ...

Debi Sou: When the Sleepers came on the scene, everybody kind of slowed down, which was kind of nice. They weren't playing particularly fast, "boom boom" punk music. They weren't the Avengers; they weren't the Dils. They had a whole new thing going.

Ruby Ray: The Sleepers were incredible. They were a different kind of sound. And San Francisco had so many different sounds. In the very beginning, it was more the hard, typical, what you would say was a "punk" sound: the Dils, the Avengers. And as time went on, more elements came in. The Sleepers had a very dreamy, psychedelic sound. I mean, they just sort of drew you in.

Rozz Rezabek: That was the *bands'* band. Everybody in every band loved the Sleepers, and we'd all go to their shows.

Denny DeGorio: I was a big fan of the Sleepers. I thought they were just the greatest fuckin' thing. I loved their sound. And the first thing I loved about Michael was his guitar tone and his style. It was like, "What *is* this fuckin' guy?" It was like Robert Fripp or something. From my perspective, it was real cutting edge, real unique, real different. It was punk rock, but it was kind of intellectual, in a way, like avant-garde jazz is.

It's just five songs, but the Sleepers' self-titled EP gives some indication of why they were so revered. It also demonstrates a range that was unmatched by any of their Mabuhay-era peers, at least on record. The opening track, 'Seventh World,' is a veritable mini-epic, careening its way through multiple tempo changes without a traditional verse or chorus to be found. 'Flying' incorporates some heavy flanger effects that give it a pronounced acid rock flavor (hardly a fashionable sound at the time). 'She's Fun' is a nasty Stooges-type rocker, only with interesting chord changes that seem to flirt with atonality at points. And the closing track, 'Linda,' is a languid, strung out ballad that showcases Mooney's swaggering drum fills as well as the singer's "crazy highwire approach," as Joe Carducci would later describe it.[41] The main guitar riff consists of literally one note, which wavers ever-so-slightly out of tune as it hangs in the air.

"Howie Klein, who had a radio broadcast on Friday nights, would play that song, and it would just come out of nowhere," recalls Connie Champagne, referring to 'Linda.' "I remember thinking, 'That's the weirdest thing I've ever heard.'" The song is apparently directed to an ex-girlfriend, although, as with most of Ricky's lyrics, it's less about narrative than it is about fleeting phrases and images—"Your mother's okay till she starts taking drugs again," "I'm so tired of trying," "It's just a look in your eyes"—that take on a life of their own thanks to his haggard, disheveled style. Says Champagne, "When I heard that as a teenager, I just went, 'I know exactly how you feel.' And I believed he knew exactly how I felt. There was something so haunting and so magnetic about it."

"I mean, nothing *touched* that," says Tim Lockfeld of the EP. "And that wasn't just because of Ricky; that was because of that combination of people. And that includes Paul, and that includes Tim, and that includes Michael, and that includes Ricky. And that includes the *time* that everything was bubbling up from. I'm sure everybody thought, 'This is just the beginning, and we'll look back and say, *This is terrible*.' But that shit was gold. They would play things differently all the time, and they'd have different versions of these songs and different incarnations of them. And certainly, lyrically, Ricky would go off on tangents all the time. But he kind of got the essence of each one of those songs."

For all that, the EP might not have seen the light of day if not for the efforts of Draper, who started his own label, WiN Records, in order to release it. He also made use of the photography lab at the Stanford Research Institute, where he held

---

41 In his book *Enter Naomi: SST and All That* (Redoubt, 2007), Carducci notes that it was none other than Rozz Rezabek who turned him on to the record. Both of them were living in Portland at the time, and Rozz would frequent Renaissance Records, the store where Carducci worked. "I remember the only record he ever bought at Renaissance was the Sleepers EP. He was so stoked to see it and said later he'd played it all day long, so I checked into it more seriously and saw he was right. I still listen to it often." (p. 166).

a day job as a graphic designer, in assembling the cover art. "He was like the dad sort of figure," says Champagne. "He made the first single for them happen. He definitely kept it together." In his own words, Draper was "like the Johnny Ramone of the band. I kind of get in trouble because I'm not really left wing."

"He was kind of the odd man out back then," adds Lockfeld, a close friend and unofficial roadie for the band in those days. "He was the only right-handed person in the band. But he was also a little bit older than us. He was the only one who actually had a job. He was the one who put up money for basically everything. And Paul held things together to make that record happen. It never, never, never, never would have happened without Paul."

SISTER BANDS

Like Negative Trend, the Sleepers were haunted by a combination of bad luck, bad karma, and at times plain old bad decision-making—traits that would continue to haunt many of the key band members well into the future. The superstitious among us might even reckon that they were cursed, or perhaps that they were channeling a sort of dark energy that was more powerful than any of them could have realized at the time.

In any event, the fates of these two bands would remain closely intertwined for years to come, long after they'd broken up. "They were kind of like a sister band, in a way," says Draper, referring to Negative Trend. Part of it was timing: both bands made their Mabuhay debuts in December of 1977, and they went on to share the stage with one another on several occasions, including a June 1978 appearance at the Whisky a Go Go in LA (as part of "Mabuhay Night"). Apart from Draper, they were also younger than many of the other bands on the scene, with several of them—including Belfer, Mooney, and Craig Gray—still in their late teens at the time. Besides, as Gray notes, "There weren't a lot of bands then, so we all knew each other and all went to the same parties after gigs."

Many of those parties took place at 1183 Howard Street, where Gray and Debi Sou had recently moved (after they and the rest of the Negative Trend crew were

THE PUNK ERA

evicted from their one-bedroom apartment on Pine Street).[42] The leaseholder at 1183 Howard, Brian Campbell, was an Art Institute dropout-turned-speed dealer who cohabited with his girlfriend, a six-foot-tall, roller-skating goddess who went by the name Suzi Skates. There were also plenty of visitors, invited and otherwise. "It was next to a detox center," notes Debi Sou, "and sometimes the alcoholics would walk up the stairs, thinking that it was the detox center." A few doors down, at the corner of Eighth and Howard, was Club Baths, a gay bathhouse that would feature in some sordid headlines during the height of the AIDS crisis.[43] The apartment's basement—which may have inspired the lyrics

---

42 The apartment at 1183 Howard was directly upstairs from the Safes, where Grand Mal played their first show in October of 1977.

43 A January 15, 1984, article in the *San Francisco Examiner* noted that "gays jokingly refer to the 8th & Howard site of the libidinous facility as 'AIDS and Howard.'" It is also mentioned in Randy Shilts's book *And the Band Played On* (Penguin, 1987): "About 3,000 gay men a week streamed to the gargantuan bathhouse at Eighth and Howard streets, the Club Baths, which could serve up to 800 customers at any given time" (p. 23).

to Negative Trend's 'Meathouse'—had evidently played host to some decadent activities in the past as well.[44]

Joann Berman: I got that house through my uncle's friend. I remember he told me, "Never to go to the basement." And then we broke the door open, and there was like a gay torture chamber down there.

Debi Sou: Downstairs was a fetish room. It had been fixed up. I remember there was some kind of bed, but almost more like a hospital bed. There was all this laughing gas there, so we would go and do the rest of the laughing gas.

Craig Gray: One bathroom had a special shower thing with places to put manacles, so you could handcuff people in the shower. Apparently, before, it was owned by some rich gay doctor. There were even little foot places in the shower to put your feet up—I guess for … spreading the cheeks. I don't know.

Debi Sou: Craig and I were always in the bedroom fucking, and it would drive Brian crazy. He would pound on the wall. One time me and Craig were in bed. We weren't loud, but it was pretty obvious what we were doing because the walls were so thin. And Brian shot a fucking sawed-off shotgun through the wall. It was high in the ceiling, so it was over our heads because we were in the bed on the floor. But Brian—that's the meth.

Joann Berman: Brian was dealing crystal meth with the Hells Angels. On the radio, it said that Sonny Barger, who was the head of the Hells Angels, had just

---

44 According to Bruce Loose, "The place below that [apartment] was a fuckin' sex shop, for the first fisting stuff. The stuff that all the swingers are into nowadays. Will used to look through a peephole and watch them fisting each other. I cannot imagine having that as your entertainment—to go and look through a peephole and see these people doing these outrageous sex acts. People are gross enough as it is. That's the type of shit that made him write 'Meathouse.' These are some of the influences. Because he saw that as an extreme, and then he saw his own scene as an extension of that." While some of the details here don't line up with others' recollections (namely, no one else recalls actually seeing people down there, let alone people engaged in sex acts), the gist of the story still makes sense in light of the song's lyrics.

gotten out of jail. I was making eggs, and Suzi was making coffee, and Brian had this fucking sawed-off shotgun at the kitchen table. And Brian got really nervous because he owed the Hells Angels money. And then the radio comes on and says, "Sonny Barger's been let out of Alcatraz"—or San Quentin or wherever he was.[45] And Brian got nervous.

Suzi Skates: There was always a Hells Angels mist surrounding Brian. I never knew exactly what it was; I just heard about it. The whole thing was just crazy. You never knew what was real and what wasn't. I can verify that Brian was a speed dealer, and he dealt with all kinds of shady people. And there was always a lot of drama—but stuff I didn't want to know about.

Craig Gray: Brian's room was painted all black with a silver ceiling. I think it might have had a black carpet. Then our room was red with a red carpet. There was a long staircase that came up. It was a big flat. There were a lot of parties there after the Mabuhay.

Joann Berman: Scott Covert had lived there before. Scott was doing these paintings where he'd go through magazines and cut out—all the people in the magazines, he'd cut their eyes out and do collages with the eyeballs. So it was Chinese red with eyeballs everywhere.

Craig Gray: One of the rooms had a great big table in it, and everybody would sit around that table doing little projects. Brian would give everybody some speed, and they would sit around doing little projects all night. And then me and Michael would disappear into the Chinese red room and play guitars with each other while everybody else was making projects. That's how we wrote [the Sleepers'] 'She's Fun.'

By the summer of 1978, Belfer and Will Shatter had moved into an apartment on Bayshore Boulevard in the remote Bayview neighborhood. At first, the scene was

---

45 Barger was released from Folsom Prison in early November of 1977. ("Uncertain Future for released Sonny Barger." *Berkeley Gazette,* November 4, 1977.)

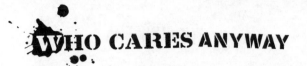

idyllic (especially compared to 1183 Howard, where the "Hells Angels mist" was growing a little too thick). As Belfer recalls, "Will's father was the vice president of Schilling-McCormick spices at that time, and as a housewarming present, he had bought us this super-deluxe spice rack that contained all the Schilling-McCormick spices. We used to play records and hang out and have listening parties. It would go late into the night—people just discussing music and politics and culture. It was a really great hangout for a while." Before long, however, things took a darker turn, culminating in a series of events that resembled the climax of a true-crime thriller.

Suzi Skates: There was an incident that happened at that place that was *really bad*. It involved guns and hostages. It was really bad.

Craig Gray: One night, me and Will were sitting, having dinner, and some dude kicked the door in—this giant dude, named Tiny, of course—and he had a gun. He goes, "You guys are cool. Don't worry. I'm just looking for Michael's stuff." They said, "Where's his guitars?" And they picked up some guitars. I said one of Michael's was mine, so he left that one. He said, "Oh, that's cool, man, don't worry." I mean, he was pretty cool to us. You know, he had a gun—he could do whatever he wanted. And then he just took Michael's stuff and left the front door in pieces.

Suzi Skates: Nobody really told me the details of what happened. But every time I drive by there, it brings up a darkness in my head. It makes me shudder. I know that Michael's girlfriend was going to nursing school, and she had a job at Silver Crest Donut Shop. She was still allowed to go and do her shift at Silver Crest, but she had to return. They were like being kept *hostage*.

Paul Draper: Well, I think there was like a drug deal gone bad, basically. That's what I recall. I think they stole Michael's Les Paul to pay for the drugs, and then he stole their car back in retaliation. That's how I remember it. And then they came looking for him, and he had to go back to Canada—where he's from,

Toronto.[46] Tim and I left, and that pretty much broke up the band. Because the drugs were out of control. It gets kind of exhausting trying to take care of Ricky and then, you know, getting Michael away from heroin dealers and stuff. I never really had any problem with Tim. Maybe Tim wanted to get away from the drugs. I'm not sure how many drugs Negative Trend was doing, but probably less than the Sleepers.[47]

The Sleepers' loss was Negative Trend's gain. Right around the time Belfer left town for Toronto, Mikal Waters quit Negative Trend.[48] The singer's departure, in turn, led Gray to make another move. "Mooney was not playing with anybody," he explains, "and there was *no way* I was gonna not play with Mooney if he was available. So I took the opportunity to make that change when Mikal quit."[49]

Both Mooney and Steve DePace were above-average drummers by punk standards, but their styles could have hardly been more different. DePace would eventually find his true calling in Flipper, where his dependable backbeat provided a foundation for the chaos swirling around him (especially live). Mooney, on the other hand, had a looser, more fluid style and an almost painterly touch.

46 The exact dates are hazy, but it would have been after August 12—when the Sleepers and Tuxedomoon shared a bill at the Mabuhay—and before October 27, 1978, when Pere Ubu played the Horseshoe Tavern in Toronto (a show that Belfer recalls attending). *Slash* mentioned the breakup in a September 1978 gossip column, noting that the Sleepers "may have chucked it quits because the band got fed up with Icky Ricky hitting them on the head with his microphone stand" (p. 5).

47 Less than the Sleepers, perhaps, but still quite a bit. Rozz offers a telling anecdote, one that takes us back to late 1977, when the early Negative Trend contingent was in the process of moving out of their apartment on Pine Street. "I go in there, and I look, and the entire inside of this one-bedroom apartment—I mean every square inch— is spray-painted, written on with marking pens and Marks-A-Lot pens, down to ink pens: 'GIVE WILL SPEED.' 'GIVE WILL SPEED.' 'GIVE WILL SPEED.' Spray-painted in five different colors across the big wall. I swear, the entire apartment, down to the hardwood floors. Will got in there and must have taken some herculean dose and had nothing to do."

48 Waters went on sing for a few other bands, including the short-lived Fillmore Struts (with guitarist Fast Floyd, formerly of the Offs and, before that, Mink DeVille) and the Soul Rebels (with Hilary and John Hanes, aka the Stench Brothers, on bass and drums), before moving back to Australia.

49 Evidently, Gray did not explain the move to DePace. "I thought everything was going great, but then, and I still don't know why, Craig decided to break up the band," the drummer admitted in a 2019 interview with *Fear and Loathing*. "I asked Will about it, and he just said, 'I don't know, but every so often, Craig likes to clean house and start over again.'" http://www.fearandloathingfanzine.com/flipper.html

A DIRKSEN - MILLER PRODUCTION

SLEEPERS
STRAYS & NOW

Thurs May **4** 11pm

MABUHAY
Gardens

TICKETS CAN BE PURCHASED AT ALL BASS OUTLETS and AQUARIUS RECORDS   443 Broadway San Francisco

"Mooney was a *stylish* drummer," emphasizes Bob Gaynor, who played drums in the Palo Alto band Half Church and briefly tried out as a replacement for Mooney in the Sleepers. "He was almost like a cross between a sloppy Bill Bruford and John Bonham in some ways." There was also a little Keith Moon in Mooney's extended fills on songs like 'Linda' and 'Sister Little' (the latter of which appears in a live version on the *Miners' Benefit* CD and in the short film *Louder! Faster! Shorter!*—the only existing footage of this lineup). "The drum breaks that Tim does on 'Sister Little' are above what anyone else was doing," gushes Draper. "That song is written so we have these dynamic pauses where the instruments aren't playing, except for the drums."

Mooney and DePace were also rather different personalities. As part-time Flipper bandmate Bruno DeSmartass puts it, "DePace was mostly interested in trying to get from one song to another, and one gig to another, with the least amount of hassle. 'Cause he plays 'the pace.'" Mooney, in contrast, was soft-spoken and often unpredictable. "Tim was very sensitive," says Tim Lockfeld. "At the same time that he was buying the Clash, he was buying Fleetwood Mac, *Rumors.* He was really open to all kinds of music. And he would show his feminine side. At his memorial, I said, 'The closest thing I ever had to a romantic relationship with another man was my relationship with Tim.' Tim was that way with everybody." Adds Debi Sou, "Tim Mooney was such a creative drummer, such a good drummer. He always came late; he never came to rehearsal. You never knew if Tim was coming or not. But when he was there, he could work his magic like nobody else. He could just come in and do it."

As for the Sleepers, they would reemerge in 1979 and again in 1980 (see Chapter 14), but the premature breakup of their original lineup still feels like a great loss of potential. "There were so many records we could have made. It's just like, 'woulda, coulda, shoulda,'" laments Draper. "We wrote so much stuff that never got recorded," adds Belfer. "We would just be writing constantly so that by the time we would go to our next show—if it was like two or three weeks later—we would have a whole bunch of new material written. We were always playing new material at our shows."

Jello Biafra: I saw whole Sleepers albums come and go, as the band got tired of old songs and wrote new ones.[50]

---

50 Liner notes to the Sleepers compilation *The Less an Object* (Tim/Kerr, 1996)

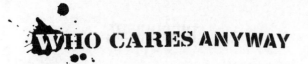

WHO CARES ANYWAY

Boris Zubov: The first time around, they were very volatile. They bordered on performance *art* as opposed to music, if you can understand what I mean. They might have done really well if they were in New York and discovered by Andy Warhol.

Tony Kinman: They were an awesome band to watch live because you literally never knew what was going to happen. It wasn't like performance art; in fact, it was hardly performance at all. It was real. They were mesmerizing to watch because their music was fantastic, and you knew every time you saw them play, something was unfolding from the moment they stepped on stage to the moment they left, not in a conscious way but in an unconscious way.[51]

Joe Rees: They had a lot of talent. And the shows that I videoed and went to of the Sleepers, I loved 'em. [Pauses.] Too many drugs and too undisciplined. I mean, that's just what happens. You can't get fucked up all the time and fight with each other and keep it together. It's a problem with every band. You gotta keep your shit together.

Paul Draper: Most people will tell you that the band with the most raw talent was the Sleepers. I'm not saying for myself, but everyone else in that band—the raw talent was exceptional. The thing is, we didn't really realize that we had all this raw talent at the time, or else we maybe would've taken things more seriously and not been such screwups with the drugs and personality clashes and fights and all that stuff.

51 In David Ensminger, *Left of the Dial: Conversations with Punk Icons* (PM Press, 2013), p. 39.

5

PUNK, ART, ANDANTI-ART / THE MUTANTS

Joann Berman: The thing about San Francisco that made it different from New York and LA was that it came from a visual art background because of the Art Institute.

Ruby Ray: The first *Search & Destroy* address, 3426 Jones, was an apartment that was right across the street from the Art Institute. There was a total interaction between the Art Institute and the punk scene.

Sally Webster: A lot of people were at the Art Institute. Bruce Pollack, who had another sort of performance space around the corner called the A-Hole. And Sue White. Jill Hoffman from Target Video. I went to the College of Arts and Crafts [in Oakland] for one year, and then we decided San Francisco just seemed better. It was a great school. Great teachers.

Stephen Wymore: David Hockney was teaching there. So was Bruce Conner. It was very inspiring to us because those guys were heavyweights.

Carol Detweiler: It wasn't very structured, really. It was really pretty open-ended. Some people weren't even taking classes there, but they would maybe sit in or just sort of infiltrate.

Sally Webster: You could just show up at school and go. You didn't even have to be enrolled. People would sleep on the ledges of the Art Institute. They'd live in the closets. There was no security, really. And then eventually, if you showed up enough, they'd give you a scholarship and just enroll you. At that point, I think it was $2,000 a year, and I could pay for it working in a movie theater making popcorn or waitressing. Easily.

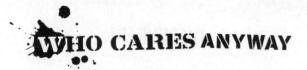

WHO CARES ANYWAY

Bruce Pollack: I lived at the Art Institute—literally lived at the Art Institute for two years.

Matt Heckert: I had never really imagined being in a band before. But then I was going to the Art Institute, and then all of a sudden, I was hearing about the Mabuhay Gardens. And, of course, I'm seeing punks around school. I didn't really know anything about punk before I moved out there. And I went, "What is *this* about? This is crazy." We just started to go over to the Mabuhay and see the bands and hang out, and we realized that people were just doing this stuff, and anybody could be in a band.

The other thing about school is that I basically went there for two years, and then I left. In retrospect, I realized that I went there long enough to gain connections into the underground of the city. And once I had that, I didn't need school anymore.

Located in North Beach within walking distance of City Lights and the Mabuhay, the Art Institute acted as the main conduit between the punk scene and the highbrow art world. For a brief time, those two worlds blurred together, with several bands—including the Mutants, Avengers, and Pink Section—forming thanks to connections made at the SFAI.[52]

At the same time, more credentialed visual artists—not just from the Art Institute but also CCAC and even the for-profit Academy of Art College—found themselves drawn to punk, seeing it as a refuge from the more established art scene. "I totally got into the whole punk thing because it made so much *sense,*" says Target Video's Joe Rees, who was teaching at the Academy of Art in those days. "It was an opportunity to do your thing, to live your life being creative. And what was the alternative in those days? Those stinky, stodgy museum shows and all those godawful art openings with that cheap wine. It just was no good."

Boundaries were being broken, not only between the art world and the live-music scene but also within the art world itself. As filmmaker Craig Baldwin

---

52 Two of the four Avengers—singer Penelope Houston and drummer Danny Furious (Daniel O'Brien)—were SFAI students. Original bassist Jonathan Postal also attended school there, though he left the band early on to form the Readymades.

THE PUNK ERA

explains, "The San Francisco Art Institute may actually be able to claim it was the first art school that had this—they call it 'New Genres,' which is a stupid name because, of course, it's not new anymore. But they didn't know what to call it. And it was basically video, performance, and installation. This was another *kind* of sensibility in the art world—the idea that there wasn't a 'high art' and a 'low art,' and that you could make video, and then it could be interesting for all sorts of reasons, but not necessarily because it's *beautiful*. They would do all sorts of weird things with installation and light and smoke and mirrors that broke with the earlier ideas about what art-making is, what performance is, and what sculpture is. Those ideas came onstage, for sure, during the punk years."

PUNK AND SURREALISM

From the beginning, there were those who saw punk as an heir to earlier art movements such as Surrealism and Dada. "[N]othing better validates the surrealist perspective on life than the emergence of new wave, in which outrage and art combine to provide means for revolt to claim new terrain," proclaimed Nico Ordway in a 1978 essay for *Search & Destroy*, which was particularly keen on emphasizing these connections.[53] In addition to Vale and Ordway (né Stephen Schwartz), the zine's staffers included Ricky Trance (Richard Waara), a "militant surrealist" in the words of photographer Richard Peterson. "In the beginning, he was just as important as Vale," says Peterson. "He was trying to push a lot of surrealism into the punk scene and *Search & Destroy*." Then there was Bruce Conner, the multi-faceted artist who had been operating out of North Beach since the Beatnik era. Already in his forties at the time, Conner nonetheless leaped headfirst into punk and came onboard as a sort of celebrity guest photographer for the zine.

Most of the *Search & Destroy* brain trust was a good decade older than the members of bands like the Sleepers and Negative Trend. As such, they qualified

53 *Search & Destroy #1-6*, p. 111.

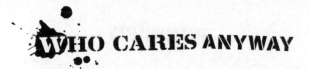

as elder statesmen relative to these younger musicians. "Vale acted kind of like this uncle," says Michael Belfer. "He would explain things to us. 'Andre Breton wrote *The Surrealist Manifesto*. You should look into it.' 'I didn't know there was a surrealist manifesto, but I do like surrealism. Okay, thank you, Vale.' So he would steer us towards different things to read."

Then again, not everyone embraced this guidance, and some actively rejected it. "All the shit that's written, like some connection between surrealism and punk, makes me sick," protested Craig Gray in a *Search & Destroy* interview. "There is no such thing as surrealism in punk. If it is surreal, then it can't be punk because what we do is the most alive and real thing to us. It's not a 'theater of illusion,' as Dirk is so fond of saying. It's our life. Broken, smashed, destroyed."[54]

Joe Rees: The first time I ever saw Negative Trend, they were playing at a place called the Longbranch in Berkeley, and there were probably about twenty people in the bar. Rozz was wearing a pair of torn Levi's, and painted on his Levi's— along the leg—it said, "I HATE ART." And when I saw that, I just about fell down! Because what the hell does art have to do with it? First of all, you had to know something about art to hate it.

Rozz Rezabek: What I like about it is, it gives people something to think about. You can't *not* think about it. "Wait a minute? You hate *art*?" We might as well have been saying we hate music, but we showed that with our actions—by the way we played.

Will Shatter: When I think of art, I think of sterile environments like museums and galleries. All that stuff's for rich people. It's removed from day-to-day life. The artist is creative by proxy for all the people who do shit jobs all their lives, people that scrape just to survive. They rely on the artist to be creative and intelligent for them.[55]

The Trend's anti-art stance didn't bother Bruce Conner, whose photograph of

54 *Search & Destroy #1-6*, p. 119.
55 *Slash*, July 1978, p. 14.

THE PUNK ERA

Rozz wearing the "I HATE ART" pants has since made its way into the New York MOMA, among other highbrow collections. For that matter, Shatter was also a visual artist of sorts. "He did a brilliant collage that's in the *StreetArt* book," says Peter Belsito, the book's editor, referring to a piece entitled 'Today a Piece of Me Died.'

In hindsight, the attitude wasn't so much anti-art as it was anti-authority. "At the time, we were *kids*," emphasizes Gray. "All we cared about was what was immediate and what was now and happening at the moment. In a way, it was Zen, but, you know, Zen on speed. It was like, 'Who gives a shit about surrealism? We're dealing with *right now*, and right now is all very real to us.' I mean, all these guys were trying to teach us stuff. Like Nico Ordway. And then Will got in with those freakin' stupid-ass revolutionary dudes, Upshot. It's just like, 'Fuck off, man. Let us be idiots on our own. If we're gonna make mistakes, let *us* make 'em, and then we learn the lessons. We don't need new parents.'

"We're talking about 'Art' with a capital 'A,'" he clarifies. "Art with a small 'a' is everyday stuff—you know, what people do every day. But art with a capital 'A' was exactly what we were trying *not* to do. The whole idea of fine art or art as an elitist thing—you know, fuck that shit."

THE MUTANTS

The Mutants were more at peace with the Art World, capital "A" or otherwise. Along with the Avengers, the Mutants had the highest quotient of art students among the Class of '77 SF bands. In addition to singers Sally Webster, Sue White, and Freddy "Fritz" Fox (all of them SFAI alums), rhythm guitarist John Gullak and drummer Dave Carothers were also former art students.

"We met at CCAC," says Gullak, recalling the band's origins. "We were roommates, and we had just gotten a nice new warehouse in West Oakland. So we had a party. It was called 'country and western versus rock 'n' roll.' At one end of the building, we had hay bales and country music playing, and then in the other room, we had a disco ball and rock 'n' roll music playing."

WHO CARES ANYWAY

A DIRKSEN-MILLER PRODUCTION

MUTANTS

MABUHAY Gardens
443 Broadway San Francisco
956-3315

PLUS SPECIAL GUEST • STEVE WEIZZER •

THE SLEEPERS   NEGATIVE TREND

11pm
Thurs
March
23

Sally Webster: We were having discussions with friends about whether country and western music or punk rock was better. We go, "Well, we're just gonna get a band and do it that way."

John Gullak: Sue and Sally and Fritz and Dave and our first bass player, Jeff Brogan—we all decided that night we were going to start a band. I was going to play guitar, and Jeff was going to play bass. Dave already played drums—he was a drummer in high school. And Fritz was already an accomplished vocalist and harmonica player. So actually, all we really needed was a guitarist.

Sally Webster: It was not like we were interviewing. We were working at a sandwich shop out in the Sunset. It was called Viking Sandwiches. That's where we met other musicians. We had to wear Viking hats. And then all our friends would just come eat there for free.

John Gullak: Sue and Sally worked with Brendan Earley and found out that he played guitar. They asked him if he wanted to play with our band. I don't think

THE PUNK ERA

he knew anything about the punk rock movement or anything. He was actually more of a bass player at the time, but he also played guitar. So we got together at First Street.

First Street was the site of the Mutants' South of Market headquarters, which also went by a few other names (including "Terminal Fun" and "Terminal Drugs"). "It was across the street from the AC bus terminal in San Francisco," explains Gullak. "So everything in that neighborhood was called 'Terminal This,' 'Terminal That.' Sue and Sally had two floors—big floors in a commercial space. They called their place 'Terminal Concepts.' Before the Mutants ever started, they would have regular poetry readings called 'Terminal Concepts Poetry Readings.'"

"There was a bar called the Wagon Wheel right next door that had martinis and Manhattans *by the jug* for a dollar," adds Webster, who moved into the space circa 1975. "There was an arcade, Fun Terminal. And then, right across the street, was the bus station. There was nothing else really down there at that time if you can imagine that. There was like one little tree, and then it was pretty much a wasteland. I rented that building—like the whole building—for about $600 for all the years that we were there. I don't think the landlords really cared. I think they were what you call 'warehousing' that block to sell at a later date. We had no restrictions. We could do anything. It was kind of great."

OPPOSITE WORLD

When the Mutants formed in 1977, starting a rock band was hardly seen as a noble pursuit for a group of art students. "I remember people saying, 'How can you abandon your art career and go into this stupid music?'" says Webster. "I also thought at that time, 'I don't like being in the art world. It's too bourgeois and boring.'"

For Webster and Sue White—both of whom sang, danced, designed costumes, and wrote lyrics—the transition wasn't too difficult. For Gullak, though, it was more of a challenge. "I had never played guitar before," he says, "and my friend Jeff had never played bass before. But he did get a bass guitar

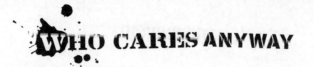

and an amp, and I got a guitar and an amp. And then poor Brendan comes to this rehearsal and says, 'Okay, what do you wanna do?' 'Well, first, you have to teach us how to play guitar.' Which he did. 'Okay, this is an E chord, this is a C chord … ' We were just playing barre chords, basically. 'Hold your hand like this, and put it on that fret, and then move it up to this fret.' I think one of the first songs we did was E-G-E-G-E-G through the whole song. It was a good learning experience. It came together."

Musically, the Mutants were perhaps the most conventional of the Mabuhay-era bands. They didn't set out to rewrite the rules of music theory or to play faster and louder than the competition. Nor did they wear their art school backgrounds on their collective sleeve. Nonetheless, something about it worked—and reflected the spirit of the times. "They were just so funny," says Peter Belsito. "And the songs were melodic. They had that kind of slight 'off'-ness that made it perfect in a way."

It helped that Earley was a talented songwriter and Fox a distinctive vocalist (often recalling Mott the Hoople's Ian Hunter, minus the Bob Dylan affectations). Equally important, however, was the balance of musicians and non-musicians (or, at least, less experienced musicians). And it was indeed a balancing act, as Webster admits. "There was always a tension between the musicians and the artists. Because just the ideology is different. For them, it was like, 'What the fuck?' You know, why they had to dress up in some stupid fuckin' costume that's sort of vaguely humiliating. But it was a great combination, and we got big audiences. Whereas I think if they were on their own, they'd be on their own. You need the two elements."

COSTUME PARTY

The Mutants are remembered first and foremost as a live band, including a legendary gig opening for the Cramps at the Napa State Mental Institution in June of 1978. But even their "ordinary" gigs at the Mabuhay and (later) the Deaf Club could be spectacles in their own right. "Freddy had incredible stage presence," says Joann Berman, a fellow Art Institute alum and First Street resident. "And then topping it off were Sally and Sue, who were both off-the-chain nuts." Adds Bruce Pollack, "Every week they'd come up with a new scheme. One time it was garbage bags—everyone was wearing garbage bags. Another one was throwing fish—actual real live fish—at the audience."

Needless to say, those aspects don't translate onto the band's recordings. That said, their 7-inch EP from 1979 stands up just fine on its own, with a couple of bona fide anthems in 'New Dark Ages' and 'New Drug' (sample lyric: "I'm sick of your politics / I don't care if you are a comm-u-nist"). In sound and spirit, the record feels much closer to 1977 than, say, 1980, which is to say that it wasn't absolutely cutting edge given the rapidly evolving standards of the underground. Then again, that wasn't the goal. As Chris Desjardins put it in a review for *Slash*, "You see pix of the Mutants, and you might think their music would be full of gimmicks and cute effects. It's not true. All three of these are straight ahead, instantly memorable in a hummable way. This stands alongside the Sleepers EP as being one of the best records to come out of San Francisco."[56]

An LP, *Fun Terminal*, was recorded and released in 1982, but it came a little too late in the game. "The problem was, I think [producer] Paul Wexler was trying to shape us into something that we weren't really," says Gullak. "He saw us as more of a B-52's or Go Go's-type act, where we really were more of a garage band." Adds Webster, "They wanted to do a very commercial-sounding record and sell it and make a lot of money. You know, people were delusional, basically." On top of that, the label—Berkeley-based MSI Records—was a fly-by-night operation that seemingly knew (or cared) little about marketing or distributing records. "You couldn't find it in any of the stores," laments Gullak. "The excuse that the record company used is that they had the whole shipment on a truck, and the truck got hijacked, and they don't know what happened to the records. So only a handful of the records ever came out. And then we would start seeing them in grocery stores in the cutout bin. I remember one of my relatives saying, 'I just found your record here at the A&P in Ironwood, Michigan. I got it for a buck!'"

In punk terms, 1982 was practically a different century compared to the late 1970s, when the Mutants were at their peak—an era still remembered most

56 *Slash*, September 1979, p. 33.

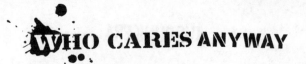

fondly by their peers. "If we're going to think in terms of the punk genre per se, I think they were the *definitive* San Francisco punk band," exclaims Jorge Socarras, who saw the Mutants play on multiple occasions before starting his own band, Indoor Life. "And I mean that in its richest sense. They had their own sound, and I think they do fit the genre, but not in an imitative way. They met all the requirements that a serious punk fan would demand, but they brought their own terrific energy and their own irony to it all. They made a big statement, I think. And I think they were one of the most loved bands in San Francisco. Everybody liked the Mutants."

"I just felt like they embodied the whole thing without the big political overlay," adds Belsito. "They were about the party, and I think initially it was a party. It was a bunch of misfits who found their place. You could be yourself and not feel ostracized. I think that's what it was at the start. It was a costume party at the beginning."

6

TERMINAL FUN

Denny DeGorio: A lot of us came from various sort of dysfunctional family systems or whatnot, and I kind of feel like we created our own little family, our own little group, where we were accepted by each other and able to do whatever we wanted. There was a lot of freedom. It was almost utopian, in a sense.

Bob Hoffnar: It was just these super creative, kind of nutty people who didn't fit in anywhere else. A lot of it was because of the gay scene. You could be gay in San Francisco before you could be gay anywhere else, so it was totally fun and open. Everybody else kind of got a free pass. It was kind of an island.

Mark Hutchinson: It was an amazing confluence of all these cultural things. I think it beat out anything in the Weimar Republic. Even in the punk scene, all the Beat poets were there. It was just like a continuum of art history, in the best way possible.

David Swan: I had been creative in the past, but I had no outlet for it. Then all of a sudden, there was an outlet for every single thing I wanted to do. And if you were in SF at that time, if you wanted to start a band, you started a band. Or you could submit something to one of the magazines. And then maybe you'd be involved in a film or video project, or it could be something to do with fashion.

Judy Gittelsohn: In '78, when we sort of found one another, it was like, "Oh my god, we are the *zeitgeist*! This is a *movement*!" And when you're in the middle of a movement, there's such energy. It was just marvelous.

The utopia of the early punk scene was juxtaposed against a city that often seemed on the brink of madness. Over the course of the 1970s, San Francisco

WHO CARES ANYWAY

had witnessed a series of strange, mysterious, and frankly dark events, from killing sprees (the Zodiac and Zebra murders) to bombings, assassination attempts, and other acts of political violence. A November 1978 article in the *Washington Post* cited a "pervasive atmosphere of terrorism that has enveloped the region since the early 1960s."[57] As Supervisor Quentin Kopp put it in the article, "We have here some very socially bizarre people."

The city was also at a low ebb economically, with its population at its lowest total in decades.[58] "I mean, if you look at films or anything from that period, there'd be like three or four cars on a block," says Noh Mercy's Esmerelda. "There were hardly any cars; there were hardly any people." Yet it was precisely these social and economic conditions that allowed punk to thrive. "You have to have a very interesting mix of an eclectic, troubled past with a depressed economy," notes Bruno DeSmartass, who moved out west from New York at the tail end of the seventies. "Coming out of the seventies and into the eighties, San Francisco was depressed. It was funky."

Ron Morgan: It was relatively inexpensive to live in the city at that point. It was why all of us moved there. You could cobble together a Victorian house with a bunch of other people and rent it for 300 bucks a month. You didn't have to work. I mean, I remember that when I first moved to San Francisco, I was in these coffeehouses in the middle of the day. They were packed. I'm going, "Don't these people have to work?" I wasn't working, but I assumed everybody else had to do it.

Sally Webster: It's probably the last time you can say anybody wasn't doing shit for money. You didn't have to be about the money because we had really no rent to pay. No overhead. That was not a factor. We could do whatever the fuck we wanted. If we wanted to say, "Fuck you, I don't need your money,"—hey, no

---

57 Joel Kotkin and Paul Grabowicz, "San Francisco: A City of Violence." *The Washington Post*. November 29, 1978.
58 The 1980 census recorded a population of 678,974, down from a peak of 775,357 in 1950.

problem. You didn't need it. No student loans back then. Nothing. And the social services were very good.

Bob Hoffnar: We all would get food stamps. We'd pool our food stamps and have some food. There were ways to get food, and if you didn't have a place, you could stay at the Club Foot. There was always somebody kind of looking out for you. A hundred bucks a month, you could have a place. Fifty bucks a month, you could have a room somewhere. It was easy. You could get by.

Jorge Socarras: San Francisco had terrific social services and social welfare programs. I would say at least half of everyone I knew in that scene, including myself, managed to get on some kind of social welfare—which we kind of treated like art scholarships. That was very particular to San Francisco, what was called SSI. There was a whole subculture. The Cockettes and the Angels of Light, who preceded a lot of the San Francisco music scene, were all on social welfare programs.

The way you'd get on them—and I think this is definitely an essential part of that zeitgeist—was that you just had to prove that you were crazy. And it really didn't take much because most of us were willing to wear pajamas on the street and act crazy just for the fun of it, much less if we were going to get paid for it. You can never really separate a zeitgeist from the politics of the time and the economics of the time. It certainly was not in a vacuum.

ANALOG CULTURE AND WORD OF MOUTH

"All we had was word of mouth, getting together with other people, being out on the street meeting other people, meeting other people at clubs."—Lisa Wooley

San Francisco is unique among American cultural centers for its compact geography. At roughly seven by seven miles, it is a far cry from sprawling Los

WHO CARES ANYWAY

UXA'S DE DE TROIT AND MICHAEL KOWALSKY IN EARLY 1978. PHOTO BY JAMES STARK.

Angeles, the only other West Coast city with a bona fide punk scene at the time.[59] "San Francisco felt quite assimilable to me as a European, really, in a way that LA didn't," recalls UK music journalist Jon Savage, who encountered both cities for the first time during the summer of 1978. "LA is a complete mind-fuck, whereas San Francisco was on a different scale to LA. It's on a more European scale in a way, so it felt easier than LA."

That smaller scale was key to the blossoming of punk culture in San Francisco, especially given that so few of the participants could afford to own a car. Given the lack of media coverage—and the nonexistence of internet, cellphones, or social media—word of mouth was everything, whether that meant phone trees, fliers, or a serendipitous meeting at a neighborhood café or theatre.

---

59 With apologies to Seattle and Portland, both of which had smaller scenes in those days and tended to serve as feeders for San Francisco or LA.

THE PUNK ERA

Tom Wheeler: One of the really great things about San Francisco in the late seventies is that it had this extremely developed repertory theatre scene, where you could see silent films, you could see documentaries, you could see surrealist films, you could see foreign films from all over the place—odd, completely weird, creepy Hollywood movies.

Sally Webster: On Market Street, there was the Strand, the Egyptian, and the Embassy. You could see four B-movies for like two dollars. So we would work there. It was very easy to get a job there, obviously. You could go really hungover or tired. And then everybody would go there and go to the movies. We would just be in the movie theater all day, recuperating.

Michael Belfer: You could go to the Strand for a dollar—fifty cents if you went before noon. Just getting exposed to so much incredible art and film and literature during that whole period, it really facilitated having lots of ideas and being inspired to do different projects.

Tom Wheeler: A lot of the musicians that were playing in these bands were getting a lot of their inspiration and source material from going and watching movies. And it was kind of a social thing because you went out and did it and ran into people and went out and got coffee afterwards and talked about what you just saw. That's what it was like in '76 when I arrived in San Francisco, and it lasted until about the mid-eighties when that stuff started closing down. It's the social part of it because you ran into people.

Handmade zines and fliers were also key in getting the word out. "The new technology we had then was Xerox," notes Ruby Ray, "and that's how fanzines started. Or just zines. And that's why posters became such a big thing because you could make something and reproduce it and make hundreds of them, and it would be cheap." The cut-and-paste aesthetic was no mere affectation, either. "We had to make all the posters and everything by cutting out letters and pasting them with glue on paper and taking them to the local Xerox place," says Esmerelda. "That's why those posters look like that because that's all we had to do it with. We wanted 'em to look like ransom notes."

WHO CARES ANYWAY

Also noteworthy was Ivey's List, a meticulously handwritten calendar of upcoming shows and events produced by one Barbara Ivey, a friend of Ruby Ray's. The list was mailed out to subscribers and handed out at cafés each month for nearly two years, from early 1979 to late 1980.

Finally, there were the phone trees. As Ray explains, "Somebody would call you and say, 'So-and-so is playing tonight.' The phone tree was the big thing. The phone tree and Xerox. You had to search it out back then to find out anything."

The word-of-mouth aspect went hand in hand with punk's status as a genuine underground subculture. That lent it a sense of community and solidarity, at least in the beginning. "I think for a long time, it was like a hundred punks," says Debi Sou, with only slight exaggeration. "So if you saw a punk a block down the road, you automatically acknowledged each other, and you almost automatically were friends because there weren't that many punks. But when the scene got a bit bigger, it got really cliquey."

"Bigger" is a relative term here, but a few landmark shows serve to illustrate how quickly things were changing. When the Ramones played the Savoy Tivoli in August of 1976, they drew a few dozen people. The following summer, they played Winterland (capacity: 5,400) to around 1,500 fans.[60] In January of 1978, the Sex Pistols sold out the same venue in a show that many cite as a pivotal event, for better or worse. In *Punk '77*, James Stark begins the closing chapter (entitled 'Dissolution') with a mention of the show: "What was a fresh and experimental scene through most of 1977 began to change in early 1978 after the Sex Pistols played America."[61] "It was kind of depressing," adds Ray, "because the people who came to see the bands, they were just idiots. They were spitting at the stage, and that wasn't the kind of thing that the punks did, the real punks. We used to call them the 'weekend punks.' On the weekend, they'd come from the suburbs, and they'd wear some safety pin or something stupid that they thought represented punk."

---

60 "The 'New Wave Music' show with Dictators, The Nuns, Widowmaker, and the Ramones failed miserably. Only 1,500 seats were sold," wrote one Evan Hosie in a live music roundup for the Berkeley Gazette (August 5, 1977). "That means you won't be seeing many shows of that nature around here (sigh of relief)."

61 p. 91.

THE PUNK ERA

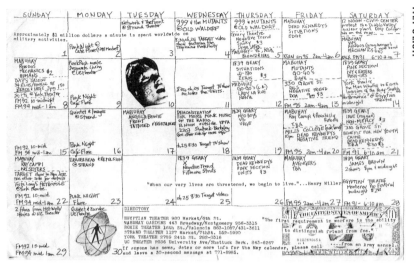

At the same time, there were plenty of newcomers who saw the show not as an ending but as a beginning. "That show was a game-changer," says drummer John Surrell. "That was like the start button.'Now we can make a band.'" Rachel Thoele had a similar awakening that night: "I was fourteen. I went from disco to punk rock in one show. I saw the Sex Pistols. I was into Earth, Wind & Fire before that."

EXCESS

Above all, San Francisco in the late seventies was a place of excess: politically, creatively, sexually, and chemically. Artist Joann Berman recalls a telling scene from the night of the Sex Pistols concert when guitarist Steve Jones and drummer Paul Cook wound up at an afterparty at the A-Hole, the SOMA loft where she lived along with fellow Art Institute student Bruce Pollack and a host of others.[62] "We had, in the A-Hole, these columns that were holding up the

---

62 Pollack describes the scenery in and around the A-Hole: "When we got in there, there was all this drug paraphernalia in the walls and just scum everywhere. We were near South

71

floors. And Bruce got really drunk or high—I don't know which—but he had his chainsaw going, and he was trying to chainsaw the pillars apart. Everybody was jumping around and partying, and I was in the bedroom with Steve Jones. It was a madhouse."

"A lot of it's blurry," she adds. "Because we did a lot of drugs. We did *tons* of fucking drugs. *Tons* of drugs."

Jorge Socarras: I can't reiterate enough how drug-fueled it was. Sometimes when I want to emphasize it to young people, I'll say to them, "It's not just that styles were different and we listened to different music. It's as if *the very fabric of reality* was different, if you can imagine that." Like when you read science fiction, and you get a picture of an alternative world, an alternative reality—it was *that* different.

Esmerelda: The excess in this town was *unbelievable*. On every level. It was just *tremendous* excess. It killed a lot of people. Tons of people died. *I* almost died.

One of the first casualties of this excess was Michael Kowalsky, who died of a heroin overdose in April 1978 at the age of twenty-five. Kowalsky's band, UXA, had just been featured in *Search & Destroy* for the first time that March; the next month's issue concluded with an "R.I.P. Michael" tribute. "Michael's last words were as if he was going to the biggest party of his life," wrote UXA singer De De Troit.[63]

Tommy Antel, who was with Kowalsky and De Troit that night, recalls the scene in more detail: "The last thing he said to De De was, 'I've never felt this high before.' He put on Dillinger—'A knife, a fork, a bottle and a cork / That's the way you spell New York.'[64] We both OD'd. She called the paramedics. I came back, Michael did not. So when they took us away, they took me to General Hospital, and they took him to the morgue. He was right above me in the ambulance."

Park. There were a bunch of bums, and there was a fire going twenty-four hours. They had a pit, and these bums would just sit there with a fire and keep going. And across the street was the unemployment office. That just closed when we started the A-Hole."

63 *Search & Destroy #7-11*, p. 28.
64 Dillinger, 'Cokane in My Brain'

THE PUNK ERA

Suzi Skates: It was really sad. He was a beautiful person. And loved. He was fucked up, though. I remember him often being really intoxicated on whatever it was. But he always had this wonderful sweetness about him. And he was a very kind, sweet *poet*. He was a poet. He was a poetic soul. And it really was weird and sad when he just was gone.

De De Troit: He felt that he knew so much about, like, Communists, Nazis, and all of the government's secrets, or a lot of the government's secrets, that it really was dangerous for him to be around. He felt that he was one of the victims, and eventually, they'd catch onto what he knew, or whatever.[65]

Michael Belfer: It was a huge loss because he was very influential in the music scene, even though he didn't play any instruments.

Suzi Skates: Things got dark after Michael Kowalsky died, in my opinion. Things started getting really dark when that happened. There was more drugs. It started out light and fun in the beginning, and then to me, it got darker.

Joann Berman: The mood in San Francisco went from being like happy and creative and "do your own thing" to dark and sinister.

DARKNESS DESCENDS

Things got even darker toward the end of 1978. On November 18, over 900 members of the San Francisco-based Peoples Temple died in an apparent mass suicide at their compound in French Guyana. Eight days later, on November 26, Mayor George Moscone and Supervisor Harvey Milk were gunned down at City Hall by a disgruntled ex-cop, Dan White. Pink Section's Matt Heckert still recalls that day's events vividly. "I was picking up Charly [Brown] and Judy [Gittelsohn]

65 *In the Red.*

73

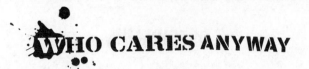

WHO CARES ANYWAY

to go to Sproul Plaza to see the Talking Heads play an outdoor free concert, and there were freaking *tons* of cop cars around the block. We did not know what was going on. We put the radio on as we were driving over the Bay Bridge, and we heard the news that Moscone and Milk had been assassinated. And then we went to Sproul Plaza and listened to 'Psycho Killer' by the Talking Heads. It was a *very* fucking strange day."

Judy Gittelsohn: That fall of 1978 was like, "*Whoa*, did the world tip on its axis?" The Jim Jones thing—it was just *such* a hard turn in our personal life, from what had been just *glorious*.[66]

Bond Bergland: It was surreal almost in a way that it is again now. It feels like a time not unlike today when we just can't believe what's happening in the world. But California seemed the center of all that weird shit back then. It was crazy to be here.

Joann Berman: The Jim Jones thing was really frightening, but we were like, "Whatever. Let's go to the next party." But no one could believe it because it was all from San Francisco.

Richard Edson: Well, for me, there was that feeling in the air for me in San Francisco anyway, so it just made it thicker. But nobody really talked about it. It was just like, "Wow, that's fucked up." But then, the attitude in that scene was, "Yeah, the *world* is fucked up. The culture is fucked up. Society's fucked up."

Esmerelda: Nowadays, everybody knows that that level of insanity goes on every day. But *then*, it was *outrageous*. It was still such a pure time. We still had a modicum of innocence.

---

66 At the time, Heckert and Gittelsohn were dealing with the fallout from another recent calamity: a five-alarm fire that burned down the North Beach apartment building where they were living, along with Pink Section bandmate Stephen Wymore. The November 15 fire also damaged the Dante Hotel and the Condor, where topless dancer Carol Doda performed.

THE PUNK ERA

Joe Rees: I think it was fuel for the fire. It certainly was in my work. I used a lot of that imagery in my video montages. It was a big deal to me. In fact, in some ways, it seemed to be easier to be deal with *then* than it is now. Now it's so commonplace.

Both the Jonestown and Moscone/Milk incidents would provide fodder for SF bands in the years to come, from Tuxedomoon's 'Special Treatment (For the Family Man)' and Noh Mercy's 'Furious' (both of which express outrage with the Dan White verdict) to Factrix's 'Final Days' and the German Shepherds' 'Mr. Tupper' (both of which make use of Jim Jones samples).[67] As chance would have it, the Peoples Temple was located next door to the Temple Beautiful, a former synagogue-turned-concert venue that had recently started hosting punk shows.[68] Not long after the Jonestown Massacre, performance artist Monte Cazazza managed to sneak into the Peoples Temple, where he discovered a series of primitive skull paintings on the walls. "That's scary shit, man," says Bond Bergland of Factrix, who used the photos in the artwork for their 1982 album *California Babylon.* "It affected us a lot. I mean, it was ... exciting. Because everybody was still thinking it kind of tied everything back to Charles Manson days in a really weird way. I don't know why all that became so important artistically, but it did."

The impact of these events wasn't just psychological or spiritual, though. There were also tangible consequences that made life more difficult for those in the punk scene, starting with the appointment of Dianne Feinstein as interim mayor. "The city changed," notes Bob Hoffnar. "The vibe with the cops got totally different. Her husband's a big real estate guy, and suddenly, everywhere you were living was a method for some ultra-wealthy guy to make a lot more money." Adds Judy Gittelsohn, "Milk and Moscone were such lights. Dianne

---

67 In addition, the cover of the Dead Kennedys' *Fresh Fruit for Rotting Vegetables* uses a photo from the "White Night" riots of May 21, when thousands of protesters swarmed the area around City Hall to protest the Dan White verdict.

68 The Peoples Temple was located at 1859 Geary, in a grand building that was previously known as the Albert Pike Memorial Temple. The Temple Beautiful (also referred to as the Geary Temple and later as Rat's Palace) was next door at 1839 Geary, which previously housed the Temple Beth Israel. Both buildings were right down the block from the site of the original Fillmore (1805 Geary), which closed in 1968.

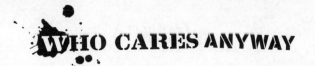

Feinstein was not pro-entertainment or pro-'gathering of young people.' She didn't like us doing all those fliers that everyone put up all over. She just was not a supporter of that at all."

As the mood of the city darkened, the mood in and around the punk scene followed suit. "When the punk scene first began, it was a very small group of people, and we weren't harassed," summarizes Ruby Ray. "Maybe when you were walking down the street, people would call out things to you and stuff, but the police were not bothering us. In the beginning, it was so conducive and free, but once the police started bothering everybody, you know, it just changed the whole atmosphere."

THE POST-PUNK ERA

7

IN THE MISSION:
THE DEAF CLUB, NOH MERCY,
AND PINK SECTION

By early 1979, much of the action had shifted from North Beach to the Mission District, where the Deaf Club emerged as an unlikely refuge for the rapidly evolving punk scene.

Part of it had to do with changes afoot at the Mabuhay, which was becoming a victim of its own success. A series of police raids beginning in November of 1978—almost immediately following the Moscone/Milk murders—led the club to start cracking down on underage patrons. The increased police scrutiny may have also influenced Dirk Dirksen's efforts to rebrand the Mab as a new wave venue ("new wave" being "a high energy music without the punk attitude," as he explained in a local newspaper article).[1] In response to the changes, a "Death of Punk" protest was staged outside the club by a group of underage punks (including a young Bruce Calderwood). In addition, several bands began boycotting the venue, led by the Dils and Negative Trend.

Meanwhile, the Mission had plenty of cheap real estate available, ranging from empty storefronts to abandoned warehouses. By the end of 1979, a network of alternative spaces had set up shop within stumbling distance of the Deaf Club. Chief among them was a veritable compound at 678 South Van Ness, which served as headquarters for Target Video; a new zine, *Damage*, which debuted in August; and a new label, Subterranean, which released its first record later that fall.

1   *San Francisco Examiner.* December 24, 1978.

THE POST-PUNK ERA

Joe Rees: In the late seventies, the Mission was a different world. It was like living in Little Mexico. I loved my neighbors; everybody was cool. It was just a great place. And you could be yourself. No one ever gave me a hard time for having green hair or whatever.

Peter Belsito: A lot of people felt like it was dangerous out there. Certainly, I saw enough gunplay myself—you know, the Latino gangs. They didn't really give a shit about us. But there was always gunplay going on down there for a while.

Bob Steeler: The scene was pretty tense because we were invading Mexican territory down there.

Joe Rees: There wasn't a specific thing against punk rockers, necessarily. I mean, sure, when you were walking the street at night, or you were going to my studio for an event, you had to be careful because there were gangs of Hispanics that were picking on people. But basically, they wanted to beat up *gay* people. They just got 'em all confused because everyone was wearing leather in those days. Plus, we were so close to the Castro District. But for one thing, punk rockers are gonna fight back. That's why you wore all those studs and stuff: to try to defend yourself.

Esmerelda: Valencia Street was the lesbian Castro. There were women's bars and women's bookstores. There was a restaurant where only women could go. But it was really dangerous, still. It was a really dicey kind of neighborhood. And then it became more and more punk rock. There was a place called Tool & Die right down the street. And then the Deaf Club, of course, was on Valencia. More and more places popped up. It was a little world. It was really fun.

Tony Hotel: The Deaf Club was totally quiet because it was down on Valencia Street, a residential neighborhood, where, during the day, you didn't even know it was *there*. Deaf people went there; it was their clubhouse. So they liked this kind of music because the deaf people could *feel* the vibrations through the floor, and they could move to it and respond to it. That's why they let us start playing

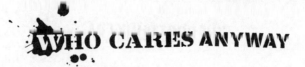

there because our music was real loud. It would vibrate through the floorboards, and the deaf people *enjoyed* it.[2]

992 VALENCIA AND NOH MERCY

A few blocks down from the Deaf Club was 992 Valencia, a converted storefront where both Esmerelda and Tony Hotel—the two members of Noh Mercy—lived and rehearsed. "I'd gotten the place from the Cockettes, and that was before punk rock," says Esmerelda, referring to the infamous drag queen theatre group. "It had these six-foot Art Deco ceiling chandeliers that were incredible. And the balconies were all open—everything was open. The walls were all mirrors. There were ballet bars on both walls. It was phenomenal. It became a rehearsal space for Japanese butoh dancers and a gay theater group and other kinds of dancers." By 1979, the basement there also served as a rehearsal space for Tuxedomoon, whose manager, Adrian Craig, was among the other residents of 992 Valencia.

Both Tuxedomoon and Noh Mercy had roots in the Angels of Light, the underground gay theater collective that spun off from the Cockettes in the early 1970s. Though scarcely documented, the Angels of Light represent a point of convergence between several distinctly San Franciscan subcultures from that decade. "If you were looking for some kind of family tree, what bled through from the hippies to punk came through the Angels of Light," notes Peter Belsito. Indeed, Esmerelda, who sang in some of the Angels' productions, first caught wind of punk through a friend and fellow Angels of Light member, Gregory Cruikshank. "He had been working in Malcolm McLaren's shop with Vivian

---

2   The Deaf Club's live music offerings were booked by Robert Hanrahan, who also managed several bands at the time, including the Dead Kennedys, the Offs, and Pink Section. All three of them appear on the live compilation LP *Can You Hear Me Now? Music from the Deaf Club,* along with Tuxedomoon, the Mutants, and KGB. "There were a lot of shadowy, influential figures in those days who didn't have official roles but were really important people," says Scott Davey. "People who would just put other people together. Hanrahan was one of those."

DEAF CLUB®

A WALKING DEAD EVENT

D E A F
C L U B ©

530 Valencia at 16th
ONE BLOCK FROM 16TH & MISSION BART

ALWAYS UNDER $3.99
FOr BOOKING AND IMFO · 863-6069 OR 221-0838

FEBUARY:

14 TUXEDO MOON, NÖH MERCY
    PINK SECTION

17 CRIME, VS., V.I.P.$, BLOWDRIERS

21 SPECIAL DEBUT NIGHT

24 X, BAGS, SUBURBS MINN.

28 ZEROS, BELFAST COWBOYS,
    VKTMS, VANDALS

Minors Always Wellcome

666   PRINTED
           IN U S A

Westwood—the Sex shop. He brought it to San Francisco—all the music and everything—and we just went nuts."

Esmerelda originally moved to San Francisco as a teenage runaway during the Summer of Love. By the time she discovered punk rock, she was already in her late twenties and a divorced mother of two (the father had custody of their kids at the time). Meanwhile, her duo mate took a similarly circuitous path to the Deaf Club. A jazz drummer from Dayton, Ohio, Tony (née Janet Ogg) moved out west in the early seventies and finally settled in San Francisco after a stint in Southern California. She had grown weary from several years' worth of toiling on the fringes of the male-dominated jazz scene when she first encountered her eventual partner:

> She was doing a play on Church Street with the Angels of Light. It had a set with like a two-story Spanish-type building. It was a Spanish scene, and there was a window in the second story. Then at a certain point, a window flung open, and Esmeralda flung her head out of the window. She had this long, red, fiery hair. And then she started singing this song, and it was fantastic. I was really floored by her talent. So I found out where she lived.

81

 WHO CARES ANYWAY

The next morning, I got up *real* early—like six o'clock in the morning—and I went over to there [to 992 Valencia]. I knocked on the door, and one of her roommates came to the door. I said, "Is Esmeralda here?" She said, "Yeah, she is. Come on in." She showed me where her room was, and I went up there, and she was in bed asleep. I said, "Esmeralda! Esmeralda!" And she rolled over, and she opened her eyes and looked at me and said, "What the hell are you doing here? Who are you at 6:30 in the morning?" I told her my name and said, "I'm a drummer, and I wanna play with you." She goes, "Well, come back later." So I left, and later on, I brought my drums over and set 'em up, and we played together in her main room there where the piano was. And that was how we started.

Musically, they were an immediate fit, even if they made for an odd couple in another sense. "I was coming from the gay world, but I wasn't gay," explains Esmerelda. "Tony *was* gay, but she wasn't coming from that gay world. It's funny, but at that time, gay men and gay women had *nothing* to do with each other. *Nothing*. I mean, you would get screamed off the street if you were a woman if you weren't a straight fag hag-type woman. And we just mindfucked everyone all the time, which was part of the fun of Noh Mercy, was just trying to keep people guessing. They didn't know *what* we were."

While there were other all-women bands in San Francisco at the time—including the Urge, the Contractions, and VS—it's safe to say that Noh Mercy was the only all-women drums-and-vocals duo. It helped that both of them were gifted musicians, and not just by the anyone-can-do-it standards of punk. "Tony was a musician, and for me, it was like a paintbox," says the singer. "She could do *anything*." The admiration was mutual. "Esmerelda was such a great singer and a great talent, plus she had the words, which were perfect for the time," says the drummer. They were also visually striking, often appearing in matching outfits, from Japanese kimonos to "these orange fifties-like Beatles-style suits," as Tony puts it.

As for the words, the most memorable—and controversial—were the ones for 'No Caucasian Guilt.' "I don't wanna be politically correct / I don't need no Caucasian guilt," sneers Esmerelda over a staccato drumbeat before rattling off a list of non-apologies (sample lines: "I never made no Black my slave / I never

82

dug no Latino graves"). The song is barely a minute long, but it has something to offend everyone within earshot, including women and gays. "People were *so* shocked by that song," Esmeralda recalls. "It was the most popular song we sang because nobody could believe that anybody would say that. But then I think that *some* people took it in a completely other way, and it's really hard for me to even acknowledge it out of context at all now."

Admittedly, the context has changed, but it's worth noting that 'No Caucasian Guilt' was just one of several songs from turn-of-the-1980s San Francisco to address the topic of race in one form or another. Others included VKTMS's '100% White Girl' ("I'm just a little white girl / I get hassled every day"), the Offs' 'Everyone's a Bigot' ("Blacks are bigots on the 22 bus / If you look different they'll put you down"), the Fuck-Ups' 'White Boy' ("White boy, can't you see / You're a minority"), and even Flipper's 'Lowrider.' Apart from a shared desire to shock and to upend taboos, these songs also reflected the realities of life on the margins of a multi-cultural city—especially in neighborhoods like the Mission.

That said, the context for 'No Caucasian Guilt' had less to do with street hassles than it did with the singer's lingering sense of disappointment about the hippie era—"this loss of romantic vision of the sixties into complete cynicism," as Esmerelda puts it. "I mean, if you listen to it, it's like, 'Who *cares*?' It's like, '*I* never did any of that stuff. I never put no Jap in a camp.' But it was the irony of showing every single horrible thing that white people have ever done to everybody. And people were *shocked* by it. Which was the point! The point was to be as shocking and confrontational and as thought-provoking as humanly possible. And that's what that song embodied. It was saying 'fuck you' to gender lines, 'fuck you' to *everything*."

TOMMY TADLOCK

Along with 'Revolutionary Spy,' 'No Caucasian Guilt' was one of just two Noh Mercy songs released while they were still active. Both of them appeared as part of a double 7-inch compilation, *Earcom 3*, on the UK label Fast Product (home to early singles by Human League and Gang of Four, among others).

"There was always the promise of recording and a label and all this stuff," notes Esmerelda, "but it never came about because everybody was so messed up on drugs and alcohol."

The duo actually recorded an album's worth of material (eventually released by Superior Viaduct in 2012). The recordings were made in the basement of 992 Valencia with the help of Tommy Tadlock, yet another key figure in the Angels of Light/Tuxedomoon axis. "He was just this brilliant genius guy who was *so* perverted," says Esmerelda. "He was also in the realm of John Waters—just *completely* twisted and *crazy.* Just totally crazy. And loved young boys. But he could fix anything. If you were performing on stage, and the amp blew, he'd fix it with a cigarette butt somehow. He was just a genius."

Tadlock had a past life as an avant-garde video artist in 1960s New York City, where he collaborated with Fluxus artist Nam June Paik and taught classes at NYU. While there, he invented a device called the Archetron, which allowed the user to "compose on a TV screen constantly moving and changing colorful kaleidoscopic images."[3] He made his way to San Francisco in the late sixties, evidently abandoning his video work after hearing that color TV tubes were a cause of cancer.[4] By the mid-seventies, he had joined the Angels of Light as a stagehand and sound engineer; by 1977, he had set up shop in the large communal house at 3645 Market Street that served as Tuxedomoon's unofficial headquarters early on.[5] It was there that Tadlock recorded Tuxedomoon's first single and most of their first EP, *No Tears.* "To say Tadlock was a pivotal all-important first member of Tuxedomoon would be an understatement," said founding member Steven Brown in an interview with Simon Reynolds.[6]

While Tadlock was instrumental in helping several bands get off the ground, he was also famously eccentric. "He had this thing going on where he was

3   Brochure for *TV as a Creative Medium* exhibit, 1969. http://www.vasulka.org/archive/Artists8/Tadlock,ThomasCarter/general.pdf

4   Isabelle Corbisier, *Music for Vagabonds* (Openmute, 2008), p. 20.

5   *Music for Vagabonds* details some of the strange happenings inside the house during this era, which included an outbreak of hepatitis and various bouts of drug-induced psychosis. After they were evicted in the fall of 1978, Tuxedomoon moved their rehearsals to the basement of 992 Valencia.

6   http://totallywiredbysimonreynolds.blogspot.com/2009/03/totally-wired-runner-up-transcripts-1-q.html

trying to clean out his system or something," recalls Tony Hotel. "He was eating charcoal—I remember that. But he was a guy who could fix or do anything. He was really inventive on musical equipment or electrical things or things of that nature. And he would *do* things. He wasn't lazy. You know, he wasn't just sitting around getting high or whatever. He did stuff. And he had a good personality, and he was a good-hearted person. You know, he was a friend."

PINK SECTION

Pink Section was another Deaf Club-era band that worked closely with Tadlock, at least early on. The quartet—Matthew Heckert on guitar and vocals, Judy Gittelsohn on keyboard and vocals, Stephen Wymore on bass, and Carol Detweiler on drums—formed in 1978 around the Art Institute, where all of them were enrolled at the time. As Wymore recalls, it was his interest in tinkering with electronics—including a cheap Magnus organ that he'd taken apart and rewired—that first caught Tadlock's attention.[7] "It was just a funky little organ, but it was overdriven, so it sounded kind of like some kind of fucked up synthesizer. So when Tommy Tadlock saw us using that, he said, 'What is that?' I said, 'It's a fuckin' Magnus.' He said, 'Oh my god.' He was a tech person, so he kind of embraced us because of our little thing." As he'd done with Tuxedomoon, Tadlock built a customized mixer for the band's shows, including a stereo dual amp setup for Wymore's bass guitar.

Pink Section also had a connection to Noh Mercy, as it was Tony Hotel who helped teach the novice Detweiler how to play drums. "I just was learning drums by rote from her and then listening to records, like the Buzzcocks," Detweiler says. She learned quickly, although like Ricky Williams in Crime, she would occasionally drop a beat (see the second chorus on 'Jane Blank' from the group's self-titled 1980 EP). Even so, she played with such energy that her

---

7   He might have also been drawn to them for other reasons, as Gittelsohn suggests. "Tommy Tadlock was really a difficult guy for me because he was interested in the boys and not so interested in me."

bandmates didn't seem to mind, especially since they were largely novices themselves. "Carol was probably the most accomplished musician, knew the most about music," says Wymore. "She had never played the drums, but she knew more about music than any of us."

Stylistically, Pink Section was the quintessential arty post-punk band with its mix of scratchy guitars, cheap synthesizers, and squeaky boy/girl vocals. They were also visually compelling, what with the petite, stylish Detweiler behind the drum kit and the animated Gittelsohn out front (to say nothing of Heckert's wholesome Ken doll appearance). Writing in *Slash*, Vale described them as a "1979 band," one that "eschewed the now-cliched raw-power guitar approach in favor of a more play-experimental, multi-instrumental context for their subliminal social criticism."[8] For much of 1979, they were practically the house band at the Deaf Club, where they played on a near-

8   V. Vale, "Search & Destroy Supplement with Pink Section." In *Slash*, May 1979, p. 9.

weekly basis for stretches.

That same year, they recorded a 7-inch ('Shopping' b/w 'Tour of China') in the living room of the 3444 16th Street apartment where several of the band members resided. The self-released, Tadlock-produced platter somehow made its way to Glenn O'Brien of *Interview* magazine, who gave it a glowing review. "We were just like, 'What the fuck?'" says Wymore. "We hadn't sent it to him, but he got a hold of it, and he reviewed it. And that was a big break for us." That fall, they toured the Northeast on the strength of that single (and O'Brien's review), playing New York, Boston, and a handful of other cities. Geographically speaking, that was farther than any of the early Mabuhay bands had gotten to that point, with the exception of Tuxedomoon (another band championed by O'Brien). "The lucky thing we had was, there was this *scene* that was very intense," says Wymore. "It was very supportive. Bands were competitive with each other in a certain way, but we also supported each other."

NOH MORE

As with Pink Section, Noh Mercy's tenure as a band was brief but intense. In Noh Mercy's case, the intensity was amplified by the fact that Esmerelda and Tony were not only bandmates and housemates but also a romantic item.[9] Then there were the drugs, which served to magnify the sense of foreboding already in the air. Along with Jonestown and the Moscone/Milk murders, Esmerelda cites the King Tut exhibit that came to town in 1979 as a contributor to the ominous vibes. "There's always been this curse of King Tut. People are *not* supposed to look at that stuff. But it was like a curse—the whole city was cursed. And it was while we were escalating and getting more and more out there. So everything seemed very mythical and mystical—like the end of the world. At the end—and by that, I mean full-on addiction—we lived with our dealer. Tuxedomoon didn't live there,

---

9   "I think something that should be brought up is that Tony and I are not just a band, but we are lovers doing a band," Esmerelda said in an interview. "That really makes a difference." (*Damage*, July 1979, p. 34)

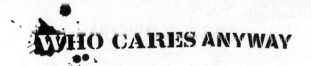

but some of the people around them lived there. It was like the headquarters, the big headquarters. There were a lot of drugs coming through there. Let's just put it that way."

"It was cocaine," clarifies Tony Hotel. "There was so much of it. It became a problem. I didn't really like cocaine. It didn't suit me well, but I was doing it all the time because I'm an addict. Everybody was doing it." Both of them wound up getting off drugs, but only after breaking up (as both a band and a couple). "It was New Year's Eve, 1979," recalls Esmerelda. "It was this really clear vision that I needed to get sober for something that was coming. And it scared me awake, to where that that's all I did, was just follow that vision after that. And what was coming was the AIDS crisis. I needed to get my life back together for my children. They'd gone to live with their father. I mean, I had lost *everything*. So I really needed to get well. Tony and I were like gasoline and fire. We weren't good for each other at all when it got like that."

8

1979: THE PUNK SCENE AT A CROSSROADS

1979 was a pivotal year, one that saw many of the early Mabuhay bands—including the Nuns, the Dils, the Avengers, and Negative Trend—call it quits, and many new ones take shape. This transformation was accompanied by a growing sense that punk, at least in its initial incarnation, had run its course, that it was time to either get serious or move on. "It was like, 'Who's in it for the long haul?'" says Rozz Rezabek, who returned from his sabbatical in Portland early that year. "There was going to be a shakeout. And in the second wave, you really had to have talent."

The Belfast Cowboys were indicative of that shakeout. Fronted by Rezabek, the quartet also featured a couple of ex-Avengers (guitarist Jimmy Wilsey and drummer Danny Furious) as well as Offs bassist Denny DeGorio. They played just a handful of shows—most of them at the Deaf Club—but they were legendary affairs, with the band serving up free shots of gin to audience members along with covers of glam rock hits by the likes of Slade and T-Rex.[10] Explains Rozz, "We get to our first rehearsal, and Jimmy Wilsey has this idea: 'Fuck all these people and all these political songs. Let's just do some songs and let people say, "It's okay to have fun again." Just do the silliest songs we can think of.'" Inveterate scene chronicler Caitlin Hines would proclaim them "this city's best punk band ever in that they never in their sweet short life played a single punk song"—a sentiment that reflected

---

10 The album was eventually released in 1998 as *The Pop Sessions*. It was originally credited to "Rozz & Negative Trend" and later corrected to "Rozz of Negative Trend," though the band was actually an earlier version of the Belfast Cowboys.

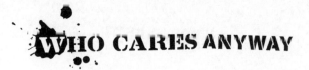
WHO CARES ANYWAY

both the celebratory vibe of their shows and the growing sense of fatigue with punk rock as the seventies drew to a close.[11]

Craig Gray: The punk rock thing—I mean, by the end of '78, as far as most of us were concerned, it was over. We were all trying to do something *more* and not just be stuck in that. It was already starting to turn suburban by then. The seeds of hardcore were starting to show up. That sucked. Too many dudes.

Tim Lockfeld: I think there was a feeling that "punk rock's over," in a way. I remember there was a good quote about, "If one person threw a punch at the Mabuhay, everybody fell down." To me, the whole LA scene that started coming up and inviting skinheads and a lot of violence kind of really—for me, it ended it.

Bob Hoffnar: Basically, when things changed was when the Dead Kennedys showed up. They were pretty much like a punk band being a punk band. That was when it kind of started becoming more segmented and codified, in a way.

Craig Gray: As soon as everything started getting really fast, it got really boring because not much can happen at that speed. And it became codified, and that's when you started to get bands like Flipper, and some of the bands who were originally punk rock started to go off and do other things. By '79, they'd already decided what punk rock was and how it was supposed to be. Even Tuxedomoon was called punk rock in '77. It's a much different thing.

The Dead Kennedys made their live debut at the Mabuhay on July 19, 1978, opening for Negative Trend and the Offs. They quickly rose to prominence thanks to the combination of singer Jello Biafra's animated stage persona and the musicianship of bassist Klaus Flouride and guitarist East Bay Ray—both of them veteran players who turned to punk after having spent years toiling in more conventional bands.[12] In this sense, they were closer to, say, LA's Fear—another

---

11 *Slash*, October 1979, p. 8.
12 Before forming the Dead Kennedys, East Bay Ray played in a rockabilly band called

band with a provocative lead singer backed by a cast of ringers—than any of their Bay Area peers.

For many onlookers, the Dead Kennedys were the band that put Bay Area punk on the map. They were the first SF punk band to tour Europe and the first one to release an LP—1980's *Fresh Fruit for Rotting Vegetables*—with overseas distribution. In his book about that album for the 33⅓ series, author Michael Stewart Foley calls the Dead Kennedys "the archetypal California punk band."[13] Yet to the extent that there was such a thing, the DKs were not it. Rather, they offered a polished, at times cartoonish, take on the genre. They put on a good show, but it didn't take long to devolve into a shtick—as Will Shatter noted as early as 1980 when he griped about "Nazi salutes and goosesteps every time the Dead Kennedys play 'California Uber Alles' for the hundredth time, the same way every time."[14] (The Dils' Tony Kinman would make a similar observation years later: "Jello, like the Dickies down in LA, was the mainstream media's idea of what punk rock was. 'This guy's name is Jello Biafra, his band is named the Dead Kennedys, and he takes his pants off on stage, wow.'"[15])

CRASS COMMERCIALISM

The Dead Kennedys may have been opportunists, but they were still a do-it-yourself proposition, operating largely outside of the established music biz machine. By 1979, that machine was looking to make inroads into punk—or at least its more sanitized cousin, new wave. A key figure in this regard was Howie Klein, an industry veteran who wore many hats in those days: journalist, DJ, manager, and record label executive. Klein's label, 415 Records, debuted in 1978 with 7-inches by the

---

Cruisin'. Meanwhile, Klaus Flouride's career as a professional musician dated back to the late sixties, when he played alongside a young Billy Squier in a band called Magic Terry & the Universe.

13 Michael Stewart Foley, *Fresh Fruit for Rotting Vegetables: 33⅓*, p. 1.
14 *Creep*, No. 5 (Fall 1980), p. 9.
15 In Ensminger, *Left of the Dial*, p. 42.

WHO CARES ANYWAY

Nuns and the Offs.[16] Along with the Mutants 7-inch from 1979, these records are still among the most sought-after ones on the label—which ultimately focused more on courting crossover success than on developing genuinely underground bands. Indeed, Klein's enthusiasm for the likes of SVT, Pearl Harbor and the Explosions, and the Readymades—commercial new wave acts that were more AstroTurf than grass roots—came at the expense of other, better bands.[17]

Peter Urban: The Readymades really didn't fit in with most of the punk scene because they were very poppy, and they did come across like the Knack or something—something that the industry created. And I think it's because of Howie. Because Howie was really kind of an animal of the industry. They did a couple of demos that were produced by Sandy Pearlman. And Klein, who was like the only establishment journalist in the punk scene, didn't acknowledge that he was managing them, but he'd write these articles and say, "Oh, they're the biggest band in the San Francisco punk scene." So it was a real bitter thing for many of us in the scene. Howie was a manipulative bastard, in my opinion. But some of the bands, because he signed them to his record label, they see him as a positive figure.

Sally Webster: People can say negative things about Howie, but he is who he is. He's bright. I'll put it that way. He's got a sharp mind. And also, he's very gay, and he was very gay at the time. I think it was off-putting to a lot of musicians.

Peter Belsito: He was kind of a curmudgeon. He was a businessman. He had seen a lot. He didn't wanna fuck around with kids. He was serious.

---

16 Klein was actually one of three founders of 415 Records. The other principal founder was Chris Knab, who owned Aquarius Records and (along with Klein) deejayed at various underground radio stations under the cringeworthy pseudonym of "Cosmo Topper." The third founder, Butch Bridges, was a silent partner who sold his share in the company in 1980 to Queenie Taylor, a veteran of Bill Graham Productions who went on to manage the Old Waldorf and the Kabuki Theatre after Graham acquired them a couple of years later.
17 In his 2018 memoir *Siren Song: My Life in Music* (St. Martin's, 2018), producer/executive Seymour Stein remarks, "Although Howie was a great talent in many other ways, I felt he didn't have the ears to run a label" (p. 283). A few pages later, he adds, "Klein was not a star at A&R. He had strengths, but that was not one of them" (p. 290).

THE POST-PUNK ERA

Ruby Ray: The thing was, the people who considered themselves the hardcore punks were slightly antagonistic to the people who already had a name and were trying to look at punk and say, "Oh, I'm gonna be cool with it too." But they're still being whatever they were before—commercial promoters or whatever. And so, I think Howie was that kind of a person. He put out that record by the guy who was in Jefferson Airplane. SVT. But we didn't consider that punk.[18] I mean, the guy [bassist Jack Casady] was in Jefferson Airplane! So that was the kind of thing that Howie would promote: these other outside bands trying to say that they were punk, but they weren't. And then the real punks just basically would get ignored.

Craig Gray: Oh God, he hated Negative Trend. We did everything possible to annoy him. And he hated the Midgets. He thought we were a bunch of useless drug addicts.

Michael Belfer: I never had any problems with the guy, but I'm sure Ricky was verbally abusive to him at one point or another because Ricky was verbally abusive to *anybody* who was in any kind of position of power who could help us.

Brad Lapin: There were many people in the San Francisco scene who distrusted Howie and who believed that he was a collaborator, if you will, with the major record companies and the very forces that we felt it was the whole purpose of the scene to resist. We were there to *resist* commercialization—to have our *own* scene, create our *own* magazines, our *own* record labels, our *own* radio shows, our *own* TV shows—not become part of everybody else's.

---

18 Drummer Bob Steeler, who played with Casady in Hot Tuna from 1974 to 1977 and went on to play with the Offs around the time that Casady formed SVT, makes a similar distinction. "The Offs were a genuine punk band; SVT wasn't. I mean, the band was good, but it was kind of like, they were *playing* punk music—they weren't punks. Or they were trying to play punk. It verged on metal."

BILL GRAHAM PREVENTS

Klein may have been the most powerful music biz figure hanging around the SF punk scene, but his stature paled in comparison to that of Bill Graham—still the most powerful name in San Francisco rock music. Unlike Klein, Bill Graham had little time for punk, especially after the Sex Pistols show at Winterland. "I liked some of their songs," Graham later said of the Sex Pistols, but that was about as far as he went. "Would I have wanted to earn a living putting on bands like that? *No*. They were an expression of an attitude which I abhor to this day."[19]

"Bill Graham and their whole ilk—Journey people, Herbie Herbert, Nightmare, all of them—I believe they were threatened by this music, and they wanted to make sure that it didn't happen," says Connie Champagne. "And in San Francisco, there was no *friend* like Seymour Stein, who signed the Ramones and Blondie. There was no Sire Records. Howie Klein tried to do 415 Records, but Howie Klein, I think, was more interested in meeting young men rather than really understanding or promoting what would work at that time. And he didn't have the *resources* that a Seymour Stein had. Those people had a lot of money. They could afford to have the first three Ramones albums not make any money."

The combination of Klein's dubious instincts and Graham's outright hostility posed some significant hurdles. The Clash's first appearance in the Bay Area, in February of 1979, offers a telling example. "I remember when the Dils were going to open for the Clash [in Berkeley], Howie steered Pearl Harbor to do the Berkeley Community Theatre show," recalls Peter Urban, the Dils' manager at the time. "So we had to go down to Los Angeles to open for them. We were frankly annoyed by the whole thing. Nobody had ever *heard* of Pearl Harbor and the Explosions, really, within the punk scene."

On that same trip to the Bay Area, the Clash were booked to headline a benefit show at the Temple Beautiful, but they had to do so unofficially, under an alias ("The Only English Band That Matters"), due to contractual restrictions imposed by Graham's organization. "Part of the backstory to that was this kind of iron grip that

---

19 *Bill Graham Presents: My Life Inside Rock and Out*. Bill Graham and Robert Greenfield. pp. 418 and 421.

Graham had," explains Tom Wheeler. "If you went and saw Patti Smith or Blondie at a Bill Graham place, you had to see these *horrible* kind of corporate new wave bands that somebody who was associated with Bill Graham and that whole scene had put together, trying to jump onto the new wave thing. It was really obnoxious."

According to Jon Savage, this lack of synergy between underground and mainstream contrasted starkly with the situation in the UK. "In Britain, punk rock groups had already a sense of privilege, which was, they were fairly certain that they would have access to national media straightaway. So they would get a review in the music press after a couple of gigs; then, after ten gigs, they would get a record contract; and then they'd release a single, and if the single flew, they'd get on *Top of the Pops*, which was seen by about a third of the country, and so on. In San Francisco, certainly, there was no sense of that. There just wasn't the money or the funds or even the expectation that anybody beyond a very small clique would take any notice of them or that they would get any access to mainstream media."

WHO CARES ANYWAY

NEW YOUTH AND THE TOWN HALL MEETING

The Clash's Temple Beautiful performance wound up raising over $3,000 for New Youth, a nonprofit whose efforts at alternative scene-building anticipated those of later, more successful ventures like *Maximum Rocknroll* and the Gilman Street Project.[20] Alas, the Clash show turned out to be the highpoint of New Youth's brief existence. While the group did manage some other successes—including a printed directory of bands, venues, and other DIY resources—their plans seemed to fall through more often than not, whether it meant losing money on subsequent shows or coming up empty in their quest to establishing a permanent venue and community center.

By the end of 1979, a sense of demoralization had set in among some of the true believers. "[T]his is indeed shaping up to be the winter of our discontent," wrote New Youth member Caitlin Hines in one of her invaluable scene reports for *Slash*, noting the demise of venues like the Deaf Club along with the emergence of "new wave discos," among other recent developments.[21] "But this is San Francisco, don't forget, and we don't take things like that lying down," she added. "We sit around and talk about them and organize things." She wasn't kidding, either.

"We decided that we were going to have a town hall meeting to discuss the threats to the scene," recalls *Damage*'s Brad Lapin. Among those in attendance were Vale, Dirk Dirksen, Peter Urban, Joe Rees, and representatives from several bands. "Mainly what we were concerned about was threats from the big record companies and from the big promoters, like Ken Friedman and Graham and others, who we felt were kind of trespassing, with the notion that this was going to be the next way that they could make their newest million dollars." There were also discussions about the future of punk itself, both as a musical genre and a sociocultural movement. As Urban recalls, "My position in the group was,

---

20 Among the members of New Youth were co-founders Sarah Salir and Sadie Deeks, Subterranean Records founder Steve Tupper, Vince Deranged of the Animal Things, Peter Urban, Bruce Lose, and "Pam and Jane from Portland" (the same Pam and Jane who moved to the city along with Debi Sou and Rozz in 1977).

21 *Slash*, December 1979, p. 10.

THE POST-PUNK ERA

'We should just destroy it. It wasn't designed to be long-term. It was designed because we didn't like what was going on around us. If what's going on now is taking us back towards where we didn't want to be, we should just destroy it and be done with it.' 'Leave a good corpse,' I guess was my attitude."

As Lapin admits, there was something distinctly San Franciscan about the meetings, whatever the disagreements between participants. "After it was over, I thought to myself, 'This is the funniest thing in the world.' We had a town hall meeting, and it was all about building community and protecting the community, the scene, from interlopers. Today, it seems incredibly quaint and silly, but at the time, we were very serious about it, very serious. I think we had two or three of these meetings. But only in San Francisco could you have this happen."

9

"NO GOING BACK":FROM NEGATIVE TREND TO FLIPPER AND TOILING MIDGETS

For all the hand-wringing over the state of the scene, there was plenty of activity brewing beneath the surface. Much of 1979 resembled an extended game of musical chairs, with band members commingling, lineups changing, and new bands forming left and right. "The scene was wild like that," recalls Offs drummer Bob Steeler. "There'd be bands starting and stopping and just all this great energy." Some of these new bands, like the Belfast Cowboys and the one-off Negative Dillingers, were short-lived; others would persist for years or, in a couple of cases, even decades.[22]

"1979 was really a year, in San Francisco, of post-punk bands," emphasizes Peter Urban. "Punk rock fundamentally was over by that time." The idea that there could have been such a thing as "post-punk" as far back as 1979 still boggles the mind, as punk itself had gone largely unnoticed by the mainstream. "From '77 to '79, it's only two years," acknowledges Faith No More's Bill Gould, who was still a high school student in Los Angeles in those days. "But you've gotta think about how things went from here to *here* in twenty-four months. It's crazy. Everything was just 'boom boom boom boom boom.'"

In the UK, it was John Lydon's transition from the Sex Pistols to Public Image Ltd. that epitomized the shift from punk to post-punk. In San Francisco, that shift was echoed by the more gradual transformation of Negative Trend into

22 The Negative Dillingers were Craig Gray on guitar, Tony Kinman of the Dils on bass, and Danny Furious of the Avengers on drums. They played one show, a March 4 gig at the Deaf Club.

two separate bands: Flipper and Toiling Midgets. Like the Sex Pistols, Negative Trend emitted a destructive kind of energy; like PiL, the Trend's offspring were looking to chart a way forward. And while there was little agreement on what that way forward looked (or sounded) like, there was at least a shared sense that punk had served its purpose.[23] "The one thing that punk rock did—and was originally supposed to do—was tear down the idea that rock music had to be this specific thing or that specific thing," says Craig Gray. "But it quickly *became* a specific thing. The original idea was that it could be *anything*, done by *anybody*. We started with that premise, and the whole idea was to destroy rock music as it was and then move on to something else."

CAPTAIN TED, PT. 1: "THE GUY WAS IN ANOTHER ERA"

Ted Falconi was an unusually late bloomer as rock guitarists go. Although he had taken accordion and piano lessons as a youngster and briefly studied classical guitar later on, he didn't pick up an electric guitar until he was almost thirty.[24] By that point, he had already done time in Vietnam, graduated from CCAC (where he focused on sculpture), and taken a job as an instructor at the Academy of Art, where he worked alongside his friend Joe Rees. He was known for wearing a trench coat, driving a Pontiac Firebird, and occasionally camping out at a golf

23 Urban also cites the example of the Kinman brothers, who moved on from the Dils—and San Francisco—to start Rank and File, an early exponent of cowpunk. "And then the Kinman brothers go on to do Blackbird, which is pretty avant-garde, and then they finally wind up in Cowboy Nation, which is doing not even country and western, but literally cowboy music. All of that, though—that trajectory, the trajectory of the Midgets, of Flipper—all represent things that *without* the punk scene would have been pretty much unimaginable. You just couldn't see those bands emerging without there having been the background of the punk rock scene, which sort of came in and said, 'All of this sucks. We don't *want* to listen to this prog rock. We're tired of musicians who are full of themselves and their egos, and we want to return this to something where we can just go and hang out and feel like we're a community.' That's what punk rock did. And there was sort of no going back after that."

24 Falconi began work on a master's degree in music at Laney College in Oakland—"that was like synthesizers and performance," he notes—but ran out of money before he could finish.

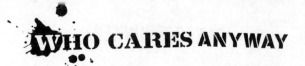

course in Berkeley; he even owned a set of golf clubs. "Ted was kind of the real deal, man," summarizes Tommy Antel. "One time we were talking, and he was telling me about just watching this ammo dump explode for, like, four days. All he did was take acid and watch it blow up. The guy was in another era."

John Gullak: He used to have a little basement apartment on Broadway across the street from CCAC [in Oakland], and I would go hang out with him there. This is way before Flipper. People would come in, and he'd make Turkish coffee, and you'd sit in his kitchen and smoke cigarettes and talk. Both Ted and Joe Rees—they were friends before the Mutants and all that. They really would pick our brains about the whole punk scene. Ted was very interested and was trying to figure out how he could get a foothold into it. And the same with Joe Rees.

Joe Rees: We went to the California College of Arts in Oakland. That's where we met. We were both in fine arts. And having similar backgrounds—we were both ex-veterans from the military, and we were into rock 'n' roll music and all that—kind of conceptual art, performance art, and sculpture. We had a lot of things that we could communicate about. So we started spending a lot of time together. I almost lived at his place for a couple of years while I was going to college.

It was thanks to his friends from CCAC that Falconi had his conversion experience with the electric guitar circa late 1977. As the guitarist explains, "I was over at Rees's—over at Joe's—and John Gullak from the Mutants was over there, and he had his guitar and stuff set up onstage. Joe had these big-ass Voice of the Theatre PA speakers. The guitar was plugged into those things directly. So it was like more electricity than to run a refrigerator. I mean, it was, like, *loud*. And I'd never played an electric guitar before. They plugged me in, and it was like, 'Wow! Wow!' A week later, I had a guitar and an amp, and I was startin' a band."[25]

---

25 Falconi's first band was called SST (no relation to the record label). They recorded one 7-inch, which was produced by Tommy Tadlock and released on his short-lived Tidal Wave imprint. SST were among the dozen or so bands who played the Miners' Benefit in March of 1978. Falconi's patented guitar sound was not yet in evidence at this point; the band was largely a vehicle for performance artist and non-singer Irene Dogmatic

THE POST-PUNK ERA

The budding guitarist had already started (and ended) two bands when, sometime in early 1979, he made the acquaintance of a 6'6" Hungarian fellow known only as "Jim." "He had a studio down below Hayward," explains Ted. "Had a huge warehouse. He's over here; he's working as a welder. So he'd weld, buy a guitar. He'd weld, buy another guitar. He'd weld, he'd buy an amp. He'd weld, he'd buy a PA. It was he and I, and then we needed a bass player. Then I got Will." Will, of course, was Will Shatter, who had just recently left Negative Trend, having played his last gig with the group on March 15, 1979. (The group would break up altogether a month later, more on which below.)

It was Will, in turn, who summoned a nineteen-year-old by the name of Bruce Calderwood to try out on vocals. A San Francisco native and recently reformed Deadhead, Calderwood discovered the Mabuhay not long after graduating from high school in 1977. "I used to go there with long hair, and I'd watch Negative Trend, and I'd sit there, and I'd read Nietzsche and Kafka and shit like that," he recalls. "I'd take a table and set it up right in front of Negative Trend's stage, like where a dancer would be, and I'd sit there in a chair with my feet up on the table while they were playing, reading this incredibly intellectual book while Negative Trend was rioting. Well, of course, Will was enamored by that."

Bruce was among the contestants who tried out to take Rozz's place in the spring of 1978. "Biafra was there, and a whole bunch of other people were there," says the singer, who by this point had adopted "Bruce Lose" (later to morph into "Bruce Loose") as his *nom de punk*. "What it boiled down to was that I was real close, but I hadn't had enough experience. I was totally fresh, and these other guys had had a little bit of experience."[26]

(sample lyrics: "You're a nothing, a total zero / You're the void, you're a real hero"). Falconi's subsequent band, Rad Command, didn't make any recordings.

26 A couple of months before his Flipper audition, Loose was seen onstage at the Deaf Club performing an impromptu version of 'I Wanna Be Your Dog' with a pickup band that included UXA singer De Troit on bass. *Slash*'s Claude "Kickboy Face" Bessy saw fit to mention it in a concert review in the zine's April 1979 issue. He describes the then-unknown vocalist as "a super-charged skinhead kid" and raves about his impromptu performance: "the crowd went ape [and] the kid went more ape, singing with more vibrancy than Iggy has shown in ages."

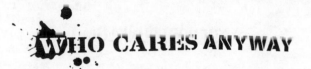
WHO CARES ANYWAY

Joe Rees: I knew Bruce when he was a teenager. He hung out in the scene. He wasn't performing. He was always a pain in the ass, but I didn't even realize he was that talented. And boy, was he. It was a beautiful thing.

Ruby Ray: Bruce Loose and Jello Biafra were some of the original punks who would always be at the front of the stage watching the bands. And then they formed their own bands and became incredible. That's how creatively intense the early scene was. It seems like everybody that was part of it in the early beginning stages went on to do something, whatever it was. Something creative.

Bruce Loose: So there it was, April '79. And Will was like, "Hey, I've got this guitar player, and he's got some songs. You wanna come down and sing?" And I said, "Sure." And there was some other weird guy, a Czechoslovakian guy named Jim. Now, Jim's idea was that he wanted to start a band that just kind of free-form jammed. He had a big old Mack truck with a generator on it, a drop-down side panel that turned into a stage, and enough Marshall stacks to blow away Ted Nugent. And he wanted us to hit the road and go around crashing the outside gates of county fairs all around America. He always tried to get us to jam to this Jimi Hendrix song, 'Night Train,' which had a certain progression of chords or notes or whatever. He was the only one who ever played it that way. Ted played something different; I tried singing it as best I could, and Will was there. There was never a drummer.

Jim had this whole thing about having me come out on a cross upside down, and because I had a shaved head, he wanted to call me "Nazi Dog." He wanted the band to be named "Five White Guys with Dicks Bigger than Niggers'." I said, "Forget that. I'm out of here. I don't want anything to do with that, and I don't want anything to do with our band name being that." So I disappear. I split, went to Portland, bought a bass, tried to do a band up there.[27]

---

27 In his book *Enter Naomi: SST and All That*, Joe Carducci recalls meeting Bruce in Portland that summer. "Diane was one of the hippest girls up there; she went down to SF and came back with her boyfriend Bruce, who intimidated most of the Portland punks, but he'd hang out at the store to listen to records and told me that he was in a band called Flipper. He wasn't in a hurry to get back there, so I figured it for a kind of loose set-up" (p. 166). Carducci later moved to the Bay Area briefly before moving to Southern California to work for SST Records.

102

THE POST-PUNK ERA

RICKY RETURNS

This brings the Sleepers back into the picture. Right around the time Flipper started rehearsing in April of 1979, Sleepers guitarist Michael Belfer returned to San Francisco from his self-imposed exile on the East Coast and was in the process of reforming his old band—only without Ricky Williams on vocals. "There was a while when Rozz was the lead singer," recalls Paul Draper, "because we kicked Ricky out for bad behavior." Thus, with Rozz taking Ricky's spot in the Sleepers, Ricky was available to step in for Bruce.[28]

The still-unnamed band played its first show at Golden Gate Park sometime in early June. On drums was Bob Steeler, who had never even rehearsed with the group before. "Things were pretty loose," he says. "We just showed up and played." It wound up being a one-off gig for the veteran drummer—who, before joining the Offs a few months earlier, had spent several years with Jefferson Airplane spinoff, Hot Tuna. It was an adjustment, as he readily admits. "I mean, I was really new to the scene. At the time, that was when they were spitting on people in punk bands and stuff. And some guy was squirting toothpaste on me, and I thought the guy was spitting on me, so I didn't want to do it anymore. Guys were gettin' hepatitis and stuff."

Musically, however, Steeler liked what he heard that day. "Crime were the only guys who played slow, other than Flipper. Everybody else was real fast. So I *really* liked the groove in Flipper. I thought it was killin'. I mean, it was a different kind of music from what a lot of other people were playing." Artist Bruce Conner, who was on hand for the occasion, concurred. "I think the last hot show

28 The Sleepers played at least two shows with Rozz on vocals, one of which was "in the living room of my parents' house in Los Altos Hills," recalls Sari Gordon, a friend of the band. "They were in Hawaii, so I had a party. Rozz was on vocals. Came into the kitchen with a big baggie of various unidentified pills, saying, 'Who wants some?' I think he had to duck to get through the door, and I couldn't believe this giant wearing makeup was standing in my parents' kitchen. It was the first best day of my life." The Rozz-fronted lineup was also scheduled to play at a June 17 show at 330 Grove Street along with the Middle Class, the Tools, and "The Band with Will & Ricky" (i.e., Flipper). However, the concert "was shut down by the cops because of some stupid dance permit infraction" according to Caitlin Hines, who mentioned the show in the September 1979 issue of *Slash*.

WHO CARES ANYWAY

I saw was Will Shatter and Ricky Sleeper and this strange Hungarian Vadar and Ted and Steeler playing at the band shell in Golden Gate Park," he raved in an interview with *Damage*. "It was chaos; it was beautiful. I talked to Joe Rees of Target Video the other night, and he said that he had a tape of that, and we agreed it was the last really hot show we'd seen … They pulled the plug fifteen minutes before the scheduled end of the permit."[29]

As Falconi remembers it, the band came up with the name "Flipper" immediately after that first show. "We were at Golden Gate Park in the band shell. Looking out down the field is the King Tut show at the de Young Museum. The line is like fifty blocks long. Everybody's wearing coats and ties. Hot summer afternoon. Everybody looks totally uptight and tired and hot. On the side of the stage was the aquarium. All these little kids comin' out: 'Flipper! Flipper! I wanna go back and see Flipper!' Will said, 'That's what I want people to be saying about us. Let's call it Flipper.' And then I did the logo the same day.

"And it was perfect," he adds, "because Ricky had a dog whose name was Flipper; he had a cat whose name was Flipper; he had a fish whose name was Flipper. He had all these other animals; they were all Flipper." Indeed, Williams had been fond of the name Flipper for some time. "He liked that television show—that's why he called it that," notes Connie Champagne, his girlfriend at the time. "There wasn't a big intellectual meaning behind it." Meanwhile, Belfer traces the singer's obsession with the name to a late-night encounter with a dolphin carcass on the beach during an acid trip. "Everything was 'Flipper' after that," he says, including all of Williams's various pets. "So he wanted to name the *band* 'Flipper.' And I told him that that was a dumb idea because I thought we would get sued by the TV show. I had no idea that nobody would have cared."[30]

As for Ricky's influence on Flipper's musical direction, things are hazier.

---

29 *Damage*, August/September 1979, p. 8. As for Steeler, he didn't even realize that the band's singer was the same person he'd seen onstage a year earlier singing for the Sleepers. "The guy who sang with me in Flipper sang with the *Sleepers*? Oh, man. He was amazing!"

30 "The Sleepers are an intense young band from Palo Alto (south of San Francisco). They decided not to call themselves Ambulance, the Teeth or Flipper." (*Search & Destroy #1-6*, p. 137)

THE POST-PUNK ERA

Apart from the aforementioned (and still unreleased) video of the first show, there are no recordings from his summer with the band, and as far as anyone can remember, none of his lyrics stuck with any of the songs. That said, it's likely that his fondness for slower tempos had at least some influence on Flipper's subsequent direction. Here, his uncredited contribution to Crime's 'Murder by Guitar'—released in 1977 as the B-side of their second 7-inch—is relevant. "He basically wrote that song, that opening part, which has the weird chord changes," recalls Paul Draper. "Because I was with him when he was fleshing out parts of that."[31] That song—or at least its slow, grinding intro section—can be heard as a key proto-Flipper moment, especially given what Champagne recalls of some early behind-the-scenes discussions between Williams and Falconi. "Ted would come over to my apartment, and he would be like, 'Yeah, we're gonna do these songs really fast.' And Ricky was like, 'No, man. *Everybody* does things fast. We have to do things *really slow*.' And he really had to sell Ted on that."[32]

Then there was Ricky's penchant for improvisation. "He made everything up on the spot and never sang the same thing twice," says Bruce, with only slight exaggeration. "He would've been perfect for Flipper, except he also never took the same handful of drugs twice, so you never knew what condition he was going to be in. It was a little much." Given their later exploits, the idea that Flipper would have to fire someone for taking too many drugs is, shall we say, a bit ironic. Yet it was part of a recurring pattern for the singer, who had already been booted from Crime and (at least temporarily) the Sleepers for similar reasons. "There were a lot of people who just wouldn't deal with him at all," says Belfer. "They would have been attracted—'This guy's fantastic!'—and then after one session with him, they would just pack up their gear and walk away."

Connie Champagne: Ted was bugging me: "You've gotta get him to rehearsal on time." I'm thinking, "Why do I have to do that? I'm not Nancy Spungen. This is not *my* life here." But I got him there. I mean, he was a small person, Ricky

---

31 Belfer has a similar recollection. "He wrote 'Murder by Guitar.' They never credited him properly for a lot of that stuff."
32 In a 1983 interview in *Ego*, Williams made a similar comment about his role in Toiling Midgets: "I always tried to slow everything down. Slower."

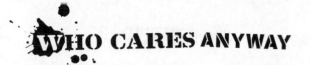

was, but he was quite a bit bigger than I was. So I got him on a dolly. And I got Ian Cartmill, who was this big Canadian guy. He saw my plight, what situation I was in. So we just stuck him on the dolly, and I rolled him in, and I said, "Here's your singer. I have to go."[33]

Ted Falconi: After Ricky had a couple of ODs—OD'd a couple of times—we did a show at the Deaf Club, and Ricky didn't show.[34] Bruce just got back from Portland. We had an open mic auditioning for singers. Bruce stepped up, and it was like he was never gone.

Bruce Loose: I came back, and here's this band, and they're playing at the Deaf Club. This guy Jim was out of the way. Steve [DePace] was there, which I wasn't in the best approval of, but he was a drummer, and he showed up, and he played.

Steve Tupper: I knew Bruce at that point, just from hanging out and stuff, although I didn't know that he was in this band, and I was kind of surprised to see him up there onstage.

Bruce Loose: It came down to me and Vince Deranged because Ricky didn't show up to sing that night. So the two of us took turns, one after each other, singing along, ad-libbing to whatever Flipper was playing. And we had the audience vote at the end. They voted me back in, even though they didn't

---

33 As for Jim, he apparently fell off the map not long after the Golden Gate Park show. "I was hoping that he would re-contact us," says Falconi. "I saw him at the Ramones show over the park in San Francisco, across from the Civic Center, and that was the last time I've ever seen him." The Ramones concert took place on June 9, and Flipper's next show was evidently the June 17 show at 330 Grove Street, alluded to in an earlier footnote.

34 In a later interview, Ricky gave his own version of what happened regarding his time with Flipper: "Me and Will started it … but then it became a joke, a little bit too much of a joke, and I quit" (*Ego*, #7). His last appearance with the group most likely came on August 18 at the Loma Linda, a short-lived venue in the Mission. Down the street, the Belfast Cowboys headlined at the Deaf Club, "with numerous indecisive dayglow kids haplessly wandering back and forth between the two gigs," wrote Caitlin Hines. "A weekend to restore one's faith in this teenage wasteland we quaintly refer to as the scene." (*Slash*, September 1979, p. 12).

know they were voting me *back* in. They just thought they were voting me *in*, versus Vince Deranged.

Steve Tupper: Mike [Fox] from the Tools and I were both total Negative Trend fans. We cornered Ted in the back room [after the show] and said, "Hey, would you like to be on this record that we're putting out?" And Ted was totally grinning from ear to ear. I don't think they'd even done a demo at that point.[35]

That record, a four-song 7-inch entitled *SF Underground*, would mark the first release on Tupper's Subterranean Records. Issued on November 17, 1979, it featured Flipper's 'Earthworm' alongside more conventional punk rock fare by VKTMS, No Alternative, and the Tools. The caustic, lumbering dirge stuck out like a sore thumb, which is to say, it was by far the highlight of the record. A reviewer in *Slash* called it "[t]he best thing out of San Francisco since that sulfate that came down here a while back"—an apt comparison given the coded references to speed freak culture in the Will Shatter-penned lyrics ("I live in the dark … and no one sees me, ever").[36]

Yet as Tupper recalls, not everyone was on board with it. "I remember playing

35 Boulware & Tudor, *Gimme Something Better*, p. 101.
36 *Slash,* January 1980, p. 45.

the Flipper track for Tim Yohannan at the time, and he got this really grave expression on his face: 'That's not Maximum Rock 'n' Roll.' He liked the rest of the record really well, but that track he just could not stomach."[37]

MUSICAL CHAIRS, PT. 2:FORMING THE MIDGETS

By the time Negative Trend played its last show in April of 1979, the band had already begun morphing into something different.[38] Another singer, the talented but mercurial Rik L. Rik, had come and gone, and with Will Shatter's departure the month before, guitarist Craig Gray was left as the last original member standing.

"It was kind of hard for Craig when Will went to do Flipper," remembers Debi Sou. "And he had such a hard time with singers. Because Rozz only did a few months, and then he took off. And then Mikal Waters came. And he was quite good—both Rozz and Mikal Waters were good. And then came Rik L. Rik. That was *horrible*. He was with his agent Posh Boy [Robbie Fields]. That was just dreadful."

"Negative Trend had a *horrible* relationship with Rik L. Rik," agrees Peter Urban, the band's manager at the time. "We had *big* expectations when he was brought in as the singer, and he was just a real pain in the ass. So when they booted him, finally, I think Craig and the others were just sick of singers."[39] Sick of singers and, according

---

37 At the time, Yohannan was hosting a local radio show by the name of Maximum Rock 'n' Roll, but he had not yet started the zine of the same name.

38 Negative Trend's last show took place on April 27, 1979, at Mills College in Oakland. The Dead Kennedys headlined, and Ricky (who was living in the closet of girlfriend Connie Champagne's Mills dorm room) stood in on vocals for part of Negative Trend's set.

39 The Rik L. Rik/Tim Mooney version of Negative Trend recorded a handful of songs together, but the discographical details are rather convoluted. Two of the songs—a re-recording of 'Meathouse' and a new song, 'I Got Power'—were released by Posh Boy in 1979 as a Rik L. Rik single. Meanwhile, 'I Got Power' and a re-recording of 'Mercenaries' appear together—this time credited to Negative Trend—on the Upsetter Records compilation *Tooth & Nail* and again on the soundtrack to the 1983 horror movie *Nightmares*. Finally, all five of the songs (i.e., the above three plus 'Atomic Lawn' and a re-recording of 'Black and Red') appear—once again as Rik L. Rik songs—on

THE POST-PUNK ERA

to Gray, sick of punk rock in general. "By the time we had Rik L. Rik in Negative Trend, being labeled a 'punk rock' band was kind of limiting. And we started to write the songs that would be Toiling Midgets songs with Rik in the band."[40]

The Midgets came together in late 1979 after Gray returned from a summer in his hometown of Vancouver. The lineup was essentially a continuation of the last installment of Negative Trend, with Tim Mooney on drums and Shatter's replacement, the seventeen-year-old Jonathan Henrickson (aka Nosmo King), on bass. The final piece of the puzzle was guitarist Paul Hood. He and Gray originally met in February of 1978 when Hood's band, the Enemy, played the Mabuhay; the next month, Negative Trend played the Bird, a punk clubhouse in Seattle operated by Hood and his bandmates. Along the way, the two bonded over a shared admiration for Mick Ronson's guitar playing, setting the stage for a chance encounter that both of them still recall vividly.

Craig Gray: Early 1980, late 1979, he moved down here. He had just bought a guitar at Guitar Center. My girlfriend and I ran into him in the street. And he asked me about Tim Mooney and the Sleepers, and I said he was our drummer and "would you like to play with us?" He says, "Well, I play guitar now." And I said,

---

the Posh Boy compilation *Beach Blvd*. "But the weird thing is, someone else redid my leads because I know I fucked up," says Gray. "I can't remember who did it—maybe the guy from the Adolescents [Rikk Agnew] or somebody. For the *Beach Boulevard* record. Not for the single. Which is weird."

As for *Nightmares*, "It was one of those chapter-like horror movies, four little, short stories," explains the guitarist. "Emilio Estevez was a punk rock kid in one of them. He listened to punk rock in his headphones, and they used two Negative Trend songs, but they were re-recorded at the Universal Studios with session dudes." The session dudes were Leslie Bohem (bass), David Kendrick (drums), and Bob Haag (guitar) of the LA band Gleaming Spires (who, incidentally, also made up the backing band on Sparks' early 1980s albums, including 1982's *Angst in My Pants*).

40 "I think 'Destiny' was written with Rik in the band," says Gray, referring to the first song on the Midgets' *Sea of Unrest* (see Chapter 18). "Negative Trend played that once or twice. Rik L. Rik actually does his own version of 'Destiny' with his own lyrics. He also does [the Sleepers'] 'She's Fun' and rewrites the lyrics. It's kind of sad. When you know the originals, you kind of feel sorry for him. It ain't Ricky, and Rik was never Ricky." Both of these songs can be found on the Rik L. Rik compilation *The Lost Album* (Posh Boy, 1991). 'Destiny' appears here as 'Teenage Destiny.' The album also includes a solo version of Negative Trend's 'Meathouse,' with Rik singing and playing acoustic guitar.

WHO CARES ANYWAY

"That's fine." And it kind of started from there.

Paul Hood: When I met Craig and those guys, I never imagined for a second that I would be playing in a band with him. Because my musical thing is crazy, and his was very rock 'n' roll, power chords, punk rock, fast but very melodic. But I bumped into him after I'd been there for a while. I had just bought a guitar—I'd traded in my bass. And he said, "Oh, hey, what're you doing?" And I said, "I was at Guitar Center. I just got a guitar." He goes, "What else is going on?" "Well, I heard this band called the Sleepers, and they have the most amazing drummer in the world. I gotta get this guy. Have you ever heard of Tim Mooney?" And Craig said, "Oh, yes. He's in my band." [Laughs.] I said, "What?" And he said, "Yeah, you wanna join?"

I seriously didn't even really know how to play guitar. I was more of a bass player than a guitar player. And Tim—amazing drummer, left-handed drummer— and Craig, they were very tight. I mean, Tim was really a floppy, sloppy drummer, but he could still play tight. Strange. And they just let me play with them. I would squeal and squawk and make noise, and they let me do it. They didn't complain about my guitar playing. And I just loved playing with them because we would make these sounds that I'd never felt before playing with anybody else. And they didn't want me to leave; they didn't tell me I couldn't play with them anymore.

Debi Sou: I think, personally, it was the coming together of Paul and Craig that got the Midgets going. That's when the spark happened: the vision of these two guitars—Craig on rhythm and Paul making noise—and then a steady bass. Although Paul never thought that Jonathan could handle the bass that he wanted. And then they had Tim on drums, and Tim was fucking *amazing*.

Craig Gray: Ricky didn't really show up until much later. Well, he would show up at shows. He would show up at shows on various drugs and either pass out halfway through our set or just do what he wanted. We just kind of ignored him.

Though Ricky would eventually join the band in a more official capacity, the Midgets were originally conceived of as an instrumental band. "I think being instrumental was real important at that time," says Gray, "because there were no bands that were actually playing just music in a rock format—around here anyway." It also fit the band members' personalities, which were, on the whole, introverted and averse to the spotlight. "I mean, I didn't really want to be the front man," says Hood. "Craig didn't want to be the front man. Tim didn't want to be the front man. Jonathan wanted to be the front man, but after looking at Craig and looking at Tim, he said, 'Okay, I don't want to be the front man either.' So we didn't have a front man."

In the meantime, they would make the acquaintance of another key contributor, though he wasn't a front man or even a band member. This was Tom Mallon, a twenty-three-year-old UC Berkeley dropout and music junkie who was operating an eight-track recording studio out of his apartment in the Upper Haight. Hood found about him through a mutual acquaintance and went to pay him a visit. "And I mean, literally, he's built himself kind of a control room, but then all around the house, the different rooms have gear set up. And I started listening to what they'd been doing, and it sounded like Motown or Stax or something. I mean, it was a big, beefy sound with horns. It was crazy."

"So then I asked Tom if he did demos and what he charged, and it was ridiculous," Hood continues. "It was so cheap. So that's what we did: we went to Tom's house and set up all over the place. And that's where we did our first recordings."[41] Those recordings, which circulated as a demo tape and were later released digitally under the title *Do the Incendiary*, reveal a band still figuring out its identity. There are halting attempts at dub ('Aquadub One' and 'Aquadub Two') as well as a brief blast of something resembling hardcore (the middle section of 'Do the Incendiary'). The songs are also rather compact, with the longest one clocking in at 2:19. For the most part, though, it already sounds like the Midgets—which is to say, it's guitar rock for the world after punk or guitar rock without guitar heroes.

---

41 The demo was recorded on April 27, a year to the day after Negative Trend's last show. Gray describes the scene: "Tim, Paul and I arrived at about 11 a.m. Tom set up Paul in the bathroom, the rest of us in a back room." (https://web.archive. org/web/20160623212611/http://toilingmidgets.com/beginning.html). Singer Paul Casteel, whose band the Woundz also recorded at Mallon's home studio that year, recounted a similar scene: "The guitarist would record in the bathroom, and the vocalist would be in the kitchen, and the drums would be set up in his bedroom. And he would be mixing down at the kitchen table."

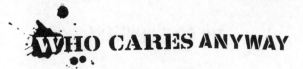

PUBLIC IMAGE

Along with Flipper, the Midgets were one of two bands to open for Public Image Ltd. when the British trio made its highly anticipated Bay Area debut on May 10, 1980. The show amounted to a do-over for Gray and Shatter, two years after Negative Trend had been offered and then denied a slot on the Sex Pistols' Winterland bill. It was also a do-over for PiL's John Lydon, who was determined to avoid working with Bill Graham. Hence the location of the show: the South of Market Cultural Center, a seldom-used venue at 934 Brannan Street "whose dingy obscurity is rivaled only by its authenticity as a counter-cultural elephant graveyard," as Shoshana Wechsler put it in a *Damage* article on PiL's visit.[42]

The show was such an event that Lydon and PiL guitarist Keith Levene actually came to town two months beforehand for a press conference (organized by the omnipresent Howie Klein) at The City, a dance club on Broadway. There, the band members "fielded a series of particularly obtuse and self-serving questions from a crowd of about seventy people [in] one of the great non-events in recent memory," according to another writeup in *Damage*.[43] It wasn't entirely inconsequential, though. As Bruce Loose recalls, "A bunch of delegates showed up there and just *demanded* that Flipper play with PiL." Evidently, it worked.

The Midgets, on the other hand, were a last-minute addition to the bill. "Peter Urban called us the day of the show and somehow had finagled us onto the bill," explains Gray. "And then we had to call Tim because we just found out that day, and I think he was at work. He had to drive up from Palo Alto. When it came time to go on, he wasn't around. So a friend of Paul's who was at the show, Bill Rieflin, did a quick little soundcheck with us. And then, just as we're going on, I looked out the back door, and Mooney was pulling up. And he ran in the back door and up onto the stage, and we started playing."

By all accounts, the show itself was a success. "They had no security, not any, and there wasn't even a fight," says Bob Steeler. "It was fantastic. Amazing playing, too. Flipper killed it, and so did Public Image." Arkansaw Man's Stephen

42 *Damage*, July 1980, p. 9.
43 *Damage*, March 1980, p. 38.

presents...

PUBLIC IMAGE LTD.

JOHN LYDON   KEITH LEVENE   WOBBLE

-Formerly-
Johnny Rotten
of the
SeX PISTOLS

south
of
market
cultural
center

934 BRANNON/eighth st.

(in S.F.)

(this!)
SATURDAY,
MAY 10th
at 8 PM

..plus more...

tickets: $8. in advance
at all bass outlets

$9. day of show
at the door

Clarke recalls a volley of beer cans being thrown on stage during Flipper's set. "At one point, Will was playing the bass and staring out into the audience, and one of them hit him right in the forehead, and he didn't even fucking blink. I thought, 'Oh my god. These guys—they're for real.' It was really nice. Public Image wasn't even interesting after I saw Flipper. So there.'"

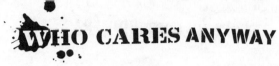

10

DARK CABARET: THE RESIDENTS, TUXEDOMOON, AND SUBTERRANEAN MODERN

Flipper and Toiling Midgets represented the "rock" end of the spectrum in post-punk San Francisco. While not artless by any stretch, they were still using basic rock instrumentation—guitar, bass, and drums—and their music had both a volume level and a visceral impact that made it more suited to rock clubs than art galleries.

Yet the city was also home to a number of groups that were less ambivalent about their artiness—groups that employed synthesizers and other newfangled electronics and often eschewed live drums in favor of drum machines. It is this thread—exemplified by the Residents, Tuxedomoon, and Factrix—that garners the bulk of attention in Simon Reynolds's chapter on San Francisco in *Rip It Up and Start Again.* To this trio, we can add Minimal Man and Indoor Life, both of whom made their best music in San Francisco before relocating elsewhere, along with the more pop-oriented Voice Farm and the more experimental German Shepherds and Pre Fix.[44][45] While distinct from each other, these groups shared

---

44 Pre Fix left behind one 7-inch, 'Underneathica' b/w 'Ectomorphine' (Subterranean, 1981), which evidently didn't make waves at the time but is now a pricy collector's item. Guitarist/multi-instrumentalist Johnny Glenn also had a hand in another Subterranean obscurity released that year: the *Arizona Disease* 7-inch, which features a couple of bands (Jr. Chemists and Les Seldoms) from the Phoenix/Tucson area, where Pre Fix also originally hailed from.

45 The German Shepherds were mostly a studio act. As vocalist/multi-instrumentalist Mark Hutchinson recalls, the duo played a total of six or seven shows during their lifespan. Their 1985 LP *Music for Sick Queers* (M&S) lives up to its name in the best possible sense.

some family resemblances, including an embrace of new technology and an emphasis on immersive, multimedia live performances—"a tendency shaped partly by the living legacy of the city's gay radical theater groups," writes Reynolds, "and partly by the 'total art' ideas emanating from the city's Art Institute."[46]

THE RESIDENTS

The Residents warrant a place in any discussion of experimental music in San Francisco, although they were an anomaly even by the city's generous standards. They predated punk by half a decade, releasing their first record (the *Santa Dog* EP) in 1972 and their first LP (*Meet the Residents*) in 1974. Though more an extension of late sixties experimental rock in the Zappa/Beefheart tradition than a true precursor to punk, they were embraced by many within the punk scene. In fact, it was thanks to a feature in *Search & Destroy* that they caught the attention of Jon Savage, who, in turn, featured them in an article of his own (alongside Kraftwerk, Devo, and Throbbing Gristle) for the influential UK weekly *Sounds*. Before long, John Peel was playing their records on BBC radio, and by late 1977, the group found themselves actually selling records instead of just making them.[47]

By this point, the Residents had established their new and improved headquarters at 444 Grove Street, a large brick building that housed a sixteen-track recording studio, a film studio, and the offices for their label, Ralph Records. The building—which they purchased for $100,000 with money from a band member's inheritance—was a mere block away from the Gay Community Center, an occasional punk venue during the era. "We would go by the Residents' studio almost once a week trying to find them, banging on their doors and all this other shit," recalls Bruce Loose of his pre-Flipper days circa 1978. Not surprisingly, they didn't answer the door. "They were pretty mysterious," notes Blaise Smith.

---

46 Simon Reynolds, *Rip it Up and Start Again: Postpunk 1978–1984* (Penguin, 2005), p. 199
47 "Whereas previously The Cryptic Corporation had literally not been able to give the records away, they were now inundated with orders, and demand even began to outstrip supply," writes Ian Shirley in his book-length history of the band, *Never Known Questions: Five Decades of the Residents* (Cherry Red, 2016, p. 60).

"I had a good friend who was in them, so I knew them and all that. But they were actually literally really secretive about it." Adds Cole Palme of Factrix, "I think if I went around and asked people, a lot of friends of mine would go, 'You know, remember that dude?' I don't know; I can't say with any certainty about that."

Given their anonymity—and the fact that they didn't perform live until 1983—one could argue that the Residents were less a San Francisco band than a band that happened to live in San Francisco. "They were in their own world," admits Tom Wheeler. "And they were influential, but it was more through a combination of their records and the films. If you went to the Roxie or the Art Institute or various places where they would show collections of music films, they always had one of the Residents' pieces in there." Those films included a striking black and white promo video for *Third Reich 'n' Roll*, with the band members clad in pointy newspaper hats, along with a series of aggressively weird "one-minute movies" released in conjunction with their 1980 LP *The Commercial Album*.

These (pre-MTV) music videos, in turn, represented just one facet of the Residents' more general penchant for media manipulation, which they employed to both conceptual and promotional ends. In addition to the one-minute movies, they promoted *The Commercial Album* by purchasing forty one-minute radio ads—one for each song—on local pop station KFRC. Then there was the intrigue involving the Cryptic Corporation, the umbrella organization that encompassed both the Residents and Ralph Records and spoke to the media on their behalf, as it were. Thanks to some winking cooperation from members of the music press, they were thus able to promote the band while also maintaining their mysterious aura.[48] Finally, there was the saga surrounding the album *Eskimo*, which was "delayed" due to a purported conflict between the Residents and the Cryptic Corporation. In place of *Eskimo* came another album with its own elaborate backstory, *Not Available*, which had supposedly been recorded and shelved a few years earlier. When *Eskimo* was finally released in 1979, it sold more than 100,000 copies—an astonishing figure for an album of faux-Inuit soundscapes.

---

48 Those paying close enough attention were probably able to figure out that the Cryptic Corporation's spokesmen essentially *were* the Residents (and vice versa), but it would have been gauche to emphasize this in print.

THE POST-PUNK ERA

SUBTERRANEAN MODERN

Thanks to the surprising commercial success of its flagship act, Ralph Records had enough resources at its disposal to start signing other acts. As a first step in that direction, they curated a compilation LP, *Subterranean Modern,* which featured several tracks each from Tuxedomoon, Chrome, MX-80 Sound, and the Residents themselves. Notably, all of these groups had a significant pre-punk element: Tuxedomoon with their British art rock influences and Angels of Light connections, Chrome with their acid rock leanings, and MX-80 with their roots in heavy prog rock à la King Crimson. Moreover, the cover art was designed by Gary Panter, who had recently designed a trio of Frank Zappa album covers. As experimental as the Residents were, their sensibilities were anchored in an earlier era—understandably so, given that their core members were already in their mid-thirties at the time.

Unlike the contemporaneous *No New York* or *Yes LA* compilations, *Subterranean Modern* doesn't document a "scene" so much as a collection of SF-based bands that the Residents found interesting. Like the Residents, Chrome was still strictly a studio project as of 1979, one that already had a couple of albums under its belt by this point. The group's futuristic acid punk had one foot in psychedelia and one foot in the sort of science fiction dystopias that *Search & Destroy* favorite J.G. Ballard conjured up in his novels. In this sense, Chrome's music was very much of its time and place, though as Tuxedomoon contributor Michael Belfer recalls, they were largely an enigma around town. "They didn't do any live shows, so nobody knew anything about them."

Meanwhile, MX-80 were transplants from Bloomington, Indiana, and self-described outcasts who had a frosty relationship with the local punk scene. "SF totally, absolutely hated us," recalled guitarist Rich Stim years later.[49] And the feeling was mutual. "We were shocked at how fundamentalist the music scene was here," said guitarist Bruce Anderson. "I took a lot of solos, and that made

49 Kevin L. Jones, "MX-80 Recapture Their Sound: SF's Noisy Art-Rockers Talk Old Days, New LP." KQED blog, November 28, 2015. https://www.kqed.org/arts/11115041/mx-80-recapture-their-sound-sfs-noisy-art-rockers-talk-old-days-new-lp

me 'old wave.' Artistically, San Francisco is very cliquish and provincial, which in turn creates cults of mediocrity."

TUXEDOMOON

Tuxedomoon was the one band on *Subterranean Modern* with extensive connections to the punk scene, if only by default. "The thing about the punk rock scene in San Francisco was, it wasn't only *punk*," explains saxophonist and keyboardist Steven Brown, one of the group's two founding members, along with violinist and guitarist Blaine Reininger. "Anything could find an audience. That's how Tuxedomoon snuck in the backdoor of punk because you could do *anything*. There was a guy in a wheelchair ranting and raving onstage at the Mabuhay. And there were all kinds of different configurations. That's how *we* fit in, and Patrick Miller/Minimal Man, Factrix—all this stuff. It was wide open. That's what made San Francisco different, maybe, was because it *was* open to these other formats—not only punk rock."

From the beginning, Tuxedomoon operated on their own terms, indifferent to any established rock norms. Their first-ever performance in June of 1977 took place not at the Mabuhay but at a café, Just Desserts, where their original idea was to provide "aural wallpaper" for the patrons there.[50] It was not until December that they first played the Mabuhay, but when they did, they made an instant impression on Dirk Dirksen, who handpicked them to open for Devo a few weeks later. As Isabelle Corbisier notes in her extensive Tuxedomoon tome *Music for Vagabonds*, the Devo gig "was a catalyst in the band's metamorphosis into a 'rock group' rather than a willfully esoteric artists' collective" (p. 62). Yet deep down, they were never *really* a rock group—punk or otherwise. As Brown put it, "When we first started, we had this idealistic, missionary idea of making electronic, avant-garde music out of the usual

---

50 This description comes from Tuxedomoon friend and associate, Gregory Cruikshank (*Music for Vagabonds*, p. 36). One of the pieces they played at the debut gig, 'Litebulb Overkill,' later made its way onto the *No Tears* EP.

highbrow, egghead type of environment and playing it for quote 'normal' people, making it more accessible, as opposed to other routes we could have taken, like the Stockhausen route, or the John Cage route … On the other hand, we didn't want to be a rock band and fall into the syndrome of playing

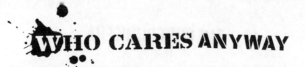

in bars every night."[51]

This urge to avoid repeating themselves—to make each show a unique event—gave them something in common with the Angels of Light as well as some of the performance art emanating from the Art Institute. Former Angel of Light (and part-time Tuxedomoon vocalist) Winston Tong was a key figure in this regard, as was film projectionist Bruce Geduldig. Along with drummer Paul Zahl and guitarist Michael Belfer, they were part of a rotating cast of characters that gave Tuxedomoon an unusual degree of range in both their live performances and studio recordings. "We were always *experimenting*," emphasizes Brown, "and every single show was different; every record was different. The *exact* opposite of what everybody else was doing."

"They were on one side of the scene," agrees *Damage* editor Brad Lapin."There was this definite division, if you will, in the scene between the sort of hardcore punk side and then this art side. They were on the most artistic side you could ask for. They were unabashed, card-carrying artists."[52] They certainly had their detractors, as exemplified by a bit of graffiti left outside a local venue circa 1980: "Tuxedomoon is a redundant, artsy-fartsy, bland fag band, but your record is nice dinner muzak."[53] Yet, as Brown points out, the divisions weren't always so black and white. "A lot of these hardcore punks, they *liked* Tuxedomoon. They wouldn't say it publicly, but they liked what we were doing, and whenever they had the opportunity, they would try to collaborate."

Michael Belfer: The guys who were more into the hardcore punky-type stuff, like the Avengers and Negative Trend, they didn't like them so much. They called them 'art fags' and kind of put them down. But I was always into prog rock. King Crimson and Robert Fripp and Roxy Music and Eno—that stuff had a big influence on me. So I just saw what Tuxedomoon was doing as an extension of that. And they had really great songs. I saw nothing but things to like about them.

51 Corbisier, *Music for Vagabonds*, pp. 65–66.
52 Ironically, they did not have any connections to the Art Institute. Instead, Brown and Reininger met at an electronic music class at City College of San Francisco.
53 *Damage*, September/October 1980, p. 16.

THE POST-PUNK ERA

Tom Wheeler: I was certainly into Eno and Kraftwerk and stuff like that, and I'd *never* seen a band play anything like that live until I saw Tuxedomoon. It was like something you heard on record, but you never walked into a club or performance space and saw anything like that for years. They had this kind of multimedia thing, where they'd have film projections. Winston had this kind of mime-ish theatrical thing that he did. And then they also had that kind of fifties artist outlaw druggy kind of thing.

Bond Bergland: They were probably the most experimental local band, just theatrically and stuff, and just stretching the boundaries of what a show was, more than most other people. Because Chrome was around, but they weren't performing—they were just recording. So as far as live shows, I'd say Tuxedomoon was pretty inspirational. Winston was just an incredible performer, and Michael Belfer was playing with them for a while. That was really inspiring. They were really good when Belfer played with them.[54]

Indeed, the guitarist had a hand in two of the group's standout tracks from this era. One of them is 'No Tears,' the title track of their first EP and, not coincidentally, the only song on it to feature a live drummer. The song was actually written before he joined the group circa May 1978, but his contributions help push it over the top, much like Fripp's guitar work on Eno's *Another Green World*. Belfer was an early adopter of the EBow, which he uses to create the sustained feedback sounds heard during the song's instrumental breaks. "I think that solo on 'No Tears' is one of the best guitar solos ever recorded," raves Bob Hoffnar, himself a guitarist and occasional collaborator with Tuxedomoon during this era.

The other standout is 'Crash,' an instrumental recorded during the December 1979 sessions for the band's debut LP, *Half-Mute*, but relegated to the B-side of that album's lead single, 'What Use?' Inspired by the J.G. Ballard novel of the same name, 'Crash' evokes the same sort of feverish night-driving atmosphere. Claude Bessy aptly described it as "[t]echnology in the service of unashamed

---

54 In addition to these two songs, Belfer performs on all four tracks of the 1979 *Scream with a View* EP and two of their three contributions to the *Subterranean Modern* compilation.

romanticism" in a review of the 7-inch for *Slash*. "Never thought I'd use the adjective 'lovely' in connection with Ralph Records," he added.[55] Once again, 'Crash' was the only song from those sessions to use a live drummer, which explains Belfer's involvement with it (and his absence from the rest of the album).[56] "I vacillated because I really liked being in a band with a drummer," he says. "And playing with a drum machine would only go so far with me. I started missing the ability to rock out a little more, and that's not what they were about at that time."[57]

Indeed, with *Half-Mute*, Tuxedomoon pretty much abandoned whatever musical connection they might have had to punk and/or rock. Much like its cover (designed by friend and art director Patrick Roques), the music on *Half-Mute* is austere and suggestive. Most of the tracks are built around minimal drum machine beats and synth lines, along with Peter Dachert's nasal-toned bass guitar. Brown's soprano saxophone and Blaine Reininger's violin lend an air of sophistication as well as a feeling of unease. As the album's title suggests, about half of the tracks are instrumental, and while there are a few more immediately accessible songs (highlighted by 'What Use?'), the album functions largely on an atmospheric level. As *Damage*'s Brad Lapin put it in a review at the time, "This is Muzak to commit ritual suicide by. Music of our time, of our places, of our abandoned hopes and drug-induced fears."[58]

By the time *Half-Mute* was released in March of 1980, Tuxedomoon were already on their way out of town. They spent much of that year in New York and England before eventually settling in Brussels, Belgium, in 1981. In hindsight, the move made perfect sense. Despite their connections to the Angels of Light and other aspects of SF underground culture, there was always something distinctly

---

55 *Slash*, March 1980, p. 44.
56 The drummer on 'No Tears' is Paul Zahl, an early member of the group who also lived in the house at 3645 Market Street along with Brown, Reininger, and Tommy Tadlock, among others. The drummer on 'Crash' is Jeff Raphael, formerly of the Nuns. At the time, he was playing drums in a short-lived version of the Sleepers.
57 In *Music for Vagabonds*, Reininger—who co-wrote the song with Belfer—expands on this point. "There was always this tendency, probably mostly from Steven and Winston, I suppose, to pull the band away from being rock. I wanted to rock. I came out of rock music, and I played guitar, and I like rock" (p. 80).
58 *Damage*, July 1980, p. 35.

THE POST-PUNK ERA

European about the band: it's no coincidence that critics often used words such as *ennui*, *noir*, and *angst* to describe their music. Dachert himself said the band members envisioned making "easy listening music for the dark, depressed *nouveau poor* [who] would be sitting in a cafe, just listening to *Half-Mute,* and drinking a Campari."[59] If this sort of thing rubbed some of the leather-and-spikes crowd the wrong way, then too bad, says Brown."Generally speaking, Tuxedomoon were considered kind of poseurs," he laughs. "The funny thing was the *punks* were the poseurs. I mean, the whole punk thing was such a *pose*."

Whatever criticisms one might lob in their direction, Tuxedomoon made some of the more lasting music from this era in San Francisco. That includes *Half-Mute* as well as the *No Tears* and *Scream with a View* EPs and a handful of singles (many of which are compiled on the *Pinheads on the Move* CD, which also includes the *Subterranean Modern* tracks). Also worth emphasizing is their role as "elder statesmen" who mentored or otherwise lent a hand to a number of other local acts, including Noh Mercy, Factrix, Minimal Man, Indoor Life, and Pink Section."We always looked up to them," says Pink Section's Stephen Wymore. "We knew them, and we were impressed with them. You know, they were real musicians. They were also pretty quirky and cool. They could play well, and they had a good concept, and they were serious. And they went somewhere. They didn't win any Grammys or anything, but they're still to this day playing music for a living, which I've gotta give 'em credit for. It's not easy to do that."

---

59 Corbisier, *Music for Vagabonds*, p. 95. The instrumental 'Urban Leisure Suite,' recorded just a few months after *Half-Mute*, offers another take on this concept. Bob Hoffnar of the band Indoor Life plays cello on it, replacing bassist Dachert, who was out of town at the time. The four-part suite was initially credited to Tuxedomoon's occasional alter ego Joeboy and included on the LP *Joeboy in Rotterdam/Joeboy in San Francisco* (released in 1981 on the Dutch label Backstreet Backlash). It was later included on the Tuxedomoon CD *Soundtracks/Urban Leisure Suite* (LTM, 2002).

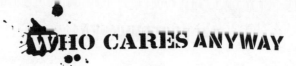

11

CALIFORNIA BABYLON: FACTRIX AND "INDUSTRIAL CULTURE"

J.C. Garrett: There was a place called the Café Flore, a funky little gay cafe on Market Street near Castro. They would have this thing they called "punk night," which was Monday night. So they would DJ punk music. Which really didn't mean specifically punk rock. They had some punk, and they would also do a lot of reggae and other stuff, but it became a draw for people. Everyone would go to the cafe, to the point where even if there was no room, the street would be full of people. That would be where Ivey would distribute, at the beginning of the week, her list for the next week.

Bond Bergland: Everybody was at the Café Flore every day. We saw Tuxedomoon every day. We saw all these people who were just around. So even if we weren't necessarily doing performances together, we were drinking coffee at the same place and just kind of hanging out.

Cole Palme: Bond was working there, and Joseph Jacobs was working there for a little bit. A bunch of people we knew were working there on and off. It was a central hub in the Upper Market/Castro. And people just hung out and drank coffee and talked, and they played all the good music there. That was the big draw. We were hearing all the new records—stuff coming from England and stuff from New York. Punk rock stuff and all the new post-punk stuff. That's when we first heard PiL, *Metal Box*. It was a good place to hang out. Tommy Tadlock was right across the street, and we came to find out that he was helping out those bands that we liked: Tuxedomoon, Pink Section, Noh Mercy.

THE POST-PUNK ERA

When they met in early 1979, Bond Bergland and Cole Palme were both recent arrivals to the Bay Area with music school backgrounds and restless dispositions. Bergland was a recent graduate of the prestigious Berklee College of Music in Boston; he settled in San Francisco after a brief stint in New York City. "I was a serious musician, and then all of a sudden, punk and all that stuff happened," he explains. "It wasn't necessarily punk, but all that new music—it just freed up all this energy. And then it was kind of like everybody was sick of all the old stuff, including me." Palme, meanwhile, had briefly studied electronic music at Santa Barbara City College while also witnessing some of the early convulsions of punk at LA venues like the Masque and the Whisky a Go Go.[60]

Using the name "Minimal Man," they made their live debut that summer at the Eureka Theatre—which, in those days, was housed in the basement of a church.[61] The church, in turn, was located across the street from the Café Flore and next door to the communal Angels of Light house where Tommy Tadlock was living.

It was Tadlock who introduced the duo to Patrick Miller, another recent arrival to the city who shared an interest in electronic music. "I think we played with him two, maybe three times," recalls Palme, referring to the group's earliest configuration. "It was me, Bond, and Patrick, and Tommy was helping us mix sound.[62] And then, I don't remember how it happened—we just sort of felt like we were going in different places." Adds Bergland, "It was fun, but Cole and I knew it wasn't really quite what we wanted to do. And at that point, Minimal Man

---

60 For Palme, it was actually his second stint in San Francisco; the first one ended prematurely in 1977 after a semester at the Academy of Art. "I remember that half of the instructors had been striking, so they brought in replacements. In Film Appreciation class, the new guy had us watching *Behind the Green Door.*" While back in Southern California, he collaborated with Christian Lunch, an electronic musician affiliated with the LA Free Music Society. He appears on Lunch's 1979 EP *Product.*
61 This was the Trinity Methodist Church at 2299 Market Street. The church burned down on October 11, 1981, and the Eureka Theatre relocated several times after that.
62 Michael Belfer, who was among those in attendance that night, recalls the trio's performance. "They had this incredible set, with these incredible film visuals behind them. They did this song called 'Prayer Works in Mysterious Ways,' and they had these film loops of hula girls dancing in the surf with palm trees behind them. It was all like super-faded Kodachrome movie film." He remembers Tuxedomoon associate Winston Tong headlining that night, which puts the likely show date sometime around late July or early August of 1979.

just seemed like a perfect name for him, so we kind of gave it to him."[63] In need of a new name for his own band, Bergland stumbled across the word "Factrix" (definition: "a female factor") in the *Oxford English Dictionary*. Somehow, it fit.

LIVE AT TARGET

Factrix emerged at a time when the boundaries between post-punk, industrial, and even performance art were still somewhat blurry. "There was this whole

---

63 As for Tadlock, his involvement with the group was both informal and short-lived. "Tommy helped us get set up because he knew electric gear, and he mixed sound for some of the early shows," says Palme. "But we just went our own ways." Adds Bergland: "He would just lay around on the floor while we made music for the first six months or so. He gave us this thing called an Optigan. We made a lot of background tapes with that that we played over. And he was just a funny, funny guy."

industrial and noise kind of thing happening," notes Steve Tupper. "There was a certain amount of crossover with the Flipper crowd, to a degree, especially back then." Factrix themselves occupied a sort of middle ground between the cool sophistication of Tuxedomoon and the more visceral approach of Flipper (both of whom they opened for early on) without fitting neatly into any one camp. "It was just for a short period that it *was* that way," says Palme. "But in the early days, it was real mix-and-match."

The *Live at Target* LP offers a snapshot of this brief period of cross-fertilization. Recorded in February of 1980, the album features live recordings of four different acts—Flipper, Factrix, Uns (an alter ego of Stefan Weisser, aka Z'ev), and LA synth-punks Nervous Gender—with a shared penchant for feedback and electronic noise, as well as a mutual disregard for such niceties as vocal melodies. For Flipper, the contrast with the previous year's *SF Underground* is striking. There, they were the oddballs; here, they are the most down-to-earth band, although the crusty bass distortion and overall bad vibes on 'Falling' are enough to rival any industrial band. "In my mind, Flipper kind of transcended punk," says Bergland. "They were just like a great San Francisco band. And that's how we all thought of ourselves, as just San Francisco bands."

INDUSTRIAL

In video footage of the *Live at Target* performances, the members of Factrix— Palme, Bergland, and bassist Joseph Jacobs—are seen clad in all black, rocking out along with a drum machine on 'Night to Forget' and looking rather severe in the process. The song ends with a bloodcurdling scream ("a night ... to forget ... to forget!"), as if to emphasize that Factrix wasn't there to give people something so mundane as a "good time." They were dark, almost comically so at times, but so were their influences. "We were way into Throbbing Gristle, of course," says Palme. "And when Cabaret Voltaire came to town, we really connected to what they were doing." In addition, one of Factrix's Bay Area collaborators, Monte Cazazza, had been a friend and co-conspirator of Throbbing Gristle's since the mid-seventies.

It was Cazazza who coined the term "industrial music," which, thanks to the influence of Throbbing Gristle and their record label, became the name of an entire genre and subculture. "I never used that term," says Palme of the "industrial" moniker. "I never have, really. But at the time, we were diggin' what they were doin'—no question about that." Certainly, Factrix embodied many of the hallmarks of early industrial music, including modified and/or "broken" equipment, taboo imagery, and references to unsavory characters like Jim Jones and Charles Manson. There was also their use of Middle Eastern instruments such as the saz, doumbek, and zither, which they incorporated into trance-like drones ('Silver River,' 'Burning Sand') that prefigured later efforts by bands like Savage Republic, Sun City Girls, and Bergland's post-Factrix outfit Saqqara Dogs. "We were using things from all over the world that we would find," explains Bergland. "Joseph had a lot of instruments. He played a lot of different Middle Eastern music and instruments just a little bit."

Whether it came to electronic gadgets or exotic instruments, the members of Factrix were less interested in what their equipment was designed to do than in what they could *make* it do. "There was a lot of modified stuff," says Bergland. "We were into things that were broken, so we liked shoddy electronic equipment that had taken on some kind of broken character that we could utilize creatively. Our main tool, other than guitars and basses, was the tape recorder. We used that to slow down the drum machine, and that was kind of the Factrix sound. We recorded a lot of stuff at our rehearsal space and would play over that. But then we'd slow it down to quarter speed and transfer it to cassette to play over. Manipulating time was kind of the idea."

SCHEINTÖT AND SLAVA

The slowed-down drum machine gets a workout on *Scheintöt*, the group's lone studio album, recorded in 1980. The word *scheintöt* is German for "suspended animation," an apt title given the ephemeral, ghostly quality of the music. While there are distinct songs, they are secondary to the overall mood of the album. The melodies are almost subliminal at times, while the vocals drift in and out of focus and the more traditional instruments (like Bergland's guitar) are often unrecognizable as such. It is a hazy, nocturnal sound, one that differs from the more aggressively rhythmic sounds heard on both *Live at Target* and their debut 7-inch ('Empire of Passion' b/w 'Splice of Life'), also recorded earlier in 1980. "We were restless," says Palme, explaining their continually evolving sound. "We were just really trying things out all the time and not much into rehearsing a set. We kept changing it. We'd never do the same set twice, and we were always trying to figure out new kinds of sounds."

Scheintöt was recorded at the home of Slava Ranko, one of the many unlikely figures to rub shoulders with the punk scene during this era. "He was another very colorful character, and he influenced us slightly just because he was so super-eccentric," says Palme. "And he was a Factrix fan, so he basically let us use his studio free of charge." Adds Bergland, "He came to see a show at the Savoy Tivoli, and he just came running up to me afterwards and said, 'You've gotta make a record at my house.' I was like, 'Okay. Don't twist my arm.' So a couple days later, we went out there, and … I don't think he gave us keys, but he might as well have."

Ranko, whose real name was Donald Philippi, was fifty years old at the time—older than most of the Haight-Ashbury hippies, let alone the Mabuhay-era punks. As he told an interviewer years later, he became a punk rock convert after noticing, "in 1977, that something was happening at a place called the Mabuhay Gardens on Broadway … I began to go down there and, of course, immediately understand what was happening. It was a sort of revolution, and you know how well I relate to revolutions. It happened to lots of other people I knew, too: Steven Brown, Esmerelda, Patrick Miller, and many, many others."[64]

Eric Paul Fournier: A member of Factrix brought me Slava. That's how we met—at a recording session at Slava's house. And then Slava was working on his own record, called *Arctic Hysteria*. It was a difficult record. You really had to listen to it and give it a moment to get into it. It might have been a little bit too

---

64 Frederik L. Schodt, "Interview with Donald L. Phillipi." http://www.jai2.com/dlpivu3.htm

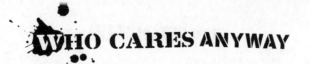

WHO CARES ANYWAY

hardcore for its time, for the noise market even. It certainly wasn't rhythmic in the way Western music was. We didn't press many of them—a couple thousand. I think I had 1,500 left after sending out 300 of them to various college radio stations. It wasn't a playable record. But I quite liked it.[65]

Esmerelda: He was just a gay San Francisco freak like everybody who used to live there. He had lived in Japan as a woman, and he was a very big man—there was *nothing* feminine about him. His head was gigantic, and he was very tall. He had vertical lines coming out of his eyebrows up to his temples. He was an incredible force of a man. He wore all black. But in Japan, he was in the midst of getting a sex change, and he dressed in women's clothes, which I'm sure had to be specially made for him. And he was very fey. He looked like this very foreboding presence, like somebody who had been in the cabinet in the USSR. But he spoke in this little voice. And then when the punk rock thing started, he just got so into it. He had all these records sent from England, and he *loved* it. He supported punk rock. He supported those boys—he supported Factrix—and he loved Noh Mercy. He and I were friends from the Angels of Light period.

Bond Bergland: The first time I saw Slava, he was performing with Noh Mercy at the Mab. He was in a Noh costume with a giant headdress. It was the first time I'd heard of him. And he was very nice to me. He was just the nicest man. That was the only time I ever saw him perform, and it was with them. And it was the only time I ever saw anybody play with Noh Mercy, but he did.

Tony Hotel: We played several songs with him on the synthesizer. We got together quite a few times with him. He was really nice, a real gentleman. A wonderful guy. I think he had money. He always looked good.

---

65 *Scheintot* and *Arctic Hysteria* were two of the three LPs released by Adolescent Records, along with the Sleepers' *Painless Nights* (see Chapter 14). The label began in late 1979 as a collaboration between Fournier—an Art Institute student and North Beach bon vivant—and Vale. "But except for bringing the bands to us—more like the A&R director—Vale had very little to do with it," explains Fournier. "He didn't finance it; he didn't produce it. I lost so much money from my inheritance putting those records out. I didn't do it as a business decision; I did it because I liked the music."

Bond Bergland: He translated Japanese manuals, technical manuals—really, really precise stuff. And he also translated Inuit poetry. That was really his thing. He was really into Inuit poetry and writing.

Esmerelda: Japanese, Russian, and Arabic were his three main translation languages. And he had this unbelievable library—this huge room, floor to ceiling with books.

CALIFORNIA BABYLON

Factrix had some other colorful collaborators in addition to Slava. In December of 1980, they played the Kezar Pavilion with their friend Monte Cazazza strapped to a rotating swastika for part of the set. In June of 1981, they staged another multimedia event—billed as "The Night of the Succubus"—this time with help from Cazazza as well as Mark Pauline of Survival Research Laboratories. Video footage from the show—released years later on a DVD along with the CD reissue of *California Babylon*—includes a stomach-churning scene in which the band members perform some unauthorized dental work on a mechanized cow skull that Pauline had assembled for them ("He bought the cow at the Piggly Wiggly," recalls Bergland). References to Antonin Artaud and the Theatre of Cruelty can be overdone, but in this case, the term is applicable.[66] "I would say that was the peak of darkness, that show," notes Ruby Ray. "Factrix could really dredge up some spirits when they were playing."

Granted, there can be a fine line between dredging up spirits and indulging in transgression for its own sake. Like some of their more infamous peers, Factrix walked that line with all the risks it entailed. "They were very, very dark," says Indoor Life's Jorge Socarras. "But to quote Andre Breton, 'Beauty will be

---

66 "I *was* totally obsessed with that at the time," Palme says of Artaud's writing. "In fact, I was just carrying it around with me when I was traveling through Europe. We were gonna go over to do some shows, 'cause our record was coming out. That was the one book I was carrying with me on that trip. It was a big thick anthology. I think I'd lifted it from the library by mistake. So I was all into Artaud at the time."

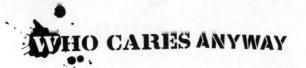

convulsive or not at all.' I think that was one of the mantras of that period. And I think Factrix is very exemplary of that. I'm not talking about conventional beauty. It was just this sense of a strong aesthetic that had a gravitas, that was more than just a reaction or trying to invoke a stance or just be ironic or just be fun. Factrix had a lot of gravitas."

Even if it wasn't ironic, the darkness wasn't entirely humorless—although, as with SRL and Cazazza, it can be hard to tell where the darkness ends, and the humor begins. "They hold hands, and I don't think they often let go of one another," says Olga Gerrard, who booked Factrix to play at the Savoy Tivoli on several occasions. "There was a very dark but very humorous group. It was a cadre there." She mentions Boyd Rice and Throbbing Gristle among the others involved in this loose cadre (which, in years to come, would also include the likes of Feral House publisher Adam Parfrey and *Lords of Chaos* author Michael Moynihan, who in 2003 produced a two-disc Factrix retrospective for his label, Storm).

"We were a little darker than others, I think," admits Palme. "There was sort of this voodoo thing. We were just playing with that. Just playin' with it! I thought we always saw the humor in it as well, though. It was just about putting yourself out there, sometimes having no idea what you were gonna do that night. We were doing a lot of fairly regular amounts of psychedelics at the time, too. Sometimes that would be part of it—if not the night of the show, a few nights before, where you're just sort of getting imagery."

As for the voodoo element, it was no laughing matter. Palme recalls a telling anecdote from Cabaret Voltaire's performance at the Savoy Tivoli. "They had some technical difficulty in the middle of their set. All their instruments started crapping out. And I remember Louis Sullivan, the soundman, was pulling wires out and stuff like that. But it all came together in a few minutes. After the set, Joseph was telling me that he was having a vision in the middle of their song, like he saw some kind of dark entity. He was describing it like the archetypal witch creature, doing some kind of weird dance in front of the stage. That's when the sound started getting weird. And he locked eyes with this creature while the sound was wigging out, and then the witch went 'poof.' And right when that 'poof' happened, Mark Pauline jabbed it in the ribs real hard. Then the sound went back on. But that was just kind of the vibe."

"DECONSTRUCTED ROCK"

The audio portion of the Night of the Succubus show formed the bulk of *California Babylon*, which was credited to "Factrix/Cazazza" and released on Subterranean in 1982. While there are parts of the performance that don't

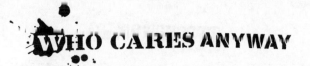

quite translate without the visuals, the album works well enough as a kind of proto-noise album, with its combination of piercing feedback ('Death by Hanging') and electronics gone haywire. It was also a fairly representative document of the trio's later sound, as Bergland explains. "The stuff that's on that record is basically what we became as a live band for about the last year that we played. We kind of just tried a *million* things and then finally found this thing that we thought worked really well, when it was basically just … deconstructed rock."

By the time *California Babylon* came out in mid-1982, Factrix had already broken up, following a winter holed up in Vermont (by which point Jacobs had already left the group). "We were completely snowed in, so you couldn't really get out to the city," remembers Palme, who made the trip to Vermont along with Bergland and Ruby Ray. Plans for both a second studio album and a spring 1982 tour with Australian industrial outfit SPK fell through (although some of the recordings from this period later surfaced on the *Artifact* compilation). "We spent the good part of the winter working on recordings," says Palme. "That was the last stuff we did. And then I came back to San Francisco, and everything was all different."

12

HE WAS A VISITOR: PATRICK MILLER AND MINIMAL MAN

"Minimal Man has always created problems for me because it's so personal … For about two years, I became the character and went through an intense drug trip and became just fucked up." — Patrick Miller[67]

"Just to be around him, your reality slipped. He'd gone so far over with drugs that he came back … different or something." — Bond Bergland

In hindsight, the decision to split the fledgling, pre-Factrix Minimal Man into two separate groups was a prescient move — a case of the proverbial "creative differences" becoming apparent sooner rather than later. Factrix, after all, was less about individual personalities than it was a collective cloud of sound. In contrast, Minimal Man was intensely personal: both the band and the character were ultimately reflections of Patrick Miller and his complex, troubled psyche.

"Minimal Man is Patrick," summarizes Blaise Smith, a member of several different Minimal Man lineups. "Honestly, no matter what the credits are, it's Patrick. He's running the show."

67 *Unsound*, Vol. 1, No. 3, p. 39.

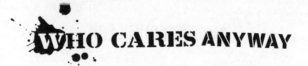

"YOU'RE NOT A MUSICIAN!"

Like so many of his peers, Miller came at music from a background in visual art, having studied at Sonoma State before moving to the city in 1978. "When I first knew Patrick, he was a *painter*," emphasizes Tuxedomoon's Steven Brown. "He had a big studio in his apartment where he was doing silkscreens and painting. He had a girlfriend who was a painter. He was completely into the plastic arts." Indeed, Miller had no musical background whatsoever prior to Minimal Man. "I never sang or played anything in my life before August of '79," he told *Breakfast Without Meat* in a 1984 interview.[68] "What I can do is I can manipulate tape recorders [and] do tape composition, just from listening to music for so long."

That interest in manipulating sound gave him something in common with many in the burgeoning industrial movement, but evidently, he didn't feel a connection there. "More or less, I didn't know how to do anything else," he explained, "and it just happened to coincide with the so-called industrial movement of the time—Throbbing Gristle and other bands out of England. I had no knowledge or interest in that."[69] Instead, his inspirations were closer at hand. "I think he was inspired by me and Blaine in the beginning days of Tuxedomoon," says Brown, a housemate of Miller's during those days. "He saw what we were doing, and he wanted to experiment with that, too. And I was a little bit put off. I go, 'What are you doing? You're a *painter*. You're not a musician.' But little by little, he started drifting that way until finally he basically stopped painting."

For a non-musician, Miller had a remarkably clear sense of what kind of music he wanted to make. It also helped that he had a couple of capable helpers in Brown and Stephen Wymore. "We got a place on Oak Street—the third floor of this big, big Victorian," recalls Wymore, who was still playing bass in Pink Section at the time. "We had a back porch that was enclosed. Tuxedomoon would rehearse there, and Minimal Man would rehearse there."[70]

---

68 *Breakfast Without Meat*, No. 4.
69 *Unsound*, Vol. 1, No. 3, p. 40.
70 This was the same apartment where the Sleepers' 'Mirror'/ 'Theory' single was recorded circa the summer of 1979, with Wymore playing bass and Brown making an impromptu appearance on saxophone near the end of 'Mirror.'

It's this version of the group—with Brown and Wymore on synthesizers and Miller on vocals—that appears on the early 7-inch 'She Was a Visitor' b/w 'He Who Falls' (Subterranean). Recorded live at the Deaf Club in October of 1979, it already sounds like Minimal Man: gritty, agitated, and, yes, minimal. The A-side is a radical makeover of a then-recent performance piece by avant-garde composer Robert Ashley; it consists largely of the phrase "she was a visitor" repeated over and over, with a couple of synthesizer loops going haywire in the background. 'He Who Falls' is similarly spartan, with just a pitter-pattering drum machine

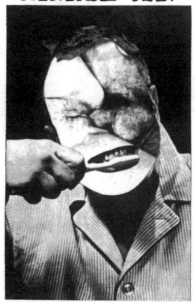

MINIMAL MAN

NEGATIVLAND + AND FILMS
FRIDAY NOV. 21 10:00 PM
SOUND OF MUSIC 885-9616
162 TURK ST. S.F. $3.50

and fractured synth melody backing Miller as he recites variations on the title phrase ("He who falls in love with himself shall have no rivals").

Though Brown never considered himself a full-fledged band member, Wymore would serve as Miller's main foil through the summer of 1980, when they embarked on a brief Pacific Northwest tour opening for DNA and Tuxedomoon.[71] Though the timeline is hazy, it was likely later that year when Miller connected with Andrew Baumer, a key collaborator who wound up being the only one besides Miller to

---

71 A review in the *Vancouver Sun* (August 12, 1980) described Minimal Man's set as wavering "between disturbing [and] unbearably arty." Wymore left soon after this tour, moving to Seattle, where he briefly joined the Blackouts (which, in turn, later morphed into Ministry, although Wymore was long gone by that point).

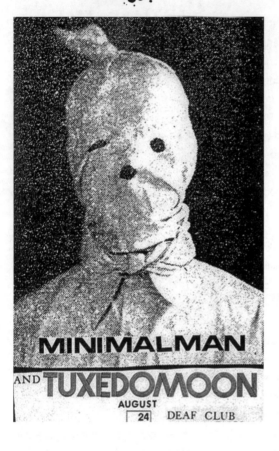

MINIMAL MAN

AND TUXEDOMOON

AUGUST 24 DEAF CLUB

appear on both of Minimal Man's San Francisco-era LPs. "Andrew would play bass, but it was almost chordal," recalls drummer Lliam Hart, who played alongside Miller and Baumer in a trio version of the group circa 1981. "He was almost covering the bass and the guitar at the same time."[72]

Baumer's fuzz bass features prominently on 'Loneliness,' the opening track on Minimal Man's debut album, *The Shroud Of* (Subterranean, 1981). It is perhaps the quintessential Minimal Man track, as well as a prime example of Miller's seat-of-the-pants approach to recording and arranging. The track opens with an extended sample from what sounds like a 1950s-era public service announcement about depression ("I hurt all over inside / I feel like crying most of the time, but I … I can't"). Baumer then enters with a lurching bass riff, followed by Hart's garage band drumming. The basic track is clearly recorded live, but the final mix includes multiple layers of

---

72 Baumer's last name is sometimes misspelled "Braumer" in album credits (Miller had a habit of misspelling his band members' names). He went on to become a restaurateur in Oakland during the 1990s before passing away in 2001 at the age of forty-nine. It's unknown whether he continued to play music after Minimal Man, but he doesn't have any other official recording credits.

distorted bass along with Miller's wavering sci-fi synths. The tempo waxes and wanes, with various instruments falling in and out of sync. As for Miller's vocals, they are not so much sung as they are delivered. "Shadows are my only friend / And ghosts are all I see / Ronald Reagan, I agree!" he exclaims at several points. He might be playing a role, but as portrayals of mental illness go, it's a little too convincing to qualify as "just acting."

'Loneliness' sets the tone for what follows on *The Shroud Of*, and while the lineup varies throughout, it hardly seems to matter. Likewise, with the distinction between live instruments, tape loops, and other sounds. The sound is so consistent, in fact, that Miller is able to "cover" Robert Ashley (a new version of 'She Was a Visitor') and Mr. Rogers ('You Are') in the space of a few tracks without either of them actually sounding like a cover.

"I SEE THINGS THAT ARE NOT THERE"

By 1981, Miller had moved into 992 Valencia, the same storefront space where Noh Mercy had previously lived and rehearsed. The space would serve as Miller's base of operations for the rest of his time in San Francisco, with the basement rehearsal studio providing the setting for a telling anecdote that drummer Hart recalls in detail:

> One of the interesting things about this room is—you know, usually you have locks on the outside to keep your equipment safe. He had the locks on the *inside* so that when he was playing or doing his practice thing, "they" couldn't get him.
>
> The first time I remember Andrew quitting the band was—we show up to rehearse and go down to the lower part where the studio is, and it's *locked*. And Patrick's in there—you can hear him fooling around. He had this weird metal box that he'd process his vocals through. There was some horrendous sound coming out of there, and we were pounding on the door.
>
> Finally, Patrick emerges. He lets us in. And Andrew's bass cabinet is

nailed shut. *Nailed* shut. Andrew looks at his amp, and all the knobs are turned to ten: the volume, treble, bass, gain—everything's on ten. And he gets really upset. "What the fuck, Patrick? What's going on?" Patrick said, "Well, I was working on music here, and there was somebody inside of your amp, and he was yelling at me, and I didn't want him to get out. So I nailed the cabinet shut, and then I turned all the knobs up to ten and plugged in the guitar and tried to kill him.

It's funny how age works because I didn't think anything of it. When you mature, you go, "That's really fuckin' crazy!"

Unfortunately, it wasn't an isolated incident. Miller suffered for most of his adult life from paranoid hallucinations, evidently the result of his heavy narcotic use. The unwanted visions were a recurring theme in his lyrics (e.g., 'Loneliness' and 'High Why' from *The Shroud Of* and 'What's Not There' from *Safari*), and tales of Miller's hallucinations are legion.

Blaise Smith: We were doing a show over in Oakland. We're going over the bridge, and the van's loaded with equipment. Halfway across the bridge, he just stops the van right on the bridge. He doesn't even pull over. I'm like, "What are you doing?" He says, "I hear something in the back of the van." I'm like, "Patrick, forget it, forget it." "No, no, no. I really hear it." He goes back and takes *every* piece of equipment—two huge PAs, all my guitar amps, everything—he takes 'em all out and brings 'em out on the bridge. Like in the street. And then he goes, "It's in there." And he's lookin' at my cabinet, which has a solid back. He gets a screwdriver, and he starts taking the cabinet apart because what he's hearing is inside the cabinet. Meanwhile, cars are just backed up. Finally, he was like, "Hmm." I said, "Yeah. Let's kind of put that back thing on there and go to the show."

Michael Belfer: Poor Patrick—he was the first person in the world who I've ever seen with rug burns on his knuckles. He would become convinced that he had spilled coke into the rug, so he would just keep searching and searching through this rug—this shag carpet—so as a result, he would get these rug burns on his knuckles. It's a phenomenon that happens with people who smoke cocaine.

MINIMAL MAN
& PINK SECTION
MACHINE STEADY TOUR

B 22 EVERGREEN STATE OLYMPIA WASHINGTON

R 23 SHOWBOX — FINGERPRINTZ SEATTLE

U 24 ROSCOE LOUIE'S SEATTLE

A 28 UNIVERSITY OF BRITISH COLUMBIA VANCOUVER

R CANADA — 8 EYED SPY & THE BLACKOUTS

Y INFO — M—MAN PO BOX 11654 SF CA 94101

They keep thinking that they're spilling it on the floor, and every time they see anything white in the rug, they're convinced that it's cocaine. So they go digging for it in the rug. And, of course, it's never there, but in the process, they end up completely mutilating their hands.

Esmerelda: He got really out there. That house was really haunted, and there's a lot of negative spirit energy in that house. That's part of why we went crazy, was the negative spirits in the house. And when we left, it had gotten so bad I think they all glommed onto Patrick.

Blaise Smith: He did so much coke; it was just out of control. But then it was weird, too: sometimes he just wouldn't do it. He never seemed addicted to anything. It just seemed like he'd do it, do it, do it, and then all of a sudden, for a couple of months, he wouldn't talk about it. Then I'd say, "Hey, let's do some … " "Nah." I don't know; he was just a strange cat. Really strange.

Stephen Clarke: He was a pretty creative guy and a really sweet guy. I did once go into his place on Valencia, really early. It must have been 1980. It was just me and him hanging out. He offered if I wanted to shoot—I'm pretty sure it was cocaine. I said no, I hadn't really done any of that. So he just shot his cocaine, and we just hung out talking. He kind of stalked around the room a little bit. And it was fun. I wasn't scared, like he was going to do anything crazy.

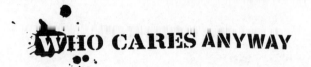

Gregg Turkington: I would go over to his house and hang out there till like three in the morning. He'd just play interesting music for me and show me art books. Clearly, clearly on drugs, but never anything weird was going on.

Kristin Oppenheim: He was incredibly fit—mentally fit; he was very intelligent and used to read constantly. And he had a very sharp, creative mind. But he did a lot of drugs, and it slowly but surely just completely destroyed his brain.

Lliam Hart: Patrick was always a very good person to me. He had a lot going on in his head. I think he was doing a lot of drugs, which I was oblivious to because I'd never seen anything like that. I mean, in hindsight, he was a real fuckin' intense drug addict. But he was always—in my mind, he saw my innocence and youngness, and he respected that. It's an intuitive thing. I never felt scared or in danger. He was a good guy, a good soul.

JERRY-RIGGING

The drug use and ensuing paranoia became bound up with both Miller's personality and the Minimal Man character—though, over time, the distinction between the two grew increasingly blurry. As he told Neil Strauss years later, "I invented Minimal Man as this wild person, and then I actualized it and took all kinds of drugs and stuff because I felt guilty for not living up to this fiction."[73] Even so, the character wasn't entirely autobiographical. "Minimal Man was supposed to be a negro-type character," he told *Unsound*'s William Davenport in 1983. "He was 'jerry-rigging' life to survive, and rather than fixing a problem the correct way, he would make up his own delusions to get by."[74]

This jerry-rigging extended into Miller's own day-to-day life in the Mission District, a topic he expanded on in his interview with Gregg Turkington in *Breakfast*

---

73 Neil Strauss, "The Pop Life: Drugs, Demons: A Man in a Mask." *New York Times*, January 8, 2004.
74 *Unsound*, Vol. 1, No. 3, p. 38.

THE POST-PUNK ERA

Without Meat. Miller alludes to unspecified legal issues (including a "couple warrants out for my arrest") and a raft of unpaid parking tickets. "I tried to take care of it for a while," he says, "but living in the Mission, you have no choice. What it does instantly is, besides being like a political terrorism, it's a really psychological *terror* the police play on you, because if they fuck with you, what it mainly means is, they're either gonna put you in jail or fine the shit out of you."

Somehow, Miller was able to maintain Minimal Man as a functioning band despite often resembling the protagonist of a Philip K. Dick novel. He managed the band himself—a rarity in those days—and evidently had a knack for the business side of things, as much he claimed to dislike it. "Patrick would just somehow magically get all the shows, and he'd get all these albums made," says Blaise Smith, who played guitar in a four-piece version of the band that opened shows for the likes of Killing Joke, the Birthday Party, and Fear during 1982.[75] The following year, Miller embarked on a brief tour of Japan, where, among other things, he encountered legendary noise artist Merzbow years before almost anyone in the US had even heard of him. "He just had this weird thing of just accomplishing things," Smith marvels, "but he always seemed completely fucked up."

Ron Morgan, the recording engineer on Minimal Man's second LP, *Safari,* echoes the latter sentiment. "He would go for stretches where he would be unworkable. He would inject coke and just go into a psychotic fugue and couldn't do anything. He'd come into work, and he would just spend the studio session hiding behind a chair. So I introduced him to heroin, and then he became more tractable. You know, I knew where he'd be every day, and he'd come in, and he would be calmer. But even so, it was hard. It was a rough go."[76]

---

75 Minimal Man opened for the Birthday Party and the Meat Puppets at the Keystone in Berkeley on February 28, 1982. On July 16, they opened for Killing Joke at the Stone on Broadway, and on July 28, they opened for Fear at the Old Waldorf.
76 The Valencia Tool & Die opened at 974 Valencia around the time Miller moved into the space at 992 Valencia, just a few doors down. In December of 1981, drummer John Surrell's hardcore band Bad Posture started using the basement of the Tool & Die as a rehearsal space. This was how he got to know Miller.

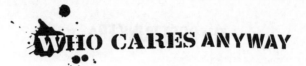

SAFARI

Unlike *The Shroud Of*, *Safari* was the work of a single lineup—the 1982 live band with Smith on guitar, Baumer on bass, and John Surrell on drums. "He brought them in, and he laid down a bunch of basic tracks," recalls Morgan. "And then, as soon as he was satisfied with the basic tracks, he fired 'em. And then we just sort of delved in. We did a lot of work on his vocals and treatments and whatnot."

Morgan was engineering the album as part of an arrangement with Subterranean, which gave its artists free recording time at the in-house studio on South Van Ness.[77] Yet, after a lengthy recording process (Morgan recalls the sessions dragging on for more than a year), Miller wound up taking the master tapes to CD Presents, a dodgy outfit run by longtime Bay Area promoter/impresario David Ferguson. (It would not be the last time Subterranean was burned on a handshake deal.)

For all the behind-the-scenes drama, *Safari* proved a worthy successor to *The Shroud Of*. Whereas that album alternates between relatively structured songs and more abstract ambient/noise collages, *Safari* is entirely song-oriented, with most of the tracks clocking in at around three minutes and sporting bona fide hooks. In short, *Safari* is Minimal Man's "rock" album.

The opening track, 'Show Time,' offers a good example of what that entails. The main riff, doubled on synthesizer and fuzz bass, calls to mind Killing Joke's 'Requiem,' although according to Miller, the influences were coming from elsewhere—namely, the late sixties acid rock bands he'd listened to as a teen, bands like Iron Butterfly, the Seeds, and the Music Machine. "I like the old basslines. They're real simple," he told *Breakfast Without Meat*.[78] "That's basically why *Safari* came out sounding poppy, and it also sounded sixties almost, in a

---

77 Morgan's own band, Bay of Pigs, had gotten free studio time to do some earlier recordings for Subterranean, and his engineering work was a form of repayment. As Morgan explains, "Richard Kelly [of Club Foot] and Mike Fox [of Subterranean Studios] worked out a deal when the Club Foot folks got signed to Subterranean and sort of like did a trade: studio time for engineering time. I was part of that deal. I was the designated engineer. So I would do work for free basically for Mike, and then we would get studio time out of it."

78 *Breakfast Without Meat*, No. 4.

way, 'cause I was listening to so much of the old shit." The song's lyrics, meanwhile, were adapted from the opening of a trashy paperback novel that Miller received from a fan. "I read it, and my interpretation, right away, was [that] this was just one analogy for entertainment and sex," he said in the same interview.[79]

Though it wasn't as overtly experimental as *The Shroud Of*, *Safari* was hardly commercial. Decades on, it still doesn't fit neatly in any genre—industrial, noise, post-punk, or hardcore—

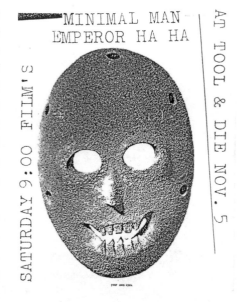

MINIMAL MAN
EMPEROR HA HA

S FILM'S

9:00

SATURDAY

AT TOOL & DIE NOV. 5

but the same could be said of Minimal Man in general. "One thing that was so spectacular about his work, I think, is that he was able to straddle punk rock and new wave simultaneously," says David Swan, whose own group, the Longshoreman, was recording at Subterranean Studios during the same period. "Because what he did had a rough edge, yet it also had a conceptual edge. The word's thrown around a lot, but I think he was a bona fide genius. I mean, his pores were just filled with creativity."

BIG HEADS AND NAIL DOGS

This brings us back to Miller's visual artwork which remains legendary among his peers, if largely unseen by the rest of the world. "He worked construction like

79 The novel is *Hollywood Hustlers* by Ferenc Bartok.

WHO CARES ANYWAY

I did," recalls the German Shepherds' Mark Hutchinson. "I was a painter, but he was just like a framer. He was doing a *shitload* of fuckin' speed. He had one of the first nail guns, and he made these things called 'nail dogs.' He got pieces of scrap lumber and just shot these nails through them. Man, they looked great. They really looked great."

"He did hundreds of these things," recalls Wymore. "What he would do, he'd take two-by-four scraps, and he would pound nails into them—different configurations of nails—then dip them in joint compound. He'd get these gigs, and they would do some work, but then they'd get really high on the job. So instead of doing the work you're supposed to do, he would do like twenty, thirty nail dogs during the day." Over time, Miller amassed quite a collection of them. "He didn't throw shit away," explains Wymore. "He was very organized; he was a packrat. He didn't do those nail dogs to toss 'em. He kept 'em. And that was part of the beauty. It's like any art thing: if you see one, it's kind of cool, but if you see like thirty of 'em, you say, 'Oh shit, this shit is real.'"

Then there were Miller's "Big Heads"—the disembodied, mask-like faces he would stencil on everything from his own record covers and fliers to walls and sidewalks all over San Francisco. "I mean, they were everywhere," recalls Hart. "Everywhere." Miller attributed an occult quality to his Big Heads. "Some are good hexes, and some are bad," he explained.[80] "I kinda think of them as, like, karma accelerators. Whatever's going to happen to you, it exaggerates it and makes it happen faster." In the same interview, Miller boasts sardonically of stenciling a Big Head on the outside of the Jefferson Airplane mansion on Fulton Street, not long before band member and resident Paul Kantner suffered a stroke. Scoff, if you will, but there was something about Miller and his Big Heads that seemed to attract the paranormal.

Blaise Smith: He was up one night at like three in the morning doing Big Heads. He did about 500 of 'em. He would go off and just do those all night long with spray paint and stencil. And finally, at four in the morning, he just decided he had to get out of there. So he *ran* out of the front of the window and shattered the entire panel, and ended up in the middle of Valencia Street covered in blood. That was kind of like his thing. He was just that way.

Ron Morgan: He leaped over the rail of his loft, landed on the floor in full stride, and continued to run right through one of the storefront's plate-glass windows and on down Valencia Street. He was unscathed. I think he may have turned his ankle, but he wasn't cut and, probably, most remarkably, turned up a little while later as if nothing had happened.[81]

Bond Bergland: Years later, we did a tour together, and you would see those things [Big Heads] everywhere. He would order a hamburger and open the

80 *Breakfast Without Meat*, No. 4.
81 Marcella Faustini, "Echoes Are All I See." September 10, 2015. https://www.artpractical.com/feature/echoes-are-all-i-see/

hamburger up, and it would look *exactly* like that—you know, it would have holes where the eyes and the mouth are. Or we'd pull up behind a tanker truck going down the highway, and the dents on the back would be such that it would look exactly like one of those. I mean, this happened over and over again. It must have happened fifty times on this tour. He was that kind of guy.

TIRED DEATH

The tour with Bergland took place in the summer of 1986 after Miller had split town and spent a couple of years bouncing back and forth between New York City (where he lived with his girlfriend Kristin Oppenheim) and Brussels, Belgium (where his old friends in Tuxedomoon had settled a few years earlier). "He was there, but he wasn't there," recalls Steven Brown of Miller's time in Brussels. "Like many Americans, he never bothered to learn any languages, so he was always kind of an outsider, as we all were, but he was *way* outside. You know, he didn't fit in at *all*."

Miller continued recording under the name Minimal Man, enlisting the help of Tuxedomoon members Peter Dachert and Luc Van Lieshout, among others. By the end of the decade, he had recorded a total of five LPs (including the two he made in San Francisco), along with a handful of EPs and 7-inches—not bad for a self-professed non-musician."That was his lifeline: he would make these records and get an advance from them and live like that," says Brown."But it was kind of strange. I could never figure out what exactly he was trying to *do*. Maybe he thought he was gonna be a successful musician or have a hit with one of his records. But he eventually just burned out on the scene and went back to the States and left the music thing altogether." After another stint in New York, he retired to Southern California, where he passed away in 2003 at age fifty-one from complications related to hepatitis.

But that's not where the story should end. For a proper ending, we need to go back to San Francisco circa early 1985. Miller and Blaise Smith had just finished recording an EP, *Sex Teacher*—the last Minimal Man record to be made in San Francisco and the first to be released on his new label in Brussels. "We did that record, and the next thing I knew, he was gone. He had to get out of the country, kind of," explains Smith. The reason had to do with the lease on 992 Valencia, which Miller had taken over several years prior. "What he did was, he made copies of the lease, and then he sold the lease to two different people. So they both came at the first of the month to move in, and they're both there with these official signed leases. And he charged 'em both—whatever, three grand or something. That was a fiasco. But that's just typical Patrick."

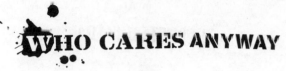

13

THE SAVOY SOUND: INDOOR LIFE AND "BEAUTIFUL MUSIC"

Jorge Socarras: There was a chain of bakeries in San Francisco—there were two or three of them—called Just Desserts. They had just started. Everybody got jobs there. Well, I didn't because I was lucky enough to get SSI. But those people who needed to work, a lot of them got jobs there. And there was all this opium dealing going on behind the scenes at this bakery. So we'd get together after work with boxes and boxes of cakes and baked goods and opium and go to the Strand and watch three horror movies for a dollar, eating cake and high on opium. And this was just a normal day, like a weekday in San Francisco.

Bob Hoffnar: They hired anybody. They sort of left the keys to the truck around, so a lot of the early bands would just borrow the Just Desserts truck to get their stuff around. I worked there. Joe Sabella, the drummer from Indoor Life, did too. That's how we started the band. I was in the punk rock scene, and Joe was a drummer in the free jazz world. We were both bakers there. We were cutting brownies together one night, and I said, "Joe, I think we could get away with playing some real music and do something fun and get some money."

Indoor Life came together toward the end of 1979, and though their time in San Francisco would be brief—just over a year—it coincided with the peak of what might be dubbed the city's "art-punk era." In addition to Tuxedomoon, Factrix, Minimal Man, and a revamped Sleepers lineup (see Chapter 14), there was the scene surrounding Club Foot—an avant-garde performance space on a remote stretch of Third Street—spearheaded by the enigmatic

THE POST-PUNK ERA

Richard Kelly (see Chapter 16).[82]

Meanwhile, the Savoy Tivoli in North Beach was emerging as a welcome alternative to the increasingly passé Mabuhay Gardens. "We were in love with Indoor Life, and Voice Farm, and Ultrasheen," recalls Olga Gerrard, who booked the Savoy in those days along with then-husband Gerry Gerrard. "There were some really remarkable artists that, although they weren't punk, there really weren't too many other places they could play other than what were primarily punk clubs. There was punk, and then there was 'punk.' In my lexicon, it was more like art rock."

Indoor Life front man Jorge Socarras has no problem with this characterization. "Even in New York, when we got written up, very often we'd be labeled as 'art rock.' I was absolutely fine with that because I *was* an artist. 'Yeah, we're artists making music.' And I think, certainly now, in retrospect, one could say there was a lot of art music in San Francisco—as there was in New York and London as well. It was kind of an ongoing joke that every artist, or anyone who came out of art school, had to have a band. It was such a natural progression at the time. I mean, Bowie, David Byrne, Bryan Ferry—everyone went to art school and then started a band."

Socarras knew those other cities well. Though he first moved to San Francisco in the early 1970s, he went on to spend time in London and then New York—where he briefly attended the School of Visual Arts—before moving back to SF in 1979. "I was a painter," he explains, "but I felt very limited by painting. San Francisco State had one of the best and most progressive and only interdisciplinary art departments in the country. So I went from visual art to performance art."

While in London, Socarras had witnessed the initial explosion of punk firsthand and felt inspired to start his own band. Yet by the time he enrolled at SF State, he had largely given up on the idea. "And as ironic as life is, I met Bob at a party—Bob Hoffnar. And I told him, 'I've just been in London and New York the last couple of years trying to start a band, and nothing's happened.' He says, 'Oh, me and these guys are starting a band. In fact,

82 Indoor Life made its live debut at Club Foot on April 18, 1980.

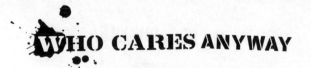

why don't you meet up with us tomorrow? We're looking for a singer.' It was that casual. And sure enough, it was Bob and Joe Sabella, the drummer, and Richard Kelly, the guitarist."

"We didn't do any recording with Kelly," clarifies Hoffnar. "We barely could play shows. He was a little nuts. We rehearsed a bunch, and then he couldn't make it—he got sick, which happened a lot, and then disappeared for a little bit. And then this guy Dino showed up—J.A. Deane. He was a free jazz trombone player."

For Socarras, who describes Deane's trombone playing as "the sound of Martian elephants," this was the missing link. "I felt like that really gave me the freedom to just express myself in any fashion that felt natural and intuitive, without trying to meet any standards of what was fashionably punk. I think we were playing more on that before Dino, looking for a sound. But I think with Dino, the sound just happened. It just emerged."

VOODOO

As with Tuxedomoon, Indoor Life would eventually migrate elsewhere in search of a broader, more receptive audience. That said, it's hard to imagine either band coming of age anyplace else. "I think we had a very strong affinity," says Socarras. "Tuxedomoon was a similar mix of well-seasoned musicians and multidisciplinary artists. And I think we recognized that in each other, and I think audiences connected us because there was that sense of—you know, what some would call the 'art bands.'"

Tuxedomoon also figures into the backstory behind Indoor Life's signature song, 'Voodoo.' Clocking in at over thirteen minutes, the song features an unusual blend of live drumming, squishy analog synths, and dub-like sound effects, topped off by Socarras's oddly crooned vocals, which bring to mind Bryan Ferry doing an Elvis impersonation. The main riff—an R&B-style bassline played on the synthesizer—repeats for the entire duration of the song.

"J.A. Deane came up with that," says the singer. "He used to call it a 'Shortenin' Bread' riff. And it's true. I mean, fundamentally, that's what it is. Dino came from

an R&B and soul background. He had played with Ike and Tina Turner." The lyrics, meanwhile, were inspired by Tuxedomoon's 'Jinx,' a brooding tango-esque number that was part of their live set at the time.[83] Socarras: "Winston Tong sings it, and the refrain is just, 'It's a jinx, it's a jinx.' It's a beautiful song, and Winston's vocals on it are perfect. 'Voodoo' was my response to that song. Even the supernatural element. Because Winston was talking about something dark: the idea of a jinx, a curse."

'Voodoo' occupies side one of Indoor Life's self-titled EP, which was recorded in 1980 with help from an aspiring producer/manager who went by the name Luther Blue. "That was the only name he ever told us," says Hoffnar. "He ran a kind of punk/new wave clothing store south of Market Street that was also called Luther Blue," adds Socarras, who initially thought the Residents' Ralph Records would have been a natural fit before Mr. Blue

---

83 A live version of 'Jinx' appears on the compilation LP *Savoy Sound: Wave Goodbye*. The studio version appears on Tuxedomoon's 1981 album *Desire*.

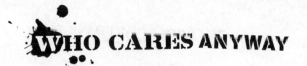

came along. "We were happy to work with him because he was an individual, and he was so dedicated to the band."[84]

The record also benefited from the efforts of producer Patrick Cowley, with whom the group shared a small rehearsal space on Minna Street in South of Market. Better known as an electronic dance music producer, Cowley had been friends with Socarras dating back to 1974, when the two began collaborating on a recording project during the singer's first stint in San Francisco.[85] Cowley's contributions to Indoor Life represent a rare instance of crossover between the city's gay disco scene and the art punk underground. "It was a different world," Socarras says of Cowley's more typical milieu.

Cowley remains best-known for his collaborations with disco diva Sylvester ('Do You Wanna Funk?') and his own openly homoerotic dance tracks ('Menergy,' 'Megatron Man'), but he had broader interests. He was particularly fond of Brian Eno's ambient albums and the new age synth music being made by the likes of Vangelis, Tomita, and Jean-Michel Jarre. "When we first met, we turned each other on to so much music," says Socarras. "He turned me on to Wendy Carlos when she was still Walter. He turned me on to Tomita; he turned me on to George Crumb. He was very interested in all music and in emulating. I think I was much more of a snob in that I would decide what was cool and what wasn't. Whereas Patrick, he really listened to *sounds*. So whatever the music was, he could extract from it what was interesting and novel to him and work with it. Really, ultimately, he was a true postmodern."

He was also, alas, among the earliest casualties of AIDS. Cowley died in November of 1982 from "one of the mysterious diseases now plaguing the gay community," as the *Examiner* put it in a lengthy obituary at the time.[86] In the years

---

84   It's unknown whether Luther Blue made any other forays into music production, but he was the subject of a couple of newspaper articles in the late 1980s after he opened a water bar—The White Room with a Blue Glow, as it was known—near Haight and Fillmore.

85   The recordings were eventually released in 2009 as a duo album, *Catholic*, by the German label Macro. "Even though now it's often called post-punk, the truth is, we were actually making it *pre*-punk," says Socarras of their collaborations.

86   "He really developed and fueled that Hi-NRG sound that became the backdrop for so much of the dance/gay sex scene," notes Socarras. "And of course, he was simultaneously making music for gay porn. So it was perfect. So in a way, he was orchestrating so much of the music of the gay sexual revolution, at least in San Francisco."

to come, AIDS would decimate the gay nightclub scene that Cowley's music had provided the soundtrack for.[87] In his case, it also cut short the potential of a more wide-ranging producing career. "He would have loved, I think, as his reputation grew as a producer, to have been able to work with a greater diversity of bands—you know, beyond Sylvester," says Socarras. "And I'm sure he would have gone on to. Because a great producer can adapt to almost any sound, and I think Patrick had that capacity."

CELLULOID HEROES

For Indoor Life, the self-titled EP wound up being a ticket out of San Francisco. The record was picked up by Celluloid, a New York-based label that was also handling the European distribution for Ralph Records. "They were putting out a lot of interesting artists and music," notes Socarras. "Little did we know then that they would turn out to be a notorious pirate label." Adds Hoffnar, "Celluloid basically bootlegged the EP." Ironically, the bootlegging meant that they actually had overseas distribution, unlike most of their peers in San Francisco.

Celluloid also booked them on a March 1981 tour of France alongside Ralph/Celluloid acts Tuxedomoon and Snakefinger. They weren't quite prepared for the reception they got. "There were about 5,000 people there," says Hoffnar of their first show in Paris. "We were used to playing the Mudd Club and the Savoy and stuff like that. We thought we were just a tagalong opening act. But we start playing, and 5,000 people start singing along to the tunes and going bananas. We were like, 'What the fuck?' We didn't even have a record out. Then it turned out we *did* have a record out because Celluloid had bootlegged it. Then we'd walk around Paris, and we would see our pictures on the freaking cover of *Actuel*. It totally caught on. It was wild. At that point, there were actual regional markets. It wasn't so global. And what had happened was, things from San Francisco became totally the hip thing in France."

---

87 Michael Snyder, "Producer's Quest for Death with Dignity." *San Francisco Examiner*, December 5, 1982.

WHO CARES ANYWAY

As the art bands were finding a footing in France, the Savoy Tivoli's brief run as a hub for the local art punk scene was winding down. "The audiences were too big," explains Olga Gerrard. "The Savoy Tivoli was a restaurant, and we were encroaching. Not just encroaching gently, but just taking over the place. It was time to move on. And we were heartbroken about it, but we totally got it." The club commemorated its closing with an LP of live performances recorded during the last week of February 1981, just before the Tuxedomoon/Snakefinger tour.[88]

It was around this time that Indoor Life decided it was a good time to move on from SF. "I never personally felt really 'in' with the inner sanctum of San Francisco bands," explains Socarras. "That was a good thing for us. I felt like that freed us a lot more because there were bands that—as interesting as they might have been—really never escaped the gravitational center of San Francisco." As with Tuxedomoon, there was a certain irony to Indoor Life's relationship with the city that spawned them. "We formed in San Francisco, and it was the right time and place, and there certainly was a zeitgeist. But at the same time, a lot of the influences and things that were propelling us really led us elsewhere."[89]

Expanding on this thought, Socarras mentions a writeup of Indoor Life by *Interview*'s Glenn O'Brien, who described the band as "one of the leading practitioners of beautiful music." "He nailed it," says the singer. "It was like, 'Thank you.' That is what I felt we were trying to do. I think part of the affinity that I felt, and Bob felt, and Dino and Joe felt with the folks in Tuxedomoon and the Sleepers, for example, was that we were concerned with the ideas of beauty and of making the beautiful. Not to say that we didn't deconstruct those ideas and play with them, but I think so much of punk was a *rebellion* against classical notions of beauty. And rightly so. Music needed to go through this revolution. But I don't think it's a coincidence that a lot of the bands that were more concerned with ideas such as that (as many as there were) also

---

88 Oddly, Indoor Life isn't on the record, but the bands that are—including Tuxedomoon, the Sleepers, Ultrasheen, and Snakefinger, among others—offer a representative sampling of the time and place.

89 Tuxedomoon's Steven Brown echoes this point: "Most people don't think of San Francisco as a small town, but it *is*. That's why *we* left. We had gotten to a certain point, and it was like, 'Okay, what next? We have to move out of here, or we're just gonna become a local novelty.'"

were able to garner wider audiences. Because there are things that translate. It was that sensibility, I think, that translated to a bigger audience, and this is what I wanted."

Yet that search for a bigger audience came with its own costs. "We got the proverbial hit record in France and spent a bunch of time over there and did a couple of big tours," says Hoffnar. "Then we settled into New York and started getting record deals. Then we just got thrown into the gaping maw of greed and avarice of the music industry, and it ate us up. They start sending you stylists and producers and all that shit, then the next thing you know, music's not fun. We did pretty good for a while, though."

Indoor Life carried on for a few more years, minus drummer Joe Sabella (who stayed behind in San Francisco). They released an LP in 1983 and a couple of records—a single and an EP—through Elektra a few years later, albeit with diminishing returns. "The downside was this increasing pressure to make something more commercial, more radio playable," admits Socarras. "It's definitely identifiable as one progresses through our recordings. There are certain songs where I listen to them, and I think, 'Who is that? Who were we trying to be?' And they're pretty, but one could say—going back to San Francisco— that the most raw, kind of pure, magical, and forceful music came out of that initial sphere. So even though we got out of there, I would never discredit San Francisco because of those creative roots."

14

PAINLESS NIGHTS: THE RETURN OF THE SLEEPERS

Eric Fournier: Vale came to me with the idea of the Sleepers because he knew them—he loved the band. At that time, the band had been broken up for a while. They were famously dysfunctional because of Ricky and his bipolar insanity and Michael's drug problems. But they were really wonderful guys. Vale wasn't sure anyone could wrangle them and get them into the studio and get anything productive out of them. I met with them, and Michael Belfer and I hit it off right away. For a couple of years, he was sort of like my little brother.

It was the spring of 1980, and a wayward Michael Belfer had just returned to the West Coast after an ill-fated season in New York City. While convalescing at his parents' house in Palo Alto, he started hanging out at KFJC, the radio station at Foothill Community College in Sunnyvale. It was there that he met Ron MacLeod, a DJ at the station who not only played bass but also had a younger brother, Brian, who was a teen prodigy on the drums. Without looking for it, then, Belfer had stumbled on the rhythm section for what would become version 2.0 of the Sleepers.

The other new addition was Mike White, who contributed much more than just a second guitar.[90] He wrote 'Zenith,' a futuristic guitar instrumental that made up part of the showstopping space-rock odyssey 'Zenith'/'Theory'

---

90 The Sleepers briefly re-formed in late 1979, with a lineup of Belfer, Williams, Paul Draper, and drummer Jeff Raphael (formerly of the Nuns). They played a few shows in November and December of that year but didn't record anything together. Earlier that year—probably in the late summer—Belfer and Williams recorded a couple of songs together with a rhythm section consisting of a drum machine and then Pink Section's Stephen Wymore on bass. The resulting single, 'Mirror' b/w 'Theory,' was the first release on Fournier's label.

(heard on both *Painless Nights* and the live *Savoy Sound* compilation). Perhaps just as importantly, he had a rehearsal studio in the garage of his Palo Alto home as well as an arsenal of Electro-Harmonix guitar pedals. And as if that weren't enough, there were also his pharmaceutical connections. "He was a telephone operator all his life for Pac Bell," recalls Belfer. "They had these in-house doctors who would write prescriptions for amphetamines to keep them awake and alert, and then valium to calm their nerves when they needed to come down after being so wired for so many hours. And boy,

CABARET VOLTAIRE
THE *SLEEPERS*
YOUNG MARBLE GIANTS

FRIDAY **24** OCTOBER | SUNDAY **26** OCTOBER
TENTH STREET HALL | KEYSTONE-PALO ALTO
220-10th St., SF 864.1639 | 260 California 324.1402
9 PM $6 | 9 PM $5 Advance $6 At Door

when Ricky discovered that Mike White had bags of these things in his freezer, Ricky started pilfering them."

Predictably, the pills fed into the singer's erratic behavior, which showed no signs of slowing down. He was still in fine form creatively, though, so his bandmates did what they could to manage him—whether that meant hiding White's stash of pills or, in one case, "kidnapping" the singer and dropping him off at his grandparents' house so that he wouldn't go AWOL in between recording sessions. With Belfer at least temporarily clean and the rest of the band rounding into form, things were looking up.

By the fall of 1980, the new lineup was wowing local audiences. "I thought they were going to be big; their live sound was massive!" wrote Joe Carducci of the band's October 24 appearance at the Tenth Street Hall, where they opened

for Cabaret Voltaire and Young Marble Giants.[91] *Creep* fanzine's Johnny Myers offered a more detailed account in a review of a show from a week earlier, this one a headlining gig at Rock City in North Beach:

> Strict taskmaster Michael has honed his new crew ... to that thin line which separates a "tight" band from one that is slick (i.e., Major Label "Product") ... The new songs are well-written, and the set is well-paced. It's really hard to believe this band has only been practicing for a matter of months ... An interesting diversion would be to compile a list of bands that have made a smooth and intelligent transition from head-bashers to '80s pop-moderne without losing most of their fans. That the Sleepers have accomplished this sleight of hand is a testimony to the collective genius of Michael and Ricky.[92]

By this point, the new-look Sleepers had already finished recording *Painless Nights*, though it would take almost another year for the album to surface.[93] Produced by Jim Keylor at his basement studio in Noe Valley, the album reflects the newer, more streamlined sound described above by Myers.[94] Much of this had to do with Brian MacLeod, whose uncluttered, metronomic style was a departure from that of Tim Mooney, yet well-suited to the band's new material. "Brian was just such a great drummer," raves Belfer. "He enabled us to put together real minimalist parts. I was always leaning towards having things be very minimalist."

Opener, 'When Can I Fly?' neatly encapsulates this approach. The song

---

91 Liner notes to *Painless Nights* reissue.
92 *Creep*, Fall 1980, p. 30.
93 Two of the album's nine tracks, 'Walk Away' and 'The Mind,' were recorded earlier that year in Southern California with the B-People's Alex Gibson and Tom Recchion on bass and drums, respectively. The B-People were associated with the LA Free Music Society, a loose collective of bands that Factrix's Cole Palme had also briefly been involved with before moving to San Francisco.
94 Located at 4326 Army Street, this was the same studio where the Dead Kennedys recorded their first single, 'California Über Alles' b/w 'The Man with the Dogs,' in 1979. Keylor also did the on-location recording for the 2LP compilation *Can You Hear Me? Music from the Deaf Club* (also recorded in 1979). In a previous life, Keylor played bass for Blue Cheer, appearing on their 1971 album *Oh! Pleasant Hope*.

is built on a pair of two-bar riffs—one that repeats for the entirety of the verse and another that does likewise during the intro and chorus. As with several other songs on the album ('Holding Back,' 'The Mind'), the key changes that occur between sections are both surprising and subtle. "He had the vision and the ears for doing something different, with a really strong pop sensibility, but still cutting edge," notes guitarist Kirk Heydt, referring to Belfer's songwriting.

The open-ended song structures also provide an ideal backdrop for Ricky's free-ranging vocals. The most dramatic example

FLYER BY DIAN-AZIZA OOKA AND MARTHA GEERING.

comes with the closing track, 'Los Gatos,' another song based around a minimal minor-key riff. The song climaxes at around the two-minute mark, with the singer pleading his case to some unspecified "you" before letting out an unintentional burp, apologizing, and then resuming his tirade—all without missing a beat. It is a Zen moment that reveals, in the space of a few seconds, both a profound sense of anguish and a self-aware sense of humor.

Michael Belfer: I was standing next to him when he said that. I was there with him holding his tall can of beer. That's why he burped. I was like, "Oh my god. [Pause.] Okay, fine, we're gonna keep that in there." But my first reaction was, "Goddammit, Ricky! Can you just sing one version of the song?" And of course, we didn't have Pro Tools to comp tracks back then. If you were gonna do that, you had to have a really good engineer who could cut tape and do his editing magic.

Connie Champagne: That was one of the things I thought was funny—I mean, that Ricky would do that. That he would burp and then say, "excuse me." Why did he say, "excuse me"? And *he* probably thought that was funny. They *did* think a lot of his hijinks were funny, though, even when they were leading into a direction that was potentially not that funny.

Decades on, *Painless Nights* stands as the most accomplished studio LP by any of the early Mabuhay-era punk bands—even if it wasn't the original Sleepers lineup, and even if they were no longer a punk band by that point.[95] "I think it would be hard to pigeonhole that record, genre-wise," says Champagne. "It didn't sound like anybody else when it came out, that's for sure." Indeed, the album is too dark and disturbing to qualify as new wave, too polished for punk, and too weird to resemble anything approaching mainstream rock. If there is a reference point, it would be Joy Division, a comparison that at least a couple of critics have invoked: Jon Savage later called *Painless Nights* "the deepest drive into the late '70s unconscious that you can find outside Joy Division,"[96] while Joe Carducci likened the Sleepers to "what Joy Division might have developed into had they the balls."[97]

While intended as praise for the Sleepers, the dig at Joy Division is a little gratuitous, given that *Painless Nights* was at least partly influenced by the Manchester quartet. Belfer credits Patrick Roques, a friend of his from the Tuxedomoon orbit, with turning him on to the band. "He had his ear to the ground and would get all these really great records. I just remember when *Closer* by Joy Division came out, we would listen to that endlessly." Champagne, who

95 Granted, most of those bands didn't stick around long enough to make an LP, and the ones that did (the Nuns, the Mutants, the Offs) did so a couple of years too late.
96 Jon Savage, "Buried Treasure: The Sleepers." *Mojo*, 1999. https://web.archive.org/web/20090721222358/http://www.jonsavage.com/journalism/sleepers/
97 This description appears in Carducci's *Rock and the Pop Narcotic* and was reused in the promotional materials for the 2012 vinyl reissue of *Painless Nights* on Superior Viaduct.

was dating drummer Brian MacLeod at the time, adds, "Patrick had the first Joy Division album, and he also had the first Psychedelic Furs album. So we were listening to it, and Ricky was there. I remember Patrick Roques saying to Michael, 'What do you think of this?' And Michael was sort of talking to Ricky about, like, 'What do you think about this music? This is sort of the direction that we should go in.' I remember that."

ADOLESCENT

Whereas Joy Division had the support of Factory Records—one of the definitive UK post-punk labels along with Rough Trade—the Sleepers' backing came from a far less established label in Adolescent. Label head Eric Fournier was committed to the band but also inexperienced at running a label, let alone dealing with a band as unruly as the Sleepers. "He was friends with artists like Fetty who were also very enamored with Ricky until they realized how much of a handful he was gonna be," recalls Champagne. "It's like, you hear about people like the Gettys, and they invite some artist, and they take a shit on their floor or steal something." Fournier's North Beach apartment was the site of many such parties—where, in Belfer's words, "the Summer of Love could be found still partying and mixing ever so slightly with the punk scene." Guests recall such high-end accoutrements as a zebra skin rug and a sterling silver demitasse filled with a certain white powder. "But he was bankrolling the whole thing," adds Champagne, referring to Fournier's financing of the latter-day Sleepers. "He paid for *everything.*"

Trouble arose not long after the recording of *Painless Nights* when Belfer brought in Roques to serve as the band's manager. "Patrick and Michael had started hanging around together, and Michael had gotten back into heroin," says Fournier. "Then Patrick and him came up with this idea that they were going to go on tour, so he booked a tour for them of New York, Boston, Philadelphia, and Washington, DC. And I asked them to not do it because I thought it was silly for them to go on tour two months before the record was going to be released and that they should go on tour when it could help sell the record. Well, they went on tour anyway, and I followed them basically to protect my investment."

The April 1981 tour was an almost unmitigated disaster. During the second show—a headlining date at Hurrah in New York City—Ricky passed out onstage after overdosing on barbiturates.[98] As Fournier recounts, "It was a packed house, and by the second song, he had literally started to slide down the mic stand and ended up sleeping on the floor. Mike White was kind of trying to nudge him with his foot to wake him up. But the band kept playing. And then, I don't know—I think it was the *Village Voice*, the title of their review the next day or the day after was like, 'The Sleepers: No Misnomer Here.'" Demoralized by their singer's behavior, half of the band—the MacLeods and a more recent addition, saxophonist Benjamin Bossi—quit the next day and flew back to San Francisco.

Bloodied but unbowed, the remaining trio managed to recruit a new rhythm section and secure a temporary rehearsal space in Manhattan. It was during this emergency retooling period that another debacle ensued, although the precise details are still a matter of some dispute. According to Belfer, his girlfriend and her friend pawned Fournier's guitar for heroin money; according to Fournier, it was Belfer himself who pawned it. Whatever the case, the saga ended with Fournier taking possession of the left-handed Belfer's guitar for the remainder of the tour. "I wanted to teach him a lesson," explained Fournier. (Alas, the lesson wasn't appreciated. "I had to finish the tour playing an upside-down right-handed guitar," laments Belfer.)

"They had a disastrous show at the Mudd Club," recalls Suzi Skates, who had relocated from SF to Manhattan by this point. It was her boyfriend, Plasmatics bassist Chosei Funehara, who lent the Sleepers the use of his rehearsal space; he was also the sound man at the Mudd Club. Adds Ms. Skates, "Ricky was completely obnoxious. I just remember him yelling at Chosei about the sound. And Chosei was just kind of laughing because it's like, 'Puh-lease. This guy is ridiculous.'" (Richard Edson, who was part of the pickup band that night, has

98 As (bad) luck would have it, this show is the source of one of the only two video clips of the Sleepers performing live (the other being the performance of 'Sister Little' from the Miners' Benefit concert in March 1978).

164

his own Ricky anecdote. "He turned and hit my trumpet *while* I was playing, and it went right into my lip. And I was like, 'I hate this guy.' I was gonna kill him. I shoulda. I shoulda punched him in the face. But I didn't.")

CLOCKS OF PARADISE

Still licking their wounds from the disastrous trip east, the Sleepers played a few more shows in San Francisco with another makeshift lineup before hanging it up.[99] "The record came out a few months later without any support or any shows to go behind it," laments Fournier. "Once again, they lived up to their dysfunctional name. But I loved that band, and I loved Ricky and Michael, and I was really sorry that things turned out the way they did."

The band members scattered in several directions: Ricky joined Toiling Midgets (see Chapter 18), while Belfer and Brian MacLeod formed the Clocks of Paradise, a short-lived band that briefly appeared on the verge of bigger and better things.[100] "Michael was so talented, and he was easy to write with," recalls Connie Champagne, the group's lead singer. "And all of a sudden, we had this incredible band. Everything was coming together very, very fast." Peter Belsito, who booked the group at the Valencia Tool & Die, remembers their gig as a highlight of his tenure there. "I remember the Clocks show as kind of being perfect. It was just one of those moments. There weren't a lot of people there. It was a good crowd, but not shoulder to shoulder or anything like that. I just remember it being the right fit for that room. It was just right."

---

99 Denny DeGorio recalls sitting in on bass for one of these shows: "We had a show at the On Broadway where Ricky sang. I think it was billed as the Sleepers if I'm not mistaken. And Ricky showed up late. So we had already played two or three instrumentals. I was blown away by Michael's playing, as usual. But then Ricky showed up, and Ricky sang a song. And I remember him doing this pirouette. He did this little whirling dervish dance step, and then he fell flat on his face and was completely out cold. They had to call an ambulance. And people thought this was part of our show. The paramedics came and actually carried Ricky out on a stretcher, right down the middle of the fuckin' venue. It was the craziest thing. And that was the last gig we played with Ricky."

100 Ron MacLeod also played bass for the Clocks of Paradise early on before being replaced by Denny DeGorio. As for Mike White, he was apparently never heard from again.

WHO CARES ANYWAY

Bassist Denny DeGorio, meanwhile, remembers his brief time in the group as a last gasp for both himself and Belfer. "We became friends, and we had a couple of things in common—our sense of humor, for one thing. And he also had a similar struggle with heroin as I did. We became friends and dope buddies." Before long, DeGorio decided it was time for a change of scenery. When his old friends Chip and Tony Kinman—formerly of the Dils—came through town that summer with their new band Rank and File, he hopped in the van with them and moved to Austin.[101]

The Clocks of Paradise weren't finished just yet, though. They found a more than adequate replacement for DeGorio in Patrick O'Hearn, a veteran of Frank Zappa's *Sheik Yerbouti*-era band. At the time, O'Hearn was playing with Group 87, a slick jazz-fusion outfit whose lineup included trumpeter Mark Isham (who would also briefly join the Clocks of Paradise). It was this version of the group that found itself opening for New Order and Simple Minds at a sold-out Market Street Cinema that November. According to Belsito, the upstart opening act wound up "rendering the headliners totally forgettable."[102]

"This was a *huge* deal," says Champagne, "to be able to do that within six months of putting a band together, to have that happen that fast. I think we were sort of kidding ourselves that the drug situation with Michael wasn't going to be a factor. You know, because you just don't want it to be. He was so talented." She pauses. "We had this really great gig, and the next day, Michael disappeared. Years later, he said to me, 'God, our band was so great: you and me and Brian and Pat. What happened?' I said, 'You don't remember? You took all the money from the gig, and you went to New York the next day.' And I swear, his face—it was that kind of realization of like, 'Oh my God, I *really* fucked that up.'" Belfer remembers the details differently (he went to New Orleans, not to New York, and he didn't take all the money from the gig), but regardless, the band was finished. In hindsight, he chalks up his sudden departure to a lingering inferiority complex. "I didn't understand why Mark Isham and Pat O'Hearn wanted to play in a band with

---

101 DeGorio, who remained in Austin, wound up joining Alejandro Escovedo and his brother Javier (formerly of the Zeros) in the True Believers, who signed with EMI and released a self-titled LP via that label in 1986.

102 *Hardcore California*, p. 111.

me. I just felt like such a hack compared to these guys."

The eighties were largely a lost decade for the guitarist, who tried his hand with a couple of other San Francisco-based bands in 1982 before departing for Belgium. There, he briefly rejoined Tuxedomoon, then collaborated with Blaine Reininger on the excellent *Night Air.* Released in 1984 as a Blaine Reininger solo album, it is one of just two albums Belfer would appear on for the rest of the decade post-Sleepers.[103] The guitarist returned to the States after a year in Belgium, but drug problems continued to haunt him for several more years, as did the lack of a consistent songwriting partner à la Ricky Williams.

As with so many things involving the Sleepers, the sense of lost potential is palpable. "I think Michael was a *tremendous* talent that, in some ways like Ricky, got thrown under the bus," says Champagne. "On the other hand, if

THE SLEEPERS WERE ORIGINALLY SCHEDULED TO PLAY THE FIRST EASTERN FRONT FESTIVAL IN BERKELEY ON JULY 25, 1981. WHEN THEY BROKE UP THAT SPRING, TOILING MIDGETS TOOK THEIR PLACE ON THE BILL. (RICKY SANG.)

---

103 The other was Rhythm & Noise's 1985 album *Chasms Accord* (Ralph). Belfer plays guitar on one track, 'Schismatic.'

WHO CARES ANYWAY

Michael hadn't been the kind of punk rock outcast that he was, would he have come up with the sound that he came up with? Would he have played the music that he played?"

Suzi Skates: Michael's a serious guy. He was serious about music, serious about the band. When I first met him, he had kind of like a teen-doll or teen-painting innocent beauty. He had these big eyes. He had an innocence, but like a poetic intelligence. But he also had drive to musically make it. And holding bands together is hard, with girlfriends and, you know, all the different people. All the personalities.

Connie Champagne: Michael really is one of the most original talents. And everybody who met him, especially at that time, would agree. There are many people, and I'm one of them, who are fairly certain that the Edge borrowed quite a bit from Michael. It's possible that it was kismet or synchronicity that they came up at the same time with the same influences. But I doubt it. Because Michael already had a record out that was really popular, which was *No Tears* by Tuxedomoon.

Eric Fournier: I remember when I first started hearing the Edge get really good. I thought, "Michael was doing this *years* before you, dude." But it takes more than just talent to make it in the industry.

15

"TWO SIDES TO THE COIN": FROM PINK SECTION TO SURVIVAL RESEARCH LABORATORIES AND INFLATABLE BOY CLAMS

SPRING 1980

Matt Heckert: Everybody was saying, "We're not commercial and not trying to make money here. We just wanna do shows and have fun and be able to go to different places and see different places." But in the meantime, some people were getting picked up. Like, you heard X all of a sudden had a record deal. So in the back of your mind, you were thinking, "Well, maybe we could have an even bigger success." But of course, that's not really gonna happen with something like Pink Section. It was just too rinky-dink, really.

Stephen Wymore: We recorded our EP in this new studio [Triangle Studios in Seattle]. We were just very elated—you know, we thought we'd somehow made it. So we were living in Seattle while we were recording it. And we finished it—finished the tracks, finished the album. We hadn't mixed it. And they had a party. It was a brand-new studio, and they had kind of like a celebration.

Judy Gittelsohn: It was the first party, like "welcome to this great recording studio," and it burned down.

Stephen Wymore: Someone had left a burning cigarette in the couch, and the fuckin' studio burned down. That kind of took the wind out of everything. Because we were gonna mix the record, but we couldn't mix it, so everything went on ice for a while.

Then we were gonna tour. We got back down to San Francisco, and we did a whole big thing where we made all these rhythm tracks to play along with live. Kind of a new thing for us. And we were going up to Seattle to play, and Judy got in a car accident. She left before us and it was raining one night, and she got in an accident. She was in the hospital. That put the kibosh on everything.

Matt Heckert: By the time we finished playing our last show, we were all kind of bored with it. The thing is, with Pink Section, we wrote a few songs, we developed for a little while, and then we *stopped*. And we didn't have like a songwriter or routine or method or way of coming up with stuff that we were all interested and together. We were excited to be in the band for a while, but musically, there was nothing compelling about it. It just got to be, "Oh Christ, we've gotta play that song again?"

Carol Detweiler: The whole thing was a really peak experience, but it seems like it didn't last all that long. We just went *boom*, arrived on the scene, and just played really hard and did all these gigs—and then we kind of burned out, and it was hard to keep it going. So we sort of splintered off into other groups.

By the time Pink Section played their last shows in the summer of 1980, the band members were already turning their attention elsewhere. For Detweiler and Gittelsohn, that meant the Inflatable Boy Clams, the whimsical act they'd put together with performance artist and fellow Art Institute alum JoJo Planteen. Meanwhile, Wymore was serving as Patrick Miller's right-hand man in Minimal Man, while Heckert had taken up a similar role alongside Mark Pauline in Survival Research Laboratories.

The contrasts were stark. "Pink Section was very much on the Boy Clams end of that spectrum," observes David Swan, who collaborated with Detweiler and Gittelsohn in another group, the Longshoremen. "It was playful and colorful, and it really was new wave as opposed to punk." Yet as he points out, the light-

and-dark contrast between the Boy Clams and SRL or Minimal Man wasn't without precedent. Rather, it could be seen as a natural outgrowth of the broader gestalt shift brought about by punk. "There was a new worldview that was open for creative interpretation, and it had two sides to the coin. Like if you look at psychedelia, there was a sort of funky, old-fashioned, natural side, and then there was a high-tech, futuristic side, in a sense."

SRL

Survival Research Laboratories epitomized that high-tech, futuristic side, staging massive, often horrifying spectacles—many of them in public spaces—involving primitive robots fashioned from scrap metal and discarded machinery. "Those are basically the most terrifying events I've ever been to in my life," recalls Brandan Kearney, who saw several of SRL's performances during the 1980s. "I think the last one I went to was somewhere down near the Bay Bridge. They had this cannon that was shooting fluorescent light tubes onto the freeway. It's a miracle the city even let them do it."

At times, it was less a matter of the city *letting* them do it than it was SRL taking it upon themselves and doing it anyway, consequences be damned. "A lot of the early SRL stuff, we just did in lots that we kind of picked out," explains Heckert. "We didn't even really get permits. Which is something you could never do nowadays." Other times, they strategically omitted certain details about their plans in order to get the green light. "We would just basically lie about what was gonna happen," he admits. "I mean 'lie' from the standpoint that we'd say something was gonna happen, but we would *completely* under-describe it. 'Oh, there's gonna be a small flame over here.' We didn't say, 'It's gonna make a twenty-foot-tall flame.'"

Not surprisingly, their guerrilla performances often left onlookers dazed and confused. "Residents in the quiet Richmond District neighborhood rubbed their eyes and stared out of their windows in disbelief last Saturday evening,"

WHO CARES ANYWAY

wrote a reporter in a June 1980 article for the *Examiner* after one such show.[104] "Here in the outdoor amphitheater of sedate Cabrillo Elementary School, where young children play innocent games, was a scene out of Dante's *Inferno*." A neighborhood resident quoted in the article called it "too sick for words."

That said, the idea wasn't just to shock people for the sake of it—or, as Pauline put it in the same article, "to do some kind of anarchistic mish-mash." As with Factrix, there was an undercurrent of dark, even macabre humor, along with a genuine sense of danger. The robots could be unpredictable, and even though there was plenty of choreography involved, each performance was a

---

104 Ivan Sharpe, "Machines That Go Punk in the Night." *SF Examiner*. June 10, 1980.

one-off event. The results were genuinely beyond category at the time. "You can say it was seminal," notes filmmaker Craig Baldwin."That is to say, it started something that will not die in our lifetimes—this kind of machine art."

The aforementioned Richmond District show took place not long after Heckert joined SRL as Pauline's second-in-command. "I originally started working with Mark under the premise of doing soundtracks for the performances," Heckert says. Before long, however, he was also assisting Pauline with other duties, from constructing robots to, shall we say, procuring equipment from nearby factories and bringing it back to the Junkyard, SRL's aptly named headquarters at 15th and Carolina. "It was just this big wooden fence around this corner lot that had some very kind of ramshackle-y wood building structures on it, a couple of garages," he recalls. "It was *really* cheap to live there. I was paying $70 a month, I think, to have this sort of boxed shape of a room with no insulation and just some Romex running along the wall that you tapped into for electricity."

IBC

The Junkyard provided the inspiration for an Inflatable Boy Clams song, 'Boystown' (their nickname for the SRL compound). The song itself was a bit like a round of playground teasing, with the girls poking fun at the boys for, well, being boys. "There was some tension over that," admits Heckert, "because Mark was so macho, and we were like the macho guys, ridin' our motorcycles around, stealin' shit out of old factories and blowin' up things. What Carol and Judy were involved in was much more fashion and dance and stuff. There was a lot of gay culture in there. And we were not that at all."[105]

---

[105] As Wymore notes, this masculine/feminine dichotomy also played out within Pink Section."We had some kind of idea—you know, Matthew and I—that we were rockin' a *little* bit. We were influenced by Wire and the Sex Pistols, so there was a little of that—I don't wanna say 'machismo,' but there was a rock thing. You wanna turn up and play loud and have some kind of power behind what you're doing. I was always into sound—how did this actually *sound*. I think Boy Clams and stuff like that was more concepts, lyrics. They're hilariously funny and clever, Judy and Carol."

WHO CARES ANYWAY

Like SRL, the Boy Clams defied categorization, though they were as unapologetically feminine as SRL was masculine. For Detweiler, that was part of the appeal. "I found it to be just really comfortable and intimate, and it was a lot less loud. Between JoJo, Judy, and me, it just seemed like such a natural evolution." That evolution unfolded over the course of a half-dozen or so shows—mostly at alternative, lower-decibel venues such as the Eureka Theatre, Club Foot, and the Hotel Utah—over the course of 1980 and 1981. There were also separate performances by Planteen (both solo and together with Detweiler), one of which—a September 1980 appearance at a secluded pop-up venue called Art Grip—was recounted in detail by artist/critic Richard Irwin:

> It begins with a black and white film by Bruce Geduldig projected
> on the screen above the main stage. Carol [is] wrapped in
> virginal/surgical/medical/funeral white arranged horizontally
> behind veils of gauze. JoJo and Alan Brown drink and chew
> chocolates campily while fondling each other in front of the
> (corpse?), ending in a weird ménage-a-trois on the bed.[106]

Among the Boy Clams, Planteen was the only one with a real background in performance art, having come out of the same late 1970s Art Institute milieu that gave rise to the likes of Karen Finley. (As Irwin put it in another article for *Damage*, "Performance literally took over at SFAI, evoking a resurgence of energy unlike anything there since the heyday of abstract expressionism in the late '40s and '50s."[107]) Prior to the Inflatable Boy Clams, Planteen was a member of the Don'ts, a performance art group that billed itself as "the world's first band without instruments." At one rather infamous Don'ts show, she got a little carried away during a piece entitled 'Hot Cross Buns' and, according to David Swan, "sliced up [bandmate] Phil Huyser's ass so bad that an ambulance had to take him away."

---

106 *Damage,* December 1980, p. 8. This performance was part of an all-night event called Son of Mayhem, which, in turn, was the sequel to something called Night of Mayhem, held earlier that year.
107 Richard Irwin, "Performance Art in San Francisco." *Damage*, May 1980, pp. 14–15.

THE POST-PUNK ERA

The other members of IBC had a more ambivalent relationship with performance art. As Detweiler said of Pink Section in a 1979 interview, "We're reacting against 1970s 'Art Performance,' which seemed to be about boredom and endurance—real cruel, in a way, to the audience, but a big joke, too!"[108] Gittelsohn offers a similar perspective: "Performance art kind of takes itself a little too seriously, maybe, for what I did. The schooling that I had, I think, was little enough that I didn't get too intellectual or too cerebral about it."

Whatever their misgivings, the Boy Clams' record nonetheless stands as one of the few tangible documents of this period of cross-pollination between the punk scene and the performance art world. Released by Subterranean in 1981, the self-titled EP—actually a double 7-inch—sold out its initial pressing of 3,000 copies and went on to become something of a cult classic (as evidenced by the eventual appearance of a fan website, inflatableboyclams.com). The "hit single," so to speak, is 'Skeletons,' which features the loopy-sounding Planteen on lead vocals and the elegantly named Genvieve Boutet de Monvel on alto saxophone.[109] Gittelsohn handles the spoken-word vocals on 'Marin,' reprising a comically accented voice she'd previously employed on Pink Section's 'Cars Don't Wait for Love.' Gittelsohn and Detweiler take turns on another spoken-word piece, 'I'm Sorry,' which finds the two trading insincere apologies for various appalling faux pas.

JAPANESE WEEKEND

Like Pink Section, the Inflatable Boy Clams had a brief lifespan. They had no ambitions of a career in music, and they weren't particularly enticed by the idea of touring or even playing in rock clubs. "I do remember having a conscious thought that, 'Ew, alcohol and bars—it's not my thing,'" recalls

---

108 Quoted in V. Vale, "Search & Destroy Supplement with Pink Section." In *Slash*, May 1979, p. 9.
109 Minimal Man's 'Two Little Skeletons' (heard on both *Safari* and the A-side of a 1983 7-inch) is actually a response to IBC's 'Skeletons.'

WHO CARES ANYWAY

Gittelsohn. "And I certainly wasn't a musician. I was a *performer*, but not exactly a trained musician who knew an instrument. So I sort of winged it a little bit that way."

Along with Detweiler, Gittelsohn joined up with Barbie White, a mutual friend who had recently started a boutique clothing company called Japanese Weekend. "They started out silk-screening really trendy clothes that they would sell at specialty shops," recalls Swan, who lived in the three-story house at 22 Isis Street where Japanese Weekend was headquartered. "And then they turned to making maternity wear—which at first freaked me out; I thought, 'Oh God, this is gross'—but they started making so much money that they bought the house at 22 Isis." By the end of the decade, Japanese Weekend was grossing several million dollars a year—making it one of the few commercial successes to emerge from punk-era San Francisco.

For Detweiler, the appeal of Japanese Weekend wasn't so much the business aspect as it was the "positive vision" the company represented. This, she says, contrasted with what she saw coming out of both the Art Institute and parts of the underground music scene. "I did feel like at the time that it had a really sort of self-destructive edge. I remember thinking that that was sort of a trend that I didn't particularly like, and it was not what I was after. It was kind of concerning."

ALTERBOYS INTERNATIONAL, SUBTERRANEAN RECORDS
& MODERN MASTERS MUSIC

ARE PLEASED TO ANNOUNCE THE RELEASE OF THE LONG-PLAYING ALBUM

CLUB FOOT

THE HONOR OF YOUR PRESENCE IS REQUESTED AT A

COCKTAIL RECEPTION FOR THE ARTISTS

A SHORT CONFERENCE FOR THE BENEFIT OF THE PRESS WILL ALSO BE HELD

AT OUR NEW CORPORATE HEADQUARTERS
453 MINNA STREET (BETWN. 5TH & 6TH STS.)
SAN FRANCISCO

SUNDAY, MAY 10, 1981
RSVP BY 5/6/81   BLACK TIE OPTIONAL

12-3 P.M.
777-3255

16

CLUB FOOT

"He was slick, charming, cold, egotistical, cool, crazy, tortured, obsessive, *brilliant* beyond belief." —David Swan on Richard Kelly

During its brief heyday, Club Foot was many things: an avant-garde performance space, a rehearsal studio, a crash pad for local artists and touring bands. There was also a nonprofit (Alterboys International), a record label (Modern Masters), a theme song (performed by the original Club Foot Orchestra), and a *Club Foot* LP. It wasn't quite a plan

for world domination, but it was a bold venture at a time when DIY was still a new concept and much of the necessary infrastructure had yet to be built.

The roots of Club Foot actually stretch back to Albany, New York, circa 1976. In those days, the quiet state capital served as an unlikely haven for avant-garde music, thanks to the presence of SUNY-Albany and its Electronic Music Lab. "Because it was fairly close to Manhattan and Woodstock and other places, a lot of pretty interesting people were regularly coming and going," notes J.C. Garrett, one of the eventual Club Foot founders. "I got to hang out with John Cage and David Tudor. Phill Niblock was doing his stuff there, and George Crumb."

Duly inspired, Garrett got the idea to rent out a storefront space and form his own artists' collective. "I printed a thousand posters," he says, "and I just wallpapered the town, advertising the event and that people who were interested should come." Among the other members of the Workspace collective, as it came to be known, were Richard Kelly—a music major who met Garrett through the Electronic Music Lab—and Richard Edson, a fledgling jazz trumpeter and fellow SUNY-Albany student. As Garrett puts it, "We were kind of the big avant-garde fish in the very small pond of Albany."

Despite the proximity to New York City and CBGB's (roughly a three-hour drive from Albany), punk was barely on the group's radar screen in those days. "J.C. was much more into the avant-garde/conceptual art scene in New York," recalls Edson. "And Kelly was more into experimental music, composed music." Photos from around the time of their journey west find the group—and Kelly in particular—looking more post-hippie than pre-punk. "Kelly was kind of new age," admits Garrett, "and he was into all this Indian mysticism, and he was a vegetarian."

SNUKY TATE AND THE ALTERBOYS

It was Kelly's decision to attend graduate school at Oakland's Mills College—a sort of West Coast equivalent to SUNY-Albany in terms of its music program—that prompted the group's trip west in August of 1978. The others—Garrett, Edson, and Kelly's girlfriend Cindy Buff—were initially just along for the ride. As Edson explains, "Back in those days, there was this thing called Driveaway.

THE POST-PUNK ERA

There were these agencies, and people wanted their car driven from coast to coast, and you would sign up and take somebody's car and drive it. So we got one of those."

The quartet arrived in San Francisco to find the Mabuhay era still in full swing. And it was there at the Mabuhay that they first encountered the legendary Snuky Tate, a self-described "singer-songwriter/crazy person" and one of the very few African-Americans in the local punk scene.[110] Tate was known for his impromptu performances in between sets, wherein he would take the stage with an electric guitar and a cheap practice amp and rattle off a few songs (sometimes while clad in a gorilla suit). On the night in question, Tate took the stage, not in-between sets, but during a set by the Readymades. "He jumped on the stage and poured a bottle of beer onto the lead singer's head," recounts Edson. "I mean, it happened really quickly. The bass player unsnapped his bass, and he was swinging it from in back of him, over his head. He was gonna kill Snuky. The other guitar player reached up at the last possible minute and just deflected it and held onto it as Snuky was jumping off the stage back into the audience. That was my first introduction to Snuky."

Before long, Tate was crashing on the floor of the Mission District apartment where Edson, Garrett, and Kelly had landed soon after arriving in town. ("We couldn't get rid of him," laughs Edson. "He stayed for four months. It was gonna be three nights.") The three-bedroom flat—located at 3579 18th Street, just a stone's throw from the Deaf Club—was home to as many as seven or eight residents at a time, including members of Inflatable Boy Clams and Factrix. The "house band," though, was the Alterboys, a loose collective that got its start one night in the spring of 1979, almost by accident. Garrett recounts the episode:[111]

Snuky Tate, Richard Edson, and myself wanted to go to the Geary Temple to see some show. At the time, most of these places would have four or

---

110 *Flipside*, No. 13, January 1979.
111 A partial roll call of Alterboys who lived at the 18th Street apartment at some point: Garrett (vocals/percussion), Kelly (organ/guitar), Edson (trumpet/drums), Tate (guitar), Karl DeLovely (tenor saxophone), JoJo Planteen (vocals), Genvieve Boutet de Monvel (alto saxophone), Georgia Anderson (guitar), and a French woman named Martine (poetry reading).

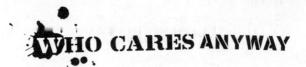

five bands in one night. So we went up to the Temple with this idea that if we showed up with a guitar at the door and claimed that we were on the bill, that we could probably talk our way into getting in. Which we were attempting to do when Jello came along and vouched for us. He said, "Yeah, those guys are on the bill. You don't have them on the list? Yeah, they're performing tonight." That's what he told the guy at the door.

So then we went in, and Jello said, "Well, now you're gonna have to perform. You're gonna have to do something." So now we were on the spot. And we sat down in what was the makeshift dressing room and created a song, which we performed about four times in a row because we had nothing else. And the rhythm was me with a drumstick banging on a beer bottle. Snuky Tate played guitar, and I think Edson borrowed a trumpet from somebody.[112]

This make-do approach was practically the only constant with the Alterboys, whose lineup—much like the list of occupants at 3579 18th Street—was a revolving door affair. "We had different people for every performance," explained Kelly in a 1980 interview.[113] "And nobody *had* to be there. If somebody wasn't there who was needed for a song, we'd just write another on the spot."

Among the Alterboys' more memorable shows was a Christmas-themed performance at the Art Institute in December of 1979. For the occasion, Kelly and Garrett went so far as to construct an elaborate living room set (complete with fireplace and easy chair) out of cardboard. "They spent a lot of time," recalls Edson."I thought, 'Okay, they're going way overboard.' And then I think some of the guys in Flipper tried to burn it down. I remember Kelly and J.C.; they were furious; they were just out-of-their-minds furious. And I thought it was hilarious."[114]

---

112 Garrett recalls that the song in question was 'Frank Sinatra' (which appears in a studio version on the *Club Foot* LP), though Edson remembers things differently. "I remember writing the lyrics [to 'Frank Sinatra'] and showing them to the guys, and they were like, 'Oh, let's write a song.' I think Kelly came up with the basic song. You know, that's not a rock song. That's the kind of thing Kelly was really good at—these kind of weird structured songs."

113 *Creep*, No. 3, 1980.

114 Though he was a founding member, Tate (né Lionel White) only played with the Alterboys for a few months. He moved to New York in the late summer of 1979, which

THE POST-PUNK ERA

RICHARD KELLY IN LATE 1979. PHOTO BY J.C. GARRETT.

RICHARD KELLY IN LATE 1979. PHOTO BY J.C. GARRETT.

"A DUMP THAT I LOVED"

By this point, Garrett and company had begun shifting their attention from the Alterboys (Christmas decorations notwithstanding) to another, more ambitious undertaking. Drawing on their experience back east in Albany—and motivated in part by the recent demise of the Deaf Club—they set out to create their own

---

is why he doesn't appear on the *Club Foot* LP (recorded in the summer of 1980). He did, however, record a solo 7-inch while still in SF, a four-song EP with contributions from the Mutants' Dave Carothers and Brendan Earley on drums and lead guitar, respectively. Tate went on to score a minor club hit in 1980 with 'He's the Groove' ("He's the groove / He's the man / He's the pope in the Vatican"), which began life as an Alterboys song.

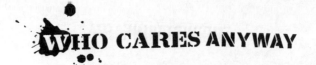

venue. After scouring the classified ads in the *Chronicle*, they found a cheap storefront space for rent at 2520 Third Street and got to work on renovating it. While doing so, they realized it would need a name—preferably something less austere than Workspace. "I thought a name could be Club Sandwich," recalls Edson. "And then I thought of Club Foot. As soon as I said it, both Kelly's and J.C.'s eyes opened wide, and they were like, 'Yeah, that's pretty good.'"

Club Foot was one of a handful of DIY performance spaces to emerge in SF at the dawn of the 1980s; others included the A-Hole in South of Market, Club Generic in the Tenderloin, A.R.E. (Artists for Revolution in the Eighties) and Jetwave on Market Street, and the Tool & Die on Valencia Street.[115] Of all these locations, Club Foot's was the most remote. It was across the street from a former American Can Company warehouse where several musicians lived and rehearsed but far removed from most of the scene's more familiar haunts.[116] "Nobody had ever thought of putting a club *way* out on Third Street," says Matt Heckert, a member of the club's board of directors. With the words "CLUB" and "FOOT" proudly emblazoned above the windows on either side of the entrance, the space would have been hard to miss, but the neighborhood itself was anything but an entertainment mecca. The surroundings included a soul food restaurant on one side and an empty lot on the other; a few doors down was Tugboat Annie's, a longshoremen's bar that offered the only semblance of nightlife nearby.

Tom Wheeler: Garrett hates when I say this because they put a lot of work into trying to fix up this storefront. But they didn't have a lot of capital, and it was in a weird part of town, and it was a little bit of a dump. A dump that I loved.

---

115 The club opened its doors to the public on December 1, 1979, with an opening-night party that featured musical performances by Romeo Void and the Dickheads (both making their live debuts) and non-musical ones by Karen Finley and JoJo Planteen.

116 Suzi Skates recalls the setup inside the American Can Company building: "It was almost like a dorm the way it was set up. I mean, you could rent rooms. There were like [school] bathrooms, like with stalls and stuff ... A lot of people had rooms there. Even [concert promoter] Ken Friedman had a room there. And there was another guy who jumped off the Golden Gate Bridge who lived there and other people who lived there who videotaped it. There was dark, crazy shit that went on that wasn't even the punk bands."

THE POST-PUNK ERA

J.C. Garrett: I think we paid $700 a month for the building, which was three floors with a storefront and a backyard. It was on what, at that time, was the periphery of San Francisco. It took a little bit of effort to get there. There was a bus—a public bus, of course—but a lot of people at that time didn't have enough money in their pockets to have a car. It was a pretty hardcore neighborhood. You know, I'd be stepping over bodies and such. There was a lot of gang sort of stuff. And so the police, I think, were happy to see a couple of college white kids. They didn't really care that we were distributing alcohol, as long as we didn't bother anybody.

David Swan: The Club Foot vibe was kind of like pop art/performance art, and there really was no venue until Club Foot for all those years that really was more conceptual than rock 'n' roll oriented, even though some new wave bands were conceptual.

183

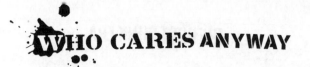

Richard Edson: J.C. was certainly not a punk rocker. Kelly wasn't. Cindy wasn't. So we were definitely part of the more art rock/post-punk attitude. And that definitely was Club Foot's attitude because that was Kelly and J.C.'s thing.

David Swan: When Club Foot first started, the first few months, every single event there was the end of the world, or the beginning of the world, or something unbelievable. Every single event. It wasn't just like a typical club where all this shit goes through, and no one really cares. There was a group called the Bachelors, Even. I still remember the night of the performance. Everyone I knew was there, and we all went crazy over it.

Tom Wheeler: They had these little cheap phonographs, and they had records that they had broken and glued back together. They would put them on, and they would have all these clunky sort of rhythm sounds because of the cracks where they had glued them back together. And then they would do things like pouring lighter fluid on the records, lighting them on fire while they were turning around on these turntables, all plugged into a sound system, emitting godawful sound. That same night, I saw Philip Galas, Diamanda Galas's brother. And he did a performance piece—this very complex, long monologue about art, life, being gay—talking to a high-heel shoe.

THE CLUB FOOT STYLE

Above all, Club Foot provided a home base for the cadre of bands spearheaded by Kelly and friends. In addition to the Alterboys, there were the Longshoremen, fronted by the gregarious Swan (aka Dog); Naked City, a short-lived instrumental group with Heckert on guitar and Kelly on keyboards;[117] and Bay of Pigs, an

---

117 Not to be confused with the later John Zorn-led outfit of the same name, this Naked City played just a handful of gigs, all of them during 1980. For Heckert, the band's tenure overlapped with the end of Pink Section and the beginning of his involvement with SRL. As he explains, the group's lineup—which also included Stefano Paolillo on drums and George Wescott on bass—was not a recipe for longevity. "Kelly knew lots

avant-punk outfit that counted Kelly, Factrix bassist Joseph Jacobs, and later Minimal Man associate Ron Morgan among its members. There was also the Club Foot Orchestra, led by Kelly and including members of all the above bands.

All of these groups appear on the *Club Foot* LP, which was recorded in the summer of 1980 and released the following year on Subterranean. The face on the record cover is Edson's, but much of the music is Kelly's, as he either wrote or co-wrote all but one song. "It's Richard's record, in a way," notes Garrett.[118] Musically, the record stands apart from what was happening elsewhere in San Francisco at the time, owing to the mix of jazz and Beat sensibilities that figure into most of the contributions. "A number of the things that we were doing with some of the bands was a kind of fusion of sort of punk attitude, to some extent, and free jazz," says Garrett. There was also a detached, ironic sense of humor that was distinctly Club Foot.

To find an apt reference point, one has to look to downtown New York, where John Lurie's Lounge Lizards were exploring a similar mix of "fake jazz," 1950s noir, and post-punk sensibilities in those days. Coincidentally, the Lounge Lizards' first album was also recorded that summer. "I think it was just spontaneous generation," says Swan. "It was just something that was in the air that made sense. Because if you think about it, even though the Sex Pistols didn't have a particularly late fifties/early sixties thing going, punk rock really did—obviously with the skinny ties and small lapels. It just kind of followed that the other side of that coin would be the cool jazz and the Beatnik thing."

Though not part of the Albany contingent—he'd actually moved to SF from Seattle in the mid-1970s, pre-punk—Swan quickly became a key member of the Club Foot contingent. His voice is heard on the album's opening track, the Longshoremen's 'What Does It All Mean?' "Sick … beat … cool … jazz" go the

---

about music, which really none of the others did. I mean, George Wescott had *never* played an instrument before, so we were teaching him how to play bass. Richard, of course, knew diatonic scales and what-have-you. I had been playing the guitar for a number of years, but I didn't really know anything about music per se. I couldn't really read sheet music at all or anything like that. It was a strange club of people doing this one little thing. It couldn't have really lasted that long."

118 Steve Tupper: "Our first intention was to release singles by each of the bands on the LP before the compilation was out. For one reason or another, Bay of Pigs were the only ones to actually record the two additional songs for a 7-inch."

opening words, which Swan delivers in a spoken-word style that feels at once like a parody of, and homage to, Beatnik jazz poetry. The track sets the tone for the rest of the LP, though, as Swan notes, the song was actually written before he'd met any of his eventual Club Foot compatriots. "The second Longshoremen show was at Club Foot, and then Richard Kelly came up to us afterwards and said, 'That one song should be on the *Club Foot* LP.' So unbeknownst to us, being into this late fifties/early sixties Beatnik jazz vibe—all the other groups on *Club Foot* were into it, too. All of a sudden, there were all these groups that were kind of 'new wave jazz' or something, and it just *happened*."

That shared sense of style extended beyond their music. "Garrett, Kelly, Dog, Cindy, and Kippy [Robinson, Garrett's girlfriend at the time] all had this kind of fifties/early sixties look, like they had stepped out of Godard's *Alphaville* or something," remembers Tom Wheeler. "The way they styled their hair, their clothes, some of the music that they were doing in their bands—that was reflected. There was a certain romance around Burroughs, Genet—you know, that kind of outlaw literature. And there was also the Chet Baker, Art Pepper kind of white, cool jazz thing as well." Adds Stephen Clarke, "They always seemed really erudite, socially aware, and a little bit aloof, to be frank. But lovely."

"DESTROY WHAT DESTROYS US"

After encountering a series of delays, the *Club Foot* LP was finally released in April of 1981. To celebrate the occasion, a "cocktail reception for the artists" was held at the organization's "new corporate headquarters" (i.e., the apartment at 453 Minna Street in SOMA, where Kelly and Buff had recently moved). It was all very much in keeping with the overall Club Foot vibe. "If you look at that invite," notes Swan, "it's tongue-in-cheek—it's totally tongue-in-cheek—and yet simultaneously, it was grandiose. But the grandiosity was kind of ironic." The event itself included a mock press conference with "flashbulb-style cameras and people that were acting as journalists and asking them questions about political intrigue," as Tom Wheeler recalls. "You know, it was all kind of like this goofy hoax. But they treated it as if they were super serious about it. It was kind of a posture, kind of a goofy construct."

That ironic grandiosity also made its way into Club Foot's fliers—which, in true Situationist fashion, blurred the boundaries between advertising and conceptual art. Garrett, who worked in a print shop, was responsible for most of the visuals, as well as the elliptical slogans that adorned many of the fliers: THE MEANS TO ESCAPE THE LIFE WHICH IS NOT WORTH LIVING ... NOT A NEGATION OF STYLE, BUT A STYLE OF NEGATION ... WHERE EVERYTHING IS BAD, IT MUST BE GOOD TO KNOW THE WORST ... The club's motto, "Moving in the Direction of History," conveyed a similar blend of brashness and ambiguity.

For Kelly, this ambiguity went hand in hand with the postmodern condition, even if he didn't use that exact term. "It isn't the important work of an artist to be creating new frontiers," he told Peter Belsito in a 1980 interview. "The people who think they're the Beethovens and Stravinskys are ignoring the fact that the rest of us are being consumed. Everything is being consumed. Artists should be dealing with the problems of living in a consumer society. Destroy what destroys us."[119]

"We were like a response to corporate America by being kind of 'corporate,'" adds Garrett, elaborating on the "direction of history" motto. "But we were deluding ourselves. We were really just a bunch of jokers. I mean, we actually used to have meetings and take minutes. We really thought of ourselves as some sort of 'organization,' which was hardly the case." Swan echoes this sentiment. "We were all young and naive, and we felt like we had something new going on in SF. In the board meetings, we thought we were building an empire. And it started to crumble fairly quickly. Because there was the Club Foot venue with its rehearsal studio, then Minna Street with *its* rehearsal studio. And Richard and Cindy became involved in bringing out these other albums on Modern Masters. And as time went by, people started to lose interest, or things got more complicated in everybody's lives. I remember at one point Richard Kelly looking at me and going, 'From now on, it's every man for himself.' Which I thought was one of the funniest things I'd ever heard. Then it all just fell apart."

119 Peter Belsito, "The Club Is a Record." *Another Room*, September 1980. http://www.o-art.org/history/Groups/Clubfoot/RKelley.html

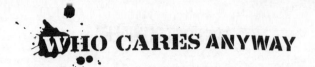

Part of the problem was simply the financial reality of producing shows and putting out records that lacked a ready audience. "It was not very marketable, that's for sure," says Garrett of the LP. "It was hard to package it and put it out there. I remember the disappointment I had when I first spotted it in the cutout bins, and it was shortly after it came out. You know, so somebody got rid of the review copy over at Aquarius. 'It's available for two dollars. Wow. That's disappointing.'"[120] Likewise, the Club Foot venue struggled to make ends meet, with a typical door price of three dollars and much of the audience coming from within the artistic community. "It never felt quite like there was an audience because everybody had something," says Garrett. "I'd be onstage, and everybody watching us perform—they all did *something*. So it wasn't like we had 'consumers,' per se. It was sort of like everybody was endorsing everybody else's activity. It never felt like 'us and the audience.' It was more like 'us and all the other us' that was there. We were struggling every day to keep it happening. We applied for nonprofit status at one point and incorporated as a nonprofit. We were doing all kinds of things—acts of desperation—just so we could pay the bills."

In Kelly's case, those acts of desperation included procuring and selling narcotics. The drug dealing paralleled his own descent into addiction—which, in turn, was intertwined with some unspecified mental health issues. There may have also been an element of romance, however ill-conceived, surrounding the outlaw/junkie artist archetype embodied by the likes of Jean Genet, William Burroughs, and Chet Baker. ("I wasn't interested in any of that and never was," Garrett says bluntly. "He took Genet seriously, and I didn't.")

Peter Belsito: He was another brilliant person, but he was tortured. He was very articulate, but he obviously had some emotional issues that nobody else knew about, except for maybe his girlfriend.

J.C. Garrett: He had psychological issues, which I was never fully aware of, but I knew that he was kind of volatile. But he had a history, and his dad did as well. So

120 Subterranean eventually sold out of the original pressing of 2,310 copies. In 2009, there was a second pressing of 500 copies, which were issued with original album sleeves and inserts (left over from the first pressing and kept in storage for almost thirty years).

it was some congenital thing. And he was experiencing some antidepressants that were not very good. There were legal issues involved. There were some busts and things.

Joe Pop-O-Pie: The way Cindy told it to me was like, "Richard was allergic to work." So what Richard did was he started to sell drugs, and he started to sell *hard* drugs, and he started to sell more and *more* hard drugs.[121]

David Swan: Somehow, in a short amount of time, Kelly became known to the vice cops. Richard was not being as smart as he thought he was and was makin' too much noise. Because also, opium hit town, and everyone was on opium for like a month. And I think Richard was the main purveyor of that if I remember correctly.

J.C. Garrett: He was certainly living an unhealthy lifestyle, and he was trying to change that, actually, because there had been a significant arrest, and he was under observation. But a lot of people were dealing shit. I didn't approve of that myself, but that's how some people made money.

Tom Wheeler: There was some stuff around the law and the police. They were looking for him. I didn't hear it from Richard, but I would hear, "Okay, the police are looking for Richard."

David Swan: I remember one night him telling me he felt like he was in a cop movie, and he was acting kind of paranoid.

Ron Morgan: I knew that he had been struggling. I'd known about the incident where he went to a party, and he snorted what he thought was heroin, and it

---

121 Michael Belfer recalls making a transaction with Kelly at the Minna Street apartment: "I knock on the door, the door opens, and here he is, sitting at this desk with this bright light on you. I mean, it was something out of a noir film. And he wanted it that way. He's in there acting like Joe Friday from *Dragnet*, sitting at this big desk with this light on you in this dark room. I just remember going in and putting the money on the table; he slides this envelope to me."

turned out to be angel dust, and it triggered a psychotic episode. And I'd known about his struggles with mental health after that. But it was pretty low-key.

In late July of 1983, Kelly—not yet thirty years old at the time—was found dead in the bathtub of his Minna Street apartment, the result of an apparent suicide. Though tragic, it was not the kind of rock 'n' roll death to make the pages of *Rolling Stone*; evidently, it didn't even make the *Chronicle* or the pages of local punk rag *Maximum Rocknroll*. One of the few publications that did see fit to comment on Kelly's passing was *Puncture*, whose Stephen Braitman remarked somewhat bitterly that "Kelly lived and played (and died) within a rigidly defined social and musical circle."[122] He then used the occasion to comment on the pitfalls of "cult genres" and "cults of personality."

Yet, for friends and associates like Swan, there was no question about the magnitude of the loss. "He was slick, charming, cold, egotistical, cool, crazy, tortured, obsessive, *brilliant* beyond belief. Even though he had that New York personality where he could be kind of insulting, everybody really loved the guy because he was so impossibly brilliant and was a real character and had a lot of energy and a lot of ideas. It was no joke when he died. People were just torn apart by it, actually."

"Unfortunately, it was also the time of AIDS," adds Garrett, "and we lost a lot of very good people to AIDS. In Cindy's case, I think she ended up taking care of a mutual friend of ours through hospice. It was almost immediately afterwards, so it was sort of a double-barrel with her. And then she was in a pretty horrendous car accident, and it took her a long time to recover from that. So she had a couple of really difficult years. And after having buried Kelly, I had other people to bury from AIDS. So the eighties was sort of a funky time."

For the original Club Foot crew, Kelly's death marked the end of an era, though, in truth, that era had been winding down for some time. The face of the *Club Foot* LP, Richard Edson, had long since settled into life in New York City, where he joined Sonic Youth as the band's first drummer and also formed the group Konk; he then went on to a successful acting career, with roles in such

---

122 *Puncture*, Vol. 1, No. 6. Reprinted in *Puncture: The First Six Issues*. p. 209.

movies as *Ferris Bueller's Day Off* (as the sleazy valet parking attendant) and Jim Jarmusch's *Stranger Than Paradise* (as a co-star alongside Lounge Lizard John Lurie). Swan kept the Longshoremen going, eventually releasing a couple of LPs on Subterranean before going on to host his own public-access variety show, *The Doghouse*, in the late 1980s. Modern Masters, the record label founded by Kelly and Buff, folded after releasing just three records.[123] Meanwhile, the Club Foot Orchestra continued on under the leadership of yet another Richard—Richard Marriott—though this version of the group bore little resemblance to the original in either sound or personnel.[124]

Leadership of the Club Foot venue also changed hands. "It kept going," says Garrett. "But the basic focus of the club as Club Foot was pretty much over by '81, '82. It fell much more to Tom Wheeler at that point, who was kind of managing it and then ended up taking it over. Cindy pretty much pulled out after Richard was gone, though she stayed in that building in Minna Street for a long, long time and continued to rent the Club Foot building."

123 Along with the Arkansaw Man EP, there was a self-titled mini-album by Danny & the Parkins Sisters and a 1983 LP by the Phantom Limbs. (The Inflatable Boy Clams EP lists Modern Master Music as the publisher, but it was released by Subterranean.)
124 The new, Marriott-led version of the Club Foot Orchestra got its start not long before Kelly died. As Marriott recounts, "I formed an orchestra to perform at a Club Foot music festival in June of 1983 ... Our band included three members from Kelly's earlier group: Opter Flame, Karl DeLovely and Bruce Ackley of the ROVA Saxophone Quartet." (http://clubfootorchestra.com/history.html)

THE HARDCORE ERA

17

GENERIC FLIPPER

Bill Gould: When I moved here, it was '81. Flipper were pretty much like the subcultural kings. Because you couldn't pin down what they *were*.

Roddy Bottum: Flipper was sort of like that band you *could not* escape. Anyone in San Francisco who did music knew Flipper—hated Flipper or loved Flipper. I loved Flipper. I saw 'em a million times.

Joe Pop-O-Pie: For those of us who got into punk rock in the late 1970s—by 1981, it was just something totally different. We were already beginning to challenge that original aesthetic by 1981. And I thought they did that really well. I thought that they were probably the first band that I saw that I can honestly say was unpretentious and honest about what they were doing—as opposed to a band that rehearses stage moves, a band that rehearses the jokes, a band that rehearses the attitude. Like, "We're supposed to be angst-ridden." It was just more honest, which is what punk was originally. And it wasn't anything like the Sex Pistols or the Ramones.

Ted Falconi: At that time, it was all the "1-2-3-4," LA/Washington DC, punk rock. We all had bands before that were doing formula, and nobody wanted to do formula—like where we'd play a song two years later, and it'd be note-for-note exactly the same. I mean, Will didn't even like to have that much structure that you could actually even *do* that. So, we would set up a bassline, a drumbeat, a verse, a chorus, but that would be, like, the starting point. The vocals are doing, "Where's Will?" "Oh, he's at the bar." "Oh, right—thanks." [Laughs.] So you'd do two or three more verses. From one show to the next, things might be totally different—one time it might be three minutes, the next time it might be twelve. Songs like 'The Wheel' or 'Kali': one riff, goes on for fuckin' ever. 'Sex Bomb,' same thing: one riff, goes on forever.

FLIPPER

PET ROCK IS

1. Punk/Existential/Terrorism
2. Pure/Energetic/Trouble
3. Petulant/Empty/Thoughts
4. Primitive/Enthusiastic/Torture
5. Properly/Exploited/Trends
6. Private/Entertainment/Totally
7. Public/Erosion/Terminates
8. Putrid/Embryonic/Trash
9. Primarily/Explosive/Tendencies
10. Previously/Exhausted/Talents

IT'S NOT A JOKE -AND
IF IT WERE IT WOULDN'T BE FUNNY

Ed Falconi — *guitar*

Bruce Lose — *vocals*

Steve De Pace — *drums*

Will Shatter — *bass*

Garry Creiman: The first time I saw them was at the Victoria Theatre in '80. They were second bill to the Darby Crash Band.[1] I walked in on one of their

---

1   The likely date of this show would have been September 26, 1980, a few months before Darby Crash's fatal overdose that December.

ten-minute dirge songs. As I looked for a seat, I remember thinking, "This is the worst band I've ever seen." After about two more songs, I "got it" and was thinking they were the *best* band I'd ever seen. Or at least the band that was the most serious about not being serious. They finished with a great version of 'The Wheel.' Will had forty or fifty people on stage swinging their arms, screaming "I am the wheel," and wouldn't stop until they finally cut the power to the stage.

Bruno DeSmartass: The first time I saw Flipper was at the Sound of Music at the [1980] Halloween show where everyone was on acid. There were smoke bombs, and there was a big pool of beer and water because the toilet had overflowed. People were running through the puddle and just sliding through on their back. The band was just standing onstage, just feeding back because they were so fucked up. So people came up and started playing. And it was the scariest thing I ever saw. It just scared the fuck out of me, and I shouldn't have done acid anyway. I went, "Oh, these guys—this isn't rock." But then I started to get it, and they turned into one of my favorite bands.

Steve Tupper: Sometimes, it seemed like they would go out of their way just to try to annoy an audience. It was part of the whole punk thing: either confront your audience or annoy the fuck out of them. The Pop-O-Pies had the same kind of aesthetic.

Rachel Thoele: Will and Bruce were extremely charismatic people. Ted, too. And that's a visual thing. And it's also a back-and-forth with the audience. But then there'd be lots of baiting, too. Which I thought would be a huge part of the stage show—all this conversation between the audience and the singer, whether it be Will or whether it be Bruce. Which pissed Steve off.

Ruby Ray: Part of the thing was yelling at the band. But that didn't mean you didn't like them. It meant more that you were friends and you were trying to egg 'em on.

That (mostly) friendly antagonism between band and audience even made its way onto Flipper's early singles—the first of which, 'Love Canal' b/w 'Ha Ha Ha,' was recorded the day before the above-mentioned Halloween show. As Steve

WHO CARES ANYWAY

Tupper recalls, "The crazy, warbling FX on 'Love Canal' were inspired by the sound man at Berkeley Square, who fucked with their sound one night, totally without permission, just to see if he could piss them off. Apparently, it didn't work since they invited the guy to help produce the record."

The next single, 'Sex Bomb' b/w 'Brainwash,' was just as idiosyncratic. The A-side is an early version of the group's best-known song with some elaborate post-production courtesy of Mr. Falconi. "I added in thunderstorms, rain, police cars, firetrucks, people screamin' in the crowd," recalls the guitarist. "It would be like if you were in a club—like the Fillmore, sitting on the windowsill—and the window is open, and you're lookin' out in the street, and you're seein' a car accident, cop cars, people screamin', a thunderstorm goin' on."

'Brainwash,' meanwhile, is an aberration even by Flipper's standards. Originally a short hardcore-like burst with rapid-fire lyrics shouted by Bruce Loose (sample line: "Psycho-politics is the hierarchy's gun / If they point it at you, you had better run"), it morphed into something else altogether during the recording process. "It was 30 seconds exactly, and my vocals kept being like 32-and-a-half seconds, 31.2 seconds, 31 seconds," explains the singer. He eventually gave up on the original lyrics and replaced them with the halting, self-negating spoken word bit heard on the record: "Never mind. Forget it; you wouldn't understand anyway." With the help of legendary mastering engineer George Horn at Berkeley's Fantasy Studios, they wound up looping the song over and over—thirteen times in all—ending with a locked groove that repeats the "never mind" tagline unto eternity. There's even a video for the song, produced by Oakland artist Liz Sher, featuring a parade of grotesque found footage synced up to the music.

Needless to say, that video didn't make it onto MTV, but the song still made its way around. "I had recorded that off the radio," recalls Trey Spruance, then a teenager living in remote Humboldt County, six hours north of San Francisco. "I used to listen to that all the time and would piss my pants laughing. I loved that thing. Then I found out it was Flipper. It's one of the things that sticks in your brain."

CAPTAIN TED, PT. 2: "I PLAY THE AMPS"

Joe Pop-O-Pie: The very first Flipper show that I saw was a benefit for a rent strike at the Victoria Theatre on 16th and Mission. The one thing I was thinking when I left there was, "How was that guy getting that guitar sound?" It was the wildest guitar sound I'd ever heard.

Stephen Clarke: He really didn't even have any imitators because no one knew what the fuck he was doing. He was like a blacksmith up there fucking banging on an anvil.

Bruno DeSmartass: I've made a study of it from watching him from across the stage. I absolutely, positively *cannot* do what he does. I absolutely cannot.

Craig Gray: I've never heard Ted play anything but noise, which is fine. But if he's playing something inside there, I can't hear it. And live it was way worse.[2]

Mia Simmans: I get the way he plays guitar. He'll take the chord and just *do* shit to it. And whatever he does—who knows. He just plugs into this subconscious thing that he does, and it's really cool. But it only works when DePace is going "boom-boom-BAP," and the bass is going "duh-duh-duh-duh."

Kirk Heydt: I remember one show at the American Indian Center.[3] It was one of the first times I sat in with them. I was right in front of Ted, and then I turn around, and Will's girlfriend Jeri is playing guitar—and it sounds exactly the same! And she doesn't know how to play the guitar! It's like he had it dialed into just the right distortion/wall-of-sound setting. Maybe it was just the tune, and maybe it was just for a second, but I turned around, and I was like, "Wow, that's Jeri playing."

---

2   Untitled interview with Craig Gray, Winterviewz blog, November 2016. https://winterviewz.tumblr.com/post/153424185763/craig-gray-toiling-midgets
3   Located at 225 Valencia Street—a few blocks down from the site of the Deaf Club—the American Indian Center was an occasional punk/new wave venue during the early 1980s.

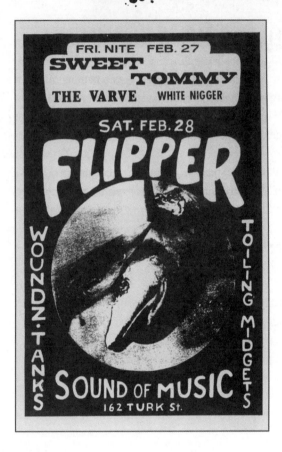

Falconi's guitar playing was just one of the elements that distinguished Flipper from their peers, but from a purely musical standpoint, it is perhaps the hardest element to wrap one's head around. In Falconi's hands, the guitar was less of a rhythm or melody instrument than it was a noise generator. Mind you, he wasn't just playing random noise, but the way he attacked the instrument gave it a genuinely chaotic sound. As he explains, it's a matter of "where you pluck your string: you can do it in the open space down below the fretboard, or you can do it *on the neck* and use the harmonics that you would hit at those spaces while you're playing. So you get a harmonic overtone on top of the note that you're playing."

That was part of it, anyway. The other part was his custom amplifier rig, which was the product of endless tinkering and re-engineering on his part. "Ted's a real techie," notes Bruno DeSmartass. "He's a mechanist, as opposed to a spiritualist. You know, he'll talk about electrons and this and that." Adds Kirk Heydt, "He liked to take things apart, I know that. He would be on speed just taking apart radios and taking apart TVs, makin' things out of things. I mean, he just sat up all night long. He worked on his own amps and stuff all the time."

THE HARDCORE ERA

Heydt, who occasionally sat in with the band on saxophone, recalls "very little conversation when I played with him. He just basically said, 'I play the amps.'"

Asked to expand on this remark, Falconi helpfully elaborates. "An *acoustic* guitar is playing the guitar. Playing an *electric* guitar, you're playing an amplifier— and whatever other kinds of stuff you can do to make the signal be more than where you started. Flangers, phase shifters, wahs, and all that type of stuff is all the *amp*, not the guitar. For a while, Flipper was real effects-laden. Now they have pedalboards; I had 'em spread out all over the place. Bruce would come over and start fuckin' with all the knobs while I was playing. So, it was like, when a new effect came out, I was able to get it. I had a cash flow at the time that allowed me to, you know, pick up a hundred-dollar this or a hundred-dollar that."

"I used two amps. One I ran really dirty; the other one I ran a little cleaner, so I could hear what I was doin'. I'd build up a wall of sound on one amplifier and then have enough definition that I could hear what I was doing in the second amplifier. And we did the same thing with the bass—ran two bass amps all the time, one totally dirty to get a wall of sound and then the other one where you could hear the notes. And with two people and four amplifiers, you sounded like four people. You could definitely fill up a stage with sound. And they weren't like super-powerful amps; they were only like 100-watt bass amps—like practice amps for most people."

ALBUM: GENERIC FLIPPER

As they'd done for their first two singles, Flipper sought out the facilities at Hyde Street Studios for the making of their first LP. Under its previous ownership— when it was known as Wally Heider Studios—the same facility had played host to the Grateful Dead, Jefferson Airplane, Santana, and countless others since its founding in 1969. Even after its sale in 1980, the studio was beyond the budget of most of the punk-era bands. However, Steve Tupper was willing to pony up the money, although the band members also chipped in by helping out with some studio renovations in exchange for additional recording time. (According to Bruce, "Will did the least work, I did the second least, and Ted and Steve did the most.")

As always, Flipper recorded the basic tracks live in the studio, with strategically placed overdubs (such as the handclaps on 'Ever' and the bleating saxophones on 'Sex Bomb') added after the fact. There were also some unusual post-production touches, like the mutant octave effects added to Bruce's vocals on 'Life is Cheap.' "They were always into experimenting and wanting to do new things," says Tupper. "It's not real *obvious*, but it is *there*."

"There were actually two versions of the record," he elaborates. "We did them both at Hyde Street. The first one, there was some guy named Yves—some French guy—who didn't know what the hell he was doing. So we basically threw that out. And then, at that point, we brought in Garry Creiman." Although Creiman had been working at the studio as an engineer for a couple of years, *Album* was his first-ever production credit. As he recounts, his approach was simple: "We tried to make it as live and as much a party as we could. If you turn it up loud, it's not too hard to imagine you're in the Mab. But it's impossible to convey the 'wheel people,' or a show where they hand off their instruments to members of the audience that jump up on stage, or any of a number of unplanned, drunk, spontaneous things that would usually happen."

Joe Pop-O-Pie: Most bands sound better in the studio than they do live, but Flipper was just the opposite. They sounded ridiculously better live. And I think that was probably because the technology at the time couldn't really capture the distortion as well as someone could today.

Ted Falconi: Well, the live stuff was unpredictable. Whether everybody was doing the same drug that night. Whether everybody was mentally there that night to begin with.

Garry Creiman: Their live shows certainly had to be seen and are difficult to capture on tape. But then, some of things that happened in the studio environment were pretty out there in their own way.

Steve Tupper: They did add in a whole lot of stuff, like the saxes on 'Sex Bomb,' and there was other stuff in there that you're just not gonna hear. But it was there

THE HARDCORE ERA

because I was there the whole time. It was done on sixteen-track, so we were able to isolate instruments and tweak them a little bit here and there.

For all the debate about the relative merits of Flipper live versus on record, *Album* more than holds its own, capturing the offhanded spontaneity of their shows while taking advantage of the fact that it was, after all, a studio recording. The lyrics, meanwhile, strike a balance between hard knocks philosophizing and dark humor, while the alternating lead vocals (Loose handles five of the songs, Shatter four) make the best out of the singers' admittedly limited ranges. The result is punk at its most poetic, without any of the pretentiousness that might imply.

The final touch was the minimalist album cover—a solid yellow background with black lettering and a bar code prominently displayed in the upper left corner.

Bruce credits Ted with the "Generic" concept, which was not limited to the LP release. "There was a Flipper T-shirt that says 'SHIRT' on it instead of 'ALBUM.' And then we had a poster that said 'POSTER.' Ted was really into pushing the concept of a generic product." (Apparently, John Lydon was into the concept too, as he would later appropriate it lock, stock, and barrel for Public Image Ltd.'s 1986 full-length.)

Ironically, *Album* received a better review in the *New York Times* — where veteran critic Robert Palmer covered it alongside LPs by Toiling Midgets and Romeo Void — than it did in local hardcore rag *Maximum Rocknroll*, which reviewed it rather unceremoniously (in between records by the Fartz and the Fuck-Ups). "The hype surrounding Flipper has already reached nauseating proportions, and I have no intention of adding to it," wrote Jeff Bale in the zine's debut issue.[4] "Flipper was much better back when this album was recorded, before they started taking themselves too seriously." Palmer's review offered a less jaded perspective, though he couldn't help but view the album through the lens of the Haight-Ashbury era, quoting a line from 'Ever' ("Ever look at a flower and hate it?") and noting its "special resonance in a city where flowers, beads and long hair used to be a way of life."[5] Fifteen years on, the Summer of Love still cast a long shadow over the SF music scene — or at least the outside world's perception of it.

Granted, there *were* connections (or, as Palmer put it, resonances), and not just because of the studio they happened to be using. As a teenager, Bruce would go see the Grateful Dead at Winterland; as a soldier in Vietnam, Ted (allegedly) took LSD while watching an ammo dump explode. In other words, they — or at least half the band — came of age in that era. There was also the undercurrent of psychedelia running through their live performances, which had a very real chemical basis. "Flipper used to constantly trip together when we played," divulges Bruce. "We'd take one hit, cut it in four, and each take a quarter hit. A perfect amount. And that's what gave us that bond that made that

---

4   *Maximum Rocknroll*, July/August 1982, p. 40. *Album* was released several months earlier, on March 31.
5   Robert Palmer, "Rebellion Rules Rock in Young San Francisco." *New York Times*, August 25, 1982. http://www.nytimes.com/1982/08/25/arts/the-pop-life-105911.html

stuff so … whatever it is." Yet for all that, the contrasts between Flipper and hippie-era psychedelia stood out more than the similarities did.

Gregg Turkington: In an hour-and-a-half set, they played five songs, which was completely the opposite of all these punk rock bands. And it was weird because the songs would just drone on and on and on and on, but it wasn't like a Grateful Dead hippie sort of jam. It was more like you kind of just plugged into this thing and went with it.

Carlos Willingham: I think they *were* what represented San Francisco punk at the time. Or whatever you want to call it. When Plastic Medium started, we were a jam band that made a lot of noise and screamed and hollered. Then I saw Flipper and said, "Yeah, that's what we're doing. This is it." And just going to Flipper shows, it felt like, to me, not so much that I wanted to *be* like them, but it was like, "Yeah, I'm home. This is where it's happening. This is what I want. This is definitely the spirit that I was hoping to be involved with."

Bill Gould: It was so open—probably something like the Grateful Dead in a weird way. There was a psychedelic element about it. Kind of like a more contemporary version of Grateful Dead/psychedelic music. Because you could be tripping on acid, but you weren't all "peace and love and flowers." You were more like edgy, street, broken glass, and chains.

Gregg Turkington: It was almost like good times music for people who were naturally just absolutely pessimistic or cynical or suicidal. It would give you some real hope and inspiration while still staying true to that sort of negative viewpoint about things.

Bruno DeSmartass: There's a pessimistic optimism. What's the phrase? "The pessimist knows how sad a place the world can be. The optimist is forever discovering that fact."

18

SEA OF UNREST

I n many ways, Flipper and Toiling Midgets were a study in contrasts. Whereas Flipper's music was the soundtrack to a sort of apocalyptic celebration, the Midgets made music for solitary listening. A Flipper show might end with audience members onstage; the Midgets could play a whole show without even addressing the audience. And whereas Flipper had two front men, the Midgets had none—at least in their early days.

There was also a bit of a sibling rivalry, given their common ancestry in Negative Trend and the Sleepers. "We were always getting stuck on bills with Flipper because of mine and Will's relationship," says the Midgets' Craig Gray. "Flipper, man—what can I say about Flipper? One riff and beat it to death. I mean, I'm not a big Flipper fan." Adds Paul Hood, "Some people kind of thought it was like, 'Oh, they're nemeses. They don't like each other. They're the antithesis of each other.' But we still seemed to appeal to a lot of the same people, for some reason."

There was one other thing they had in common: both bands employed the services of Ricky Williams, at least temporarily, although he turned out to be a better fit for the Midgets. And it was with their new singer (and old friend) in tow that the band seemed to come into their own, forging a kind of moody, introspective guitar rock that didn't fall in line with any of the prevailing trends—hardcore, new wave, goth, or otherwise. "No one else was like them," says artist Kim Seltzer. "They were more *metal* than they were ever punk. Of course, at that time, nobody listened to metal. If you listened to metal, you were a dork."

They certainly weren't metal in the sense of, say, Metallica, but there was a menacing quality to Midgets songs like 'Destiny' and 'Trauma Girl' that you don't hear in many of the "louder/faster" hardcore bands from the same era. Yet there was also a looseness to their playing that ran counter to the more regimented attack of most metal. "We never seemed to be of our time," admits Gray. "I don't know if it bothered me. I don't know if I've thought about it that much, but in retrospect, it seems to me that we were never of our time and what was going on around us. We were not part of even the mainstream of the whole post-punk, post-rock, whatever-you-wanna-call-it movement. No one was paying any attention to us. Well, then we could do what the fuck we wanted."

This sense of being out of time and disconnected from "the scene" extended into the Midgets' everyday lives. Living and rehearsing amid the warehouse spaces of South of Market, they would spend hours wandering around the docks, train tracks, and abandoned buildings in the area. In 1950s-era Paris, members of the Lettrist International—the precursor to the Situationist International—coined a term for this sort of spontaneous urban wandering: the *dérive*, or "drift."[6] The Midgets, however, drew inspiration from an earlier decade of twentieth-century Paris: the 1920s, as depicted in Geoffrey Wolff's *Black Sun*. The book is a biography of Lost Generation poet, publisher, and *bon vivant* Harry Crosby, an American expatriate who eventually, in the author's words, "killed himself to make his life a work of art." Though Crosby wasn't a musician, the tragic arc of his life's story finds parallels in the lives of several of the Midgets' peers in early eighties San Francisco (among them Will Shatter and Richard Kelly). "Craig was obsessed with stuff from the twenties and thirties, and he was obsessed with that whole lifestyle," recalls Seltzer. "That was a big influence on us at the time," admits Gray. "That was Mooney—Mooney brought that to us."[7]

Images of the Midgets' South of Market surroundings featured heavily in their fliers as well as their live performances, where Seltzer would often project slideshows of her drawings of the band members. The cover of their first album, *Sea of Unrest*, features one of these drawings, along with a sketch of a smokestack atop the nearby MJB coffee factory. The factory was visible from

---

6 One of the Lettrists, Ivan Chtcheglov, likened the dérive to psychoanalysis, noting that too much of either activity could lead to "dissolution, disassociation, disintegration." He claimed that he and his associates once "drifted" in such a manner for months at a time, noting, "It's a miracle it didn't kill us." (Greil Marcus, *Lipstick Traces*, p. 336)

7 It may have been Jon Savage, in turn, who introduced it to Mooney. The author recalls reading the book on his trip into San Francisco from LA in 1978. "When you're young, you're open to all sorts of bad ideas," he says of the book. "That was probably one of them. I can't remember where I heard about it. I might have heard about it from Throbbing Gristle, but I might have actually discovered it myself."

WHO CARES ANYWAY

a window in the A-Hole, the Third Street space where the band rehearsed (and where both Gray and Hood lived at different points during this era). "Everything outside was pretty what she painted," says Gray. "That was kind of what South of Market was like back then. Much more exciting. Much more interesting. That was back when all that was post-industrial, totally empty. You could wander around down Third Street and not see anybody and go down by the train tracks and the water, and there was just nothing but those old buildings."

"It was kind of the tail end of industry being in San Francisco," adds Seltzer.[8]

---

8   Kim Seltzer: "The coffee plant was there, and it was still being used, but those businesses were starting to move out of San Francisco. I think a lot of the buildings were just empty. But there was a lot of industry down there still. The Hostess factory was there, and the Hellman's mayonnaise factory was there. There was a steel plant, and there was a concrete company."

THE HARDCORE ERA

"It was more like the San Francisco of the Beats at that time. And of course, there were the hippies and all that, but it still had a lot of the feeling from the fifties and sixties because there were a lot of old bars, and there were actually nightclubs that had been jazz nightclubs in the fifties and sixties. So you still had a sense of San Francisco's past. Not like now. And especially South of Market, it did have that feeling of bleakness, but a wonderful bleakness that I think we're losing quickly."

"SILENT CEREBRALISTS IN BLACK"

Seltzer, who was dating Hood at the time, describes the Midgets' internal dynamic as a sort of camaraderie among introverts. "My focus was always the visual, and their focus has always been sounds. So a lot of the time, that's how we would communicate. We would talk about the sounds that they were making, or we'd talk about the pictures I was making. We were comfortable with each other, but I don't think we were real comfortable with a lot of other people. I'm probably more extroverted than they are, but I'm still a pretty big introvert myself."

That introversion was reflected in their live performances, where, apart from Mooney and Williams, the band members would play with their backs to the audience. According to Gray, this practice began at a later Negative Trend gig: "Rik L. Rik pulled a no show, so I tried to sing a song. I was so embarrassed I couldn't look at the audience, so I quit singing and turned around. We finished the set instrumentally, and I haven't turned around since."[9] Hood offers a different explanation. "For me, it was basically so I could watch Tim. He was holding it together for me." Either way, the band's habit of literally turning their backs at the audience created a peculiar dynamic at their shows.

Tim Lockfeld: I thought, "If you don't have vocals, and you turn your back on the audience—well, you're supposed to be *performing*."

9   "Q&A with Craig Gray." *Pig State Recon* (webzine), January 2010. https://web.archive.org/web/20100305104859/http://mrowster.wordpress.com/2010/01/22/qa-with-craig-gray

WHO CARES ANYWAY

Craig Gray: We weren't exactly showmen, and we were very insular on stage as an instrumental band. A lot of audiences—there used to be like a gap. Like, no one would come to the stage. They'd stand about ten feet back, for some reason, when we played like that. It was very, very strange. They'd come up when Ricky was singing. But when nobody was singing, they'd just stand back from us a ways. And I'd like to think that's because they were actually listening to us.

Paul Hood: I was very proud of the fact that we didn't play show business. It didn't bother me at all that we turned our backs to the people. We weren't putting on shows for the people. My dad, as a player, used to say, "I don't write music for anybody else. I'm not there to wiggle my bum and make people feel good. That's not my job." And I always took that to heart. So, for me, if I had to be a bike messenger for eight hours and then do speed and go to rehearsal for another four hours—fine, I would do it.

Kim Seltzer: It was very romantic; it was very much like the idea of nineteenth-century romantic poets—that commerce is beneath art. The Midgets definitely came from that school of thought—that a pure poet is just removed from anything to do with commerce or self-promotion. The people who came to Midgets shows were really into the Midgets. That was part of their whole mystique, and they cultivated it. I don't think people were turned off by it.

A *Puncture* fanzine review of an August 1983 Midgets show at the On Broadway, post-Ricky, describes the audience as a mix of "the usual deathly Toiling Midgets crowd of Flipper-ish creatures, skate-punks, and silent cerebralists in black," along with "a good number of 'normal' people who seem to have found it a sneaking pleasure to crawl out of the grave for some fresh air."[10] The reference to skate-punks might seem incongruous, but the group actually had a strong contingent of skateboarder fans—including members of the infamous Jak's Team (a skateboarding crew of which bassist Jonathan Henrickson, aka Nosmo King, was a founding member). "I remember certain shows where Jak's Team would come, and they would skate around the dance floor in a big circle," says

10 Patty Stirling, "Toiling Midgets: On Broadway, August 19, 1983", *Puncture*, Vol. 1, No. 5. Reprinted in *Puncture: The First Six Issues*. p. 153.

THE HARDCORE ERA

PAUL HOOD (LEFT) AND CRAIG GRAY. PHOTO BY KIM SELTZER.

Seltzer. "They loved Toiling Midgets, especially before Ricky, when they were just instrumental." Gray recalls a large contingent of skaters seemingly materializing out of nowhere during an instrumental set they played in Sacramento, opening for the Dream Syndicate. "All of a sudden, all these skater dudes showed up and just started rollin' around on the floor and sitting out on the stage with their back to us while we were playing with our backs to them. And then soon as we stopped, they all left. It was a very weird scene."

MAKING SEA OF UNREST

The Midgets began work on *Sea of Unrest* in the summer of 1981, not long after Ricky—still fresh off the Sleepers' disastrous East Coast tour and ensuing

WHO CARES ANYWAY

breakup—had come onboard. As Hood recounts, they were prepared to record an album of instrumentals until Ricky literally showed up at their doorstep. "I was on my way to Mallon's, opened the door to leave the flat, and there's Ricky, right there. He's like, 'Oh, hey.' I said, 'Hey Ricky, I'm going to Tom's. You wanna come?' So he followed me, and he did three vocals for 'Destiny,' and we ended up using the first one. And it was improvised. He had to listen to it and write it down because it was off the top of his head."

Most of the other vocals on *Sea of Unrest* were recorded in a similarly off-the-cuff fashion, which might explain the recurrence of certain phrases (for example, "you might as well give up," which appears in three different songs). "Ricky would come in maybe with a couple of scraps written ... *maybe*," recalls Gray. "But more often than not, he would just improvise over and over in the studio until he had some lyrics. And he would figure it all out afterwards, and then he would pretty much sing that live. Some of the live versions are pretty faithful to the recorded versions, but when they were faithful to the recorded versions, it's always him singing 'em *after* they were recorded because he'd figured it out afterwards." (Williams later said of his lyrics, "I can improvise them the same way, every time. I try not to, especially in the live shows."[11])

It's not unheard of for singers to come up with their own parts after the rest of the music has already been written. Mike Patton did so on Faith No More's *The Real Thing*, and Morrissey routinely did likewise with the Smiths. But examples of rock singers improvising lyrics *and* melodies in real time are harder to come by. "The fact that he could even sing *tunes*—I mean, it's not like some guy who's singing speed-metal monotone or anything," marvels Hood. "He's got these weird melodies going on. And he's creating these really strange, disembodied sort of stories of psychic phenomena and power and technology." Granted, the precise details of those stories can be hard to decipher, but they were evidently very real to Williams. "I remember watching him talking—or singing at, gesturing at, whatever—whoever was in the room with him," says Gray. "Which was nobody we could see. Almost seemed like someone possessed. It was interesting to watch. And Tom would laugh his ass off at Ricky. He found Ricky hilarious."

11 *Ego Magazine*, No. 7, 1983.

THE HARDCORE ERA

There isn't much humor on *Sea of Unrest* itself, at least on the surface. Rather, there is a thoroughgoing sense of bleakness, from the charcoal-gray album cover to the song titles ('Shooting Gallery,' 'All the Girls Cry,' 'Late Show') to the understated guitar riffs that underpin most of the songs. Some of them, like 'Trauma Girl' and 'DJMC,' have an almost metallic chug; others, like the title track, threaten to come apart at the seams, with Hood's guitar howling like a wounded animal and occasionally landing on what, in music theory terms, can only be described as "wrong notes." Meanwhile, Ricky's stream-of-consciousness vocals—alternately spoken, sung, and grunted—create an almost voyeuristic feeling in the listener.

Suffice it to say, it isn't the easiest album to penetrate, especially the opening sequence, which showcases the singer at his most unhinged. It does, however, reveal itself on repeated listening, with side two in particular featuring a succession of concise, even accessible songs before concluding with the harrowing title track. And as usual, Tim Mooney's drumming is enough to hold one's attention in its own right, with the instrumental 'All the Girls Cry' offering a particularly clear showcase of his unique approach to the kit.

"What we set out to do on that record, I think we achieved, far better than I ever hoped," says Hood. "And thanks in large part, I think, to Mallon because he put up with us. He put up with Ricky, who almost ruined his mixing board by spilling a Coke on it." Kirk Heydt, who later played alongside the singer in the band Recoil, recalls Mallon's skill at splicing together parts from different vocal takes ("this was tape and a razor blade," he emphasizes). "Amazing ear. And he *loved* Ricky. Ricky was his Nick Cave, I think. Because he'd come up with these *great* things all of a sudden—these big, dramatic parts."

"WHERE WAS RICKY?"

The Midgets' live recordings from the same era offer an interesting vantage point on the *Sea of Unrest* material. While they weren't the kind of band to play solos or launch into Grateful Dead-style jams, they didn't try to replicate their recordings onstage, either. Not surprisingly, the biggest variable was Ricky, who

would often change lyrics or even entire vocal parts on the spot—with wildly unpredictable results.

For example, video footage from a July 19, 1982, show at the I-Beam shows him struggling to find his way into a song ('Get an Answer') that the rest of the band seems to know far better than he does. Simply put, it doesn't work, and the results are almost painful to listen to. Yet an audio recording from two nights later finds him improvising a completely different vocal—lyrically, melodically, and rhythmically—over the same instrumental backing, this time with much better results. Never mind that he had just wandered onstage midway through the song, his bandmates wondering if he would show up at all that night.

Paul Hood: We were opening for Nico, and it was being recorded for the radio.[12] And … where was Ricky? It was like, "Fine, we'll start without him." He had an armful of magazines; he walked up to the stage, dropped the magazines, dropped the coat, and started singing. That's it. I mean, you never knew, with Ricky, what you were gonna get. It could be amazing or amazingly bad. It just depended on so many different factors.[13]

Michael Belfer: A lot of it was really repetitious. At that point, Ricky had really kind of exhausted his themes for what he was singing about, and you'd find him repeating things like "It's your reputation." There'd be certain catchphrases that he would just repeat over and over again.

Connie Champagne: He got into doing this extemporaneous stuff, which was great when it worked, but it was terrible when it didn't work. It's like watching your grandma who's got dementia, sort of just howling. It doesn't go anywhere. When he was on it and could really tap into it, he did some really interesting things.

---

12 The song is the opening track on *1982 Volume 2*. In this version, it is entitled 'India.' In the video from the July 19 show, it's entitled 'Get an Answer.'

13 For Gray and Seltzer, the night was also memorable for their brief encounter with the headliner. "Nico showed up with no money at the door and asked the door guy for money to pay for her cab," says Gray. "Then I played pool with her, and she beat me. Then some people showed up with drugs, and she disappeared into a room. I didn't see her again for the rest of the night until she played." Seltzer: "We watched her kick his ass at pool, just in awe."

The problem was that he was unwilling and undisciplined to write anything down, so when he got to places where people expected him to deliver it, *his* deal was like, "No, I'm not gonna deliver it. I'll just make up everything off the top of my head." Well, that's not how you become successful in the recording business. Because they expect you to be able to replicate that live when you do it, and you can't just make up a new song every time.

Sea of Unrest surfaced in April of 1982 on a one-off label called Instant Records—a subsidiary of Rough Trade,

which had recently opened a satellite office in San Francisco. "It was originally supposed to come out on Rough Trade US," explains Gray. "But Rough Trade UK didn't like it and were pissed because Rough Trade US had supposedly signed us instead of REM. So they created a new label, one called 'Instant' just to get the record out."

That August, the *New York Times* published a glowing review of the record, courtesy of Robert Palmer (in the same article where he reviewed Flipper's *Album*). "The Toiling Midgets sound like a band with a future," he raved, before once again invoking the Haight-Ashbury era. "It may be difficult to imagine a group with such a silly name going on to make more albums, but remember, Grateful Dead and Jefferson Airplane had silly names."[14]

In the end, it wasn't the band name that did them in—it was their mercurial

14 Palmer, "Rebellion Rules Rock in Young San Francisco." *New York Times*, August 25, 1982.

singer. Mere days before Palmer's review appeared in print, the band had returned from a brief Pacific Northwest tour—two shows each in Seattle and Portland—with Ricky in tow. Gray describes it as "an *absolute* disaster" and recalls having to drag the singer out of his motel room before one of the Seattle shows because he wanted to sleep instead.[15] "That was pretty much the last time we did anything with him," he adds. "There was just no way we could've taken Ricky on any kind of long, long tour."

15 The show was recorded and later released as *1982 Volume 1.*

THE HARDCORE ERA

19

"WHAT IF?" ARKANSAW MAN, RED ASPHALT, AND G.O.D.

By 1982 or so, the "punk scene" was no longer one scene but many. From post-punk to new wave to hardcore, the sheer number of underground bands had grown exponentially since the early Mabuhay days. Even so, the LP remained an elusive benchmark for most of these bands—something that's easy to lose sight of in an age of easily accessible music production software and practically unlimited hard drive space.[16] "Hardly anybody thought about doing albums," recalls Subterranean's Steve Tupper, "and the cassette thing really wasn't happening at that point."

Subterranean, which was the city's most prolific independent label during this era, released just three single-band LPs through the end of 1982: Minimal Man's *The Shroud Of,* Flipper's *Album,* and Factrix/Cazazza's *California Babylon*. Yet a deeper dive into their catalog reveals plenty of intriguing, even vital music by bands that never graduated to the LP format. The same goes for a smattering of other bands that likewise never released anything more than a poorly distributed 7-inch or a couple of obscure compilation tracks.[17] In this pre-digital, pre-

16 Apart from Flipper, Toiling Midgets, the Dead Kennedys, and the cast of commercial new wave bands on 415 Records—bands like Romeo Void, Translator, and Wire Train—few acts had graduated to the LP format. One other LP that warrants a mention is Black Humor's *Love God, Love One Another* (Fowl, 1982), an experimental hardcore/noise record. Black Humor in this incarnation was essentially a studio project led by the duo of George Miller and Dan Houser, along with an assortment of guests. Unlike Flipper, they managed to garner a positive review in the first issue of *Maximum Rocknroll,* which described them as "lunatics [who] swing from music for nightmares to rhythmic jungle rock." The album was reissued in 2011 as the first release on Superior Viaduct.

17 Speaking of compilations, the *Red Spot* LP (Subterranean, 1982) offers perhaps the best snapshot of the wild array of sounds emanating from this portion of the underground—sounds that were too unkempt for new wave, too abstract for

215

Internet era, their fates were not the exception but the rule. As such, their stories reveal much about the tenor of the times and the obstacles involved in "making it" as a band, even in the most modest sense of the term.

ARKANSAW MAN

Arkansaw Man was a case in point. The trio, which formed in early 1980, played a kind of intricate, mostly instrumental music that would have been considered "post-rock" had it come along a decade later. Though none of them actually came from Arkansas, they were all recent arrivals to the Bay Area, with guitarist Stephen Clarke coming from Long Island, bassist Patrick Lovullo from Buffalo, and drummer Glenn Sorvisto from Houston (where he played in a proto-hardcore band called the Hates). The three of them met through a day job working as bike messengers, a popular if also dangerous gig among local musicians in those days.

Clarke and Sorvisto both took up residence in the Tenderloin, the notoriously seedy neighborhood just north of Market Street. "The place was oozing," recalls Clarke. "You know, alcohol, needles, people throwing up, sex." On the plus side, there was the cheap rent (Clarke rented a studio at 370 Ellis Street for $150 a month) as well as the proximity to both the Sound of Music and Turk Street Studios, two key locales that warrant a brief digression.

"The Sound of Music was a big deal," explains John Surrell. "It was just like another little hellhole, but it was a very key place to the underground scene back then." Adds Bill Gould, "It was the shittiest place in town, right next to a Black transvestite bar. But that was a *great* place." Like the Mab, the Sound of Music was run by a Filipino, in this case one Celso Ruperto, "who was really nice and

---

hardcore punk, and too grimy for the respectable avant-garde. Highlights include the Animal Things' 'Wanna Buy Some?' (Flipper-approved P.E.T. Rock with warped funk undertones), the Fried Abortions' wonderfully amateurish 'Joel Selvin,' and a pair of tracks by the Woundz, a Vallejo-based outfit featuring the talented Paul Casteel on vocals. The best-known artist on the record is Minimal Man, whose *Psycho*-themed 'Shower Sequence' opens the record. Several of the other bands—including Micon, Arsenal, and Research Library—are seemingly lost to the sands of time, and only a few of them managed to release any other recordings.

sort of ineffectual," notes Alistair Shanks. "But he had this booking policy where pretty much anybody could play there. To be perfectly honest, every scene needs a place like that. It became a hangout for us. We would go there after rehearsal and just hang out, so we would go and watch whatever band was playing that night."

Shanks's band Tragic Mulatto, which played its first-ever show at the club on Easter Sunday of 1982, rehearsed across the street at Turk Street Studios. "It was in the basement of a hotel," notes Mark Bowen, whose band Tanks also rehearsed there in those days. "This guy named Francisco built a whole bunch of little cubicle rooms and then rented them monthly—maybe $300, $350 a month. Back then, it was a lot. There were probably twenty rooms in there, making this cacophony of noise. In any other neighborhood, it would've been shut down. But it was the Tenderloin, so none of the local residents were cognizant and together enough to be able to complain about it." Adds Clarke, "Some people ended up staying and living there, even though there were no windows, no nothing. Just like one bathroom. That was a great place. It was like a little strange underground community."

The grittiness of their surroundings didn't seem to filter into Arkansaw Man's music, which was more playful than angst-ridden. "It was always a little bit off-kilter and arty," Clarke says of the group's sound. "I mean, if there's 'art punk,' that's probably us." As a guitarist, Clarke avoided distortion and power chords, opting instead for cleanly picked lines that weaved in and out of Lovullo's nimble bass playing and Sorvisto's agile drumming. The result was jagged, heavily contrapuntal music that didn't resemble *Trout Mask Replica* or any of the other more obvious precursors. "Basically, what we did was experiment," says the guitarist. "If you're going to really experiment and throw away the blueprint, you'll end up with something that's a little chaotic and maybe not as smooth. Although we would hear something like Gang of Four and think, 'Wow, they're doing a completely organized version of what we're doing, and they're also doing it very beautifully.' But we weren't using their blueprint." The guitarist mentions the Fall and DNA—the latter of whom he saw at CBGB's before moving out west—as other influences.

Thanks to an early gig at Club Foot, the trio made the acquaintance of Richard Kelly, who quickly became a supporter. "He thought it was kind of hilarious," recalls Clarke, describing Kelly's reaction to their set. "I remember him cracking up at one point. That was kind of nice." Kelly offered to produce a record for them, a four-song EP that wound up being one of the only releases on the short-lived Modern Masters imprint. (Kelly also provided horn arrangements on one song and played keyboard on another, meaning the record was also one of the few that he appeared on as a musician.) A Tom Mallon-engineered 7-inch ('Mark Twain' b/w 'Every Job') followed on Subterranean a couple of years later. Along with their contribution to a live Sound of Music compilation, that was the extent of Arkansaw Man's official discography: seven songs totaling less than half an hour.

"We basically broke up after we toured in '83," explains Clarke. "We bought a van, left on July 19, 1983, and played twenty-four shows. We made it to Toronto; we played in Buffalo. Our closest gig wasn't until Denver, and that was on the way back. So nothing west of Denver. By the time we got to New York, I was, like, having a nervous breakdown. There wasn't even anything going on to precipitate it. It was just all these gigs, not getting a lot of money. Some of them, like Milwaukee—ninety-five degrees, three people show up, they gave us five bucks. By December of '83, Glenn had split. Which was fine because I was done anyway. I was like, 'No, I won't do this. I'm going crazy.'"

While Arkansaw Man was not cut out for pop stardom, the trio had enough talent—and enough original ideas—that it's hard not to engage in a little "what if?" speculation. "You know, I used to think about it a *lot*," admits Clarke. "Like, 'Oh, we could have done this and that, and what if we had taken *this* direction?' But it was only possible to do what we did and take the direction we took."

RED ASPHALT

Much like Arkansaw Man, Red Asphalt wouldn't have sounded out of place in early 2000s San Francisco. By then, synthesizers—particularly analog synths of a 1970s vintage—had come back in style; in Red Asphalt's day, they'd yet to go *out* of style, partly because they were still hard to come by. "Keyboards didn't sound corny yet," notes Scott Davey, one of the band's three founding members. "They sounded fresh, especially with people who weren't experienced keyboard players. I bought an Oberheim Two Voice, and I bought it with an inheritance. It

THE HARDCORE ERA

wasn't cheap at the time."

Even before Red Asphalt, Davey had been an important behind-the-scenes figure on the local scene. In 1976, he opened Iguana Studios, a South of Market rehearsal space where bands could rent studio time by the hour. Countless bands made use of the facility, from the Avengers and Negative Trend to the Dead Kennedys and Flipper. As a performer, Davey's experience actually predated the punk era, including stints with the Cockettes as well as Mary Monday and Her Bitches (the first vaguely punkish band to play the Mabuhay, before even the Nuns).

As Davey recalls, it was Deaf Club impresario Robert Hanrahan who introduced him to guitarist Ron Hanik and drummer Ted Johnson, his eventual bandmates in Red Asphalt. Fittingly, the band would later become a part of Deaf Club lore after a nearby resident jumped from a Valencia Street window and splattered onto the

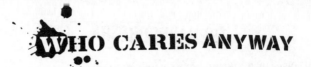

sidewalk outside the club—on a night when Red Asphalt just so happened to be playing. "He was lying there in a pool of blood," recalls the keyboardist. "We were all milling out on the street. It took a while for anyone to come get him."

The band's signature song, the eponymous 'Red Asphalt' ("Blame it on Red Asphalt / It's nobody else's fault"), could be interpreted as a response to rumors surrounding the incident.[18] Yet, as Davey clarifies, the song had already been written by that point; moreover, the incident didn't happen *during* Red Asphalt's set, but after it.[19] The song originally appeared on a 7-inch EP that the band self-released in 1981. "We actually got a great review in the *New Musical Express* in England, but we didn't know how to follow it up," laments Davies. "We didn't know anything about distribution or the fact that we should have had records there for people to buy. We just sent 'em out for review and thought things would follow. We thought people would contact *us*. But nobody actually did."

The singer heard on 'Red Asphalt,' Megan Mitchell, quit the band not long after the record was released and evidently fell off the radar screen. She was replaced by Trina James, a similarly elusive figure who came to the band via an ad in the *Chronicle*. Her tenure as lead singer is highlighted by the song 'Human Capital,' a hidden gem that still sounds fresh decades later. Built around a lurching bassline in 7/4 time, the song finds James reciting a monologue that depicts one side of an imaginary telephone conversation. Her delivery is nonchalant yet somehow in sync with the odd rhythm of the song. "I'm trying to be reasonably detached / With my fingers crossed," she deadpans, conveying a sense of cautious optimism

---

18 The song has since appeared on a few different compilations, including the Bay Area-focused *Bay Area Retrograde* (Dark Entries, 2014) and the bootleg comps *Homework #101* (Hyped to Death) and *Killed by Synth, Vol. 1*.

19 There are conflicting accounts on exactly what happened. A chapter-length oral history on the club that appears in David Ensminger's *Left of the Dial* includes a few such recollections. As Noh Mercy's Esmerelda recalled, "I was really stoned standing outside on the sidewalk smoking and talking when a dead body fell out the window from the whore hotel upstairs and scared the fuck out of me! It was already dead when it fell, they reported." However, another witness, one "Lu Read," remembered things differently: "I assumed it was a mannequin or such since many musicians also attended art school. As I approached, I realized it was a dead body, splayed in a very strange way since the neck/spinal cord broke from the fall; the way the body lay on the sidewalk did not look human at first. Thick cerebral fluid surrounded the head. It was intense! I hurried upstairs, somewhat nauseated from the sight. I returned to the sidewalk to watch until the police and fire department pushed us all back. 'I guess he didn't like the band that was playing,' I said."

that's echoed by Davey's layered synth melodies. It sounds like the early eighties, but in the best sense: streamlined and futuristic, not cold or inhuman.

Alas, the song would remain unreleased for another twenty-five years, along with the rest of the album it was supposed to be a part of. "We sent it out to a lot of companies," says Davey. "We came kind of close with Ralph Records. We were friends with them. But this was right when they started putting out a whole lot of records, and they told us that they just weren't getting paid for the records. They overextended themselves, so we kind of missed the window." The album eventually saw the light of day in 2008 as a CD entitled *UnReleased*, while an LP containing much of the same material was released in 2014 via the Italian label Synthetic Shadows. "I'm *extremely* proud of it because it's got some really weird stuff," says bassist Bruno DeSmartass, who joined the band after the earlier EP was released. "Every time I hear it, I fuckin' cry. Just because of Trina, because she was such an ethereal being."

Discouraged by the lack of response from record labels, Red Asphalt dissolved in late 1982, not long after Davey closed down Iguana Studios. Trina eventually drifted off to Oregon—where, in August of 2000, she perished in a head-on collision after swerving into oncoming traffic, apparently while driving under the influence.[20] "She always had an addictive personality, let's say," admits Davey. "As did many of the people on the scene."

G.O.D.

Bruno DeSmartass: "G.O.D." stood for "Girls on Drugs," or "Girls Overdrawn," or "Girls on Dogs"—who knows what it stood for? But they were *super*-arty, with some *mythically* talented, creative, and fucked-up women. It was sort of Flipper-ish, in a way—in the sense of an anarchic noise. Totally the thing that girls are not supposed to do.

20 "One Killed, Five Injured in Collision." *Statesman Journal* (Salem, Oregon). August 21, 2000.

WHO CARES ANYWAY

Susan Miller: I loved G.O.D. Because, hell, who wouldn't love a band called "Girls on Drugs"— G.O.D.—right? They were amazing.

Mia Simmans: It was just completely unacceptable on just every level as far as society was concerned in the early eighties.

G.O.D. lived up to its name in more ways than one, for better *and* for worse. "I remember one time staying up for five days and then doing two shows on the last day," says guitarist/keyboardist Lisa Wooley. "We were just so wired and wild."

A Seattle native, Wooley moved to SF in 1978 out of frustration with the state of affairs in her hometown. "There were these clubs here," she notes, "but every time you'd turn around, they were getting shut down." While hanging out at the Bagel on Polk Street, she made the acquaintance of a pre-Dead Kennedys Jello Biafra (still going by the name Eric Boucher at the time) and moved into the crowded flat where he was living at 29th and Mission. "He was a good roommate," Wooley recalls. "Because we liked weird music—the weirder shit, the better." She actually turned down an invitation to try out for the DKs on keyboards, feeling she wasn't quite ready to play in a band. "I was just going to tons of shows at first. And then I started meeting other musicians and hanging out at Iguana Studios. That's when it started for me, when I met Susan Miller. And then I got Mark Bowen to come down from Seattle."

Along with bassist Michael Davis and drummer Ben Cohen, they formed the group Tanks in 1980. They were named after a T-Rex album but more often drew comparisons to X due to the ragged male/female harmonies of Davis and Miller. Wooley co-wrote 'March of the Slugs,' the B-side of the group's only 7-inch, but she had already moved on by the time they recorded it. "She was just like, 'No, my musical muse is going in a different direction,'" recalls Miller. "Because we were kind of like a rock band, and she wanted to be more avant-garde and more *out there*. And Tanks was really more rock 'n' roll."[21]

---

21 The record ('Bongo Congo' b/w 'March of the Slugs') was released on manager Ian Cartmill's "Capital Records" (not to be confused with Capitol Records, although that was precisely the idea, as the label borrowed the original Capitol logo and merely

THE HARDCORE ERA

By the time she started G.O.D., Wooley had moved into the A-Hole on Third Street. Like Toiling Midgets, G.O.D. also rehearsed there, at least early on. "We would jam till all hours of the night," Wooley recalls. "We were driving our roommates *nuts* because we didn't know how to play very well yet. So it was like this cacophonous insanity. We were trying to make something out of it, being high on speed and stuff.

"But actually, we *did*. We played gigs all over the city, but we never had a car. I remember a few times, taking all of our equipment on the city bus— you know, my guitar and amp, and then Rachel's trying to get her bass amp, and I'm trying to help her. And Crawford's trying to get all her drums on there before the bus driver gets too frustrated. We were right there on Third Street, so we could take the bus all the way up to Broadway and play at the Mabuhay Gardens. It was really *fun*. I really enjoyed playing with them. It was great until Crawford died."

Anne Crawford was yet another in a long line of casualties from this era. It happened after a June 18, 1982, show at Club Foot, where G.O.D. shared a bill with the Pop-O-Pies and Sharp Young Men. Carlos Willingham, who was helping manage the club in those days, recalls a telling anecdote from before the show. "All of a sudden, someone said, 'There's somebody out in the backyard.' I went down, and it was Crawford. She was all cut up and scraped. I said, 'Crawford, what are you doing?' She said, 'I'm trying to sneak in to see the show.' I said, 'Crawford, you're *playing* tonight.' That's how fuckin' out of it she was."

Lisa Wooley: After we played, they all wanted to go to this big party, and I said, "I think I'm just gonna go back. I'm cool. I've done enough tonight, and I don't really feel like doing anything else right now. So you guys have a good time. Bye."

Joe Pop-O-Pie: She was doing uppers and downers at the same time. And she turned to somebody, and the last thing she said was, "If I don't get some speed pretty soon, I'm gonna die." And she meant it.

---

replaced the "o" with an "a").

WHO CARES ANYWAY

Susan Miller: She fell asleep at the party. I was sitting next to her, and before I knew it, she wasn't breathing. We had to call the ambulance, and it was just a nightmare. So, you know, things like that are hard to deal with. But Crawford was kind of the heart and soul of that band, along with Lisa Wooley.

Rachel Thoele: It affected me deeply because she was my best friend.

Lisa Wooley: She was really creative. I mean, she was a real creative force and a very unique individual, but somebody who couldn't really find her place in the world. And I remember, six months before she died, she said, "I don't think I'm gonna be around much longer. I really don't think I am." I remember her telling me that.

She was thirty. She was older than us. She was into drama. She did plays. And then she'd come up with these little profound sayings. She'd focus on one sentence in the song and just try to—I don't know, kind of be in the moment with that one sentence. It was really cool. She had a presence. She definitely had a presence and knew how to relay it out there.

Like Richard Kelly and Michael Kowalsky, Crawford was a lost soul who left a big mark on those around her but little to posterity. That said, her voice can be heard on 'In Jail,' one of four songs the group recorded during a December 1981 demo session at Tom Mallon's studio. Though still officially unreleased, the songs have the makings of a lost cult classic. Wooley sings lead on the other three songs, whose titles—'Pits of Hell,' 'Nuthouse,' and 'From Here to Depression'—give a sense of the overall vibe. "I guess it was pre-goth or something," says Wooley. "We called it 'psychotic rock.'"

G.O.D. continued on for a short while after Crawford's death before eventually splitting up, with Thoele going on to play drums in an early version of another all-woman band, Frightwig. For Wooley, Crawford's death was one sign that a more drastic change of scenery was in order; the strange death of Luis Gomez, a friend and roommate at the A-Hole, was another one.

Bruce Pollack: He was going out with this girl, and she was a real sexy girl, but she was a real character. He went back to Colombia to visit his mother and then came back two weeks later, and she had slept with his best friend. He started drinking and doing drugs because he was a big speed dealer back then.

Lisa Wooley: Supposedly, he was playing Russian roulette in the room with his girlfriend and shot himself in the head. Then she was found cutting his hair, probably trying to cut the blood out or looking to see what was going on with his head.

Bruce Pollack: Apparently, she said that he took the gun and put it to his head and clicked the gun once and then did it again and clicked in his mouth and shot himself in the mouth. But when I listen to this story, my friend Gomez had a .38 automatic. Not a gun that twirls around, six-chamber. Her story was like a six-chamber story. If you take an automatic and put a bullet in the chamber, you don't get a click with nothing happening. But I wasn't there.

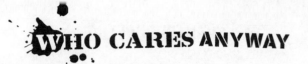

Kim Seltzer: After Gomez died, we were spending a lot of time with her. I was doing all of these paintings—like Midgets paintings—but there were a lot of ghostly figures in them: people looking in mirrors and ghostly figures looking back. And every one of those paintings, she bought. Like, I would paint one, and she would buy it. And it was just getting weird. I mean, I was happy for the money, but I was really struck by it. And then one day, I had this epiphany—and I could be completely wrong, but I had this epiphany that the reason she was buying them is because she shot Gomez, and she was seeing something in those paintings, and it was really upsetting her, so she was just acquiring them all. She probably shot him by accident.

Paul Hood: After that, you didn't know what was really happening. I just got the feeling like, "I don't really know what's going on after all." So I was just gonna put as much distance between myself and that as possible.

Lisa Wooley: After that happened and Crawford had died, I don't know—something hit me, and I just said, "I don't know. I don't think I wanna be around here much longer."

20

HARDCORE

The rise of hardcore coincided with the demise of art punk. Many of the key bands in this respect—Tuxedomoon, the Sleepers, Indoor Life, Factrix, and the Club Foot bands—had either left town or broken up by 1982, and the ones that stuck around were left to navigate an increasingly hostile environment. Some of them, like Flipper, took these changes in stride, developing a love-hate relationship with hardcore audiences. Others found themselves increasingly alienated by the more aggressive, less open-minded crowds. Either way, hardcore represented a fork in the road.

Peter Urban: You started having two scenes emerging there, and the sensibilities are very different. And for the first year or two, I don't think any of us really recognized that it was really emerging as a distinct animal. But by 1980, '81, you definitely felt it. And the Kennedys were part of that emerging group that the rest of us from the early days really didn't want anything to do with.

Denny DeGorio: A lot of the bands and kids from the suburbs were coming into the city with their own ideas. It seemed like they were a little more separatist, in a way—the hardcore scene. The early scene was really unique, real open-minded, real accepting of everything. It was kind of just like "do your own thing." We really didn't have any hard-and-fast rules, whereas later, the hardcore scene was more strictly defined.

Paul Casteel: In '78, '79, you'd go to shows, and there would be art bands playing with bands like the Dils and the Avengers, and also reggae bands. And then it really changed over about the same time the LA punk rock scene changed from the older bands like X and the Weirdos and the Screamers and the Bags. But when Black Flag—later versions of Black Flag—and Adolescents

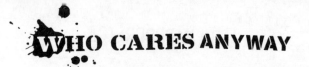

WHO CARES ANYWAY

and TSOL got really big, it changed a lot. It became the slam dance thing, and it really sectioned off the different types of music. A lot of the old-school bands, they started playing at offbeat clubs, and the more hardcore stuff played at the Mab or the On Broadway. There weren't as many shows like the Deaf Club or that kind of thing where there were really diverse billings.

Bruno DeSmartass: Certainly, the seventies stuff had a foot really deep in art rock. Even bands like Crime were more conceptual, the way they dressed. And the Mutants certainly came out of art rock. The Sleepers, definitely. And by extension, Flipper was more about the concept. But what ended up happening is, just right around the time Bad Posture started, there were a lot of unknown bands coming up that were more hard-edged. And I don't know where that came from. Certainly, there were the beach bands—we always referred to them as that. They would come on up here, and they'd be like thugs with their chains and whatever. It was silly, but it was definitely a different energy than, say, going down to the Mab and seeing Tuxedomoon. But that was the beginning of thrash, and I guess that was around '82. Bad Posture fit right in. I mean, we were just yahoos and just liked to stir shit up.

Bad Posture was an interesting case. On the one hand, they were almost the prototypical hardcore band: loud, fast, aggressive, and snotty. On the other hand, the band members themselves weren't hardcore purists by any stretch. At the time, drummer John Surrell was also playing with Minimal Man and the Black Dolls, a goth outfit. Guitarist Bruno DeSmartass played bass in Red Asphalt and later filled in on both guitar and bass in Flipper. And bassist Emilio Crixell would later go on to play with Will Shatter in his post-Flipper band Any Three Initials.

That said, the music they played as Bad Posture was no-frills hardcore, with a metal edge to boot. "I was always a Motörhead fan," says Crixell, "so in my way, I was trying to do Motörhead-type stuff inside of punk rock—which some people thought was cool and other people didn't like." In their own way, Motörhead represented a merger of punk and metal sensibilities, but generally speaking, these elements did not tend to coexist peacefully. "At that point, there was a metal/punk rock divide," notes Surrell. "You were either on one side of the street or the other. The big heavy metal scene was the new thing. But for us, I wanted us to have the big metal sound—the great big sound—but I wanted the anarchy. I wanted the rebellion thing."

In North Beach, the punks and the metalheads were often literally on opposite sides of the street—Broadway Street, to be precise. The scene there was once again picking up steam with the emergence of the On Broadway (located directly upstairs from the Mabuhay) and the Stone (across the street at 412 Broadway).[22] "The Stone was where the metal bands played—the hair bands, they called them back then," says Crixell. "They hated punk rockers, and the punk rockers hated them, for some reason or other. On any given night, there would be beer bottles flying over the cars on Broadway. It was crazy, stupid shit. When Metallica came around, they kind of brought those two worlds together. They really weren't together back then. Really, they were at odds."

"The Broadway strip was just an incredible scene back in the early eighties on a Friday or Saturday night," adds Surrell. "*All* the action was happening. There'd be the barkers from the strip clubs, and then there'd be bumper-to-bumper traffic, but it would be lowriders, with the cars jumping up and down. Then there'd be the Hells Angels, and then there'd be the punk rockers, and then across the street, there'd be the metal kids at the Stone. It was just such an incredible scene. The Broadway strip—it *rocked*."

Broadway was not the only hardcore hub in those days. On Valencia Street, there was the Tool & Die, which had opened a couple of years earlier as an art gallery and occasional performance space before gradually morphing into a more hardcore-friendly venue. "Somehow, those landlords let us in," marvels Peter Belsito, who co-founded the venue with his friend Jim Stockford in 1980. "They didn't have a fuckin' clue what we were doing. The rent at Tool & Die was

---

22 Located at 435 Broadway, the On Broadway was a converted theater that began hosting punk shows in 1981 and soon became the premier hardcore-era venue in SF—somewhat incongruously given the decor. "It had red velvet and theatre seats and a nice stage and curtains and all of that," remembers Olga Gerrard, who did some of the early booking there after moving on from the Savoy Tivoli. "It was at the end of its tenure as an actual theatre. It was a little bit bordering on seedy, which was really quite charming and appropriate for what we were doing." Both the Mab and the On Broadway were regular venues for Bad Posture. Surrell: "I remember one night we did the early show at the Mabuhay, then we dragged our stuff out through the fire escape and played a show at the On Broadway."

650 bucks for 3,000 square feet—and a basement. It had an apartment in the back, so I lived there. When Stockford and I did our first shown there, the fire department showed up the next morning and said, 'You can't do that.' We said, 'Well, we're just having a rent party.' And the fire department said, 'Oh, okay. In that case, it doesn't matter.' So we kept on for two years, and I never saw one cop, one fire department guy."

Much like the Sound of Music, the Tool & Die was literally an underground venue. Shows took place in the basement, which also functioned as a rehearsal studio by day. "They tore up the floors of the Tool & Die, and they reinforced the ceiling down in the basement," explains Surrell, who rehearsed there in the early days of Bad Posture. "They came in with something like two tons of sand to make it soundproof. And then they put the floorboards back together. They really did this construction so they could have live music down in the basement and get away with it." That made the venue safe from the cops but not necessarily safe for concertgoers, as Blaise Smith explains. "The only way you could get into a show was, you would go into the main floor—like the street level—and then there was a hole in the ground with a ladder. And you'd climb down there, and that's where the shows were. And I mean, it was so dangerous. I took one friend there, an older cat, and he was just like, 'I'm not goin' down there. You guys are all gonna die.' It was completely illegal and dangerous."[23]

Then there were the Vats, one of the more vivid examples of DIY ingenuity in post-industrial San Francisco. Housed in an abandoned Hamm's brewery in the no-man's-land between SOMA and the Mission, the Vats consisted of a couple of dozen empty beer vats that bands could rent for $200 a month. "The vats were ten feet in diameter, tiled, and maybe thirty feet long with a hatch on the end," explains DeSmartass, who rehearsed there with his post-Bad

---

23 Belsito, who went on to author the San Francisco half of the 1983 book *Hardcore California*, was not enamored with hardcore as a genre. "I was using 'hardcore' more in the sense of *how* we got there, and also, hardcore in the sense of, 'These people *can't* do anything else.' It's kind of like the migratory patterns of birds: you gotta go where you're goin'." Belsito bowed out of booking the Tool & Die in 1982 as hardcore was taking over. "I liked some of those people," he says, "but it kind of got too young for me at that point. The last hardcore show I did was, I think, Bad Posture and Tanks. And I just couldn't take it anymore after that. I had to get out of there."

Posture band, the Sluglords. "Some enterprising outlaw ended up leasing the building, and they would cut doorways. And then people would live in there or turn these cylinders into living spaces. Then on the ground floor, they had proper studios. But that spawned a particular type of sound that was more hard-edged. Maybe just a little bit more violent and rocky. And bands that did have a political bent to them, like MDC. They were sort of the kings of down there."

MDC (originally an acronym for "Millions of Dead Cops") was one of several hardcore bands to migrate to San Francisco from Texas around this time; others included DRI and the Dicks, whose members also took up residence in the Vats. Meanwhile, Bay Area hardcore and skate-punk bands were sprouting left and right, many of them scarcely distinguishable in sound or message—as evidenced by the double-LP compilation *Not So Quiet on the Western Front*. There are a few outliers, such as Flipper's 'Sacrifice' and the Church Police's 'Oven Is My Friend,' but for the most part, the album is a monochrome blur of distorted guitars, thrashing tempos, and shouted vocals.

The release of *Not So Quiet ...* , in turn, coincided with the debut issue of *Maximum Rocknroll*, which was included as an insert with copies of the LP. The package was an ambitious undertaking that, much like the Vats, highlighted the resourcefulness and initiative of the early hardcore scene. Yet much like the record, the zine's contents also reflected the sense of orthodoxy that was already coming to define the genre. And no one embodied these strengths or weaknesses more vividly than *MRR* head honcho Tim Yohannan.

Peter Urban: Tim had actually, in former days, been with the Communist Party. At the same time, he was like a super rock 'n' roll guy. So he was a bit of a contradiction himself. But his politics were pretty mainstream communist—like Soviet-style communism.

Eric Cope: Tim Yohannan had problems with so many people out there, and I'm surprised he didn't get killed, seriously. If it was hip-hop, Tim Yohannan would have gotten shot, for real, because he had so many problems with so many good bands. He was so narrow-minded about music and the whole political, communist, "this-this-this" idea.

WHO CARES ANYWAY

Alistair Shanks: It became this dogmatic, narrow thing, with the beach punks and hardcore, and if it didn't fit into that category, then it wasn't "punk rock." And that was the absolute antithesis of what punk rock was, in a way, because there was no room for any kind of change or mutation. I mean, that was one of the original punk rock phrases: "Mutate or die." And here, people like the *Maximum Rocknroll* people took it all and shoved it in this little box. It was like the new orthodoxy.

William Davenport: I was never a huge fan of the magazine because I just thought it was kind of strange how they were doing it. It kind of reminded me of punk, being the same thing over and over and over again, and sort of too much of it. But I respected the work. They reviewed everything.

"THE FOOTBALL PLAYERS CAME IN"

As *Maximum Rocknroll* was attempting to push punk politics in one direction, the music itself was attracting a different element—one that was seemingly less concerned with politics than it was with physical confrontation. Even for many who didn't share *MRR*'s ideological commitments, the increasing violence at shows was becoming hard to ignore.

"The shows were getting bigger, the bands were getting more aggressive," recalls John Surrell, who had the pleasure of being hit in the head with a flying bottle during a Bad Posture show at the On Broadway. "In the very beginning, when we were playing, there was no such thing as the pit, where everybody went around in a circle. It used to annoy me. It was like, 'Will you children sit down? Sit down! I'm trying to play some music. You're not listening.' That used to bother me.

"And all of a sudden, it became this thing. Every time we'd start a song, they'd start going around in a circle. All of a sudden, the fistfights would start. Then all of a sudden, people are climbing up on stage and diving off into the audience. That kind of nonsense. It was like, 'What are you guys doing?' After a while, you just accepted it. But in the beginning, it was like, 'What the hell is *this*? You're not listening to the art.' That was my point of view—like it was art."

232

THE HARDCORE ERA

Ruby Ray: The first thing people were doing was the pogo. And we actually used to do that. You know, you're just jumping straight up and down. And then the pogo just got more wild, and then slowly they started thrashing and bumping into people. And then, just little by little, it became more aggressive, until then when those all-guy sort of hardcore bands started, they encouraged that kind of thing, and it just took over. And I think a lot of people stopped liking it at that point because it was just too aggressive.

Bill Gould: There was also a period where you had a lot of kids who went from being football linebacker to punk overnight. They still had a Lynyrd Skynyrd sticker on the back of their pickup truck but had a Mohawk.

Tom Wheeler: I like to say the football players came in. Because from '77 to '80, you had a bunch of skinny, somewhat druggy poets and artists—acting a little tough, but they weren't really. And it evolved into something in which you had big, bulky guys in a mosh pit, pushing everybody around. And it was kind of like a uniform developed, where if you were quote-unquote "punk," there was a much more limited way that you were supposed to look. Whereas if you look at bands like Patti Smith or Television, it doesn't look anything like that.

Mark Bowen: It wasn't so much that San Francisco was full of people like that, but there was a certain type—Joe [Pop-O-Pie] used to make comments and snide remarks to them. Brand new leather jackets, new boots, shaved head, bangin' into each other, kind of like a little army. They all looked more or less the same. Trying to be punk rockers, saying, "We're punk rockers, and you're not." We didn't care. We just thought they were a little obnoxious. That's not to say that lots of our friends didn't have leather jackets and boots—they all had leather jackets and boots. It was more like kids from the suburbs would come in and dress up as punk rockers and cause trouble.

Meri St. Mery: I didn't understand hardcore. I didn't really get where things got super violent or weird at a show because life as a teenage girl, surviving by yourself—it's hard enough as it is. You didn't need to make things hardcore. And what I liked so much about the punk scene was, it was the first time I

233

ever felt beautiful, and it was the first time people ever said that. It was just a bunch of misfits.

Peter Urban: I hated the hardcore scene. I just hated it with a passion. And most of the people I know who were around in '77 or '78 felt the same way. The hardcore scene, for us, was pretty much representative of everything that we had tried to get away from back in those years. What I mean by that is that it was very macho. There was a lot of uniformity to it. Everybody looked the same. The violence of the mosh pit was not the same as the sort of good-natured ramming into each other that occurred in the earlier seventies punk scene.

21

'GET AWAY,' GONE FISHIN' AND A SEASON IN NEW YORK

Flipper always had a complex relationship with hardcore. "If you looked at us on the street," says Ted Falconi, "you'd say, 'Ah, that's a hardcore punk band.' The lyrics—if you read the lyrics, you would say the same thing. 'Love Canal' and all that."

Yet, in many ways, Flipper was really the anti-hardcore band. They played slow while almost everyone around them was playing fast, and they made a habit of taunting audience members and even other bands on occasion. "I like all the bands that opened for us," proclaimed a sarcastic Bruce Loose between songs during a 1983 show at CBGB's. "'1-2-3-4!' All the songs sound the same." (Though, he was quick to add, "So do ours.") He wasn't just being provocative in the moment, either. "That fast hardcore stuff is some of my least favorite music in the world," he says today. "I despise it."

The feeling was often mutual. Audiences would heckle them back, and the hardcore rank-and-file was outright hostile to them at times, as evidenced by their ongoing feud with *Maximum Rocknroll*. "They're fuckheads," said Will Shatter of the hardcore bible in a 1982 interview with *SMASH!* fanzine. "Some of these people out there are just [trying] to make bucks off of you." *MRR* responded with an "Open Challenge to Will Shatter," in which Jeff Bale (who had penned the zine's negative review of *Album*) and Tim Yohannan protested Shatter's accusations before imploring him to "take the needle out of your arm and investigate things before you go around slagging people off."[24]

For some, this sort of allergic reaction was a sign that Flipper was doing

24 *Maximum Rocknroll*, January/February 1983.

something right. "Really, part of the appeal of those guys for *me* was how much all of these people didn't like them—didn't like Flipper, didn't understand it," says Brandan Kearney. "That was definitely a selling point from my perspective. They had that sort of attitude of just sort of trying to undo their fanbase or make it difficult for whatever acclaim they were getting to necessarily stick." Gregg Turkington echoes this sentiment. "Basically, people who were really the oddballs and that never really fit in would go for Flipper, and the people who gravitated to punk rock because they liked torn jeans and Mohawks—they're the people who would not like Flipper. I think Flipper was hip to this trend. That's why they were such a thorn in the side of this whole crowd. They were really into taunting these people, and that was part of what made them so exciting, too."

MISTAKES

As Flipper chafed against the strictures of hardcore, they also struggled with their own identity. The period in between *Generic* and their second studio album, *Gone Fishin'*, was a time of existential crisis for the band, both onstage and off. Live, Flipper seemed less concerned with performing their songs correctly (whatever that meant) than with creating situations, spectacles, psychodramas.

From a purely musical perspective, their shows could be train wrecks at times. Yet the band also had an uncanny ability to play through mistakes and even incorporate them into the fabric of their performances. That ability, in turn, went hand in hand with their approach to rehearsing (rule number one, according to Loose: "*Do not* fucking practice a song to perfection") and their Zen-like attitude toward mistakes in general. "A mistake is something you don't do," says Bruce. "What you do when you have an issue when you're playing a song onstage is either, you make a big spectacle out of it and say, 'Okay, stop. This one's all messed up. Let's get it right'—or you fuckin' play through it. And you have to have confidence the whole fucking time you're playing through it. Or confidence in exploiting the buffoonery. Either way. It's really simple."

THE HARDCORE ERA

THIS BUD'S FOR YOU. L-TO-R: BRUCE, WILL, TED, STEVE. PHOTO BY VINCE ANTON STORNAIUOLO.

Matt Hall: It's probably not a great formula for most bands. You know, they'd collapse in a big mess and then start again and not be able to finish it again. Eventually, they'd have a half-hour or forty-minute set. And there'd always be a few people pissed because of the lack of professionalism. But it was all kind of part of the experience with them.

Lizzy Kate Gray: I *loved* Flipper's lackadaisical feeling—their approach to concerts. There'd maybe be some half-assed soundcheck that would last way too long, and then they'd half-assedly start to play. And Will would just banter and apologize for being so lame. And they'd never really play any songs. And yet you knew they *could*. There was this sort of Situationist feel to all of it, where it was just funny that there was a band onstage, and a lot of time would pass, and nothing would happen. The whole result of that was this crazy conflict going

237

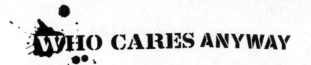

on onstage—of fuck-ups and people angry about it being a fuck-up, including some people in the audience who were throwing things or whatever, and then Will being his abstract self, making a commentary on it all. And that would just put me in seventh heaven.

Brandan Kearney: They had this thing where it was equally okay to play the song right or to play it wrong or to stop it halfway through, or to not play it at all and just argue about the *possibility* of playing it. With those guys, you didn't really get the feeling that there was this line between success and failure anymore or between competence and incompetence.

Flipper's 7-inch from this period, 'Get Away' b/w 'The Old Lady Who Swallowed the Fly,' illustrates this blurring of the lines between success and failure, competence and incompetence. 'Old Lady' is an adaptation of the old nursery rhyme, recorded at a rehearsal sometime in 1982 and (apart from the lyrics) largely improvised. It starts out tentatively, with Bruce halfway-singing the first couple of verses while Steve DePace attempts to lay down a steady beat, even as Ted and Will seem to ignore both him and each other. Not until the end of the third verse do they start to converge on a recognizable riff. Once they do, they gradually build up a head of stream behind Bruce, whose vocals grow more and more animated with each additional verse. What starts out as an utter mess winds up as a veritable clinic in conjuring order out of chaos.

'Get Away,' a hard-luck anthem in which Will name-checks an assortment of down-and-out friends and acquaintances, has its own quirks. Most notably, Will sings the entire second verse a full four bars ahead of the rest of the band. It's the kind of mistake that would cause most bands to stop the song right then and there. Shatter and company, however, play on without batting an eyelash; when the third verse rolls around, he reenters at the correct time like nothing ever happened. That said, it's one thing to play through this sort of mistake before a crowd at the On Broadway and another thing entirely to release this version of the song as the A-side of a single. Yet that sense of oblivious invincibility is part of what makes it compelling.

"I hadn't ever really heard anything like it," recalls Kearney, who bought the record around the time of its release in late 1982. "It wasn't something that just any musically naive or inept schmuck could just pick up and do at will. It still had this weird type of arc to it, or some sort of intuitive expertise to it, which I think was what seemed the most interesting about that. I can't really think of too many other things that gave you that same sense of new possibilities. Maybe *Metal Box*, but apart from that, I can't really think of anything else."

GONE FISHIN'

In contrast to 'Get Away,' *Gone Fishin'* sounds like a record that was labored over—and it was, at least off and on, for nearly two years. The basic tracks were actually recorded in the span of a single weekend session in September of 1982 (the same session that yielded 'Get Away'), but the album wasn't released until the late summer of 1984, by which point it had undergone an extreme makeover. "That was just one of those problematic records, where the mixing just went on forever," says Turkington, who was working at Subterranean in those days. "Bruce would go in and do his own mix, and then Steve DePace went in and did his own mix. And everybody was going in and overdubbing instruments, and the whole thing kind of got away from them a bit, I think. Because it was a much artier record. It's a great record—I wouldn't knock the record. But the final version is really different from the rough mixes."

Bruce recalls adding many of the overdubs during an all-night session with engineer Garry Creiman."We were all supposed to show up, but nobody showed up besides me," he recalls. "We snorted speed the whole time and drank, and I went to town—played piano parts, played bongo parts, played clavinet parts. All this shit. And everybody came in and freaked out." Some of those overdubs, like the clavinet on 'The Lights, the Sound, the Rhythm, the Noise' and the schizophrenic backing vocals on 'You Nought Me,' made it onto the album; meanwhile, the piano and percussion parts were redone by DePace, and the rest were vetoed for being too over-the-top.

As Creiman explains, the band actually recorded enough material for a double album. "We tracked a bunch of stuff. They proceeded to overdub on the tracks that they seemed to have the most interest in. We mixed what seemed

to be the best and most balanced for *Gone Fishin'*. There are still about an album's worth that needed to be mixed. Although a lot of what remained was, shall we say, a bit indulgent? A ten-to-twelve-minute version of 'Kali.' Will's spoken 'I Want to Talk.' 'In the Garden,' which we all referred to as 'In the Garbage.'"

The unreleased tracks are admittedly uneven, and a couple of them—'Flipper Blues' and 'In Your Arms'—would eventually surface in alternate (live) versions.[25] But there are also some lost gems amid the outtakes. Falconi singles out the extended version of 'Kali,' which was augmented with "sitars and tablas and saxophones and Bruno on lead guitar. I mean, it was like a real menagerie."[26] For Kirk Heydt, who played sarod on 'Kali' as well as saxophone on the album track 'First the Heart,' the highlight was 'In Your Arms.' "It's a brilliant song. I think it's his nod to Lou Reed's 'Heroin.' I think it's right there with it, and it's really poignant with the lyrics."

Though it doesn't mention her by name, 'In Your Arms' is addressed to Will's then-wife Jeri, and it speaks to the dire state of their lifestyle.[27] At one point, he rattles off a list of illicit substances (quaaludes, Dexedrine, heroin, PCP, MDA,

25 'Flipper Blues' appears in a superior version on the live *Public Flipper Limited.* 'In Your Arms' appears on the live *Blow'n' Chunks*, though in this case, the studio version is the definitive one.
26 Lyrically, 'Kali' echoes the apocalyptic themes expressed in another song that did make the album, 'One by One.'
27 Jeri is credited with the lyrics for the *Gone Fishin'* track 'First the Heart' as well as the A-side of Bruce's solo 7-inch, 'What's Your Name?'

DMT …) that, one surmises, the two had indulged in together. It is not a happy song, nor is it a harbinger of good things to come.

It was Jeri who persuaded Will to sit out Flipper's big East Coast tour in the spring of 1983. As Ted recalls, "We're getting ready to leave. Jeri is hangin' out the window: 'You leave, and everything you own will be out the window in three hours.'" Rather than canceling the tour, they went on the road without him, enlisting the versatile Bruno DeSmartass as a last-minute replacement. "I don't think Jeri wanted him to leave, but I don't think he wanted to go, either," says Bruno. "So it's like, 'Sorry guys, maybe you can get somebody else to go,' but with the hope that everything is canceled. So I went, and we had an *epic* time."[28] It was indeed an eventful tour, one that included a graduation party at a Princeton frat house, a stolen bass guitar, and a night in a New Jersey jail after a leaky gas tank gave police an excuse to pull them over and inspect their graffiti-covered van.(The cops found some spiked wristbands and an unmarked bottle of pills, though the charges were eventually dropped.)

Shatter rejoined the band when they returned to San Francisco that May, but by then, things were fragmenting. "In reality, Flipper kind of broke up in '83, '84," says Bruce. "We were all kind of pushing our own things." By this point, Ted was living part-time in Southern California, where he played in an early version of the infamous SWA, the brainchild of ex-Black Flag bassist Chuck Dukowksi. He commuted to San Francisco for occasional gigs and other band business ("It's like only 350 miles," he shrugs), including the ongoing work on *Gone Fishin'*. "We were in the middle of mixdowns when I got a call from LA: 'Get down here

---

28 One show from this tour—a May 14 gig at CBGB's—would later be released in its entirety as *Live at CBGB's* (Overground Records, 1997). Allegedly, Steve DePace brokered the deal without the other band members' knowledge, making it a quasi-bootleg (though accounts were later settled). "That show was like a gathering of the San Francisco tribes," recalls Bruno. "All of the Bad Posture guys were there. That's actually a really exemplary live recording. It's too bad there wasn't a DVD of it because it was fairly chaotic." According to Bruce, the May 14 recording was originally earmarked for release on the NYC-based cassette label ROIR—at least until Johnny Thunders, the ex-New York Dolls guitarist, tipped off label head Neil Cooper to the fact that Shatter wasn't on the recording. Flipper returned to CBGB's that November for a do-over, this time with Shatter in tow, to record the live shows from which their eventual ROIR release, *Blow'n' Chunks*, was compiled. Even with this delay, *Blow'n' Chunks* came out well before *Gone Fishin'*.

immediately.' It was during one of the biggest storms in LA. I got down to there, and I was baggin' sandbags for the next three days."

FROM MISSION-A TO ALPHABET CITY

When in San Francisco, Falconi would hole up at Mission-A, a legendary hardcore-era crash pad at 2448-A Mission Street. The two-story apartment building was a step up from the Vats but still far from luxurious. "It could have been a boarding house at one point, but it kind of became a punk rock household," says Anna-Lisa VanderValk, one of the tenants. "Because it had so many bedrooms, at any given time, there could be anywhere from eight to twenty people living there."[29] Among the other denizens of Mission-A were DePace, the Dead Kennedys' D.H. Peligro, Patrick O'Neil (a roadie for Flipper and the DKs who later went to jail for armed robbery and wrote a book about it all), Susan Miller, and several members of Bad Posture.

By 1983, both Miller and the Bad Posture contingent (minus Bruno DeSmartass and drummer John Surrell) had relocated to the Lower East Side of Manhattan, hoping for a change of scenery. By October of that year, Bruce had joined them, taking up residence in the basement of Miller's Third Street apartment. A period of feverish activity ensued—fueled by a plentiful supply of drugs, which were somehow even more prevalent in Manhattan than they were in San Francisco.

Emilio Crixell: It was pretty insane. It was wide open. Everywhere you went, it was right in front of you. We were living in the Lower East Side, near Alphabet City and all that. There was heroin being sold out of abandoned buildings. Our alarm clock on Avenue B was a guy selling heroin every morning at nine in the

29 Emilio Crixell was among the first of the more hardcore-friendly inhabitants of Mission-A. "At that time, when I first moved in, it was kind of a hodgepodge of kind of art students from the Art Institute who were kind of into punk rock but a little leery of it, too. A guy named Robert Sweeting—we called him 'Sweet'—he was kind of a patriarch there."

morning. He would be downstairs from us yelling. Every drug had a brand name. This one was called "The Mad." He would be there going, "The Mad is open, open and smokin'. Pass me by, you don't get high." Over and over. That was our alarm clock every day.

Susan Miller: It was grimy and dirty and crazy, like *Taxi Driver*. It was more *Taxi Driver* as opposed to being FAO Schwarz/Tom Hanks. So the kind of music that we made kind of reflected that pulsing energy and that insanity.

Bruce Loose: It was the old New York. It was the New York that you see in the seventies films. There was one film that was made during that time called *Alphabet City*, made between '83 and '85. A lot of the graffiti artists were into us. And in this film, you go through this one part where this young kid is walking along, and you see this huge "ASOA" graffiti along the whole side of the building.

"ASOA" was short for Altered States of America, an ephemeral band whose lineup included Miller and Loose along with free jazz saxophonist Daniel Carter and drummer Mike Ludlow (who took Surrell's place in the NYC incarnation of Bad Posture). There was also a singer, Philip Overbay, about whom little else is known. As the personnel might suggest, ASOA's sound was a mix of punk and jazz influences—not unlike Flipper's 'Sex Bomb' or 'First the Heart,' but by no means a carbon copy.

There were other fleeting projects from this era, such as Pure Schism, a band with five bassists (including Miller and Crixell), a drummer, and "this weirdo Puerto Rican guy named Manuel on vocals," as Miller puts it. "We could clear a room faster than anybody, man," says Crixell. "We had crazy ideas. The drugs were really good—what can I tell you?" ("It was a great band," adds Miller. "It was one of my favorite bands, quite frankly.")

Bruce's 1983 solo record, 'What's Your Name?' b/w 'Waking to Sleep' (Subterranean), actually predated his move to New York, but it's still representative of this mini-era and the altered state of mind that went along with it.[30] The B-side

---

30 The record is credited to Bruce Lose (without the second "o"), as he was still known at the time.

WHO CARES ANYWAY

is admittedly something of a mess, with Loose rapping over a collage of primitive cassette loops and other assorted noises. Much better is 'What's Your Name?' which features Miller's arpeggiated guitar along with lyrics by Jeri Wilkinson. Bruce supplies the fuzz bass (the only Flipper-ish aspect of the song) and sings near the top of his range with his voice cracking at times; more than one reviewer compared it to Neil Young.

Much like Altered States of America, 'What's Your Name?' might have signaled a "new direction for Flipperites," as one reviewer optimistically put it at the time.[31] Yet ultimately, neither project went anywhere. Loose wound up reconnecting with his Flipper bandmates upon the release of *Gone Fishin'*, while Miller was recruited to join Frightwig around the same time.[32] "I had fun with Bad Posture," she explains, "but the minute Frightwig came along and said, 'let's go,' I quit. Because it really wasn't me, you know? It wasn't me."

Thus ended a brief chapter in the Big Apple, one that yielded precious little in the way of documentation, apart from a few rehearsal tapes and some long-lost four-track recordings in the vein of 'What's Your Name?' "Bruce and I could have made some really amazing music together," laments Miller. "And we *did*. We had little tape recordings and everything, but that shit goes away. You can't capture those moments in time, in history, and really adequately explain them if you don't have recorded documentation. And a lot of it is not documented."

31 *SMASH!* Fall 1983.
32 As for Bad Posture, they recorded a 12-inch EP, 1983's *C/S*, while in New York. The lineup included three-fifths of the San Francisco version of the band, with Susan Miller and drummer Mike Ludlow taking the place of Bruno DeSmartass and John Surrell, respectively. The EP was later included on the CD compilation *G.D.M.F.S.O.B.* (Grand Theft Audio, 1996), along with studio and live recordings by the San Francisco lineup.

22

DEMORALIZATION

Meanwhile, back in San Francisco, Will Shatter was finding himself adrift as Flipper's future grew increasingly uncertain. Then again, at least some of that uncertainty stemmed from his own wavering commitment to the band. "Around late 1983, I think that Will was kind of sick of doing it," says Gregg Turkington."I think he found that limiting," agrees Craig Gray. "I think he was getting bored with it and the whole scene."

Even before sitting out the spring 1983 tour, Shatter had shown signs of restlessness. Turkington recalls seeing Flipper in Phoenix, Arizona, that March, a few weeks before the start of the East Coast tour. One of the opening bands that night was Sun City Girls, and Shatter evidently took a liking to them. "That was really early on," notes Turkington, "and they were really a strange group, but he totally saw the appeal—even though, basically, nobody liked the Sun City Girls for years. They were just one of those bands that was just *despised* around Phoenix because it didn't follow the punk rock rules—it was just a weird band."

"Will was very friendly," recalls Sun City Girls' Alan Bishop. "He and Charlie [Gocher, drummer for Sun City Girls] were hanging out drinking in the back somewhere. And I think he wrote him and stayed in touch with Charlie because Charlie gave him his address." As Turkington remembers, Shatter actually wrote a letter to Gocher and asked if he could join their band. "I never heard that," says Bishop. "Maybe it was true—maybe he wrote it to Charlie, or maybe he told him. I don't know how it would have worked. We weren't moving to the Bay Area at that point, and I don't think he was coming down to Phoenix, so I think it was maybe just some kind of an idea. But he was a very interesting character. Who knows?"

There were other signs of weariness, like 'I Want to Talk,' one of the unreleased tracks from the *Gone Fishin'* sessions. The song finds Shatter doing just what

the title suggests, addressing the audience in uncharacteristically direct fashion and offering some eerily accurate premonitions:

> Don't put us on any kind of pedestal
> Because if you do, and we're up there
> It's really gonna hurt a lot when we fall
> And sooner or later, we're gonna fall

Flipper had actually been playing 'I Want to Talk' live since at least February of 1982 (before *Album* was even released). Along with Loose's 'Flipper Blues,' the song illustrates a self-reflexive streak that would only become more pronounced over the next couple of years. "They were doing all these shows where they were criticizing Flipper during the show," recalls Turkington. "Which I thought was great. Because the music, I thought it sounded just as good as ever, but there was just this weird edge to it where they would come out and say, 'We're frauds. You've been had.' It was almost like the more popular they got, the more Will seemed to think that they had become this commercial entity that wasn't as pure anymore and that the live shows were just sort of a cash grab and a scam. Which was crazy to me because I thought the shows were as pure as they could get."

"The thing is, his being tired of it made the act wonderful," adds Lizzy Kate Gray. "Just that he would stand up there and talk about how bad they were and how sold out they were *as* a part of the performance—whether he really was separate from it and offering commentary on it, or whether he knew that was part of the act—*I* interpreted it as part of the act and just enjoyed it. Erving Goffman, the sociologist, talks about 'frontstage' and 'backstage' and about how we're all putting on some sort of show for each other. And the great thing about punk was that it mixed those two things—or at least Flipper did—where they'd have arguments on stage. They didn't present a united front. And he'd offer that commentary *on* the band."

THE HARDCORE ERA

60 SIXTH STREET

At the time, Will was living with Jeri in a converted warehouse space at 60 Sixth Street, amidst one of the seediest, most decrepit parts of South of Market. Apparently, that suited the couple just fine. "They were total drugged-out punk rockers," says Kim Seltzer, an occasional visitor in those days. "They kept the cat's litter box on the fire escape, and they never cleaned it. I remember looking out the window one day. It was a very punk rock moment." Yet despite the drab surroundings, the apartment became a popular hangout—one that resembled a cross between a French salon and a shooting gallery.

247

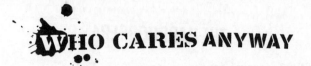

Gregg Turkington: Will would talk about heroin all the time, and I'd hang out with him. We'd go back to his place at five in the morning, and he'd shoot up. Or Craig would come over, or these lowlifes would show up, and they'd be doing heroin. Jeri would be sick all the time up in this loft—like really sick and just looking like *death*. It was clear it was some drug shit. But at the same time, that did feel like just a small part of his thing because, generally, he'd just be enthusiastically talking about music and art and philosophy and this and that. It was weird.

Lizzy Kate Gray: Jeri would be in a loft in the back of the warehouse, and you could hear her coughing and coughing. And somehow, I thought of *Camille*. I just remember thinking I was in an atelier in Paris, and Camille had consumption. I remember he had rats, and one of their names was "Egon," as in Egon Schiele, the artist. And the other one had some other name—it was something like "Rimbaud" or "Voltaire." But I do think he must have been reading European literature. And I think he would occasionally drop remarks about it, too.

Kim Seltzer: He was a really smart guy. He was a really lovely guy. It's funny: when you look at pictures of him, he was kind of all-American and almost preppy. Of course, he wasn't, but he could have been easily.

Lizzy Kate Gray: I mean, Will really *was* an intellectual in a way—in a good way, with a sense of humor. I think he fancied himself an intellectual, and maybe that's what people picked up on. But it wasn't offensive.

Paul Casteel: Onstage, he was a completely different person. He was really wild and stuff. But if you read his lyrics, you can get an idea of what he was like. Bruce had a little bit more bitter outlook and a drier sense of humor. Will was like Lao-Tzu. He was, like, Zen or something.

Despite being deep into drug addiction, Shatter acted as a sort of mentor to the likes of Casteel, Turkington, and a friend of Turkington's by the name of Grux—who, like Gregg, was still just a teenager at the time and not at all interested in drugs. "Grux and me and Will would just go do stuff," recalls Turkington."A lot of dumpster diving and just a lot of chatter about art and all this kind of shit. Will turned me on to a lot of great stuff, like Leonard Cohen. His idol was Leonard Cohen.

"And then Will was really into this collage art," he continues. "He would get all these old books out of thrift stores or dumpsters or whatever, with really detailed black-and-white line drawings, and then he would sit there with the Exacto knife at four in the morning and just piece together these really amazing little collages. He was just really into just doing art for the sake of it. Like, he'd find dead pigeons in the neighborhood and take them into the house and bleach the bones and then make these mobiles out of them. Just really strange projects."

Shatter's punk rock lifestyle was a far cry from his childhood in nearby Gilroy. His family, it seems, held out hope that it was all just a phase that he would eventually outgrow. "Will wasn't like a spoiled brat or anything," explains Debi Sou. "It was nothing like that. But if Will's father came to visit, he always gave him money. If Will had a problem, his father would be there for him. But Will never asked.

"I did meet Will's father once," she continues. "He was a very nice man, and he loved Will very much. And yes, he was very sad that Will was living an anarchist lifestyle. But he wasn't *mad* at Will. He was very sad. He thought that he had done something wrong—that he didn't do something sufficiently enough—so that's why Will was living on beans for three days a week and that kind of stuff. But I think that Will had a really good connection with his father."

GENE

Perhaps Shatter's strongest connection to his past was an old friend from back home by the name of Gene Benczak. Among other things, Benczak was the inspiration for 'The Wheel,' whose first four lines ("**G**oodness won't help you / **E**veryone knows / **N**othing can help you / **E**verything is mine") make up an acrostic for his first name. "He used to work construction," explains Joe Pop-O-Pie, "and in order for him to get all psyched to go into work, he would do this thing—he'd crack

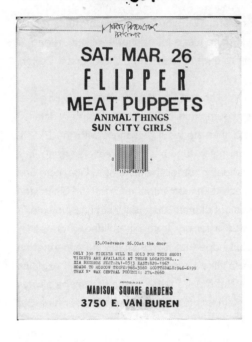

MARTY PRODUCTIONS
PRESENTS

SAT. MAR. 26
FLIPPER
MEAT PUPPETS
ANIMAL THINGS
SUN CITY GIRLS

0 11240 48770 4

$5.00 advance $6.00 at the door

ONLY 350 TICKETS WILL BE SOLD FOR THIS SHOW!
TICKETS ARE AVAILABLE AT THESE LOCATIONS...
ZIA RECORDS WEST:241-0513 EAST:829-1967
ROADS TO MOSCOW TEMPE:968-3860 SCOTTSDALE:946-6199
TRAX N' WAX CENTRAL PHOENIX: 274-2660

PRINTED IN U.S.A.

MADISON SQUARE GARDENS
3750 E. VAN BUREN

open a beer in the morning and look in the mirror and say 'I am the wheel! I am the wheel!' and swing his arm around. And Will used to see this and laugh."

To Will's friends and associates from the Negative Trend days, Gene was not such a benign influence. "He was kind of a rich kid," says Peter Urban. "Will had been a rich kid. So he'd grown up in rich circles, if you will, but had rejected it. But when Gene came back into town, he sort of fell in with him. And Gene was a major alcoholic, but he also used junk, and that's how Will got into doing it. But just the fact that he was hanging out with his childhood rich-kid buddy seemed very unlike the Will that I knew." Craig Gray has a similar recollection. "When I first met Will, we were really close. We wrote songs together; we lived together. But then Will got more involved with Gene. And they started coming up with the concept of Flipper, and we kind of grew apart."

Despite their growing differences, Gray and Shatter made an attempt to reconnect musically around this time. "Will wanted to do something that sounded like Leonard Cohen," says Gray. "So the guitars weren't noisy. I think there was actually an acoustic guitar on one song. Will hadn't really learned how to sing to that kind of music yet. He was still trying to do the Flipper shout, rather than more talking." They recorded some songs together, but they were never released, and the two of them never played any shows together as a duo. "We were gonna try to do something," says Gray, "but we were both doing lots of drugs, and things got in the way, as they do. It really didn't go anywhere."

DEAD BEATS

Toiling Midgets were having their own struggles around this time, and as with Flipper, drugs were a big part of the story. The sense of desolation that comes through on parts of *Sea of Unrest* and, even more so, on 1983's cassette-only *4-Track Mind* was evidently a reflection of their collective state of mind.[33] "Everybody was doing speed—speed and acid," recalls Kim Seltzer. "You'd do speed for three days, and then you'd drop acid. That accounted for a lot of ghosts—seeing a lot of ghosts."

For a brief time during this era, the Midgets were managed by Adam Parfrey, better known for his later role as head of controversial indie publisher Feral House.[34] Seltzer again: "Adam used to say to me, 'You know what you're doing—taking speed and then taking acid to come down off of speed—that's exactly what the Nazis used to do to brainwash people.' But we were constantly in this kind of liminal state, where you'd start to see other dimensions."

One anecdote, in particular, captures the paranormal aura that surrounded the group in those days. As Seltzer recounts:

> I come over one night, and Ricky's sitting there, and he was just being a *dick.* He was irritating me. So I said to him, "I know what you're thinking, Ricky." He goes, "You don't know what I'm thinking." I go, "Yeah, I *do* know what you're thinking." He had a magazine in his hands. "You're thinking *tank.*" And he opens up this magazine. He had been looking at

---

33 Several of the songs on *4-Track Mind* appear elsewhere in different versions. The instrumental 'Aaron's Song' appears (with vocals) on *Live 1982 Vol. 1* as 'Dream on Jesus' and on *Vol. 2* as 'Walk on Jesus.' The instrumental 'Trust' appears on *Dead Beats* in a different instrumental version (with live drums instead of drum machine) under the title 'Before Trust'; it also appears (this time with vocals) as 'Before Trusting Ricky' on both of the 1982 live albums. The instrumental 'Train' eventually resurfaced (again, with vocals) as 'Train Song' on the digital-only *Little Ricky*, recorded in 1991 but not released until 2017.

34 Peter Urban managed the Midgets in their early days before exiting the music scene to focus on political activism. Parfrey went on to co-found the zine *EXIT* with Seltzer and George Petros.

a picture of an Israeli tank, and I just somehow picked up on it. I don't know how it happened. And after that, he thought I was like a psychic— he thought I could read people's minds.

Ricky was out of the picture by the time the Midgets went back into the studio to record the material for their second LP, *Dead Beats*.[35] In the meantime, they had added a third guitarist, Annie Ungar, whom they'd met while on tour in Portland in 1982. Her slide guitar playing on tracks such as 'Black Idol' and 'Night Science (Preludes)' has a vocal quality to it, filling at least some of the empty space created by Ricky's absence.

It wasn't a happy time for the band, though. Ungar and Tim Mooney soon became an item, and, like Gray, the two of them were descending deeper into drug addiction. "I was doing speed; they were doing heroin," summarizes guitarist Paul Hood. "And you can't get somebody on speed and somebody on heroin to agree on very much." Adds Gray, "Those recording sessions were full of … strife. Everybody was doing their fair amount of drugs, dividing into camps—all that dumb rock shit. Rock band shit. And things usually end when they're that intense."

By the time *Dead Beats* finally came out in 1985, the band had long since broken up. As Hood explains, "Aaron Gregory was playing bass, and he and I were like Mr. Happy, Mr. Perky, and those guys were kind of like the downers. So it got more and more friction-y, to the point where we just said—or I said, and Craig said—'Annie's gotta go.' And then Tim said, 'Fine, well, I'm going, too.'"

Gray picked up and moved to London, where he spent the next several years clearing his head. "I needed to clean up myself, get a whole new look at life," he says. "No one knew anything about the Midgets over there. No one gave two shits." Meanwhile, Hood moved back to Seattle, and before long, Mooney

---

35 He does appear on two tracks on the original LP—a version of the Sleepers' 'She's Fun' (which Gray co-wrote with Williams and Michael Belfer) and 'Funk Song,' a bizarre misstep and the only time the Midgets ventured anywhere near funk territory. Both of these tracks were outtakes from the *Sea of Unrest* sessions, and Gray left them off of the digital-only reissue of *Dead Beats*, which was pared down to five songs. Also omitted from the digital version are 'Incendiary' (known elsewhere as 'Do the Incendiary') and 'California' (actually an instrumental version of *Sea of Unrest* track 'Big Surprise').

followed, along with Michael Belfer, who was having his own struggles post-Sleepers. "The theory was, they wanted to get a fresh start, and they didn't know anybody, and they wouldn't have any drug dealers to get in their way, etc., etc.," says Hood. "And that didn't last too long." All of them would eventually wind up back in San Francisco by end of the decade, but for the time being, they just needed to get away—from the city, from each other, and from the lifestyles they'd been leading. "The whole drug train can be a real rut," says Gray. "For the music to develop, we need to evolve."

FROM SPEED TO HEROIN

The drug train had already claimed its share of casualties by this point, and it showed no signs of slowing down. In 1983, Don Vinil—Shatter and Gray's bandmate in the short-lived Grand Mal—died of an overdose in New York City, where his band, the Offs, had relocated a few years earlier.[36] The cumulative effects of years' worth of hard living were rearing their head.

Mia Simmans: It's hard to imagine now, but in the early eighties, everybody was taking whatever there was. And then some people got hooked. Because I think people are either born with the addictive thing or not. And those of us who are end up getting into it, and that really changes your priorities a lot.

Speed was always around. And after a few years, you're ready to relax a little bit. Which is where heroin came in. That's a really boring drug, frankly. You just exist on this really singular plane that makes your life really simple in some ways because you're just dealing with this one thing. That's your priority. And all these

---

36 Their one and only studio LP, *The Offs' First Record*, was already in the can when he died. "It was a pretty good record," says drummer Bob Steeler. "It wasn't quite as crazy as the earlier stuff, so I don't think it got the same kind of marks. But I liked it because it was groove-oriented, and it was fun for me to play on the drums." The record, which features a cover by artist Jean-Michel Basquiat, came out in 1984 and has since become a collector's item. However, it received little attention at the time, as the band had already broken up, electing not to continue without the charismatic Vinil.

other things don't affect you; they don't touch you—like normal life things. It's just kind of a tunnel vision sort of existence.

Ted Falconi: If it wasn't for speed, I don't think the music scene would've been what it was. Being up at two o'clock in the morning, you know, for the last band that goes on at midnight or one o'clock. They would close the club down at two, and everybody's still, you know, "Let's go out and get something to eat." And all that would have never happened if people were straight.

Debi Sou: Especially in the San Francisco scene, because of the drugs—because of the Methedrine—there were a lot of people quite busy with the political side and organizing things, being busy, being active. And I think that heroin has another effect on people. It just makes you lazy. You're just not even functioning. You can't deal with anything. You just want to be in that one sedated energy because it's just all too much for your feelings.

Denny DeGorio: In '77, '78, '79 maybe, heroin wasn't that accessible in San Francisco. And when it was, it was Turkish dope and Persian dope and occasionally China White. Later, there started to be an influx of Mexican tar and dope cut with fentanyl, and then it started to become a lot more accessible, and everybody was getting strung out. By then, I was out of there. I mean, that shit followed me around my whole fuckin' life. I was afraid it was gonna kill me. I got out of there with my life still intact.

Peter Urban: I saw it as a period of demoralization, where people who had been shooting meth started shooting heroin. And the Midgets were part of that as well. It was when a lot of the original bands were breaking up, and we had a lot of people who weren't part of the original scene come in from the suburbs. In the early days, it felt like a community of rejects who were happy in each other's company. And then it started becoming—you know, there were rivalries, and people started getting worried about whether they were gonna get signed. It just wasn't what it had been, so I think the demoralization was a natural thing to set in.

But the way in which part of the scene responded to it was by getting

THE HARDCORE ERA

into junk. And Will was one of them. I just kind of felt that he was a stronger personality than that, so I kind of held it against him, in a manner of speaking. I thought it was an easy out for Will, is I guess what I thought. I thought he caved in too easily to the pressures. He was an in-your-face kind of person.

Tommy Antel: At the end of any scene, like the Haight-Ashbury, it kind of gets weird. A lot of people turn to dope. A lot of the creativeness that people saw from the meth, it was really a mirage. I think people, especially addicts, don't realize that they can be just as creative without the medication; a lot of people I know didn't get a chance. Their fear was that they couldn't create unless they were in that kind of situation. There's this fantasy where you need to have a dimly lit closet, a lightbulb, and a spoon to write poetry, good poetry, or something. It's not really necessarily the case. It can get dark in there.

Joe Pop-O-Pie: One thing you've gotta realize about a lot of the alliances that are formed artistically is that the people are into the same kind of drugs. They even attract an *audience* that's into the same kind of drugs. It's like this metaphysical vibe.

Craig Gray: I don't think the drugs influenced the sound. It influenced the places our heads went. But the sound was something that was always there. I mean, it's been there and evolved slightly all the time, through taking drugs and not taking drugs. Whether it would have evolved exactly like it has, I don't know. It's always hard to say with that because you can't make the comparison.

But I think we might have taken a lot more risks, which is more our personalities. We were willing to risk taking the drugs; we were also willing to risk doing those things musically. They might go part and parcel. But what we tried not to do was let them take over the band, and usually, when that happened, the band broke up. So in that respect, the only way I would say it affected the music is that it caused us to stop playing it sometimes.

THE MID-EIGHTIES

23

THE POP-O-PIES:IN GOD WE TRUCK

Most of the bands that you go out to see
Save the hit till the end, and it's all real cheese-y
But there's only one group, and it comes from San Fran
That will play you the hit over and over again
– The Pop-O-Pies, 'Pop-O-Rap'

Elementary penguin, singin' Hari Krishna
Man, you shoulda seen the Pistols in '78
—The Pop-O-Pies, 'I Am the Walrus'

When the Sex Pistols played Winterland, Joe Pop-O-Pie was still Joe Callahan, an undergraduate music major at Glassboro State College in southern New Jersey. And while the Winterland show was indeed a pivotal moment for many young punks and punks-to-be, it wasn't until a year or so later that year that Joe—who until that point had been preoccupied with the works of twelve-tone composers like Webern and Schoenberg—had his own punk rock epiphany.

"I thought it was magical because it healed all these stress-related diseases I had," he says of the music of bands like the Pistols, Ramones, and Devo. "I thought, 'There's something to this, so I gotta get into it.' So I just became a punk-rock-o-phile and found a punk rock element, which in 1979 was about a half a dozen people at this college in New Jersey."

Several of those friends were on hand for Callahan's senior recital, which created enough of a stir to warrant a full-page spread in the *Philadelphia Inquirer*. "Imagine the Philadelphia Orchestra having a pie fight in the middle

of Beethoven's Fifth, and you get a small idea what Joe Callahan's recital at Glassboro State College was like," wrote one Frank Rossi in the March 23, 1980, edition of the paper.[1] The performance included one piece, 'Fascists Eat Donuts,' that would later resurface as a Pop-O-Pies song; Rossi describes the recital version as "a baroque piece in which Callahan played piano nimbly and well." More controversial, however, was the finale, in which Joe took the stage "wearing a devil mask and a white lab coat and carrying a machine gun" and then proceeded to mock the chair of the music department—who subsequently brought the budding composer up on disciplinary charges and even threatened legal action.(The charges were ultimately dropped, and Callahan graduated later that spring.)

It was not long after the recital that Callahan hit upon the idea for what would become the Pies' signature song: a punk version of the Grateful Dead's 'Truckin'.' As they did with 'Fascists Eat Donuts,' the Pop-O-Pies were known to perform entire sets consisting solely of 'Truckin'' (played "over and over again," as the bandleader boasts in 'Pop-O-Rap'). "The original version was real squeaky like the Buzzcocks were playing it," he explains. "We started off playing that version of it, and then we began to do an improvisational thing where we'd kinda take it *out there*, so by the end it would sound like John Cage was sitting in with the Pop-O-Pies—like the Residents doing '(I Can't Get No) Satisfaction.' You'd think

---

1   Frank Rossi, "Composition (Burp) in Un-Natural from a Zany Glassboro Musician." The Philadelphia Inquirer. Sunday, March 23, 1980. Another choice excerpt from the article: "Some of Joe Callahan's teachers say he is a talented young composer. A few even call him a genius. Then there are those who angrily dismiss Callahan's work as junk."

that might be boring to hear a band play the same song over and over. But it *wasn't* because it was different every time."

With a demo tape of 'Truckin'' in hand, Callahan moved out west in the summer of 1980, first landing in San Jose before eventually moving up to San Francisco. It would take a year or so for the first Pop-O-Pies lineup to come together—they made their live debut on September 26, 1981, at the Berkeley Square, opening for the Waitresses of 'I Know What Boys Like' fame—and even then, it was a revolving-door affair. Indeed, the bandleader would often facetiously claim that the group played only one song because that's all they had time to learn, and besides, the sound systems in most clubs were so bad that most people wouldn't notice anyway.

THE WHITE EP

The Pop-O-Pies' first steady lineup coalesced around a backing band that included Tanks' Mark Bowen and Ben Cohen on guitar and drums, respectively. Cohen recalls his first encounter with Joe:

> I was at this warehouse party, and this weird guy approached me, and
> he was kind of tweaky. I've forgotten if he knew I was a drummer or if he
> just said, "Do you play drums? Do you want to play in my band?" And
> I said, "Sure." No idea who he was. "We're playing at Le Disque next
> week." "Okay, great." "So, here's what I want you to do. Come over to
> my house at this time." So I go over there, and it's just him. And I didn't
> have my drums. So he just tells me, "Here's what we're gonna do. Here's
> how the songs go." So he just starts telling me. "Okay. What the fuck?"
>
> So at the appointed time at Le Disque, I show up with my drums,
> and then there's some guy playing guitar and someone playing bass—I
> couldn't tell you who it was now. So we set up, and he goes, "Okay,
> we're just gonna play." And I think it must've been 'Truckin',' because
> that's the only song that the guitar and bass player knew. I don't think
> they had met either. "Okay, let's all play 'Truckin'.'" So we start playing,

and Joe has a can of spray paint, and he goes up and starts spray painting "Pop-O-Pies" on the wall. The owner came running out, and she was *livid*—she was enraged. "Get out of here!" She tells us to "get out!" That was it. The show lasted about, you know, two minutes. "Get out of here!"

They had better luck with radio. The 'Truckin'' demo made its way to Howie Klein, who in those days was deejaying at KUSF, the radio station of the Jesuit-run University of San Francisco. "I didn't really know what the hell I was doing when I got here," admits Pop-O-Pie. "I just wanted to hear my music on the radio, like a couple of times—I thought it would be fun … and it got to be the most requested song on KUSF for three months running or something, toward the end of 1981." Sensing he might have a novelty hit on his hands, Klein set about trying to contact Joe—an elusive figure in those days, as he lacked a permanent address, much less a telephone number. "He finally caught up with me in early 1982, and he said, 'Hey, do you wanna do a deal?'"

By September of that year, the Pop-O-Pies were setting up shop in the Automatt—perhaps the most upscale recording studio in town in those days—to put the finishing touches on *The White EP* for Klein's 415 Records. Released later that year, the record featured not one but two versions of 'Truckin'': a revamping of the original demo, plus a rap version in the then-current style of Sugarhill Records. Rounding out the mini-album were a couple of topical songs in 'The Catholics Are Attacking' and 'Timothy Leary Lives' as well as a (relatively) abbreviated version of 'Fascists Eat Donuts'—a one-chord anthem that rivals Flipper's 'Brainwash' as an exercise in high-concept tedium.[2] Of the Forty Minutes of 'Truckin''

A few months before *The White EP*'s release, Klein and company had signed a distribution deal with Columbia Records. Next to 415's stable of well-coiffed new wave bands—Romeo Void, Translator, Wire Train, and the Red Rockers—the Pop-O-Pies were veritable black sheep. Still, they benefited from the label's promotional muscle, which helped land them a tour of the East Coast in early 1983.

Evidently, audiences there didn't quite know what they were in for. "People had a certain expectation," recalls Cohen."You know, 'This band's got a record out, they might be on college radio, so let's go see them'—not really knowing what to expect." Unfortunately, there were no video crews on hand, but an audio recording from a March 4 show at Zappa's in Brooklyn gives some idea of the madness that ensued. At one point, a delirious fan takes the mic and begins

---

2   Like the original 'Truckin',' the *White EP* version of 'Catholics Are Attacking' was originally recorded back in New Jersey before Callahan moved to San Francisco in 1980. "For the recording of *The White EP*, I felt it would be a good idea to get Jeff Ruzich, who was one of my music major buddies from Glassboro State College in New Jersey (now known as Rowan University), to come out to California and record the album with us," explains the bandleader. "I did this because I wanted the same bass player through all six songs for the sake of having a more consistent sound. It worked. Jeff Ruzich went back to New Jersey right after the recording of *The White EP*." Because Ruzich wasn't available for the photoshoot, a stand-in was needed. Enter Rachel Thoele (Mark Bowen's girlfriend at the time), who appears on the back cover wearing a paper bag over her head.

chanting, "Get this *shit* over with!" and then "Play somethin' different! Play somethin' different!" as the band chugs along behind him.[3]

"The most hostility we got was playing in Providence," adds Cohen."I think it went on for two hours. Because they wouldn't turn the power off, and we just kept playing, and people were just … hating us. I mean, *actually* hating us—not just mad. I think they really wanted to hurt us. And we just kept playing. In that particular case, it ended with people screaming at us—you know, 'Fags, go back to Frisco.'"

As with Flipper, the audience reaction was often as much a part of a Pop-O-Pies show as the band's actual performance was. "They were really kind of testing the audience's patience or tolerance for what they were doing, to the point where it was kind of cartoonish and funny," notes Tom Wheeler, who booked them at Club Foot on multiple occasions. "And this is in a context where you had the remnants of the hippie scene. So when the Pop-O-Pies would go to a venue and do forty minutes of 'Truckin',' it's because most people in San Francisco had had their fill of the hippie thing and the Dead and all of that kind of stuff."

David Katz: The first time I saw them was at the Stone. And I recall that the UK Subs had just played, like the night before or something, and they were in the audience at the back. In those days, the whole show would just be 'Truckin'.' You know, it could be forty minutes of 'Truckin',' or an hour, or more. So, I remember the lead singer from UK Subs at the bar saying to me, basically, "These guys would never get away with this in England. They'd skin them alive."

Lizzy Kate Gray: You could say that they played 'Truckin'' for half an hour, and no incredible solos happened or nothing happened. But something about being there and seeing this whole thing unwinding in such an absurd way—I mean, it was absurd that they played 'Truckin',' and while you were there, it became increasingly absurd with every minute that they *continued* playing 'Truckin'.' I

---

3 Bowen was unable to go on the tour because of an illness. His place was taken by Mike King, a close friend of Joe's and a frequent stand-in on guitar and/or bass for the Pop-O-Pies in the years to come. Cohen: "I just remember, the few times I actually heard him play guitar on that tour … it had nothing to do with the song we were playing."

THE MID-EIGHTIES

★☆ **AT THE KABUKI** ☆★

Sun., Dec. 26/9 PM **OINGO BOINGO**
Plus MUTANTS/POP-O-PIES

just would reach this level of bemused nirvana, somehow.

Ben Cohen: We got this good show with Flipper at the On Broadway.[4] It seemed like it was our first high-profile show where there were a lot of people. We started doing the 'Truckin'' thing, and at first, people were laughing. And then Joe would announce, "Okay, we're gonna play a different song now," and we'd start playing 'Truckin'' again. "No, this time we're *really* gonna play a different song." And we'd play 'Truckin'' again. At first, people were laughing, but then after about six times, people were *pissed*—like, *really* pissed. Whatever people could grab, it was coming on the stage. Beer. A lot of beer.

Joe Pop-O-Pie: We just played 'Truckin'' over and over again. And we were really insulting the audience, just taking no prisoners, saying things like, "You kids think you're so individual. Well, you're all wearing the same leather jackets and have the same haircuts. It looks like a goddamn military school out there." And they were just attacking us. I mean, they were throwing glass. It was the

4 The likely date of this show was February 6, 1982, as this is the only time Flipper and the Pop-O-Pies are known to have played on the same bill.

real deal. They were aiming to hit us. I had to hide behind amps, and there were just bottles cracked everywhere. It was exciting.

Ben Cohen: And we wouldn't get off the stage—you know, we just kept playing. And whoever is on the side of the stage [whispering]: "Come on!" We'd just say, "Okay, we're gonna stop now." And they'd say, "Okay, great." Joe would always start off the song by counting it off—his trademark "1-2-3-4!" So he'd count it off—we'd start playing it again.

Joe Pop-O-Pie: Eventually, they just cut the power off. After I picked up one of the bottles and tried to throw it, one of the stagehands grabbed my hand and grabbed it out of it.

The Pop-O-Pies were in their element playing to hostile crowds, and their brief tenure with 415 gave them plenty of opportunities to do so. On December 26, 1982, for example, they opened for Oingo Boingo at the Kabuki Theatre—a Bill Graham venue, "so it was very organized and machinelike," says Bowen. "We had union roadies. We couldn't adjust the angle of our equipment. They had to come up and move it for us. That kind of stuff."

Ben Cohen: Oingo Boingo had all their stuff set up on the stage, and they didn't want to break it down, so we had to set up in front of it. And part of the whole Pop-O-Pies thing was that we were throwing beer everywhere. And Oingo Boingo didn't like that, so they were kind of standing by the side of the stage watching us.

Mark Bowen: They were a fine band, but they were the kind that spent fifteen minutes getting the tone on their electronic hi-hat just right. And we were the kind that went up and we hadn't practiced for two months, so we'd use the soundchecks to practice. [Laughs.] Kind of like that. So they weren't happy about us.

Ben Cohen: Anyway, so we started playing 'Truckin',' and all these people in the audience just had no frame of reference for this kind of idiocy. They just stood there. I think we played it three times. In the dressing room, they had given us a fifty-gallon garbage can full of beer. So we had dragged it out onstage. And at first, Joe was starting to throw the beers out in the audience, and then he started selling them. So people started throwing money on the stage, and he was throwing the beers out, and all of the sudden, he said something like, "More! I want more money!" And there was this deluge of change. At that point, he dropped the mic, and he was on his hands and knees scrounging for money. Then the curtain came down.

The Pop-O-Pies were playing with house money, having turned a would-be novelty song into the basis for an extended conceptual joke whose punchline kept evolving. At one point, they enlisted a Jerry Garcia lookalike to serve as pre-show emcee. ("Of course, people didn't *know* that it wasn't him," says Cohen of the doppelganger.) Before long, they were posing for a *Rolling Stone* photographer with the real Jerry Garcia—another result of the Howie Klein publicity machine in action. Cohen: "They whisked us in and took the picture, and then, 'Get outta here, you assholes!'"

ENTER FAITH NO MORE

By the time the *Rolling Stone* article hit newsstands in September of 1983, much had transpired. "I just remember thinking how ridiculous it was. It was *after* the scene, more or less," says Cohen. "You know, *Rolling Stone*, of course, in their utter cluelessness, is writing about something after it happens."

Indeed, a changing of the guard was underway, not only with the Pop-O-Pies but with the proverbial scene in general. Flipper was on the verge of breaking up, and Romeo Void—the third band featured in the *Rolling Stone* piece (along with Flipper and the Pop-O-Pies)—was in the process of being chewed up and spit out by 415/Columbia after a couple of minor hits. Joe himself had spent the summer couch-surfing through the Northeast US following the Pop-O-Pies' East Coast tour. Needing a place to stay (and a new rhythm section) upon his return to San Francisco, he reached out to his pals in an obscure local band known as Faith. No More.

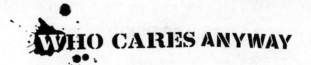

WHO CARES ANYWAY

As it happens, FNM was also in a state of flux at the time. They had recently changed their name (from Faith. No Man) and jettisoned guitarist/front man Mike Morris, a founding member and their primary songwriter up to that point.[5] That left bassist Bill Gould and drummer Mike Bordin—both of them undergrads at UC Berkeley who'd met upon joining Morris's band in 1981—and keyboardist Roddy Bottum, a childhood friend of Gould's from LA who was taking film classes at SF State.[6] What ensued was a sort of temporary merger between the two bands, with Callahan and Pop-O-Pies guitarist Bowen (the lone holdover from the *White EP* lineup) both contributing to FNM over the next year and Gould, Bordin, and Bottum doing likewise for the Pop-O-Pies.[7] They even shared living arrangements for a time, in the form of an old Victorian apartment at 109-A Shotwell Street in the Mission.

Joan Osato: It was very typical for that time, in terms of cheap housing. Certainly, at all the houses where we lived together, we had more people than we had room for. That house was probably like a one-bedroom, and Roddy and Bill and I were living there.

Bill Gould: We had a thing at that house where we weren't gonna clean the house. No matter what, we wouldn't clean anything. And we didn't have any furniture, so basically dirty clothes just sat on the floor, and you'd sleep on the dirty clothes and use that as a bed. Roddy had a couple of mice living *in* his dirty clothes, so you'd wake up in the morning and see mice running around in the house. That was really fucked up.

---

5   Bottum joined Faith. No Man during the summer of 1983, replacing original keyboardist Wade Worthington. It wasn't long before Gould quit, with Bordin and Bottum soon following suit. It was at this point that they re-formed under the name of Faith. No More, though it would take them another year or so to drop the period from their name and sort out the rest of their lineup.
6   As Joe recalls, he met the two of them after his band's set at the aforementioned Flipper/Pop-O-Pies show at the On Broadway. At the time, the Pop-O-Pies' bassist was Joe Hornof, a dorm mate of Gould's at UC Berkeley.
7   Bottum appears (under the name Roddy Cougar Mellencamp) on a couple of tracks on *Joe's Second Record,* but he was not part of the live band.

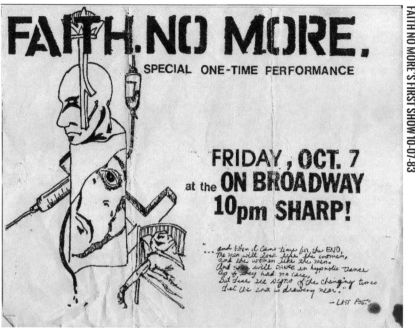

FAITH NO MORE'S FIRST SHOW 10-07-83

Joe Pop-O-Pie: I was crashing on Bill and Roddy's floor until I could find a place when one day Courtney Love walked through the door, and I said to her, "Hey, I know you—you're that gal I met in Portland when we were touring with Iggy Pop." So, at that point, it was me *and* Courtney crashing on Bill and Roddy's floor.

The trio of Gould, Bordin, and Bottum would spend the next year publicly auditioning an array of singers and guitarists—beginning with an October 7, 1983, appearance at the On Broadway featuring none other than Joe Pop-O-Pie on vocals. It was a short set—about twenty minutes, the entirety of which was recorded and later released as side one of FNM's first demo tape. Joe doesn't sing so much as talk and occasionally shout over the music, at one point referring to the new combo (in the third person) as "the best band to come out of Frisco since the Pop-O-Pies."[8] (As Gould recalls, the singer's initial idea was to read the newspaper while they played. "And we were like, 'Come on, man, we're fuckin' playin' hard up here—put *somethin'* into it! Let's get something out of you. I don't care what you do, but just don't read the fuckin' newspaper!'")

In the meantime, the new Pop-O-Pies lineup was up and running. A mere week after Faith. No More's live debut, they played Los Angeles, where they earned a special kind of rave review from the *LA Weekly*'s Craig Lee:

> We can all relax now: The search for absolutely the worst band in California was abruptly ended Wednesday night when San Francisco's Pop-O-Pies took the stage at the Music Machine. The twist is that the band would probably relish the honor of that title. For forty-five minutes, the quartet alternated between two songs: 'Truckin'' and a piece that featured a non-stop chord and a singalong chorus about making doughnuts for the chief of police.[9]

Evidently, the new lineup was just as polarizing as the previous one, even if they had now expanded their repertoire to include two different songs. They would soon pare it back down to one, playing entire sets of nothing but 'Fascists Eat Donuts' (instead of entire sets of 'Truckin''). "It was just one chord, and we did whole sets—like an hour—of just one chord," recalls Gould. "That was actually one of the highlights of my life. That formed what I expect out of an audience as a musician. Because it goes through these periods where it's *real* audience interaction."

As with the earlier lineup's versions of 'Truckin',' performances of 'Fascists Eat Donuts' elicited a full spectrum of audience reactions—reactions that became part of the spectacle that was a Pop-O-Pies show. "In the beginning, people are waiting for the change," recounts Gould. "Then, after five minutes, they realize you're not gonna change, and they're starting to laugh with each

---

8   As offhanded as those contributions seem, some of Callahan's lyrics would later resurface, in altered form, on later records by both the Pop-O-Pies (two different versions of 'The Words of Jamal') and Faith No More ('Why Do You Bother?' from *We Care a Lot* and 'Spirit' from *Introduce Yourself*).
9   Craig Lee, "Pop-O-Pies Puts an End to the Search" (sic). *LA Weekly*, October 21, 1983.

THE MID-EIGHTIES

other. Then after about ten minutes, they're going, 'Okay, the joke's over. It's not funny anymore.' And then you keep playing it, and after about twenty minutes, people start getting pissed off and then start throwing stuff. And from about twenty minutes to about forty minutes, they start screaming at you: 'Stop!' And you keep doing it, and you break through this wall, where it's kind of like all the stages of death. And then there's just acceptance, passive acceptance when people just realize it's not gonna end," he laughs. "Then it kind of ends after that. It was an amazing thing.

"There was this one show we did at this warehouse in Dallas, Texas, where we played 'Fascists Eat Doughnuts' for so long that I was actually starting to hallucinate. I was starting to hear new melodies and new songs because it was just this drone that was going on relentlessly. That stands out the most."

JOE'S SECOND RECORD

It is this version of the group that appears on the aptly titled *Joe's Second Record*. Clocking in at just under sixteen minutes, it's technically just an EP. Yet, in Borgesian fashion, the Pop-O-Pies manage to condense more ideas into a quarter-hour than most of their peers could have fit on a C-90 cassette.

The record opens with a lumbering version of 'Truckin',' with the Gould/Bordin rhythm section resembling a cross between Flipper and Killing Joke, and Mark Bowen (the lone holdover from the *White EP* lineup) adding his own brand of caustic noise guitar. This is followed by a succession of short, topical songs: the self-referential 'Pop-O-Rap'; 'Industrial Rap,' which takes aim at both top forty pop and political hardcore; the sarcastic 'I Love New York,' which is built on a purposefully dumb 1-4-5 chord progression; and yet another dig at hardcore, 'A Political Song':

We don't want your apathy
No fuckin' government gets down on me
Can you spare any change?
Can you spare any change?
(Anti-Reagan and stuff, man—yeah.)

269

The "song" lasts all of ten seconds, including three seconds for the spoken punchline. It is then repeated three more times as if to emphasize the monotony of it all. As punk parodies go, it's both funnier and more convincing than, say, Frank Zappa's 'Tinseltown Rebellion,' not only because Joe had actually observed the phenomenon firsthand but also because Gould and Bordin had previously played together in a hardcore band (the short-lived Police State) back in 1982.

The hardcore-themed material was partly inspired by the bandleader's impressions of New York City, where he spent some time following the Pop-O-Pies' East Coast tour. The city also inspired the record's closing track, 'The Words of Jamal'—a song whose origins are worth recounting given its role in the lore of both the Pop-O-Pies and Faith No More. As Joe explained in an interview for the FNM fan site faithnoman.com:

> I was crashing at a friend's place in Alphabet City (the Lower East Side of New York). This friend of mine, who was also a boyhood friend of Bill and Roddy, is named Mark Stewart. Mark was subletting his apartment from this guy named Jamal. It was a hot summer night in New York City in the wee hours of the morning, and Mark was talking with his housemate about how silly this Jamal guy was and saying, "Ya notice how Jamal always uses these same phrases over and over again, like *spirit*?" And his housemate said, "And *excellent*." And Mark said, "And *good stuff*." And then they both said at the same time, *"Further on down the road!"*[10]

Musically, the song offers the clearest example of a link between Flipper and Faith No More. Though it was written by Joe—who came up with the chord

---

10 Adapted from www.faithnoman.com/joe-pop-o-pie.html. The song has a complicated genealogy. A different version (same refrain, different music) was performed at Faith. No More's October 1983 On Broadway show with Joe on vocals; this version appears on their first demo cassette as 'The Words of Jamal.' The same words resurface at the beginning of Faith No More's 'Spirit' (from 1987's *Introduce Yourself*), which also uses the same music as the live/demo version of 'Jamal.' Finally, a sequel to the Pop-O-Pies' version with new lyrics and a new backing band appears on *Joe's Third Record* (see Chapter 27).

progression while fooling around on guitar during an early FNM rehearsal—it could be mistaken for Flipper, at least if not for the vocals. The lyrics, however, are pure Joe, as is the deadpan delivery with which he rattles off his observations on the Big Apple. "New York is a place where middle-class white kids come from all over the world to live out their groovy comic-book fantasies of being a junkie like Lou Reed," he says at one point. There are also gripes about the high cost of living and the low quality of produce in New York. In sum, "You get the feeling like you're privileged to live in a shithole where nobody gives you a break."

In a post-punk year marked by ambitious double albums like *Zen Arcade* and *Double Nickels on the Dime*, the compact *Joe's Second Record* might have seemed like a trifle in comparison. In truth, it's a meta-punk concept album (or mini-album) masquerading as a flimsy novelty record. It doesn't announce itself as a Serious Work of Art in the way that, say, *Zen Arcade* does, but that's part of its charm—a charm that wasn't entirely lost on critics at the time. As one of them put it, "*Joe's Second Record* is all tongue—sometimes sticking out to razz, sometimes panting in ain't-I-artistic indulgence, and sometimes tucked severely in cheek. It has no commercial potential, and no doubt will someday be a much sought-after cult item by people now not even four years old."[11]

11 *Allentown Morning Call,* February 9, 1985.

24

WE CARE A LOT

They were on drastically different career paths, but the Pop-O-Pies and Faith No More maintained a symbiotic relationship from the fall of 1983 through much of 1984. There were a few reasons why it worked. For one thing, the bands weren't in competition with one another: the Pop-O-Pies were always more about the concept and the spectacle, while FNM was more focused on a sound. Moreover, they were still searching for that sound—or at least the missing puzzle pieces needed to help them fully realize it—and they were willing to take their time in order to find it. In the meantime, their tenure in the Pop-O-Pies amounted to a kind of apprenticeship for Gould and Bordin. As an added bonus, the Pies weren't the kind of band that spent hours in the rehearsal studio, so there was no conflict on that front, either.

The connection between the two bands drew even closer when Mark Bowen came onboard as FNM's guitarist in February of 1984. Bowen holds the honor of being their first guitarist to last for more than one show, even if he never considered himself a full-fledged member.[12] "They never said, 'Hey, come join our band,'" he explains. "It was more like, 'We have these gigs—you wanna come and play with us?' So I did." As he notes, it was a period of trial and error for all those involved. "I played what I played, and they liked it, or they didn't. I mean, they never said, 'Oh, that sucks.' They'd say things like, 'Try playing a more screechy chord on this,' but it was all very friendly."

It was an unusual configuration for a rock band, with the bassist, drummer, and keyboardist forming the core of the lineup and the other two spots up for grabs. Several of the songs in their setlist at this point would later make

---

12 The list of guitarists includes Jake Smith (October 1983), Mark Stewart (December 1983), and Paula Frazer (January 1984), who also sang in her one performance with the band.

it onto the band's first couple of albums, but at the time, they were still works in progress. "There were no lyrics and no guitar parts—just Roddy, Michael, and Billy," recalls Bowen. "They were very riff-heavy, and they kind of developed them into songs depending on who the singer was and who showed up to play." For most of Bowen's tenure, that singer was none other than Courtney Love. [13]

Steve Tupper: She was so hilarious. She was just like kind of ranting and raving onstage. She was either like totally drunk—stoned, whatever—and could barely maintain her composure, or else she was acting that way just for effect. I don't know which one it was, but that was the way it came off. I was having a hard time not falling off the chair; it was so funny. The songs were okay, but really, the draw was basically Courtney at that point.

Eric Cope: I really liked them when they were with Courtney Love. She was just *weird*. And I loved Courtney Love because she was just *out there*. She was just … oh, man.

David Katz: Courtney was really good with them, as long as she wasn't too high—you know, too smacked out. And if she was too high and smacked out, then she would be terrible and kind of ruin the night. So they kicked her out of the band before too long because she was just too unreliable and too much of a junkie.

Bill Gould: The one thing I can say about her that was good was, she was so obnoxious with a microphone that where beforehand nobody really cared whether we played or not, she would get people's attention between songs by talking so much shit. Then people would start talking about, "Who is this band with this obnoxious singer?" [Laughs.] So in that way, she did us really good. But as far as singing goes and the music side of the band, it wasn't happening at all.

---

13 Ms. Love had some other connections to the San Francisco scene in those days. In addition to an on-again, off-again relationship with Rozz Rezabek, she also co-starred in a low-budget music video for Toiling Midgets' 'Night Science (Preludes),' a track from their *Dead Beats* LP.

WHO CARES ANYWAY

RODDY BOTTUM (LEFT) AND MIKE BORDIN PHOTO BY JOAN OSATO.

NEW BEGINNINGS

For all of the mixing and matching on guitar and vocals, the basic elements of Faith No More's sound—Bordin's tribal drumming, Gould's looping basslines, and Bottum's goth-tinged keyboards—were already in place early on. This much is evident from their first demo tape—not just the On Broadway set with Joe Pop-O-Pie on vocals, but also side two, an extended instrumental recorded at the Vats in late 1983 and referred to informally as "The Opium Tape."[14] The

---

14 As Bottum clarifies, they rehearsed at the Vats, but not in an actual beer vat. "On the upper floors, there were just regular big studios. And we had one of those. Not because we had more money. I think we coveted—everyone coveted the vats. But that's what we

unvarnished recording offers a window into their methodical song-sculpting process. "We started by doing loops, heavy loops," explains Gould. "We had a keyboard, so it was kind of ambient. We'd have these washes of sound, and we were doing these grooves that just played over and over again. So in that way, it was kind of like Flipper. And it was kind of like Killing Joke because that was the only band at the time that was kind of modern but heavy at the same time. It was kind of like a dub version of Killing Joke in a weird way."

It's no coincidence that the group's two best-known songs, 'We Care a Lot' and 'Epic,' are built around minimal bass/drum patterns. Many of their songs started that way, with just Gould and Bordin in the studio together. "I wouldn't call it jamming," clarifies Will Carpmill, a friend and fellow UC Berkeley student who often sat in on their early rehearsals.[15] "It was more like grooving for like an hour and a half on something really heavy and dirgey and repetitive. Then maybe the next time they would go in there, they'd get Roddy in there, and he'd come up with a keyboard line on it, and they'd kind of build on songs like that."

Even if they came later in the process, Bottum's contributions—rendered on an Oberheim Matrix 12 he'd bought from *Flashdance* soundtrack composer Duane Hitchings—were no less central to FNM's distinctive sound. Essentially, he was the yin to Gould and Bordin's yang. "It was a challenge, at the time, to sort of jump into that realm—into a scene of bands where keyboards were *not* very cool," Bottum admits. "But we kind of used it to our advantage." In addition to Kraftwerk and Psychic TV, he cites the British synth-pop duo Yaz[16] as an inspiration.

It was Yaz's 1982 LP *Upstairs at Eric's* that led to an epiphany one night after he put it on the turntable at the 16th Street apartment he was sharing with Gould, Carpmill, and others.[17] "I remember Will was like, 'I don't know, that sounds really *gay*,'" laughs the keyboardist. "We were all so open-minded and such liberal kids. But being sort of closeted or wherever I was with my sexuality, hearing that made me go, '*Ooh.*' It was kind of shameful. Like, 'Oh, that's *not* a good thing. You shouldn't *sound* gay.'" So there was kind of a period of figuring

---

were rehearsing in, was just a big basic room up on the fifth or sixth floor."

15 Carpmill is the younger brother of Olga Gerrard, who booked the Savoy Tivoli during 1980–1981 (see Chapter 13). She went on to manage FNM for a couple of years.

16 Known as Yazoo in the UK.

17 This was before the move to 109-A Shotwell.

that out for myself and coming to terms with, 'Yeah, that's a pretty powerful and effective tool, especially to throw into the mix of what we did. There was no heavier drummer than Mike Bordin, and Mike and Billy's riffs were these *heavy*, intense things. And I guess looking back on it—in a reactionary way, throwing some gay into that mix, if you will, kind of formed the sound."

Much like Killing Joke, the early Faith No More fell somewhere in between post-punk, goth, and metal. What that meant in terms of the San Francisco music scene circa 1984 was that they didn't really fit in anywhere. As Bordin told one interviewer years later, "There was a hardcore scene (not us), a metal scene (not us), a college radio scene (not us), a pop and dance club scene (also not us) ... you get the idea, and most of us were coming from different backgrounds ourselves as well."[18]

Even those who liked the band were not quite sure what to make of them in those days. "They were really a different band depending on where they played and depending on who the sound man was," notes Brandan Kearney, who saw them play often during this period. "If Roddy was coming through really loud, then they were kind of a weird post-punk band, whereas if he was drowned out and it was just the guitar coming through, then they were more in the Metallica vein, I guess. In some clubs, what they sounded like depended on what side of the room you were on."

ENTER CHUCK AND JIM

The Metallica comparison was not unfounded. Bordin grew up in the East Bay town of Castro Valley, where his best friend in high school was eventual Metallica bassist Cliff Burton. The two played together in a couple of bands during the late seventies, one of which also included a guitarist named Jim Martin. By the summer of 1984, Burton had already recorded a couple of albums with Metallica. Knowing that FNM was looking for a guitarist, he suggested Martin. Bordin was

18 http://faithnoman.com/mike-bordin

skeptical—the two of them didn't get along the first time around—but he took his friend's advice and decided to give Martin another shot.

Singer Chuck Mosley entered the picture around the same time—the late summer of 1984. There was another childhood connection here, as Mosley and Gould had previously been bandmates in the Animated, an LA new wave act that made it as far as releasing an EP in 1981 before Gould moved away for college. [19] By 1984, Mosley was singing and playing guitar in his own band, Haircuts That Kill—though, as he explains, he didn't really consider himself a singer. "The whole time that band was around, we were always looking for a singer, but we could never get one or never get lucky enough to have one that would stick around for more than a few shows." Ironically, then, Faith No More found its new front man by plucking a reluctant vocalist from another band that was having its own problems finding a singer.[20]

Both Martin and Mosley would contribute greatly to the band's sound as well as their motley image. Along with Bordin, Martin was largely responsible for the band's metal quotient, which only came to the fore after he joined. As Gould explains, "It was kind of a weird experiment to see what would happen. It was kind of like having a pet—you know, like a mascot. And what happened was, he started attracting these metal people, and we started becoming this rock band. And it was kind of a hoot to make ourselves a rock band and see what it would be like." As for Chuck, he served as a necessary irritant, providing a kind of SoCal skate-punk insolence that meshed with the band's (or at least Gould and Bottum's) sarcastic streak.

Personality-wise, it was a different story. Part of the issue was that neither of the new additions elected to move to San Francisco. "I just would go up for

19 Mosley played keyboards in the Animated, having grown up taking piano lessons: "My parents had me starting at three years old, playing classical piano, until I was around fourteen or fifteen. That's the one thing I *can* play good. I can't sight-read, but I can read music."
20 The timeline is hazy, but Chuck's first appearance with the band was likely a September 22, 1984, show at Club Foot, where FNM wound up closing out a marathon bill that went on late into the night. Among the other bands on the bill were the Pop-O-Pies, Caroliner, Glorious Din, and Hello Kitty on Ice, who were originally scheduled to go on last. As Hello Kitty guitarist Kirk Heydt recalls, "I show up with all my gear, and we're sitting out there for like five hours waiting to play. Well, it turns out the joke's on us. Faith No More does this *loong* set, and then the cops come and shut it down."

THIS PHOTO OF FNM'S MIKE BORDIN APPEARED ON THE COVER A 1985 ISSUE OF THE ZINE WIRING DEPT. PHOTO BY JOAN OSATO.

their shows and stuff and hang out while we were recording," explains Chuck. "That was probably one of their pet peeves because I *wouldn't* move up there. It was like a reverse Metallica when they got Cliff. Because Cliff lived up there, but they all lived down south [in Los Angeles]." Meanwhile, Martin still lived with his mother in the East Bay town of Hayward, which was closer to San Francisco geographically, though not necessarily culturally.

To some onlookers, there was a clear discrepancy between the core trio and the two new additions. "Roddy and Bill and Mike—who were the core of the band, who had always been doing it—those guys were really part of a community, at least as I saw it," notes Brandan Kearney. "Jim and Chuck always seemed to me to exist in their own weird, individual bubbles." Joe Pop-O-Pie offers a similar take. "Those guys were all college-educated, well-read, worldly-wise, open-minded, and had been around the block a few hundred times," he says, referring to the Gould/Bordin/Bottum triumvirate. "And Jim Martin was like this guy who'd been living in his mom's basement for his whole life and never been out of Castro Valley. So he was limited in his worldly wise-ness. He was about as deep as somebody that worked in a convenience store. I just said, 'What is he doing playing with Bill and Roddy and Bordin? This guy does not fit psychologically with these guys.'"

WE CARE A LOT

It would take a couple of years for the interpersonal friction to fully rear its head. In the meantime, things were working out well enough musically for the band to consider booking some studio time—despite the lack of interest from any of the more established local labels. As Bordin explained in an interview with the zine *Wiring Dept.*, "We felt like we weren't getting anywhere just kicking around hoping that Howie Klein or the dude from Subterranean Records or Rough Trade, who had a big profile in San Francisco, would sign us." Thanks to their friend Will Carpmill, a tape of some rough mixes from their first studio session made its way onto the stereo at Rough Trade's retail store on Sixth Street, where he was working at the time. One of his co-workers, Ruth Schwartz, liked it enough that she decided to start a new label, Mordam Records, in order to release it.[21]

With the newly-formed label behind them, the band went back into the studio to record the remaining handful of tracks for what would become their debut LP, *We Care a Lot*. Today, the LP is best known for the title track, which became an early calling card for the band despite being something of a red herring. After all, it's the only song on the album to incorporate rap ("Run-DMC had just happened, and we were super into that," notes Bottum) and the only one with overtly topical lyrics.[22] Yet, in other ways, it was fairly representative, from the tribal bass/drum groove that opens the song to the gauzy keyboards to the obnoxious sense of humor on display in the lyrics (which were inspired by the recent barrage of celebrity charity anthems such as 'We Are the World').

"I thought it was great," recalls erstwhile vocalist Joe Pop-O-Pie, who first heard the song on a local college radio station."I hadn't talked to Bill in a year or something, and we hooked up again in like '86. I said, 'Yeah, I heard that, that 'We Care a Lot.' That's really a happening song.'" Critics at the time also singled it out. "The title track … is easily one of the best songs I've heard in the last few months," wrote Len Righi in a review for the *Allentown Morning Call*, adding, "The LP's other nine songs … aren't quite as good, but several come close."[23]

One of those honorable mentions would have to be 'As the Worm Turns,' which hints at things to come with its combination of metallic heaviness and unabashed melodicism. It opens with a dramatic series of keyboard arpeggios before launching into another patented Gould/Bordin riff. Jim Martin's guitar is low in the mix, but he manages to sneak in a few nifty wah-wah leads. Once again, the lyrics are key, as is Chuck's spoken/sung delivery, which straddles the line between empathy and mockery as he sings to a down-and-out friend.

In the years to come, *We Care a Lot* would end up being relegated to footnote

21 Mordam had already been in business for two years as a distributor, with its main clients being *Maximum Rocknroll* and Jello Biafra's Alternative Tentacles label.
22 With the possible exception of 'Arabian Disco,' which alludes to ongoing violence in the Middle East, with Mosley barking out commands like a choreographer-turned-drill sergeant ("Put your guns … up / Feet … down / Forward … march!"). As for Mosley's non-singing style on some of the other tracks, he clarifies, "They call it rap, but with me, it was just ranting because I was never a rapper."
23 *Allentown Morning Call*. March 22, 1986.

status in the band's discography, with many of FNM's 1990s-era fans unaware of its existence (or at least unable to find it in record stores). It wasn't a big hit at the time, but it did garner some positive reviews, including one from the *LA Weekly*'s Craig Lee (the same writer who, just a couple of years earlier, had christened the Pop-O-Pies the worst band in California). First, there was his near-perfect description of the band's sound: "You take your basic punky, snotty teen attitude, mix it up with a little post-druggie San Francisco art damage, throw in a few Killing Joke riffs, add a touch of thrash and some gloom-rocker melodicism, and you get an idea of what makes this a pretty swell mix-and-match genre album."[24] And then came the kicker: "As soon as this band forgets about San Francisco, the Pop-O-Pies, and Flipper, they may even be great."

Mark Bowen: I first saw them at the little clubs when my bands were playing, when they were "Faith. No Man." Before I even met them, and before Joan was my girlfriend, I saw them, and I just went, "Wow." Especially Mike Bordin. I said, "This guy is gonna go somewhere." I could just tell by the way he played. Looking back on it, he must have been about nineteen years old at the time.

Joan Osato: I knew it when I met them. I could see that ambition. Billy's a person who you can always tell is thinking, even when he's not speaking. So they had that combination of ambition and faith and, certainly, musical talent to make that jump. They also risked a lot to do what they did, and I appreciate that. I remember the year Billy quit school. It was a big deal—you know, like, eighteen, nineteen years old and going to college. I remember going to Los Angeles to support him when he told his parents.

David Katz: You could see from early on that Faith No More were gonna be big—that if anybody was gonna break out of that little scene, it was gonna be them.

24 *LA Weekly*. January 30, 1986.

25

"SAN FRANCISCO AS MANCHESTER": THE WIRING DEPT. ERA

Bill Gould: Flipper was an earlier generation; they were more like forefathers. We were the younger kids coming up on the second, maybe third wave, fourth wave. There's always a layer of kids who play all the misfit places and start sticking together and building a little community. And that's what this was, really. I mean, people did a lot of really brash, obnoxious stuff, but it was a *community*. In a way, there was nothing inviting about the music in a lot of these bands, but people kind of shared the fact it was *their thing*. And the people who played in the bands were very close with the people who came to their shows.

Jay Paget: There are always subcultures and factions, or just different people with different sounds that gravitate toward each other. So you'd have the *Maximum Rocknroll* crowd that I more or less watched from a distance, like Code of Honor and Fang. Flipper was completely in its own universe, as everyone, I think, rightly recognizes, and the sound was just completely their own. Not derivative. Then you'd have a range of campy, new wave and songcraft kind of bands, like the Mutants and Romeo Void and Translator. But by the time I came to town, that felt more like an old guard and not something that we were interested in repeating. But we recognized it.

And then—I don't know if "goth" is the right word, but you had some of the darker English bands come along, and I think our ear was tuned somewhat to that. And we wanted to use that as a jumping-off point. Faith No More, back then, felt really kind of mysterious and dark. They used to burn frankincense and stuff at their shows. It was sort of dark, heavy trance music. Glorious Din was what we were; Trial was what they were. It felt like we were sort of akin to each other in that respect. David Katz was in Thought Factory, and they had that vibe. And Brandan [Kearney] was just a friend of all of us, and his tape experiments were in that vein, although somewhat different, too. But personally, we were sort of traveling in the same circles.

THE FOG IS ROLLIN' IN

Faith No More didn't emerge from a vacuum. Circa 1984, they were one of a handful of bands absorbing the same sounds from post-punk England and breathing the same air in post-industrial San Francisco. These bands shared a rehearsal space in Hudson Street Studios, a converted warehouse off Third Street that was not far from Club Foot but not close to much else. They also shared a tireless advocate in Eric Cope, a Sri Lankan-born Joy Division enthusiast whose zine *Wiring Dept.* documented this era in a uniquely stylized fashion.

"*Wiring Dept.* was bold and very much in accord with the factory neo-industrial aesthetic," says Trial's Desmond Shea, whose Xeroxed likeness appears on the cover of the first issue. "His stark photography and graphic sense combined with that oblique interview structure yielded such a chilly intensity. He illustrated San Francisco as Manchester and created mysterious, insightful artists out of ne'er-do-well, hippie-punk dropouts."

Like his portrayal of San Francisco, Cope's idea of Manchester—the home of Joy Division and Factory Records—may have been mythical, but there were some parallels between the two cities.[25] "Previous to the eighties, San Francisco *was* an industrial town and a maritime town," notes Will Carpmill. "When we showed up, it was a dying industrial town. The port had just closed."

---

25 Jon Savage offers a dissenting view here: "I always saw Manchester as being like Cleveland, in that it was a very obviously degraded industrial city, which I didn't think that San Francisco was. San Francisco was too cute, whereas Manchester is just not cute, nor was Cleveland. There are cute bits of San Francisco, which there just aren't in either Manchester or Cleveland."

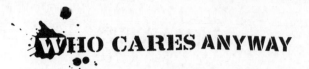

WHO CARES ANYWAY

Then there is the climate—in particular, the damp air and gray skies that are common to both Manchester and parts of San Francisco, including the Club Foot/Hudson Street area. "I've never been to England, at least if you don't count the airport," says Matt Hall, an early member of Glorious Din. "But that was one thing that depresses most normal people about San Francisco, is the fog. And I loved it. I think most people associate that with being gloomy, but it just feels right to me."

Joan Osato: There was a lot of bleakness. You have to understand, back then we weren't living in, like, livable housing by anyone's standards. And also, none of us made any money. I'm talking about, like, ninety dollars rent a month was hard to come up with. In that way, the industrial influence was really there.

Roddy Bottum: Billy and I, we were kids from Los Angeles. We were brought up in sunny, sunshine, entertainment-industry Los Angeles. And we moved to San Francisco, and it was a marked difference. "Oh wow, this is really foggy and dark and serious, and there's people on speed, and bicycle messengers." Just the vibe was so different and so much darker. We would never be exposed to anything like the Vats in Los Angeles.

Joan Osato: I mean, we knew people who lived in the Vats or in abandoned shipyards over by the piers. I wouldn't call it "romantic" because people definitely had to compromise comfort for the sake of doing what they did. In that way, I can look at all of us when we were like eighteen and say, "Wow, what a bunch of ballsy little kids." I mean, just so *bold,* and really risking a lot, I think.

Carlos Willingham: There were all these warehouse spaces that were just basically open spaces that we could use for rehearsal studios and for underground clubs or whatever. That was basically where we could afford to live, where we could afford to play, where we could put on shows and charge two dollars and put on six bands.

William Davenport: I had a space that people would die for now. It was a storefront that was 700 square feet maybe, and we had an apartment attached

284

to it, and then we had a basement where we had a rehearsal studio, and then next door to that I had a recording studio.[26]

Carlos Willingham: They call it the Dogpatch now; we called it Dogtown back then. That was some pretty heavy-duty territory. I mean, that's where you buried the bodies back then. So the locals were pretty tough. They felt kind of like we were infringing.

free free   ✝ FrEE SHOW ✝   free free

HELLO KITTY ON ICE
FAITH. NO MORE. ✝
GLORIOUS DIN
PARANOID BLUE
CAROLINER RAIN PROBLEM
·THOUGHT FACTORY·
MJB ·· NO HEADS
Plus guests - all for FREE!

Thoughts

At: CLUB FooT   Sat. Sept 22   8 pm
2520 3rd St.

STOP AND THINK

William Davenport: I found it to be kind of isolated and nice. It was definitely very desolate, and it was funny because you were in the city, and Potrero Hill was right there—you could just drive up to Potrero Hill. But it was nice, because it was cheap rent, and you could really make some noise there, too. Nobody would bother us.

---

26 Davenport published the industrial zine *Unsound* and also recorded music under the name Problemist. *Unsound* started in 1983, the same year that RE/Search published its *Industrial Culture Handbook*. Though *Unsound* wound up covering many of the same artists, it did so through a different lens. "I didn't connect with Vale, really," admits Davenport, "especially when the *Industrial Handbook* came out because I felt like what it was doing was simplifying what we were doing in many ways. It kind of made it like, 'Okay, you've got to read this book, you've got to listen to this record.' Just these lists that they had, I didn't like,"

GLORIOUS DIN

It was against this backdrop that Glorious Din came together in 1983, although their story actually begins a couple of years earlier—in Davenport, Iowa, of all places.[27] It was there that Eric Cope found himself following a series of travels that had taken him through Dubai, the Netherlands, and Alaska, among other far-flung locales. Cope's life story could fill a book or two on its own, and much of it would read like fiction: childhood years spent exploring the jungles of his native Sri Lanka and studying with a shaman; teenage years spent engaging in petty thievery, getting expelled from school, and doing jail time for allegedly assaulting a priest.[28]

That propensity for troublemaking carried over into Cope's first band, a rudimentary hardcore outfit called White Front. The band name alone was enough to make them unwelcome at most venues, but Cope's appearance was also jarring, especially given the time and place. "I think he had his head shaved, and he had, like, 'PIGS EAT SHIT' with red duct tape written on the back of his jacket," remembers Matt Hall, an Iowa City native who was booking punk shows at a local Unitarian church in those days. "This was the kind of thing that could get you beaten up in Iowa. I said, 'Well, who the hell is this guy? I've gotta know this guy.' He was a little bit scary to me at the time, actually. But eventually, I went up to him and talked to him."

As fellow outcasts, the two of them hit it off ("He had the tallest Mohawk I have ever seen," recalls Cope), though the budding friendship wasn't enough to keep either of them in Iowa for much longer. "It's a kind of small-town thing," explains Hall, "where you feel like, after a while, you've seen every corner of the town and gotten tired of getting beer bottles thrown at you by rednecks or whatever. Chicago seemed too close, and New York seemed a little too hard

---

27 His connection to Iowa came via an exchange student who stayed with his family in Sri Lanka. As a return favor, the student's family helped arrange for him to travel to the US.

28 For more on Cope's early life, see David Katz, "Who Was Eric Cope: The Story of '80s Punks Glorious Din." June 2016. https://www.factmag.com/2016/06/08/glorious-din-eric-cope/

THE MID-EIGHTIES

to make it, so a lot of us ended up in the Bay Area."

Eric Cope: There was a guy from near the Bay Area called Tim Tanooka, who had this magazine called *Ripper*, and somehow I found it in a record store. I wrote to Tim, and he said, "Yeah, come down." At that time, I was into Joy Division and Gang of Four and the Fall, but still I was into skinheads and Crass and all of that stuff, too. So I came to San Francisco, and I'm telling you, I was so excited. In Iowa, if you went to a club to see punk, it would be us and hardly anyone else. But when I came here, I was so excited to see all these punks and bands like Crucifix and Urban Assault and Flipper. It was an exciting time.[29]

---

29 White Front actually relocated to San Francisco as a group—minus their original
     drummer—in the summer of 1982. They found a new drummer, Pete Herstedt, and

WHO CARES ANYWAY

Brandan Kearney: I first knew Eric Cope as this guy who would come up and try to sell you copies of *Maximum Rocknroll* at shows, and you'd say, "Get away from me—I don't want that rag."

David Katz: Eric was crucial to that whole scene. The reason why he was selling *Maximum Rocknroll*—he was living in the rehearsal space in Hunter's Point, in a place that had no windows, that had about six or seven different bands' equipment in a tiny room. He was *living* there. I went there to rehearse a couple of times, and even just going there at first, you feel like you can't breathe after about an hour.

Matt Hall: Me and Eric ended up living in the practice space down on Hudson Street. I didn't have a job. We were living off of welfare at the time, I think. We'd spend all day playing music and trying to make something out of that. In some ways, it seemed like the perfect life. In other ways, it's like, you're at a practice space and you wake up, and there's some shitty band playing next door, and there's zero light in the room, and you have no idea if it's seven in the morning or two in the afternoon. And sometimes you'd wake up, and you'd hear somebody working outside, and you felt like you couldn't leave because they weren't

---

briefly gave it a go in San Francisco before disbanding in early '83. (Not surprisingly, the band name didn't go over any better in SF than it had in Iowa.)

supposed to know we were living there. We had a hotplate that we'd cook bowls of ramen on, and then we'd buy a bag of oranges with our food stamps at Safeway or whatever.

As Cope and Hall were separately making their way out west, Jay Paget was in the midst of his own westward journey. "I was bumming around, basically, after high school," says the Boston native. "Landed in a couple of places on the West Coast. Tried college but really didn't like it. At that time, you could hitchhike around pretty easily, so I just disconnected and hitchhiked all over the west for a couple of years, really—'80 to '82. When I was on the road, someone gave me a guitar, and I would pluck out songs. But I didn't have any musical background. I didn't have lessons, and I didn't play when I was in high school."

Undaunted by his inexperience, he put an ad up on the bulletin board at Rough Trade. Cope answered it, and despite some initial reservations, Paget agreed to give it a try. The two of them worked on songs together for a couple of months—with Cope singing and playing acoustic guitar and Paget accompanying him on electric—before Hall eventually joined them on bass.[30] A drummer friend from Iowa came and went, but the rest of them forged ahead as a trio. "Eric would write a song," says Hall, "and he'd play us his simple chords on the acoustic guitar, and then we'd come up with our parts. Then he took the acoustic guitar out and started playing stand-up tom-toms. So the final version of the song would not have his guitar anywhere."

Hall's tenure with the band would be brief, but he was responsible for both the band name and their distinctive bass guitar sound. "Basically, he set a certain kind of a sound for Glorious Din," explains Cope. "And even when Doug Heeschen came and started playing bass, on our first record, most of the songs were bass parts that came from Matt Hall. He created the bass parts."

---

30 Hall spent some time living with a relative in Orange County before finally moving up to San Francisco. "I think I had this impression that it was gonna be a cultural mecca or something after growing up in Iowa," he says of Southern California, "but it didn't really feel like that when I was there. I remember taking a bus to LA and going to some punk rock shows. At that point, it seemed like every punk rock show would get shut down by the police." After moving to SF, Hall briefly lived with Cope at a house in the Fillmore before the two of them moved into the rehearsal space on Hudson Street.

WHO CARES ANYWAY

GLORIOUS DIN'S PETE HERSTEDT (LEFT) AND FNM'S BILL GOULD. PHOTO BY ERIC COPE.

"I was just really into trying to figure out how to make a wrong note sound right," says the bassist. "I just remember, that was my main idea with Glorious Din: trying to find a really sour note and make it work—*the* most wrong note—and just insist on forcing it in there."

Hall's bass guitar—drenched in chorus and played with a pick—figures prominently on the first Glorious Din recording, a five-song demo engineered by Matt Wallace in December of 1983.[31] "It's *completely* different from the first record," notes Paget. "It's fast and frenetic, and Matt's bass playing is just sick. He's completely unique. And then Eric's pounding on the drums, and I'm trying

---

31 The demo was eventually released, sans identifying information, as part of a digital-only compilation entitled *Was It Mouth Poison, Suicide or Murder?* The five songs are 'Words People,' 'Factory Salt,' 'Narrow Streets,' 'Silence,' and '4 O'clock in the Morning,' none of which made it onto either of the band's LPs.

to figure out the guitar."

It was Glorious Din's new acquaintances in Faith. No More who referred them to Wallace, a fledgling engineer who had recently started his own studio in the East Bay. Wallace had produced an earlier single by Faith. No Man, and given that Glorious Din was mining similar territory, the connection made sense. As Roddy Bottum recalls, "Eric was a very intense person, and he came to some of our early shows. And we saw Glorious Din right when they were getting started. They were super dark and very serious and had a sort of somber musical statement."

The two bands would go on to play numerous shows together over the next couple of years, beginning with a February 27, 1984, appearance at the Mabuhay. By this point, Hall had already exited the band, having left San Francisco and headed back to the Midwest shortly after the demo was recorded. ("It's hard to remember what I was thinking at the time," he admits. "It seemed like, 'Well, I could keep doing this, but maybe I don't want to live in this practice space forever. I should go back to Iowa and go to school.'") With Hall suddenly out of the picture, Cope enlisted Doug Heeschen—formerly the guitarist in White Front—to play bass, and he brought in another former White Front bandmate, Pete Herstedt, to take over on drums.

Evidently, the new lineup clicked right from the start. "Billy and Mike were running around in the audience with incense when Glorious Din came on, and they were totally into it," recalls David Katz. "And Glorious Din were astoundingly good. They were kind of unbelievably impressive. And the leader of the band was that little scrawny guy who used to always shove Maximum Rocknroll in my face." Writing about the show years later, Katz would add, "The debut show immediately marked them out as strikingly different, with the skinny, dark Cope standing stock-still at the microphone, murmuring his unknowable lyrics from another place."

"TO SELL KEROSENE DOOR TO DOOR"

Together with his distinctive visual sensibility, Cope's mysterious yet strangely evocative lyrics and song titles helped define the Glorious Din aesthetic. He designed the band's fliers and album covers, which, not coincidentally, bore a strong resemblance to the visuals found in *Wiring Dept*. Taken together, the words and images—with their odd juxtapositions ('Factory Salt,' 'Empty Milk Bar') and frequent references to trains and factories—conjure up an eerie gestalt. And while his bandmates didn't always understand exactly what they meant, Cope's lyrics were nonetheless a welcome anomaly in the days of "anti-Reagan and stuff, man." As Hall puts it, "I'm not usually a lyric guy, but there's a few of his songs where I have a hint that something's going on—I can't quite figure out what it is, but it's like looking through a keyhole at some horrifying scene in a room that you're not sure you should be looking at, and you can't quite see the edges to really get a clear picture of what it is. It's like some kind of terrible crime scene or something, but sort of beautiful at the same time."

Eric Cope: For me, what's really important when you write a song is, okay, when you sing the song, it sounds nice, but I want to see those words on paper, and I want to see the image that it creates. If you have a phrase like "to sell kerosene door to door," it creates an image. And to me, it was important that people get an atmosphere and a feeling—more than information, that they get this atmosphere and a feeling from those lines. And that was the whole thing.

Desmond Shea: I remember he worked in a kitchen and took inspiration from culinary tools and devices. The song entitled 'Danger, Rotating Knives' was a reference to a Cuisinart! He just had a stoic and stylized engagement with his art that was terribly genuine and wholly committed. He would make an absolute phony of anyone with his abstract and earnest sensibility.

Brandan Kearney: The other thing he did that was really, really weird—at least in my case; I don't know how many people he did this to—but he would review things of mine that didn't exist. There's all these reviews of World of Pooh releases, and they just describe this sort of mood, but there's never a reference to any songs because they don't exist. He's just making this stuff up off the top of his head.

Granted, there were some moments of frustration between Cope and his bandmates. For as much as he'd immersed himself in punk culture, he was still coming from a different world, a different culture. As Cope puts it, "It's like we were talking two different languages, and I understood their language, but they did not understand my language."

That didn't stop them from trying, though. "I remember, he'd say things that, to other people, wouldn't be really great advice," recounts Hall, who would eventually return to San Francisco in the late 1980s and collaborate with Cope in a couple of post-Glorious Din side projects, Beetle Leg, and Highway Iguana Car. "He'd say, 'Play something green,' or something like that. And somehow, I'd try to figure out what he meant. And it would kind of work—better than you'd think it would. You'd have to just try to open up yourself to whatever you think that might mean.

"Eric was always a really interesting guy to play in a band with because, in a lot of ways, he was completely primitive," adds the bassist. "He knew his five chords or whatever, but in a way, I think he's way more of an advanced musician than any Berklee-trained guy I can think of, just because his songs all had such a strong mood to them. And to me, that's advanced music: when you can get across a feeling so efficiently, so well. For someone halfway across the world from me, we seemed to have a similar take on what music was for, I guess."

LEADING STOLEN HORSES; TRIAL

While Glorious Din were frequent openers for Faith No More throughout 1984 and '85, their first LP, *Leading Stolen Horses,* actually predated *We Care a Lot* by a few months. Both albums were produced by Matt Wallace, and when listened to side by side, the similarities—booming drums, repetitive basslines, and a generally chilly atmosphere—are readily apparent. Then again, so are the differences. For one thing, there is the guitar playing: Jim Martin's playing on *WCAL* already has a pronounced metallic chug, whereas Paget eschews distortion and power chords altogether in favor of sparse single-note lines, often with a Middle Eastern tinge. Another difference is that for all their moodiness, Faith No More had a sarcastic sense of humor that was seldom too far from the surface. Glorious Din, on the other hand, doesn't crack a smile. Indeed, at no point on the eight-song *Leading Stolen Horses* do they even venture into a major key.

The same thoroughgoing sense of solemnity also permeated the music of Trial. Even more so than Glorious Din, Trial's music had a ritualistic quality to it, often featuring chanted background vocals, tribal percussion, and ambient keyboard washes. Over time, their concerts grew to encompass black-and-white video and slide projections that further underscored the apocalyptic mood. "They were just this ultra-goth band—goth beyond anything anyone's ever seen, really," says Brandan Kearney. "They made Bauhaus look like the Partridge Family."

Along with Crucifix, Sleeping Dogs, and a few others, Trial were part of the so-called "peace-punk" movement, an offshoot of hardcore that preached vegetarianism, environmentalism, and anti-war politics.[32] The Bay Area peace-punk scene, in turn, connected with a network of like-minded British bands, including Crass (the movement's originators) and Chumbawamba. "It was a very deep message, and it wasn't just talking about changing political leaders," notes Cyrnai (née Carolyn Fok), who joined Trial on bass in 1985. It was a far cry from the flippant tone of 'We Care a Lot,' if not out of step with a general feeling in the air.

"At the time, it was so serious," recalls Roddy Bottum, who performed live with Trial on a couple of occasions.[33] Cyrnai echoes this point. "The live shows were so cathartic that after every show, I couldn't talk to people." Yet she also emphasizes that for all of its somber aspects, Trial's music wasn't about bleakness for its own sake. "Certain musics are just pure bleak, like death metal. But I think with Trial, there's a sense of personal hope. If you read the lyrics, it's actually hoping to connect. It wants something more than what it is. It's not saying that everything's gonna get destroyed and everything's horrible. So

---

32 Trial had connections to several of these other bands. Their drummer, Christopher Faith, also played in Crucifix. Meanwhile, Crucifix bassist Matt Borruso was the brother of Trial vocalist John Borruso, and their sister Sara was the singer in Atrocity. Finally, Cyrnai played in a couple of other peace-punk bands, including Treason and A State of Mind, before joining Trial. Members of several of these bands lived in New Method, a legendary East Bay warehouse that also hosted shows during the era.

33 One of these shows was a December 8, 1984, benefit for squatters' rights that took place outside the Civic Center. Also on the bill were the Dicks, whose drummer, Lynn Perko, went on to play with Bottum in Imperial Teen.

there's a light to it. There's a glimmer of light even if you're in the prison. There's a piece of that."

Musically, Trial were the most ambitious of the Bay Area peace-punk bands, and this was reflected in some of the other company they kept. Guitarist Desmond Shea put in a brief stint with FNM (in between Mark Bowen and Jim Martin) and also worked with industrial performance troupe Rhythm & Noise during this era. Cyrnai had a parallel identity as a solo artist, recording experimental electronic music in the living room of her parents' house in the East Bay. (She had already recorded her first solo LP, 1985's *Charred Blossoms*, before joining Trial.) Like Shea and singer John Borruso, she eventually joined Rhythm & Noise and even put in time as a studio intern at the Compound, R&N's headquarters and occasional performance space a few blocks from Hudson Street Studios.[34]

It was there at the Compound that Trial recorded their lone LP, *Moments of Collapse*, with R&N leader Naut Humon co-producing. Alongside *We Care a Lot* and *Leading Stolen Horses*, the record offers a representative time capsule of the *Wiring Dept.* era, evoking the cavernous spaces and foggy skies of Eric Cope's mythical San Francisco-as-Manchester.

Like those albums, *Moments of Collapse* was the first release on a new record label; unlike those records, it was also the last. The label, Communications Syndicate, was set up in conjunction with Rough Trade, which still had a presence in San Francisco as of 1986, the year the album was released. "Honestly, their involvement was somewhat of a hands-off travesty," laments Shea, who is critical of the album, though he looks back on it as a valuable learning experience, given his later work as a recording engineer. "Some of our writing is cringeworthy, to say the least, if not adorable in retrospect—and probably twenty-five percent of the performance execution and production experimentation actually works. But for a few wide-eyed teenagers, it was a life-changing experience banging on metal ducting with mallets or utilizing the 'cutting edge' technology of tape-splicing and digital effects."

---

34 An unreleased R&N demo tape from 1990 includes contributions from Shea, Cyrnai, and Borruso, as well as wayward Sleepers guitarist Michael Belfer and (on one track, 'Without Your Eyes') Ricky Williams. 'Without Your Eyes' later surfaced on the CD reissue of R&N's 1985 LP *Chasms Accord* (Asphodel, 1996).

WHO CARES ANYWAY

Cyrnai takes a similar view, not only in terms of *Moments of Collapse* but also the close-knit peace-punk scene in general. "It's kind of like we were in a self-created school back then. We learned from each other: techniques, whatever it took. It's kind of the Harry Potter school of magic, where you're developing this magic, and then you leave and go live in the world." While Trial were never the cheeriest bunch, this sense of lost innocence might have contributed to the album's despondent tone. "It was the death of an era, and it turned into something else," she says. "And I think we felt it, like a prediction. That's the bleak part."

For some, like Faith No More, that "something else" was a welcome challenge: an opportunity to graduate from the DIY realm and insinuate themselves into the mainstream. For Trial and their anarcho-punk comrades, there were more sobering realizations about the limits of youthful idealism. "Ultimately, the system was too hard to really fight," concludes Cyrnai. "You're not gonna take over the system. Eventually, you're gonna succumb; you're gonna surrender. And that's kind of what happened. San Francisco became corporate, and it closed up all of those holes. You end up working for the tech companies."

26

"O": ENTER GREGG AND GRUX

By the mid-1980s, Subterranean Records was practically an institution in local underground terms. Yet the label's release schedule had begun to wane, along with founder Steve Tupper's enthusiasm for the local music scene. "People are not open right now to anything different," he told Eric Cope in a 1985 *Wiring Dept.* interview. "When punk sort of started, it was so very different from what had been happening before that a lot of people became inspired by it and opened up the perception to what they could listen to. Right now, I don't see a widening of perception. I sense it narrowing down."

Tupper's own attempts to widen perceptions met with some mixed results. The label still had Flipper and the Pop-O-Pies, but new LPs by the likes of Wilma, Longshoremen, and Muskrats fell largely on deaf ears. Of the label's newer signings, only Frightwig managed to garner much attention, and this had as much to do with their provocative shows as it did the quality of their recordings.

Even so, Subterranean remained an important presence. In 1982, the label relocated its headquarters to a storefront at 577 Valencia Street (across the street from the old Deaf Club), and in 1984, Tupper opened up a small retail area in the front of the space. Although business was often slow, the store served as a crossroads for a variety of characters from eras past and present.

Lizzy Kate Gray: You could work there and be paid in records, but then you'd have to go peddle the records somewhere. So it wasn't lucrative. But it was a nice thing.

Kirk Heydt: It was a so-called "job." I don't know how I got a job there. I was working there with Gregg. He's like, "You can do this, and he'll pay you five dollars an hour."

297

WHO CARES ANYWAY

Bill Gould: Subterranean put out the Pop-O-Pies record, and Gregg used to work there. So we were stuffing Pop-O-Pies records with Gregg. That's how I met Gregg, actually—at Subterranean. It was a really cool thing because there were a lot of really *different* people who were just naturally kind of interesting. Like, Gregg is an interesting guy. He doesn't *try* to be an interesting guy; he just does what he does. And there were a lot of people like that.

Kirk Heydt: People would pop in. Bruce would come in. Gregg was there, and he'd make a lot of really funny jokes. And then Joe would come in and really goad Tupper: "Hey Steve, you wanna go dutch on a cup o' joe?"

Dog Swan: There was a sort of attic that Tupper kept product in. And at one point, Tommy Tadlock moved into the attic, and we couldn't get him out. And he was a sweetheart, but he was psychotic. He could fight three men at once and win. He was just unbelievable.

Gregg Turkington: I would come into Subterranean, and he'd be up there asleep, and then he'd come down out of the hole onto the table, in his underwear, and go on these insane rants—just these drug-fueled, annoying, manic sort of rants. I just started dreading it and not wanting to be alone with him because he was so crazy. He was friendly, but he just didn't feel like a safe guy to be around.[35]

But he was working on this album the whole time. Steve was always like, "When are you gonna finish the album?" I was just thinking, "Nobody fuckin' cares about this album! Who cares? A Tommy Tadlock album that no one is gonna buy?" But Steve was always really into it. Then in later years, I started realizing, "This guy was like a genius producer, and this album probably would have been pretty incredible."[36]

---

35 Details on Tadlock's later years are hard to come by, but according to *Music for Vagabonds* author Isabelle Corbisier, he passed away in 1995 at the age of fifty-four. "He ended up getting real sick," recalls Cole Palme. "He got sick with AIDS. And he ended up moving up north—somewhere up in Washington. It was the Radical Faeries retreat, out in the woods."

36 The Tadlock LP never saw the light of day, but there was a Tadlock 7-inch ('Body Ad' b/w 'Poker Keno') that hints at what it might have sounded like. Released in late 1982 in an edition of 1,200, it was a slow seller, even by Subterranean's modest standards.

THE MID-EIGHTIES

Ron Morgan: He had a song cycle, basically, and he recorded everything. He had probably twenty songs that were recorded and could have been released if there was a market for it. It was queer exotica. Tommy had his obsessions, and he wrote his songs about it. It's difficult to contextualize out of the moment.

HELLO KITTY ON ICE

On Saturday, March 17, 1984, the Sound of Music played host to what was, in retrospect, an all-star cast. Along with headliner Minimal Man, the bill featured a Courtney Love-fronted Faith No More as well as an unheralded new band called Hello Kitty on Ice.

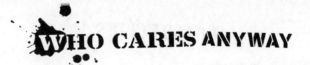

That said, it probably didn't feel like an all-star cast at the time. The crowd was sparse, and apart from Minimal Man, none of the bands had any official recordings to their name. Tupper was there to check out Hello Kitty on Ice, which featured two of his Subterranean employees in guitarist Kirk Heydt and vocalist (not quite singer) Gregg Turkington. As Tupper recalls, "Will [Shatter] and I went and sat at the bar and listened to it and shook our heads and said, 'No, this is not happening.'"

It would take Hello Kitty a few more shows to figure things out. The group had existed in a previous configuration as an instrumental free jazz trio. "I wanted to do kind of a cross between what Prime Time was doing—you know, Ornette [Coleman] with Prime Time—and then Flipper," recalls Heydt, a multi-instrumentalist who had already recorded with both Flipper and free jazz saxophonist Sonny Simmons by this point.[37] The new version of Hello Kitty, however, was as much a vehicle for Turkington's comedic stylings as it was for Heydt's guitar playing. "He used to come out with a Darth Vader helmet on, with a mannequin's hand taped to the back of the helmet with, like, KFRC stickers on it," recalls Joe Pop-O-Pie. "And he'd talk in other accents, like English accents—just really campy stuff. And Kirk would be there playing like the dickens."

Kirk Heydt: It was undeniable that Gregg was genuinely funny, even as a sixteen-year-old, and brilliant. So I was like, "This is a win." I wasn't a front man.[38]

Lizzy Kate Gray: Gregg was sixteen years old, but he had a strange, wizened quality. It was like he was an old man—a fucked-up old man with weathering life experiences. And his voice was like that, too. Just this roar.

---

37 Heydt: "I met Will through Sonny because he [Sonny] was going down to get some dope. So I went down to the warehouse, and I met Will, and then he said he had this band, Flipper."

38 The lineup was rounded out by drummer Bob Witsenhausen and bassist Otto Waldorf (aka Evil Otto). Witsenhausen replaced an earlier drummer whose name has been forgotten, although Heydt can still vividly recall his persona. "He used to wear these gold chains, and he had kind of like an afro, and he wore the big lapels with the gold chains with his shirt open. Tight pants. He was like Mr. Rocker Dude. And Gregg's like [whispering], 'Where'd you get this drummer?' Because he was kinda scamming on the punk rock chicks. 'Hey baby, what's happenin'?' And they're all like, 'Ew! Gross.'"

THE MID-EIGHTIES

Kirk Heydt: His lyrics were great. I mean, he was still discovering even what a tone is. But given a little time to develop a little more tonality, it could have been interesting, vocally. I mean, his lyrics are hilarious and brilliant, but he wasn't really a singer, per se. He was still kind of figuring stuff out.

Gregg Turkington: I don't think Hello Kitty on Ice ever drew more than fifty people. We played a lot of shows to eight people or whatever. Joe Pop-O-Pie put us on opening for them, and that really helped. We opened for the Meat Puppets.

Kirk Heydt: I remember when we opened up for the Meat Puppets [at the Mabuhay]. Ness came out and said, "You guys so terrible, we shouldn't even pay you any money! You terrible—so awful!" And we're like, "Ah, come on." It was one of those things. I don't know if he gave us a hundred bucks. Grux played bass. We couldn't find a bass player, and he said he knew the songs. He didn't.

Lizzy Kate Gray: Ness was talking to Gregg and saying, "Who book you? I no book you! You terrible! You terrible!" [Laughs.] Even Ness, who booked punk rock bands, was wanting nothing to do with Hello Kitty on Ice. But you know, Kirk was a real musician. It wasn't that they didn't have any skill.

Joe Pop-O-Pie: They didn't have a real sense of managing themselves. But they did great shows. I think I saw every show they did. It was just so entertaining. Kirk was a great player, and Gregg is a real good showman, so it was a real good time.

Gregg Turkington: Hello Kitty on Ice was pretty short-lived. It was right when we started having people coming to our shows that the band broke up. Hello Kitty on Ice had a total of one headlining show, and it was our last show. It was kind of a young, struggling, up-and-coming group that fizzled too soon.

Kirk Heydt: It's a shame that we couldn't have given it a run. Because it could have been really a lot of fun. But whatever—that's why there's so many bands that nobody hears of, because it's so hard to keep something together, even if it's good or even decent.

301

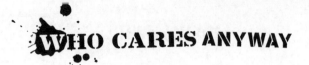

BEAN CHURCH

Hello Kitty on Ice disbanded in late 1984, not long after their non-appearance at the same marathon Club Foot gig where Chuck Mosley debuted with Faith No More. (Hello Kitty was scheduled to go on last, but police shut things down before they could take the stage.) In the meantime, Turkington—still just a junior at Washington High School—had his hand in a few other pies, including a home recording project called Bean Church.

Gregg Turkington: In 1984 or '83, when Grux and I were living at my dad's house on Steiner, some flier came in the mail for this Angel Trumpet Tapes in Anaheim. Grux goes, "These people seem cool." So he sent them his fanzine, and then they sent back a bunch of tapes and said, "We love your fanzine, Grux— you're great." And he loved their tapes, which were just really lo-fi recordings of basically drugged-out jerks fucking around.

So they said to Grux, "Do you have a band we can put on one of our cassettes?" This was pre-Caroliner. He goes, "Gregg, we could be on this compilation cassette called *Ugly California*!" So we took my grandmother's ukulele, which was in the house, and took a cardboard box and just banged some things around and sent them the tape. Robert Omlit, the guy from Angel Trumpet, wrote back and said, "Bean Church are geniuses! You've gotta do a full fuckin' release for Angel Trumpet Tapes!"

Brandan Kearney: Around the time I first met Grux, he left a tape for me at Sub when it was on Valencia and 16th, and I went in to get it from Tupper. I said, "Yeah, Grux, who works here, he left me this thing." He's like, "Grux doesn't work here. He comes in once in a while and causes more trouble than anything else."

Lizzy Kate Gray: I think I met them both [Gregg and Grux] through Kirk. He talked about them as his crazy young friends, and he tried to describe them to me. And Grux and Gregg were really best friends for a really long time there. Gregg lived in the attic of his dad's house for a while, and I think Grux lived there, too.

THE MID-EIGHTIES

Gail Coulson: When I first moved to town, Grux and Gregg were both living in the garage where Will was living.[39] Grux was like fifteen at the time, and Gregg wasn't much older. These two little kids just living with this guy and totally fascinated by it—not participating in any of the drug stuff but hanging out there and observing everything. It explains a lot about Grux and Gregg, too.

Bruce Loose: Gregg actually asked me—Will was getting ready to pop him up with a big hit of good fuckin' speed, I could tell. Because he came up to me at Subterranean and said, "Is it worth even trying drugs, Bruce?" And I just said, "*No*. Don't do it. Forget it. What happened? Did Will offer you some speed?" "Yeah." I said, "Don't do it." That was it.

Gregg Turkington: At some point, we recorded the first Bean Church cassette while Hello Kitty was going, but there was never any Bean Church show or anything. Kirk would do anything and was a great musician, and was up for a good time. So I just said, "Kirk, why don't we record this album today for this stupid label?" "Yeah, come on by, guys." We recorded this tape at his apartment.

Kirk Heydt: They came over to my house. I picked up my saxophone that I hadn't played in a long time, and then they were pickin' up instruments. I don't even remember—I'm sure it's pretty goofy.

Gregg Turkington: We turned the tape on and sat there with a room full of instruments and just played and talked for ninety minutes, and then turned it off and sent the tape to this guy and called it "Bean Church." That was it. It was like one genius professional musician playing with two retarded kids, just wailing and hitting cardboard boxes while this guy pulls out a cello and pulls out all these fucking instruments. It was kind of a compelling sound. We sent that to Robert Omlit, and he pronounced it the "album of the decade" and released it on his tape label.

---

39 According to Turkington, the two of them didn't actually live with Will, though they did spend a lot of time there.

WHO CARES ANYWAY

So then he came out to visit, and we went for a walk with him in the park. He was pretty creepy. He talked all the time about how great drugs were, and LSD, and eating mushrooms, and how we were stupid for not having gay sex and being fucked up twenty-four hours a day on drugs. So we sat on the bench in the park—we went over there on Steiner Street and talked about this stuff for a while and, you know, bade him farewell.

So I eventually took the Bean Church tracks from the great *Men's Suits/ Men's Sluts* cassette [i.e., the original ninety-minute cassette] and took the best twenty-five minutes of 'em and reissued it as *The Best of Bean Church*. So much of it was garbage, but because Kirk was such a good musician, some of it was kind of interesting …

And then, around 1991, Robert Omlit from Angel Trumpet Tapes blew his brains out with a gun, and that ended the sad story.

As for Bean Church, the ending was somewhat happier, if less dramatic. Since they were never exactly a functional band with a fixed lineup, there was no breakup to speak of. Still, Bean Church did manage to put on a handful of shows during its roughly three-year lifespan, including a June 20, 1986, gig opening for Sun City Girls and Caroliner at Club Foot. Reviewing the show for *Wiring Dept.*, David Katz wrote, "They began with a rambling rap set to fuzzy guitar and wah-wah organ, exposing the A-I-D-M conspiracy and its relevant links to Kenny Rogers's beard. Then they treated their audience to many of their great hits from the '50s, '60s, and '70s, like 'Stayin' Alive' and the great tearjerker, 'Garden Party.'"[40]

As for Bean Church's recordings, it would be pointless to analyze them in any detail, given both their extreme rarity (all of them were cassette-only releases, none of which have been reissued) and their general air of absurdity. Suffice it to say that they contain the blueprint for much of what Turkington and company would release later on through Amarillo Records: prank calls, irreverent covers ('Dream Weaver,' Black Flag's 'Rise Above,' multiple Bee Gees songs), and head-scratching originals ('Taxi Bus,' the aforementioned 'A-I-D-M'). Or, as Turkington

40 *Wiring Dept.*, Summer 1986.

himself puts it in the track 'O'—a prank call in which he asks a bewildered lady to help his band come up with a song title—"It's like rock 'n' roll … like, eighties rock 'n' roll."

BREAKFAST WITHOUT MEAT

In much the same spirit as Bean Church was *Breakfast Without Meat*, the zine Turkington started in 1983 and, together with Lizzy Kate Gray, continued publishing through the end of the decade. Like Bean Church, *BWM* had one foot in the punk/hardcore underground of the day and another in the thoroughly unhip realms of easy listening and showbiz-friendly pop. Early issues of *BWM* included interviews with Patrick Miller, Bruce Loose, and Frightwig; later ones would feature Wrecking Crew drummer Hal Blaine, songwriter Jimmy Webb, washed-up boogie rock outfit Canned Heat, and 101 Strings producer Al Sherman. This is to say nothing of the publishers' ongoing obsession with the likes of Richard Harris and Frank Sinatra, Jr.

As with many of Turkington's later creations, it could sometimes be hard to tell which parts of *BWM* were sincere and which were ironic, or where the parody ended and the homage began. Regardless, the zine's sense of humor set it apart from several of the more prominent local underground publications. "You know, we were just a tiny Xeroxed magazine," says Gray, "but we—our magazine—had a big ego, in a sense. Because it was the bigger, supposedly transgressive publications that we wanted to take the piss out of. They were all dark and published stuff about child molesting and just this nasty pseudo-intensity. And I do think we combatted that with a lot of absurdism. So the people who liked it must have enjoyed this kind of absurd goofiness and taking the pompous darkness out of a lot of the punk stuff. Not that what we did didn't have some dark aspects to it, but it wasn't this 'we are the spooky, dark punk people' kind of thing that those zines really seemed to have."

Much of the inspiration for *Breakfast Without Meat* came from scavenging the bins at thrift stores and out-of-the-way record shops. Some of the duo's finds would later go on to become expensive collector's items, but at the time,

these records were dirt cheap because hardly anyone was interested in them. As Brandan Kearney puts it, "Both of them were really good at finding the stuff in this ostensibly square culture that was actually a lot more daring and confusing—and really, in a lot of ways, artistically free—than the stuff that a label like SST or Homestead was churning out at the time."

The appeal of *BWM* lay in its blend of absurdity and pathos. It was smart and funny but without being mean-spirited or condescending. "It wasn't what a lot of people were doing," says Gray, "which was finding kitschy stuff and laughing at it. I never had the feeling that Gregg had that what they call 'ironic distance' from things like Canned Heat. He's not making it seem alien and stupid. He's kind of pointing to the pain and feebleness of it. But with heart." As she notes, his tolerance for the likes of Dora Hall—an elderly woman whose records were given away for free with proofs of purchase from Solo Cup packages—often exceeded her own."He could really wallow in the poignancy and the failure of a bad vanity pressing. And he had more of a capacity to stay with something that was painful. Whereas to me, it could sometimes be intolerable. I don't know if I thought that the aesthetic it embodied was contagious or just depressing."

ZINE CULTURE

Though its voice and subject matter were unique, *Breakfast Without Meat* was just one of countless low-budget zines emanating from the underground circa 1985. Many of them had little or nothing to do with music, at least not directly.

Such was the case with *Lobster Tendencies and Closest Penguins*, a pair of early "punk-lit" zines that were the brainchild of Denise Dee.[41] A veteran of

---

41 *Lobster Tendencies* was co-edited by Michael Kaniecki, Dee's boyfriend when she first moved to San Francisco. The zine ran for a couple of years, after which Dee decided to start a new publication. Of the zines' funny-sounding monikers, she explains, "Lobsters try to escape, and the other lobsters pull them back in. And *Closest Penguins*, the meaning of that is, one penguin tests the water for the rest of the penguins. So it's a big shift from being a little bit nihilistic, I'll say, to, 'Okay, I want to start involving more people. I'll be the fool—I'll be the person who goes out and does this stuff and then see what happens.'"

the small underground scene in late-1970s Pittsburgh, Pennsylvania (where she sang for an all-girl punk band, Hans Brinker and the Dykes), Dee moved out west in 1982 and began publishing *Lobster Tendencies* soon thereafter. "I remember going to Rough Trade," she says, "carrying in this little xeroxed, cut-and-paste, stapled-in-the-middle magazine and asking them if they would carry it." The first issue sold out, and word of mouth spread—at least enough to justify making another issue, and then another. "And then I started to meet other writers," recalls Dee. "But I didn't know anyone doing anything like that at the time. People have told me that it was like this seminal punk-lit magazine. I can't prove that, but I do believe we were one of the first, if not the first."

Before long, Dee met Factrix's Cole Palme through a job at the Strand, a movie theatre on Market Street where they both worked. The two of them put together a benefit show for *Lobster Tendencies* sometime in 1983, and before long, their shows became a semi-regular occurrence. "We started doing this thing where it was more of a literary café thing," says Palme. "We ended up doing more variety shows and then doing it with bands. Caroliner was one of the bands, and Wee Doggies, Fuck Bubble, then Tragic Mulatto later on. We were setting up a show like that once every couple of months." Other performers included Trial, a solo Roddy Bottum, American Music Club's Mark Eitzel, and the seemingly indefatigable Turkington."He did solo things and then things with Grux," recalls Palme. "Pretty spontaneous little performance things, or just starting I guess what maybe later became Neil Hamburger material. He was hilarious, always."

Denise Dee: I like some performance art, but with some of it, you need to have the context—you have to know what they're referring to and all that. But someone like a Grux or a Gregg Turkington or a Bill Gridley, they're just standing up and creating these things.[42] To me, that's a form of performance art, though it

---

42 Along with friend Bobby Ray, Gridley was an early member of Caroliner. The two of them also played together in several other bands—Wee Doggies, Junglee, and Fuck Bubble—none of which officially released any recordings. Even so, they are still fondly remembered by some of their peers. "In the mid-eighties, Wee Doggies was the house band at the Sound of Music," recalls Cole Palme. "I think they were one of the few bands that had a regular gig. Tuesday night was theirs. They would stuff all

might not fit the standard definition of that. But I mean, they were fully taking on characters, just going in, *all the way* into it. You couldn't tell if they were putting it on or not. You really couldn't tell if Gregg was those people or not. I think now with Neil Hamburger, maybe he's a little bit more "polished" in that sense.

Lizzy Kate Gray: Gregg and I would go to these actual comedy open mic nights, and he would do some comedy to a very unreceptive audience. And in this one, he got a slightly more receptive audience. And I got heckled by prostitutes. [Laughs.] But I think that he was starting to develop his act, even at a couple of the Denise Dee events.

Denise Dee: People are always talking about "like-minded people." I'm not a fan of that. I thought it was more interesting to get DIY people, but not necessarily doing it exactly the same way.[43] That's what I moved to get away from—doing anything in the same way. Why would we want to repeat that in the punk scene?

One thing that always stayed in my mind was when Michael [Kaniecki, a *Lobster Tendencies* contributor] said, "If writing doesn't stop you from going crazy, it will at least slow it down." So I was always looking for people to publish who had something that they couldn't express, even to punks—even to other people who might seem like they were people who were "like" you. It wasn't okay to be really sensitive or to have certain types of feelings in that punk movement.

---

their instruments in shopping carts and go halfway across the city and set up their instruments to an empty room. There'd be like ten of us or twelve, fifteen at the most, ever."

43 Dee found some of these "DIY people" through an unlikely source: her job as a supervisor at Research and Decisions, a market research company located near Union Square. "Denise Dee was fairly high up in that organization, so she served as a portal for losers like us," recalls Brandan Kearney, who worked there along with Turkington, David Katz, and Joe Pop-O-Pie, among others. "My job was basically to call random strangers and ask them how recently they'd had anal sex, or rimmed someone, or been fisted, and stuff like that." Adds Dee, "In the beginning of those social health surveys, it was so early that AIDS was still called GRID: Gay-Related Immune Deficiency. We were randomly opening a phone book, counting down ten names or whatever, and calling people out of the phone book. We were getting yelled at all the time by the people we were calling: 'What the hell's wrong with you?'"

THE MID-EIGHTIES

Lizzy Kate Gray: I think Denise Dee was very important to the scene. She came at it from a literary side. But to me, she was very much the essence of "do it yourself." She made a space for a lot of people to perform or read poetry. And just as a reminder, Gregg was around sixteen in these early punk years. He was just a kid. And the fact that Denise Dee kind of drew him into her circle meant that she was—I just think that she was a solidly good person in a way and recognized what a lot of people had to offer when your average person wouldn't.

27

CREATIVE LANDMINES: JOE'S THIRD RECORD, TRAGIC MULATTO, AND THREE DAY STUBBLE

"One must likewise dig up the garbage dumps near old prisons, comb the trash cans as well as other rubbish receptacles, ferret through stores of wastepaper; it would also be well to examine carefully dunghills and sumps, mainly their fossils, since it is precisely there that one finds everything humanity has held in contempt and swept beyond the perimeter of existence."
—Stanislaw Lem, 'Odysseus of Ithaca'[44]

In the annals of rock history, *Joe's Third Record* is admittedly something of a curio, a footnote. At first glance, the very idea of a third record by a band known for playing only one song might seem preposterous—like the musical equivalent of a *Weekend at Bernie's III*. Yet first glances can be deceiving, and given its role as an important puzzle piece in our narrative, the album warrants a closer look.

As with *Joe's Second Record*, *Joe's Third* uses a new backing band—in this case, one focused around guitarist Kirk Heydt. He also brought along a couple of songs from the Hello Kitty on Ice repertoire, including the stripped-

---

44 'Odysseus of Ithaca' appears in Lem's *A Perfect Vacuum* (Northwestern Univ. Press, 1971), which consists entirely of reviews of nonexistent books. This one recounts the title character's search for "geniuses of the first order"—that is, "creators of truths so unprecedented, purveyors of proposals so revolutionary, that not a soul is capable of making head or tail of them."

THE MID-EIGHTIES

down arrangement of 'I Am the Walrus' that opens the record.[45] This turns out to be one of the highlights, along with a new version of 'The Words of Jamal' that finds Joe's droll, deadpan musings sharing the spotlight with Heydt's molten guitar leads.

As for the rest of *Joe's Third Record*, it is in some ways more straightforward and in other ways more perverse than *Joe's Second*. There is no 'Truckin'' and no one-chord rock à la 'Fascists Eat Donuts' this time around; two of the songs, 'Bummed Out Guy' and 'World-O-Morons,' could almost pass for normal as far as punk rock goes. Meanwhile, two of the others—'In Frisco' and a cover of the Grateful Dead's 'Sugar Magnolia'—are presented backwards. All in all, it's the kind of record that gratifies and perplexes in almost equal measure—although, for Heydt, it was more of the latter.

"At one point, Joe was pushing real hard to release the whole album backwards—everything backwards," recalls the guitarist. "He goes, 'Oh, that's brilliant!' I said, 'Fuck you, Joe. I'll kick your fuckin' ass if you do that.' So then I was banned from the studio. And they went back some night in the middle of the night and just mixed it in two hours or something, using only the basic tracks." (Engineer Garry Creiman offers a more measured take on the backward versions: "I think the reverse mix of 'Sugar Magnolia' worked good, probably helped it. 'In Frisco' was a really rockin' track with great lyrics. It's too bad it didn't get released as a single forward."[46])

The decision to include the de facto single as a backward track reflects a

---

45 Kurt Cobain included this version of 'I Am the Walrus' in a list of favorite songs that appears in one of his posthumously published diary entries. Though he was too young to have seen the Pistols in '78, he may have seen the Pies in '85 when they played Seattle (where Heydt remembers "teenagers with those little plaid shirts running around"). Coincidentally, the Pies' version of 'I Am the Walrus' includes a reference to Seattle: "Sitting in a Frisco garden waiting for the sun / And if the sun don't come we'll get a tan from standing in Seattle rain." The other song from the HKOI is 'Ripped Off and Promoted Lame,' which is Hello Kitty's 'The Answer' with different lyrics. There are no recordings of HKOI's version of 'I Am the Walrus,' but a studio recording of 'The Answer' can be found on the B-side of the group's (very) posthumous 7-inch single, released in 2016 on Burger Records.

46 A non-backward version of 'In Frisco' was recorded with a different backing band in 1993, but to Creiman's ears, the original was superior. "The nineties version is totally different. The track is called 'Frisco Inn' on the third album, but it was 'In Frisco' before we mixed it backwards. If you have a way of doing it, listen to 'Frisco Inn' backwards, and you'll hear the original 'In Frisco.'"

penchant for self-sabotage, intentional or otherwise, that was a hallmark of many of the bands discussed in this book, from the Sleepers to Flipper and beyond. In the Pop-O-Pies' case, it wasn't a result of drug use or abuse: while Joe enjoyed an ice-cold beer as much as anyone, he eschewed hard drugs, and in several songs ('The Words of Jamal,' 'World-O-Morons'), he spoke disparagingly of them. What it *was* is harder to pin down, other than perhaps a deeply ingrained contrarian streak.

"I didn't get Joe," admits Heydt. "I just wanted to get *recorded*. To be honest with you, on the Pop-O-Pies album, if you listen to what I'm doing, I'm thinking about John Coltrane's *Interstellar Space* with the solos that I do on a couple of those things where they're really stretched out. It's more like [Miles Davis's] *Agartha* or Coltrane's *Interstellar Space*. It was definitely coming from a free jazz thing, and then obviously Hendrix. I did some cool stuff that never got put on," he laments, referring to some guitar overdubs that were recorded but left out of the final mix. "It got to the point where he ran over the budget, and Tupper pulled the plug on the project. Joe was intentionally trying to run up a budget on Tupper for some reason. He was mad at Tupper because Tupper didn't promote him the way he did Flipper, or ... I don't know."

There are no audible signs of creative tension on *Joe's Third Record*, perhaps because it was recorded in a single all-night session—too fast for any second-guessing or overanalysis to set in. That said, the disagreements between guitarist and bandleader reflected a dilemma that other bands were also grappling with in those days—namely, how to progress beyond punk without backsliding into progressive rock. As Heydt recalls, "This period up until like '85—the second wave of punk rock—people had these principles. They were like, 'You gotta do it this way! You can't know your instrument. You just gotta have some angst and get out there and play.' But I guess people learned to play their instruments, and it started becoming progressive rock again or something." Yet despite his guitarist's virtuosity (and his own classical training), Joe was wary of this trend:

> When I was a kid just starting to play music in rock bands, I thought, "Wow, wouldn't it be great to play in a rock band that people would want to come see and put out records and stuff?" And then I got into

THE MID-EIGHTIES

this whole attitude of, "I've matured and grown up from rock 'n' roll. I'm playing serious classical music and jazz, and I'm learning how to write music and orchestrate properly and all this stuff." And by the time I was a senior in college, when I discovered punk rock, I realized, "You know, all that advanced, highly technically competent stuff—that's *not* what music is about, and that's not what it's about for me, and that's not what I'm doing it for."

When I was a music major, you would spend more than five hours a day in a practice room, and I think there's more to life than that. I think that just because you *could* play something that sounds like Chick Corea doesn't mean that you *have* to play that. I think it's better to be able to play really well and write really well but not sweat the small stuff. In other words, being able to play really well but not be like, "Oh, we

spent forty hours a week practicing so we could get every little note in place." I think, one, that alienates people, and two, it eats up a lot of your life. I mean, I *like* mistakes. That shows that people are human. That's the spice of it, when the note is a little flat, or the guitar entrance is a little slow, or you don't all start and end at the same time.

IAN CARTMILL

Joe's Third Record is rife with references to SF punk lore. 'I Am the Walrus' alludes to the Sex Pistols' appearance at Winterland; 'In Frisco' name-checks Dirk Dirksen and fellow concert promoter Paul "Rat" Backovich ("Rat is fat / In Frisco / Dirk is a jerk / In Frisco"); and 'The Words of Jamal (Rainbow Bridge Version)' includes a tip of the hat to the band's manager, Ian Cartmill:

A long, long time ago
The manager of an aspiring underground San Francisco rock group
Moved to Reno and opened up a burrito stand
Now he's making more money than he could have ever dreamed of in the music business

At the time, Cartmill hadn't actually moved to Reno, but he would do so a few years later. As his sister Cari recounts, "Ian took some of his money, he got married, and he got out of the city and moved to Reno and opened Eatos Burritos, which was a great success, and got into gambling too much. He used to say, 'You could make a lot of money if you opened a burrito restaurant in Reno.'"

Before making his exit, Cartmill was an important behind-the-scenes figure in the local underground. He operated a rehearsal space, Secret Studios, where he often gave discounted rates to musicians he liked. He also managed several other bands in addition to the Pop-O-Pies, including Flipper, Frightwig, Chris Isaak's Silvertone, and even lesser-known acts such as Tanks and G.O.D. "He

THE MID-EIGHTIES

was our out-front guy," says Ted Falconi of the burly ex-hockey player.[47]

One envisions Cartmill wielding a hockey stick in much the same way that Spinal Tap manager Ian Faith wielded a cricket bat. Alas, he didn't, but he also didn't hesitate to play the role of enforcer when it was necessary. "Back in that day, bands would get terribly taken advantage of by the club—usually the club manager, but sometimes the owner and the manager were the same thing," explains Cari. "At the end of the night, the cashbox would suddenly disappear, or the band wouldn't get paid properly, period. So Ian was really good at making sure that they got money from people coming in the door."

While he was good at making sure his bands got paid, Cartmill wasn't in the music business to get rich. "Ian was like an old-school patron of the arts," says Cari. "If he had made a lot of money 300 years ago, he would have been one of those great people who just promoted and helped and appreciated and treated artists well. Artists and musicians. He was different in that way, unlike Howie Klein, who went on to become president of Reprise Records. Howie Klein was not nearly as altruistic. But you know, A explains why B is true."[48]

TRAGIC MULATTO

The Pop-O-Pies weren't alone in struggling to find a way forward through a post-punk, post-hardcore terrain littered with creative landmines and booby traps. As Simon Reynolds put it in *Rip It Up and Start Again*, the independent record charts in those days offered a "smorgasbord of the stale and second-

---

47 Cartmill is mentioned by name in Flipper's 'Ice Cold Beer,' which appears on the CD version of the live *Blow'n' Chunks* ("So I yell out the monitors / Towards Ian Cartmill / And I say I want an ice cold beer / And I want it right now!"). The song is actually just "You Nought Me" played at a slower tempo, with Bruce ad-libbing the vocals. "That was one of my beer callouts," he explains. "I used to do that all the time. We'd start up a song; we had nothing to drink; everybody would be thirsty. So they'd just sit there and play, and I'd go, 'We're not gonna continue any further than this if you don't bring us some fuckin' beer.' And I'd just go on and on until they brought us some beer."

48 Cartmill died in November of 2006 after a boating-related accident in Sausalito Yacht Harbor. "He didn't have a yacht, but that's where his boat was slipped," explains his sister Cari. "He passed away accidentally and drowned."

315

rate: past-its-prime Goth, rancid psychobilly, third-wave avant-funk," and other dead ends.[49] With new frontiers becoming harder to identify, many bands found themselves looking back to previously neglected eras for inspiration. To wit, late sixties psychedelia and acid rock were improbably creeping back into style, thanks to bands like the Meat Puppets, Dinosaur Jr, and the Butthole Surfers— all of whom emerged from the hardcore scene, only to start growing their hair out and embracing guitar solos, among other previously forbidden excesses. Meanwhile, there was also something of a trend—at least in certain corners of the underground—towards transgressive, over-the-top, and often just plain gross performance antics, as exemplified by such otherwise disparate acts as GWAR, GG Allin, the Mentors, and (once again) the Butthole Surfers. In these realms, the pursuit of excess was a perpetual frontier in its own right.

It was in this context that the rebooted version of Tragic Mulatto reemerged in 1986. "We got accused of being a Butthole Surfers copy band a lot," laments bassist Alistair Shanks, one of the band's two mainstays, along with singer and horn player Gail Coulson. There were indeed some parallels: the two bands briefly shared a label in Alternative Tentacles and also shared the stage on a few occasions (including a November 1984 show at the Mab). That said, they had little in common musically early on. When Tragic Mulatto formed in 1982, they were an arty, guitar-less quintet with a deadpan male vocalist and a horn section that wouldn't have been out of place on the *Club Foot* LP. With Coulson taking over on lead vocals a few years later, they morphed into a full-on rock band with a flamboyant singer who elicited comparisons to Grace Slick and Janis Joplin. They would go on to add a guitarist and a second drummer (which gave them something else in common with the Buttholes). Before long, they were covering songs by Led Zeppelin and Slade, alongside provocatively titled originals like 'Underwear Maintenance' and 'Fist of the Fleet.' The transformation was striking.

Gregg Turkington: I knew Gail because she had volunteered at Subterranean a few times. She just seemed like this low-key, nice, dorky, horn player girl. But then, like fuckin' three years later, I saw them opening for Will [Shatter]'s other

49 Reynolds, *Rip It Up and Start Again*, p. 390

TRAGIC MULATTO AT THE A-HOLE. L-R: ALISTAIR SHANKS, GAIL COULSON, MARC GALIPEAU, JEHU GODER, BAMBI NONYMOUS. PHOTO COURTESY OF A. SHANKS

band, Any Three Initials, and she's graduated to the lead singer. The band has become, like, this metal band. She came out wearing just Saran Wrap, wrapped around and around and around. And sure enough, the Saran Wrap's coming off, and the songs are just *filthy* and repulsive, and she just had so much charisma!

Lizzie Kate Gray: It might have been more repellent to a guy. I mean, Gail was generously, amply fleshy. I remember she was naked, and then she took these two coconut puff cakes and put one over each breast, and then wrapped herself (or had someone wrap her up) in Saran Wrap. And that's how she was dressed for the show.

Brandan Kearney: Of all the bands that tried to do that sex/grunge stuff, they really did leave you feeling like you needed to take a bath, unlike a lot of these bands.

Rebecca Wilson: Gail from Tragic Mulatto was one of the really strong, powerful women. And a lot of the girls in the music/punk scene weren't like that. People were in awe of her, but they were intimidated by her.

Lizzy Kate Gray: Gail was just totally the epitome of the *completely* unselfconscious performer who *did not care*. I mean, she was no-holds-barred. She was *inspiring*. I don't know if it comes across on their records, but she was one of the brilliant lights to me. She just did things that were so far outside what most women could do onstage. I thought it was good musically, too. Somehow the antics were right on target for me—the interplay between her and Alistair.

At least part of that interplay involved their creative use of props. "We did a lot of stuff with animal parts," admits Shanks, who credits original lead singer Patrick Marsh with some key innovations in this department. "Pat was really good with duct tape. One of the things we liked to do is we'd get these pig ears, and he would cut a hole in them, and he would make a headband out of duct tape and thread it through and fit it to our heads. So these ears would sit perfectly in front of *our* ears." Other favorites props included turkey necks ("from a distance of a few feet, it looks so real and so much like a long, disgusting cock that it's amazing," notes Shanks), razor clams ("they have this appendage that sticks out of them, and it looks exactly like a horse penis," adds Coulson), and pig intestines. The group also had a penchant for performing in various stages of undress, which caused a minor scandal in 1989 when a cable access show in Austin, Texas, aired a video of them "playing in the buff," according to a local newspaper report.[50]

"So from this, you may be getting a sense of maybe why people tended to overlook our music," says Shanks. "But it was always secondary—it was always like, 'What are we gonna do to make this really funny or entertaining *while* we play?'"

The onstage antics may have been secondary, but they were consistent with the basic thrust of the music and lyrics. Take, for example, the first song on 1987's *Locos Por El Sexo*, 'Freddy,' whose lyrics were inspired by a safe sex poster on the wall of their Turk Street Studios rehearsal space. "It was like a cartoon image of a guy," he explains. "And one of the rules was, 'Jacking off is hot and safe.'" Coulson adds, "I think that the whole thing was, 'Don't let him come in your ass; don't come in his. Don't come in his mouth; don't let him come in yours. Jacking off is hot and safe. Don't rim.'"

Taken together, it amounted to a concentrated dose of filth and depravity, albeit mixed with a sense of humor and at least a modicum of intelligence. For a band with essentially no major label prospects—indeed, they were too raunchy for even most college radio stations—they did remarkably well for themselves, releasing three LPs between 1987 and 1990 and touring the country several times. "We had gotten in a pretty good groove of putting out an album a year and doing a national tour or two every year between '88 and 1990," says Shanks. "And actually, at the time we broke up, we had people in Amsterdam setting up a European tour for us that I had to cancel, which I actually still kind of regret, because I never got a chance to play in Europe."

"We actually came home with money on the last tour," adds Coulson. It was quite the contrast from their first tour, a summertime slog through the Southwest in 1984 that nearly left them stranded in Phoenix after a club owner refused to pay them.[51] Or their second tour, when the tour van broke down outside of

50 Pete Szilagyi, "Clothes-Optional Music." *Austin American-Statesman.* August 8, 1989.
51 Shanks describes the incident in more detail: "Before we went to the club, it was six,

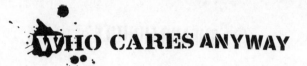

Portland, leaving them stuck in a house full of "disco queen skater-punks," this time in the midst of a winter storm. Yet they persevered. "Most of our audience at the beginning was people who were in bands like us," reflects Coulson. "Kind of experimental-type bands—that was most of our audience. But at the end, we'd just be getting Joe Punk Rocker off the street coming in. And people would be dancing. That was the fun thing at the end when we were packing houses, would be getting the whole place dancing, and moving your arm and having the whole audience ripple in that direction."[52]

THREE DAY STUBBLE

Then there was Three Day Stubble, one of a handful of bands to relocate to the Bay Area from Texas during the 1980s, but the only one specializing in self-proclaimed nerd rock. They formed in Houston in 1980 and played San Francisco for the first time in 1984 when they left a lasting impression on Mark Bowen:

> Billy Gould, when I was hanging out with Faith No More, was the one
> who said, "Three Day Stubble's coming to town, man. We've gotta go

---

seven in the evening, and it was still ninety-eight degrees. I remember seeing the thermometer in the supermarket parking lot. And we were eating cold refried beans out of a can that we had bought with the last of our money. We didn't have any money for gas to get back. And we went, and we played this show, and the owner refused to pay us because he claimed we weren't a 'real band.' Probably because it was just bass, drums and saxophone—and you know, we didn't have a guitar. So he claimed we weren't a real band. And I sat, and I argued with him, trying not to lose my temper and be really reasonable, but I argued with him for a long time—close to an hour, I think it was. And finally, he gave us like seventy bucks. We were supposed to have a $100 guarantee, and finally, he came up with about $70. I think we wore him down."

52 Members of Tragic Mulatto populated several side project bands during the late 1980s, including the punk-polka outfit Polkacide and the bawdy Pennsylvania Mahoney & Her Safe-Sextette. "They were kind of like big band-style jazz, with Gail's amazingly projective voice," says Joan Osato of Pennsylvania Mahoney. Adds Bill Gould, "Gail was an *amazing* torch singer. And they would go to a place like the Paradise Lounge and make it like an open bar for the band—they'd sneak behind the bar while they were playing and steal drinks and just get so trashed they'd vomit on stage. But they were *excellent* players—they were fantastic."

see these guys!" So we went to see their show up on Haight, and I was floored. I thought they were retarded. I mean, it doesn't sound very PC, but they had such a retarded-looking, nerdy sort of sound and look that I thought, "How are these people managing to even tour?" I literally thought that they were developmentally disabled. And then I figured out that it was just a show—it was their thing.

Bowen would later join the band on drums after they moved to San Francisco in 1985. Other members came and went, with the exception of guitarist Brently Pusser and vocalist Donald the Nut—who, according to Pusser, was "tone-deaf and rhythm unconscious." Onstage, Donald's excruciating vocals were accompanied by an arsenal of convulsive dance moves and a heavy-handed persona that makes the characters in *Revenge of the Nerds* look measured in comparison.

Paul Casteel: I remember one time at the Art Institute—it was one of their first shows, I believe. And I was there with Will Shatter. And we ended up in an elevator with Donald. And he's dressed, like, real geeky—you know, like double-knits and stuff—but then he had on this pair of, like, super nice cowboy boots. So Will pushes the stop button between floors and goes, "Gimme those fuckin' cowboy boots." [Laughs.] And he scared the shit out of the guy. The guy kept reaching for the button, and Will kept putting his hand over it, going, "Hey, you've gotta explain yourself. Nobody's that nerdy. I know this is all a fuckin' act. So come on, break with the fuckin' act and just tell us who you are!" At one point, I almost had to say, "Come on, Will, give him a break." He was just pushin' the guy's buttons to see what he would do, see if he would break character.

As premises go, Three Day Stubble's wasn't the most durable, but that didn't stop them from landing plenty of choice opening slots or making fans out of everyone from Germs drummer Don Bolles (who deemed their 1983 live debut in Los Angeles a "religious experience") to the members of Tragic Mulatto. "They had this whole sensibility of really kind of attacking the whole rock thing, which is really how Tragic Mulatto started out, too," says Shanks. "We wanted

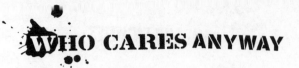

to do everything kind of the opposite of what regular rock bands do."[53]

Along with Bolles, Shanks later wound up joining the group in the early nineties. "I'm not trying to take *credit*," says the bassist, "but I think that my sensibility changed the band a little bit, and I think that things normally evolved in a certain way. And it got to be more—in a way, more conventionally musical. So you could blame me for that."

53 According to Pusser, the feeling was mutual. "When [Tragic Mulatto] would come to Houston, we would all just open our homes and our hearts. And they would stay with us. They were like family. We loved them so much. They were our favorite band."

28

"INSTITUTIONALIZED DYSFUNCTION": FLIPPER AND FRIENDS IN THE MID-EIGHTIES

Meri St. Mary: I came up with the line, "Flipper can ruin a wet dream." Because they could. They were just, like, *miserable.* What happened is that everybody was on different drugs. But basically, they would do shows just to get money. They were in limbo. They weren't really a band.

Bruno DeSmartass: I think it's the institutionalized dysfunction again. I really think that Ted was a fuckin' boiling mess. Stevie would play, but he wasn't elemental. And Brucie was a mess. And I think that it really got to the point where they just couldn't progress.

Steve Tupper: They were just not communicating very well for a while there. So that's why after that you had, like, basically the singles and compilations album [*Sex Bomb Baby!*], and after that, you had the live LP that was basically assembled from just a bunch of miscellaneous live stuff. They weren't really functioning. Sporadically, they would scrape themselves together and do a tour. But at that point, that was mostly to raise money for their living expenses.

By the time *Gone Fishin'* finally saw the light of day in August of 1984, almost two years had passed since work originally began on the album. And while the finished product was by no means slick, it didn't exude quite the same charm, the same devil-may-care attitude, as its predecessor. A writeup in the *Boston Globe* called *Gone Fishin'* "a polished album that's more ambitious, yet less

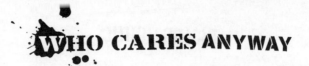

powerful" than *Generic*.[54] The *Allentown Morning Call*'s Len Righi offered a similar take: "Only one song, 'In Life My Friends,' has the resonant, liberating din of such singles as 'Love Canal,' 'Ha Ha Ha,' 'Sex Bomb,' and 'Get Away' or the band's excellent debut."[55] The reviews were also sprinkled with rumors—not entirely unfounded—that the band had broken up, along with references to the elaborate album art, which included a cut-and-fold model of the infamous Flipper tour bus, and its role in delaying the album's release.

In other words, a lot of momentum had been lost since 1982, when *Generic* rated as the only independent release in the top twenty of the *Village Voice*'s annual Pazz & Jop Poll. In comparison, 1984's list included four such albums in the top twenty: the Replacements' *Let It Be*, Hüsker Dü's *Zen Arcade*, the Minutemen's *Double Nickels on the Dime*, and *Meat Puppets II*. Considering that three of those bands (all except Hüsker Dü) had opened for Flipper at some point in the not-too-distant past, it would have been understandable if they'd felt one-upped by the competition. Yet as Bruce Loose recalls, that was probably not the first thing on anyone's mind. "I mean, there were so many drugs being used in the band at that point, it's really hard to say where anybody's real feelings were."

WEASEL CONTINGENT, MERI ST. MARY, AND HOUSECOAT PROJECT

It was the *Gone Fishin'* tour that brought an end to Bruce's sojourn in New York City, although due to a complicated situation with a girlfriend, he wound up returning to San Francisco midway through the tour. Once again, an emergency call was put in to Bruno DeSmartass, who had already filled in for both Will and Ted on previous occasions. (Ted recalls the gist of the phone call: "How 'bout we pick you up tomorrow at the airport in Memphis, and … what are you doing for the next three weeks after that?")

54 Ariel Lipner, review of Flipper, *Gone Fishin'*. *Boston Globe,* November 1, 1984.
55 *Allentown Morning Call*, March 16, 1985.

THE MID-EIGHTIES

Back in San Francisco, Bruce put together another new band, Weasel Contingent, which included his childhood friend Bill Burgess on guitar, plus Carlos Willingham on vocals and a succession of drummers. "It was really a good band, but it still was raw as hell," says Willingham. "It had that wall of sound, kind of Flipper-ish wall of sound, but it had a lot more tightness to it. I was so fuckin' happy to be in that band."

It was not long after his return to SF that Bruce met Meri St. Mary, a singer-songwriter and LA punk scenester who had moved to the city a few years prior. A whirlwind romance ensued, and by December of 1985, Meri was informing friends and family that she was pregnant. Wanting to sidestep the temptations of city life, the couple moved up to the Humboldt County ranch house where Loose's mother and stepfather lived. That meant the end of Weasel Contingent, as Willingham ruefully notes. "I remember Bruce said, 'We're gonna give it a break for a while. When the kid comes around, I'll come back.' I said, 'I don't think that's gonna happen.' Which it didn't."

St. Mary's own band, Housecoat Project, went on hiatus around the same time, though her pregnancy wasn't the only factor. While she and Bruce were off visiting family in LA, Housecoat Project guitarist Eric Yunker suffered a freak accident on stage at the Mab, where he was performing with another band on the night of December 20, 1985. "I thought he had a heart attack," recalls Joe Bonaparte of Any Three Initials, who also played that night. "All I know is, we were playing next, and we were standing around, probably drinking beer. We just hear this 'crash, boom.' It's like, '*Damn*.' Then the ambulance came and took him away. And the show continued, which is kind of fucked up. We played, then the Mentors played."

Yunker (aka Eric Rad) was a multi-talented artist who also wrote screenplays and designed custom guitars out of found objects like radiator pipes and car hood ornaments. (One of these guitars was purchased by ZZ Top's Billy Gibbons and featured on the cover of *Guitar Player* magazine; another can be seen on the cover of Flipper's *Sex Bomb Baby!* compilation.) Yunker was reportedly testing out one of his new creations on that fateful night at the Mabuhay, and one newspaper report even blamed his death on the guitar (though others have blamed the wiring in the club).[56] "I still don't know to this day how he died," admits St. Mary. "It was tragic and weird. But then again, I thought it was a great way for him to go because he was a musician, and he loved to play guitar."

Housecoat Project eventually regrouped after Yunker's death and then the birth of Bruce and Meri's son in June of 1986. They went on to make a couple of LPs for Subterranean, the first of which, 1988's *Wide Eye Doo Dat*, was funded in part by a check from ZZ Top (as payment for the aforementioned guitar). Taking Yunker's place on guitar was Jay Crawford, who had the unenviable task of filling in for St. Mary's former right-hand man. "Jay was good," she says. "He did some of Eric's stuff verbatim, as best as he could. But that dynamic of writing songs with Eric was, of course, over. So we took what we could and went from there."

Thanks to her relationship with Bruce, Meri St. Mary's band became part of the extended Flipper family, though she had mixed feelings about the association. "I wasn't a person who felt like I needed to be a part of Flipper to be an artist," she says. "I was my own person before I even got with Bruce." As for other parties involved, the feelings weren't even mixed. "I think my band did not appreciate Bruce. They didn't want him anywhere near. And Flipper—definitely those guys didn't want me anywhere near." Nonetheless, Housecoat Project often wound up on bills with Bruce's Weasel Contingent or Will Shatter's Any Three Initials, and they also opened for Flipper on a few occasions. Moreover, one of the songs on *Wide Eye Doo Dat,* 'Gilroy,' is about Will:

He's just a guy from Gilroy
He'd shoot up his brother, probably sell his mother
To get some dough, to buy some drugs, to get laid
By a girl who ain't even pretty

"I thought it was hilarious," she says of the song, "and so did Bruce, and so did Will."

---

56 *The Sacramento Bee*, January 12, 1986. "Also deceased is guitar designer Eric 'Rad' Yunker, thirty-two, who was electrocuted December 20 while testing a guitar for ZZ Top's Billy Gibbons."

ANY THREE INITIALS

Any Three Initials was Shatter's own attempt at coping with the Flipper Blues. The story of how A3I came together brings Bad Posture—the remnants of which had recently returned from New York—back into the picture.[57] As bassist Emilio Crixell recalls, "When they had heard that we weren't doing Bad Posture, his girlfriend, Brenda Sheehan, approached us about that. She was kind of his manager. And we said, 'Sure.' Ever since Negative Trend, I was always kind of a fan of Will's. I thought he was a really great songwriter."

They added a guitarist, Joe Bonaparte (aka Joe Dead), formerly of a local hardcore band called the Emetics. For him, the big draw was the Bad Posture connection."I really liked Flipper and had seen them play a bunch, but I listened to Bad Posture tons," he says. "We would play them before all our [Emetics] shows."[58] And as for Will, he was looking to play the part of the rock 'n' roll street poet, or at least his version of it. "He just wanted to be up front," says Crixell. "That was his thing. I don't recall him ever really picking up an instrument once, at all, like playing bass."

Stylistically, the band was nothing exotic. "We were kind of just a rock band," says Bonaparte. But they weren't generic, either (no Flipper pun intended). The basic template was not unlike that of Lou Reed's 1980s albums—half-spoken, half-sung vocals backed by a workmanlike band—but the sound was at once post-hardcore and pre-grunge. "I think we felt in some ways we were kind of ahead of the curve," says the guitarist, "if you look at some of the things that were happening by 1990. You know, the loud part, the quiet part—and they were longer songs. There were definitely dirgey aspects to the music, but it wasn't thrash, which is what everybody was doing at the time."

---

57 The comings and goings are hard to keep track of, but here is a brief rundown: Three-fifths of Bad Posture (Crixell, guitarist Eddie Galvan, and singer 4-Way) moved from SF to NYC in 1983. While there, they added Susan Miller on guitar and Mike Maurer (aka Mike Ludlow) on drums to replace Bruno DeSmartass and John Surrell, respectively. When they disbanded in 1984, it was Crixell, Galvan, and Maurer who returned to SF.
58 Bad Posture guitarist Eddie Galvan was initially a member of A3I, but he left relatively early on and was not replaced.

WHO CARES ANYWAY

For much of 1985 and '86, A3I was a functioning band that played out regularly and even went on tour—a brief jaunt through the Southwest in March of 1986. By this point, Shatter had taken to wearing a cowboy hat onstage, a somewhat incongruous sight given the band's sound; only one song they recorded, 'The Worst Thing (I Ever Saw),' hints at anything resembling country. "I don't know what that was about," admits Bonaparte. "But he definitely was wearing one on pretty much the whole tour. He wore that a lot. He was losing his hair pretty young, around thirty. So he was embarrassed. I think that had a lot to do with the hat."

A few months before the tour, A3I recorded material for an LP at Tom Mallon's studio. Entitled *Ruins of America*, the album was slated for release on Subterranean in 1986 before encountering a series of delays. In the meantime, the band broke up.

Joe Bonaparte: Me, Emilio, and Mike had become very close, and Will always kept a little distance. He was more intellectual, more of an artist than us. He would want to listen to Leonard Cohen, and we would want punk or metal. A rift started to happen. Will could have the "lead singer" attitude sometimes, and it was not going to fly.[59]

Steve Tupper: There was just a lot of confusion back then. And at the same time, we were having a lot of money problems, too. All these distributors were dying out. Thousands and thousands of dollars went down the drain.

Gregg Turkington: There were test pressings, the artwork was done, and everything. It was all ready to go. The test pressings had been sent out to distributors; the PR sheet was done; they had the catalog number. It was listed in the Subterranean catalog for years after that as "coming soon." And we were even taking advance orders at one point, but the money all got refunded, and nothing ever happened.

---

59 https://web.archive.org/web/20130507015240/http://mekaprods.com/A3I_bio

THE MID-EIGHTIES

Joe Bonaparte: It's in the *Trouser Press Alternative Record Guide*. There's people out there who say they've seen it, but I've never seen it.[60]

Ruins of America is not quite a lost classic on par with, say, the Beach Boys' *Smile,* but it does have its moments. Foremost among them is the ten-minute closing track, 'Don't Turn off the Light,' an ode to juvenile delinquency that

---

60 The Subterranean release never materialized, although bootleg versions of the album have circulated for years, and in 2011, a semi-official CD version of the album came out—in a very limited edition—on the French imprint Meka Records.

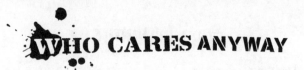

echoes earlier Flipper songs like 'Get Away' and 'Shed No Tears,' in sentiment if not in sound. The song name-checks Brenda Spencer—who, in 1979, went on a shooting spree that killed a school principal as well as a janitor. Asked what motivated her actions, she told a reporter, "I don't like Mondays. This livens up the day."[61] He then goes on to dedicate the song to "all the sons who shot their fathers," "all the daughters who can outdrink their mothers," "all of you fifteen-year-old junkies and whores," and "the kid with the matches burning down the church." It is a gut-wrenching song, one that's both rousing and deeply unsettling. As the last song on the last album Shatter would record, it serves as a fitting enough summation of his personal philosophy and all of the "pessimistic optimism" it entailed.

61 The song also mentions Tina Walker, a sixteen-year-old who, in 1985, spent time in jail for hitting her math teacher. For Shatter, the anti-teacher sentiments were a recurring theme. Other examples include 'Shed No Tears' as well as A3I's cover of Leonard Cohen's 'Teachers' (which appears in a rough rehearsal version on the Meka CD). As for the reference to Brenda Spencer, one is reminded of Andre Breton's infamous declaration that "[t]he simplest Surrealist act consists of dashing down into the street, pistol in hand, and firing blindly, as fast as you can pull the trigger, into the crowd" (Second Manifesto of Surrealism).

29

SHATTERED

"In his heart he lived a dangerous metaphor: Art is magic. The magician is a god. Gods can do anything, and never mind the cost."[62]

Peter Urban: Will and I had kind of drifted, mostly because Will got into junk heavily, and I didn't like what it did to his personality. Other people said that he was in the process of cleaning up, but it seemed to me that he had checked out sometime earlier. He was giving into sort of his worst impulses. Others, I know, continued to see him as a heroic figure.

Denny DeGorio: During the early period, I was real tight with Will. He had a lot of enthusiasm, and he was really funny. We would do just anything and everything we thought of. We would go down to Fisherman's Wharf and set up these little street bands, and we would play just crazy shit—old country songs and whatever. I remember Will would even tap dance. One time we stole a boat out of Fisherman's Wharf. It was just a rowboat. We untied it off the pier and just took off into the bay. We just did all kinds of crazy shit like that.

The last time I saw Will was in Austin, and he wasn't like that anymore.[63] He seemed darker and a little more negative. I couldn't tell what was up. Later, I learned more about him. I guess he was using a lot more than I realized during that period. Maybe it was depression—I don't know—but he got a little more somber, a little more serious, a little darker.

---

62 Geoffrey Wolff, *Black Sun* (New York Review Books, 1976), p. 12.
63 This would have likely been either January of 1985—when Flipper last played Austin—
    or March of 1986 when Any Three Initials played there.

Rozz Rezabek: He was always very cynical. That was the nature of his humor, 100 percent. He said to me one time, "My girlfriend's pregnant, but when the kid realizes that I'm his father, he'll probably spontaneously self-abort."

Denny DeGorio: When he came out to Austin, that's when I really noticed the darkness. Because I was really enthusiastic about the music and art scene here, and he was just unmoved by everything, I think. And that was part of it. I think it must have been kind of depressing to go through that period of being stuck—you know, being creatively stuck. And I think that happens to a lot of artists and musicians. You go through a period where you get creatively stuck, and it's a kind of chicken-or-egg thing. I don't know if it's the depression that causes you to be stuck, or if it's the being stuck that gets you depressed. It's like they feed off each other, and I think that kind of happened to Will.

Michael Belfer: The last time I talked to Will, it wasn't pleasant. He was very much down on the whole idea of being clean and sober, and he was ridiculing me for being in a halfway house. But I'd really hit a horrible bottom living in New York [in 1986] and being clean was the only hope for me to live. I was gonna die if I didn't get clean. When I tried to explain that to him, he just mocked me. He was very cruel the last time I talked to him. He wasn't supportive at all. As far as he was concerned, I'd become one of "those people." I remember him saying something like that to me. I'd become one of those "clean and sober people." He was making it out like it was trendy.

Rozz Rezabek: I saw him really close to when he died. He showed up with a basketball and said, "Do you wanna go play some ball?" And I just figured he must have been up all night on speed or something. And we went over to the courts at the Panhandle for a while. He was terrible at it, though. He couldn't play basketball; he couldn't even *dribble* a basketball.

THE ACID SHOW

On August 9, 1987, Shatter made an impromptu appearance during an event at the Art Institute. Referred to by many as "the acid show," it was officially

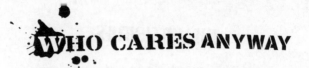

the opening night of The Holy Transfers of the Rebel Replevin, an exhibit of LSD blotter art curated by collector Mark McCloud. Several bands played, including Caroliner, Bond Bergland's post-Factrix outfit Saqqara Dogs, and Tragic Mulatto, whose Alistair Shanks remembers the night vividly:

In between performances, Will took the mic and started haranguing the audience about what punk rock was and what art was. I think he even said something like, "Punk rock's not just dressing up in costumes or strapping milk crates to your penis," which is what I had done. And the audience was kind of heckling him back.

It was kind of amazing and kind of annoying both at the same time, so there was this tension about it. Like, at first, it was sort of funny, but then he kept going. Will was the kind of guy who sometimes you might not be able to tell how serious he was, but he just started getting into it more and more, and it seemed like he was really serious after a while. And it created a weird vibe. A lot of people were on acid already, and he was putting out this really sort of negative energy. It was sort of like, "Oh, here's this guy who used to be in this great band, and now he's just haranguing people for getting a little weird." To me, even though Flipper was never part of that orthodoxy, I hated that idea that you had to *do* or *be* a certain way in order to conform to some idea of what punk rock was. To me, punk rock was about really pushing boundaries and exploration and always trying to change. Any kind of good idea, people are always trying to pin it down and codify it and computize it. That was happening a lot, and I just really hated it.

The other thing was, I recall him being either high or drunk or both. So it wasn't like it came across as some sort of incisive critique of anything; it was just some drunken guy mouthing off, and it was kind of easily dismissible.

HARD COLD WORLD

On November 23, Flipper played the I-Beam in what would turn out to be Will Shatter's last performance. In a video clip from the concert, the band is seen playing a ramshackle version of 'Way of the World' that takes several minutes to get going. At one point, Will complains to the sound man, "I can't hear any vocals in the monitor." Bruce goads him: "Maybe that's because we're not *singing* any vocals!" It's funny, but Will's reaction registers somewhere between annoyed and disinterested.

But maybe they were just getting warmed up. An audio recording of the full show has since made its way onto the internet, and while the band does at times sound bored with the material (most of which dates back to *Album* or earlier), there are some inspired moments toward the end. The last song is an extended version of 'Ha Ha Ha' that concludes with a free-form noise duet between Shatter and DePace. Bruce waxes poetic about it: "Will takes off on the bass and just—I mean, he goes to Saturn, Jupiter; he goes out to the fuckin' novas that are exploding all over the universe. I mean, he's just everywhere. And then, at the end, he pulls it right back into fuckin' place. Even with the break [in the recording] and that missing segment of five minutes, ten minutes—whatever it was—you still get the idea of the insanity, the chaos, the brilliance of what Will was as a bass player."[64]

Just over two weeks later, on December 9, 1987, Shatter was found dead in the kitchen of his Mission District apartment. He was thirty-one years old.

Joe Pop-O-Pie: I mean, it wasn't terribly shocking because everybody knew he was an IV drug user. But when I would see him at shows, he seemed pretty healthy. So it was a shock in that sense. But it was not a shock in that it was so far-fetched that you couldn't believe it.

---

64 Evidently, there were multiple recordings made that night. Bruce has his own (still unreleased) recording from the soundboard, and the break he's referring to was a result of the tape running out and needing to be turned over. The recording that has circulated on the internet does not have this interruption.

WHO CARES ANYWAY

Gregg Turkington: I was pretty shocked by it. The last time I talked to him, he sounded like a changed man. He was excited because he was about to have a kid, and he'd been working on cleaning up.

Meri St. Mary: When Will died, he had cleaned up. He had a new wife, who was pregnant. He was gonna have a kid, and he was gonna move out of the city, and, you know, he was *done* with all that. And then he did a shot and died. And that was all too common.

Tommy Antel: Will was really trying to do a new life. He was going to move to Sonoma or Napa or something to start a new life with the kid. You just stay clean for about two weeks, and then you do your regular shot, and you pretty much go out. Your tolerance level is gone. Most of us, we think we can go right back to where it was, and a lot of people died that way.

Ted Falconi: He was kind of like in a rehab thing. But Will's problem was that he couldn't give up his connections. Because every time that somebody would come to him and want Will to cop, he would cheat—he'd, like, take a little piece. So it was his way of getting high without spending money.

Janette Emery: He was supposed to pick me up from work. There was no answer. I walked home. It was raining. The lights weren't on in his studio. He was on the kitchen floor, dead. Our four cats were sitting next to him. The burner was still on (from Shatter preparing his fix). It had to have been instantaneous.[65]

Emilio Crixell: He died in our kitchen. I was out of town at the time, but I got a phone call from my girlfriend, who lived there, and she told me that Will had died.

Peter Urban: When Will died from an OD, I just sort of was angry at him, frankly, as opposed to feeling a sense of loss. I just felt really a sense of anger.

65 D'Arcy Fallon."Shattered." *San Francisco Examiner.* February 28, 1988.

THE MID-EIGHTIES

Ted Falconi: I was kinda pissed on the way that he left. I wasn't shocked about the fact that he OD'd.

Joe Pop-O-Pie: I've noticed that sometimes people have issues with other people when they're alive, and then, as soon as they die, they're like, "Oh, what a nice guy he was." And no one says a rude word about them. I noticed a lot of that going on when Will died. But I noticed that Bruce was very careful not to fall into that trap. He'd say, "Yeah, that fucker still owes me twenty bucks." [Laughs.] He was just very realistic about Will's past. And I think Will would have wanted it that way. I think Will wouldn't have wanted people to get all weepy and sappy and not discuss his good *and* bad points. Because Will was a down-to-earth guy, and the thing about the whole Flipper attitude was that it was not romantic. For people to become all sappy about Will, he wouldn't have liked that.

Peter Belsito: Will Shatter's been sainted by the early punks. I didn't know him, but I know he's been sainted. Which makes me skeptical. The dead people I know from that scene—not too many of 'em were saints.

Rozz Rezabek: In a lot of ways, I don't want to say this because you know how much I love the guy, but Will was pretty pretentious and pretty insecure underneath it all, too. Like we all are. We are all born wounded animals. We're looking to belong to something.

Connie Champagne: That's the curse of a lot of those guys. They were really smart, but they also had a lot of pain. They came into a city, even a country, that wasn't terribly supportive of any of the new art forms that they were trying to do.

Alistair Shanks: Will was the kind of guy who did believe in things. I think that's why he died. There are still people who believe in an idea like "punk rock"—they buy this image, this identity, this whole concept. They buy into it; they can't let go of it. Then if it changes, it becomes confusing to them. And I'm not saying that's necessarily what happened to Will, but I think Will was the kind of guy who really passionately believed. And believers can be fragile entities when things don't work out the way you want.

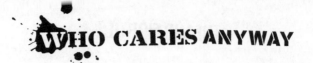

I should also say that Will Shatter was a very, very sweet guy, and I really liked him, and I respected him. So anything that I'm saying about him that's critical of him doesn't change the fact that I did have a lot of respect for him. I liked him as a person. Because there were a lot of people who would get up and spout some kind of politically correct, "You should do this, that, and the next thing," and they were shitty human beings. And Will wasn't. Will was a really sweet human being.

Michael Belfer: I had a lot of love for Will. Russell Wilkinson. He was a really amazing human being. And he was a hell of a good cook. He taught me how to use cucumbers in making salsa. He also certainly taught me a hell of a lot more than that. He taught me about a lot of music and art.

Rozz Rezabek: *He* should be the one that is on all the T-shirts. It shouldn't be Sid Vicious. Sid Vicious, once we all met him, was a loser and a moron and smelled like urine, and he's nothing to be idolized, and he's nothing to be cherished. I always thought it would be a much better world if people were walking around wearing Will Shatter T-shirts instead of Sid Vicious.

Ted Falconi: You know, I always thought, if I would've stayed with that business, I would've gotten into selling Narcan.

DON'T TURN OUT THE LIGHT

Will Shatter's death came almost ten years to the day after Negative Trend's live debut at the Mabuhay. Fittingly, a memorial show was held upstairs at the On Broadway on New Year's Day, 1988, as the Mabuhay itself had closed about a year earlier. ("I'm tired," owner Ness Aquino told the *Examiner* in a March 1987 article. "I want to take it easy for a while. I'm stuck here all the time, and it's sort of a dead end."[66])

---

66 Joel Selvin, "Tired Mabuhay Owner Sells Epochal Gardens." *San Francisco Examiner.* March 8, 1987.

THE MID-EIGHTIES

In reality, things had been bleak for some time, at least for veterans of the early punk scene. "Punk has degenerated severely," lamented Steve Tupper in a 1986 interview in the zine *Puncture*. "1986 is to 1977 as 1975 was to 1967. That is, just as the hippies degenerated into boring nothingness by the mid-70s, the punks have now gone the same way. A lot of people are just waiting for something new."[67]

This sense of malaise wasn't unique to San Francisco. Years later, Simon Reynolds would offer a similar perspective from the other side of the Atlantic: "The post-punk years felt like one long rush of endless surprise and inexhaustible creativity … By 1985, though, it seemed like almost all of that energy had dissipated, as every trajectory from punk reached an impasse or petered out."[68] That said, the cumulative effects of a decade's worth of hard-partying and drug use took an especially heavy toll on Flipper and their circle of friends. "The end of the eighties was ugly," recalls Anna-Lisa VanderValk, a resident of the infamous Mission-A. "That's when everybody was going down. From '85 on is when it started to just really get bad."

"It was the end of an era," adds Tommy Antel. "It was very lonely and depressing at that time. A lot of people started dying." One of those people was Janie—the younger sister of Will's ex-wife Jeri—who passed away in February of 1988 from drug-related complications.[69] "When Janie died, there was this whole ring happening of someone going to Vietnam and shipping drugs back to California," remembers Meri St. Mary. "And she collected these exotic birds. There was this place on 11th Street. She was doing a lot of drugs. She was by herself. Her birds were dying, and she got all these infections. I think we took her to the hospital. We visited her in the hospital, that's for sure. But what was very odd is that her family came out, and they had no clue—*no* clue. I mean, they were just like, '*What?*'"

Still another casualty was A3I/Bad Posture drummer Mike Ludlow, who died of an overdose on New Year's Eve 1987, just weeks after Will. "Emilio called me

---

67 Patty Stirling, "Subterranean: A Label's Story." *Puncture*, Fall 1986. http://www.subterranean.org/press/puncture.html
68 Reynolds, *Rip It Up and Start Again*, p. 389.
69 After Will died, Jeri reportedly moved back to her hometown in South Dakota and quit heroin cold turkey. The couple had gotten divorced circa 1985 or 1986.

both times," recalls Joe Bonaparte, who had moved back to his home state of Texas by this point. "I remember he called me and was like, 'Man, Will … ' And then he called me again, and I'd just seen Mike a month earlier, a month-and-a-half earlier. That was pretty fucked up. Mike was a sweet guy."

Emilio Crixell: At that time, I also found out that I was gonna have a kid with Susan. So that just really turned my life around. At that point, I gave up all the drugs and everything. I could see where that was going, you know? So that was just a real sad time, and kind of was instrumental in changing my life around, too.

Susan Miller: The real fundamental change for me was when I got pregnant. When I got pregnant, I almost literally walked out one door and into another life and said, "Fuck it. I'm not having a child and raising it in that craziness. I'm not doing it." That just completely derailed my punk rock nihilism, "what the fuck?"/"who cares?" kind of existence. When you have a baby growing inside of you, it really changes you.

Emilio Crixell: After Will died, I probably was in the punk rock scene a few more years, but I was kind of on my way out. Things were getting pretty repetitious at that point. You know, you went downtown, and secretaries at financial brokers were wearing Mohawks. [Laughs.] It started to become more mainstream.

THE LATE EIGHTIES

30

I'M ON THE WRONG SIDE: FROM GLORIOUS DIN TO WORLD OF POOH

FEBRUARY 9, 1985

David Katz: Jay Paget put on a show called the Dry Show, which was at the YMCA, right in the heart of the Tenderloin. It had this kind of monster lineup with all these different acts, all from that same little scene. It had this guy Walter Alter, who had hooked up these computer monitors to a keyboard, and he was in the basement typing this stuff that was on a huge screen at the back of the venue. Then they had these guys onstage who were painting on this big canvas behind the band while they were playing. I mean, it was a real art happening, and it was pretty damn neat.

Jay Paget: Walter Alter was a sort of installation artist. He had the whole room lined with old TVs with gels on them and different things being projected. So that set some atmosphere. And Doris Boris Berman was a photographer, and she was doing a self-photo booth where you took your own picture with a little trigger thing. Chel White was a filmmaker back then, and he and a couple of others did short films. Connie Harris, who was a friend of my partner at the time, was at the Art Institute, and she had a bunch of students painting a mural on some cardboard I got from the packaging store where I worked. So they were on some scaffolding above the bands, painting a mural while the evening went on. Paranoid Blue played, and we played. It was a nice spot, really. Sound was good in there, too.

THE LATE EIGHTIES

David Katz: But unfortunately, what happened on that night was that Eric got very, very drunk. The first inkling that we had that anything was up was midway through the night; before Glorious Din went on, some music was playing in between bands, and Eric went up to the mixing tech and just grabbed the volume slider and cranked it so loud that literally people were clamping their hands over their ears and half falling down. It was way, way too loud, and thankfully the mixing engineer was there and pulled it right down immediately. But it was like, "Whoa, what are you doing?"

And then when Glorious Din played, because there'd been so many acts— and that place had a curfew because it was right there in the middle of a neighborhood—somebody said to Eric that they had to cut a couple of songs out of the set. And Eric got very upset onstage, and he went totally berserk. He started swinging the mic stand around and trashing the drum kit. He went completely ballistic, to the extent that it literally took about five different people to get him off the stage. And then they kind of passed him through the crowd, and he was just completely flailing like a maniac the entire time. A whole group of people had to literally carry him out the building and throw him out onto the street, where he puked his guts out. He was beyond the point of no return, and it brought out some kind of demons. That was scary as hell.

Seymour Glass: At the end (or what turned out to be the end) of the only live performance I've seen of them—it was at the YMCA, I believe—the singer, Eric Cope, kicked over a conga drum and started swinging a mic stand back and forth in such a manner that Einsturzende Neubauten would want him in their band, except that he wasn't swinging it at the audience but at the other band members. A bunch of people leapt on him, de-miking him in the process, forming what we used to call in college a "pigpile" until he convinced them that he would be submissive for a while. They let him up, and he went berserk again. Finally, they dragged him out into the foyer, where he sat until I passed him on my way out. I remember thinking, "What the hell do you say to the guy? 'Good show'?"[1]

1   Seymour Glass, review of *Leading Stolen Horses. BravEar*, 1985.

WHO CARES ANYWAY

THE DRY SHOW

ART INSTALLATION
CONNIE KEANE HARRIS

MUSIC
GLORIOUS DIN
PARANOID BLUE

FILM
CHEL WHITE. JOHN MARSIC

T.V.CI5
WALTER ALTER

PHOTO AKTION
DORIS BORIS BERMAN

GLORIOUS DIN

220 GOLDEN GATE

FEB.9.SAT
8-12-PM
Y.M.C.A

In Glorious Din lore, the Dry Show is remembered as the beginning of the end. Chronologically, though, it was closer to the middle, taking place in between the recording and the release of their debut LP, *Leading Stolen Horses*. Still, it was a sign that the differences between the enigmatic Cope and the rest of the band ran deeper than either party had previously acknowledged.

Those differences would grow more pronounced over the next year and a half, with tensions again coming to a head during the 1986 recording sessions for their second LP, *Closely Watched Trains*. There were no pigpiles or swinging mic stands this time, but rather a more philosophical disagreement over how to mix the album. Cope wanted the drums turned down (the opposite of the approach used on *Leading Stolen Horses*), while Paget wanted the mix to more accurately reflect the band's live sound. "It's only a three-piece band, for God's sake," Paget says with a laugh. "I wanted to hear everybody. You know, it was like, there's not *that* much going on. So I think I was in a huff, and I just said, 'Okay, Matt Wallace and Eric are fine with mixing it that way, and I'm hearing something different, so you guys go ahead and mix it.'"

In Cope's defense, the finished product does make for a nice contrast with the more overtly Joy Division-style production heard on the debut album. There is also more variety in both sound and mood. Paget plays dobro instead of

344

electric guitar on several songs, one of which, the nostalgic 'Stilt Walkers,' is actually in a major key. It is one of the album's highlights, along with 'Cardboard Boxes,' which encapsulates the band's gloomy, minimalist trance-rock as well as anything in their catalog.

The recording of *Closely Watched Trains* followed a nationwide tour in the spring of 1986 that played its own role in the band's eventual demise. (As bassist Doug Heeschen would later put it, "We limped home, and no one talked for a month or two."[2]) As if spending six weeks cooped up together in a 1971 Ford Econoline van weren't enough, there were also external pressures. For one thing, it was getting harder for independent bands like Glorious Din to operate in an underground music landscape that was growing increasingly competitive and business-minded. Whereas their friends in Faith No More had significant backing—first from Ruth Schwartz's Mordam Records and then from Slash, which signed the band in early 1986—Cope and Glorious Din were truly on their own. Both of their records were self-released and self-financed through Cope's own label, Insight Records. He even booked their tour himself—no small task in the pre-internet, pre-cellphone era, especially for a non-native English speaker. "These people in the clubs, man, they could not understand a damn word I was trying to explain to them about Glorious Din," he laughs. "I could not get a show. Just imagine calling a club. It's like, 'Who is this guy? He's talking about punk rock, and he sounds like a foreigner.' Right away, they say, 'No, no, no.' We had a hard time."

Cope himself was surviving on a shoestring budget, living in a van with his girlfriend, Mary Downs, outside of the Marina District restaurant where she worked. He credits Downs with helping keep Glorious Din afloat during those years: she not only fed him with leftovers from her restaurant job but also helped fund several Insight releases, including *To Sell Kerosene Door to Door*, a double LP featuring a constellation of bands involving Cope, Paget, and others from the *Wiring Dept.* orbit.

Ultimately, it wasn't a lack of funds that led Cope to pull the plug on Insight and *Wiring Dept.* (both of which continued for another year or so after Glorious

2   Katz, "Who Was Eric Cope: The Story of '80s Punks Glorious Din." June 2016. https://www.factmag.com/2016/06/08/glorious-din-eric-cope/

Din's breakup). Rather, it was the influx of money from major labels hoping to land the next REM. The result was a flood of mediocre college rock. "At that time, people who had a little commercial sound started getting signed," explains Cope, who liked REM and even spent a brief period living with a friend of the band in Athens during a break from Glorious Din. "But because of REM and a few other bands, the doors got opened. And people would start changing their music to fit into radio and getting signed. That was the end of it—that was *all*."[3]

---

3   Cope's post-Glorious Din adventures are, like his childhood in Sri Lanka, almost the stuff of fiction. Toward the end of Glorious Din, he developed an interest in the writings of Malcolm X and other Black nationalists. One thing led to another, and by the end of the decade, he and Downs had gone to Sri Lanka to (in his words) "join the revolution" unfolding there. "I had all these discussions with Eric about politics," remembers original GD bassist Matt Hall, who had moved back to San Francisco from Iowa by this point. "He got really into Black politics—Black nationalism and stuff—for a while. I had some sympathy for that, but not as much as he did, I guess." Cope returned to the Bay Area in the early 1990s and eventually settled in Vallejo, where he started the successful gangster rap magazine, *Murder Dog*. Writing under the pseudonym "Black Dog Bone," he published *Murder Dog* from 1993 to 2014. He speaks of the Bay Area rap scene of the 1990s with the same enthusiasm that motivated him to start *Wiring Dept.* "If you listen to E-40 or if you listen to Too Short, no one sounds like that. Same as that music that was going on here in the eighties. I don't know what it is about the

THE LATE EIGHTIES

WORLD OF POOH

Glorious Din's last show took place on December 14, 1986, as part of a quadruple bill that also marked a debut of sorts for the opening act, World of Pooh. Originally started as a four-track recording project by Brandan Kearney and a friend circa 1983, World of Pooh eventually morphed into a makeshift live act, playing its first show in May of 1985 (also an opening spot for Glorious Din). Kearney tried a couple of different lineups, including one with David Katz on bass and a singer named James Dillon.[4] "I think we only did three or four gigs or something like that with that lineup," recalls Katz, "and then Brandan kind of said, 'This isn't happening,' and split it up."

The new World of Pooh lineup came together in late 1986, with Glorious Din's Paget on drums (a new instrument for him) and a relative newcomer to the scene, Barbara Manning, on bass. A recent graduate from Cal State Chico, Manning already had a bit of musical pedigree when she arrived in San Francisco earlier that year. While in Chico, she fronted the jangle pop trio 28th Day, whose self-titled LP on Enigma Records was a minor college radio hit in 1985. The story of how she wound up in World of Pooh brings Eric Cope back into the picture.

Brandan Kearney: I'd been recording all this stuff on cassette, and somehow—I think in really early '85—I got suckered into doing some improv show with people from Glorious Din and some other people. But I had played the clarinet. Eric Cope saw that, and he was just absolutely thrilled because, for some reason, he really liked the clarinet. So Eric started out having me play clarinet while he sang and played guitar. And then he hired Barbara to play cello along with us. So Eric ended up kind of fixing me up with Barbara, in a way.

Bay Area, but it was unbelievable; it was so exciting."

4   Along with Paget, Dillon and Kearney would later end up as bandmates in Archipelago Brewing Co., whose tenure as a band ran parallel to that of the later World of Pooh lineup with Paget and Barbara Manning. ABC's collected works—a trio session recorded in 1987 and then a 1989 session with an expanded lineup—are compiled on the CD *Drill Ye Terriers Drill* (Brinkman). ABC also landed a couple of tracks on the *To Sell Kerosene Door to Door* compilation.

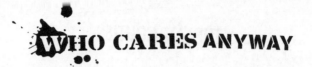

WHO CARES ANYWAY

Barbara Manning: I think I was twenty-one, turning twenty-two. I wanted to test the waters. I wanted to learn about people. I wanted to meet people. And because I worked in this print shop, I was able to meet musicians in the South of Market area, which was the place where people were renting because it was so cheap back then. So I couldn't have fallen from the sky at a better time and into a better place.

Eric Cope: There was a copy place on Mission owned by an Indian guy, and Barbara Manning was working there. And Barbara loved Glorious Din. So I would go there, and I'd say, "Hey Barbara, I need some fliers." So what she would do is, she would make, like, a thousand fliers and charge me for 200. She would do *all* this stuff for free, and then we became great friends.

David Katz: So Eric had this idea: it would be me and Eric doing this kind of singer-songwriter balladeer stuff, and Barbara Manning would play the cello, and then Brandan would play the clarinet, and then "Dave, you can play guitar." And I was like, "Eric, man, if there's one instrument I will never be able to play in the world, it's guitar." He said, oh, it didn't matter; I could play the guitar scraping the strings with a knife and just make noise. And he called that band Wednesday Morning 3 a.m. It was completely terrible; it never got off the ground. I think we did two gigs, and they were both total disasters. Nothing went right, and it sounded terrible.

Eventually, Brandan decided that he wanted to draft Barbara Manning into World of Pooh. Brandan had already been dating some woman who I had come to know at SF State, who as far as we all knew was a lesbian, but somehow she started going out with Brandan. And then he kind of left her because he was getting involved with Barbara Manning.

By that time, Brandan and I were having a bit of a falling out. At one point, I was actually playing in two different bands with him [World of Pooh and Wednesday Morning 3 a.m.] and living in the same flat with him, but we weren't speaking to each other. And it was funny, too, because he lived in this one bedroom close to the kitchen, and I lived in this other one at the other end of the hallway. And James Dillon was in the middle. You could reach James's room from the rooms on either end, and James was really close friends with both of us at the same time. It was kind of a funny little dynamic.

THE LATE EIGHTIES

"WORLD OF CRAP"

On paper, Manning and Kearney might have seemed like an odd match, given the contrast between her folk-pop songwriting sensibilities and his predilection for noisier, more confrontational fare (two of his favorite bands were Flipper and Throbbing Gristle). And it did take some time for things to come together, as Kearney explains. "I was initially really nervous playing with her because she seemed like kind of a pro by my standards. I just figured, 'I can't possibly measure up.' She'd say herself that none of my songs made any sense to her and didn't even seem like music and just seemed random and incoherent."

Some of her old fans back in Chico had similar reservations, as evidenced by a scathing review in a local paper after a homecoming show there. "World of Crap might be a better name for the San Francisco band World of Pooh, which played a disappointing set—to say the least—at the Burro Room Saturday," the review began."Material from Manning's *Lately I Keep Scissors* LP is topping the KCSC Livewire Top Ten list, so interest was somewhat keen in the World of Pooh performance … But it was a waste of brain cells, eardrums, and $3 for those fifty or so [in attendance]."[5]

In truth, there wasn't such a wide gulf between World of Pooh and Manning's solo material, some of which eventually made its way into the trio's repertoire. Manning was responsible for almost half of the songs on their records, with Kearney writing the rest of them. Granted, one can usually tell them apart, with Kearney's generally being more agitated, dissonant, and unorthodox in their structure. Still, there was common ground, including their fondness for obscure post-punk bands like 100 Flowers (whose song 'Strip Club' WoP covered on a later 7-inch). Moreover, Manning was eager to avoid being pigeonholed as a singer-songwriter, and her experiences with the local acoustic folk scene only reinforced that feeling. As Kearney summarizes, "The weird thing about Barbara is we sort of saw eye to eye on a lot of stuff. I think for all of our differences, we clicked in terms of allowing this space for disasters to happen on stage—for songs to fall apart, for things to go wrong, for nothing to work, and just for bizarre interactions."

Adding to the bizarreness of the interactions was the fact that Kearney and Manning were a romantic item. This detail colored audience perceptions of the trio, eliciting comparisons to Richard and Linda Thompson more so than, say, John and Yoko. The perceptions weren't entirely inaccurate, admits Kearney. "I feel like we were people with a weird relationship portraying people with a really

5 Paul Harrar, "World of Pooh is Full of It." *Grass Valley Union*, 1989 (precise date unknown).

weird relationship," he told *Dynamite Hemorrhage* in a 2016 interview. "Over time, the distinction vanished." At times, they actively blurred the distinction, like the time Kearney hit Manning over the head with a fake beer bottle onstage. "I felt like the audience went cold," Manning later recounted. "They were mad to see a girl get hit by a bottle. I remember feeling, 'Oh, I really shouldn't have played it up.'"[6]

THE LAND OF THIRST

The trio recorded their lone LP, *The Land of Thirst*, with the help of Greg Freeman, a budding engineer who had just opened his own studio, the aptly named Lowdown."At the time, my studio was *really* filthy," he recalls. "It was just this horrible, like, carpet-tacked-up-on-the-walls, kind of gross former practice space in the South of Market." In the years to come, Freeman would emerge as a key behind-the-scenes figure for numerous local bands (much as Tom Mallon had done earlier in the decade), but World of Pooh were among his earliest clients. "I put up an ad at Rough Trade, saying, 'Studio—$8/hour for eight tracks.' And two people responded. One of them was Jay Paget, who was doing a project called Harry's Picket Fence.[7] That was one of the first sessions I did. So I met Jay, and then I met Brandan Kearney. And at that point, everybody kind of knew everybody: Barbara Manning, the Thinking Fellers, and all that stuff."

Freeman's production on *The Land of Thirst* is deliberately understated, much like the group's songwriting. Musically, the album seems to draw equally on late sixties folk rock and the more minimalist strains of early post-punk, though other elements are harder to place, like the dissonant chords on 'Laughing at the Ground' and 'Mr. Coffee-Nerves.' The lyrics have their share of black humor,

6   Jay Hinman, "World of Pooh: The Oral History," *Dynamite Hemorrhage*, No. 3. 2016.
7   Harry's Picket Fence was Glorious Din minus Eric Cope plus a second guitarist. They recorded material for an LP album circa 1987, but the only two songs they officially released are found on the *To Sell Kerosene Door to Door* compilation.

as with the dark singalong chorus on 'Coffee-Nerves' ("Seems that fear always closes our eyes as we connect the dots / Fa-la-la-la la la-la-la-la") and the almost cartoonish violence alluded to in 'Playing One's Own Piano' ("Go take a board / Put nails in it / Beat father over the head with it").

With just a thousand copies pressed, *Land of Thirst* was never destined to reach a massive audience. Still, it connected with those in the know. Writing in *Spin*, Byron Coley praised the album as a "Scrambled, druggy version of what folk rock might've evolved into if all the world were the Haight."[8] A couple of decades later, Andrew Earles included it in his book *Gimme Indie Rock: 500 Essential Indie Rock Albums*, comparing it favorably to the work of New Zealand bands such as the Bats and the Clean: "That's right—the greatest album of Flying Nun-style indie pop didn't even come from New Zealand."[9]

As for the "indie" tag, it's accurate up to a point. *Land of Thirst* ticks off several of the boxes on Simon Reynolds's checklist of indie rock hallmarks, which include "scruffy guitars, white-only sources, weak or 'pale' folk-based vocals, undanceable rhythms, lo-fi or Luddite production, and a retro (usually sixties) slant."[10] That said, the terms "indie pop" and "indie rock" were not yet in vogue at the time, and Kearney himself resists being lumped in with those genres. "That whole thing was so alien to me, and it's weird because, on the basis of the one record, I get lumped in either with that or a proto version of that. Maybe it's the vanity of small differences, but all that stuff is of no conceivable interest to me."[11]

Even so, *Land of Thirst* was independent in the sense of being DIY. Apart from the recording, the band did indeed do everything themselves, with Kearney releasing it as the first LP on his label Nuf Sed (the label's previous releases were cassette-only). For Manning, who already had a solo album to her name by this point, the DIY approach was a revelation. "Brandan was the first person who made it clear to me that that's possible," she says. "Because I had been with 28th Day

---

8   Byron Coley, "80 Excellent Records of the '80s." *Spin*, January 1990, p. 82.

9   Andrew Earles, *Gimme Indie Rock: 500 Essential American Underground Rock Albums 1981–1996*, p. 360.

10 Reynolds, *Rip it Up and Start Again*, p. 391.

11 An early version of the album was released on cassette in 1988, and a couple of the songs ('Scissors' and 'Somewhere Soon') also appear in different versions on Manning's 1989 solo debut, *Lately I Keep Scissors*. The LP was reissued with different cover art by Starlight Furniture Co. in 2017.

and was always chasing the label: 'What label can we get on, and how can we make this work?' But Brandan was just like, 'Yeah, I'm gonna make my own.' And I watched him put that album together so fast and so amazingly. I didn't know you could make up your own label name. I didn't know you could print up your own label and put it all together and decide exactly how it's gonna be, and you don't have to have a barcode stamp. I didn't know you could walk into a distributor on your own and just say, 'Hey, I've got this record,' and then they like it so much, they'll take half, and then you get all your money back—just like that."

While the album was a success, the ensuing tour—a weeklong excursion through the Northeast in March of 1990—was not so much. It wasn't because of their awkward encounter with Henry Rollins at CBGB's (on a night when WoP found themselves on a bill with both the Rollins Band and Helmet) or even the quality of their performances. "I mean, we had some bad shows, but Barbara and I weren't getting along, to put it mildly," says Kearney. "It was extremely tense. And basically, I think it was only seven days' worth of shows, but it was hard to get through."

The last show of the tour found the trio opening for Yo La Tengo at Maxwell's in Hoboken, New Jersey. Much like the Glorious Din's Dry Show, this one would live in infamy. "It was just horrible to watch, and of course completely enthralling," wrote blogger Elisabeth Vincentelli years later.[12] "It didn't feel like a put-on but like the raw implosion of a couple right in front of us, *Scenes from a Marriage* punk rock–style."

Yet as enthralling as it might have been to watch, this wasn't the kind of show World of Pooh intended to put on, nor was it anyone's idea of a sustainable working relationship. By the time they made it back home—following a harrowing drive through a snowstorm, a mad dash through a Chicago train station, and a three-day train ride from there to San Francisco—it was understood that things had run their course. "You are so right," wrote Barbara in a letter to Brandan a few months later. "We are a very dangerous mix, and it was daring and fun for a time, but now it needs to be left alone and perhaps even forgotten."

---

12 "Scenes from a Break-Up." March 17, 2008. http://determineddilettante.blogspot. com/2008/03/scenes-from-break-up.html

31

HELL RULES: GILMAN STREET, TFUL 282, AND BANANAFISH

Through no fault of their own, World of Pooh's lifespan coincided with a lean period for underground music in San Francisco. At least, it seemed that way to many observers. "For years, I've been carrying on about the virtual flushability of San Francisco's musical output," wrote Byron Coley in a 1989 issue of *Spin*.[13] A year earlier, critic Gina Arnold had weighed in with a similar opinion. "Ever wonder why San Francisco's underground music scene is so bad?" she asked. "I don't know why it is, but bands from San Francisco just aren't very good. Maybe because it's so easy to reach a low level of recognition here: you don't even have to have a record out before you can get booked, played constantly on cart at KUSF, be … treated, anyway, as if you were already somebody."[14]

Esmerelda: San Francisco's like a laboratory. It's where people try things and where people who aren't even talented but want to perform can get notoriety and encouragement and become famous, even if you're not that great.

Barbara Manning: People feel very free—at least they did back then—to be themselves in San Francisco. I was shocked when I first moved there in '86 because I remember a woman just walking around topless, not being harassed. [Laughs.] People were dressed to an extreme just to show that's what they cared about, which was pretty strange back in the '80s.

---

13 *Spin*, July 1989, p. 120.
14 *Vinyl Propaganda*, May 1988, p. 24.

THE LATE EIGHTIES

Brandan Kearney: In the last issue of *Wiring Dept.*, I interviewed Steve Albini because Big Black came through town, and he was just saying, "This is the worst city for music in the history of the world. You people are idiots. All the worst bands on Earth come from here. Maybe in the seventies, you guys had a couple of good bands, but basically, you've sucked ever since, and everything that comes out of here is terrible, and this town oughta be wiped off the face of the Earth with a neutron bomb." And, of course, Eric and I were arguing with him about that, so he finally said, "Okay, well, I can admit maybe there's some stuff going on that's decent that I don't know anything about, but it's sure not what gets popular."

Seymour Glass: The standard line among outsider blowhards was that there were no good bands from San Francisco at the time, and given what they were hearing about, it's easy to see why they'd say that. There *were* a lot of goofy, sort of lame bands from San Francisco, but there was a hell of a lot more going on than dismissible joke bands.

Margaret Murray: It just depended on what you were listening to. If you were really listening to all the Subterranean stuff, then there was some of that that was drifting away. But something else was going on and building up at the same time.

Mark Davies: There was a lot of really cool stuff going on in the late '80s, but it was all very underground. None of it was getting much attention. I mean, I guess what I considered great stuff just wasn't that commercially viable to get a lot of attention.

GILMAN STREET

In hindsight, there was plenty happening in 1989, just as there had been in 1979 — the same year that many were openly lamenting the death of punk. Undoubtedly, the signal-to-noise ratio was lower in 1989, if only because there were so many more bands, venues, and record labels than there had been a decade before. But it's also fair to say that within rock music, there wasn't the same sense of urgency or of new ground being broken at the end of the decade as there had been at the beginning. After all, punk began as a wholesale rejection of the hippies, whereas much of the activity in the late eighties was still building on the efforts of the early punks.

Berkeley's Gilman Street Project was a case in point. The all-ages venue opened its doors to the public on December 31, 1986, following a volunteer-heavy renovation effort spearheaded by Tim Yohannan and others associated with *Maximum Rocknroll*. In one sense, the venue marked the fulfillment of an idea originally conceived of by Steve Tupper and other members of New Youth in the late seventies. There were a couple of key differences, though. For one thing, Berkeley wasn't San Francisco, either geographically or culturally. For another, punk rock as it existed in 1987 was no longer a cutting-edge, urban phenomenon as it had been in 1979 but a largely suburban one that had been dulled and often dumbed-down by successive waves of newcomers.

There was also a big difference in the sort of mindset cultivated by *Maximum Rocknroll* as opposed to, say, *Search & Destroy* or its LA counterpart *Slash*. In particular, there was the aura of political correctness that hovered over *MRR* and, by extension, Gilman Street. Whereas the early punk scene was largely self-policing, 924 Gilman had a strict code of conduct (no drugs, alcohol, racism, sexism, homophobia, ad nauseam). In the early days, the club also prohibited bands from posting fliers in advance of their appearances there, the idea being that audience members should show up and support whichever bands were playing.

From a purely organizational standpoint, however, the club was a success. Within a few years, 924 Gilman would become known as ground zero for the early 1990s pop-punk explosion, spawning the likes of Green Day and Rancid. For the time being, it would also serve—at least some of the time—as a refuge for more experimental and unusual bands. "It was *the* place to go," says Seymour Glass, who was an early volunteer (or "shitworker") at Gilman Street.[15] "Saturday night

---

15 Glass (Chas Nielsen) also played Gilman Street as a member of Idiot (The), and he has only good things to say about his experiences in that role. "You knew you were

THE LATE EIGHTIES

ANNE EICKELBERG (LEFT) AND MARK DAVIES ONSTAGE AT 924 GILMAN, CIRCA 1988. PHOTO COURTESY OF M. DAVIES.

was for the big hardcore punk bands, and Friday night was for whatever else. So Vomit Launch would play there on Friday night. Negativland and the Thinking Fellers, Friday night. So we were always there on Friday night, too. The first time I saw the Thinking Fellers was at Gilman Street, opening for Negativland. I loved them right away."

---

never going to get screwed out of your allotted time or that someone was going to pull a shitty maneuver where you end up forced to play before your friends arrive or after everyone's on their way home. And whatever you wanted to do with your time was fine, whether it was conceptual or theatrical or less-than-musical. If no one liked it, that was your problem, but I never got the sense that they would shut you down if they disapproved."

ENTER TFUL

The Thinking Fellers—officially Thinking Fellers Union Local 282, or TFUL 282 for short—are not a band one typically associates with 924 Gilman, but their origins were somewhat intertwined. The Fellers made their live debut at Gilman Street on July 3, 1987, and before that, they rehearsed there as well.

Gilman Street was also where they met Greg Freeman, one of several candidates for the title of "unofficial sixth Feller." "At the time, I was living in a house in Oakland with some people who put out this magazine called *BravEar*," he recalls. "In the kitchen at the house, they just had this huge box full of records and tapes, and you could just pull stuff out and review it for the magazine. And there was a tape by this band Horny Genius." Freeman wrote a glowing review of the tape for *BravEar*, and the band's guitarist, Brian Hagemann, responded with a thank-you note, informing Freeman of his impending move to the Bay Area.[16] "And then I actually ran into them at a show at Gilman Street," adds Freeman, "probably in '87 or something, after they'd moved out. I told 'em, 'Hey, you know what? I have a studio.'"[17]

Freeman would go on to engineer almost all of TFUL's studio recordings,

---

16 It was not until after moving out west in 1986 that Hagemann—along with friends and fellow Iowans Mark Davies and Anne Eickelberg, Hugh Swarts, and Paul Bergmann—formed the Thinking Fellers.

17 As for how they ended up in the Bay Area, Mark Davies explains that it had more to do with their general impression of the Bay Area than with any specific bands or trends. "I had visited San Francisco once with my family in high school, and I thought it was a cool place. It just seemed like a *weird* place. I had never seen homeless street people—you know, people walking around who were obviously crazy, just doing weird things, and no one really paid much attention to it. I was really struck by that, coming from the Midwest—you know, a pretty conservative background. There was something kind of liberating about San Francisco, just the few days we spent there. And there just wasn't a lot of opportunity in Iowa if you wanted to try to seriously have a band and actually get shows somewhere. There was a really cool scene in Iowa City when we were there, but it was very small and limited. So it was natural for everyone, when they finished school, to try to look somewhere else. A lot of people came to San Francisco, a lot of people went to New York, some people went to Chicago. I mean, we liked some stuff from the Bay Area, like some of the Ralph Records bands: Snakefinger, the Residents, stuff like that. But it was kind of arbitrary—it wasn't that connected to what was going on musically. We weren't very aware of that."

THE LATE EIGHTIES

beginning with 1988's *Wormed by Leonard*, a self-released cassette issued on their own Thwart imprint. The opening sequence of *Wormed …* offers a glimpse of the group's peculiar *modus operandi*. There is a grating noise improvisation ('It's Seven'), followed by a gorgeous electro-folk ditty ('Hell Rules') and an abrasive noise rock hoedown ('Leaky Bag'). It was a sign of things to come. From the beginning, the group displayed a knack for intricate, inventive guitar interplay and unexpected melodic twists. They also had a predilection for inscrutable inside jokes, along with a seeming reluctance to give audiences too much of what they wanted. More accessible fare (like the countryish 'Narlus Spectre') would be followed by head-scratching interludes ('KLTX'), and their nods to pop music were buried in deliberately lo-fi production or slowed down to half-speed (as with their cover of the Carpenters' 'Superstar').

In any event, they were a talented bunch, and their peers took notice. "I mean, that just changed everything so much," says Brandan Kearney of the group's arrival. "They were the best thing in town, hands down, as far as I was concerned, when I would see them live," adds Jay Paget. "I was totally impressed. Loved 'em."

BANANAFISH

During their first year as a band, the Thinking Fellers would often find themselves booked alongside acts that were more typical of the 924 Gilman scene, such as Operation Ivy (precursors to Rancid) and the Mr. T Experience. "At that time, there was a lot of hardcore going on," says guitarist/vocalist Mark Davies. "I felt like hardcore punk was congealing into this really specific thing—that all these bands were trying to get that same kind of sound, and that was what people were looking for. And there was this interesting stuff going on that didn't fit into it, and then for a while, people just weren't interested in that."

It was Glass's zine *Bananafish* that helped give a sense of shape to this other music happening in the Bay Area during the late '80s, much as *Wiring Dept.* had done a few years earlier. *Bananafish* debuted in August of 1987, a month after TFUL's first show and a couple of months before Glass first saw them play. Glass

WHO CARES ANYWAY

himself had arrived in the Bay Area from Chico in 1984, a year or so before his old friend Barbara Manning, and he lived in the same Oakland house as Greg Freeman and others involved with the zine *BravEar*. It was a small world.

Bananafish wasn't a local music zine per se, but early issues included interviews with TFUL 282, World of Pooh, Caroliner, Tragic Mulatto, Three Day Stubble, and Greg Freeman (an amusing exposé focusing on his past life as a bassist with rock band the Call). There was also a lengthy reviews section in which Glass offered his takes on dozens of new albums per issue, championing the likes of the Dead C and Merzbow years before even most underground listeners had heard of them. The publication's tone was highbrow, if sometimes ironically so. If it felt a little exclusive at times, well, it kind of was. But it's not as if anyone else was covering this stuff at the time, and if people didn't like it, there were plenty of other zines out there. As Glass puts it, "I was used to being the only guy in the room who liked what I liked," a sentiment that many of the zine's readers could probably relate to.

As the years passed, *Bananafish* would devote less and less coverage to artists from the Bay Area. However, the first half-dozen issues—spanning 1987 to 1991—went a long way in alerting outsiders to the existence of a new cadre of smart, funny, hard-to-classify bands, even if there wasn't really a name for what they were doing. "It was just a lot looser then," says Mark Davies of the underground landscape at the time. "There wasn't this defined thing that was 'indie rock' or 'alternative rock.' We just kind of called it 'underground rock' because it was stuff that just wasn't really getting above the radar. There *was* kind of a network of people around the country, different small clubs and little zines and stuff that you could kind of connect to other local scenes that way, but it wasn't a phenomenon like it became in the nineties."

32

"I'M ARMED WITH QUARTS OF BLOOD": INTRODUCING CAROLINER

Caroliner's origins date back to either 1983 or sometime in the 1800s, depending on which version of the story you prefer.

"If you wrote about Caroliner," suggests one former band member, "it would go, 'Caroliner is the singing bull from the 1800s, and the reason for all the crazy patterns and the Day-Glo lights and all that is this representation of ergot poisoning.' So it's like this psychedelic experience but in the 1800s. And the singing bull is channeling this time period in the lyrics."

As the legend has it, a book containing transcriptions of the singing bull's lyrics was found in 1983 (it isn't clear where) by one of the eventual band members. The group formed soon thereafter with the aim of bringing the bull's songs to life—which meant coming up with music that would do justice to the hallucinatory and often grotesque lyrics.

Officially, Caroliner exists solely in the artistic realm—on records, in concert, and (occasionally) in the text of interviews with the band members, who never break character and seldom say anything that can be taken at face value. The members' names are not credited anywhere on the records, and when they've appeared in interviews, they've always used pseudonyms—absurd, unwieldy pseudonyms such as "Cottypearile Weddingforke," "Obsidian Skeleton," and "Akkoblutten Knobones." The only permanent member of the group is known among friends and acquaintances simply as "Grux." As for his legal name, no one else seems to know it.

As convoluted as the Caroliner's mythology is, it's possible to establish a few basic facts about the group. They did indeed form in 1983, emerging from the same grubby hardcore-era underground as Tragic Mulatto, Glorious Din, and even Faith No More—all of whom they shared bills with in their early years. At various points, their membership has overlapped with that of dozens of other bands, including Frightwig, World of Pooh, the Thinking Fellers, and Faxed Head. "Caroliner was a clearinghouse of different musicians who went through that scene and did other stuff," summarizes Alan Bishop of Sun City Girls. "It's an immense legacy, in a way."

"WHAT THE HELL IS CAROLINER RAINBOW?"

Caroliner's records are like incursions from a parallel world, evoking comparisons to fellow American outsiders such as Captain Beefheart, Sun Ra, Harry Partch, and, yes, the Residents. Yet none of these comparisons get at the actual sound of the music, which could roughly be described as 1800s Americana refracted through a prism of industrial noise, low-budget electronics, and any number of unorthodox recording techniques. If Caroliner has anything in common with the likes of Partch or Beefheart, it is drawing on quintessentially American musical forms while creating dense sonic pileups that are at once avant-garde and primitive.

Grux won't speak on the record about his background, musical or otherwise. "It's a real mystery," admits Trey Spruance. "Nobody really knows. I don't know how a person could become like a Harry Partch of weird experimental Bay Area music." That said, Grux is known among friends as an avid record collector with an encyclopedic knowledge of various obscure subgenres—"everything from weird fifties garage-type music like Hasil Adkins and vanity records and Mrs. Miller to some weird early punk stuff," according to Rebecca Wilson. "He was really into Helios Creed and Chrome." Others recall his enthusiasm for the Butthole Surfers, Flipper, and the early version of Frightwig (whose rehearsals he sometimes attended circa 1983). In interviews, however, the only influences Grux will cop to date back to the 1920s or earlier, such as Dock Boggs, the Skillet Lickers, and the (possibly fictitious) Barrel Gordon Trio.

It's also unclear how much of Caroliner's concept was in place from the start

WHO CARES ANYWAY

CAROLINER IN REHEARSAL. PHOTO COURTESY OF B. KEARNEY.

and how much of it was improvised as they went along. Documentation of their early years is scarce, but by all accounts, it took some time—and multiple lineup changes—for the band's sensory-bombarding aesthetic to fall in place. Early on, they were primarily known as a collective nuisance, if they were known at all. The original lineup was a bare-bones trio consisting of Grux on bass, Gregg Turkington on drums, and Mia Simmans of Frightwig on guitar. "We would do things like take a motorcycle battery and put it in a shopping cart and go down to Powell and Market and just make a ton of noise," recalls Simmans, who, like her bandmates, was still a teenager at the time. "I had a little amp that would run off of the battery. We'd just like pound the sidewalk with coffee cans and make a lot of noise."

David Katz: I remember before I met Grux and before I'd actually seen them, you'd see on the bus—particularly on the number 28 bus that goes down 19th

Avenue—these handmade stickers: "Caroliner Rainbow." I thought, "What the hell is Caroliner Rainbow?"

Cole Palme: The early fliers, I remember I saw them. Because I'd been so disenchanted with the whole [music scene]. I wasn't going out to shows hardly at all. That was just something that totally grabbed my attention when I saw them play. I just felt a certain kind of kinship, for sure.

David Katz: Caroliner had an endlessly revolving lineup because most people couldn't really tolerate Grux's extremities for too long. At that time, Grux was living in this place in the Western Addition. He used to have these mummified rats hanging from the ceiling.

Tom Wheeler: There were a couple of bands like this, in which they reveled in being as non-musician-y and amateur and crude as possible. There was a band called the 12 Yr. Olds who were very much like that as well. I even think there was some crossover between members of the 12 Yr. Olds and Caroliner. Because there was Grux, who was always there, and it seemed like every time Caroliner showed up, they would come in with five or six people I'd never seen before. It always seemed to be kind of a rotating, different group of people around him.

Caroliner played Club Foot often in their early years, though they occasionally made their way onto bills at places like the On Broadway and the Mab, where they played to mostly unsuspecting audiences. "The room would be empty really quick," laughs Palme. "Most times, people just weren't havin' it. And then they got more and more visual, and people would be intrigued. It was fun."

A *Wiring Dept.* review of a November 1985 show in nearby Danville offers a vivid description of some of the visual (and otherwise non-musical) elements of their live act. "Caroliner played with cowboy hats, a black light, and in their socks were what looked like tomatoes (or something red and puffy)," wrote the reviewer, "Stringut" (likely a pseudonym for Grux).[18] "Some of the songs were knocked out

18 *Wiring Dept.*, Summer 1986.

365

HOTEL
UTAH
OCT 19

CAROLINER
RAINBOW DELAW COW
MERCHANTS OF THE NEW BIZARRE
WE DON'T CARRY SKULLS OR HAIR SPRAY - STINK NATURALLY

by a hammer instead of drums, and the most graphic song they did was 'Mud Cup Monocle,' where a band member quit playing guitar and shook out a shirt full of manure and waved bright fluorescent flowers that had little booger ghosts on top of them."

"There was garbage, animal heads, whatever," recalls Wheeler. "It's sort of a performance art kind of thing. I mean, you have to put this in the context of people like Karen Finley, Johanna Went. So you had this whole performance art thing that was based around bodily functions and garbage and grossing people out, pushing stuff into the audiences—ways of making the audience feel a little bit less than comfortable."

Katz remembers a specific incident along these lines from one of the Club Foot shows. "You could kind of smell something before you saw him," he says, referring to Grux. "He came into the venue wearing this garbage shirt that had like a sack of rotting compost on his back—like rotting orange peels and just half-decomposed muck. And he did this staggering kind of movement up to the stage, and by the time he reached the stage, Karl [Danskin, who managed Club Foot after Wheeler] can kind of see where this one is headed. And lo and behold, he just dumps it all over the floor. And he did the gig shirtless, wearing a kind of a hula skirt, and he kept running into the audience with a chair over his head as though he was gonna smash the front row over the head with the chair. He was pretending that he had taken bad acid, and you never were really that clear if he was actually gonna do it or not."

RAINBOWS MADE OF MEAT

Despite the group's hallucinatory aesthetic, Grux himself was not a drug user. "Oh, he was absolutely 'no mind-altering anything,'" notes Lizzy Kate Gray. "He's never had a beer in his life," adds Rebecca Wilson. Evidently, he didn't need chemical enhancements in order to be creative, eccentric, or just downright weird. As Denise Dee recalls, "He was always in some kind of ... 'costume' may be too extreme of a word, but he made all these great shirts—hand-painted shirts—sometimes hats, sometimes they would have scrims with things painted on them. Always a lot of props. Just his *mind*—I didn't know anybody who was that fertile. I don't think that he ever went a minute, maybe, without creating something."

David Katz: Grux used to do this thing where—if he wanted to contact you, he wouldn't phone you. I think he didn't have a phone. What he would do was, he would write you a letter, but he would address it to himself and put your address as the return address and put no postage on it, or put, like, a one-cent stamp on it. So most of the time, the post office would redeliver it to the person he was trying to deliver it to, but with a stamp on it that would say, "Post office will not deliver without correct postage."

Denise Dee: He used to color-Xerox Muni fast passes. Who would think of that? I think that's what he was living off of for a while. I just thought, "What a fantastic idea." I don't know if he ever had a "job" job.

Dame Darcy: He was extremely cheap. He would buy a big thing of oatmeal and then eat it for every meal of the day, every day of the week. Then he sometimes would splurge and get a two-dollar burrito. And he was on SSI, and that's how he basically didn't have to have a job. So he could work full-time on the band and the props.

367

WHO CARES ANYWAY

Over time, the band's repertoire of props grew to include everything from masks and appendages to a full stage set that included a cardboard windmill and other scenery, most of it painted in Day-Glo colors. By the late '80s, their act had evolved into a handmade multimedia spectacle rivaling anything done by SF forerunners such as the Angels of Light or the Residents. "The first time I saw Caroliner, it was like seeing fireworks for the first time when you're a little kid," says *Bananafish*'s Seymour Glass. "I'd never seen a band with that many props, and the Day-Glo lights." Dee had a similarly awed reaction. "I've never seen anything like that in my life. I remember I went to one show, and they had clouds hanging from the ceiling. His mind is just so fascinating. Like, where do you get that? I've been to a lot of great shows musically, but I've been to probably under ten shows where you feel like you're *fully* in that person's world."

"Their live shows were amazing and immersive and insane," adds Alicia Rose, who often booked them to play at the Chameleon on Valencia Street in the early 1990s. "They'd spend days and weeks making all these poster boards and banners. And if you went over to Grux's house, it would just be *filled* with all of these insane props all over the place that would then get turned into costumes and stage setups. It was all sort of this blacklight fantasy world with this just insane music going on."

According to Gregg Turkington, who left the band toward the end of 1984, the props weren't initially part of the live act. "You know, the band was so terrible when I was in it—so utterly worthless—that when I *wasn't* in it, I had no reason to go see them play," he explains. "It may have only been a year before I saw them again—I don't remember. But I just know Grux would always tell me to go to the shows, and I wouldn't go to them because I didn't expect much. And then when I did go, it was really impressive. It was this huge blacklight extravaganza with all these costumes and all these other members. I don't know how gradual the change was because when I was in it, it sure wasn't anything like that."

THE LATE EIGHTIES

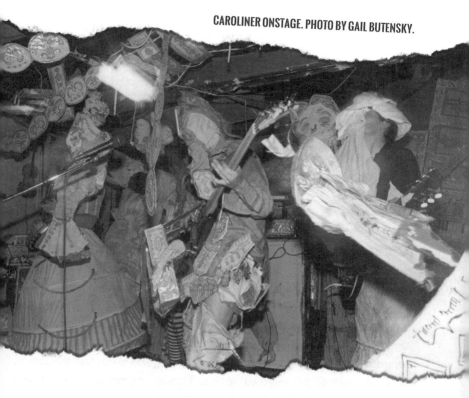

CAROLINER ONSTAGE. PHOTO BY GAIL BUTENSKY.

QUARTS OF BLOOD

Aside from Grux, Caroliner's longest-serving member was Brandan Kearney, who joined in 1986 (around the same time the trio version of World of Pooh with Barbara Manning and Jay Paget came together). He initially joined on drums ("which pretty much drove everyone else out of the band," he quips), then switched to guitar, though he played a variety of instruments on the records— everything from dulcimer to clarinet to glass harmonica. For nearly a decade, he would function as a sort of right-hand man to Grux, co-producing many of the albums, teaching parts to new band members, and handling much of the band business. "Grux leaned on Brandan," says Eve Bekker, a member during the late '80s.

Another important piece of the puzzle was Greg Freeman, who entered

369

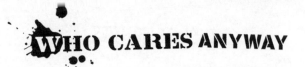

the picture not long after Kearney did. "Grux was always looking for a good deal," notes Freeman, "and he found a really cheap recording studio—namely, me. I was probably charging twelve bucks or fifteen bucks an hour then." With Freeman as engineer and Kearney as de facto musical director, the band developed into a well-oiled machine, cranking out seven LPs (one of them a double) between 1990 and '94, beginning with *I'm Armed with Quarts of Blood*. (Caroliner's first album, *Rear End Hernia Puppet Show*, predated Kearney's and Freeman's involvement.)

"It was a challenge, aesthetically and also just from a technical perspective, because of how they did things," recalls Freeman. "The first sessions, when we recorded live, they would set off firecrackers and stuff in the studio. There was also a teasing thing—they just liked to give me a hard time. Grux would sort of insult me whenever possible—in a friendly way, but he was still kind of a dick sometimes," he laughs. "But as far as having them in the studio—I mean, I've had a lot of other sessions where I just wanted to kick people out. They were never like that."

Freeman took on a more traditional producer's role in the studio with the Thinking Fellers, but not so much with Caroliner. "I had very little input," he admits. "They had a pretty good idea of who was going to do what that day, so Grux just would say, 'Okay, you: it's time to do the track where you put your head in the bucket and sing,' or whatever. And then he'd have whoever go and stick their head in the bucket. And then I'd go and hit 'record,' and they'd have one chance, and that was it."

None of Caroliner's albums make for pleasant background listening, and *I'm Armed with Quarts of Blood* is no exception. It is relentlessly abrasive, with clattering percussion, high-pitched vocals (sung by Grux in what sounds like a helium-induced falsetto), and an array of strange noises and sound effects whose origins (rubber band, washboard, broken accordion) are mostly indiscernible to the naked ear. Several of the songs feature the infamous "Goddamn Girl Drummers"—Bekker, Dame Darcy, and Lynne Porterfield—who played (or attempted to play) while jumping up and down on trampolines. Yet for all the surface-level chaos, there are recognizable songs hiding underneath; occasionally, as on the title track and 'For Bread and Ax,' the result even resembles something akin to rock music, if only by accident.

THE LATE EIGHTIES

Quarts of Blood was released through Subterranean, an appropriate pairing given the label's history with local experimentalists such as Factrix, Minimal Man, and, for that matter, Flipper. Like all of Caroliner's records, it comes with handmade cover art, though Kearney recalls the process of making covers for *Quarts of Blood* as being exceptionally tedious:

If you wanted to get a cover printed in those days, it would cost you roughly in the neighborhood of a thousand bucks, all told. Grux was always trying to figure out ways we could "save money," so for the second album, I was like, "Well, why don't we get a bunch of records out of the dollar bin at Revolver?" Because I worked there, and I could just take them at a discount instead of payment. So we got a thousand of these, and I had to sit there shucking them like peas until I had four-foot-tall stacks of vinyl at the top of my stairs—which we ended up pushing down the stairs because it was the only way to get them down there easily.

And then we had to go all the way down there to Subterranean with these fucking heaps and piles of covers. I didn't have a car in those days, and neither of us would spring for a cab, so we had to take them down there in shifts on the bus. And again, a thousand record covers takes up space; it's heavy—it's a pain in the ass.

So then we had to get paint, but Grux isn't willing to buy paint. So we had to find people who had paint they were going to throw away. And then we had to find the other stuff, like rollers and paint pans and all of this other crap. Then we'd have to lay them down in the hallway, and you could maybe fit thirty at a time. It was really labor-intensive. And you have to wait for 'em to dry in between, and the fumes are just fucking horrible. On top of that, Grux wanted dirt on them, and dust. So we'd have to go sweeping the floors and digging up all this fucking dust and dragging it over and sprinkling it over the records. We were just breathing these paint fumes and dust and dirt.

I swear to God, putting those records together—for the initial batch, it must've taken us three weeks of just backbreaking, miserable, poisonous labor to get them done. And of course, every re-press, we've gotta go through it all over again. We had to shrink wrap 'em

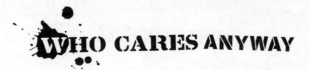

too because Tupper was like, "I don't want them touching any other record." And then they'd start to grow mold under the shrink wrap, under the plastic.

The resulting album cover—painted brown and covered in dust and dirt, with a photocopied black-and-white drawing pasted on the front—may or may not have been worth the effort. Even so, it's illustrative of the lengths that Grux and Co. were willing to go to in order to translate his vision into something tangible. That the payoff often seemed meager relative to the amount of work involved was one reason for all of the lineup changes the band endured. That the albums exist at all is a testament to both the members' dedication and the bandleader's charisma (some would call it "megalomania"). "To get your vision across," summarizes Denise Dee, "you have to be a little bit of a control freak, I think."

33

INTRODUCE YOURSELF

Roddy Bottum: I have the utmost faith in the record industry. They haven't really let me down yet. I think that everybody in the charts today has at least something that's worth listening to or looking at.

Bill Gould: Yeah, it's not that easy to get on the charts. If it was, any simpleton would be doing it.[19]

Grux and Caroliner had one set of ideas on how to position themselves in relation to the music industry; Faith No More had another. As existential strategies go, they could have hardly been more different. Where Caroliner was determined to exist outside of the system, Faith No More was equally determined to infiltrate it and subvert it from within.

Even in the days when they were gracing the cover of *Wiring Dept.*, FNM showed an interest in pop music—an "affection and revulsion," as Gould would later put it—that set them apart from their peers.[20] Their faithful cover of Van Halen's 'Jump' (never recorded but included in their live sets circa 1984) was a case in point, as was their perverse fascination with MTV. "It was just when MTV started," recalls Bottum, "and I remember we were really bold and brazen and proud about the fact that we took all our money and we got cable TV so we could watch MTV. And then we were championing all these ridiculous things we saw on MTV, like Cyndi Lauper and Madonna. We were really about embracing that culture in an obnoxious way, mostly because we were just provocative and wanted to push people's buttons. And San Francisco took that

---

19 *Wiring Dept.*, "Empty Milk Bar" issue.
20 Harte, *Small Victories*, p. 147.

so seriously—like, the crass commercial world of music would be considered so distasteful."

Granted, it might have been an ironic gesture to proclaim their "utmost faith in the record industry" while still an unsigned band playing dive bars like the Sound of Music. But that sense of irony reflected a desire to have their cake and eat it too—to subvert the conventions of the music industry while achieving the kind of success that necessitated playing along with at least some of those conventions. "We wanted to be able to tour and make records," says Gould. "I come from LA, so I have a little bit of that damage, I guess. I was a little more ambitious. And Roddy came from LA too."

Even so, Gould and company were committed to making it on their own terms as opposed to just mimicking what was already popular. "He was always looking to forge new ground like that," recalls Chuck Mosley. "That's his personality. Billy was ready to take over the world. He had that mindset from the time he left LA. They were really into Killing Joke and stuff, but they were gonna take it to the next level. And right from the beginning, when they started that group, they were like, 'Oh yeah, this is the new sound. It's gonna just take over.' And he was right."

SELLING OUT

We Care a Lot wasn't a massive seller at the time, but it caught the ear of an A&R rep at Slash Records, the LA label that grew out of the punk fanzine of the same name. Slash had signed a distribution deal with Warner Brothers in 1982 (the same year 415 Records signed one with Columbia), making it a de facto major label. They signed Faith No More to a five-album deal in May of 1986, and while the band's subsequent stardom was hardly a foregone conclusion, they were well on their way.

For some, it was a jarring move. "Ruth Schwartz was deeply disappointed that Faith No More got management (hello)," says Olga Gerrard, the former Savoy Tivoli booker who, along with husband Gerry, managed the band during this era. "And when we took them to Slash, that was just against all that she stood for. There were those diehards—she and *Maximum Rocknroll* and Tim Yohannan, et al.—who really didn't want to see anybody ever go mainstream. They wanted people to be successful, but they didn't want to see people go mainstream. Slash was considered very corporate. Faith No More *always* wanted to be signed to a major label. They might not have told Ruth that, but that's all they ever wanted."

Others, however, were not so much disappointed as they were puzzled. "I liked Faith No More—I thought they were great," says Gregg Turkington, "but I just remember thinking, 'Wow, what is Slash thinking? This band doesn't have a commercial sound at all. They're gonna lose so much money on this fucking band.' I just never thought of them as a band with commercial potential."

In the meantime, Faith No More was outgrowing its old scene, or at least what was left of it. The band played their first out-of-state shows in March 1986 as part of a rambling, two-month-long tour that took them through pockets of the Southwest, the Southeast (including a lengthy stopover in Atlanta, where they were temporarily stranded with no shows and no gas money), and the Northeast (including an opening gig for Ministry in Trenton, New Jersey, where they were thrown out of the club after Chuck spilled a beer on one of the headliner's fancy synthesizers).

Back home in San Francisco, they still played out often enough, but the vibe was changing. "One minute these guys are playing in a room full of people you know and it's this sort of little scene, then the next minute it's this kind of big crowd of people," remembers Brandan Kearney. "It got to the point where, for the most part, you couldn't get into their shows. It was incredibly crowded and kind of a weird audience—a bunch of people you didn't recognize. It may not even be that they changed that much. I think it's just that their audience probably changed, or at least perceived what it meant to be at one of their shows differently."

Part of that change had to do with their growing appeal to metal audiences, and part of it had to do with the demise of the *Wiring Dept.* scene, with bands like Glorious Din and Trial busy recording and touring before eventually petering out in 1986. "After a while, we didn't play here very much at all," admits Gould. "And to tell you the truth, after we got out of here and started touring, people kinda weren't so interested in us here, either. There was a real stigma about

FNM CIRCA 1985. "THEY'RE STILL IN THE STREET-LEVEL, PUNK-ROCK, SAN FRANCISCO BOHEMIAN KIND OF THING." – JOE POP-O-PIE. L-R: RODDY BOTTUM, MIKE BORDIN, CHUCK MOSLEY, JIM MARTIN, BILL GOULD. PHOTO COURTESY OF B. GOULD.

people leaving town. People already were saying that we were sellouts because we were going on tour. So the way we looked at it was, 'Well, if we're already there anyway, then fuck. If there's no loyalty to us, then we don't have to build anything here and be guilty.' It's a very small-town mentality here for a big city."

INTRODUCE YOURSELF

The quintet recorded *Introduce Yourself*, their debut album for Slash, toward the end of 1986. Released the following April, the LP marks a natural progression from *We Care a Lot*. Production-wise, it is brighter and more metallic than its predecessor; it sounds less British and more Californian. Even so, it is still unmistakably Faith No More, with the Gould–Bordin rhythm section sounding as powerful as ever and the other elements—Bottum's synth washes, Mosley's sneering vocals, and Jim Martin's increasingly prominent guitar—somehow peacefully coexisting in the mix.

Apart from a remake of 'We Care a Lot' with a slightly altered (and more DJ-friendly) drumbeat, there were no obvious concessions to the mainstream marketplace. Videos for 'We Care a Lot' and a second single, 'Anne's Song,' did make their way onto MTV, but just barely, as airplay was mostly restricted to the late-night show *120 Minutes*. The former video, in particular, offers a good reflection of the band's love/hate relationship with the new medium. With its bright colors and gratuitous rock poses, it comes across like a parody/homage of mid-eighties MTV tropes. As such, it makes for a revealing contrast with another "college rock" video from the era—namely, the Replacements' 'Bastards of Young,' which consists of an extended black-and-white shot of a stereo speaker. Both bands were demonstrating a sense of self-awareness in terms of what it meant to graduate from the underground to the major label scene, but whereas the Replacements were staging a kind of half-hearted protest, FNM were reveling in the crassness of it all.[21] As Bottum puts it, "We never made any

---

21 As different as they were, the two bands were perceived—at least at the time—as part of a broader phenomenon. As Bob Mehr writes in *Trouble Boys: The True Story of the*

pretense about *not* selling out. Which is so obnoxious."

The video for 'Anne's Song' is more straightforward, but the song itself was an idiosyncratic choice for a single. Chuck spends the first minute of the song casually talking over a bouncy bass/drum vamp, with the chorus not entering until around the 1:20 mark. There is also a rare Jim Martin guitar solo (harmonized in Thin Lizzy/Iron Maiden fashion, no less). As a single, it went nowhere, but as a song, it showcases the band's increasingly sophisticated arrangement skills as well as their vocalist's distinctive ragamuffin charm. As one reviewer put it (speaking of the album as a whole), "The lyrics careen between offhanded, brainless, clever and sophomoric, but their casual feel of being assembled on the spot is belied by the airtight ensemble work."[22]

Other critics were less attuned to the nuts and bolts of the music than they were the novelty of the total package. "Faith No More is contributing to a new West Coast sound … that draws in different measures from funk, hard rock, punk, or reggae," wrote critic Tom Harrison in the *Vancouver Province*.[23] A review in the *Louisville Courier-Journal* described the album as "a bizarre but riveting assemblage of seemingly incompatible styles: techno-pop, heavy metal, rap and punk" before concluding, "*Introduce Yourself* is one of the few albums this year to prove rock 'n' roll can continue to take new directions and remain the potent force it was meant to be."[24] Then again, not everyone was enthusiastic about where this all seemed to be heading. Joe Carducci, for example, characterized the band as "crossover profit-takers" (along with the likes of Jane's Addiction and Living Colour) and exponents of "Neo-Mofo" (along with Fishbone and the Red Hot Chili Peppers). It was one of many unflattering genre tags that would be applied to the band in the coming years as their popularity grew.[25]

Replacements, "Just as the Replacements released *Tim*, Warner Bros. A&R woman Karin Berg signed Hüsker Dü to the label. Hüsker Dü was the beginning of a wave of 'alternative' American rock bands that Warner would sign over the next few years: Faith No More (via a partnership with Slash Records), Jane's Addiction, and Throwing Muses among them."

22 "Faith No More brings heavy rap to Metroplex." Bo Emerson. *The Atlanta Constitution*. July 8, 1987.

23 "Faith Back in Power." Tom Harrison, *The Vancouver Province*. June 3, 1987.

24 Review of Faith No More, *Introduce Yourself*. *The Louisville Courier-Journal*. June 20, 1987.

25 Joe Carducci, *Rock and the Pop Narcotic*, 1994 edition. The quotes come from pages

Novelty aside, the album captures the essence of the band as well as any of their studio recordings do. "*Introduce Yourself*, to me, is kind of the ultimate Faith No More record," says Mike Hickey, who, like many other listeners, came to the album only after having heard its platinum-selling follow-up, *The Real Thing*. "It's the record that, from beginning to end, sounds the most like what I think of as Faith No More—to *me*. No one else really sounds exactly like them."

CHUCK

As FNM was introducing itself to new audiences across the country, Chuck was slowly inching his way out of the band, whether he knew it or not. Tensions with his old friend/adversary Gould played a part, although he also clashed with the others at times. "I was still acting my same old punk self," Mosley admits, "just doin' shit just because I thought it was funny and stuff. Everybody didn't always think it was so funny. For instance, when we did that 'We Care a Lot' video, I had on all these layers of clothes, and the last layer was a T-shirt that just said, 'FUCK YOU.' They were going through the video frame by frame, and all of a sudden, I'm doing jumping jacks, and my shirt opens up, and you can see it real clear. And everybody stops and looks at me, and I'm just like, 'What?' And they're like, 'Well, "what" is we gotta spend a thousand dollars to edit that little frame out.'"

At the same time, Mosley's substance abuse issues were coming to the fore, and while he wasn't quite on a par with, say, Ricky Williams, he had his moments. "We had one show in LA when we were signed to Slash, and everybody in LA came to check us out," recalls Gould.[26] "Like, 'Okay, they just got signed to this label—what's their deal?' All the press people came. We were totally primed to play, and he showed up totally drunk and fell asleep on stage. Nobody would write about us for two years after that. They were like, 'This band sucks. I'm not doing anything on 'em.' We had a lot of experiences like that, where it's

35 and 382, respectively.
26 The show in question took place at Club Lingerie on May 16, 1987, a few weeks after the release of *Introduce Yourself*.

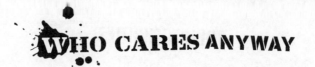

WHO CARES ANYWAY

just, 'Enough.' He just made it difficult." (Years later, Bottum would laugh off the same incident: "What a memorable presence! Someone who actually fell asleep onstage. Amazing."[27])

Chuck Mosley: By that time, me and Roddy were really close because we have the same mentality. Everything's kind of funny. Roddy was maybe more business and professional, but we were always getting into trouble together. He was a peacemaker, and he was way more mellow about stuff.

Olga Gerrard: I'm just gonna put it this way: Roddy has been an absolutely darling, wonderful, creative, talented person with actual strains of kindness. The others—when things started to turn was when they set Chuck Mosley on fire in a rehearsal. That was when I started to think, "This is maybe not the best fit for me." They were *assholes* to Chuck. It was difficult for him. Chuck is a doll. I'm not saying he was easy, but he was a doll.

David Katz: I remember Mike [Bordin] telling me a story, which I hope is apocryphal, from the early days. They were rehearsing in one of their garages, and they kept telling me a story about some Scottish neighbor they had whose wife just had a newborn baby. That day they were in there cranking it up, doing their version of 'Iron Man' or something, kind of cranking it up to eleven. And that the guy kept coming and knocking on the door saying, "Oh please, my baby, my baby—you're upsetting the baby." And then they kept saying, "Oh, sorry," and they'd turn it down for three minutes and then turn it back up. And then, eventually, Mike said something about how some ambulance came and took the poor baby away because they'd upset the baby so much that it had to go to the hospital. I don't know if that's true, but he did tell me that story.

Bill Gould: We were all pretty tight—my group was pretty tight. And I think we pretty much respect each other. We definitely butted heads a lot. We were very creative in how we tortured each other. But I think the thing was, when we were

27 Harte, *Small Victories*, p. 99.

380

THE LATE EIGHTIES

together, we were really strong. And when I look back, when people like to write about us now, they like to really find the bad quotes singling the others out. And there's truth to it. We all look kind of bad in our own band, the way the former band members talk about each other. But the overall vibe is, we pretty much like each other. It makes more interesting reading, I guess. Character assassination's always interesting reading.

34

THE REAL THING

"We looked at it like we were hackers: Imagine if we could actually get through that. How would you crack that?" —Bill Gould[28]

Chuck made his last appearance with Faith No More on May 24, 1988, in London, the final stop on a month-long tour through Europe and the UK. By June, he was officially out of the band, and the search for a new singer was on. That search occupied them for most of the summer and included trips to LA and Seattle, where they held an informal audition with Soundgarden's Chris Cornell. Local music rag *BAM* even rumored that Cornell was officially joining the band, although, in retrospect, it's hard to imagine the combination working out. (As Gould would later put it, "Great, great voice, but not for us."[29])

By this point, Gould was living at the Pet Hospital, a converted animal hospital located near the intersection of Fell and Market (a stone's throw from the eventual site of Twitter's corporate headquarters). As friend and housemate Will Carpmill notes, it was a unique living situation, though hardly a luxurious one. "There were x-ray machines, and it smelled like frightened animals. It was two stories. It had an elevator shaft and operating rooms. Hardly any facilities. We ended up having to build even the vestiges of a kitchen." Joan Osato, another Pet Hospital resident, recalls helping out with the renovations, which included a makeshift home studio for Gould and some other more basic improvements. "Will and I tore up the bathroom and made an actual shower. You're doing plumbing, and probably none of it is legal. We were knocking out walls with a sledgehammer.

---

28 Harte, *Small Victories*, p. 172.
29 Harte, *Small Victories*, p. 116

THE LATE EIGHTIES

Now that I think about it, it's like, 'Man, were those supporting walls we were knocking down?' Who knows."

Gould would end up spending most of 1989 and '90 on the road instead of at the Pet Hospital. At the time of his move-in, though, the band's future was up in the air. "Bill was all stressed out and crazy because Chuck was suing him, and he had ulcers and was self-medicating with Quaaludes," remembers Joe Pop-O-Pie, yet another denizen of the building in those days. "It was a messy situation." It was messy enough that, according to Joe, Gould was briefly considering *him* as a possible replacement for Mosley. "Bill was really trying to talk me into it, going, 'Come on, you were number one on college radio, and where the fuck did it get you? How long have you been doing this Pop-O-Shit for? Shit, Joe—you can't even pay your rent.' He was giving me the hard sell. And I was like, 'Okay, okay—you don't have to push me. I'm up for it.' But we never discussed it again." (Gould remembers things differently: "He didn't like loud noise, and his ears started getting more sensitive, so he was definitely not the right guy for the band. We were a little more *edgy*; he was more *funny*.")

ENTER PATTON

It was the late summer of 1988 when Gould and Co. decided to summon Mike Patton, then a college student at Humboldt State University in Arcata, for an audition. Patton wasn't their first choice, as they'd already tried at least a handful of others before giving him a shot. That said, they'd been vaguely aware of him for a couple of years, thanks to a demo tape of his other band, Mr. Bungle.

This takes us back to October 4, 1986, when Faith No More played an otherwise routine show in Arcata at a venue called the Depot. Along with Patton, Mr. Bungle guitarist Trey Spruance was among the small crowd in attendance. "There were like two other people watching them besides me and Mike," he recalls. "But it was really good. It was a fucking *amazing* concert. It was *incredible*. I loved it; I was shitting my pants. Roddy had dreadlocks and was wearing an army helmet. But the drums—the drums were just un-fucking-believable. So loud and so heavy."

383

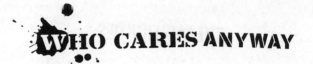

Kris Hendrickson: So we go to the show, and Mike takes a demo tape—a Mr. Bungle demo tape—with him, and they play their show. We visit with Mike Bordin and then kind of meet a couple of people in the band, and Mike hands them the Mr. Bungle demo tape. They keep it for years. Eventually, Chuck Mosley is out of the band, and they're looking for a new singer. They called Mike and asked Mike if he wanted to audition. And that's kind of how that all happened.

Bill Gould: We didn't know what he looked like; we just got a Mr. Bungle demo, and it was like a death metal tape. So our guitar player, Jim, was going, "We want the Mr. Bungle guy!" And I thought, "Oh God, some big fat guy with a leather jacket—some macho dude."

Chuck Mosley: When I was still in the band, my friend April worked at Restless Records. We were out hanging out, and she goes, "Check this out." And it was Mr. Bungle. But it was not like the Mr. Bungle everybody's familiar with. It was like *metal*. It was literally like Germs meets Metallica meets Corrosion of Conformity. And it was just *hard*. Just all hard and fuckin' badass and full of time changes and fuckin' relentless. I said, "Whoa! This shit is fuckin' insane! You guys should sign 'em." And then, next thing I knew, I got fired, and then next thing I knew, he was gonna be the singer for Faith No More, and then *next* thing I knew, every time I'd see a picture of him, he had a Mr. Bungle shirt on. And then I went, "Oh, I get it. Now I get the connection."

As Gould recalls, things worked out musically from the get-go, even if Patton wasn't the most natural fit in other ways. "He had maybe come to San Francisco once in his life before, so he was just freaked out. We were living in the Pet Hospital, and there were holes in the walls, beer on the floor, and we were thinking, 'This is not gonna work.'" We went to practice, and we already had the songs written. We played him a song, and he said, 'Here's some ideas—can I just sing them?' So we turn on the tape recorder, and he just sang. I went away with Jim for the weekend, and we took the tape and listened to it, and it was like, 'He fuckin' nailed it.' This one song on the record, 'Underwater Love,' he basically nailed it the first time he heard it. We're like, 'Hey, he's really naive. I almost feel like a cradle robber to get this kid in the band, but he *gets* it; in a musical way, he kind of gets it.'"

Carpmill can attest to his friend's enthusiasm. "We were sitting in the living room at the Pet Hospital, and Billy came running up the stairs with this cassette tape. He goes, 'I'm gonna be rich!' Me and Mike Canavan were like, 'What?' He pops this cassette in, and it was a practice tape that they'd done with Mike Patton. He played one song, and I said, 'Yep, you've found your vocalist.' Because he was insanely talented."

THIS IS IT

Like him or not, Patton was a quick study. He made his debut on November 4, 1988, at the I-Beam—his only appearance before heading into the studio with his new bandmates that December to begin work on *The Real Thing*.

As the story goes, the music for *The Real Thing* was already written by the time Patton joined, which left him with the task of writing lyrics and devising vocal parts to fit the existing music. This sort of sequential division of labor—write the music first, then find a singer—was a microcosm of Faith No More's first year as a band, only instead of publicly auditioning vocalists at dives like the Sound of Music or the On Broadway, they were doing so behind closed doors, in the recording studio. Then again, the stakes were higher this time.

On the surface, *The Real Thing* feels like a drastic departure from *Introduce Yourself*—not just due to the vocals but also because of the more elaborate song structures and the glossy, widescreen production.[30] A few of the songs,

---

30 Gould attributes the differences between *Introduce Yourself* and *The Real Thing* to a few different factors. "We had more money to record, so it sounded slicker. And the singing made a lot of difference. But we pretty much wrote the way we always wrote. I mean, we were the same band otherwise. Maybe we got a little better." As for the more complex song structures, he says, "I think it's because we had a period when we were writing, and we didn't have a singer, and we just went to practice and kept working on the songs."

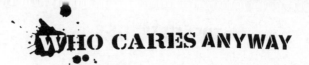

including 'Zombie Eaters' and the eight-minute title track, border on progressive rock. Meanwhile, the metal elements are more pronounced, especially on the Jim Martin-penned 'Surprise! You're Dead!' and the cover of Black Sabbath's 'War Pigs.' In contrast, the closing track, 'Edge of the World' (which directly follows 'War Pigs'), verges on contemporary R&B and is devoid of guitars. As Bordin would later summarize, "The heavier stuff is getting heavier, the aggressive stuff is getting more aggressive, and the melodic stuff is getting more properly melodic."[31]

In that sense, the versatile Patton was the right man for the job. He delivers an agile, almost athletic performance, and the fact that he wrote all of his parts in just a couple of weeks makes it all the more impressive—whatever the occasional lapses in taste. In terms of discipline and work ethic, Patton was the anti-Chuck, the anti-Ricky Williams. He also projected a different demeanor—that of the talented whiz kid instead of the lovable loser. Indeed, it's hard to imagine *The Real Thing* with Mosley in place of Patton. The only direct point of comparison is 'The Morning After,' which appeared in an earlier version (as 'New Improved Song') with Chuck on vocals.[32] Apart from a slight difference in tempo, the music is the same, but the lyrics and vocal melodies are entirely different. Patton's version is admittedly more dynamic and attention-grabbing, but it's also slicker. In comparison, Mosley's crooning approach feels offhanded, almost lazy in spots. Yet it also has a charm to it that Patton, for all his bionic virtuosity, seldom exudes.

Ultimately, it's an apples-to-oranges comparison since the decision was never about Chuck versus Patton; rather, it was first about Chuck versus Not Chuck and then about Patton versus the other potential replacements. That said, when one listens to 'The Morning After' and 'New Improved Song' back-to-back, it becomes clear that the only thing the two vocalists really had in common was that they happened to sing for the same band.

Lizzy Kate Gray: Chuck has a little more of the feel of what was San Francisco about the band—the sort of punk/lackadaisical approach. Whereas Mike

---

31 *Small Victories*, pp. 132–133.
32 'New Improved Song' was originally released on a flexi-disc included with a March 1988 issue of *Sounds*.

Patton's so damn impressive, you just sit there being impressed. And that's not exactly entertainment.

Mike Hickey: I don't want to sound like a naysayer. I mean, Mike Patton was a great singer, but it wasn't like, "Oh, the Mike Patton band." I didn't give a fuck about that. He was an amazing singer. And I also thought, conceptually, in the earlier days, extremely funny. But when I heard the records with Chuck, I mean, I loved those just as much. I've always loved those records.

Chuck Mosley: Okay, let me put it this way: I can play piano way better than I can sing or play guitar. But I found what works for me. And I've always had this voice that I have. I can't do many different things with it. I can go falsetto; I can go higher—a little bit—and go lower. But it's my voice, and you can pretty much tell all the time. It ain't perfect, but it's got character and a unique quality. And when I'm in tune, it's actually good. But as far as being trained, he's trained on vocals like I was trained on piano. I don't want to say he's better or worse or whatever.

WHAT IS "IT"?

Like Faith No More in general, *The Real Thing* was hardly an overnight success. The album was released on June 20, 1989, but it took another year to break through to a wider audience in the US. (It did find a more receptive audience in the UK, where *Kerrang!* readers voted it album of the year for 1989, ahead of titles by Aerosmith, King's X, and Skid Row.)

In the meantime, the band toured relentlessly from June 1989 to December 1990, including stretches opening for Metallica, Billy Idol, and even Robert Plant along the way. They played nearly 200 shows in 1990 alone, including multiple trips through Europe and the UK. There were also plenty of low-profile, out-of-the-way headlining gigs throughout the US. "We got a new agent," notes Gould, "and he was one of these more rock agents. So all of a sudden, we'd play in Austin—where we knew there would be like 200 people who would come to see us—and there'd be five people there. 'Cause they booked us in

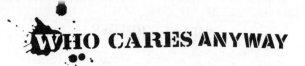

some *fuckin'* strip club in the end of town, with no promotion."

Somewhere along the way, the video for 'Epic' began picking up steam on MTV—first garnering a few plays a week and eventually making its way into heavy rotation. According to *Small Victories* author Adrian Harte, the video aired every hour of the day for an entire week in late May of 1990. Here it is worth recalling the outsized role that MTV played in breaking new bands in those pre-internet days—back when the channel still actually showed music videos. And at a time when hair metal, R&B, and teen pop still dominated the playlists, 'Epic' was something different. It was modern, even arty, yet still accessible to headbangers, mall rats, and other denizens of suburban America.

As Harte's book recounts, MTV programming director Rick Krim made a big behind-the-scenes push for the video well before the song (or album) had made a dent in the charts. "I feel like I went out of my way," he told Harte, "feeling like this is really something that could become a big thing."[33] This might seem to bear out Chuck Mosley's contention that the band's commercial breakthrough was a *fait accompli*, one that would have happened regardless of the singer. "Me getting fired was just incidental," he says. "It was gonna go that way anyway. Who knows how long it might've lasted? But whatever—they would have had one hit that they shoved down people's throats on MTV, and it would have been big. At least for a year, or fifteen minutes." Perhaps. Yet FNM's previous video— an awkward clip for lead single 'From out of Nowhere' that looks like a Guns 'n' Roses parody—didn't make any headway. 'Epic' was the second video for *The Real Thing*, and according to Gould, if it had gone the way of the first one, the label would have pulled the plug on promoting the album.

Even with the big push from MTV, it took until late July of 1990 for 'Epic' to make its way into the top forty. The song eventually peaked at number nine on the Billboard Hot 100 in September, with the band joining the likes of MC Hammer, New Kids on the Block, Poison, and Jon Bon Jovi in the top ten. *The Real Thing* peaked at number eleven on the Billboard 200 album chart that October—fifteen months after the album's release and seven years to the month after FNM's debut performance at the On Broadway.

33 Harte, *Small Victories*, p. 171.

THE LATE EIGHTIES

But the ride wasn't over yet. Touring continued through the end of the year, culminating in a memorable appearance on *Saturday Night Live* that December. By this point, delirium had long since set in. "I used to see Faith No More when they would come through town," recalls David Katz, who had moved from SF to London by this point. "And I remember one time seeing Billy at the Columbia Hotel, and he just looked … morbid. He was going around, saying to some A&R woman, 'Julie, give me a hug.' I remember coming up and saying, 'Hey Billy, man, what's the story?' He says, 'What's the story? We've been on tour for eighteen months straight. There is no story.' And he just looked totally miserable and completely exhausted."

Joan Osato: They didn't take the path that was an easier path or the one that was laid out for them, but it was certainly worth the risk. Some of us probably didn't feel like we had that much to risk in terms of where we come from or what we were doing. We didn't really envision a future for ourselves. So what risk is it to live on the edge? But for Billy and Roddy, *I* know that there was a risk involved. So I always really admired them for that. Karma's like that: you do things with intention, and stuff happens with it.

David Katz: You know, for a while, it was funny for me: "How did I get to know those guys?" They played at my student union as a trio. They were just some guys, you know? And then they play over here [in England], and they're booked into five-star hotels under a secret name, and they would literally have fans trying to break into their tour bus. I mean, it was just kind of unbelievable how huge they had become.

Will Carpmill: Everything that happened after that, you could sort of see why it happened. Everybody had their own issues that they carried into it, so those were going to have to be dealt with (or not dealt with). But everybody also had their talents. Billy and Roddy both have this Hollywood sensibility. They knew how to handle fame and how to handle interviews and how to handle the exposure, and make the most out of it.

INTO THE NINETIES

35

HAZTECH, THE EASY GOINGS, AND THE ZIP CODE RAPISTS

"It's like, what if fuckin' Ringo hadn't called McCartney at midnight? Where would we all be, right? We'd all be listening to the Dave Clark Five!"—from 'I'm in Your Band' (*Great Phone Calls*)

John Singer: The first time I met Gregg, I saw him on the steps there with Grux. He kind of went, "Eh, who are you?" I said, "Oh, I live here now."

Gregg Turkington: I was just like, "Ugh, who's this hippie?" I really was not very friendly.

It was late 1987 when John Singer moved into the downstairs unit at 639 Steiner Street. Upstairs from him was one Robert Turkington—who, unlike his son Gregg, took an immediate liking to his new neighbor. Mr. Turkington had recently started his own business, a chemical testing company by the name of HazTech, and he was in need of some help around the office, so he decided to offer his new downstairs neighbor a job.

And it was there in the cramped offices of HazTech that Singer had his second encounter with the younger Turkington, who was working at the company part-time, filling bottles of hydrochloric acid and shipping mail orders. And as two of just a handful of employees at the company, they had no choice but to get to know each other. "And he turned out to be more open-minded than I thought," admits Gregg. "Eventually, we got into this game where we'd bring in an album from our collection to trade, and the game was to see who

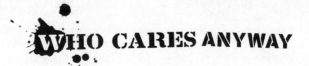

could bring the worst record. So we got into that." As rock 'n' roll origin stories go, it may not rank with Mick and Keith's chance meeting on a train platform (or "fuckin' Ringo calling McCartney at midnight"), but the hand of fate was at work, nonetheless.

THE EASY GOINGS

Singer originally moved out west from upstate New York in 1980, settling in San Jose, where he played guitar in a "top new wave band" that achieved middling success. "We did demos and shopped them around," he says, "and there was interest, but not enough interest to get signed to anybody."

It wasn't music, but marriage, that prompted Singer's eventual move to San Francisco. That said, the move did open up a broader range of opportunities for the versatile guitarist, who soon found himself playing in the Spiritual Corinthians (a black gospel group based in Oakland) as well as a "queer band, for lack of a better word" whose bassist would later go on to play in 4 Non Blondes. Meanwhile, he was also delving into the acoustic singer-songwriter scene that had coalesced around venues like the Albion, a bar on 16th Street in the Mission."Having come from just playing electric, trying to learn how to do stuff with a single guitar—get up and play and sing a song—was really worthwhile," he notes.

And as if that weren't enough, there was the Easy Goings, the first of many bands to emerge from the back offices of HazTech. The group, which initially formed with the modest goal of providing some wholesome entertainment for a friend's birthday party, took its name from a master list that Turkington and Co. had been compiling at work. (A few names they passed over from the same list: Broken Hand Rock, July Fourth Toilet, and the Slow Drippings.) The drummer-less, bass-less quartet—rounded out by guitarist Gary Strasburg and keyboardist Stephen Hanson—played a brief set for the party and then, for some reason, decided they were ready to make a record.

The resulting 7-inch is undoubtedly one of the more inscrutable records released in 1989—though, to be fair, it could have been released anytime

INTO THE NINETIES

between, say, 1972 and 1995 and still felt equally out of step with the times. The cover art offers the first clues that something is, shall we say, a little "off" about the record. The front cover features a Xeroxed image of a smiling young couple from a Benson & Hedges cigarette advertisement. The back cover includes a dedication to *Breakfast Without Meat* favorite Dora Hall, along with an informational blurb about something called "Phase 44 Stereo," which is touted as "a marvel of sound, a radically new and dramatically potent concept in the art of high fidelity reproduction."

Both front and back cover seem incongruous with the contents of the record itself: surprisingly well-played covers of moldy oldies 'The Straight Life' and 'Most of All There's You,' along with one original, 'Hoboes Need Lovin''—a catchy ode to truck stop sex that commingles religious references and jarring profanity to great comic effect. Turkington even offers a preemptive apology at the end of the song ("We hope you've enjoyed it and that you'll tell your friends, and if the sound quality isn't quite up to your standards—well, sorry"), as if objections to sound quality were going to top anyone's list of concerns. The cumulative effect of all of these disparate elements is at once disorienting and deeply funny.

At the time, Turkington and Lizzy Kate Gray were still publishing *Breakfast Without Meat*, which provided a ready outlet to advertise the record—which they did, enthusiastically and shamelessly.[1] They also placed ads in the classified sections of a couple of local newspapers (example: "**NUDE VIDEO** of The Easy Goings is not available. But their sick-a-delic 7-inch EP is!") and even managed to sell a few copies this way. But while *BWM* readers who purchased the record likely had some idea of what they were getting into, newspaper readers did not—and they were not always amused. "I believe I'm *among* those to whom you owe an apology," wrote one angry customer, who returned the record and demanded a refund.[2] A sampling of critics' reviews in a subsequent issue of *BWM* is equally amusing, with the assessments running the gamut from "horrifyingly bad" to "very swinging in a crippled sort

---

1   The record was released via *BWM* subsidiary, Bee-Fast Records.
2   The letter is reproduced in full in issue #6 of *Bananafish*.

WHO CARES ANYWAY

L-R: GARY STRASBURG, GREGG TURKINGTON, STEPHEN HANSON, JOHN SINGER. PHOTO BY STEPH PORTER; COURTESY OF G. TURKINGTON.

of way."[3]

For Turkington, such puzzled reactions had been par for the course since his days in Bean Church and Hello Kitty on Ice. For Singer, however, it was a change of pace, but one that he took in stride. "What was really attractive for me was the lack of attachment to outcome—like, if people are gonna like it or

---

3   A subsequent 7-inch followed in 1992 on Nuf Sed, featuring equally irreverent covers of Black Flag's 'Scream,' Bruce Springsteen's 'Born in the USA,' and the Brian Wilson-penned 'Life Is for the Living' (an unreleased Beach Boys track from the mid-1970s). Other items in the Easy Goings' scant discography included a cover of another Beach Boys oddity, 'Johnny Carson' (issued as part of a flexi-disc that came with issue #14 of *Breakfast Without Meat*); 'Bigfoot/Popcorn Medley,' which appeared on a 7-inch included with issue #6 of *Bananafish*; and 'My Compromise,' which surfaced in 1994 on a two-CD compilation on the noise label RRR. Unreleased covers of King Harvest's 'Dancing in the Moonlight' and Joe E.'s 'Come on Sign' round out the band's discography, the sum total of which would fit neatly on a single LP.

they're not gonna like it," he says. "Not caring too much about that provided a super amount of freedom that you couldn't have if you were trying to get people to buy your new record on whatever label."

"IT WAS HORRIBLE, BUT IT WAS WONDERFUL"

Like Bean Church, the Easy Goings were not exactly a working band, as they didn't tour and didn't play any shows outside of San Francisco or Berkeley. "There was a time in 1989 when it was kind of a functional group, but not for long," notes Turkington.

That summer, he moved to Santa Fe, New Mexico, along with Gray and keyboardist Hanson, temporarily putting the band on hiatus. "To this day, I don't know quite how we chose New Mexico, but I think it had somewhat to do with the painting market down there," says Gray, who was a landscape painter.[4] "And I did end up getting in galleries and selling a lot of paintings." She and Gregg published the final issues of *Breakfast Without Meat* from their temporary home in the "land of enchantment" before parting ways, with Turkington and Hanson subsequently heading back to the Bay Area in early 1991.

The Easy Goings would play a handful more shows over the next year or so, with their performances often eliciting the same range of reactions that the record did—especially when unsuspecting audiences were on hand. Alicia Rose, who booked the Easy Goings to play at Brainwash (a South of Market laundromat and cafe), recalls one such occasion:

> The owner, Susan, was like this dried-up, over-tanned kind of fancy-car-driving lady in her forties at the time. She goes, "I've been approached by MTV about doing a show based on what we're all

---

4   Turkington recalls their car breaking down on the way to New Mexico, leaving the trio stranded at a Best Western in Tehachapi, California, for several days. "I had never really been back there after that, until … twenty-five years to the day, we shot a bunch of *Entertainment* there and stayed in town a couple of nights."

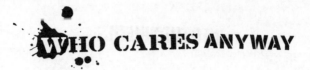

about. I'm gonna bring 'em here on a night when you're having live music, okay?" And I go, "Great!" And the night she brings them is the night that I have the Easy Goings. It was the most glorious thing. At first, they seem like a band, and then you realize it's all just a foil for Gregg's insanity. He was swigging motor oil and spitting it all over the place (but it was actually chocolate syrup) and just making this insane mockery of the place and speaking complete obscenity and talking about all of these things like burning the place down. It was horrible, but it was wonderful.

Suffice it to say that the Easy Goings never made it onto MTV, although a year later, they opened for a band that did—namely, Faith No More. Performing for a capacity crowd at the Warfield on August 19, 1992, the Easy Goings played what appears to have been an otherwise typical set, including their ramshackle covers of 'The Straight Life,' 'Born in the USA,' and Brian Wilson's 'Life Is for the Living.'[5] Video footage from that night shows Turkington berating the crowd, drinking Windex, and eventually challenging audience members to come onstage and fight him. Evidently, it was not what Faith No More's fans had in mind as an *aperitif*.

"It was hard for us to go on after that, actually," laughs Bill Gould. "We were going, 'Maybe this was a mistake!' I was expecting people to get drunk and rowdy. I was a big, big fan of the Easy Goings and Zip Code Rapists, and we didn't have an opener to play the Warfield and thought it would be kind of interesting. They were kind of confrontational. I think I really realized that we had a more traditional rock crowd than I wanted to admit because they killed the buzz! By the time we went on, the room was just frozen. We had to work real hard to get it going again. But it was great."

5　By this point, they had added a drummer in Scott Brizel, who also appears on the *Cigarettes* EP.

ZCR: SINGING AND PLAYING

The Easy Goings actually came out of retirement for the Warfield show, by which point Hanson (who flew in for the occasion) had finished grad school at UC Berkeley and taken a job as a professor at the University of Washington. In the meantime, the duo of Turkington and Singer had begun performing together

THE EASY GOINGS

LIVE! THURSDAY FREE
MAY 10 8:30 plus: THE NICE GUYS
THE MINT PLATTER, 2566 TELEGRAPH, BERKELEY

Wildness at its way-out-est, to the pitch of furious frenzy—the height, apex, acme, epitome—the living END!!! That is The Easy Goings. Singing and playing the young sounds of today. Wind up the Gramophone, turn the horn towards the action and let's dance, let's listen....it's the sound you asked for! This rocking group, with all its many knobs, buttons, and doo-dads, looks and sounds like it might launch a rocket. The sounds of "freakout" found on this record are sure to please the most discerning palate.

THE EASY GOINGS

Only 1000 copies of this 3-song, 7" EP were pressed. To assure that each and everyone gets the chance to hear the "Goings" out-perform themselves on these great songs, there is a limit of five (5) records per address. The cost for one copy of THE EASY GOINGS, delivered to your home or office by US Mail, is just $2.50, postpaid. Send payment to: Bee-Toor Records, P.O. Box 19327, Santa Fe, New Mexico 87504, USA.

under a different, less wholesome moniker.

Like so many of Turkington's projects, this one began on a whim and steadily took on a life of its own. "I got asked to do this spoken word thing," he recounts, "and I wasn't in the mood for it, so I asked John to come, and I figured we'd just do Easy Goings songs acoustically. But then we went out and had drinks and plotted out all this other crap and did the first Zip Code Rapists show." Singer recalls the same pre-show meeting: "Gregg said, 'I don't know what the hell we're gonna do. Let's just go pretend to do some songs.' We probably played for fifteen minutes, and most of it was yelling or something. I'm sure the whole reason why the band name came up is that we just looked at a list and said, 'Well, we've gotta call it something, so we'll call it this because this is so horrible that no one will ever ask us to play again.'"

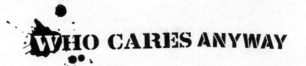

Yet they *were* asked to play again—and again, and again. "Grux was at that show and thought it was really funny, so he offered to book more shows," says Turkington. "And then he got this show at the Sixth Street Rendezvous, which was just like the worst skid row bar ever. Brandan and Grux and a couple of other friends were there, and then there were just a few derelicts who were there every night drinking at the bar. We had the tape from that show, and we'd listen to it in the car on the way to work, and we thought it was pretty funny. So we decided, 'Well, we should release this—it's got its moments.'"

The live recording—much of which consists of audience heckling and drunken between-song banter—occupies most of side two on the duo's debut LP. As for side one, it was the product of a spontaneous recording project whose origins, once again, trace back to HazTech.

Brandan Kearney: One day, Gregg and John were bickering over a new album by some band, which John liked and Gregg didn't. I don't know what band it was, but what particularly irritated Gregg was that they'd taken a long time to record and mix it; I guess this was being passed off by journalists, or the band itself, as evidence of their status as artists. Anyway, Gregg argued to John that the two of them could write and record a better album in twenty-four hours and demanded that they start recording at midnight that Friday.

John Singer: We would establish these kind of stupid ground rules for what we were gonna do, and then that would be what we'd do. A lot of times it was, "Hey, let's just do everything as quick as we can." That doesn't mean that we didn't do overdubs or think about some stuff, but we didn't go away and think about it and then come back and do something later. But the idea of it was to kind of spontaneously do things, not worry about sound quality, not worry about performance. Having played music for a long time and been in lots of bands and worked really hard to do things, there was a lot of freedom in just coming in and doing that kind of thing.

Gregg Turkington: This record-pressing company in LA had a big ad in *BAM* saying, "400 12-inches for $599 including mastering and plain covers." I just saw the ad and said, "That's so cheap; we should just fucking make an album."

INTO THE NINETIES

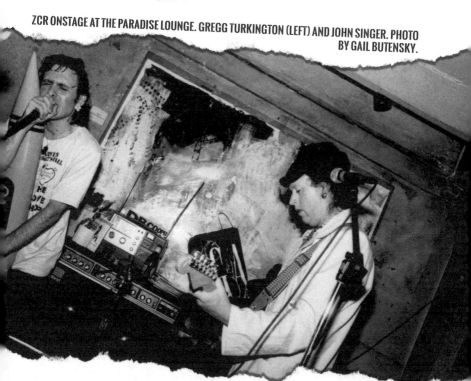

So we recorded 'Touch Me' and 'The Best Never Rest,' and then we took all the other stuff from the other recording session—the twenty-four-hour thing—and we took that live material and just pieced together this album and rushed it to the pressing plant.

The ensuing LP—*Zip Code Rapists Sing and Play The Three Doctors and Other Sounds of Today*—is even more perplexing than the first Easy Goings 7-inch, if only because the long-player format offered more room to work with. Once again, the album art is crucial to the overall experience. The front cover is completely out of step with punk/rock design standards. It includes an out-of-order track listing (including one song, 'If You Had My Eyes,' that's nowhere to be found on the record); a photo of an ice-skater pirouetting alongside a circus bear; and a proud declaration along the bottom that reads, "YOU WON'T BELIEVE THE SOUND YOU HEAR!—IT'S GREAT!!" In the top left corner is the Amarillo

Records logo, along with the official-looking catalog number "2YEF575."[6] Atop the back cover, meanwhile, is an enthusiastic blurb that begins:

> Hit sounds from Texas—"THE" Duo that is breaking all the Records! "ZIP CODE RAPISTS" outperform themselves on twelve great songs that are sure to appeal to everyone who belongs to today's thing.

One is struck by the peculiar attention to detail, down to the bad punctuation and the arbitrary use of capital letters and quotation marks.

The music is equally baffling. The centerpiece of side one is the acoustic 'President's Song,' in which Turkington casually rattles off allusions to "Richard Reagan" ("he won in nineteen-hundred and sixty-one") and "President Arthur Tony Randall Ashe" as if he were reading the phone book. Then there is 'Wired,' an up-tempo rocker inspired by the ill-fated John Belushi biopic of the same name. The studio portion of the record concludes with 'The Three Doctors,' another up-tempo rocker with lyrics that defy analysis; the chorus, for example, repeats the word "fuck" sixteen times before proclaiming, "I'm going drinking with two of the three / We're going out / We'll be free."[7]

Given its rather selective appeal, *Sing and Play* was hardly destined to become a big seller. Accordingly, only 800 copies were pressed, but they sold out quickly enough, after which the album practically vanished—suggesting that most people who bought it liked it enough to keep it. Not so for critic Greg Prato, however, who awarded the album a measly one star out of five in a review for *All Music Guide Online*. "The worst record of all time? It's definitely up there," he proclaimed. "This is the type of stuff that will clear a party in one minute flat or will offend just about everybody in hearing distances [sic]."

As usual, Turkington took the criticism with a grain of salt. "People are not very smart or very nice when they say those things, but you know, you make

---

6   The cover, like the Amarillo logo, is actually an unspoken homage to Alshire Records, the budget label that was home to the 101 Strings Orchestra.
7   The trio of doctors referred to in the song are Dr. Eugene Landy, best known as Brian Wilson's psychologist and life coach for much of the seventies and eighties; Dr. Norris, a San Francisco talk radio host; and Dr. Larry, one of Turkington and Singer's co-workers at HazTech.

a record like that, and you kind of expect that kind of thing." Given that the duo initially bonded over trying to outdo each other with bad records from their own collections, one might be tempted to speculate that Prato's reaction was precisely what they had in mind. Yet Turkington is quick to counter this notion."We weren't trying to make the worst record ever," he clarifies. "I think it was just that there was a certain amount of freedom about not caring what people thought, not being overly concerned.

"The thing about that record is, it's like an album that you can listen to, and you don't have the feeling you've listened to an album. It's like a non-album album—it just doesn't satisfy in the way that you've come to expect from a full-length album. There's something really wrong with it, but that's part of its charm."

WHO CARES ANYWAY

ZCR'S JOHN SINGER (LEFT) AND GREGG TURKINGTON. PHOTO BY ALICIA ROSE; SET DESIGN BY REBECCA WILSON.

36

AMARILLO

"**A**SK YOUR DEALER FOR THESE GREAT COUNTRY & WESTERN ALBUMS," announces a promotional blurb on the back cover of *Sing and Play*. It's unknown whether anyone ever did so, but if they had, they would have come up empty-handed for the simple reason that the albums in question—the Zip Code Rapists' *Refried Boogie* and *Touch Me*—did not exist (at least, not in the material realm).

Sing and Play was not only the Zip Code Rapists' recorded debut but also the debut release for Amarillo Records.[8] That said, both the album and the label were in keeping with the same peculiar aesthetic that Turkington and his collaborators had been cultivating since the early days of Bean Church and *Breakfast Without Meat*. That aesthetic is still hard to pin down, in part because of the disparate (and often seemingly incompatible) influences that helped shape it, from hardcore-era favorites like Flipper and Black Flag to showbiz relics like the 101 Strings and Frank Sinatra, Jr. Like *BWM*, the label also reflected a (sometimes morbid) fascination with the institution of entertainment and its various notions of success and failure. Finally, there was a prankish playfulness behind the whole endeavor. Turkington and Co. seemed to rejoice in taking far-fetched ideas, willing them into existence somehow, and then releasing them out into the wild; consequences be damned.

"He always liked to put things out," says Lizzy Kate Gray. "He got that do-it-yourself ethic early on, and working at Subterranean, he knew it was possible." In addition to the Easy Goings 7-inch, these pre-Amarillo releases included a Sun City Girls cassette (*Midnight Cowboys from Ipanema*, later reissued on Amarillo),

---

8   The label took its name from the supposed hometown of the label's flagship duo. According to the album credits, the studio portion of *Sing and Play* was recorded at "Modern Facilities Studios, 3405 Amarillo Boulevard, Amarillo, Texas."

an Easy Goings/Mark Eitzel flexi-disc (included with an issue of *BWM*), and even a Bean Church "12-inch cassette" (i.e., a cassette strapped to a 12-inch record). "And when he couldn't put something out," adds Gray, "he would just make one out of another record. He was so involved in every aspect of records that he would take a single, put a different label on it with the name of a band he'd made up and the name of a song he'd made up, and do the cover art. It was like he couldn't stop putting things out, whether he had a label or not."

For Turkington—who wasn't so much a musician or even a singer as he was a conceptualist, an idea man—Amarillo was the ideal medium. On a meta level, the label was a creative project in its own right, one with a distinctive A&R sensibility and an equally distinctive approach to packaging and marketing its records. Press releases and other promotional copy were often purposely vague, misleading, and/or replete with outmoded lingo ("Stunning packaging complements a fine selection of new tunes," went the mail-order catalog entry for one LP). Back covers were frequently adorned with cheerful blurbs like the one that appears on *Sing and Play* ("YOU WON'T BELIEVE THE SOUND YOU HEAR!"). While Amarillo was indeed a real label with (mostly) real bands and records, it often came across more like a simulation or even a spoof of one. Or maybe it was all of the above.

"What Amarillo Records did was *really complex* to understand," emphasizes Margaret Murray, who was involved in a number of the label's releases as a musician and/or layout artist. "Because if you just bought it as music, you'd go, 'This music's poorly recorded and terrible!' But if you followed the whole thing that everyone was trying to do, it just became this amazing experience. And I don't think that other people did similar things until much, much later."

"There are layers and layers of commentary on show business in everything Gregg does," adds Lizzy Gray. "And he used to read hundreds of showbiz biographies.[9] He read *everybody's* biography. And, in a way, I think a lot of what he's playing on is who gets success and who doesn't, and why they want it,

---

9   Rebecca Wilson makes a similar observation: "He can read a page of Charles Dickens in like five seconds. And the first time I saw how fast he read, I thought he was kidding. And I'm a pretty fast reader—I'm a really fast reader—and Gregg is like, '*Doot*.' He's a human computer—he processes stuff so fast."

and what's valuable in the attempt, even in failure. Of course, what we're talking about is just commercial failure and the sadness of so many people who wanted commercial success so desperately and didn't get it. And he read about every way that even commercial success can go wrong."

ENTER BRANDAN AND MARGARET

As it did with the Easy Goings and Zip Code Rapists, HazTech served as a breeding ground for Amarillo Records. This was especially true once Margaret Murray and Brandan Kearney joined the staff circa 1991, around the time Turkington returned from New Mexico.[10] Along with John Singer (their ostensible boss), the four of them spent untold hours listening to records and discussing music while filling orders and pouring toxic chemicals into small bottles. It was tedious work, admits Murray, "but with that mix of people, all kinds of creativity started. That's where Amarillo started, and it's where Brandan wrote his zine *Nothing Doing* and did a lot of his record releases for Nuf Sed as well."

The group also developed an array of odd pastimes, such as playing darts with old record covers as dartboards (Starship's *Knee Deep in the Hoopla* was a favorite in this regard) and writing album reviews based on anagrams of band names and album titles.[11] Then were the masochistic listening marathons,

---

10 Murray was another product of the Iowa-to-SF pipeline, though she had a couple of stops in between. As she recalls, "I went to school in Chicago at the Chicago Art Institute, and when I graduated from there, I moved to New York with one of my roommates from Chicago because I thought it would be fun. And it wasn't. It was kind of a nightmare. I didn't know what I was doing, and New York's a hard place to live, especially at that time, which would have been '86.

"So I wanted something that was still a city but a lot easier and pretty. And I had visited my half-sister in Berkeley many years ago, and I thought, 'Oh, San Francisco, that seems nice.' So I moved to San Francisco with a friend of mine. And then ... how did I find these musicians? Maybe through Matt Hall—I'm not really sure." Hall, in turn, had been bandmates with Murray's older brother David in Stiff Legged Sheep, the Iowa City outfit that Hall played in immediately before and after his first stint in San Francisco.

11 That particular pastime eventually culminated in an actual book, *Warm Voices Rearranged: Anagram Record Reviews* (Drag City, 2002), which was co-authored by Turkington and Kearney.

wherein the crew subjected themselves to the likes of Roger Daltrey's *Ride a Rock Horse* on a constant loop. (Mind you, they did earn their paychecks, as Turkington clarifies: "Sometimes it was really busy there—you could have a $15,000 order or whatever. But sometimes there was nothing to do, and that's when we'd just sit around and come up with these fucking band ideas.")

Another crucial part of HazTech lore was the shared obsession with vanity pressings—low-budget, self-produced anomalies, primarily from the late sixties and seventies, that made their way into heavy rotation on the office turntable. "Those guys would really like to go out record shopping," says Murray, "and they'd go to the bargain bins and find all these records and bring them in. That's how we started listening to Russ Saul and all these other vanity pressings and getting really carried away with them." Songs from vanity pressings—including Saul's *Begin to Feel* and James Lowry's *His Way*—were covered on numerous Amarillo releases, including ones by the Zip Code Rapists and their offshoots (the Zip Code Revue and the Three Doctors) as well as Murray's US Saucer.[12] Both Amarillo and Kearney's Nuf Sed imprint drew inspiration from the world of vanity pressings, in some cases packaging their records to look like old vanity pressings (e.g., Tarnation's *I'll Give You Something to Cry About* on Nuf Sed). One Amarillo release, Harvey Sid Fisher's *Astrology Songs*, was a reissue of an actual vanity pressing.

The interest in vanity pressings reflected not only a growing sense of boredom with the state of underground rock but also a genuine appreciation for the often mysterious characters who made the records. Some of them were calculating hucksters; others were desperately sincere, if only marginally talented, singer-

---

12 Technically speaking, these two records weren't vanity pressings, but they are close enough for our purposes. Turkington offered some more details on the provenance of *Begin to Feel* in the book *Enjoy the Experience: Homemade Records, 1958-1992* (Sinecure, 2012): "Not a true vanity pressing at all, *Begin to Feel* was, in fact, part of a complicated tax-scam scheme perpetrated by a few record labels in 1977, after which time the short-lived loophole in the tax code was closed. In order to make this peculiar scam work, actual 'dummy stock' had to be pressed and stored in a warehouse, though none of it was intended to be actually heard or distributed. The reason for Tribute's cavalier attitude as to how the records looked and sounded was simply that these records didn't need to be entertaining in any way—all they had to do was take up space for a set amount of time." Russ Saul and James Lowry (another Tribute Records artist) were pseudonyms; the performers' actual names are still unknown.

INTO THE NINETIES

songwriters. In music industry terms, the likes of Russ Saul and Joe E. were abject failures, yet for the HazTech crew, they were borderline heroic—in spite of their sometimes glaring flaws. "We thought the lyrics were sometimes hokey," admits Murray, pausing to choose her words carefully. "I don't know how to call them 'not very good' while still loving what they were doing. Because that's really how we felt about it."

That complex relationship with the vanity pressing material comes through poignantly in US Saucer's version of 'His Room,' which features a rare vocal turn by Murray. Credited to the pseudonymous (and ultimately anonymous) James Lowry, the song is a maudlin yet heartfelt ballad about "this lonely old man I once called Dad." On paper, it sounds hopelessly corny, and in the irony-laden nineties, it's the kind of sentiment that would have been roundly greeted with condescension. Yet Murray's performance is at once self-aware and disarmingly sincere—self-aware in that she's clearly playing a role (that of the forlorn adult daughter of the aforementioned dad), but sincere in that she could just as easily be singing about her own dad. That said, there is a moment of unintentional comedy midway through the song when one of the guitarists hits a sour note during the instrumental section, threatening to derail the take. One envisions the band members stifling a laugh, but they manage to keep it together long enough to finish the song. Much like Ricky Williams's unscripted burp and "excuse me" during the Sleepers' 'Los Gatos,' the juxtaposition of heartfelt sentiment and accidental comedy adds another layer to the performance.

The other vanity pressing covers that saw the light of day via Amarillo sometimes veered closer to the comedy side of the "tragicomedy" equation, but they were hardly irreverent. "We picked these things out, particular vanity pressings, because we felt like the people really believed what they were doing, and that mattered to us," says Murray. "That mattered to us more than technical ability, certainly. And it's why we would criticize all this other [contemporary] music because it didn't *sound* like anything; it didn't *feel* like anything. And then here's these people where it really *feels* like something. They're *really* trying to do something. And the fact that they are off-key, or their lyrics are trite or something like that—it's beside the point. It doesn't matter. It's pointless to start critiquing that kind of stuff."

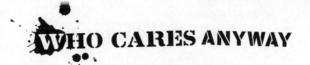

THE FLAGSHIP DUO

As Amarillo was establishing itself—however improbably—as a bona fide label, the Zip Code Rapists were doing likewise as a live act. It helped that some of their biggest fans were members of other bands, such as Faith No More, Mr. Bungle, the Thinking Fellers, and Caroliner. "Grux was really into booking us on these bills," notes Turkington, "so he kept pushing, and people started to come see it eventually because word was out that it was kind of a funny experience to watch this miserable two-person act, and it was just all about self-pity and terror and misery." There was a clear division of labor, with Singer handling the music and Turkington everything else: goading audience members, butchering song lyrics, smashing Pablo Cruise records over his head, and hauling a bizarre assortment of props on stage, from stuffed animals to bowling trophies. "I was really into the idea of these trophies," he admits. "I mean, you could bludgeon someone with them. You'd kind of be drunk, and you're stumbling around with these terrifying, heavy trophies in your hand."

Bill Gould: I went to see them at the Paradise Lounge. That was a real suburban crowd that was just kind of a captive audience. Gregg came out, and he had this blowtorch, and he turned it on. And then he's singing Doors covers. There's girls sitting in the front row, and he's going, "Come on, come on, come on, *touch* me, baby." [Laughs.] You'd see people just get up and walk away. The boyfriend looks like he's gonna punch him in the face. It was great, man. That was great shit.

Gregg Turkington: We used to cook food during the set. We had this show where we bought all these baked beans and had a frying pan and a propane torch and cooked up just like a whole mess of beans. Then we had all these industrial magazines, and we were serving them to people on these chemical industry trade magazines.

Trey Spruance: I remember one show at an art gallery. People were doing projections, and Gregg tore the goddamn screen off the wall. I didn't really know him that well, but to see him completely drunk out of his mind, screaming these horrible obscenities at these delicate San Francisco hipster types at their art opening—where they've asked him to do it because ... I don't really know why. I guess because they were "edgy, arty" people. And he turns around and pulls that shit off the walls and makes a complete ass out of himself—makes everybody there hate his guts. It was fucking great. It was amazing.[13]

Seymour Glass: Over time, it got more and more refined, from being like an Andrew Dice Clay thing to more of an Andy Kaufman thing. The concepts got more elaborate and had more layers. At a Zip Code Rapists show, you don't just watch the performers; you also stay aware of the reactions of all the people around you. I don't know how much of it they had planned.

For Singer, his partner's antics could sometimes be a bit much. Though he was secure in his role as the "straight man" in the duo, he still wanted to play the songs correctly—or at least make it past the first chorus without utter chaos ensuing. "It did get frustrating," the guitarist admits. "But on the other hand,

---

13 The show in question is mentioned in Jack Stevenson's *Land of a Thousand Balconies: Discoveries and Confessions of a B-Movie Archaeologist*, which includes a chapter on "guerrilla cinema" in San Francisco. The chapter focuses on the exploits of rogue filmmaker Jacques Boyreau, co-founder of the Werepad, a performance space at 2430 Third Street (a mere block from the site of the old Club Foot). As Stevenson recalls in the book, "The last show I did with Jacques was in the summer of 1993, another *Night of the Living Dead* theme show. The film was an ongoing obsession of his. We ran all three spools of the film simultaneously on three big screens while live bands flailed away down front. Somehow it wasn't working. Then the guitar player for the Zip Code Rapists yanked down one of the screens in a fit of punk nastiness, in turn prompting the projectionist to shine the projector beam into the face of the offending assholes. When this seemed to have no effect, he turned the projector sideways at a sharp angle onto the surviving screen, and the resultant shadowy, dream-like superimpositions were magical" (p.144).

Like Spruance, Turkington remembers things differently. "He's actually mixing up a lot of the details. Earlier in the book, he describes the show in question, a screening of Peter Fonda movies at a club called the Garage on 10th Street. That's where the screen was ripped down. A couple years later, we performed at a screening of *Night of the Living Dead*. I don't remember the screen getting ripped down then, and definitely not by John. But that's how [Stevenson] remembers it. Mike Patton was also at the show Trey was at [i.e., the Fonda show on 10th Street], and he once told me he never saw people flee a venue as quickly and in such vast numbers as he did that night, when we tore the screen down and threw an old theatre lamp (plugged in; the bulb exploded) into the crowd."

what I picked up from that period—which I've been able to take onward from it—is that it kind of took out the fear of doing just about *anything* on stage. You didn't have to worry, especially once you got past thinking, 'We want to please people musically.' Because obviously, our live shows were not gonna be *very* pleasing musically. So once you get past that, you can actually play in just about any situation and figure out a way to have fun.

"Plus, I think it was really interesting to just be able to interact in *any* direction at a Zip Code Rapists show," he adds. "A lot of it had to do with the push and pull between the audience and the band. Some shows would turn into confrontations with stuff being thrown; other shows would turn into singalongs. Within that, yes, there were some nights when it was absolutely frustrating because most of the time was spent knocking over drinks, throwing stuff, and having people yell at you. And as somebody who's played for years and years, sometimes if you do a whole string of shows like that, it gets pretty depressing."

Gregg Turkington: I think that's really the key to the group, just his total ambivalence. Half the time, he thinks it's really great, and half the time, he's really disgusted with the whole thing. And I really don't think, to this day, that he's made up his mind.

Margaret Murray: John has an amazing heart. He's a really great person. He's thoughtful; he cares about all kinds of things. He tried *so* hard to make HazTech a place that felt good to work in, and he got disturbed by a lot of the negativity. Even though it was funny, he got tired of it. He wanted to be more positive. "Can't we just listen to this record without tearing it to pieces?" Because that did get to be a habit, of being overly critical. And just his ability to play in a band like Zip Code Rapists, which played a lot of music that was antagonistic—I don't think that's naturally the kind of music that John plays.

Gregg Turkington: Sometimes he would be more obnoxious than me, just screwing everything up, and I'd just go with it. But other times, he'd get in this mood where he wanted us to try to do a better show … and then we would do just the worst, most horrific shows ever, and John would get a little frustrated with it. Or we would have rehearsals and try to learn songs, and then I would ruin

INTO THE NINETIES

them at the show by being too drunk or just not remembering the lyrics. It'd just waste any and all effort that was made.

John Singer: Overall, I think the most interesting stuff happened when we would perhaps bounce back from one of those shows and do something absolutely different—something really friendly—or just hand out lots of presents or whatever.

411

37

LIFE BEYOND EUREKA

When Mike Patton joined Faith No More, the ripple effects extended well beyond his impact on the band's own fortunes. His eventual move to San Francisco in 1991 initiated a small caravan of sorts. "It was all within that same year or two that everybody I knew was moving to San Francisco," recalls Danny Heifetz, the drummer in Patton's other band, Mr. Bungle, as well as a founding member of Dieselhed, another Humboldt County band that made the move south around this time.[14]

Much like the Thinking Fellers contingent had done a few years earlier, the Humboldt County crew brought an influx of new talent as well as a different sensibility. "What I appreciated about Mike," notes Will Carpmill, "was that he brought Northern California in. San Francisco's always been a magnet, but it was mostly pulling people from LA and the rest of the country. Northern California's actually a really cool place. So he sort of put it on the map. I don't think a whole lot of people, unless they smoked pot, had heard of Humboldt before."

"It would have been a fairly weird place to grow up," says Heifetz, who attended Humboldt State University in Arcata along with the other members of Mr. Bungle but, unlike them, did not grow up in the area. "Eureka's a fairly redneck kind of place. It's a lumber town—they have huge lumber mills there. And Arcata's a pretty liberal university town, I guess. You've got a lot of hippie elements, so there was a lot of hippie/redneck vibe going on up there."

---

14 Dieselhed originally formed in the late 1980s and then re-formed in San Francisco after three of the four original members moved there. Heifetz: "It was originally a four-piece truck-drivin' band in Arcata, where it started. It was Shon [McAllin], Virgil [Shaw], me, and Chris [Imlay] of Brent's TV. So it was Virgil and Chris from that band, and me and Shon from Bagelface—two totally different bands. And we got together and decided to write and play songs about truck driving."

INTO THE NINETIES

"There was always this rivalry between Eureka and Arcata bands," adds Kris Hendrickson, a Eureka native. "Arcata was more of an intellectual place. Eureka was more of a metal/rock kind of place. And so it was like 'the punkers versus the metalheads.'" Heifetz's old band, the Arcata-based Eggly Bagelface, fell more on the "intellectual" side of this divide (band name notwithstanding). Mr. Bungle, in contrast, fell squarely on the metal side. Their first demo, *The Raging Wrath of the Easter Bunny*, was basically unadulterated thrash/death metal, not counting the occasional satirical song title or lyric (e.g., 'Evil Satan,' 'Anarchy up Your Anus'). On subsequent demos, they abandoned death metal in favor of a ska-funk-metal hybrid. In any case, they weren't punks, musically or otherwise.

Rebecca Wilson: When I first met Trey, he was kind of like this rocker guy coming from Eureka. All those Mr. Bungle guys, their first band was like a rock band. They were wearing Spandex and doing headbanging and air guitar, and it wasn't a parody. They were serious metal guys.

Kris Hendrickson: I know Mike loved Mötley Crüe very much because he had a real Nikki Sixx kind of look going on. He and Trevor played in this band called Gemini. And there was a little of a Mötley Crüe influence in there. He would probably never admit that.

Trey Spruance: We were definitely metalheads. Instead of being punk people who are smart, literate, and socially aware, we were violent, leather-jacket-wearing heshers who were introduced to punk through crossover hardcore. We weren't into Mötley Crüe or Poison or anything like that. We were into Exciter and all these weird underground bands. We were total snobs, importing records from European death metal bands. Patton was a buyer at the local record store. That record store had amazingly well-stocked death metal. We were lucky.

But there was never any listening to the Dead Kennedys; there was never any concern of any kind for politics for us—ever. There was nothing of any real value as far as punk rock is concerned. My friends were listening to Crass or that kind of stuff; I would listen to the Exploited or something. But there was no legitimate punk rock core to Mr. Bungle at all.

413

WHO CARES ANYWAY

Danny Heifetz: You know, a lot of times when Trey's saying "we," he's talking about the core: he, Mike, and Trevor. And beyond that, probably even including all the previous members from the first demo or two, like [original drummer] Jed Watts. I definitely don't think of Bär as a metalhead. *I* was a metalhead but in a totally different era. Even though I'm only four or five years older, I was like a generation away. I really couldn't have cared less about Metallica. Didn't like Slayer. When I was fourteen, fifteen, I was listening to Judas Priest, Black Sabbath, and Richie Blackmore's Rainbow.

IN FRISCO

As Patton settled into life in San Francisco, he did so as a full-fledged rock star and teen idol. Within the past year, he'd appeared on *Saturday Night Live*, the MTV Video Music Awards, and *Yo! MTV Raps,* in addition to gracing the covers of glossy magazines from *Spin* to *Kerrang*. That said, he wasn't exactly living like a rock star. In 1991, he and Bungle guitarist Trey Spruance moved into a house in the Sunset District, a quiet, residential neighborhood on the west side of town. "I used to stay there," recalls Rebecca Wilson, who was dating Spruance at the time. "And that place was so disgusting. Talk about filthy—I mean, garbage everywhere."

One of their neighbors was the notorious Smelly Mustafa, a rural Michigan transplant who fronted the band Plainfield. "Mike and I would be watching [televangelist] Robert Tilton at three or four in the morning," recalls Spruance, "and Smelly would just show up at that time, drunk out of his mind, and climb through our fucking window. And for some reason, that was okay—I guess because our house was filled with garbage and shit-eating videos and pornography and a rotting refrigerator. It was horrible. You wouldn't believe it. This was at the height of Patton's stardom. Just living in fuckin' filth and slime, watching a television preacher and getting attacked by a punk rock redneck in the middle of the night."

Kris Hendrickson: Mr. Bungle are a boys club. They had a lot of fun together, but they were always at odds or always trying to one-up each other. I mean, "Mr.

INTO THE NINETIES

Bungle" the name and where they got it from—*The Pee-wee Herman show*—has to do with "bungling" things, throwing a stick in the spokes, fucking with people. And that was their notorious nature. And they would either have great friends because of it, or they would make total enemies.

Rebecca Wilson: There was a side to these guys that was really gross and really juvenile—really puerile, really scatological. I don't know how to explain it other than that they came from really repressed families in Northern California, and this was a big thrill to them. But they were also musically very sophisticated.

When I dated Trey, he had long dreadlocks down to his waist, and he used to wear a batting helmet all the time. I took him to dinner with my grandfather one time, and my grandfather was like, "What's with the batting helmet? Why won't he take off the batting helmet?" Because we're in some nice restaurant in North Beach, and he just kept wearing this—like a real batting helmet, you know what I mean? He wore it all the time. And it was cool; it was fun. But it's just one of those classic things. He is kind of rebellious.

MR. BUNGLE

It was thanks to the Faith No More connection that Mr. Bungle found themselves signed to Warner Bros. They began work on their debut album in early 1991, shortly after Patton's return from the *Real Thing* tour and before most of the other band members had officially moved to San Francisco.[15] Moreover, most of the songs had appeared before, in different versions, on the demo cassettes *Goddammit I Love America!!!* (1988) and *OU818* (1989). In other words, *Mr. Bungle* is less a San Francisco album than it is a summation of the band's

15 Then again, it's not as if they would have been doomed to obscurity without the FNM connection."This wasn't exactly a recording budget we couldn't have gotten elsewhere," Spruance told an interviewer in 1991. "In fact, before Mike's offer to join FNM, we had an offer from another label that we almost took. Who knows how things would have turned out? Who knows if Mike would have even ended up in FNM?" (Mike Gitter, "BUNG-HO!" *Kerrang!* July 20, 1991.)

WHO CARES ANYWAY

Humboldt County years—or, in the words of bassist Trevor Dunn, "a glimpse of Eureka through the eyes of kids who had to get out."[16]

That was part of the backstory, anyway. The other part had to do with Patton's rock star status, along with the desire of everyone involved to keep his two bands separate. Warner Bros. barely promoted the album, and when they did, they were coy about the Patton connection ("We can't tell you who's on the Mr. Bungle record. *Their contract won't let us,*" read one magazine ad). In the album credits, Patton is listed as "Vlad Drac," and perhaps in a show of solidarity, Spruance also uses a pseudonym ("Scummy"). Onstage, the band

16 https://www.trevordunn.net/mr-bungle-mr-bungle

members took to wearing masks to conceal their identities. For saxophonist Bär McKinnon, it was all part of dealing with the spectacle that was the Mike Patton Show. "I was aware that the audiences were star-struck with Patton after seeing him on MTV in the 'Epic' video, and if you took a photo from stage, you could see the bulk of the audience entranced, hypnotized with watching Patton," he told an interviewer years later.[17] "I also remember the wearing of masks to be Patton's way of dispersing that rabid attention, of downplaying his celebrity, and we were sorta playing along (although we weren't famous or dealing with the same cult-of-personality stuff that he was)."

On a strictly musical level, the similarities with Patton's other band were superficial at best: heavy guitars, garish keyboards, the occasional funk bassline, and, of course, Patton's vocals (although he largely foregoes the bratty, nasal delivery he employs on his Faith No More debut). But whereas *The Real Thing* was sleek and streamlined, *Mr. Bungle* was a study in excess, with the band gleefully piling on overdubs and stuffing sound effects into every available nook and cranny. There are arcade noises, snippets of movie dialogue, and a recording of Colonel Sanders fumbling his way through a Kentucky Fried Chicken ad. In some cases, the excess truly was excessive, as with the smutty 'The Girls of Porn' and 'Squeeze Me Macaroni' (both of which were mercifully retired from the band's setlist within a couple of years). Apart from those two missteps, the rest of the album has aged reasonably well, with songs like 'Dead Goon,' 'Love Is a Fist,' and 'My Ass on Fire' offering far more in the way of musical substance than their titles would suggest.

Not surprisingly, *Mr. Bungle* had a polarizing effect on listeners, especially those who were somehow expecting a sequel to 'Epic.' *Entertainment Weekly* gave it a D, calling it "puerile" and "unlistenable." Then again, the mere fact that it was getting reviewed in rags like *Entertainment Weekly* meant that the album was making its way to a mass audience. For at least some of those listeners—curious, novelty-starved listeners who didn't have access to independent record stores—the album was a gateway into a whole new realm. As *Trouser Press* would put it years later, "Faith No More fans, who picked

17 Carl King, "Awkward Interview with Bär McKinnon." March 2016. http://carlkingdom. com/awkward-interview-with-bar-mckinnon-of-mr-bungle

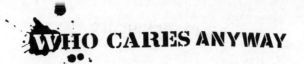

up *Mr. Bungle* on a whim to see what Patton's pseudonymous sextet was like, found themselves in possession of one of the most ambitiously random, fractious records in recent memory."[18]

Jai Young Kim: Everyone knew who Faith No More was. And you just kind of heard that Bungle was the band that Patton was extending his vocal range in. And then I went to the record store and saw the cover and thought, "This is insane." And then I took it home and opened it up, and I thought, "This is even *more* insane." I was doing a lot of psychedelic drugs at the time, like acid. And when I saw the Mr. Bungle self-titled album, I was convinced that these guys had a strong handle on the psychedelic experience and just, like, being able to manipulate people's mental spaces through music.

Mike Hickey: I went from *The Real Thing* to Mr. Bungle. When I got the first Mr. Bungle record, that was, at the time, the most insane thing I'd probably ever heard in my life. I couldn't *believe* how much was going on. I loved it. I was freaked out by the density of the sound, at the freneticness of it, at the fact that it was at one time funny and heavy and menacing. The lyrics were *fucked*. I was *all-in*.

Jai Young Kim: I played it for my older brother. I made a mixtape and put some Mr. Bungle songs on it. And he said he didn't like it because he thought it made him feel crazy. And then my brother ended up becoming a paranoid schizophrenic and killing himself. So maybe that first album was really good at identifying psychotic tendencies in people.

Trey Spruance: Often, I feel that the public that took to this album had pre-existing mental problems that the wide distribution of the CD only exacerbated. So when I hear about how this music affected these youngsters, it really just makes me sad.[19]

18 http://www.trouserpress.com/entry.php?a=faith_no_more
19 http://www.faithnomorefollowers.com/2016/11/trey-spruance-halloween-interview.html

INTO THE NINETIES

FUNK METAL

Mr. Bungle was released in August of 1991, near the height of the short-lived funk-metal craze. An article in *Spin* from January of that year reported on this phenomenon: "All of a sudden there's a virtual army of funk-metal bands, primarily centered in the San Francisco Bay Area. They range from thrashers, who lend an occasional funk edge to some of their material (Mordred, Death Angel), to straight-out funkers (Primus, Psychefunkapus, and Limbomaniacs) to those who defy categorization (Faith No More)."[20] The popularity of funk-metal and related genre mashups was also evident from The List, a weekly roundup of upcoming Bay Area "funk-punk-thrash-ska" shows that debuted in 1990. For a brief time, such mutant hybrids were practically unavoidable. "The late eighties and 1990 was just the worst for that," laments Brandan Kearney. "You'd go to a show, and you'd see a guitarist coming onstage in big baggy shorts, and you just knew you were in for a nightmarish time."

In hindsight, the collision of funk, punk, and metal was probably inevitable. Metal had first come into contact with punk in the early 1980s via crossover hardcore, but funk influences had been audible in the post-punk scene since the days of Gang of Four and the Pop Group. Flipper was known to cover Rick James's 'Super Freak' in concert, including once in a "duet" with Austin, Texas, hardcore band the Big Boys (who had their own, more overt funk leanings). Then there were the Minutemen, whose *Double Nickels on the Dime* has its share of slap bass and chicken-scratch guitar. "The Chili Peppers were out then too," adds Bill Gould, acknowledging the elephant in the room, "and they were succeeding, so it just became a certain thing that people tried to do. But at the same time, in punk rock before that, it was not cool to listen to Cameo or Parliament or any of that. That was like 'the other.' And so for somebody to say, 'I kind of like Cameo' — that was a big thing at the time. It was really weird to like funk music."

FNM actually toured with the Chili Peppers for a couple of months in the fall of 1987, and while Roddy Bottum noted a distinct difference in their fanbases

---

20 *Spin*, January 1991, p. 39. Psychefunkapus bassist Atom Ellis would go on to join Dieselhed and (briefly) the Pop-O-Pies (see Chapter 38).

WHO CARES ANYWAY

("theirs was a little more *dude*, and ours [was] a little freakier"[21]), there were at least a few similarities between the bands, as Gould acknowledges. "In a weird way, we were both a reaction against the prevailing music of the time, which was this British, depressing kind of music. We were Californians. We didn't know each other, but what they were doing in their own way in LA—kind of punk rock, not depressing, but not being just punk-by-the-numbers—we were trying to do here. So we saw each other, and it was kind of like a double take in a weird way. Because there was nothing else to compare each other to."

It was the influence of bands like FNM, RHCP, and Fishbone that prompted Mr. Bungle's abrupt turn from death metal to the kitchen sink hybrid of their subsequent demos.[22] That said, the "funk-metal" tag was largely a misnomer, given the fractured nature of the band's music. "We played some officially funk-metal functions, like the Funk Fest," admits Spruance. "But even when that stuff was going on, our relationship with it was tenuous at best. We never really got along with any of the bands, and they always looked somewhat distrustingly at us—with good reason. We weren't really doing it to make people dance or have a 'good time.' It wasn't really about having fun and drinking and partying. It has never been about that. I don't honestly know why the hell we were even doing it, other than we must have been jumping the trend at the time, being from a rural town and being clueless idiots about everything."

From the outside looking in, it might have appeared that the likes of Primus, Mr. Bungle, and Faith No More were the product of a coherent, unified scene, but this was never really the case. Despite sharing a lead singer, Mr. Bungle and Faith No More generally kept their distance from each other, and neither band was particularly chummy with Primus or any of the others mentioned in the *Spin* article.[23] "Maybe the people that liked Primus also could have liked 'Girls of

21 Harte, *Small Victories*, p. 102.
22 Spruance was open about his admiration for the early Faith No More. As he put it in a 1991 interview, "FNM were both [Patton's] and my favorite band for a long time, *Introduce Yourself* and everything. We really loved that band." The singer then chimed in, "Trey liked them better than I did." (Kim Edwards, "Interview with Mr. Bungle," 1991. http://www.negele.org/cvdb2/index.php?id=2232)
23 One exception: Mike Bordin was a friend of Primus's Les Claypool, who named the song 'Mr. Krinkle' after an alias that Bordin sometimes used. Bordin played on a few songs on Primus's 1991 album *Sailing the Seas of Cheese*.

420

INTO THE NINETIES

Porn' and 'Squeeze Me Macaroni,'" notes Jai Young Kim, "and they liked Trevor Dunn's bass playing on 'Dead Goon.' But I think it quickly became clear that just because those two bands were in the same geographical area and kind of playing music that young white-boy musicians could get into, they had very little in common and probably don't even like each other."

"It was never unpleasant dealing with them," clarifies Spruance, who notes that Mr. Bungle and Primus shared the same management office in those days. "We just were definitely not on the same team. We never had been on the same team. And I think there was a perception that we were. And that definitely changed at one show in particular."

The show in question took place on New Year's Eve 1992 at the Bill Graham Civic Auditorium, an 8,500-seat venue near City Hall. As Spruance recalls, the trouble began during soundcheck, when Mr. Bungle—a six-piece band at the time—was rushed through the process in less than an hour, while the three-piece Primus was given the rest of the day. "Then we had a problem like an amp blew or something. So we just re-strategized the whole show. We found a Santa Claus on the street; we took golf clubs to it and broke a bunch of bottles. We put a microphone inside a garbage can and broke a bunch of glass around it, and just did this horrendous performance. We played, but we were affected by the whole situation, and it was very violent. Actually, that was the night that Mike drank piss out of a boot. Somebody threw their boot onstage, and he peed into it, and then he drank his pee."

"We'd never played for that many people," adds Heifetz, "and it was our worst show ever." It wasn't a total loss, though, at least for the drummer. After the show, Heifetz followed through on a $1,200 dare to go up to Metallica's Kirk Hammett, who was socializing in the backstage area, and kiss him on the mouth. "I had to give him tongue, too—that was part of the deal," the drummer laughs. "I think he must have been onto it because he did it back to me. I just remember having his mustache in my mouth. It was the grossest thing ever. And it took me like *six months* to collect all the money for that."

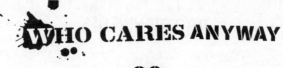

38

FAXED HEAD, DIESELHED, AND THE BRIEF RETURN OF THE POP-O-PIES

The New Year's Eve show was a one-off event for Mr. Bungle, as it came in the midst of another long stretch of touring for Faith No More. And with Patton back on the road, Mr. Bungle was back on hiatus. That meant more time for the rest of the band to devote to other projects—several of which found a home on Amarillo Records.

It was Bill Gould who first introduced Patton to Gregg Turkington, not long after Gregg had returned from his stint in Santa Fe in 1991. "Bill and I went out drinking one night at the Covered Wagon or something," Turkington recalls. "Mike was there, and they introduced me to him, and we hit it off. I said, 'I really want to hear this band you're in, Mr. Bungle.' So he called me when they were playing, and I went and saw it and thought it was fantastic. This is when they were doing these clown-terror shows. And then Mike called me when they were filming the 'Travolta' video, so I went out and did that and just got to know those guys. And I started going to every fucking show they did and just thought it was really great.

"There was no connection, initially, between those people and the scene with Brandan and me and the Easy Goings and all those kinds of bands," he clarifies. "But eventually, just because Mike would go on tour with Faith No More and all the rest of Mr. Bungle had moved to San Francisco, it started getting cross-colonized."

GREAT PHONE CALLS

A key figure in this cross-colonization was Rebecca Wilson, a writer, dancer, and all-around instigator who helped connect Spruance with some of her musician/artist friends, including Gregg and Grux. "Becky didn't really play music, but Becky was hugely influential," says Margaret Murray. "A lot of people listened to her, and a lot of people found her an exciting person to be around." Adds Lizzy Kate Gray, "She was another woman like Denise Dee who provided some of the glue that held a bunch of people together, even though she wasn't in bands. She just had a great social sense of who would get along and who might be able to work together. That's a talent."[24]

Wilson can be heard, briefly, on *Great Phone Calls*, an album of prank calls recorded by Turkington and Co. and released on Amarillo in 1992, not long after the Zip Code Rapists LP. The record went on to become something of an underground classic, thanks to the combination of Turkington's quick-witted patter and the alternately confused and belligerent responses of the unfortunate folks on the other end of the line. "That was three or four nights," recalls Spruance, who was on hand for the proceedings, doing his best to remain quiet in the background. "The first two nights, it was just Grux and Gregg and I up in the attic of Gregg's house, just making phone calls. Mostly Gregg, because Grux and I would be the first to admit that we don't even have close to that wit. Grux and I were both pissing our pants laughing. And then we went over to Becky's house to do some more."

"I said, 'Oh, we should record them—they're really good,'" adds Wilson. "We recorded that whole record, *Great Phone Calls*, at my house, on my Panasonic answering machine, because you could trick the machine into recording calls. Then Mike Patton did the last call, 'Music of the Night,' when I left the room. I was really pissed off. I said, 'Don't make any rude calls to old ladies or women or children,' and then they made this really rude call to a woman, and I didn't even know."

---

24 Wilson originally met Spruance when she went to interview Mike Patton for *The Nose*, a local magazine that both she and Turkington contributed to at various points.

FAXED HEAD

In the meantime, plenty of other ideas were brewing. Among them was Faxed Head, which marked a reunion of sorts between Gregg and Grux, who had last collaborated in Bean Church and the early version of Caroliner.[25] As with Caroliner, Faxed Head's members were officially anonymous, but their identities have long been an open secret among fans. And for anyone familiar with Caroliner, the visual similarities—down to the freakish, unwieldy costumes— are hard to miss. "It was definitely a Grux brainchild, for sure," says Spruance. "Gregg would just come back with these crazy lyrics written in the mold of this fantasy that we had all come up with. And what I was bringing to Faxed Head was just the metal aspect."

Faxed Head's lyrics center on the trials and tribulations of a group of beleaguered metalheads from Coalinga, California. Fed up with a life of sniffing glue, eating at Taco Bell, and listening to Pantera, the band members entered into a joint suicide pact. Yet instead of ending it all, they merely succeeded in disfiguring themselves—hence their grotesque costumes and bizarre nicknames ("Neck Head," "Graph Head," etc.). Musically, the concept manifested in the form of crude-sounding death metal songs interspersed with all manner of disorienting sound effects: tape dropouts, muffled instruments, wildly unbalanced mixes, and blasts of electronic noise. In essence, they were a conceptual noise band masquerading as a metal band.

Some Mr. Bungle fans who caught wind of Spruance's role in Faxed Head found themselves wondering what on earth he was doing. Some even speculated that it was all just a ruse to see what he could trick Bungle fans into buying. Not so, says Spruance, who had been dabbling in the more highbrow scene associated with saxophonist John Zorn (who co-produced Mr. Bungle's debut album) but found projects like Faxed Head to be more rewarding.[26] "This

---

25 Wilson recalls lobbying unsuccessfully for a role in the band: "I was gonna be the drummer. I thought it was gonna be one of these nonsense noise bands, and it wouldn't matter if I played drums that well, but they didn't let me do it."

26 Zorn produced Mr. Bungle's debut album, and Spruance appears (as "Scummy") on Zorn's album *Elegy*, which was recorded in November of 1991 with a cast of Bay

COALINGA'S FINEST. L-R: NECK HEAD, FIFTH HEAD, MCPATRICK HEAD, GRAPH HEAD. PHOTO BY CATHY FITZHUGH; COURTESY OF JAMES GOODE.

was just a completely different world," he says, "where I didn't really understand everything that was going on. It was totally intriguing and amazing to me. It was all such a *mystery* to me—one that just kept pulling me in. It was a mixture between feeling really intimidated and small, and also feeling like, 'Wow, it's really worth honing my craft on this stuff,' as opposed to the excessively cerebral crap that I could have been doing that whole time."

A big part of the adjustment involved fitting in with Grux, who, despite still being in his mid-twenties, was practically an elder statesman of the underground by this point. As such, he could be intimidating, especially given his sweeping, decisive verdicts on music that didn't meet his exacting standards. As Wilson recalls, "I'd put on a record, and Grux would say, 'Why do you want to listen to that? That's *rock*.' And he would make fun of anything I listened to that wasn't like Japanese noise music."

Trey Spruance: Grux is a person who would be pooh-poohing anything that was not "fucked up." So, of course, anything remotely resembling "funk metal" or anything like that's gonna be shit upon. But I think Gregg had videotapes of Mr. Bungle's first tour—some of the really, really insane shit that happened on that tour. And I remember sitting and watching that videotape with Grux, right when I was just sort of starting to get to know him, feeling a little bit weird, like, "Is he just gonna think this is stupid?" But he was just on the ground fuckin' laughing. He thought it was the most amazing thing in the world—how "fucked up" we were. So that was gratifying in a way. I felt more comfortable around Grux after that.

Gregg Turkington: See, the thing was, a lot of these people were like, "Ugh— Mr. Bungle, Faith No More. Bluh." But I was a super fan of both of these bands. So I don't think Trey was self-conscious around me.

Rebecca Wilson: Trey's very curious and smart, and when I started dating him, I was like, "You gotta hear this! You gotta hear this!" He had never listened

---

Area-based musicians. Spruance also took part in live performances of Zorn's improv "game piece" *Cobra* during this era.

to, like, Mrs. Miller or anything like that before in his life; he'd never listened to anything "confused weird."

Faxed Head's early recordings trickled forth via a string of 7-inches, beginning in 1992 with a self-titled EP on Stomach Ache (a prolific label whose roster reads like a Who's Who of obscure noise acts, both high and lowbrow). This was followed in 1993 by *Necrogenometry* (Amarillo), which marked the debut of a new band member—the aptly named Fifth Head—on electronics and sound effects. Yet another early 7-inch, 'Show Pride in Coalinga' b/w 'The Colors of Coalinga,' was purportedly released as a promotional item by the Coalinga Area Chamber of Commerce. In a sense, the records existed to serve the underlying narrative of Faxed Head, the metal band from Coalinga. As far-fetched as it was, there was enough subtlety and attention to detail—in the production, the artwork, and the lyrics—to make it seem (almost) plausible.

Mike Hickey: I went into a record store where a close friend of mine was working. He said, "Oh, Mike, you gotta check this out. It's got Trey from Mr. Bungle playing guitar on it." So I spend five dollars on this record: Faxed Head, *Necrogenometry*. I brought it home, put it on, and I was *completely* baffled. The sounds really weren't like anything I'd heard before. But the lyrics I just thought were some of the funniest things that I'd ever heard. And that's also the record with the hidden groove in it, so depending on where you dropped the needle, you would get all these weird voices that would come out sometimes when you played the record, and sometimes it wasn't there. But I loved it. I was obsessed with the record.

The next day, I went into another record store, Birdman Sound, and right on the rack in front of the store was a record: "The Zip Code Rapists." It had a really cool-looking cover, and I picked it up, and the first thing that I noticed was that it was on Amarillo Records. "Oh, same label as Faxed Head. This is crazy." And I see in the "thank yous," they thank Bill Gould. "Oh, so they know Bill Gould. That's cool."

So I bought it right then and there, having no idea that Gregg Turkington was the singer in Faxed Head as well. I just bought it because of the Amarillo connection. I put that on, and then I was *so confused*. Just so, so confused

427

about that record. The thing I was most confused about was, "Who in the hell would put this out on a record? Who is going to buy this? Who is the intended audience?" But I guess I like being confused because I was very attracted to the whole thing. I was just mystified by what all of this meant. What was the purpose? What was the point? Were these real bands? Did they play shows? Who would go see their shows? Side B was the live recording, and it just sounded totally insane! I'd never *seen* anything like this before, live. I just couldn't fucking believe it.

Those two records were my introduction to Amarillo. So for me, it went from Faith No More to Mr. Bungle, Mr. Bungle to Faxed Head, Faxed Head to Amarillo, and then that changed everything.

DIESELHED

Dieselhed was another product of the Mr. Bungle-to-Amarillo pipeline, although their music had little in common with that of Mr. Bungle or the other acts on Amarillo. They occupied a unique little niche: skewed country rock with oddly specific (and often dryly funny) lyrics, mixed with occasional detours into more aggressive yet still vaguely countryish hard rock. They weren't a comedy band, but they also didn't take themselves too seriously, unlike so many alt-country bands from the same era did.

Dieselhed was also very much a product of Humboldt County in their own way. "When I first met 'em, they were kind of like dreadlocked hippie/punk guys from Northern California," says Wilson."A lot of those guys were into, like, ska bands and stuff like that. And you know, they were a little sophomoric, and they weren't like jaded art punks like Flipper or anything like that. But they were neat, and they were nice. And then once they moved to San Francisco, they all cut off their dreadlocks and were like, 'Oh, we're not Humboldt hippies.' They all changed."

"They stood a little bit apart from the rest of the Amarillo catalog," adds Margaret Murray. "Because they recorded their music nicely, they were playing music at a pretty high level, and they had great harmonies, and they didn't do stuff that was messed up. But their lyrics were still a little bit goofy." Most of those lyrics were based on real-life characters and situations that the band's two songwriters, Virgil Shaw and Zac Holtzman, had witnessed firsthand. For example, 'M and M' tells the (mostly) true story of a shipmate aboard a salmon-fishing boat who died from an allergic reaction to peanuts. Another song, 'Brown Dragon,' tells of a camping trip gone wrong, one that ended with a friend's beard catching on fire in a bizarre smoking-related accident. "Those are all actual stories from guys they knew up there," says Heifetz.

Perhaps because they didn't tap into the heartland mythos that *No Depression* readers seemed so fond of, Dieselhed wasn't embraced by that demographic. Yet their albums for Amarillo—*Dieselhed* (1994), *Tales of a Brown Dragon* (1995), and *Shallow Water Blackout* (1997)—are full of memorable songs, even if the presentation could be jarring at times. "Every other song always bounced back and forth between, you know, a mellow one and a spastic one," notes Heifetz. "That was part of my doing, which I wish I hadn't done. I wish I'd made it more consistent—the flow of music from beginning to end. There were a lot of juxtapositions in the song styles, on those first three records, anyway."

THE RETURN OF THE POP-O-PIES

The Mr. Bungle/Amarillo connection also figured into the brief return of the Pop-O-Pies. Dormant since 1989, the group resurfaced in early 1993 after Turkington put Heifetz in touch with the enigmatic bandleader, who'd been enjoying a sabbatical from the music world. "I was just working a straight gig and coming home every night and listening to talk radio, and I was just so glad that I didn't have to think about the music business anymore," says Joe. "I mean, I was very badly burned out by the age of thirty, and I really needed to take a long time away from it. And I had thought I had left it for good. And you know, '92 and '93, they were really exciting times again. This grunge thing kind of got everybody excited about music again."

After auditioning a few other candidates, he settled on a lineup consisting of Spruance on guitar, Heifetz on drums, and Dieselhed's Atom Ellis on bass. Officially speaking, there wasn't much to show for the new lineup—a 7-inch on Amarillo (highlighted by a new, non-backward version of 'In Frisco') plus a handful of local gigs—but it was a memorable experience for those involved.[27]

Trey Spruance: I only remember one rehearsal as a band. We learned from tapes, and then we when we got together, I think it was understood that we would know how to play everything already. What we were really rehearsing was the way the show flowed. So he handed us Xeroxed setlists, and he would rehearse his in-between-song banter. And that was the most mind-blowing thing. That was when I realized that we were really in the presence of a totally unique genius.

Danny Heifetz: I just remember thinking, "Is he—is this serious? Is this really what we're doing?" He was reading a piece of paper, as I remember it. "I'm not gonna cue you guys, but you guys be ready to go." And then we'd play like the first two notes of whatever song it was. "Okay, you guys know that." But we *didn't*, really. I mean, we knew them, I *guess*. It's not like we had them really that well down; we'd never played them together.

Trey Spruance: I wasn't really sure what was going on with the Pop-O-Pies. Here's this guy who comes reemerging out of the woodwork, playing this kind of straight-ahead rock. I mean, I understood the subtlety of the music, but I still just didn't quite get it until that day when the in-between-song banter was being rehearsed. And it was nothing special. He wasn't doing any kind of posturing to make himself look good or make his delivery seem like he was this really witty person who was coming up with all this stuff off the top of his head. It's just really unspecial, very kind of banal in-between-song stuff that he rehearsed *at the rehearsal* and did exactly that way at the shows. I mean, he could have probably come up with better stuff off the top of his head. If you know Joe, you know that

27 "The guitar solos that I did were sung to me note-for-note by Joe," notes Spruance (who, like Heifetz, appears on the record under an alias). "I mean, I'm serious: note-for-note." Indeed, an early demo recording of 'In Frisco' from 1983 (later released on the CD compilation *Joe's Greatest Disasters: 1983–2009*) features Joe doing a sort of vocal "air guitar" rendition of the exact solo that Spruance played on the 1993 version.

he's a fully lucid, amazingly bright person. But what we were rehearsing was this really-not-that-interesting stuff coming out of his mouth. It was amazing.

There had always been a "meta" angle to the Pop-O-Pies, who, even early on, were as much about the spectacle of punk (and rock music in general) as they were an actual punk rock band. But a lot had happened between 1981—when the Pop-O-Pies first appeared—and 1993: the decline of punk and hardcore; the rise of grunge and "alternative" rock; and the proliferation of ever more challenging and obscure forms of underground music, from noise to gangster rap to extreme metal and beyond. In this context, the notion of three-chord punk rock felt increasingly quaint.

Trey Spruance: The context for me was, "Here's all this Japanese noise shit that's happening." You know, not just the end of rock music, but the end of *everything*. And when Joe comes out and does something like that [i.e., rehearsing his onstage banter], there was a real ghostly quality to it. I'm not sure that that's exactly what Joe has in mind. But it came across to me as definitely a simulation of the rock performance.

Joe Pop-O-Pie: I kind of know what he means about "simulating the ghostly quality." I was reinventing, almost as if stepping out of a time machine, the 1980s. So it's almost like it was a nostalgia act for a band that nobody in the audience ever saw the first time around. In other words, I was transporting the vibe of the eighties to the nineties. But somehow they liked it because it was so different.

But one of the things that kind of rung hollow to me when we actually did start to do those performances is, I realized I was living in a different time, and the vibe was not exactly with that time, which was 1993. I wasn't bitter about it, like Eric Burdon, who's still bitter that the sixties are over. I was like, "Well, I'm gonna do this because this is what rock 'n' roll is to me. And if people like it or they don't, I don't really give a shit because this is what makes me feel good, and this is the way I wanna do it."

The Bungle-era Pop-O-Pies played their last show on October 10, 1993, at the Night Break, a small club on Haight Street. "It definitely felt like an *event*," says Heifetz, who recalls playing his drums left-handed that night in an attempt to sound "more authentically punk rock." "People were there to see an event, almost like history. I remember people totally enjoying it. I remember seeing *so* many smiles on people's faces."

The drummer also remembers a telling anecdote about Joe from earlier that day. "We were rehearsing somewhere off Army Street, pretty far away," he says. "When we finished loading up after the rehearsal, he just went, 'Alright, I'll see you guys there.' I said, 'Don't you want a ride?' 'I'm gonna walk.' It's a thing he always did: he only ever walked, especially to gigs. It was a *fuckin'* long walk [roughly five miles]. He just walked to the gig, and we saw him there, and he was not tired at all. It was like, 'Fuckin' *hell*. He's a walkin' *machine*.' I thought it was so great. I just *loved* the fact that he did that."

After the show, Joe walked off into the sunset, metaphorically speaking—this time for good. He got a job as a software engineer and holed up in a spartan one-room apartment in the Tenderloin, where he was able to save enough money to retire in the 2000s and move to Reno (though, unlike his old friend Ian Cartmill, he did not go on to open a burrito stand).[28] "He was only really around for about four months before he disappeared again," says Spruance. "And during that four months' time, we would rehearse or whatever, and I would walk around with Joe listening to his ideas on things—sometimes with James Goode, sometimes just walking around with him. That was really neat because what I knew of Joe was essentially from that *Wiring Dept.* magazine, and it's not very much—just a picture of him with a fuckin' Budweiser in his hand, looking like he just woke up on the street somewhere."

28 He reemerged a few times in the 2000s—first with a CD reissue of the Pies' post-*White EP* material (*Pop-O-Anthology*) and then with an acoustic version of 'A Political Song' for a 2005 compilation CD (*Go Contrary, Go Sing*). In 2010, a one-off version of the Pop-O-Pies (with Kirk Heydt on guitar and the Dead Kennedys' Klaus Flouride on bass) opened for a reunited Faith No More at the Warfield.

39

AMERICAN GRAFISHY

"It's the most spectacular ending anybody could've ever had! Humor! Pathos! Tragedy! And it's real! It's real! Their house is *really* burning!" — Albert Brooks in *Real Life*

Whereas the Pop-O-Pies' return was both short and sweet, Flipper's would turn out to be neither.

Initially, it might have seemed unthinkable that the band would even consider reforming without Will Shatter. Then again, they'd done a tour without him in 1983, and they still had one of their two original front men in Bruce Loose. Meanwhile, they'd enlisted a new bassist (and part-time singer) in John Dougherty, a biker dude with friends in the Hells Angels. Sans Bruce, the other members jammed together at an East Bay warehouse for a few months before asking their old singer to rejoin. "It was probably the biggest mistake I think I ever made," he says, with only a hint of exaggeration in his voice.

It started out innocently enough, with an April 29, 1990, gig at the Stone — across the street from the same building that had once housed the Mab and the On Broadway. By October of that year, they were back in another familiar locale, Hyde Street Studios, to record a new single for Subterranean. "I kind of heard something that they were doing and thought it was okay," recalls Steve Tupper, "and it sounded fresh enough that I thought we should probably go ahead and do it."

The A-side, 'Someday,' finds Loose reprising the rhythmic, rap-inflected vocal stylings he'd tried out on parts of *Gone Fishin'*, and the song's chorus has elements of vintage Flipper, sounding both catchy and musically "wrong" at the same time. However, the B-side, 'Distant Illusion,' would prove to be a more accurate sign of things to come — which is to say, less *Generic Flipper* than generic

WHO CARES ANYWAY

Flipper. As Grady Runyan put it in a lengthy review for the zine *Superdope*, "Flipper is much more than a sound or a style, it is a method, a way of thinking and doing things, and all we have here is the empty shell that said band used to occupy." The similarity to Bruce's own lyrics on 'Distant Illusion' ("You're just a dead, empty, sexless soul") is hard to miss, and while it's unclear who the "you" in that song is, the lyrics speak to the singer's general state of mind.

Both songs would appear, in updated versions, on the group's comeback album, *American Grafishy*. Alas, the album is less noteworthy for the music it contained than it is for the sordid saga that accompanied the band's signing with Def American, the boutique label of mega-producer Rick Rubin. A decade earlier, Rubin was playing in the New York hardcore band Hose, which Tupper quite accurately describes as a "total Flipper copy band." (Their cover of Rick James's 'Super Freak' was essentially a cover of Flipper's own version, which they played live but never recorded.) By signing Flipper, Rubin was finally able to get his hands on the genuine article, or at least something resembling it.

From a pure business standpoint, the signing didn't make a lot of sense. Unlike, say, Faith No More, Flipper didn't have much in the way of crossover potential. *Generic* was by far the best-selling album on Subterranean, selling around 30,000 copies in its original pressing, but this was still a fraction of what they would need to sell in order to make the investment worthwhile for a major label.

In the end, it wasn't Rubin or Def American that got the raw end of the deal—it was Flipper and Subterranean."They had Rubin dangling $20,000 in front of them, saying, 'Here, sign,'" recounted Tupper in a 1993 *Maximum Rocknroll* interview. The deal included the rights to the band's entire back catalog, which wasn't entirely theirs to give away. "We never had any written contracts for the albums," said Tupper, but "[a]ccording to our verbal understanding from back in 1980, the tapes weren't supposed to be used by anyone other than Subterranean without our permission, and the band had always respected that." That changed in December of '91. "Steve [DePace] came by waving this contract. I didn't get to see much of it, but the one page he would show me very clearly had them selling all the rights to all the tapes to Def American for $20,000. There were five albums at that point, so it must have been the cheapest sale of the century." Tupper tried to intervene, but his calls to Rubin's office were ignored. "At the end

INTO THE NINETIES

FLIPPER AFTER WILL. L-R: STEVE DEPACE, BRUCE LOOSE, JOHN DOUGHERTY, TED FALCONI. PHOTO BY VINCE ANTON STORNAIUOLO.

of the three weeks, we got a fax back from Warner Bros., and their attitude was, in effect, 'We have the tapes, you have nothing, fuck you.'"

Flipper wasn't the only underground band to renege on a handshake deal with an independent label. The Butthole Surfers did likewise with Touch & Go when they sued the label in 1999 for the rights to their own back catalog, nullifying a verbal agreement that dated back to the mid-1980s. Unlike the Butthole Surfers, who by that point had improbably scored both a gold record (*Electric Larryland*) and a surprise top forty hit ('Pepper'), Flipper wasn't in a position to burn bridges. Moreover, they were Subterranean's flagship band, having grown up alongside the label from the very start. It was a bitter pill.

"When they fucked over Tupper and went to Rick Rubin, I was against it the whole way," says Meri St. Mary. "Bruce brought me to some of the meetings with lawyers. All I could say was, 'God, you know, Tupper has been there for you the *whole* time. He put out your records when nobody would touch you. And you're gonna fuckin' steal back the masters and give 'em to Rick Rubin? *Come*

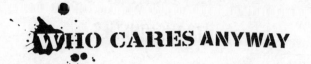

on. And actually, they got the worst deal known to mankind."

It was a sign of the times and a sign of how much times had changed. Whereas the early punk era was marked by a sense of community, the alternative/grunge era was all business. And whereas Rubin, like Howie Klein, was a creature of the entertainment industry, Tupper was anything but. "If anything, he was too innocent," says Club Foot's J.C. Garrett. "Steve Tupper—beautiful guy. He was so incredibly naive and innocent, and he still is."

Eric Cope: I was living in a van [circa 1987], and I had all these magazines and records, and I didn't even have a place to store them. And Steve Tupper kept all the stuff—all these magazines and records—at his store. And then he moved to a warehouse, and he had all our stuff in there. He did not charge me even one penny. He was just cool. I'd always go there and get my stuff, and he's like, "Fine." He's a real person. That's why he did Flipper; that's why he was hooked up with Caroliner, you know what I mean?

Meri St. Mary: There was this whole joke: "Nobody ever gets money out of Tupper except for Meri, Bruce, and Will." And the reason we got money out of him is because we would go in and talk to him. He was our friend. And he helped me—that man has helped me out of so many jams in my life. For me, that's *way* more worth it.

POST-IT NOTES

For all of the trouble they put Subterranean through, Def American took an oddly hands-off approach to Flipper. Apart from sending them out on tour and devising some clever promotional items—including cans of actual StarKist Tuna with the words "Chunk Light Flipper" on the label—they didn't do a whole lot to promote them. There were no videos or TV appearances. According to Loose, Rubin's only creative input on *American Grafishy* involved sequencing the already finished songs. "So he put 'Someday' on the record as the first song—you know, the slow song that's supposed to be at the end."

"What we should've done is had Rubin produce the damn thing," laments

Ted Falconi. "Because with us producing it, he didn't have his signature on it. So he didn't have any impetus to really push it because it wasn't him that he was pushing. And the guy—his buddy, the VP—that he turned us over to was afraid of us. Because all his other bands—the pop bands—were so *nice*." Adds Loose, "I've even heard stories that go so far as to say that the whole reason Rick Rubin signed us was to bury us in the Warner Brothers catalog and lose us because *I* wouldn't help his band Hose—in 1984, or 1983, or 1985, or whenever it was—get signed to Subterranean Records. I mean, this is how crazy the business is."

Any hope of building a long-term relationship with Rubin was quashed when Loose paid an impromptu visit to the producer's Hollywood mansion to request an advance. "We had an option to do another album, and then Bruce started getting all fucked up on drugs, big time," says Falconi. "He went and stickered up Rubin's Rolls-Royce. Got into his garage at his house, put stickers all over his car. You know, 'I want money!' 'What you want is more drugs, and you want him to supply the money you can buy drugs with.'"

"We went down one Christmas, and we couldn't even get a hundred dollars to get presents for our kid," clarifies Meri St. Mary. "I was so pissed. We went to Rubin's house, and we had a bunch of Post-Its. And there was his Rolls-Royce sitting in the driveway. So Bruce and I wrote on the Post-Its: 'Give us our money!' And we covered his car in Post-It notes. And the story became convoluted. We later heard that we scratched his Rolls-Royce. We didn't do that; we didn't deface his car. We just simply wrote on the Post-Its, 'Where's our money?' Because we wanted some money for our kid for Christmas. I think we did get some money."

BURNING BRIDGES

American Grafishy was greeted with lukewarm reviews upon its release in January of 1993, and it didn't do any better commercially. Truth be told, it isn't such a terrible album, at least not if one is in the mood for a little caustic noise rock. It's just that Flipper had always been so much more than that kind of band—more than just "godfathers of grunge" or any of the other titles that even well-meaning supporters sought to bestow upon them.

That summer, the band toured the country with the Dwarves before heading to Europe for the second time in three years. The touring ended with Loose in severe pain, the result of a lingering back injury that would continue to worsen over time and eventually require surgery. By 1995, he had quit the band, which briefly soldiered on with stand-in vocalist Brandon Cruz (former child star of the early 1970s sitcom *The Courtship of Eddie's Father,* and also an eventual replacement for Jello Biafra in a reconstituted version of the Dead Kennedys). In 1997, John Dougherty died of a heroin overdose, ten years after Will Shatter had died the same way. "It's like Spinal Tap," Loose told the *SF Weekly* in 1999, "except the bass player keeps dying."[29]

One can hardly fault them for trying, but in hindsight, restarting the band without Will was probably doomed to failure. In their prime, Flipper thrived in large part due to the delicate balance of personalities within the band. They didn't always get along, but there was a mutual understanding that enabled them to flirt with chaos and disaster without totally falling apart. Clichéd as it might sound, the whole really was greater than the sum of the parts. Yet, with Dougherty in place of Shatter, this was no longer the case. "He might have played bass better than Will," says Tupper, "but he basically brought nothing to the band. At that point, most of the creativity was coming from Bruce."

Bruno DeSmartass: Will was the poet, the one that all the girls fell in love with. Bruce was the shit disturber. Ted was the mad scientist. And DePace was mostly interested in trying to get from one song to another, and one gig to another, with the least amount of hassle. Because he plays "the pace."

Susan Miller: They're an interesting band. Falconi has his contribution. That sound that Ted made is incredible. But to me, Flipper was Will and Bruce. I'm sorry—that was the soul of that band. And if you go back and listen to their recordings, you will agree with me.

29 "Flipper Redux." *SF Weekly*. February 10, 1999. https://www.sfweekly.com/music/flipper-redux/

INTO THE NINETIES

Peter Urban: Ted is a hell of a nice guy, and his guitar playing is certainly unique. But I think Will and Bruce were always the core of Flipper. And I know Will's death hit Bruce really hard. Because Bruce was kind of a follower of Will's. And I know he was angry when Will died, but it was also a major blow to him. And then I think he kind of rebounded by sort of becoming the Bruce/Will—he almost *was* that axis by himself after that. And so it was kind of natural that he was going to be at odds with the rest of the band, I think.

In the end, there's an almost poetic quality to Flipper's slow-motion demise. Shatter foresaw it in his lyrics to 'I Want to Talk' ("It's really gonna hurt a lot when we fall / And sooner or later, we're gonna fall"), but that didn't make it any less painful when it actually happened. As much as any band this side of the Sex Pistols, they embodied what Jon Savage identified as a central paradox of punk—namely, that "to succeed in conventional terms meant that you had failed on your own terms; to fail meant that you had succeeded."[30] By this standard, they were a smashing success.

"You know, Rick Rubin tried to put Flipper records out, and they totally fucked it up," says Bill Gould. "And if they hadn't fucked it up, they could be in the part of history that everybody knows. They're notoriously fucked up. And that's kind of their charm because they're for real."

"Burning bridges is almost like a badge of honor," he adds, with an appreciative laugh. "You know, it's like you can only be judged by the quality of the bridges that you've burned. There is an element of that."

30 Savage, *England's Dreaming*, p. 140.

40

SON, EITZEL, AND THE DEATH OF RICKY

On October 17, 1989, the Loma Prieta earthquake struck the Bay Area, killing dozens and causing billions of dollars in damage. It was San Francisco's worst earthquake since 1906.

Earlier that same week, Toiling Midgets made the decision to re-form after a six-year hiatus. The earthquake may or may not have been an omen—although, given the band's history, they didn't exactly need one.

The remaining holdovers from the original lineup—guitarists Craig Gray and Paul Hood and drummer Tim Mooney—had been making their way back to San Francisco one by one over the past few years, with Gray the last to return."Craig flew in from London with the Royal Ballet because he was a prop-master," recalls Hood. "And we decided to get back together again at that point." Also back in the fold was their longtime engineer/soundman Tom Mallon, who had spent the last several years working closely with Mark Eitzel's American Music Club—first as a producer, then as a band member.[31] While Mallon had recorded literally hundreds of bands during the 1980s, the Midgets and AMC had been his two pet projects.

Mallon wasn't the only point of connection between the two bands, though. In 1986, Mooney had briefly joined AMC on drums but was "just too strung out on drugs at the time," according to Eitzel.[32] Mooney, in turn, was responsible

---

31 Mallon played drums on AMC's 1988 album *California*, which he also produced and engineered. Live, he played drums from fall 1987 to spring 1989, after which he switched to bass (following Davis's departure). He plays bass on their 1989 live mini-album *United Kingdom*.

32 Body, *Wish the World Away*, p. 46. According to Eitzel, when Mallon joined AMC on drums the following year, he would purposely imitate Mooney's style. "He'd play just

for bringing Eitzel onboard as the Midgets' new lead singer in 1990, not long after they'd begun playing out as an instrumental quartet.[33] Mooney also recruited bassist Lisa Davis, his girlfriend at the time and a former AMC member herself before quitting the band over friction with Mallon. Complicating matters even further was the fact that just before Eitzel joined the Midgets, Mallon had abruptly ended his association with AMC, having kicked them out of his studio in the middle of a December 1989 recording session.

With all of the divided loyalties and shifting alliances it entailed, the Eitzel/ Midgets marriage was hardly a recipe for stability. It did, however, help get the attention of up-and-coming indie label Matador, which had already released an Eitzel solo single. With Mallon once again at the helm, the new-look Midgets recorded the material for their Matador debut, *Son*, over the course of multiple sessions during 1990 and 1991.

As with *Sea of Unrest*, most of the music for *Son* was written without a singer in mind. This created a different kind of challenge for Eitzel, whose lyrics were usually the starting point in AMC and not something layered on after the fact. He was also coming from a different place stylistically than Ricky Williams— more Bruce Springsteen/Paul Westerberg than comatose Iggy or Bowie. There are times when it works ('Fabric,' non-album single 'Golden Frog') and other times when it almost sounds like Eitzel is singing for a different band. Apart from the vocals, the most striking contrast between *Son* and *Sea of Unrest* is the overall tone. Whereas *Sea of Unrest* was menacing and claustrophobic, *Son* is melancholic, even pretty at times, as on the mostly instrumental 'Third Chair' and 'Slaughter on Sumner Street' (the latter a nod to *Slaughter on Tenth Avenue* by Gray and Hood's mutual guitar hero, Mick Ronson).

As was often the case with the Midgets, the issue with *Son* wasn't the music itself—it was everything else surrounding it. A preliminary single, 'Golden Frog' b/w 'Mr. Foster's Shoes,' was released in October of 1991, but the album itself

---

like Tim, which made us all happy" (p. 52).

33 The Eitzel-fronted lineup played its first show on August 5, 1990, at the Paradise Lounge. A recording of the show was later released on CD-R and then on Bandcamp under the title *1990: Live at the Parasite Lounge*. It is an uneven, erratic performance. Much better is *Live at the I-Beam SF 1991*, which documents the singer's last show with the band. In both cases, he appears on only about half of the songs.

was delayed for months. "When *Son* came out, Pavement were a huge hit for Matador," explains Gray. "And our pressing, which we booked a tour for, was put on hold so they could press more Pavement records. So some of the shows on our tour were canceled because they couldn't get any records or merchandise because it wasn't gonna be ready in time."

In the meantime, Eitzel and his American Music Club were peaking. *Rolling Stone* had named their *Everclear* album of the year and Eitzel songwriter of the year for 1991. The following year, Reprise signed AMC to a multi-album deal, and by the time *Son* was finally released in July of 1992, Eitzel was long gone, having quit the Midgets before they went out on tour that May. Thus, the group was left to perform instrumentally in support of a yet-to-be-released album, one whose chief selling point—at least from the label's perspective—was the star singer. At the end of the tour, Mooney quit to join AMC full-time.[34] A decade after *Sea of Unrest*, the Midgets weren't having any better luck than they did the first time around.

RICKY RETURNS

On the plus side, Eitzel's departure cleared the way for the improbable return of Ricky Williams, who had been languishing for some time, though not entirely absent from the scene. He'd continued writing and recording music after leaving the Midgets in 1982—more out of compulsion than ambition, it seems. The introduction to a 1983 interview with the singer in the local *Ego Magazine* offered

---

34 Asked about the Midgets a few years later, Eitzel responded, "Oh, they're fucking assholes. They're like these ex-junkie rock stars who expect to be driven around in limousines all the time, and they're getting older, and they're not doing anything. Fuck 'em." (Source: Scott Carlson, "The Gospel According to Mark." *The Minnesota Daily,* May 23, 1996.) Lisa Davis echoed these harsh sentiments: "Those people were fucked up. They were not good-hearted people. Craig and Paul had just been such bad junkies. They kept all the rock 'n' roll antics, and they were in it for the wrong reasons" (quoted in Sean Body, *Wish the World Away*, p. 99). In a later interview, however, Eitzel offered a more positive assessment: "I thought it was a good experience. They are good people. Basically, I was just a guy who sang on the record. They should not even have had a singer. They don't need one" (Ibid., p. 135).

a tantalizing update on a then-in-progress solo album, which writer J. Neo Marvin described as "nothing less than an old-fashioned full-blown psychedelic classic, combining the best of *Electric Ladyland*, *The Madcap Laughs*, *Forever Changes*, and *Unknown Pleasures*."[35] Hyperbole aside, the recordings demonstrate that Ricky wasn't "just" a singer but also a versatile multi-instrumentalist who could hold his own on guitar, bass, keyboards, and various percussion instruments; even his use of the drum machine is creative. Alas, only one of the songs, 'Crawling,' was ever officially released, and that was on a compilation LP (*SF Unscene*, released in 1985).

There were occasional live performances, too, including a December 1983 show at the On Broadway, where he played bass and sang as part of a duo with guitarist Alan Korn. *Puncture*'s Patty Stirling wrote a glowing review of the show (which turned out to be the duo's only one), calling it a "mesmerizing and engrossing set that lasted twenty minutes and ended too soon."[36] In December of 1985, Ricky took part in a quasi-Sleepers reunion at the same venue as part of a double bill with American Music Club.[37] 1986 saw a couple of solo performances at the Farm, including a record release party for the *SF Unscene* compilation. But none of it seemed to go anywhere.

The singer's only sustained post-Midgets project was Recoil, the band that Kirk Heydt formed after leaving the Pop-O-Pies in 1985.[38] Sometimes billed as "30/20 Recoil," they played out locally from 1987 to 1989, and made it as far as

35 *Ego Magazine*, No. 7.
36 *Puncture*, Vol. 1, No. 6. Reprinted in *Puncture: The First 6 Issues*, p. 184. The duo appeared under the name "Piltdown Man." They also did some home recording together, as Korn recounts. "We did these two instrumental tracks or two versions of the same track, and then he just said, 'Give me a second.' And I seem to recall he closed the door and locked me out and just kind of improvised it. And it was brilliant—it was spot on, with the words and everything."
37 The details are sketchy, but given the Tom Mallon/AMC connection, the lineup likely included Tim Mooney on drums and perhaps Mallon on bass. It's unknown who the guitarist might have been, but it wasn't Michael Belfer (who was living in NYC at the time). The same group might have served as Ricky's backing band the following month for a show at the Farm. (A newspaper ad lists the headlining act for the January 17, 1986, show as "WHAT IS REAL with Ricky Williams of the SLEEPERS," and the phrase "WHAT.ISREAL" also appears on a flier for the On Broadway show.)
38 Recoil's lineup also included Hello Kitty on Ice bassist Otto Waldorf, saxophonist Jeff Grubic (a member of the earlier, instrumental-only version of HKOI), and drummer Mike Simms (later of American Music Club).

THE FARM 1499 POTRERO
SF 826-4290

FRIDAY, JAN. 17   8:30 $5
WHAT IS REAL with Ricky Williams
of the SLEEPERS
A CRUEL HOAX / ANY 3 INITIALS / HOUSE OF WHEELS

recording a demo at Mallon's studio in 1988. Unfortunately, Heydt's experiences with the mercurial singer resembled those of his past bandmates. "We played these shows, and they were good and great and horrible at times. But then after the show, it's like, 'Okay, who's gonna take care of Ricky?' Because Ricky doesn't drive. Someone's gotta take him back to Palo Alto, or someone's gotta get him on a bus." He was still self-medicating as well. "He got to the point where he could only have a creative idea with speed because speed did something to his brain that made him—you know, he could *work,*" says Heydt. "That's where he would come up with this stuff, just freestyle. But it was *insanity*, too. It was just a jumble, almost like a computer spitting out words. But really, he really needed speed. Otherwise, he would just be *drinking* all the time."[39]

By this point, Ricky was mostly living at his mother's house in the Palo Alto area. "They had an apartment on El Camino in Mountain View somewhere," remembers Michael Belfer, who had just moved back to the Bay Area himself in 1989. "They would wake up, and one of them would walk over to the liquor store and get their beer for the day. And then Ricky would just sit there and drink Budweiser all day long, watching TV."

He still made it up to the city on occasion, though, and once the Midgets reformed, he started shadowing them, just as he'd done with the original lineup back in 1980. "He would show up at shows, and it would bug Mark," recalls Paul Hood. "At one point, Mark just said, 'Well, fine—use Ricky!' I don't know what was going on with that because Eitzel quit soon after. But Ricky did just pop up

---

39 Recoil recorded a demo at Tom Mallon's studio in May of 1988, though it was never officially released.

444

onstage, and so we started working with him again."[40]

With high hopes, the Midgets unveiled their new lineup—Gray and Hood on guitars, Mallon on drums, Williams on vocals, and newcomer Erich Werner on bass—at Brave New World, a small club in the Panhandle District, on November 20, 1992. It went well enough, which is to say that nothing disastrous happened onstage. "He was super nervous about singing," recalls Gray, "because he hadn't sung for quite a few years in front of an audience. And I know he was a bit disappointed in the show afterwards."

Early the next morning, Richard James Williams passed away from what an obituary in the *SF Chronicle* referred to as "a long bout with respiratory illness."[41] He was thirty-seven.

Michael Belfer: Ricky's mom got run over one day coming back from the liquor store. It was horrible. She died. Ricky was all alone after that, and I think it really broke his heart.

Tommy Antel: Right after Ricky's mom died, Mooney goes, "Ricky's gonna die right away." And he was right. He didn't last long after his mom. They were really, really close. Ricky's mom took care of Ricky.

Connie Champagne: He went home with these kids—people in their twenties— and they had some place they lived on Haight Street. And they snorted heroin, is what I understand. And the reason I want to say this is that in my experience, I never saw Ricky shoot up anything. In fact, he had a big aversion to needles because his mom had been a heroin addict.

---

40 Williams actually sat in with the band live on at least one occasion, a 1991 show in Oakland that took place while Eitzel was away on tour with AMC. Around that time, the Midgets also recorded a studio album with a sort of parallel version of the band featuring Williams on vocals, Mallon on drums, and a two-piece "string section" consisting of Wade's Mary Redfield on violin and Paul Hood's sister Joanna on viola. The live set, which features Mooney on drums, was later released digitally as *Oakland 1991*; the studio set was released (also digitally) as *Little Ricky*.

41 The obituary was written by none other than Stephen Schwartz, aka Nico Ordway of *Search & Destroy*.

THE SLEEPERS
ricky williams ordeal

AMERICAN mu$ic Club
mark eitzel ordeal

on broadway friday dec. 20
another celso ordeal
10:00 late show

Craig Gray: He was supposed to come to my house later that night, but he didn't come. He stayed at someone else's house. Took too many drugs. The paper said "pneumonia," but he'd taken Valium, and I think somebody'd given him some heroin, and he'd been drinking as well.

Paul Draper: He was sort of like a little brother. He was the second oldest in the band [i.e., the original Sleepers lineup], but he was a couple of years younger than me. So I just felt really bad.

Connie Champagne: It's hard for me to say, but when I heard that he had died, it was a relief. Because he was incapable of redemption or rehabilitation in any way. And he has the worst karma of anyone that hasn't committed—or hasn't been *arrested* for—a serious violent crime. I thought, "This is a good thing because if there *is* reincarnation, he can just come back as something else. Like, just start over." Because he just never had a chance, in my opinion, despite all the opportunities he had, despite all the gifts he had that most people would kill for. I mean, girls *and* guys loved him, wanted to help him, wanted to do *anything* for him, but he just wasn't capable of surviving.

INTO THE NINETIES

Eric Paul Fournier: If some of these modern medications were around, Ricky could've been somethin', man. Ricky had charisma. He had a voice like David Bowie. He could be Bowie one minute, Iggy Pop the next. He was fuckin' great.

Craig Gray: I don't think Ricky would have ever been well-adjusted, and if he was, he would've been on so many meds that he probably wouldn't have *wanted* to sing. He probably wouldn't have wanted to do much.

Connie Champagne: Ricky didn't have a David Bowie to save his life like Iggy Pop did. But he also didn't have the intense self-discipline that Iggy Pop had. I mean, Ricky Williams had more musical talent than Iggy Pop does. Sang better, prettier voice, better intonation—all of it. Just no discipline. How can you have discipline if you can't function?

THE DJ IS WRONG

Somehow, the remaining Midgets managed to carry on as a band, despite the one-two punch of Mooney's departure and Ricky's death. They tried a couple of different singers before reverting to an instrumental-only format, which ultimately suited Gray and Hood just fine. "I think nobody really agreed with me that instrumental was the way to go," says Gray. "No one besides Paul. They always wanted to add a singer for the Midgets. As far as I'm concerned, only one person could actually sing with the Midgets, which would be Ricky. A lot of people could sing *over* the Midgets; a lot of people did when they sang with us. But Ricky sang *with* us."

The Midgets' brief tenure on Matador ended with *Son*, which didn't sell particularly well, especially compared to the likes of Pavement and Liz Phair. They continued playing out locally and recording in various configurations for a few more years, with seemingly diminishing returns. A 1994 profile in the *Bay Guardian* lamented the band's fate. "It may be true that prophets cannot be loved in their own country, but the fact that the Midgets cannot play gigs for a decent fee or get booked on a decent bill or get a decent album deal (in fact, have never made a penny) after fourteen years is like being dissed by your own apostles."[42]

By this point, there was no shortage of bands playing moody guitar-based instrumentals, only now there was a name for it: post-rock. As with the partially overlapping "sadcore" trend, the Midgets had anticipated and predated this one—a distinction Gray has mixed feelings about. "I just didn't feel that connected to it," he says. "I heard some things, but you can never be sure that you've influenced those people—I mean, *I* can't. And I've never felt like I influenced any of those people."

As for the rest of the bad luck that befell his band, he remains stoic. "I don't think any of us at the time thought that big success was coming our way. Even the second iteration, I had hoped for some minor success—enough to maybe get a couple of tours off. Which didn't really happen, except for one US tour. But I would have picked a different kind of music to do if I wanted to be more successful."

42 Dean Kuipers, "Lost on the Sea of Unrest." *SF Bay Guardian*, April 6, 1994.

INTO THE NINETIES

4.1

ANGEL DUST

"We're not alternative—we're a rock band, we're mainstream, and there's a little bit of shame in that."—Bill Gould in 1992[43]

In the wake of 'Epic' and *The Real Thing*, Faith No More found themselves facing a new kind of challenge—namely, that of following up a hit record and managing the expectations that went along with it. As band problems go, it was a good one to have, but in FNM's case, there were some additional complications to contend with.

Much of it came down to public perception, together with the longer than usual gap in between *The Real Thing* and its eventual follow-up. Consider that in December 1990, Faith No More appeared on the cover of *Spin*, which had just crowned them Artist of the Year. A few months earlier, an article in the same magazine touted them as the "future of rock." Yet by the summer of 1992, they were practically old news, thanks to a series of developments that not even the tastemakers at *Spin* could have anticipated.

"Somehow, when Nirvana was like the revolution that divided the future and the past, we were on the side of the past," says Bill Gould. "Which is very bizarre. I mean, I like Nirvana and everything, but I always thought that was the same period in time. Somehow, when the Grand Canyon parted, we were on the other side of the Grand Canyon. So we're perceived as an old rock band—a metal band."

In a sense, FNM were victims of their own success—and more specifically, the success of the 'Epic' video. That video had propelled them into the public consciousness, but three years later, about all that remained in the collective

---

43 Ann Scanlon, "Making a Leap of Faith." *Vox Magazine*, December 1992. http://www.faithnomorefollowers.com/2015/12/faith-no-more-december-1992-vox-magazine.html

memory were images of a flopping fish and a bunch of long haired dudes playing "funk metal."

The perception of FNM as part of an older guard was reinforced by their decision to spend much of 1992 on tour opening for Guns 'n' Roses—first on a six-week tour of Europe, where they were sandwiched in between the headliners and opening act Soundgarden, and then on a three-month tour of North America, where they were relegated to the opening slot ahead of G'n'R and co-headliners Metallica. As the third wheel on the biggest stadium rock tour of the year, FNM would typically take the stage in the late afternoon sun while fans were still filing into the stadium. They also had to deal with the ongoing three-ring circus surrounding G'n'R's embattled front man. "It wasn't very healthy for us," Gould says, speaking of that summer's tours in general. "We had a lot of days off—four days, five days a week off sometimes with no playing because Axl was canceling shows all the time. And they had these stripper club parties every night, and our guitar player was *loving* that. He would refer to us as, you know, 'You're all a bunch of fuckin' fags,' or whatever. So we had to deal with that crap and get him in the bus every night because he wouldn't wanna leave the party. It was a drag.

"And also, who were *we*?" he continues. "What were we, and why were we in this world, and how did we end up here? We weren't making that much money; we were an opening band. And we were just surrounded by this horrible scene." The band members didn't realize it at the time, but they had actually been offered a slot on the second annual Lollapalooza tour alongside the Red Hot Chili Peppers, Ministry, and a trio of Seattle grunge bands in Pearl Jam, Soundgarden, and Alice in Chains. For better or worse, their management turned down the offer without informing the band. "Personally, if I was gonna spend five months in front of a crowd, I related much more to the Lollapalooza crowd than to [the Guns 'n' Roses/Metallica] crowd," laments Gould. From a marketing perspective, it wasn't the best decision, although, as usual, Roddy Bottum managed to find a silver lining. "As a meta-art statement, it was a little bit confrontational of a gesture," the keyboardist told author Adrian Harte years later, "[and] a teensy bit cool that we were doing something so radically disgusting."[44]

"COMMERCIAL SUICIDE"

The perception of Faith No More as hard rock dinosaurs helped account for the relatively lukewarm response to *Angel Dust*. Released on June 8, 1992, it debuted at number ten on the Billboard 200 and quickly went gold, but it stalled soon thereafter and fell out of the charts completely within a few months. "There was a template that worked, and that was *The Real Thing*," notes Gould. "If we'd used that as a model for the next record, we'd have sold many millions of records because we were there. The hard part was over. And we threw the template away. And at that time, it was just perceived as this giant failure, and we took a lot of shit for it. In retrospect, I'm really glad we did it."

Artistically, *Angel Dust* was anything but a flop, though it lacked a juggernaut hit single on par with 'Epic,' and it made for a challenging listen, especially by mainstream standards. *Entertainment Weekly* called it "probably the most uncommercial follow-up to a hit record ever," a nod to both the musical content and the often unsettling lyrics.[45] It was also a difficult album to make. Guitarist Jim Martin was at odds with the rest of the band throughout the recording process, to the extent that Gould wound up writing guitar parts for around half the songs. And keyboardist Bottum—typically the peacemaker within the band—was absent from many of the sessions, in part due to a recently acquired heroin habit.

Yet *Angel Dust* doesn't sound like the work of a band in turmoil. Creatively, it marks the peak of the band's Mike Patton era, and from start to finish, the singer gives what may be the best overall performance of his career. The first couple of tracks showcase his formidable range, from the baritone crooning and smarmy infomercial sales pitches of 'Land of Sunshine' to the threatening whispers and piercing shrieks of 'Caffeine.' That range, in turn, is matched by the band as

---

44 Harte, *Small Victories*, p. 242.
45 https://ew.com/article/1992/07/10/angel-dust/

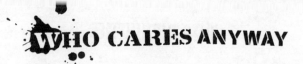

a whole, as they veer from mock-country ('RV') to unabashed pop ('A Small Victory') to the heaviest metal song in their catalog ('Jizzlobber'), without any of it sounding forced. But perhaps best of all is 'Everything's Ruined,' which alternates between a minor-key verse with a classic Gould/Bordin rhythm track and a soaring major-key chorus; there's even a vintage Jim Martin guitar solo mixed in for good measure. Finally, the production is the most intricate and detailed of their career. Together with the quality songwriting, the result is an album that stands up to repeated listening far better than either *The Real Thing* or the band's later recordings. In a feature review for *Spin*, *American Hardcore* author Steven Blush called the album "easily the grimy unit's finest hour," adding, "Faith No More might just be the greatest progressive hard-rock band since Queen in its golden age."[46] He wasn't wrong.

That an album of this caliber could get lost in the shuffle, relatively speaking, says something about the fickleness of the music industry. At the same time, a little perspective is in order here: even as a supposed "flop" by mainstream standards, *Angel Dust* still sold more copies at the time than Subterranean Records had sold in its entire decade-plus existence.[47] It has since gone multi-platinum, surpassing even *The Real Thing* in worldwide sales.

All of this speaks to the massive scale at which Faith No More was operating in the early 1990s, as well as the comparatively tiny scale at which the underground bands of the early 1980s were operating. Yet without the foundation laid by those bands, Faith No More's success would not have been possible. Gould and Bottum, in particular, were keenly aware of this. In their own way, they sought to convey some of the adversarial spirit and contrarian humor they picked up from predecessors like Flipper and the Pop-O-Pies—qualities that were seldom found in other big-name rock bands from the same era.

Bill Gould: People told us we were boxed in, like our management and our label.

---

46 *Spin*, June 1992, p. 67.
47 Subterranean's top-selling record was a one-off Dead Kennedys 7-inch ('Nazi Punks Fuck Off' b/w 'Moral Majority'), which sold over 70,000 copies. The label's top-selling LP was Flipper's *Album*, which sold around 30,000 copies. Other top sellers included the 'Sex Bomb'/'Brainwash' 7-inch (13,800 copies) and the 'Love Canal'/'Ha Ha Ha' 7-inch (9,700 copies). Most of the label's other releases sold in the low thousands, if that.

INTO THE NINETIES

We refused to recognize that. Sometimes it came off as us looking guilty because it was almost like, "We're not this kind of band." But if you look back at our history, we never really saw ourselves that way. It's that kind of thing: "Do you play for your audience, or do you play for yourselves?" And there's that fine line. I think we *were* boxed in, but I think that we tried to just not look at that and deny that.

Trey Spruance: Put yourself in their shoes: if you know that you come from at least a semi-intelligent background, musically—you know, a dignified background in some way—and suddenly you get all this huge overnight success, all of the people who you would think of as your peers are only gonna see the hype and everything that's going on around it. And that's gonna feel a little weird. You're gonna feel a bit uneasy around the people who would otherwise be your peers. They're gonna look down on you and think that you're just a lame-ass. Not even a sellout, but that you're a pandering fuckin' idiot. I do think there is a part of them that was trying to counteract a little bit of that.

Bill Gould: Okay, if I can tell you how I see it. Like, if I'd see a Flipper show, I would get fucked up out of my mind and want to see something happen—maybe somebody'd break a bottle over somebody's head; maybe somebody'd start urinating on themselves. *Something* was gonna happen that you don't see every day that kind of breaks a certain kind of social restriction. And that's where I wanted to be. And what I got out of that was some *amazing* shows. You really were going into a little area that was outside of social control.

Okay, so you're in a band, and you're playing for like 30,000 people—I mean, why not try to bring that element in? Think of the power you could have. When there were only fifty people, how amazing was it? Why couldn't you throw that random element in and snap people a little bit, and get them out of their repetitive thinking, give 'em a disconnect and watch how they react. Maybe they're gonna get pissed off. Fine! Let 'em get pissed off. If it doesn't make sense, and they don't like it, that's okay—let 'em throw a bottle at you. That's still something. At least that's something that you're doing that you're not supposed to do.

You should be able to do whatever you want in this space. It's a kind of protected environment. It isn't, "Don't stand in the line where the fire exit is," or "Give me all your money for the ticket and buy the T-shirt, and your friends will accept you." You have to break that kind of mentality. And throwing in things that are wrong—if you look at it the right way, it's actually right. It opens it up. So, I mean, it's kind of a responsibility, if you find yourself in this situation, to take full advantage of it and fuck it up. You *have* to. And you wanna survive and try to keep *doing* it, but you have to bring a random element into it.

Certainly, their decision to have the Easy Goings open for them at the Warfield—in between legs of the Guns 'n' Roses/Metallica tour—was one example of this "random element" at work.[48] Another was their low-budget video for 'Everything's Ruined,' the fourth and final single from *Angel Dust*. The video finds Bottum playing a keytar (not a regular part of his onstage arsenal) and features several scenes of the band members sarcastically "rocking out" in tandem—all set against a backdrop of cheesy stock footage that was unrelated to the song's lyrics.

Finally, there was their tongue-in-cheek cover of the Commodores' 'Easy,' which they'd started playing on the *Real Thing* tour in response to audience requests for 'War Pigs.' They recorded a version of it during the *Angel Dust* sessions, and though it didn't make the album, it went on to become a hit single overseas.[49] Musically, it is faithful to the original—apart from Patton's purposefully unctuous vocals—but as a gesture, it was very Faith No More. Which is to say, it was the kind of thing that endeared them to their diehard fans while irritating most everyone else. "I mean, you don't see that shit anymore—not that I'm aware of," says Mike Hickey, one of those appreciative fans. "I mean, everyone now is just so desperate to get their fuckin' fifteen minutes that they're sure as hell not gonna toy with their chances. But Faith No More did."

Granted, covering 'Easy' was hardly as adversarial as playing forty minutes of 'Truckin'' or forty minutes of 'Fascists Eat Donuts.' And as with the cover art for the accompanying *Songs to Make Love To* EP (which depicts a couple of

---

48 Not only did FNM's fans object, but as the Easy Goings' John Singer recalls, so did plenty of local musicians: "My wife said, 'There are bands who would kill to open for Faith No More. You guys aren't even a serious band, and you're getting to do that. That's not right.'"

49 It was a number one hit in Australia, number two in Norway, and number three in the UK, but it wasn't released as a single in the US and, therefore, didn't chart there.

rhinos in the act of fornication), the humor was admittedly a little broad. Then again, they were operating at a scale that didn't exactly lend itself to subtlety. As Bottum noted in a 1990 interview, "One of the things we've had to come to terms with this year is that the mass audience isn't as cynical and bitter as we are. They don't find the same things funny as we do."[50]

KING FOR A DAY–FOOL FOR A LIFETIME

As defiant a gesture as *Angel Dust* was, subsequent events showed even FNM was not immune to the pressures of the music business. Up to that point, they'd managed to navigate the treacherous highwire act that was "selling out" (i.e., becoming a mainstream rock band) without losing their identity. What's more, they did it with humor and style—and without any of the pious posturing of so many of the supposedly "alternative" bands that rose to stardom after Nirvana and *Nevermind*.

Eventually, it caught up with them—which is to say, they were human. In the fall of 1993, after completing their touring obligations for *Angel Dust*, they sacked Jim Martin (via fax machine, no less). This was followed by a rehab stint for Roddy Bottum, whose heroin addiction had become a serious problem by this point. These personnel issues, in turn, left a skeleton crew of Gould, Bordin, and Patton—plus guitarist Trey Spruance, on loan from Mr. Bungle—to write and record the bulk of their next album, the lackluster *King for a Day ... Fool for a Lifetime*. By the time that album came out in early 1995, they were being written off as has-beens: an unceremonious review of the album in *Spin* noted that the group's brief reign as the "king of 'alternative' rock" felt like it occurred "several thousand years ago."[51] When they finally hung it up in April of 1998, the headline in *Rolling Stone* was similarly dismissive: "Funk Metal Band Calls

---

50 *Spin*, December 1990, p. 39.
51 *Spin*, May 1995, p. 97. *King for a Day ...* has since gotten a more positive reappraisal from at least some fans and critics. In November of 2011, the band played the album live from start to finish (with Spruance joining them on guitar) before a large and adoring crowd in Santiago, Chile.

WHO CARES ANYWAY

It Quits."[52]

David Katz: I actually interviewed Billy on their 1995 tour because I was writing for this magazine over here called *Bassist*. I was like, "Damn, look at this." Billy had put on weight, and he looked miserable. He really did. The only thing that he said that he enjoyed was that he'd been to Moscow, and he'd been working with some band out in Russia or the Czech Republic. I remember asking him, "Do you guys still hang out anymore?" He said, "No way." They were kind of like at the Emerson, Lake & Palmer phase; you know what I mean?

Trey Spruance: The one thing that Faith No More had that *none* of these other bands had, including Mr. Bungle, is just this extra pressure—you know, accountants, management, the label guy coming by sniffing around. They had *so* much of that shit to think about. And I think they spent enough of their time blowing it off and saying "fuck you" to it that there was almost like a backlash—that they maybe listened a little bit too much to it after that. I'm not sure.

And they were trying to figure out their way of being friends with the people around them and not being in such an adversarial role all the time. But I have a feeling it was kind of too late. At that point, you can't really *stop* doing that midstream. I'm not really sure exactly where the psychology of it fits, but I know it was a really difficult time for them; just trying to sort that out.

By the time FNM called it quits, a new (or "nu") crop of hybrid metal bands had risen to prominence, and while many of them—including Korn, Limp Bizkit, and Slipknot—cited Faith No More as an influence, none of them seemed to pick up on the humor, the irony, or the contrarian tendencies that made FNM what they were. Even so, FNM bore their share of guilt-by-association for having helped spawn the nu-metal genre. If they got any positive coverage at all during those years, it was usually as Mike Patton's former band.

Eventually, the smoke cleared, and nu-metal wore out its welcome, making

52 Blair Fischer, "No More Faith No More." April 20, 1998. https://www.rollingstone.com/music/music-news/no-more-faith-no-more-182924/

it easier for many to step back and appreciate Faith No More on their own terms. By the time they reunited for a series of concerts in 2009, they were being hailed as godfathers of "alternative metal," with *Angel Dust*—not *The Real Thing*—at the center of their legacy. It was a long way from where they started, as Gould acknowledged in a 2003 interview. "Most people who are really interested in what I'm doing now are rock and metal people. And that's cool. It makes me realize that we were really strong that way. But I didn't come from that background. And it's just very odd to see that where we were finally accepted is kind of different from where we started out, which was more like the Pop-O-Pies school, Flipper—that scene. It's kind of weird to think about."

42

WIRE THIN SHEEP LEGS: CAROLINER, PART 2

Circa 1992, one would have found it fairly mind-boggling that Faith No More and Caroliner had ever shared a stage—and not just once, but twice, as they did in 1984. After all, the juxtaposition was about as stark as one could imagine. Yet eight years on, both of them were still going strong; along with American Music Club, they were among the only San Francisco groups to remain active throughout that timespan, long enough to build up a discography that could be measured in terms of albums rather than singles, EPs, or demo tapes.[53]

Like Faith No More, AMC had made the jump to a major label (Reprise) by this point. Caroliner, on the other hand, had no such prospects and, frankly, no such ambitions. Instead, they continued to burrow further underground, going out of their way to avoid even the most basic concessions to the music business. They stuck to vinyl at a time when the music industry was abandoning LPs in favor of CDs. They were still creating all of their album art by hand, with the Xeroxed lyric sheet inserts offering the only evidence of mass production (and even those were handwritten in their original form). They remained anonymous, at least officially speaking, and declined to hire a publicist or manager.

Even so, they were peaking both creatively and in popularity.[54] 1992 was their *annus mirabilis*, with the band releasing three LPs that year—*The Cooking Stove Beast*, *The Sabre Waving Saracen Wall*, and *Strike Them Hard Drag Them*

---

53 Disclaimer: This is not counting metal bands (obviously Metallica would fit the bill here) or holdovers from the pre-punk era like the Grateful Dead.
54 No sales figures are available, but Kearney estimates that the records from this period generally sold between two and three thousand copies apiece.

to Church—all of them essentially self-released via Brandan Kearney's Nuf Sed label. "It was like we were making a record every week," recalls Lara Allen."You're like, 'Oh, we're making another record? Didn't we just make one? Ok, I guess we're making another one.'"

There is little to distinguish one Caroliner album from the next in a chronological sense—not because they all "sound the same," but because they seem to exist out of time. (Then again, this is only fitting for a band that claimed to be channeling the words of a singing bull from the 1800s.) As *Bananafish*'s Seymour Glass puts it, "After a while, I was at least able to anticipate what I was going to get, alien and unique as they may have been. I don't hear the progression from one era to another; Caroliner's sound and style had to remain consistent by necessity, no matter who was in the band."

Even if the albums blend together, there are still standout tracks, like 'Fiddle with the Heart Stuck in It,' which opens *Cooking Stove Beast.* Built around a looping viola riff played by the Thinking Fellers' Brian Hagemann, it hobbles along for nearly seven minutes, with Grux ranting over the top in shrill, maniacal fashion. Another highlight from the same album, 'Huge Gunset,' features a menacing fuzz-bass riff that sounds like a nod to Flipper.

Cooking Stove Beast also marked the introduction of a new weapon in the band's arsenal: an old theatre organ that Kearney purchased at a thrift store and kept in a shack next to his apartment on Clement Street in the Richmond District. The organ features heavily on the next several albums, adding a carnivalesque aura and evoking images of freak shows at the county fair. Alongside the organ, the group's ever-broadening sonic palette included violins, horns, strange percussion sounds, and noisy tape loops. On a few occasions, they even took to physically altering the tapes they recorded on."We were getting very grandiose at this stage," recalled Kearney, "with talk about splicing tapes lengthwise, gluing pieces of tape onto the master in patterns, etc. Greg Freeman worked patiently at some of these daft ideas, but most weren't worth the trouble."[55]

Then again, the sounds they managed to get on tape in the first place were enough to render such post-production trickery superfluous. "From an audio

---

55 Brandan Kearney, "Caroliner.doc." Unpublished essay.

standpoint, you can't help but marvel at how all of Caroliner's sounds have been created," wrote engineer Scott Colburn, a longtime collaborator of Sun City Girls, in an essay on *The Cooking Stove Beast*. "It sounds lo-fi, but with careful listening, you will find a clarity unequaled by any other. What's more, the consistency of any Caroliner albums are indicative of a complete artistic vision, and that's what makes a great recording."[56]

"Everybody has their different opinions on Caroliner albums," adds Trey Spruance, another admirer. "I've never heard anybody say that they like *The Sabre Waving Saracen Wall* as much as I like it. I really love that record. The imagery in it is really vivid, and there are enough different kinds of sounds going on. It doesn't get locked in to one kind of fidelity as much as some of the other ones. And Grux's voice is incredible on it."

"SENSORY BOMBARDMENT"

Though their lineup remained in flux, Caroliner had developed into a reliable live attraction by this point—occasionally opening for the odd out-of-town band like Ween but more often headlining their own shows at small venues like the Covered Wagon and the Chameleon. "There was definitely a crowd that was interested in what they were doing," says Chameleon booker Alicia Rose. "It was a more in-the-know kind of San Francisco weirdo crowd."

They also toured the country several times during this era, occasionally garnering a preview blurb or even a live review in a local paper. "[T]he Caroliner's [sic] moved the audience to spasms of mashing, dancing and general mayhem," noted a review of an April 1993 show in Salt Lake City, adding that "only Kiss and Gwar can rival the Caroliner's costumed finesse."[57] Earlier that month, *New York Times* critic Alex Ross weighed in with a similarly enthusiastic review of the

---

56 "Recordings That Changed My Life" (https://web.archive.org/web/20110711123122/ https://gravelvoice.com/change/caroliner.html)
57 William D. Kinnear & Grant Sperry, "Caroliner's Club Starzz show a palatable feast of 'spiced' music." *Daily Utah Chronicle*. April 26, 1993.

group's performance at the Gargoyle Mechanique in Manhattan: "'Psychedelic' doesn't begin to describe it: this is some lost American Baroque, retrieved at rummage sales."[58]

As always, the attraction had as much to do with the immersive spectacle the band created as it did with the actual music. Yes, there were songs, but they were subject to varying degrees of collateral damage, depending on the conditions onstage. "Part of what was really interesting about the band for me was this experience of things failing, breaking down," recalls Lara Allen. "*That* was what was improvised because when you're playing with these ridiculous costumes in low-rent rock clubs, with a lot of electrical equipment, and switching instruments—you know, things go wrong all the time. You'd be up onstage thinking, 'What song are we doing?' *Sometimes*. Depending on how badly things were fucking up."

James Goode: It's like sensory bombardment, with all this noise and lights and all that stuff. Certain instruments would be out of tune, deliberately or otherwise. Sometimes it was kind of hard to tell what song it was because you couldn't quite tell where the beginning of the riff was and where the end was.

Joe Pop-O-Pie: The music has a certain sound to it because it has this kind of chaotic clunkiness to it that's recognizable, but it's really about the visuals. Grux is a performance artist; he's a live act. And his live act is very interesting to look at because it's always very asymmetrical—there's something very off about it, and that's kind of interesting because it's always different from what other bands are doing.

Alan Bishop: They got more captivating from beginning to end as time went on. There's still nothing like it. You'll never see anything like a Caroliner show. It's one-of-a-kind; it's its own universe. And you have to really admire the continuity of it and the persistence to keep it together for so long.

58 Alex Ross, "Pop and Jazz in Review." *New York Times*. April 15, 1993.

Lara Allen: You definitely had to be there for a Caroliner show—I mean, if you could stand it. I think a lot of it was awful. I'm sure now, if I saw Caroliner, I might look at it and think, "Well, that looks kind of cool, but I can't stand the way it sounds. It's so noisy." There was probably feedback going on all the time. It was *chaos*, sound-wise. Because a lot of times, people were just trying to figure out what the hell they were doing with all that equipment on them—all those costumes.

THE CULT OF CAROLINER

Caroliner's mythology remains largely inscrutable to outsiders, beyond what can be gleaned from the lyric sheets or the occasional interview. The song titles are certainly evocative—'Old Eggwipe,' 'Wire Thin Sheep Legs,' 'Hannah's Medicinal Tick Collection,' 'Rainbows Made of Meat'—but those in search of a clear, linear narrative are likely to come up empty-handed. Instead, there are images and fragments, references to what feels like a sort of parallel folklore that the band members—and perhaps *only* the band members—shared. One almost gets the sense that a certain degree of impenetrability was part of the point, although Kearney rejects this notion.

"I don't think the band is impenetrable or that impenetrability is the point. I think—and I'm probably going out on a limb here—that it represented the ordinary things in the world as they might be seen with different eyes. There's a heightening and exaggeration, especially of nature, typical of childhood or madness. I think, too, that there's a sense that, say, pioneer history is so far removed from our current experience that it's basically a fever dream. And then you have all the tall tales of that era and the mythology. I think Grux responded to that stuff with a sense of wonder and was compelled to recreate it in his own image via storytelling, much like early twentieth-century lumberjacks came up with mythological creatures like the Squonk and the Axehandle Hound."

"I think what was crucial in my participation was that this myth really rang true for me," adds Allen. "I experienced this myth through drawing, playing music, writing music. It just came out. It was channeling this myth that some of us, I think, really felt resonance with. It was very, very easy to write songs, to do drawings, to make costumes, within the context of that band's mythology. It was really fun. And I think a lot of us took to it very naturally—this sort of psychedelic ergot-poisoning, wigged-out, stream-of-consciousness, sort of hillbilly aesthetic came pretty naturally to some of us."

Maintaining the band's mythology, in turn, meant concealing the band members' identities. "We all had our own Caroliner names," recalls Dame Darcy. "I don't remember what mine was, but I wasn't allowed to be all like, 'I'm Dame Darcy! I'm in Caroliner!'" Margaret Murray, bassist during the *Cooking Stove Beast/Strike Them Hard ...* era, elaborates on this point. "It's not quite like Apple Computer, where you can't talk about anything you're doing. You could definitely say that you were at a Caroliner practice, and a lot of people knew, and your friends all knew, and your friends would all show up to the show. And they knew who was behind those costumes, for the most part. But you couldn't talk publicly about it because it just spoiled the mythology. And people played along with that. They kind of liked it."

That sense of playing along carried over into their occasional zine interviews, if only because interviewers knew they weren't going to get much in the way of mundane factual information.("My mother was a barrel-wearer from way back and tried to teach me to make umbrellas that didn't work," said one band member—presumably Grux—in response to a question about his childhood.) "It was *poppycock*, basically," says Allen."It was throwing people off the scent. In a way, it was really playing with this self-important, self-mythologizing rock-star aesthetic. Or rock-star elitism. I mean, if you think about it, that is *so* misplaced. I think that Caroliner definitely had an appeal for me because it was *not* that. It was not like your classic rock band setup. It had the utopian commune/anonymity aspect that was really, to me, extremely creatively liberating."

The communal aspect of the band, together with the dictatorial tendencies of the bandleader, calls to mind another "c" word—namely, "cult." Mind you, Caroliner wasn't literally a cult—certainly not in the religious sense—but there were, shall we say, cultish aspects to the way they operated. "Grux would definitely have been the evil genius who people would sort of be devoted to," says Greg Freeman, "and he would push them around and make them breathe

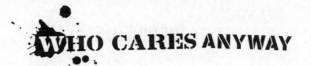

paint fumes for hours on end or whatever. He was a little demanding. You know, he would book studio time at two in the afternoon on a Wednesday and expect people to show up. And if they said, 'Well, I have a job,' he'd say, 'Well, quit your job.' [Laughs.] That's kind of what he expected from people. So it was a little cultish."

Brandan Kearney: If Caroliner was a cult, it was not a very imposing one, given that the band burned through more members than the Beach Boys and Blood, Sweat & Tears combined. I think some people looked at us and figured, "anything goes!" But artistic freedom usually entailed a roundabout, almost ascetic path. You had to give up some control, but that wasn't necessarily a bad thing.

Lizzy Kate Gray: Grux had this coterie around him, and many of them were young women, too. I think of him as a fertile mentoring area for people who went on to do other things. A lot of people would come to town and be involved in the cult of Grux and play in Caroliner and then go on to be good at other stuff—women, too. So that was somewhat unusual. And I think he must have had a supportive, tender side, silly as it sounds. I mean, he's so gruff and impossible and, you know, covered with apple cores and dead rats and so forth. But he certainly respected young women in the scene for their talents and tried to get them on board.

Dame Darcy: Grux was a very visionary person, but he was also kind of a staunch dictator. I hung in there for a while, and I helped make a bunch of the albums, which was cool. And they taught me how to self-publish and self-distribute and do all the things that I still do today. So I always thank Brandan and Grux for showing me how to do what I did for the rest of my life and how to empower me, especially as a young girl. I really think being in Caroliner Rainbow was as much of my art education as my fancy schooling.

Lara Allan: I think that for a lot of us, this whole freetarian thing that Grux was into—you know, there was something to it. Eating out of the dumpster. I guess I'm just a little bourgeois, though. I remember he made sushi this one time, and I just thought, "You know, I don't wanna eat this." Actually going into a Japanese restaurant is something that's very exciting to me. But for me, I couldn't really go into complete freetarian living and live off of government grants and things like that.

43

NOTHING SOLID: TFUL 282, PART 2

Whereas Caroliner represented the squirming underbelly of avant-weird San Francisco in the early nineties, the Thinking Fellers represented its more presentable face. Relative to the experimental noise substratum championed by zines like *Bananafish*, they were downright accessible. Then again, relative to the broader indie rock scene being curated by labels such as Matador—which signed the band to a three-album deal in 1991—they were still oddballs. They managed to carve out their own niche thanks to a rare ability to straddle these two worlds.

In many ways, TFUL 282 and Caroliner were fellow travelers during this era. Three of the Thinking Fellers—Mark Davies, Brian Hagemann, and Anne Eickelberg—sat in with Caroliner at various points, both live and on record. ("They saved our necks again and again when the band would be down to like me, Grux, and Darcy," says Brandan Kearney.) Yet the two bands were also a study in contrasts. If Caroliner was a dictatorship, then TFUL was a democracy, with the members sharing songwriting and lead vocal duties as evenly as any quintet this side of Blue Öyster Cult. And if Caroliner was cultish, then TFUL was familial. With the exception of Jay Paget, who joined the band in 1990 following the departure of original drummer Paul Bergmann, everyone in the band had known each other before moving out west from Iowa. They lived together in the same Oakland house for three years. Apart from the one-time change in drummers, the lineup remained constant. They were possibly the least dysfunctional band imaginable.

Along with Sun City Girls—who, by this point, had relocated from Phoenix to Seattle—Caroliner and the Thinking Fellers formed a triumvirate of sorts. As experimental West Coast bands that came of age in the post-punk, post-hardcore era, they naturally gravitated to one another. In the fall of 1992, SCG opened for the Fellers on a month-long US tour. That same year, the two bands

INTO THE NINETIES

shared a split 7-inch on Kearney's Nuf Sed label, with each of them covering a Caroliner song.[59] Along with openers Three Day Stubble, the three bands played a memorable Halloween show at the Great American Music Hall on October 29, 1993. (Infamously, Sun City Girls sat on the floor and told campfire stories as part of their set.) "That was like the show of all shows," recalls Stubble guitarist Brently Pusser. "I think it was *the* show of the nineties for me."

All three bands were remarkably prolific, though the Thinking Fellers had the highest profile and the largest audience. Their first two albums for Matador, *Lovelyville* (1991) and *Mother of All Saints* (1992), were sprawling affairs that had as much in common with Captain Beefheart's *Trout Mask Replica*—abrasive guitar counterpoint, strange lyrics, abrupt changes in recording fidelity—as they did with anything under the indie rock umbrella. As a result, critics often found themselves searching for (or even inventing) words to try to describe the group's sound. A 1991 review in the local zine *Superdope* called the band "light years ahead of their competitors in whatever it is they do."[60] Writing in 1993, Simon Reynolds used the term "avant-garage" to describe TFUL and a handful of other like-minded bands that he deemed "too motley to be a movement."[61] Years later, Andrew Scott Earles would describe *Mother of All Saints* as "sort of like the *Daydream Nation* of the late '80s and early '90s experimental out-to-lunch quasi-movement of noise pop" and "an excellent showcase of just how innovative, individualistic, and unprecedented this corner of early '90s indie rock could be."[62]

"We never really felt like we fit into any particular genre," says Davies. "It's just like you kind of had to hitch your wagon to some movement that was going on in order to get shows or to put out records. There's this infrastructure of labels and clubs and stuff that considers itself part of this genre. So you kind of attach that [indie rock] label to your band because those are the kinds of places you perform or put out stuff. But we never felt that much of a part of it musically or stylistically."

59 The title of TFUL's 1993 EP *Admonishing the Bishops* is also a nod to Sun City Girls.
60 *Superdope*, No. 2 (Summer 1991), p. 36.
61 *Spin,* June 1993, p. 85.
62 Earles, *Gimme Indie Rock*, pp. 328–329.

467

NOBLE EXPERIMENTS

Greg Freeman, who worked with the Thinking Fellers on all three of their Matador LPs, represented yet another point of connection between them and Caroliner.[63] "I had much more input with the Thinking Fellers," he notes. "It was more of a traditional role because, with those guys, I was labeled the 'producer,' or 'co-producer,' so I had aesthetic opinions and input. They would either listen to me or ignore me, but I was still a member of the dialogue in the studio. Whereas in Caroliner, I was just like a guy who was being pushed around by Grux, like everybody else," he adds with a laugh.

Freeman had the challenge of faithfully capturing the sound of a band known for its spirited live performances and tangled guitar interplay. They also had a penchant for group improvisation, the results of which often made its way onto the records in the form of brief interludes (so-called "Feller filler"). "They recorded tons of stuff in the practice space," recalls Freeman. "A lot of times, they would mix that stuff in on the record, but it would go back and forth between a studio thing and just a live jam or whatever. Later, when I actually did have some decent microphones, we would try to recreate their live setup with better mics. And that was sometimes successful, I think. But still, it's just different when you're in a studio, and there's a guy there who pushes the big red button and points the finger and says, 'Okay, now be creative.'"

According to Paget, much of their songwriting evolved through a similar process. "A lot of the stuff came out of just jamming. We would just play and hit the tape recorder. And then we would have these cassette tapes, and we'd just go through them and go, 'Okay, let's try that.' I can't remember anyone really coming in with songs."

That collective songwriting process might account for the unusual song structures—especially on *Lovelyville* and *Mother of All Saints*—which seldom break down into traditional verses and choruses. There are stretches where it's hard to tell where one song starts and another one ends, a result of the often

---

63 The one TFUL record from this period that Freeman did not work on was the EP *Admonishing the Bishops*, which was produced by Shellac's Bob Weston.

INTO THE NINETIES

TFUL 282 OUTSIDE OF LOWDOWN STUDIOS, SOUTH OF MARKET. L-R: MARK DAVIES, ANNE EICKELBERG, JAY PAGET, HUGH SWARTS, BRIAN HAGEMAN, PHOTO BY GAIL BUTENSKY.

jarring contrasts within songs as well as the tight segues between them. Yet as shown by their next two records—the *Admonishing the Bishops* EP (1993) and *Strangers from the Universe* (1994)—they were perfectly capable of writing concise, even catchy (if still quirky) songs when they felt like it.

If there's a knock on the band's Matador-era records, it's only in comparison to their almost mythical reputation as a live band. As *Superdope* editor Jay Hinman put it years later, "Some of their live shows, especially around 1991 or so, are among the jaw-dropping best I've ever seen. Their San Francisco Bay Area-based fans devotedly hopped from gig to gig, and for a year or two, it was absolutely worship-like at the shows themselves."[64]

---

64 Jay Hinman, "Have You Heard the TFUL282?" February 8, 2008. https://detailedtwang. blogspot.com/2008/02/have-you-heard-tful282.html

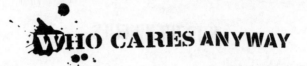

WHO CARES ANYWAY

Johan Kugelberg: Lo-fi as they were, the multi-directional super-dynamic barrage of the first four albums [*Wormed by Leonard* through *Mother of All Saints*] makes them absolute classics of their era. What TFUL282 would have sounded like all along with "proper" record production is one of those armchair quarterback shoulda-coulda-wouldas that rock fandom reverberates with.[65]

Margaret Murray: I think that their records were different than how they were live. Because live, there was a kind of energy in the way that the sounds blended that was very different. It sounded sometimes like an orchestra. You didn't know what instruments were making those sounds. And I don't think they captured that completely on the records. And they tried, you know, almost like an intellectual exercise, to do all of these things, but it just didn't have the same flow as it did live. It had a flow that you understood without having to intellectualize it. They'd be off kind of falling apart, and then all of a sudden, they would all come together, and that's when you could swear there was a whole horn section up there. But there wasn't. It was just the guitars and the bass and the drums.

Greg Freeman: They always had *amazing* ideas and just incredible sounds and everything. It was always a struggle to capture the sound either that they were doing or that they wanted to get. A lot of it, I think, was just because my studio was *so* limited and very, very basic. I'm not slighting *them* at all. It's really just a function of the process and my crappy studio. I mean, you can do a two-guitar, bass, and drums rock band with pretty basic stuff, but if you're trying to do, like, something with four vocals and all these other different instruments and different sounds, it's more of a challenge.

Mark Davies: On some of the earlier recordings with all three guitars going and drums and bass, you ended up getting so much phase cancellation that often, the more things you added, the smaller the whole thing sounded. One of the

---

65 Kugelberg, "Genre Definitions, The Second Guessing of Intent and the Killed-By-Death-style Punk Rock Rarity." *Perfect Sound Forever* webzine, August 2010. http://www.furious.com/perfect/genredefinitions2.html

strong points about the live show is the density and the onslaught of all that sound. But in the studio, it just doesn't work that way.[66]

Seymour Glass: No one's records capture what they sound like live. Even live albums. You just have to be in the room with the amps and the PA and the people screaming their beer orders at the bartender. Having seen them play live many times and listened to the records even more, I'd say the underacknowledged genius of the band was the arrangements.

MATADOR

During the Thinking Fellers' three-year tenure with Matador, the label grew from indie upstart to juggernaut within the span of a few years, thanks to the success of acts like Pavement, Yo La Tengo, Guided by Voices, and Liz Phair. In 1993, the label entered into a partnership with Atlantic Records, and while the deal only applied to some of Matador's new releases (and nothing by the Thinking Fellers), it was nonetheless a sign of the times. Meanwhile, bands as far-flung and seemingly uncommercial as the Melvins, the Butthole Surfers, and the Flaming Lips had all signed to major labels in recent years. The Thinking Fellers were not oblivious to these trends, but they were also realistic.

"We were talking to some major labels for a little while," recalls Davies. "When our contract with Matador expired [in 1994], we were trying to kind of pick up the pace, and not work day jobs and tour a lot. At that point, we were talking to a bunch of different labels, some of which were majors or like the indie subsidiary of the major label. And it *was* right around that time when there was kind of a feeding frenzy, where all these A&R guys from major labels were trying to capitalize on this surge of indie rock. So there *were* bands at our level being signed by majors. And we did talk to some labels, but nothing came through on that. I think it would've been disastrous if it had happened. I mean, I can't

66 Paul Clements, Interview with Thinking Fellers Union Local 282. *PSF*, May 2001. http://www.furious.com/perfect/thinkingfellows.html

imagine that *working*, really. I can't imagine them being able to market us the way that they would want to be able to sell enough copies to make it worth their while. I just think we were too hard to get a grip on. I mean, how would they present us to the radio market? I don't know."

Matt Hall: When I first moved back to San Francisco [in 1989], hair metal was still the thing. You'd see ads in the back of the weeklies for hair metal bands with poofy hair. Then all of a sudden, grunge was the thing, and then indie rock. And all of a sudden, it seemed like the people I knew could actually go tour the country or maybe even tour Europe. Bands like the Thinking Fellers were able to actually survive on just the band. Before, there was kind of a mentality that people like us were *always* gonna be completely marginal and have *zero* chance for any kind of commercial success. So it was kind of a weird thing when all of a sudden, for a few years there, it seemed like you actually maybe could. I'm still trying to decide how good of a thing that was, musically, for people.

Jay Paget: Nobody had ever come in and ever listened to our material and said, "Why don't you try *this* approach?" We never had a producer who was like that, or whatever they call the A&R guy. We had never worked in that realm before. Not to say that we wouldn't be open to it, but … it just didn't seem like a good fit for the type of things that were coming out.

Mark Davies: I think some of these agents from the labels saw us categorized somewhere as "alternative rock." And they saw that we were doing a lot of touring and had put records out and stuff and said, "Okay, let's consider these guys." But I think once they started to actually *listen* to the music, they were like, "Fuck, we can't sell this."

LIVE

The Thinking Fellers did get their chance to experience the world of corporate alternative rock in 1995 when they accepted an invitation to go on tour as openers for the band Live. Along with the likes of Bush, Better Than Ezra, and the Goo Goo Dolls—generic pop-rock bands that were somehow marketed as "alternative" in those days—Live were emblematic of the sea change that had taken place in the wake of Nirvana.

Mark Davies: That tour was such an eye-opener into that world. It was really interesting. It was kind of a fluke. Somehow they picked us. I still am really confused at how that came about. I think it was some kind of weird street cred, to get this obscure band. I know we talked about it, like, "Do we really want to do this corporate tour? Yet … this is a really weird thing to do. Let's check it out and see what it's like."

Jay Paget: The Live tour was just an aberration. It was probably a good way for us to see how wonderful we had it with the club scene. It's completely a different dynamic with the music on the large tours that are mainly played for people who don't listen to music as much as the people that we generally play for. So I guess it's the difference between a sort of superficial kind of pop market, so to speak, and then more of what I would consider a better-informed population in the smaller clubs. Their ears were completely different, and their personalities were completely different. So the Live thing was an eye-opener in a weird way. We'd never done *anything* like that, before or since.

Mark Davies: It was pretty comical, too, because they're coming in this fleet of buses and semis to set up the show, and then we pull up in our little van—like six of us pile out of the van with all our gear in the van. And all these roadies come up to help us unload it, and every time they were just shaking their heads at what a rinky-dink operation we were.

Anne Eickelberg: As soon as we walked out [onstage], it was just: hatred.[67]

Brian Hagemann: I stepped up to the mic once and said, "Now we're going to play a medley of selections from the theme for *A Fistful of Dollars*." And this

67 Ibid.

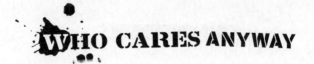

skinhead in front of me, his eyes were going crossed. He nearly broke his middle finger off giving me the finger so hard. He was screaming at me with hatred! I can't imagine anything more horrible for him than to have me walk out there and keep him from his band.[68]

Mark Davies: There were these weird extremes of being treated really well and treated really poorly at the same time. Everyone was really professional. They didn't give a shit about the music. As long as you got onstage at the right time, got off at the right time, didn't make any waves, they thought you were great. We traveled with these great chefs who made gourmet meals for everyone every night and stuff like that. But then you're playing a twenty-five-minute set to a bunch of kids who can't stand what you're doing and just want Live to get on— so we got pelted with stuff and booed.

Trey Spruance: Somebody from the Thinking Fellers was telling me how the guys in Live were amazed after three or four shows that the Thinking Fellers had played. "Wow, so you guys play a different set every night—like, you change the order of the songs and do different songs?" "Yeah, we get a little bored of doing the same thing every night." Because Live themselves weren't changing their set; they were doing the same set every single night. And so a couple of weeks into the tour, Live decides they're gonna change it up a little bit: they're gonna put some songs before other songs and try different combinations. It was a complete fuckin' disaster. It was just completely terrible. So after trying it a few times, they just stopped and went back to their original set.

Going back to the Pop-O-Pies thing of rehearsing the in-between-song banter [see Chapter 38]—what does this tell you about music that a band is gonna fall apart unless they can play their songs in the rehearsed order? Because they really *are* rehearsing the in-between-song banter, and they are doing all of that stuff the same way every fucking night, for real. And that it's shocking to them, to the point of being *intimidating*, that a band in this world would actually be writing their setlists right before they went onstage.

68 Ibid.

INTO THE NINETIES

Mark Davies: I think the most disturbing thing was, here's this huge infrastructure that goes along with producing these shows, and not one person out of that whole crew had one thing to say about the music. It didn't *mean* anything. It's just a product that had to be plugged into this slot. As long as you can come and put that out there and not cause problems for the crew, it didn't really matter what it was. And that was just weird—this cold business aspect of it. And you know if you sign to a label, that's what your career is gonna turn into. That's all that matters in that realm.

While they didn't break up as a result of the Live tour, the Thinking Fellers did start to wind down the operation over the next couple of years. "In '96, we had been touring for about six years," explains Paget. "Not all the time, but just one or two tours a year. So there was an idea at that time that we could perhaps make a living out of this. And I think we tried for about a year to try to just make money from music, but we couldn't quite get there. It felt like we had plateaued."

This feeling had been bubbling under for a couple of years, as evidenced by several entries in Anne Eickelberg's tour diaries, which she published on the band's website years later.[69] "The lifestyle and this pursuit seem more and more meaningless to me," she wrote in a November 1994 entry, adding, "I feel silly, being in a band and touring and hanging out in ugly, boring rock clubs (at my age)." "Getting the feeling that driving all day every day is a job I've done for years," she added in an entry from April 24, 1995.

TFUL's lifespan as a touring band coincided almost perfectly with the heyday of indie rock, at least in the original sense of the term. As Andrew Earles puts it in *Gimme Indie Rock*, 1996 "was a year of transformation in the underground, as indie rock was by then three or four years into a growing backlash … 1996 also marked the first full year of serious encroachment of underground hip-hop, electronica, post-rock, widescreen avant-pop, and other styles that would drive guitars deeper into the metal-and-hardcore-based undergrounds." The Thinking Fellers didn't hop on board any of these bandwagons, as their last two albums—*I Hope It Lands* (1996) and *Bob Dinners and Larry Noodles Present*

69 http://www.tful282.com/annediaries.htm

475

Tubby Turdner's Celebrity Avalanche (2001)—are basically further refinements of the band's already identifiable style.

As for the band members themselves, they quietly exited stage left after performing a few shows in support of *Bob Dinners*, having already settled down into day jobs and/or family life by that point. The last song on that album, ''91 Dodge Van,' offers a rare moment of sentimentality from a band that typically avoided it like the plague. "Looking back over our days, I know we won / Sometimes it feels like that's erased by moving on," sings Eickelberg.

"I think we did win," she told the *SF Weekly*'s Mike Rowell in a 2001 article.[70] "Even though we never achieved great fame or recognition beyond a certain level, we did what we set out to do, and we did it on our own terms."

70 Rowell, "Collective Cacophony." *SF Weekly*. May 2, 2001. https://archives.sfweekly.com/sanfrancisco/collective-cacophony/Content?oid=2141602

END THE GAME

4.4

"100 BANDS": RECORD COLLECTORS, SIDE PROJECTS, AND THE YELLOW PAINT INCIDENT

Jay Paget: There weren't any hard drugs in our sort of world. I don't think anyone was interested in it, really.

Lara Allen: There were definitely a lot of stoners and stuff. But in the whole Thinking Fellers and Caroliner scene, drugs definitely were not a part of that.

Trey Spruance: There was like no drug culture in any of this stuff in the nineties. It was not anti-drug in terms of being "clean and sober" or anything like that. But if you were somebody who had to rely on drugs to be interesting, you were just a boring fuckin' idiot. Nobody had to talk about it. It was just understood. "Oh yeah, this person needs to take acid in order to have something kind of interesting to say." Well, it's *not* interesting.

Jay Paget: When I think about Brandan and Barbara and all the folks in Archipelago Brewing Co. and then everyone in the Thinking Fellers, one thing that is common with everyone is a really great sense of humor. You know, people were pretty funny. They could be droll funny, and they could be sarcastic funny, and they could be edgy funny, and all the characterizations of funny. But people had an eye for the absurdity of things. So that through-line gives you some protection, I think, from getting sunk by everything. Sometimes the substance is another protection from it. But those groups just happened to have people in them who were pretty funny. I think the Thinking Fellers sort of embodied this, too—absurd, funny perspectives within relatively serious music.

END THE GAME

Mark Davies: There's just a certain joy in performing, and I think that that kind of bubbles out into humor sometimes, to express that. And it's one thing that bothered me about a lot of bands in that genre of, you know, post-punk or alternative or whatever—this kind of too-cool attitude, like nobody can crack a smile, and you're not supposed to look like you're having fun playing. There was a lot of that going on, and I didn't understand why anyone would want to do that. It's *fun*, you know? It's fun to play.

COLLECTORS

The Thinking Fellers were emblematic of a certain slice of the early nineties San Francisco underground. They were smart, funny, and musically literate. They didn't take themselves too seriously. And as prolific as they were, that didn't keep the individual band members from branching out into a far-flung variety of side projects. "There was a zeitgeist of music happening," says Lara Allen, "and this included a lot of erudite musicians and also people who were experienced and really *hemorrhaging* creative stuff."

Another hallmark of this zeitgeist was the prevalence of non-rock influences. Simon Reynolds has noted the onset of "record-collector rock" as a sign of creative exhaustion in the post-punk era. "Obviously, rock bands have always included record collectors in their ranks," he notes. "What changed in the mid-eighties was that bands increasingly signposted their reference points and that spotting these allusions became an integral part of the listener's aesthetic response and enjoyment."[71] While there was no shortage of record-collector rock in early nineties San Francisco—for example, the surf rock revivalism of bands like the Mummies and the Phantom Surfers—others were delving into their record collections to find a way *out* of rock.

Lara Allen: My friend Andrew Rush had this amazing collection from the sixties

---

71 Reynolds, *Rip It Up and Start Again*, p. 393.

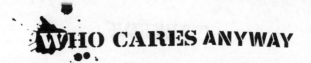

and seventies, and then there was Craig Ventresco, who has a world-class collection of turn-of-the-century pop vocal records. And you had these other people who just have *tons* and *tons* of records. And then you've got Gregg Turkington, who's like the king of vanity pressings. And then Brandan. Just a lot of people collected a lot of weird, crazy stuff.

Barbara Manning: You had Gregg Turkington's influence—heavy influence— because of *Breakfast Without Meat*. And then his world drew in Brandan and Margaret and members of the Thinking Fellers and others. He was kind of a central figure to a lot of that. People were drawn to him. People were drawn to Grux.

Alan Bishop: Trading tapes with Grux over the years and then CD-Rs and VHS tapes—I mean, he's always the winner. He's always sending me more than I could ever make for him. There's a lot of things that I was turned on to by those tapes. I would imagine it's similar the other way, but I think Grux just had access to so much stuff, and he would share it. He'd send twenty cassettes at a time, and I'd listen to 'em all. It became daunting after a while. Then he'd send me twenty video cassettes that are six hours long *each*. So I didn't have time— there's no time to process it all. I tried.

Lara Allen: A lot of things were coming in and going out. What I'm trying to say about this whole collector thing—about people and records and music— was that everybody was sharing stuff. People were passing around cassette tapes, VHS tapes. And the thing is that it was pretty democratic. When you were listening to something like Ennio Morricone, it was—maybe at another time, for somebody from a more punk rock viewpoint, maybe a joke. But that stuff wasn't a joke anymore. The easy listening stuff and all that—*all of it* became part of what people were listening to, loving, and then *doing* themselves.

Gregg Turkington: The unique thing about the particular group of folks that, in retrospect, you might call a "scene" was that rather than everyone having their one band that they were serious about and that played 100 shows, each of us would have 100 bands, each of which only played one show. There were a lot of really unique "conceptual" projects going down with interchanging members, many of which went undocumented and certainly unheralded. Which was completely fine.

It seemed like when the Thinking Fellers were really doing well, that really got a lot of stuff going. Because there were so many spinoff bands, and they were good about putting these bands on bills when they were popular. It seemed like there was just this thing where a lot of different bands were just all friends and willing to be involved in all these spinoff bands.

Brandan Kearney: I don't know why it worked out that way. I think it's probably because everyone was just interested in a lot of different kinds of music but couldn't necessarily—I mean, Mark maybe really liked that kind of material Job's Daughters did, but it didn't mean that the Thinking Fellers were gonna start playing it.

JOB'S DAUGHTERS

At first glance, Job's Daughters might seem like the kind of side project band that's at most worthy of a footnote. After all, they played just a few shows and never recorded any original material. Their entire discography consists of a couple of 7-inches, the first of which—'The Prophecy of Daniel and John the Divine' b/w 'Sinner Man' (Nuf Sed)—looked and sounded like the work of apocalyptic Christian folk rockers from the tail end of the hippie era.[72] Although the recording date (February 1991) and credits (Mark Davies, Brandan Kearney, Greg Freeman, et al.) are clearly displayed on the back cover, the combination of the front cover and the actual music was enough to cause confusion. As Kearney recalls, "The first problem was that it got delivered to Revolver, and they thought something had been mis-shipped because it had a big crucifix on

---

72 The A-side was originally recorded by the Cowsills in 1969, while the B-side, 'Sinner Man,' first appeared as the B-side of a 1956 single ('Tango of the Drums') by Les Baxter and His Orchestra.

WHO CARES ANYWAY

JOD'N DAUGHTERS, L D: MARK DAVIES, GREG FREEMAN, BRANDAN KEARNEY. PHOTO BY GAIL BUTENSKY.

it. They were like, 'Oh, we got some weirdo religious guy's record, and we've gotta return it.' But luckily, Seymour Glass [who worked at Revolver] thought to call me up."

Mark Davies: I can imagine how it would be sort of hard to know what to do with it. It was just us doing a *cover*. It wasn't a song that we wrote—it was this Cowsills song, and it was a pretty straight cover, too. I think we added our own thing to it, but it was pretty faithful. I can see hearing that and thinking, "What is the point of releasing this faithful cover of this very obscure song?" And I still don't really know what the purpose was, but it was just really fun to do. And then Brandan had a label, so he could put it out.

Brandan Kearney: A lot of stations wouldn't play it because it's like, "Well, we can't tell if this is a joke." And I gotta say, that made me extremely irritated, and it's one of the things probably that contributed to me getting out of the goddamn business. I don't know why that bothered me so much, but I just really found it irritating. Who cares if we had been sincere? What difference would it have made to anybody? No one was going to know what they should think about it until they knew whether we were kidding or not?

Mark Davies: If you really *mess* with a cover and change it into your own thing, I can see the point of recording that and releasing it. And if you do it more faithfully, then it gets into this gray area. But it's kind of interesting in itself just to make you ponder why you would do that. I think you could say that about most of the Amarillo/Zip Code Rapists stuff. It's like, "Why is this being released? What is the *point* of it? Yet I really *like* it."

I think there's a certain complexity there that is hard to pin down. Because you can obviously see the point of putting out music where *you've* written it and performed it, and it *expresses* something about you. But I'm *sure* that all these covers of vanity pressings or Neil Hamburger or whatever kind of stuff Gregg was doing—he's totally expressing himself through that. It's just less obvious for you to look at it and say, "Well, how is this expressing something about him?" It is. It's what he was driven to do, so obviously, there's some point to it just for that reason. And I think the underlying motivations behind it aren't clear to the listener, so it gets discounted.

And I guess you could apply that to some of these Job's Daughters singles, too. Like, I still don't know what the point of putting those out was, but I *like* them, and I feel pride in those, and I feel like there was something expressed through doing that. So I guess when you think of it in that way, it becomes kind of silly to feel like you have to define what your motivations were. It's sort of mysterious how your creative self operates. And if you were driven to produce it and put it out, then obviously you were trying to express something through it, or you wouldn't have had the energy to carry it through. I wouldn't feel the same way about somebody's CD-R. There's something about the actual act of putting out an album, even if those guys ended up throwing away several hundred copies. There is a financial reality to doing that.

483

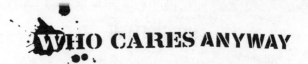

THE HEAVENLY TEN STEMS AND THE YELLOW PAINT INCIDENT

Job's Daughters eventually morphed into the Heavenly Ten Stems, a larger ensemble.[73] Like Job's Daughters, the group played only a handful of shows, but one in particular—which Lisa Carver recounted in detail in the July 1993 issue of *Rollerderby*—lives in infamy:

> On 18 June 1993, at the Chameleon in the Mission District of San Francisco, Heavenly Ten Stems sang emotional pop duets in Cantonese, Hindi, and Japanese and played instruments including trombone, violin, banjo, guitar, and keyboards, making possibly the prettiest music I have ever heard live ... Then someone threw yellow paint on the female singer [Lara Allen]. Then someone threw a full glass of beer on the person who threw the paint. Something else was thrown ... Then two Asian American females and one African American were yelling at the band members, and at one point, one of the three unplugged an effects box, and the music stopped.[74]

Fortunately, for posterity's sake, the incident was captured on video—still a rarity in those pre-smartphone days. In the footage, one of the protestors can be seen jumping onstage, taking the microphone, and yelling, "Stop it!" "This is racist bullshit!" shouts another voice. Then Grux can be heard speaking to the band from the audience: "Maybe you should explain yourself. Some people think it's a joke." Davies, wearing a cowboy hat and neckerchief, then addresses the crowd: "I don't know if there is anything I can say to explain it. When emotions get to a certain level, I don't know if I can really explain it in a way that will be taken the way I mean it. But we don't mean this as a parody. To us, it's a tribute.

---

73 The A-side, an Ennio Morricone composition, features a lead vocal turn by one "Livingstone Semakula" (who sounds an awful lot like Grux). The B-side, '静静夜雨,' is a Cantonese pop song whose title translates to "Quiet Night Rain." Davies handles the lead vocals on this one, offering a dramatic and reverent performance.
74 Lisa Carver, "The Yellow Paint Show." *Rollerderby*, No. 12. Summer 1993.

END THE GAME

HEAVENLY TEN STEMS. L-R: MARK DAVIES, ALEX BEHR (BACKGROUND), LARA ALLEN, BRANDAN KEARNEY. PHOTO BY ELISABETH SISCO; COURTESY OF LARA ALLEN.

And if it's perceived in another way, we have to take that into account ... And if we're naive, I can admit that we would be naive." At the end of the set, the protesters handed out fliers accusing the band of "re-enacting stereotypes" and "actively contributing to and ensuring the continuance of a historical tradition of white people's co-optation of other cultures."[75]

There was ensuing coverage in the *Bay Guardian* (which supported the protesters) in addition to *Rollerderby* (which aired both sides but generally supported the band). Alan Bishop, who was living in Seattle at the time, remembers hearing about the event "as quickly as news traveled in those days." He adds, "I was livid when that happened. I was going on radio stations in San Francisco ripping into them by name, calling 'em idiots. Maybe that was an overreaction, but I kind of felt partially responsible for that.

75 Ibid.

WHO CARES ANYWAY

"I mean, they were young, they were impressionable," he says of the protesters, "but they were completely ignorant of what was going on onstage. Which, of course, those guys were paying tribute to a lot of music from Asia that they loved, whether it was Erkin Koray or Bollywood or a Chinese pop song or a Vietnamese song or whatever. That's what they were doing. And we were doing the same thing, even before them. We were playing songs from other countries, but no one ever did that to us."

Indeed, Sun City Girls had been playing covers of Asian and Middle Eastern songs since the mid-eighties, but they also had the experience of playing to hostile crowds full of hardcore punks (including a 1984 tour opening for skate-punks Jodie Foster's Army), which fostered a sort of bunker mentality. "That's why I always told 'em, 'Why didn't they do that to us?'" adds Bishop. "I really would've loved to have responded to that at one of our shows. I mean, not to knock those guys for being sort of shocked when it happened, because I think they really were, and they were taken aback by the fact that some of their own contemporary friends, or their crowd, was against them and misunderstood what they were trying to do. And they acted very passively; they didn't respond. But we would have been very aggressive. Because for us back then, we weren't taking any shit from anyone."[76]

In contrast, the Heavenly Ten Stems responded to the incident by breaking up. They released a posthumous 7-inch ('Jaan Pehechaan Ho' b/w 'China Town') in 1994 via Amarillo, but the Chameleon show effectively ended the band. As Davies told *Rollerderby*, "What they did was give us two choices: be defiant and make the band into a crusade, or be intimidated and quit. It can't be just

76 One of the protestors, Windy Chien, was also the owner of Aquarius Records at the time. Given the store's championing of niche sub-genres from around the globe, the selective outrage over the Heavenly Ten Stems is ironic. As she explained years later in an interview with the design magazine *Dwell*, "I'm really into subcultures of all types. When I owned the record shop, I loved being part of all kinds of subcultures, from punk to Ethiopian jazz to Norwegian black metal." (https://www.dwell.com/article/windy-chien-home-tour-2968ba57). It's also ironic that of all the potentially "offensive" bands in the scene in those days—including the Zip Code Rapists, Faxed Head, Three Day Stubble, and Plainfield—it was the Heavenly Ten Stems who found themselves being attacked onstage. "I think it's kind of interesting that now, if we were trying to do this, it would be almost impossible," admits ZCR's John Singer. "People kind of sneered at us, but we never had that particular kind of incident happen with us—even with that name."

END THE GAME

music and appreciation anymore. It can't be innocent anymore, which I guess is what *they* wanted. I've lost all enthusiasm for keeping the band going." It was a harbinger of things to come, from political correctness to cancel culture and the rest of it.

"I wanted to keep doing it," says Allen, who bore the brunt of the attack. "We really fucked up by not doing it. I just think that—the thing that happened was bogus, so why give so much credence to it, to *stop playing*? I mean, that's ridiculous. I can say that now." For Allen, who had been ousted from Caroliner earlier that year, the incident was a nail in the coffin. She took up painting, began studying ragtime with Craig Ventresco, and quietly exited the scene. "It was at that moment when I just said, 'I'm never gonna perform again.' I was so upset."[77]

---

77 Allen sang lead vocals on a couple of Bollywood covers on *Second Grand Constitution and Bylaws*, the second album by Trey Spruance's Secret Chiefs 3 (Amarillo, 1998), although she didn't perform live with the band.

45

ACTING, THEATRICALITY, AND "JOKE BANDS"

"Indeed, carnival masks are generally hideous and most often evoke animal or demonic forms, so that they are like a figurative 'materialization' of those lower—we might even say 'infernal'—tendencies, which are allowed to be expressed."[78]

From Caroliner's Old West fever dreams to Faxed Head's handicapped death metal to Three Day Stubble's nerd rock, some strange things were happening on San Francisco stages circa 1993. There were others, too, like Miss Murgatroid, the accordion-wielding alter ego of Chameleon booker Alicia Rose, and Dame Darcy, the public persona of musician, artist, and (by this point) ex-Caroliner member Darcy Stanger. Even Mr. Bungle still wore masks and used pseudonyms in those days. "There was something of a genre," notes Faxed Head's James Goode (aka Fifth Head). "A lot of it has to do with Grux—not that he invented it or anything. There's maybe his influence of the Residents, of GWAR, of other acts. I'm not sure how he got that idea; I'm sure it just occurred to him at some point that he had to be anonymous."

Wherever Grux got the idea, the Residents must at least be acknowledged as precursors. They wore elaborate costumes and wove even more elaborate backstories, and they did it right there in "the kook capital of the world," as Residents spokesman Jay Clem was fond of calling San Francisco. At the same time, it's possible to overstate the extent of their influence. "Long before I moved

---

78 René Guénon, *Symbols of Sacred Science*, p. 143.

END THE GAME

back to the Bay Area in 1984, I remember a couple of friends rolling their eyes when their own music was compared to the Residents," notes Seymour Glass. "It seemed like they were already the name to invoke among squares trying to talk about unconventional or off-kilter music."[79]

There's also a chicken-or-egg aspect to questions about the influence of the Residents on subsequent SF bands. After all, there's a reason why the Residents chose San Francisco—as opposed to, say, Houston or Chicago—when they relocated from Shreveport, Louisiana, in the late 1960s. The city's reputation for tolerance, permissiveness, and, yes, weirdness is also what drew bands like the Thinking Fellers and Three Day Stubble to the Bay Area in the 1980s. It was a haven for oddballs and eccentrics—gay or straight, musician or non-musician. "There was always this 'going west' thing that happened," notes Lara Allen, "and usually people landed in San Francisco. You know, the freaks would go to San Francisco."

From the outside looking in—or to the innocent bystander wandering into the Chameleon on a random weeknight in 1992 or 1993—it might have all resembled one big freakshow. But that wasn't necessarily the point, and fixating on the surface-level "weirdness" of it all tends to obscure whatever nuances and subtleties were hiding below the surface. "A lot of it is perspective on who you are against the Other," notes Bill Gould, speaking more generally of San Francisco's place in American pop culture at the time. "If you're coming from somewhere in Middle America, this is all gonna kind of sound and look the same: greasy and dirty people with horrible looking hair and whatever. It all looks like one group of people. And then, when you get inside, you can start differentiating. 'This isn't like that at all.'"

---

79 Which is not to say that all of them would have resented the comparison. "We wrote them and visited them in San Francisco at their offices on Grove Street and met them, gave them cassettes, gave them eight-tracks, told them the concept of Three Day Stubble and everything," says guitarist Brently Pusser (who also played in the Heavenly Ten Stems). "And we just pretty much worshiped Ralph Records and what they were doing: Renaldo and the Loaf, Snakefinger, the Residents, and the Fred Frith records that came out on Ralph and the fact that he was playing with them." Also of note is the 1996 compilation *Eyesore: A Stab at the Residents* (Vaccination), which includes a handful of Bay Area bands (among them TFUL 282, Idiot Flesh, Primus, and Cracker) among the two dozen or so paying homage to the eyeballed ones.

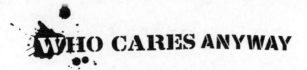

ACTING (OR NOT)

Of course, it's not as if every performer in early nineties San Francisco took the stage under a pseudonym or behind a mask. "You forget that the great majority of bands are not 'joke bands,' 'concept bands,' 'costume bands,'" notes Goode. "They're just four or five people that write songs and get up on stage and play those songs. And they don't try to pretend like they're somebody else."

Indeed, there were still plenty of singer-songwriters performing in the first-person, as it were, often to critical acclaim and at least modest commercial success: Mark Eitzel and American Music Club, Mark Kozelek and Red House Painters, Paula Frazer and Tarnation, Barbara Manning and her post-World of Pooh outfit the SF Seals. There was even some overlap between these ostensibly different spheres. For a time, the SF Seals' lineup included past or present members of both Three Day Stubble (guitarist Brently Pusser, drummer Melanie Clarin) and Caroliner (bassist Margaret Murray). Tarnation's first LP came out on Nuf Sed amidst a flurry of Caroliner LPs, as did records by countryish bands such as Virginia Dare and the Wandering Stars. And Amarillo's stable of eccentrics coexisted alongside more conventionally song-oriented bands such as Dieselhed and US Saucer.

Still, there was a fairly stark dichotomy in approaches, and Manning, for one, was cognizant of it. "I think Brently—who is by far one of my most favorite guitar players I've ever played with—was *acting* with me," she says. "And I think he was acting with Three Day Stubble. And I think with any other projects he works on, he *is* playing a role. And I don't think that's what I'm doing." She pauses to reconsider. "Or maybe I *am* doing it because I'm trying to be in the moment every day, every time I play a song. But the fact is that I'm playing *my* stuff. I'm speaking from my experiences rather than making up a story or even a whole backstory. And I think maybe that is the fork in the road where, in a way, I was not viewed as underground so much anymore when I went that direction. But I *was* still underground, absolutely. My music was not commercial—it wasn't played on commercial radio—and I made the decision to stay that way. I think that's why I retained the respect of my friends."

Ironically, her ex-bandmate Brandan Kearney was drawn to Manning in part

490

because of the drama he observed in her early solo performances. "She could be pretty confrontational and unpleasant or just weird," he says. "You never really knew what was going to happen—if she was going to get through the songs. I mean, it wasn't on the level of Flipper for that kind of thing, but it had a weird, erratic human drama to it. And whether that's 'acting' or 'not acting' is sort of beside the point, I guess. It was how she dealt with being on stage—how she dealt with presenting herself. So in a sense, it's acting.

"I'm not naive enough to think that anyone gets on stage and is themselves," he adds. "First and foremost, what would be the attraction to anyone? There's a lot of attraction in passing yourself off as *authentic*, as a sort of self-fashioning device, but I think most people go on stage because they either want to be something different or they want to be some sort of idealized conception of themselves, or they just want to experiment with what happens in the moment."

The flip side of the coin is that the bands who weren't "being themselves" on stage weren't necessarily just role-playing, either. "It definitely wasn't just acting," says Lara Allen about playing in Caroliner. "I felt like there was a lot of channeling going on. And maybe it was made up, but whatever. My mind goes to the church and how people get into this place where God is speaking through them. *I* don't know if God is speaking through them, but I know that it's pretty awesome to see.

"Part of what attracted me to Caroliner was this idea of being unclassifiable," she continues. "And of course, if somebody calls it 'costume rock' or 'art school band' or whatever—when I first heard something like that, it sort of hurt. It hurt because I thought, 'Oh, shit—this is *that*? That's not my experience of it.'"

Margaret Murray: It's something that's hard to understand, and I think it's hard for people to relax with it and just let it go. Because they want to be on top of it and in control of it, and they want to feel like there's an authentic singer-songwriter telling them what's up with life. I think that can get really tricky. But if you can really create a character and you can bring in some fictional elements to enhance the things that you want to bring out, I think it has a lot of power, and I think it is really authentic. And it helps when you're trying to communicate complex ideas to be able to create these characters to do them.

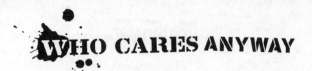

WHO CARES ANYWAY

Alan Bishop: One of the most effective ways to actually make statements about society—make political statements, make statements about justice on this planet—is to have a disguise or a mask or an altered personality. Because it *isn't* you—it's another entity. And that entity is expressing something that the audience will give the benefit of the doubt to listen to, because they're sort of hypnotized by the other character, as opposed to just some guy up there spouting some statement like "fuck the government" or whatever they're gonna say. So it's a powerful tool, and a lot of groups continue to use this. Back then, it was a viable way of performing.

Seymour Glass: Looking back, I suppose one thing all of these groups have in common is a predilection for upsetting the expectations of the audience. They certainly didn't have stylistic similarities. To me, it seems like the theatricality of it all is incidental. What they were doing sprang up as a reaction against music as an ego-worship delivery system.

"A DIFFERENT CONCEPT"

"A serious and good philosophical work could be written that would consist entirely of jokes."—Ludwig Wittgenstein

As with "costume rock," the terms "joke band" and "concept band" have been used at various points to describe (and deride) a number of San Francisco bands from the eighties and nineties, from Flipper and the Pop-O-Pies to the Zip Code Rapists and, for that matter, much of the Amarillo roster.[1] Yet as with the distinction between acting and non-acting, the distinctions implied by these

---

1   Yes, even Flipper. From an early review of *Live at Target*: "Flipper is one of the best bands going. Don't laugh. They may have started as a joke, but the joke has gotten more and more memorable, rhythmic, and good." *Damage*, September/October 1980, p. 38.

terms tend to break down upon closer inspection. After all, if there are joke bands, then there must be serious bands. And if there are concept bands, then there must be—what, exactly? As Kearney puts it, "Who the hell isn't a concept band? I mean, a band is kind of a concept from the get-go, by definition."

Admittedly, there are bands whose concepts are more explicit, more sharply honed, and more central to the overall experience—for example, Devo, Kraftwerk, or Laibach. As with Flipper and the Pop-O-Pies, these bands often toyed with and commented on the very idea of being a band and participating in the music industry. In their own way, the Zip Code Rapists and Amarillo were doing likewise with their odd juxtapositions of music and packaging, content and presentation. Yet the fact that they could be very funny in the process doesn't mean that it was all just a joke. Rather, they were playing around with ideas about authorship and authenticity ("cred," in early nineties parlance) that were often taken for granted in the realm of indie and alternative rock. In ZCR's case, at least some of this commentary was aimed at the ascendant indie rock aristocracy—the Pavements and Yo La Tengos of the world. At shows, Turkington would sometimes take to openly insulting other bands on the bill, to his partner's chagrin. "Gregg definitely did not have a large love for the indie rock that was going on at the time, whereas I liked a lot of it," admits John Singer. "It's still pretty easy to make fun of."

Turkington's persona in ZCR offers another example of the sometimes blurry distinction between acting and not acting. As he has done in the more recent *On Cinema* series with comedian Tim Heidecker, Turkington used his real name in the Zip Code Rapists but still performed in character. That said, it wasn't always easy to tell where the ZCR stage persona began or ended, and at times, he took advantage of this ambiguity to utter some forbidden truths. For example, there was the time when Matador Records invited the duo to review a batch of the label's new releases. While Singer was typically charitable in his assessments, Turkington was less so. (Sample: "Pavement targets those eager beavers who are too intelligent/skeptical to buy into the Smashing Pumpkins and Soul Asylum, but not intelligent/skeptical enough not to buy into Pavement.")

"I used to talk to these Matador people pretty often," recalls Kearney, "and a woman who worked there called me up while I was at HazTech. She said, 'Oh yeah, these great Zip Code Rapists reviews—they're really funny. That stuff

JAPAN OVERSEAS & AUGEN present

FAXED HEAD
&
ZIP CODE RAPISTS

from USA

FAXED HEAD

10/30 (MON)	OSAKA **MUSE HALL** 06-245-5389	
	with HANATARASH, MASONNA,	
	GEROGERIGEGEGE, SEKIRI	
11/1 (WED)	TOKYO **LOFT** 03-3365-0698	
	with VIOLENT ONSEN GEISHA,	
	YOSHIHIDE OHTOMO	
11/2 (THU)	TOKYO **SHELTER** 03-3466-7430	
	with MERZBOW, JON	
11/4 (SAT)	OSAKA **BEARS** 06-649-5564	
	with COA, ULTRA FUCKERS, MAJI,	
	THE PIRATE ACT (FAXED HEAD's UNIT)	

**TICKET
3300/3800**
(2800/3300 at Bears only)

**OPEN/START
6:30/7:00PM**
(6:00/6:30PM at MUSE HALL)

TICKET ON SALE
 TOKYO: PIA 03-5237-9999, LOS APSON 03-3369-9616,
  DISC UNION SHINJUKU 03-3352-2691
 OSAKA: PIA 06-363-9999, SAISON 06-308-9999,
  FOREVER RECORDS UMEDA 06-312-1663,
  TIME BOMB 06-213-5079

**10/31(TUE) 6PM
IN-STORE EVENT
at DISC UNION SHINJUKU**
(03)3352-2691

INFORMATION: JAPAN OVERSEAS/06-771-8573, AUGEN/06-312-1663

494

END THE GAME

Gregg says is so mean. But of course, he has to say that—he's got the persona to keep up. He has to say this negative stuff no matter how he feels about the music.' And I said, 'Well, yeah, he will sometimes do that even if it's something he actually loves, but when he says he really wishes that Matador had put out something good so he could express the side of himself that gets excited about good music, I think he's being sincere.' And there was just this long silence."

The occasion for those reviews was a 7-inch EP, *The Zip Code Rapists Sing and Play the Matador Records Catalog*, released in 1994. From a distance, it would have been hard to discern the intentions of any of the involved parties— including Johan Kugelberg, the Matador insider who produced the record. (It was released in Europe via the one-off label Ecstatic Piss, its name a spoof on Thurston Moore's Ecstatic Peace label.) And even by ZCR's peculiar standards, the record doesn't quite work. As Turkington admits in a spoken voiceover near the end of one song, "This record's no good … It's also not our idea." Much like a court jester hired to entertain the king, he was aware of the double bind inherent in making fun of Matador bands on what was essentially a Matador release: "No matter what we say, we're rendered impotent by the fact that they're sanctioning and paying for it."

Kugelberg, meanwhile, took it all in stride. "I think everyone was pretty amused," he says. Yet some of the bands that ZCR took aim at in those days were not so amused. At their shows, there was often heckling between band and audience—not all of it in jest. "For some of them, it wasn't good-natured at all—they really did despise us," says Singer. "Ira [Kaplan] from Yo La Tengo despised us and pretty much was telling everyone what a waste of time we were while we were playing."

Trey Spruance: Hipsters from New York would come to town and say, "You know what? I just really hate all this fuckin' Bay Area inside-joke shit." Like, people from Matador Records, who are maybe dealing with some San Francisco bands, and then they get exposed to what Gregg or somebody is doing, and they go, "Oh, I really hate all this snooty San Francisco shit." And that was always just really unfair to me. From what I could tell, these were like the least snooty people I'd ever dealt with. That was why I liked hanging around with them so much. They're anything but "snooty." And the humor is anything but inaccessible. But it

495

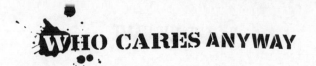

was always this thing about how they just liked to put out shit records—records that sound like shit—and they're trying to say "fuck you" by putting out crappy records. But that's never what it was.

John Singer: Let's put it this way: I *absolutely* understand the point of view because I had to hear it a lot, especially as a musician who's playing in other serious bands. Because—and this is purely in quotes—I do write "serious" songs that I do believe in. I do that, and I have done it for years and years. But coming from the point of view of somebody who does that, I absolutely understand why they hated it. Because in some ways, it feels like it's making fun of these serious bands. But at the end of the day, there's so many different ways to make music. I don't hate any particular kind. It's all good in some way. It seems kind of a waste of time, but I understand—when people tell me Amarillo's no good, I can understand why they're saying it.

Margaret Murray: Amarillo asked people to look at music in a really different way and to not be so rigid about it. I think it was confusing for people who just wanted just simple, angry answers in their music.

Brandan Kearney: I think it was cultural criticism, which, you know, could be funny, but it doesn't mean it doesn't have a point. I get that people don't necessarily like humorous music, and I get the idea that always having to have a punchline for a song can kind of be a copout. But I don't see Faxed Head or some of these other bands as being all that more conceptual than some of the people who were dumping on us for not being serious. It was just a different concept.

46

DISCO VOLANTE

Mr. Bungle spent most of 1993 and '94 out of the public eye, with the band members having scattered in several different directions while Mike Patton was off touring with Faith No More. They played a grand total of two shows as Mr. Bungle during this stretch: an improv performance with the Berkeley-based Splatter Trio in April of 1994 and another collaborative gig with the ROVA Saxophone Quartet (billed, somewhat pretentiously, as "Music for Saxophone Quartet and Rock Band") in June of that year. Behind the scenes, however, they were already laying the groundwork for their next album, even as the band members were busy branching out into an array of side projects and collaborations.[2] "We'd have months apart," explains drummer Danny Heifetz, "but me, Trevor, and Trey would all get together—at Mike's house, of all places. Because he had a little studio—like a little garage thing."

Nicknamed the Shotwell Bomb Factory, the makeshift studio doubled as a rehearsal space and even a temporary dwelling for Spruance.[3] "It was really ridiculously nice of him," says the guitarist, who was otherwise living out of his car during this period. "I was sleeping in that studio. When Mike was on tour, I would just be in that studio."

It was around this time that Spruance acquired an ADAT—a then-new piece of studio technology that allowed for the recording of eight tracks of digital audio

---

2 Dunn played upright bass in several jazz combos, including Junk Genius, the Graham Connah Sextet, and the West Coast version of John Zorn's Masada; Heifetz played drums in Dieselhed, the Pop-O-Pies, and Plainfield; and Spruance played guitar in Faxed Head, the Three Doctors, and Faith No More in addition to joining Heifetz in both the Pop-O-Pies and Plainfield.

3 The Shotwell Bomb Factory was also used for recordings by Faxed Head (*Necrogenometry*) and Dieselhed (parts of their self-titled debut album). Located at 307 Shotwell, the building was just a couple of blocks from 109-A Shotwell, where Bill Gould and Roddy Bottum lived during the early days of Faith No More.

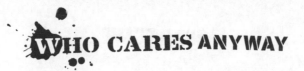

onto a VHS tape—and began experimenting with more advanced production techniques. "I started doing all kinds of shit," he says, "everything from techno music to death metal to just experimenting with ways of creating cutup compositions by recording as opposed to composing it. Which definitely found its way into Faxed Head. Sometimes Danny was helping me put weird ideas together because he was around. Some of it ended up being Mr. Bungle stuff—not very much of it."

"We'd be in there for way too long sometimes," remembers Heifetz. "We have all these ADAT recordings because we'd record a lot of the stuff we did just to get ideas down. If you've ever listened to the very, very end of *Disco Volante*— which is basically just us at band practice at Capp Street Studios—it's completely stupid because we'd get completely delirious and just do stupid shit. There'd be hours and hours of that kind of stuff from Shotwell." Bassist Trevor Dunn offers a similar recollection: "there are hours upon hours of documented experimental pieces, improvs, half-baked ideas, and crank phone calls. 'Rehearsals' usually started with a trip to the taqueria. Then we'd stay in the studio all night wasting time to the point of delirium."[4] And when they weren't "rehearsing" as a trio, Spruance was often in there by himself, tinkering with various combinations of synthesizers, sequencers, and MIDI controllers. "Trey was constantly working," remembers Heifetz.

"I mean, I had a lot of ideas—way, way, way too many ideas," says the guitarist. "I was filling up books with ideas. And then I did a whole bunch of techno—a whole bunch of weird techno shit. I had a friend—a guy who goes by the name of Adolf Nigger—from New Orleans. He's a Black guy, and when I met him, he was wearing a KKK robe—in New Orleans. This guy is a complete genius. We would talk about Penderecki, talk about Xenakis. He was really literate. He didn't have any money, didn't have a sampler, but he had all these amazing tapes—like cassette tapes of beats that he had assembled. And he would send me these cassette tapes of weird beats. So I would take these beats and add my own synthesizers and all this different shit. My plan was eventually to do a record with Adolf Nigger, but I just lost track of him."

Some of the techno elements would make their way onto *Disco Volante*

4   https://www.trevordunn.net/mr-bungle-disco

END THE GAME

(most notably on 'Desert Search for Techno Allah') as well as subsequent albums by Secret Chiefs 3 (whose 1996 album *First Grand Constitution and Bylaws* was recorded by the trio of Spruance, Heifetz, and Dunn and gives some indication of what their "delirious" Shotwell Bomb Factory sessions might have sounded like). For Spruance, the techno experiments weren't just a means of learning his way around the studio but also a response to the burgeoning rave scene in San Francisco. "I was doing sort of an echo of that rave culture," he says. "I was trying to anticipate the evil dimension of it. It started to kind of happen. There were a few months when Detroit techno went evil, but then it didn't stick, unfortunately. So, of course, my attention ended up going elsewhere."

"AIM TO CONFUSE"

As the material for *Disco Volante* started coming together, there was an unspoken consensus—at least within the band—that the album would not be a sequel to *Mr. Bungle*: no ska, no funk, and certainly no funk-metal. "I would say that after our first tour of '92, we were completely done with that music," Dunn told an interviewer years later.[5] The only holdovers from past setlists were Dunn's 'Platypus' and 'Everyone I Went to High School with Is Dead,' but even those were given radical makeovers during the course of the preliminary Shotwell Bomb Factory sessions. None of the other songs had ever been played live; instead, they were assembled from the ground up in the studio, with Dunn and Heifetz laying down the rhythm tracks first and the many layers of overdubs— guitars, synths, vocals, horns, orchestral percussion, and more—being added over the course of several months. ("I had no idea just how deep some of the parts were gonna go," admits Heifetz.)

The record label, meanwhile, was even further out of the loop. As Dunn later put it, "We never heard anything from [Warner Bros.], and by the time we were ready to record again, the entire staff had changed anyway, so nobody knew us.

5   "Mr. Bungle's *Disco Volante* 25 Years Later: Trevor Dunn Interview." https://www. fnmfollowers.com/post/mr-bungle-disco-volante-25-years-trevor-dunn-interview

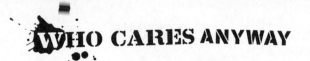

That was fine."[6] Essentially, the band had a major label recording budget without the commercial pressures that usually went along with being on a major label.[7] In that sense, they were in a very different position from Patton's other band. Yet there were some parallels between *Disco Volante*-era Mr. Bungle and *Angel Dust*-era Faith No More. Both albums were preceded by long layovers (three and four years, respectively), and both of them represented drastic departures that caught many old fans off guard.[8] Granted, Mr. Bungle didn't have the commercial profile of Faith No More, but they still had a rabid fanbase and an established template they could have adhered to if they'd been interested in pandering. As fan/critic Carl King would later summarize, "It would have been easy to continue to churn out 'Girls of Porn' for the rest of eternity and just go with the flow, pleasing the audience and quenching their adolescent thirst for songs about private parts. They had their lips around the teat. They could have really milked it."[9]

In this context, it can be tempting to think of *Disco Volante* as a deliberate attempt to defy expectations, especially given that one of the band's early mottos was "Aim to Confuse" (a phrase that appears in the liner notes to their first demo cassette). Yet it wasn't quite so simple. "We didn't have some manifesto on How to Destroy a Career in Music," explained saxophonist Bär McKinnon in an interview with King. "We did enjoy making people uncomfortable (the way young men are known to do) but even more we enjoyed cool sounds and music that wasn't either easily digested or understood."[10]

There was also the cumulative effect of four years' worth of living in San Francisco as opposed to Humboldt County, together with the spare time

---

6   https://www.trevordunn.net/mr-bungle-disco
7   According to Spruance, *Disco Volante* cost somewhere between $80,000 and $100,000 to record (http://carlkingdom.com/trey-spruance-mr-bungle-interview-1995). For the sake of comparison, *Angel Dust* cost around $150,000 (Harte, *Small Victories*, p. 208).
8   Jai Young Kim: "Everyone's like, 'Man, four years between making records—why so fuckin' long?' But then you live in San Francisco, and you kind of see what the deal is. At least I do, which is: since everyone is doing shit, they're kind of like asking friends 'come see me play' or 'come see my art opening' and 'come see me DJ.' And because everyone is doing that, there's just not as much time to work on your own shit."
9   Carl King, "An Open Letter to Estradasphere (and Their Fans)" http://carlkingdom.com/estradasphere
10   Carl King, "Awkward Interview with Bär McKinnon." March 2016. http://carlkingdom.com/awkward-interview-with-bar-mckinnon-of-mr-bungle

afforded by Patton's commitment to Faith No More. As Dunn put it, "We were hungry for different music and culture, and we used that time to research and absorb, individually finding things on our own as adults in 'the big city.'"[11] Spruance echoes this point: "We were listening to all these different records, getting hugely influenced by a lot of different music from a lot of different areas, most of it coming from just buying records. We just wanted to try to create compositions out of these different influences that we were hearing because it seemed like the right thing to do. That part of the Mr. Bungle thing has always been very pure, in the sense of being *not* affected by what our impact on anything is gonna be."

"A MIRACLE OF AN ALBUM"

The making of *Disco Volante* was not without its complications. For one thing, both Patton and Spruance had just returned from Woodstock, New York, where they spent the fall of 1994 working on Faith No More's ill-fated *King for a Day* ... Spruance, who was brought in earlier that year to replace Jim Martin, quit FNM shortly thereafter—right as Mr. Bungle was set to begin recording. There were logistical challenges, too, like finding a bandoneon player for the tango sections on Patton's 'Violenza Domestica.'

The actual recording sessions spanned two months and three different studios in town—Brilliant, Hyde Street, and Coast—not counting some earlier ADAT recordings from Shotwell Street. As Dunn recalls, "We would spend entire days and nights in [the studio] without seeing the sun." It all culminated in late January of '95 with a marathon mixing session that, perhaps fittingly, gave rise to one last bout of sleep-deprived delirium. "I remember it being like a thirty-hour session—like literally straight through," says Heifetz. "Because we just had to finish. And my ears were so fried, for the last four hours, I just said, 'I'm going upstairs. I can't do this anymore.'"

11 "Mr. Bungle's Disco Volante 25 Years Later: Trevor Dunn Interview." https://www.
fnmfollowers.com/post/mr-bungle-disco-volante-25-years-trevor-dunn-interview

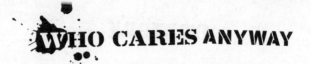

WHO CARES ANYWAY

The result was something to behold: sixty-eight-plus minutes of densely orchestrated, full-color sonic revelry, with liberal doses of organ, analog synth, death metal guitars, and exotic percussion (courtesy of Mills College professor and virtuoso William Winant). There are lengthy instrumental sections throughout, and on many tracks, the vocals are either wordless or sung in a foreign tongue.[12] While Patton delivers some showstopping performances—particularly on the fiendishly difficult 'Carry Stress in the Jaw' and 'Phlegmatics'—he does so as a member of the ensemble, not as the star of the band. As much as he remained the center of attention for fans and critics, he was very much a team player on *Disco Volante*. A glance at the songwriting credits bears this out: Spruance and Dunn share the bulk of the writing credits, followed by Patton; Bär even gets in on the action with the catchy, disturbing 'After School Special,' the only song to feature anything resembling a traditional verse-chorus structure.

Lyrically, *Disco Volante* is more mature and less scatological than its predecessor, although it does pick up where that album left off: with a song about Humboldt County casualties. The last song on *Mr. Bungle*, 'Dead Goon,' recounted the (apparently true) story of an acquaintance who died from autoerotic asphyxiation while hanging from his mother's pantyhose.[13] The first song on *Disco Volante*, the trudging 'Everyone I Went to High School with Is Dead,' is less explicit, speaking more to the general trend of violent, often bizarre deaths among the band members' former Eureka High classmates. That song, in turn, is bookended by 'Merry Go Bye-Bye,' which offers its own, more esoteric take on the theme of death, all the while veering from Beach Boys-style pop to a harrowing Slayer-meets-Merzbow interlude and back again. It's a fitting conclusion to a veritable labyrinth of an album.

---

12 'Violenza Domestica' is sung in Italian, 'Chemical Marriage' and 'Backstrokin'' employ wordless vocals, and 'Ma Meeshka Mow Skwoz' uses a made-up language. Meanwhile, sections of 'Desert Search' are in Arabic.

13 Remarkably, the protagonist of 'Dead Goon' wasn't their only acquaintance to meet such an ignominious demise. Sometime after the release of *Disco Volante*, Spruance's mother sent him the obituary of a former Eureka High classmate, one whom he'd last seen working at the twenty-four-hour supermarket in Arcata. "My ex-girlfriend tells me the story of what happened, which is that they found him dead on the floor of that market surrounded by porno magazines, with evidence that he had engaged in autoerotic asphyxiation. I mean, what the fuck is going on?"

END THE GAME

"AVANT-GARDE OR AVANT-GARBAGE?"

Disco Volante was released on October 10, 1995, to little fanfare outside of the band's (and Patton's) cult following. There were no singles or videos; evidently, Warner Bros. considered it unlikely that a video would actually receive airplay on MTV, given the channel's frosty reception for the 'Travolta' video four years earlier. ("That's the kind of support you can only get from a fungus-ridden jockstrap," Heifetz quipped at the time.[14])

The band did, however, take part in a newfangled form of promotion: a live internet chat on the fledgling America Online platform.[15] The internet was still new enough that most Americans (including this writer, an eighteen-year-old college freshman at the time) had yet to even access it. However, there was a cadre of devoted FNM and/or Bungle devotees who were ahead of the curve in this regard. In 1994, they set up a website, "The [UnOfficial] Faith No More Page (featuring Mr. Bungle)," along with a dedicated listserv, Caca Volante. A decade before social media, here was an early example of an online community, and a motley one at that.

Reviews poured into the Caca Volante mailing list as Mr. Bungle toured the US and parts of Canada in the fall of 1995. Opinions were split over the band's new direction and the dearth of older, more familiar material in the setlist. "I would say about eighty percent of the crowd was disappointed with this show," lamented one otherwise satisfied fan after a November 22 show at the Opera House in Toronto. "The thing is, the band is evolving and progressing and those people who like Bungle because of Faith No More or 'Girls of Porn' probably like them for the wrong reasons."[16] An earlier concertgoer was more blunt in admonishing her fellow fans: "BE PREPARED TO HEAR MUSIC WITHOUT WORDS. IT EXISTS…. If i sound bitter, it's because i just attended the chicago show shoulder to shoulder with 1,100 of the most intellectually

---

14 http://www.negele.org/cvdb2/index.php?id=2179
15 Also on the AOL Live docket that night were KISS, horror director Wes Craven, and professional wrestler Ted DiBiase. Newspaper readers were advised that in order to access these events, they would need "a computer, modem and appropriate software."
16 http://www.negele.org/cvdb2/index.php?id=558

challenged human beings i've ever had the displeasure of swapping sweat with."[17]

But it wasn't just casual fans who found themselves scratching their heads at what they were witnessing. "Avant-garde or avant-garbage?" began critic Katherine Monk's review of the group's December 13 performance in Vancouver. "After an hour of Mr. Bungle, the confusion remained—stuck in the quagmire of sound and noise that never once stretched out a hand ... Wearing executioner's black headgear, kabuki-meets-Mardi-Gras masks and intermittently insulting the audience verbally, Mike Patton (front man for Faith No More) and his entourage put on one of the weirdest shows this city has ever experienced."[18] Yet her initial bewilderment gradually gave way to a sort of grudging admiration as she conceded that "Patton and band are amazing players" and "there was something undeniably attractive in the swirling chaos."

Reviews of the album itself encompassed a similar range of reactions. Taken together, they read like the results from a Rorschach test. "If you listened to *Disco Volante* enough, you could probably grow to like it," wrote a reviewer in the *Allentown Morning Call*. "But by that time, it wouldn't matter—you'd be as whacked out as Mr. Bungle."[19] A writeup in the Madison *Capital Times* summarized the album as "Twelve 'songs' consisting of random, dissonant bursts of horns, organs, screams, explosions, and any other noise that might sound cool on a disc."[20]

The most violently allergic reactions, however, tended to come from the Patton-worshipping contingent, with several reviewers evidently longing in vain for a sequel to 'Epic' (a song recorded six years prior and, let us not forget, by a different band). A one-star review in the British metal magazine *RAW* sums up this sentiment: "If Faith No More's last two albums were increasingly lunatic attempts by Patton and Co. to distance themselves from the commercial sound that made them successful in the first place, then

17 http://www.negele.org/cvdb2/index.php?id=556
18 Katherine Monk, "Commodore Show Deliberately Bungled by First-Rate Rockers." *The Vancouver Sun*. December 15, 1995.
19 *Allentown Morning Call*. November 25, 1995.
20 *The Capital Times* (Madison, Wisconsin). November 16, 1995.

END THE GAME

Mr. Bungle is the sound of the singer's marbles spilling freely over onto the pavement."[21] *Kerrang!* offered a similar assessment: "*Disco Volante* revels in its utterly abstract, non-structured, chopping and changing styles like a radio dial being twisted continually. It deliberately messes with your head, which doesn't make for much fun after a while."

But the band members mostly took it in stride. "I think we all reacted differently to it," says Spruance of the dismissive reviews. "Trevor's reaction would be a little bit more to try to maintain what the musical merits of it are in the face of that. Patton's reaction would be, 'We just do what we do, and who cares what you say?' And mine would be getting some kind of a sick thrill of the whole thing—the fact that it's not being understood, it'll *never* be understood, and that it's really fun to do all of that different stuff. I definitely had this sense that by just not minding, and even enjoying, ignorant and ridiculous reactions, we'd form a really solid core of listeners—of honest listeners."

Coming at the tail end of the analog era, *Disco Volante* would have been virtually impossible to pull off without a major label recording budget. Even then, it took great daring and ingenuity to make it happen (whereas the same album today would be a relative cinch in Pro Tools, and less interesting for it). Sonically, *Disco Volante* was closer to Faxed Head or even Caroliner than it was to anything on MTV or alternative rock radio. Yet instead of merely reaching an audience of underground noise cognoscenti, it made it into the kinds of chain stores that could still be found in shopping malls circa the mid-nineties.

"That it was going out on a huge major label—that seemed totally ridiculous to us," admits Spruance. "You don't make any money on indie labels or on major labels, so who cares? It's not about that. We got this really major distribution. The only people who were listening to our music were sort of the fringes of the Faith No More crowd. And so you get all these kind of suburban kids and rural people. It becomes the weirdest thing on the shelf, all across the nation. So we picked up all these people who were alienated youth, or whatever, in these places that don't have access to Flipper and that

21 Review in *RAW* magazine, 1996. http://negele.org/cvdb2/?id=2148

505

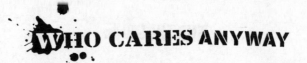

kind of shit. I think that was great, in a way. It's not a very good reflection of what we were doing, especially after *Disco Volante*, but I'm not complaining. There's a lot of opportunity for just really interesting social effects, and I think that that part of it turned out great."

47

CAROLINER IN JAPAN

Interviewer: A friend wanted me to ask, "Why are wild and crazy bands like Boredoms only coming from Japan and not the United States? Is it something about the Japanese culture?"

Eye: I say San Francisco … San Francisco is more … more, more crazy![22]

Although Caroliner wrote songs about 1800s America, their trip to Japan in late 1994 was akin to a spiritual homecoming. During their brief tour of the country, they shared the stage with the leading lights of the Japanese noise underground, including Merzbow, Masonna, and Boredoms (whom Caroliner had opened for a year earlier in San Francisco). Not only that, they were the headliner most nights.

At the time, both Caroliner and Boredoms were more popular with audiences on the other side of the Pacific than they were in their own hometowns. "Boredoms were almost completely unknown in Japan until they were asked to open for American indie stars like Sonic Youth and Caroliner Rainbow on their Japan tours in the early 1990s," writes David Novak, who spent time in both Japan and San Francisco during this era.[23] Meanwhile, Boredoms albums were being released in the US via a major label, Warner Bros./Reprise.

Caroliner didn't have major label distribution in Japan (or anywhere else, for that matter), but they did have a substantial cult following there. An illustrative anecdote comes from Deerhoof singer/bassist Satomi Matsuzaki, who first

22 *Browbeat*, Fall 1993. http://browbeat.com/browbeat01/boredoms.htm
23 Novak, "In Search of Japanoise: Globalizing Underground Music." In Alissa Freedman and Toby Slade (eds.), *Introducing Japanese Popular Culture*.

WHO CARES ANYWAY

CAROLINER ONSTAGE SOMEWHERE, CIRCA 1994. PHOTO COURTESY OF KRIS HENDRICKSON TESTANIER.

encountered Caroliner while still living in Tokyo: "Someone gave me a tape of this music by a band called Caroliner, which I later learned was part of a scene on the American West Coast. I got really interested in this and started asking around, 'What is this "American West Coast" music?'"[24] (After corresponding with Grux through the mail, she decided to visit San Francisco in 1994, and it was thanks to this visit that she wound up auditioning for and, ultimately, joining Deerhoof.)

There were other musical connections between San Francisco and Japan in those days. The Osaka-based Japan Overseas label released records by TFUL 282, Faxed Head, and Miss Murgatroid. The Tokyo-based noise-punk band Melt-

---

24 David Novak, *Japanoise: Music at the Edge of Circulation*, p. 79.

END THE GAME

Banana opened for Mr. Bungle on their 1995 US tour, and Mr. Bungle returned the favor by making a cameo appearance on Melt-Banana's 1997 album *Charlie*. Faxed Head and the Zip Code Rapists toured Japan together in 1995, and Three Day Stubble toured the country on two separate occasions. There was even a noise "tribute album" to Boredoms satellite band Hanatarash, curated by Seymour Glass and featuring a number of SF bands from the *Bananafish* orbit.

"People in the Bay Area and the Japanese noise musicians all knew each other," says Trey Spruance, "and there *was* a form of connection there on a fundamental sort of conceptual level. Not on a musical level at all. I mean, I never knew any Bay Area musicians that could really do Japanese noise or noise like that. It's *completely* different. I really learned how different it was when I went there."[25]

Regardless of the differences, Japanese audiences were especially fascinated with Caroliner. "It was out of control over there," recalls Brandan Kearney. "The reception we got over there—I think if Grux had played his cards right, he could have basically ruled the country for the next twenty years." Indeed, the tour was an unprecedented success for a band that was accustomed to operating on a shoestring budget. "We had made something like $40,000—just this *incredible* amount of money for such a marginal band," says Kearney of the Japanese tour. "When we got there, each of us got $900 spending money, which is just unheard of in my performing career, *period*. But in terms of Caroliner, you'd just fall over and faint to be handed money like that."

Alas, the tour also marked the beginning of the end for the last of Caroliner's peak-era lineups, due in large part to escalating tensions between Grux and Brandan. It began with a disagreement over how to apportion their earnings from the tour. "Our promoters just *completely* bent over backwards for us, and they got nothing in return," laments Kearney. "Grux was on his best behavior, we had a great time, everything was really fun, but one of the last nights, I was in

---

25 "What Trey says rings true," observes Seymour Glass. "To some extent, noise is an expression of frustration for the Japanese. Obligation to the group is one of the foundations of society there—whether it's your classmates, your coworkers, your family, your neighbors. The pressure to conform and do what is expected of you is ingrained, sort of how Americans have an ingrained optimism, the pursuit of happiness, and all that. I'd say American noise was more about hedonism and power."

Yokohama at this woman's house, and for some reason, I was the only one up. She came in and gave me an itemized breakdown of the money we made and where it all went, and how it was being allocated.

"So anyway, I'm looking down at the bottom of the list, and she and her counterpart in Osaka were taking home $24. I said, 'This is insane; this is completely unacceptable. I'm gonna talk to Grux, and you're gonna get more money than that—I guarantee it.' So I talked to Grux about it, and he was just like, 'You don't know the whole story; you don't know what's going on here.' 'Well, I know that they worked their asses off, and I know that the shows were a success. And I think you really need to pay them at least another couple hundred dollars each. In fact, you should probably give them a thousand each. But you gotta give them more than twenty-four bucks.' And he wouldn't do it."

Gregg Turkington: The thing with Grux is, he was becoming aggressively judgmental in an almost Tim Yohannan-like way. He was such a bully with everyone and just treating everyone so badly—after a while, we just decided to needle him about this stuff and call him on it. He'd be like, "Cars are stupid. You're an idiot for having a job and spending money on a car. You could live for free like me. You're stupid. Oh, could you drive me to this printing place and pick this stuff up?" "Uh, Grux—if I'm so stupid, are you sure you wanna get in my *stupid* car?"

David Katz: I remember coming back to California—maybe it was in 1990—and Brandan at that time kind of had Grux on a pedestal. He was like, "Grux is a genius! Grux has all this stuff, and it all means something, and it's all worked out and blah blah blah." But all I can tell you is, I came back years later, and it was like, Brandan and Grux won't speak to each other. And Grux had fallen from being the number one star in Brandan's universe to kind of the worst boil on the ass of whatever at the bottom of the pit.

Brandan Kearney: The band had started to get crazier and more difficult to deal with, or maybe I had. But the main thing was that these nice, honorable people were getting fucked over financially, as I saw it. And I felt like staying in the band was kind of rubber-stamping that—like I approved of it in some way. And if I'd had any gumption or been a reasonable person, I would've said as much. But instead, I didn't show up for a rehearsal one day and never went back. I never actually said anything.

Brandan was the first in a succession of departures, with drummer Phil Franklin and multi-instrumentalists Chris Cooper and Jess Goddard leaving soon thereafter.[26] "It was a really strong band right when I got into the band," recalls Kris Hendrickson, who joined after the Japanese tour. "But then, within a year, year and a half, it just kind of petered out. Everybody was gone." A 1995 tour of Japan with Faxed Head led to a similar falling out, only with Grux (er, Graph Head) leaving that band. (Ironically enough, it was Kearney who wound up replacing him in the role of Faxed Head's bassist.)

While Caroliner never officially disbanded, their albums and shows grew more and more sporadic over the years. Grux himself stayed busy, though, with such unmistakably Grux-ian side projects such as Spider Compass Good Crime Band (a solo keyboard/organ project) and Rubber-O-Cement (an unwieldy costumed noise duo). He also remained a central presence in the small but enthusiastic San Francisco noise scene, which congregated at under-the-radar events such as his regular "noise pancake" brunches on Sunday mornings. Well into the 2000s, he could still be found walking around the Mission or the Lower Haight, clad in homemade pants with stuffed animals and other foreign objects sewn into them.

"HE'S LIKE A CUBIST PAINTING"

As much as anyone described in this book, Grux embodies the archetype of the lifer—the uncompromising artist who dwells on the margins of society, refusing to assimilate. His former bandmates and collaborators remember him with a mixture of frustration and (sometimes grudging) admiration. Some remain on

---

26 All three of them moved to the New England area, with Franklin going on to play with the sprawling Sunburned Hand of the Man, and Goddard and Cooper starting their own duo, Fat Worm of Error, which was active through most of the 2000s.

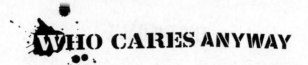

good terms with him, while others haven't spoken to him in decades. Trey Spruance is among those in the latter category, if only because of the falling out between Grux and the rest of the Faxed Head crew. "I knew so many people who had been on the Grux revolving door of friends—that once he shuts them out, that's it, and they're dead or whatever from that point on," he says. "And while some of those things were understandable, most of them were totally ridiculous."

Margaret Murray: I *love* Grux. I think he's wonderful. Of course, I'm multiple hundred miles away from him and haven't played in a band with him in forever.

Lizzy Kate Gray: I always had a sense of humor about Grux. I thought he was *incredibly* talented. I think he was conceptually talented and sort of literarily talented. And I *loved* his ink drawings. I would always try to encourage him, but he didn't want to go a regular route. But I think he might have had some success in the mainstream art world—galleries and stuff. And that's certainly not what he wanted.

He was enormously disciplined in being able to stay different. He really pared down his personality to sidestep a lot of things other people fell into. He wasn't gonna sell out. He refused to even be represented as a regular human being. He didn't seem to want to repeat *anything* that had ever been done before, which is a tall order. And he came pretty close to fulfilling it for a long time. Anything that seemed rock 'n' roll-like, like giving an interview, was just crass to him. You know, the "talking bull of the 1800s" or whatever—just the avoidance of the idea of modernity, of just how these rock bands are the latest new things: he subverted that by basing himself way in the past, in an imagined past. And his approach to absolutely everything was cultivated to be very different. Grux must have had an enormous amount of energy to keep doing that for so long and never relax into just being a regular human being.

Lara Allen: At that time, in Caroliner, what we were privileging—what we thought was this kind of moral high ground—was this anti-capitalist, anti-corporate-music-world, anti-fame thing. Those were kind of the selling points of Caroliner

END THE GAME

for me. But the irony is that the fame that Grux incurs from that kind of anonymity has, in and of itself, sort of become a trap.

Alan Bishop: There's never been an effort to popularize the band from the inside. They kept the record prices at $5 for so long. And they don't really promote themselves in a way that most bands would try to do. I mean, we were similar in that way, but they're, I think, as low profile as you can imagine.

Gregg Turkington: I really don't understand Caroliner's lack of popularity when you have things like, say, Jandek and other fuckin' things like this that people have championed. The fact that Grux wouldn't do CDs and things like that doesn't help, but you'd think the fact that Jandek won't do interviews or appear in public wouldn't help him, either.

Joe Pop-O-Pie: He is such a sarcastic, funny guy in his own way. One time, he saw me when I was temping in the early nineties, and I was wearing a suit, and I looked really square. I was coming home on BART, and he saw me there and said, "Hey Joe, I had this dream that I saw this guy, and he was wearing a suit, and he looked really square. And he looked just like you!" And then he just walked away from me.

But see, that's the way Grux is. He's like a Cubist painting. He talks to you like there's a couple of extra dimensions to the four dimensions that we live in, and he's existing in them at the same time. And I guess the whole point of that encounter when I was dressed in the suit was that he was talking to me as if I wasn't in that suit, and I'd just run into him some other place in my street clothes, and he was relating this incident of when he saw me dressed in a suit. He was mixing it all together so that it was happening at the same time. That was the joke there, and you had to think about it for a couple of seconds to get it.

513

48

LEAVING HAS HURT: THE BREAKUP, ABUNDANCE, AND BACK TO BASICS— "LIVE"

As Caroliner was quietly dissolving behind the scenes, the Zip Code Rapists were in the midst of staging their own very public breakup— even as Gregg Turkington and John Singer remained friends and co-workers in real life.

The duo went on the record about the breakup in a 1994 issue of the zine *Snipehunt*, which featured separate interviews with the (purportedly) feuding ex-bandmates alongside commentary by interviewer/accomplice Seymour Glass.[27] It is a classic piece of zine-writing: the attention to detail—down to the inclusion of some very authentic-looking legal documentation—is exquisite, and as far-fetched as it all seems, no one breaks character at any point. Turkington comes across as exceptionally petty and vindictive ("The more lawyers you have and the more lawsuits you've got going, the more likely you are to win out in the end"), while Singer is his usual calm and levelheaded self, sounding bewildered by his ex-bandmate's vitriol—and rightfully so. As Glass puts it in his introduction to the piece, "Why, one might ask, would such a two-bit act like the Zip Code Rapists, whose reputation rests on a handful of shows the quality of which is gauged in numbers of objects broken and thrown at the audience, subject themselves to the rigamarole of lawsuits and scandal?"

The article also announced the formation of two rival spinoff groups—

---

27 The interview was reproduced and included with the *Back to Basics—"Live"* LP, along with a reproduction of an official-looking legal document ordering Turkington to pay $4,825.37 in punitive damages for "malicious prosecution."

END THE GAME

Turkington's Three Doctors Band and "Therapist John's" Zip Code Revue—whose origins can once again be traced to the back offices of HazTech. "We used to have conversations about what indie rock bands would look like ten years down the road," explains Therapist John. "So the whole idea of Therapist John's Zip Code Revue was pretty much the idea that after the Zip Code Rapists, I would just be in a Motown and good-times rock 'n' roll cover band." In contrast, the Three Doctors Band would serve as an outlet for Turkington's (or, rather, the Turkington character's) delusions of grandeur: the hack bar band fronted by a washed-up has-been.

For his part, Singer recruited a cast of ringers—including TFUL 282's Mark Davies on guitar and vocals, Counting Crows' Charlie Gillingham on accordion, and American Music Club's Bruce Kaphan on pedal steel guitar—to help realize the concept. The Revue played just a couple of shows in SF (and one in the nearby town of Santa Rosa) during the summer of 1994 before heading into Tom Mallon's studio that September.

The resulting album, *Abundance*, features a mix of rebooted Zip Code Rapists songs ('Che,' 'Wired'), covers (country standard 'Making Believe,' Russ Saul's 'Leaving Has Hurt'), and a handful of new originals, highlighted by Davies's 'Doctors Are Spreading Disease.' The song is at once a coded rebuke of the rival Three Doctors and a dead-on send-up of the type of earnest country rock that was in vogue at the time, yet it also works on a purely musical level, with a rousing chorus that showcases Davies's underrated vocal chops. Speaking of coded references, Singer's 'If You Had My Eyes' makes use of a song title that was listed on the front cover of the Zip Code Rapists' *Sing and Play ...* LP, even though there was no such song on the actual record. Then there is the remarkably (some would say pointlessly) faithful remake of that album's 'Wired,' right down to the wailing, Turkington-esque lead vocals by US Saucer's David Tholfsen.[28] As humor goes, it is so subtle as to be undetectable by all but the most devoted ZCR fans.

---

28 Tholfsen was the main singer and songwriter in US Saucer, and like his bandmates Margaret Murray and Brian Hagemann, he was another Iowa transplant. "He was definitely the heart of that band," says Murray. "Some people heard in David this mocking thing because they couldn't believe that David's really like that. But that's how he sings: he wants to be a country singer. He was really hopeful that the song 'My Company Is Misery'—that Conway Twitty might hear it and want to record it. Conway Twitty! Not even like someone really huge and fancy."

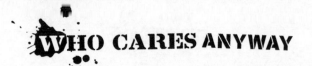

"It was a pretty big inside joke," admits Davies. "People who were into the Zip Code Rapists thought it was hilarious and really were into it, but if you weren't into that band or didn't know anything about the mythology of the breakup, I think it would be kind of lost on you. So we didn't expect much of anyone to really respond to it." Ironically, the album did garner some positive reviews based strictly on its musical merits. Writing in the zine *Surrender*, Brian Doherty called *Abundance* "a sensitive and beautiful take on San Francisco indie neo-country, maybe the only record on Amarillo that could be appreciated by someone without a sense of humour."[29] Meanwhile, Greg Prato—the same writer who nominated *Sing and Play* as a candidate for "worst album of all time"—called it "a sadly overlooked debut" before adding, "Fans of classic rock sounds, take note." Go figure.

BACK TO BASICS

Whereas *Abundance* cloaks its conceptual shenanigans beneath smooth production and professional musicianship, the Three Doctors Band's *Back to Basics—"Live"* purposely calls attention to its own shortcomings. The front cover features a poorly lit photo of a woman's underwear-clad behind, along with a typo in the band name (which appears, in iron-on letters on the aforementioned underwear, as "The Three Doctor's Band"). Equally garish is the back cover, which includes an unctuous, typo-riddled dedication from Turkington. Set in pink type against a turquoise background, the dedication reads, in part:

Working and sweating with great, soulful musicians like Trey (Faith No More), Brandan (Caroliner), and Margaret (who you may know from her work with U.S. Saucer) has been a "dream-come-true".... These last 2 months have involved hard work, sweat, and dedication but the rewards are obvious. An idea is 1% inspiration and 999% perspiration; The Three

---

29 *Surrender: A Journal of Ethics*, No. 5, pp. 13–14.

END THE GAME

THERAPIST JOHN'S ZIP CODE REVUE, AS ENVISIONED BY BRANDAN KEARNEY.

Doctors have produced that 99% both within themselves and me. Now its your turn!

The reference to Faith No More, while true, was also rather gratuitous (and purposefully so). Spruance had just recently joined FNM, and like the early, pre-Jim Martin guitarists, he was more of a short-term contractor than a full-fledged band member. But Turkington—or at least the Turkington character in this semi-fictional realm—was not one to quibble over such minutiae. Indeed, when the group played the Cafe This in nearby Santa Rosa (the only venue they ever played), they proudly mentioned the Faith No More connection on the flyer.

All of which is to say that there was a lot of subtext to go along with the musical contents of the *Back to Basics* LP: nine tracks, eight of them covers, and most of them recorded live in the studio with only minimal overdubs. To some observers, including prolific internet critic Mark Prindle, the actual music was mostly beside the point. "The joke is conceptual," he wrote in his review of it. "Turkington claims in the liner notes that his band will be experimenting and not living in the past, but then the record itself is a bunch of shitty cover tunes."[30] That's a bit harsh, though. There *is* one original song ('Three New Doctors,' a rewrite of ZCR's 'The Three Doctors'), and most of the cover tunes are well suited for the band's unusual lineup (three electric guitars and no rhythm section). As befitting a group with three members from the HazTech team, several of the cover songs are taken from vanity pressings, including 'Leaving Has Hurt' (also covered by the Zip Code Revue), the remarkably creepy 'Phobia' (sample lyric: "I envision you as naked / Is that why you're so scared?"), and the even creepier 'My Leviticus.' Parts of the record are admittedly pretty obnoxious, like the scowling cover of the Monkees' 'Listen to the Band' (itself a "cover" of the Zip Code Rapists' similarly caustic version on an earlier record) and the extended live version of 'Sweet Caroline,' which includes a cringe-inducing audience participation section in the middle. But other parts are—don't laugh— unexpectedly poignant, particularly the heartbroken 'Leaving Has Hurt' and the countryish 'By Special Request' (another of the vanity pressing covers).

The critical consensus, such as it was, held that *Back to Basics* was a mess of an album released by a bunch of smart-asses who didn't expect or even want people to like it. *Trouser Press* describes it as "an elementary effort that sounds like one talentless teenager's bedroom mirror rehearsal session, and is about that much fun to endure."[31] Prindle, who gave it a "low 6" out of 10, added, "The liner notes are the best part of the album."[32] And an exasperated DJ at WXYC-Chapel Hill in North Carolina (where this writer worked in the late 1990s) concluded an in-house review of the LP by writing, "It's funny because it isn't—or is it?"

From a more detached perspective, these assessments are understandable. Turkington comes across as awfully self-confident for a lead singer with such imperfect pitch. Meanwhile, the mere sound of three electric guitars (sans rhythm section) gives the proceedings an impoverished feel: it's as if the front man wanted to hire a full band but either couldn't find one or couldn't afford it. There are also awkward gaps between several of the songs (which, like the typos and misprints on the packaging and label, were either intentional or left there on purpose). As with the first Easy Goings 7-inch and the Zip Code Rapists LP, *Back*

30 http://www.markprindle.com/three.htm
31 https://trouserpress.com/reviews/zip-code-rapists/
32 http://www.markprindle.com/three.htm

END THE GAME

THE THREE DOCTORS. L-R: BRANDAN KEARNEY, MARGARET MURRAY, TREY SPRUANCE, GREGG TURKINGTON. PHOTO COURTESY OF G. TURKINGTON.

to Basics presents the listener with an existential conundrum—namely, "Why does this record exist?"

Mike Hickey: I mean, right there, *that* was a *monster* record for me. It was *sicker* than the Zip Code Rapists, in a way. And a big part of it was the liner notes [a reproduction of the *Snipehunt* piece on ZCR's breakup]. That was just *so funny* to me. To me, that was striking gold in terms of figuring out the thinking that was going on behind this. I don't know; it was just weird hearing Trey, who I knew was this brilliant, sort of high-minded musician, doing this stuff with Gregg Turkington. It just added to the insanity and the whole "What the fuck is this?" feeling. So *Back to Basics—"Live"* was just a monster record for me, a huge piece of the puzzle.

Margaret Murray: Nowadays, people do this all the time: people will make up a song and put it up on Soundcloud. We were doing this without the path to do

519

that. We were just sitting around making jokes all day at HazTech: "Let's release a record; let's press this into vinyl." I mean, it meant a lot to us to express this kind of stuff, but I don't think people really did that musically at the time.

The unspoken theme of the record is failure, which manifests itself on multiple levels, from the lyrics of several of the songs to the pathetic album art to the eventual fate of the album itself. *Back to Basics* sold so poorly—even by Amarillo's modest standards—that Turkington wound up depositing boxfuls of it directly into the dumpster just a few years later. Other copies were sold at a discounted price, but evidently not that many. ("More of them were distributed to thrift stores than were sold—that's a fact," notes Kearney.)

That said, *Back to Basics* doesn't wallow in failure; it celebrates it, or at least makes peace with it. In essence, the record is a tribute to the hopelessly obscure vanity pressing acts that the band members (minus Spruance) had spent so much time obsessing over at HazTech. These mythical figures—the Russ Sauls and James Lowrys of the world—likely dreamed of hit records and successful showbiz careers, and in that sense, they failed. Yet, in another sense, they succeeded in ways they couldn't have imagined.

Brandan Kearney: I think that record's entirely unlistenable. But I have to say, it sounds like you're approaching it kind of in the spirit that we were approaching the stuff that inspired us to *do* the record. Because we were at HazTech listening to these vanity pressings, and on the surface, they're horrible, but there just ends up being this compelling thing about it. Where I don't get it is, we were being these completely cynical, contrived, calculating goons, whereas the people that we were actually listening to in order to be inspired to do that seemed to be—at least in some cases—totally sincere.

Mike Hickey: To me, it's kind of a strange sort of circle here. Because, unbeknownst to me at the time, they were influenced by this entire scope of music that I didn't know existed. You know, I was a fucking kid living on a farm in Canada. I had no *clue* what was influencing these people. I couldn't imagine who was making these records, and who the intended audience was, and what the idea was. I didn't know about vanity records. I know those guys now, and I

END THE GAME

know the way they reacted to these vanity records, like, "What the fuck is this?" It's like my reaction to *their* records.

Brandan Kearney: Gregg and I have both been digging through these thrift stores since we were little kids. That feeling where you get some record, and you like it, but you have absolutely no idea what's going on with it—or maybe you don't like it, but you have no idea what's going on with it, and it's fascinating. I think that's real interesting when that happens. That's one of the things that got us so whole-hog into the vanity pressings. You just have *no idea* where these people are coming from, and you've just got this weird kind of artifact.

Gregg Turkington: Our failure was authentic. The Three Doctors records were a self-fulfilling prophecy that sold very, very poorly—and as individuals, our personal "stock" in the world of indie rock suffered because of them. But we met a few folks who were tapped into the particular aesthetic that we were mining and who were thrilled to find kindred spirits out there ... which is really the best thing you can hope for.

Trey Spruance: If you know what it feels like to fail horribly, and if you know what it feels like to be ashamed and embarrassed in front of people for how bad you are, then you get practice at it. And if you have practice at it, then you can do it with some kind of perspective on it when it actually happens. All I know is that I've had that feeling playing shows with Gregg because he's an old master at doing that. It was, in a certain way, traumatizing, but more than anything, really liberating—to be standing there, forced to cut your ties with any sense of being able to save face.

Brandan Kearney: I was driving around the country a lot, state to state and everything, and I'd just leave copies of the LP at thrift stores. And Gregg was doing the same. We'd have a trunk full of these records and just put them in these thrift store bins in, like, some horrible town in southern Idaho with a population of a hundred people. And just the thought of some kid thinking, "this record looks weird," and going home and listening to it and trying to make some kind sense out of it: that's when the whole project suddenly seems totally worthwhile—like probably the best thing I've ever done in my life.

521

49

"WHAT IF YOU HAVE A DREAM AND NO ONE'S INTERESTED?"

In 1995, the Zip Code Rapists "reunited" to make a new EP, *94124*, thus completing the saga of ZCR's breakup and reunion. This was followed later that year by a second Three Doctors LP, the faux-mystical *Archaeolgy* [sic] *of the Infinite*. As with *Abundance* and *Back to Basics*, both of these records came out on Amarillo—which, during the same stretch, also produced new recordings by the New Session People (an impossibly obscure tribute album to easy-listening organist Ken Griffin), Totem Pole of Losers (creepy novelty songs that fall somewhere in between the Easy Goings and Zip Code Rapists, with personnel to match), and a hapless stand-up comedian by the name of Neil Hamburger.

It was the last of these acts that would wind up becoming Turkington's crossover success, with over a dozen records, countless tours, and eventually a major motion picture, *Entertainment*, to his name. Ironically, only one of Hamburger's records—1994's *Looking for Laughs* 7-inch—actually came out on Amarillo.[33] Nonetheless, both the Neil Hamburger character and the bleak, loserish aura he conveyed were thoroughly in keeping with the Amarillo aesthetic. To wit, the back cover of *Looking for Laughs* displays a grueling schedule of supposed tour dates (sample entries: "Sept 2, 6: Gary, IN"; "October 1, 2: Coalinga, CA"); the B-side, which is ostensibly an interview with the comedian about the making of 'Looking for Laughs' (all five minutes of it), gradually reveals itself to be a paid promotional message for the Iowa Council for the Prevention of Incontinence.

---

33 Subsequent reissues of *Great Phone Calls* have been credited to Neil Hamburger, but the character only appears on a few of the calls, and the comedian's name doesn't appear on the original record cover.

END THE GAME

At the time, Hamburger wasn't actually doing live performances, let alone touring. The laugh track and other "audience sounds" on *Looking for Laughs* were harvested from other comedy records and spliced together by Turkington and co-producer Trey Spruance (who also assisted on Hamburger's debut album, 1996's *America's Funnyman*). The plotlines that emerge over the course of Hamburger's early albums rely heavily on the "reaction" of the imaginary audience, which consists largely of groans, heckles, and awkward silences, with the occasional laugh mixed in (usually in response to the inexplicably popular "zipper schtick"). On *Raw Hamburger* (1998), we hear Neil attempting to rationalize his surprising turn to X-rated humor: "If it offends anybody, well, I guess that's the point—is to get some laughs. [*Awkward silence.*] But we can always do something else as well." On *Left for Dead in Malaysia* (1999), the comedian finds himself in front of an audience that doesn't even speak English. He tries to go on with the show, but before long, the set devolves into a sort of onstage therapy session, with the comedian baring his soul to an audience that can't understand a word he's saying. In the process, he reveals something of his (or is it Turkington's?) worldview:

> I've long believed that if you persevered at your dream long enough, it
> would eventually come true. But here's a question I've often asked: What
> if someone's talent was at something that no one was interested in?
> They could conceivably persevere forever and get nowhere. Sometimes
> I've felt this sort of pointless struggle was my calling in life.

Turkington himself echoed this point years later in an interview with the *Washington Post* occasioned by the release of *Entertainment* in 2015:

> Often people in show business who win awards say, "I just believed in
> myself and followed my dream, and if you do that, these great things will
> happen to you." It ignores the fact that thousands follow their dreams
> just as passionately, but it doesn't work out. What if you have a dream
> and no one's interested?[34]

---

34 This remark, in turn, echoes a line from 'His Room,' the James Lowry song covered by US Saucer: "If he ever had a dream / No one knew if it came true."

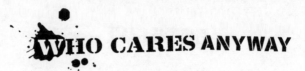

Turkington is alluding not only to Neil Hamburger, the fictional character, but also to the star-crossed, woe-begotten entertainers who inspired that character—from Frank Sinatra, Jr., to Russ Saul to Patrick Miller. ("The live show—when it was stripped down to just him with the backing tapes, it really had the Neil Hamburger/Frank Sinatra, Jr., vibe that I really like," he says of Miller's Minimal Man."Just one lonely, balding man up there.")

YOU GAN'T BOAR LIKE AN EABLA WHEN YOU WORK WITH TURKRYS

As Hamburger's career was taking off, Amarillo was winding down. The label closed shop in 1999, by which point Turkington had already moved to Sacramento. Brandan Kearney, who began winding down his Nuf Sed imprint a couple of years earlier, followed suit and moved to the sleepy state capital not long after his friend and former HazTech co-worker.

For Kearney, the Three Doctors' *Archaeolgy of the Infinite* was one sign that things had run their course. "To an extent, we were responding to this whole dreary scene surrounding private-press psych LPs, where people would clean out their bank accounts to own or reissue some lost album with a couple tracks of bumbling fuzz guitar. Like, 'Okay, that crowd fuckin' hates us, so let's do one of these stupid homemade psych records and dare them not to like it.' I love that record, but in retrospect, the one bad part of it was realizing, 'Ah, I did this in order to communicate—even in the most subtle, non-explicit way—with a bunch of freak scene collector snobs.' That's not really what you want inspiring you."

It wasn't just the HazTech crew that felt it was time to move on. By the late nineties, the once-bustling orbit that encompassed TFUL 282, Caroliner, Lowdown Studios, *Bananafish*, Nuf Sed, and Amarillo had largely dissipated. Along with the usual factors—strained relationships, creative burnout, the creeping realities of adulthood—there were other, more fundamental changes that were beyond anyone's immediate control. These included changes in the way music was recorded (thanks to Pro Tools) and distributed (thanks to the

END THE GAME

Internet). Last but not least, San Francisco itself was rapidly changing, with rents rising and the first dotcom boom on the horizon. A gradual exodus ensued.

Barbara Manning: I got there in '86, and I left in '98. By '93, I was so busy with amazing opportunities. And then by '98, it was like, "Oh my god, I'm in poverty, and I've lost my place to live, and I don't know what to do." It's amazing. I thought it was gonna last forever. By '95, I thought that this is what my life was going to be like, and then three years later, I'm like, "Holy crap." It *doesn't* last.

Matt Hall: Throughout the nineties, I remember everybody complaining about gentrification. It's sort of hard to believe that it's actually continued and gotten even crazier since I left there. A lot of the practice spaces started closing. Before I left, it seemed like a lot of people were either starting to leave town or decide that music was getting to be more of a hassle than it was worth. You'd play a show and get back at three in the morning, and there's no parking, so you have to drive around for another forty minutes.

Greg Freeman: When I started Lowdown Studios, it was *so* cheap. There was no such thing as Pro Tools. If you had music and you wanted to make a record, you had to go to a studio. I was into the idea of people who were doing cool stuff—working with *them*. It was really great. And then, as time went on, things kind of changed, and that whole music scene just sort of evaporated, for many reasons.

Rebecca Wilson: When you're young and broke, you're like, "Oh, this is fun!" But then you start getting older, and you start freaking out. Like, "I can't handle livin' in a fuckin' apartment with a bunch of people I barely get along with! And what am I gonna do in the future?"

Mark Davies: There are certain people who will continue in that vein throughout their whole life, but most people have a few years of this burst of creative energy, and then you get older, and you don't have as much of that energy or drive anymore, and it just kind of naturally peters out.

I keep wanting to do stuff musically, and I cling to the hope that I will continue to do that in the future. But it's just a natural part of aging, you know? You don't

525

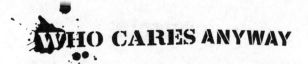

have that same drive anymore. And it takes a lot of energy and drive to keep a band together, with all the personalities and just the shit work that needs to be done and all that crap. So I think it's pretty natural that things peter out in that way.

"OH MY GOD-WHAT ARE YOU SELLING?"

Davies was one of several key players from early nineties San Francisco to essentially retire from the music business and move on to a new chapter in life. His bandmates in TFUL 282 did likewise, as did the HazTech crew (with the exception of Turkington). There have been occasional reunions, including a 2011 appearance by the Thinking Fellers at All Tomorrow's Parties (where they were invited to perform by festival curators Animal Collective). The Zip Code Rapists reunited for a couple of shows in 2005 and again in 2015, partly for the hell of it and partly because that's just the kind of thing that old, washed-up bands are supposed to do.

By and large, though, there has been relatively little in the way of organized nostalgia for this particular slice of the San Francisco underground. Perhaps it's because the bands involved were so different from each other, which meant that there was no "San Francisco sound" to speak of in those days (unlike, say, Seattle). There's also the fact that none of them fell in line with the prevailing trends of the time, whether that meant grunge, angst-ridden alternative rock, or insouciant indie rock. For a while, it seemed like everywhere you turned, there was another four-letter band: Bush, Hole, Tool, Lush, Live, Cake. Against this backdrop, gleefully weird monikers such as Caroliner Rainbow Scrambled Egg Taken for a Wife or Thinking Fellers Union Local 282 seemed downright perverse. More to the point, none of the San Francisco bands discussed here struck the requisite Gen X pose as it was being defined in the media—a pose that fell somewhere between sullen detachment and feigned boredom.

"Back in the early nineties, when the underground was becoming the mainstream, all of these people were so *desperate* to be considered cool," recalls Mike Hickey. "They wanted to *look* cool, *sound* cool, be liked by cool people, play in the cool towns. You can name any band—Sonic Youth and everything that followed suit—it was all just drenched with 'coolness.' And the thing that

END THE GAME

attracted me about these Amarillo bands and Mr. Bungle's *Disco Volante* is that they had *no fucking interest* at all in being cool and were pissing and shitting all over these quote-unquote 'cool' bands. *Mocking* them publicly. Which was *sacrilege*. You did not do that back then!"

There were others who, while not openly mocking the new indie/alternative aristocracy, were at least skeptical about where it was all heading. Barbara Manning, for example, recalls turning down an offer to appear in *Vanity Fair* at one point during her tenure with Matador:

> I was offered … not an interview, actually. It's a picture where you're wearing certain clothes, and you're sitting, looking out a window or something, and then they'll have like a paragraph. Half the information is about you; half is about what you're wearing. And I said "no." But I had seen many people do it. Jon Spencer did it. I think Cat Power did it. There were quite a few artists from Matador who did it. But I was just like, "No. *No!*" I would be laughed at by my friends in San Francisco because that's exactly what we didn't like! That's when you start going, "Oh my god—what are you selling?"
>
> Another time, I was invited to be interviewed by *Spin*, but it was by another girl artist who I didn't respect. And I didn't wanna do it, because … I don't know; it just seemed *smarmy*. It wasn't very realistic to me. So those two things, I remember very specifically saying "no," and I think soon after that was when I was let go.

In an age of personal branding strategists and social media influencers, this sort of principled stance seems almost quaint. At the time, though, there was still a sense of "us vs. them," even if the battle lines were getting increasingly blurry. "I mean, we weren't in any way a commercial band," says Lara Allen of Caroliner, "but the idea of even, say, *doing* a commercial or having your music sold—that was just *disgusting*. You were *slime* if that would have been what you had done. And now … hell, I mean, people line up to audition. They would *love* to have their music on a Google commercial or whatever it is. But that was very different then, in that scene. Being commercial versus being in the underground. And *that's* what being underground was."

THE END?

"The end of history will be a very sad time. In the post-historical period, there will be neither art nor philosophy, just the perpetual caretaking of the museum of human history. I can feel in myself, and see in others around me, a powerful nostalgia for the time when history existed."
—Francis Fukuyama[35]

In the grand narrative of punk, Nirvana's breakthrough was its own End of History. It may have been coincidence that this breakthrough happened within a couple of years of Fukuyama's notorious speech (and while the collapse of the Soviet Union was in its final stages), but in each case, the initial sense of triumph was accompanied by a hollow feeling, a sense of "What do we do now?" As Cobain biographer Michael Azerrad put it a decade later in *Our Band Could Be Your Life*, "The revolution had been largely successful, but as it turned out, the struggle was much more fun than the victory."

This is not to suggest that alternative/indie music fans were sitting around reading Fukuyama in between MTV Buzz Bin videos—only that there was a palpable shift in the zeitgeist. Whether geopolitically or culturally, the consequences of this shift would take some time to play out. Yet, with the benefit of hindsight, it's safe to say that the early 1990s marked the last real aftershock of the cultural upheaval that began a decade and a half earlier with punk. Relative to this narrative, everything that came afterward—from the mainstreaming of indie pop to the retro stylings of the White Stripes, the Strokes, et al.—was, in a very real sense, "post-historical." It was a state of affairs that Mark Fisher eloquently captured in his 2009 book *Capitalist Realism*:

35 Fukuyama, "The End of History." *The National Interest*, Summer 1989.

END THE GAME

"Alternative" and "independent" don't designate something outside mainstream culture; rather, they are styles, in fact the dominant styles, within the mainstream. No-one embodied (and struggled with) this deadlock more than Kurt Cobain and Nirvana. In his dreadful lassitude and objectless rage, Cobain seemed to give wearied voice to the despondency of the generation that had come after history, whose every move was anticipated, tracked, bought and sold before it had even happened. Cobain knew that he was just another piece of spectacle, that nothing runs better on MTV than a protest against MTV; knew that his every move was a cliché scripted in advance, knew that even realizing it is a cliché....[36]

Cobain must have felt this double bind more acutely than most, given the messianic status that was foisted upon him. Nonetheless, it was the same *kind* of dilemma that, say, the Zip Code Rapists encountered in making fun of Matador Records on Matador's dime or that Faith No More confronted in mocking MTV tropes in their own MTV videos (for example, with 'We Care a Lot' and later 'Everything's Ruined'). It's the kind of dilemma that every self-aware artist in this era had to face up to in one way or another. Short of exiting the music business (or, worse, committing suicide), it was a dilemma that didn't seem to offer any viable solutions. In light of this Catch-22, the best one could do was have some fun with it, as the Zip Code Rapists did with their mock breakup. And if one were going to commit suicide, better an artistic one like *Back to Basics* than the alternative.

Alan Bishop: I like the fact that back in the days of whatever people would call the late seventies or early eighties, whether it's punk or—I wouldn't even say "new wave," because that brings on other connotations that are less interesting to me, but experimental music or this kind of new paradigm of weird alternative directions in music, you had so many different ideas going on, and it was all sort of not available to everybody else unless you really

---

36 Fisher, *Capitalist Realism: Is There No Alternative?* p. 9.

committed to it. So everyone else was an outsider. You're either in or you're out.

Margaret Murray: It was really amazing to those of us who actually liked it. But in a broad way, people didn't really care, and they often didn't quite get it, either. It was a pretty small group of people that got it. But I think that going through that with that group of people made us feel okay about the way our creativity worked. All of a sudden, it's like I could say something, and Brandan would get it, and Gregg would get it, and vice versa. We all understood each other. And when you always feel alienated and outcast, it's pretty amazing to suddenly have even ten or fifteen people who get what you're doing and want you to do more of it and find it thrilling.

Brandan Kearney: Some of the stuff around '91—I mean, God knows, my own personal life was a nightmare, but in general, it was kind of idyllic, in terms of just having, say, fifteen to twenty people who have similar senses of humor and a similar aesthetic. Just like parties at the Thinking Fellers' house, and barbecues, and everyone's always doing stuff. It was very, very social, and there were always baseball games and brunches and—you know, all that stuff was really nice. But it's not maintainable, I don't think. If the history of all these things all through the twentieth century is any indication, there's this kind of centrifugal force, and you can't maintain that stuff.

Barbara Manning: I think that it *was* a community, and that was because people could afford to live in San Francisco and work there. And if you have a community of sort of similar aged people with similar flavors of taste, then you're gonna end up having an art community.

Margaret Murray: You see these scenes crop up, and then they pass like weather systems. They'll crop up in Chicago; they'll come up in Akron, Ohio; they'll happen in Athens, Georgia; in Denton, Texas. There'll be things that suddenly appear—they'll bubble up—because of some magic coincidence. Somehow a bunch of people get together, or they bounce off of each other like electrons in an atom, and things happen that are really interesting. But it's not

END THE GAME

in their nature to stay. They just … they dissipate, but they leave an effect on everyone who was a part of them.

50

WHO CARES, ANYWAY?

History, as they say, is written by the victors. Yet when it comes to punk and its progeny, the very idea of victory is turned on its head. ("To succeed in conventional terms meant that you had failed on your own terms; to fail meant that you had succeeded.") What this means is that standard benchmarks like record sales and chart positions are mostly irrelevant, as are endorsements and testimonials from the Dave Grohls and Billie Joe Armstrongs of the world. And as far as accolades go, designations like "Worst Band in California" (the Pop-O-Pies) and "Worst Album of All Time" (ZCR's *Sing and Play the Three Doctors*) are more reliable indicators than, say, Grammy awards or Rock & Roll Hall of Fame inductions.

Still, it seems like there should be some sort of moral to this whole story, especially given the number of casualties sustained along the way. Jon Savage provides a good starting point when, at the conclusion of *England's Dreaming*, he singles out punk's "gleeful negation" as a valuable trait. It is an apt term, internal contradictions and all. Admittedly, that book focuses on London and the Sex Pistols, and it ends just as the events in this book were getting underway. Even so, there are connections between that story and this one, including the various subplots involving the Pistols and Negative Trend, PiL, and Flipper. Certainly, "gleeful negation" could describe a decent share of Flipper's lyrics: anyone familiar with *Album* (Flipper's, not PiL's) can probably hear Bruce sneering out the words "*nothing, nothing, nothing, nothing*" right about now. The same goes for songs by Faith No More ('We Care a Lot'), the Pop-O-Pies ('Fascists Eat Donuts'), and the Zip Code Rapists ('Fuck a Duck,' and basically any of their live recordings). And likewise for several of Club Foot's otherwise cryptic slogans: "DESTROY WHAT DESTROYS US … "; "NOT A NEGATION OF STYLE, BUT A STYLE OF NEGATION … "; "WHERE EVERYTHING IS BAD, IT MUST BE GOOD TO KNOW THE WORST … "

END THE GAME

There was also the self-negation practiced by so many of the artists, which wasn't always so gleeful and at times led to outright tragedy. It sometimes took the form of outright self-sabotage (the Sleepers, Flipper) but also manifested itself in self-criticism (Flipper again), aggressive obscurantism (Caroliner), and preordained failure (the Three Doctors). Whether it was a legacy of punk or something specific to San Francisco in this era is hard to say, but there was a tendency to seek out the path of most resistance—a sense that if you weren't making things hard on yourself (or your audience), you were doing something wrong.

Along with negation, there is the related (if much abused) concept of irony. At its core, irony entails a kind of negation, or at least a contrast—between what is said and what is meant, or between what is said and *how* it's said. I would argue that much of what transpired here went beyond mere irony, being more oblique, ambiguous, and open to interpretation than that term tends to imply. That said, irony was certainly part of the toolkit, and like any tool, it can become dulled with overuse.

Eventually, a kind of irony fatigue began to set in. "For better or worse, criticism and irony are the dissenting voices of our generation," wrote Stephen Duncombe in a 1993 article in *The Baffler*. "Well, maybe for worse, because there's a problem: criticism and irony are negative ... in the sense that they can only work as negations of an already existing culture to which they refer."[37] This echoed a point made earlier the same year by David Foster Wallace, who lamented that "irony, entertaining as it is, serves an exclusively negative function. It's critical and destructive, a ground-clearing ... But irony [is] singularly unuseful when it comes to constructing anything to replace the hypocrisies it debunks."[38] And while neither of them were talking about music per se—and while one could quibble with their particular conceptions of irony—they weren't entirely wrong.

"The problem with punk is that it was very negative," acknowledges Savage, this time speaking in an interview from 2019. "The negativity was very important and very useful to cut through that dreadful kind of post-hippie, post-glitter

---

37 Stephen Duncombe, "We're Marketed, Therefore We Are?" *The Baffler*, No. 5. December 1993.
38 David Foster Wallace, "E Unibus Pluram: Television and US Fiction." *Review of Contemporary Fiction*, Summer 1993, p. 183.

miasma. You know, you needed something fairly strong to cut through all that crap because it *was* crap by '75, '76. It was *awful*. And the negativity was a reflection—a kind of prediction—of what was going to happen in politics with the right-wing regimes in the US and the UK in the 1980s. So it was an artistic movement, punk, but it was very negative. And at some point, you have to be able to turn around and say, 'Well, I don't believe in that; that's a load of fucking shit. What *do* I believe in? What am I going to say *yes* to?'"

That was indeed the question. The challenge was coming up with an answer that didn't immediately yield to the kind of merciless self-criticism that drove so much of the creativity in the first place. One of those answers—advocated by David Foster Wallace in literature and embodied in a lot of treacly emo and post-rock from the mid-1990s onward—was the New Sincerity. Yet, for those afflicted with a more critical mindset, this escape route was sealed off, for better or worse. After all, if you grew up under the influence of contrarians like PiL, Flipper, or Throbbing Gristle, it wasn't as if you could just flip a switch and decide to be Bruce Springsteen. "It sounds kind of douchey to say, 'after punk,'" admits Brandan Kearney, "but after whatever series of cultural moments happened back then in all kinds of different fields—I just don't think that you can pretend to be naive and romantic in that way. I think you have to have some kind of self-reflexive side."

That self-reflexive side, in turn, seemed to go hand in hand with the sort of existential humor that was a hallmark of so many of the bands in this book. As Bill Gould observed, "There's a certain sense of humor that—it's like, it's hard to find when it's real and when it's a joke. Flipper, Pop-O-Pies, Zip Code Rapists—they all kind of come from the same scene of people. It's a certain mentality that San Francisco produced, and that came out of here that was really good. It's like a theatrical kind of blurring the lines between reality and art, in a way." Reality and art, but also comedy and tragedy. "That's a good starting-off point," noted Bruno DeSmartass, elaborating on Flipper and the idea of "pessimistic optimism." "*God, the world's an awful place. What a fuckin' riot.*"

If it seems that all roads keep leading back to Flipper, it's because they embodied so much of whatever it is that this book is ultimately about. They were funny without being a joke. They reveled in paradoxes ("Life is the only thing worth living for") and contradictions ("Life is pretty cheap"). They had a fatalistic

END THE GAME

streak ('Way of the World,' 'Shed No Tears') but were also prone to life-as-a-game metaphors ('End the Game,' 'The Game's Got a Price,' 'New Rules No Rules'). And they seemed intuitively aware of the spectacle they were creating as well as the inherent absurdity, even futility, of it all.

Who cares anyway
Who listens to what I say
This song rhymes
And we play it in time ... [39]

I n lieu of a grandiose ending, I conclude this saga with a snippet from an interview/conversation with Bruce Loose in 2019, when I paid a visit to his remote cabin in Humboldt County. As his lyrics were the inspiration for the book's title, it seems only fair to grant him have the last word.

B: I don't even know what you're supposed to be doing here.

W: I think the point is ultimate enlightenment, right? Maybe it'll happen, but probably not.

B: Maybe that's a big joke. Maybe the ultimate enlightenment is ...

W: ... realizing that there is no ultimate enlightenment?

B: There you go.

39 Flipper, 'Living for the Depression'

WHO CARES ANYWAY
ACKNOWLEDGEMENTS

Thi**s** book has been many years in the making. Although most of the interviews were conducted between 2016 and 2020, the initial dozen or so date back to the early-mid 2000s, when I was a freelancer for the *San Francisco Bay Guardian*. My editors at the *SFBG*—first Tommy Tompkins and then Kimberly Chun—are therefore deserving of special thanks. Without their support, I wouldn't have had the opportunity to write the articles (and conduct the interviews) that wound up providing the initial foundation for the book.

Speaking of interviews, I am grateful to everyone who took the time to share their thoughts and recollections with me: Alan Bishop, Alan Korn, Alicia Rose, Alistair Shanks, Anna-Lisa VanderValk, Barbara Manning, Ben Cohen, Bill Gould, Blaise Smith, Bob Gaynor, Bob Hoffnar, Bob Steeler, Bond Bergland, Boris Zubov, Brad Lapin, Brandan Kearney, Brently Pusser, Bruce Loose, Bruce Pollack, Bruno DeSmartass, Cari Cartmill, Carlos Willingham, Carol Detweiler, Carolyn Fok, Chosei Funahara, Chris Brewster, Chuck Mosley (RIP), Cole Palme, Connie Champagne, Craig Baldwin, Craig Gray, Dame Darcy, Danny Heifetz, David Katz, David "Dog" Swan, Debi Sou, Denise Dee, Desmond Shea, Emilio Crixell, Eric Cope, Eric Fournier, Esmerelda, Eve Bekker, Gail Coulson, Garry Creiman, Greg Freeman, Gregg Turkington, J.C. Garrett, Jai Young Kim, James Goode, Jay Paget, Joan Osato, Joann Berman, Joe Bonaparte, Joe Pop-O-Pie, Joe Rees, Johan Kugelberg, John Gullak, John Singer, John Surrell, John Zerzan, Jon Savage, Jorge Socarras, Judy Gittelsohn, Kim Seltzer, Kirk Heydt, Kris Hendrickson, Kristen Oppenheim, Lara Allen, Lisa Wooley, Liz Sher, Lizzy Kate Gray, Lliam Hart, Margaret Murray, Mark Bowen, Mark Davies, Mark Hutchinson, Matt Hall, Matt Heckert, Meri St. Mary, Mia Simmans, Michael Belfer (RIP, my friend), Mike Hickey, Mike King, Olga Gerrard, Paul Casteel, Paul Draper, Paul Hood, Peter Belsito, Peter Urban, Rachel Thoele, Rebecca Wilson, Richard Edson, Richard Peterson, Roddy Bottum, Ron Morgan, Rozz Rezabek, Ruby Ray, Sally Webster, Scott Davey, Seymour Glass, Stephen Clarke, Stephen Wymore, Steve Tupper, Steven Brown, Steven Keena, Susan Miller, Suzi Skates, Ted Falconi, Tim Lockfeld, Tom Wheeler, Tommy Antel, Tony

ACKNOWLEDGEMENTS

Hotel, Trey Spruance, Will Carpmill, and William Davenport.

For help with tracking down and obtaining permission for photos and other images, thank you to James Stark, Kim Seltzer, Vince Anton Stornaiuolo, Paul Draper, Gregg Turkington, Brandan Kearney, John Singer, James Goode, Kris Hendrickson, Joan Osato, Eric Cope, Lara Allen, Elisabeth Sisco, Gail Butensky, Olga Gerrard, Gail DeMartis, Carol Detweiler, Matt Heckert, Alistair Shanks, J.C. Garrett, Ken Fowler, Phill Griffin, Scott Davey, Carolyn Fok, Joe Pop-O-Pie, Joe Bonaparte, Mark Davies, and Cathy Fitzhugh.

Others who provided valuable "material support" in one form or another (whether they realized it or not) include Joe Carducci, Hisham Mayet, Peter Conheim, Brian Doherty, Brian Weitz, Steven Blush, Owen Kline, Patrick O'Neil, Kareem Kaddah, Katheleen Landino, Mark Prindle, Gregg and Brandan (again), Eric Cope (ditto), Verna Doherty, Stefan Negele, Tom Mallon (RIP), Bruce Gauld, Mark McCloud, Carl King, Nick Tangborn, Alan Korn, Steve Tupper, Scott Ryser, Jay Hinman, Alex Behr, Harvey Stafford, Virgil Shaw, CirculationZero.com, Discogs.com, and FaithNoMan.com.

Several people helped me out by reading and giving me feedback on rough drafts of various chapters: Katie Boyle, Marcie Jaffee, Kyle Waldner, Tera Stubblefield, and Pam Puglis. Thank you all very much.

For moral support and other intangible contributions at various points along the way, I offer my thanks to Brendan Walls, Tim Flynn, Justin Farrar, Erin Weber, Ksenia Zanon, Jacqueline de Groot, Michael Weddington, Brian Turner, Tim Ward, Heather Stephenson, Hozac Books, Cornucopia Records, the staff at Lucky Tree on Hillsborough Street, my dog Alfred, and (of course) Mom and Dad.

Thanks to Jay Boronski for letting me sleep on the couch and Mike McGuirk for recommending me to Tommy.

Thank you to Dan Partridge for introducing me to Neil Hamburger and Amarillo Records at WXYC way back in 1998. For that matter, I'm grateful to everyone else at WXYC who at least tolerated me in those days, but especially Franz Kunst, David Strader, and Cy Rawls (RIP). And for being my first editor and offering my first paying gig as a writer, thank you to Greg Barbera at the *Spectator Magazine* in Raleigh.

Last but not least, thank you to David Kerekes and everyone at Headpress for making this book a reality.

WHO CARES ANYWAY
INDEX

Page numbers in **boldface** denote illustrations

INDEX

INDEX

INDEX

INDEX

INDEX

INDEX

INDEX

Stress in the Jaw," 502; "Chemical Marriage," 502n.12; "Dead Goon," 417, 421, 502; "Desert Search for Techno Allah," 499, 502n.12; *Disco Volante*, XI, 498, 499, 500-506, 527; "Everyone I Went to High School with Is Dead," 499, 502; "Evil Satan," 413; "Girls of Porn, The," 417, 420, 500, 503; *Goddammit I Love America!!!*, 415; "Love is a Fist," 417; "Ma Meeshka Mow Skwoz," 502n.12 "Merry Go Bye-Bye," 502 *Mr. Bungle*, 415, 417-419, 502; *OU818*, 415; "My Ass is on Fire," 417; "Phlegmatics," 502; "Platypus," 499; *Raging Wrath of the Easter Bunny, The*, 413; "Squeeze Me Macaroni," 417, 421; "Travolta," 503; "Violenza Domestica," 501, 502n.12

Mr. Rogers (band), 139; "You Are," 139

Mr. T Experience, 359

MSI Records, 63

Mudd Club, 164

Mummies, The, 479

Murder Dog (zine), 346n.3

Murray, David, 405n.10

Murray, Margaret, 355, 404-407, 410, 428, 463, 471, 490, 491, 496, 512, 515n.28, 516, **519**, 530-531

Music for Vagabonds: The Tuxedomoon Chronicles (book), 84n.4, 5, 118, 120, 122n.56, 123n.59, 298n.35

Music Machine, 144, 268

Muskrats, The, 297

Mustafa, Smelly, 414

Mutants, The, 8, 56, 59, **60**, 61-64, 80n.2, 92, 100, 162n.95, 181n.114, 228, **263**, 282; *Fun Terminal*, 63; "New Dark Ages," 63; "New Drug," 63

MX-80 Sound, 117

Myers, Johnny, 160

My Life Inside Rock and Out (book), 94n.19

Naked City (band), 184

National Interest, The, 528n.35; "The End of History," 528

Negative Dillingers, 98

Negativland, **137**, 357

Negative Trend, 8, 17, 18, 20, 22, **23**, 24-26, **28**, 29, 46, 48, 51, 57, 58, **60**, 78, 89, 90, 93, **95**, 98, 99, 101, 107-109, 111n.41, 112, 120, 204, 207, 219, 250, 327, 338, 532; "Atomic Lawn," 109n.39; "Black and Red," 30, 109n.39;"Groovy Terrorist," 24n.22; "I Got Power," 108n.39; "Meathouse," 30, 48, 108n.39, 109n.40; "Mercenaries," 29, 108n.39; "NWLF," 24, 30; *We Don't Play, We Riot*, 29n.27

Nerves, The, 7

Nervous Gender, 127

Never Known Questions: Five Decades of the Residents, (book), 115n.47

New Kids on the Block, 388

New Musical Express, 220

New Order, 166

New Session People (band), 522

New Wave Theatre (TV Program), 9n.11

New York Dolls, 4, 241n.28

New York Times, 142n.73, 202, 213, 460, 461n.58; "Pop and Jazz in Review," 461n.58; "Pop Life: Drugs, Demons: A Man in a Mask, The," 142n.73; "Rebellion Rules Rock in Young San Francisco," 202n.5, 213n.14

New Youth (band), 356

Niblock, Phil, 178

Nice Guys, The, 397

Nico, 212, **213**

Nietzsche, Friedrich, 18, 101

Nigger, Adolf, 498

Night Break (venue), 431

Nightmare (band), 94

Nightmares (film), 109n.39

No Alternative (band), 107

Night of the Living Dead (film), 409n.13

Nirvana (band), 449, 455, 473, 528, 529; *Nevermind*, 455

Noh Mercy, 66, 75, 80, **81**, 82, 83, 85, **86**, 87, 123, 124, 130, 139, 220n.19; "Furious," 75; "Jane Blank," 85; "No Caucasian Guilt," 82, 83; "Revolutionary Spy," 83

No Depression (zine), 429

No Heads (band), **285**

No New York (compilation LP)

Nonymous, Bambi, **317**

Nose, The, (magazine), 423

Nosferatu (film), 39

Nothing Doing (zine), 405

Not so Quiet on the Western Front (compilation LP), 231

Novak (band), 7

Novak, David, 507, 508n.24

Nuf Sed (label), 352, 394n.3,

INDEX

WHO CARES ANYWAY

INDEX

INDEX

INDEX

WHO CARES ANYWAY